www.wadsworth.com

wadsworth.com is the World Wide Web site for
Wadsworth and is your direct source to dozens of online
resources.

At *wadsworth.com* you can find out about supplements,
demonstration software, and student resources. You can
also send email to many of our authors and preview new
publications and exciting new technologies.

wadsworth.com
Changing the way the world learns®

American Public Policy: An Introduction

SEVENTH EDITION

Clarke E. Cochran
Texas Tech University

Lawrence C. Mayer
Texas Tech Univeristy

T.R. Carr
Southern Illinois University at Edwardsville

N. Joseph Cayer
Arizona State University

THOMSON
WADSWORTH™

Australia Canada Mexico Singapore Spain
United Kingdom United States

To:
Anne
Etta
Lucy
R.G.C.

Executive Editor: David Tatom
Editorial Assistant: Dianna Long
Technology Project Manager: Melinda Newfarmer
Marketing Manager: Janise Fry
Marketing Assistant: Mary Ho
Project Manager, Editorial Production: Katy German
Print/Media Buyer: Doreen Suruki
Permissions Editor: Bob Kauser
Production Service: Carlisle Communications Ltd.

Copy Editor: Christopher Feldman
Illustrator: Carlisle Publishers
  Services
Cover Designer: Sue Hart
Cover Image: Getty Images
Printer: Maple-Vail Book
  Manufacturing Group

Printed in the United States of America
1 2 3 4 5 6 7 06 05 04 03 02

For more information about our products, contact us at:
Thomson Learning Academic Resource Center
1-800-423-0563
For permission to use material from this text, contact us by:
Phone: 1-800-730-2214
Fax: 1-800-730-2215
Web: http://www.thomsonrights.com

Library of Congress Control Number: 200211312

ISBN 0-534-60336-X

Wadsworth/Thomson Learning
10 Davis Drive
Belmont, CA 94002-3098
USA

Asia
Thomson Learning
5 Shenton Way #01-01
UIC Building
Singapore 068808

Australia
Nelson Thomson Learning
102 Dodds Street
South Melbourne, Victoria 3205
Australia

Canada
Nelson Thomson Learning
1120 Birchmount Road
Toronto, Ontario M1K 5G4
Canada

Europe/Middle East/Africa
Thomson Learning
High Holborn House
50/51 Bedford Row
London WC1R 4LR
United Kingdom

About the Authors

Clarke E. Cochran is Professor of Political Science and Adjunct Professor, Department of Health Organization Management, at Texas Tech University, specializing in religion and politics, political philosophy, and health care policy. He received his Ph.D. from Duke University, and has served as Chair of the Religion and Politics Section of the American Political Science Association and Chair of Christians in Political Science. He has won the President's Award for Excellence in Teaching. Professor Cochran held the position of Research Fellow in the Erasmus Institute at the University of Notre Dame (1998–1999) and held the Shannon Chair in Catholic Studies at Nazareth College (Spring 2001). Professor Cochran is the author of *Character, Community, and Politics* (University of Alabama Press, 1982), *Religion in Public and Private Life* (Routledge, 1990), and (with David Carroll Cochran) *Catholics, Politics, and Public Policy: Beyond Left and Right* (Orbis Press, 2003), as well as numerous articles, including articles in the *American Political Science Review, Journal of Politics,* and *Polity.* His recent writings on politics and Catholic health care institutions have appeared in the *Journal of Church and State, Christian Bioethics, Medical Care,* and *Commonweal.*

Lawrence C. Mayer is Professor of Political Science at Texas Tech University. He received his Ph.D. from the University of Texas. Over his career, he has taught at California State University—Fullerton; the University of Miami at Coral Gables, Florida; and the University of Maryland. He teaches in the areas of comparative politics (especially Western industrial democracies), and American and comparative public policy. In addition to *American Public Policy,* he is the author or coauthor of four other books: *Comparative Political Inquiry, Politics in Industrial Societies, Redefining Comparative Politics,* and *Comparative Politics: Nations and Theories in a Changing World,* third edition. He has also contributed articles in such scholarly journals as *Comparative Political Studies,* the *Western Political Quarterly, West European Politics,* and *Nationalism and Ethnic Politics,* and has presented many papers to the major conventions in his field. He is currently researching the rise of parties of identity populism in Europe.

T. R. Carr is Professor of Public Administration and Department Chair at Southern Illinois University at Edwardsville. He received his Ph.D. and M.P.A. from the University of Oklahoma and his B.A. from Minot State University. He has taught at Texas Tech University and at the University of Arkansas at Fayetteville. He teaches primarily in the areas of quantitative methods and policy analysis. In addition to *American Public Policy,* he has published in various journals and has presented papers at the major conventions in political science and public administration. He is active in academic and professional associations and has served in numerous offices in state and local chapters of the American Society for Public Administration. He is currently serving as Mayor of the City of Hazelwood, Missouri, and is active in both the Missouri and St. Louis County Municipal Leagues.

N. Joseph Cayer is Professor of Public Affairs at Arizona State University. He received his Ph.D. from the University of Massachusetts and his B.A. and M.P.A. from the University of Colorado, Boulder. He has taught at Lamar University, the University of Maine, and Texas Tech University. He is author or coauthor of seven books, including *Public Personnel Administration in the United States, Public Administration: Social Change and Adaptive Management, Managing Human Resources, Handbook of Training and Development for the Public Sector,* and *Supervision for Success in Government,* as well as numerous chapters and articles on public management and policy, with an emphasis on public-sector human resources management issues. He is also active in academic and professional associations, having served in many offices in the American Society for Public Administration, National Association of Schools of Public Affairs and Administration, International Personnel Management Association, and Western Social Science Association.

Contents

PREFACE   xviii

1   Issues and Public Policy: An Introduction   1

STUDYING PUBLIC POLICY   1

What Constitutes Public Policy?   *1*
Why Study Public Policy?   *2*

DEFINING MAJOR CONCEPTS   3

Policy Analysis   *3*
Categories of Public Policy   *3*
Models for Policy Analysis   *6*
Stages of Policy Development   *7*
Aspects of Policy Evaluation   *10*

THE CONTEXTS OF CONTEMPORARY PUBLIC POLICY   11

The Institutional Context   *12*
The Economic Context   *13*
The Demographic Context   *14*
The Ideological Context   *17*
The Cultural Context   *19*

APPROACHES TAKEN BY THIS BOOK   20

Chapter Plan   *20*
National Focus   *21*
Comparative Information   *21*

SUMMARY   21

NOTES   23
SUGGESTED READINGS   24

2   Intergovernmental Policies: A New Federalism?   25

ISSUE BACKGROUND: THE FEDERAL SYSTEM   25

Issues in a Federal System   *25*
Participants in Intergovernmental Relations   *27*

CONTEMPORARY POLICY: INTERGOVERNMENTAL REALITIES   **29**

Modern Intergovernmental Relations   29
Other Forms of Intergovernmental Interaction   31

**POLICY EVALUATION: CHANGING INTERGOVERNMENTAL
RELATIONS   32**

Administrative Problems   32
Monitoring   34
Finances   35
Unfunded Mandates   36
Structural Effects   37

**FUTURE ALTERNATIVES: CONTINUING ADAPTATION
OF THE INTERGOVERNMENTAL SYSTEM   38**

SUMMARY   40

NOTES   40
SUGGESTED READINGS   42

**3   The Economy: Changing Government-Business
Relationships   43**

ISSUE BACKGROUND: KEY CONCEPTS IN ECONOMICS   43

The Free-Enterprise System   44
History of Government's Role   46
Inflation and Recession   48
Microeconomic Approaches   49

**CONTEMPORARY POLICY: CASE STUDIES IN ECONOMIC
INTERVENTION   52**

The Federal Trade Commission: Traditional Economic Regulation   52
Community Revitalization Issues: Merging Social and Economic Concerns   57
International Trade   59

**POLICY EVALUATION: ENCOURAGING COMPETITION
OR DISCOURAGING INNOVATION?   60**

Deregulation   60
International Trade   61
Assistance to Business   62
Effects of Regulation   63
Changes in Regulation   64

**FUTURE ALTERNATIVES: REFORMING THE RELATIONSHIP
OF GOVERNMENT AND THE ECONOMY   66**

SUMMARY   69

NOTES   70
SUGGESTED READINGS   71

4   **Economic Issues: Taxing, Spending, and Budgeting**   **73**

ISSUE BACKGROUND: CONCEPTS AND ISSUES   **73**

Economic Policy Obstacles   *74*
Macroeconomic Approaches   *75*

**CONTEMPORARY POLICY: APPROACHES TO MANAGING
THE ECONOMY**   **78**

Supply-Side Economics   *79*
Budget Deficits in the 1980s and 1990s   *80*
Tax Reform   *83*

POLICY EVALUATION: SUCCESS OR FAILURE?   **84**

Social Orders   *84*
Inflation   *85*
Fiscal Policy   *86*
Federal Revenues and Spending   *89*
Fiscal Policy Evaluation   *89*
Defense Spending   *92*

**FUTURE ALTERNATIVES: SPENDING, TAXES,
AND THE DEFICIT**   **93**

Taxes   *93*
Other Future Issues   *94*

SUMMARY   **96**

NOTES   **97**
SUGGESTED READINGS   **98**

5   **Energy and Environmental Policies:
Policy Complacency**   **100**

**ENERGY POLICY ISSUE BACKGROUND:
COMPLACENCY AND CRISIS**   **100**

Traditional Energy Policy   *100*
Western Vulnerability: OPEC and the Arab Oil Embargo   *103*

**CONTEMPORARY POLICY: FROM CRISIS
TO COMPLACENCY**   **105**

Energy Problems Emerge   *105*
Global Dependence on Fossil Fuels   *106*

Energy Policy after 1973   *107*
Energy Policy after 1980   *109*

**POLICY EVALUATION: CONTINUED FOSSIL FUEL
DEPENDENCE   111**

Alternatives to Fossil Fuels   111
Nuclear Power   113
Political Impact of Continued Oil Dependence   117

FUTURE ALTERNATIVES: ENERGY POLICY COMPLACENCY   119

ENVIRONMENTAL POLICY   120

**ISSUE BACKGROUND: A LEGACY OF ENVIRONMENTAL
ABUSE   121**

Air Pollution   121
Water and Solid-Waste Pollution   124
Toxic and Hazardous Waste   125
Acid Rain   127
The Environmental Legacy   128

CONTEMPORARY ENVIRONMENTAL POLICY   128

Water-Pollution Policy   129
Air-Pollution Policy   129
The National Environmental Policy Act (NEPA)   130

POLICY EVALUATION: SEARCHING FOR DIRECTION   131

Current Policy Direction and Values   131
Reduced Public Concern   132
The Politics of Regulation   132
Enforcement Problems   133

FUTURE ALTERNATIVES: UNRESOLVED POLICY ISSUES   133

International Treaties   133
Environmental Justice   134
Self-Regulation of the Market   134
Taxes and Legal Action   135
The Role of State Governments   136
Public Attitudes   137
Energy and the Environment   137

SUMMARY   139

NOTES   140
SUGGESTED READINGS   141

6   Crime and Criminal Justice: Dilemmas of Social Control   143

ISSUE BACKGROUND: THE GROWTH AND DECLINE OF CRIME   145

The Extent of Crime   145
Reasons for Crime   149

CONTEMPORARY POLICY: CONSTITUTIONAL RIGHTS AND THE DETERRENCE OF CRIME   157

Confessions and the Right to Counsel   157
The Exclusionary Rule and Search and Seizure   160
Capital Punishment   161

POLICY EVALUATION: FLAWS IN THE CRIMINAL JUSTICE SYSTEM   167

Confessions and the Right to Counsel   167
The Exclusionary Rule and Search and Seizure   168
Capital Punishment   169
Conclusion: Crime and Criminal Procedure   172

FUTURE ALTERNATIVES: POLICY OPTIONS FOR REDUCING CRIME   174

Drug-Related Crimes   174
Violence against Women   176
Crimes of Violence and Gun Control   178
Decriminalization and Deterrence   186
Strengthening the Police   187
Penal Reform, Sentencing, and Recidivism   188
Limiting the Alternatives to Punishment   190

SUMMARY   192

NOTES   194
SUGGESTED READINGS   196

7   Income Support: Security, Work, or Dependence?   197

ISSUE BACKGROUND: RESPONDING TO POVERTY   197

Defining Poverty   197
How Many Poor?   201
Who Are the Poor?   202
The Causes of Poverty   205
The Welfare State   207

CONTEMPORARY POLICY:
SOCIAL INSURANCE PROGRAMS   **208**

  Social Security   *209*
  Unemployment Insurance   *210*

POLICY EVALUATION: DOES SOCIAL SECURITY
STILL WORK?   **211**

  Social Security Successes   *211*
  The Social Security Dilemma   *212*
  Is Social Security Fair?   *213*
  Unemployment Compensation   *214*

FUTURE ALTERNATIVES: THE DIFFICULTY OF SOCIAL SECURITY
REFORM   **214**

  The Future of Social Security   *214*
  Quick Fixes   *215*
  Diversifying Social Security Investment   *216*
  Privatizing Social Security   *216*
  Pensions   *217*

CONTEMPORARY POLICY:
PUBLIC ASSISTANCE PROGRAMS   **218**

  Cash Assistance Programs   *219*
  In-Kind Benefits   *222*
  Work/Employment Programs   *224*
  Public Assistance Spending   *224*

POLICY EVALUATION: PUBLIC ASSISTANCE   **225**

  Accomplishments of Public Assistance   *225*
  Has Welfare Reform Worked?   *226*
  TANF, Children, and Work: Evaluation and Re-authorization   *229*

FUTURE ALTERNATIVES IN PUBLIC ASSISTANCE: CHILDREN,
UNDERCLASS, HOMELESSNESS, AND WORK   **232**

  Children and Poverty   *232*
  The Underclass   *234*
  Housing Programs and Homelessness   *235*
  Employment Issues   *236*

CONCLUSIONS   **238**

SUMMARY   **238**

NOTES   **239**
SUGGESTED READINGS   **241**

8   Health Care: Unlimited Needs, Limited Resources   243

ISSUE BACKGROUND: THE HEALTH CARE SYSTEM AND ITS
PROBLEMS   243

The Structure of American Health Care   243

Paying for Health Care   245

Other Nations   246

How Healthy Is America?   247

Inequities in Access to Health Care   249

High Cost   251

Quality of Health Care   255

CONTEMPORARY POLICY: HEALTH CARE
FOR THE POOR AND AGED   256

Medicare   257

Medicaid   259

State Children's Health Insurance Program (SCHIP)   261

Other Federal Programs   261

POLICY EVALUATION: HEALTH CARE AT THE CROSSROADS   262

Medicare and Medicaid   263

Questioning the Structures of Health Care   264

Managed Care Backlash   266

FUTURE ALTERNATIVES: HEALTH CARE REFORM, ETHICS,
AND LONG-TERM CARE   267

The Failure of Universal Health Care and Future Prospects   268

The Promise of Incremental Reform   270

States and Health Care Reform   271

Medicare Reform   273

Ethical Issues   276

The Moral Dilemmas of Research and Technological Development   277

Long-Term Care   278

SUMMARY   280

NOTES   282
SUGGESTED READINGS   283

9   Education: Conflict in Policy Direction   285

ISSUE BACKGROUND: HISTORICAL PERSPECTIVES AND THE
ONSET OF FEDERAL INVOLVEMENT IN EDUCATION   286

The Tradition of Free Public Education   286

The Tradition of Local Control   286

An Emerging Role for State Governments   287

Federal Involvement in Education   287

The Elementary and Secondary Education Act of 1965: Expanding the Federal Policy Role   287

The Federal Role in Higher Education   291

CONTEMPORARY POLICY: REMEDYING SOCIAL INEQUALITY THROUGH EDUCATION   291

The Issue of Unequal Financial Resources   292

Equality in Education   295

Educational Inequality Outside the United States   297

POLICY EVALUATION: EDUCATIONAL QUALITY IN THE UNITED STATES   297

Concern over Poor Student Achievement   298

Questioning Teacher Competency   301

Merit Pay and Master Teachers   302

Bilingual Education   303

Multiculturalism   304

FUTURE ALTERNATIVES: COMMUNITY CONTROL, PRIVATE SCHOOLS, A CHANGING FEDERAL ROLE, AND CONFLICTING PRIORITIES   305

Community Control and Decentralization   306

The Issue of Private Schools   307

Crisis in Education   310

Changing Priorities in Federal Education Policy   311

Education Priorities in the Twenty-First Century   312

Unresolved Education Issues: Teachers and Curriculum   315

Unresolved Education Issues: Structural Questions   318

Issues in Higher Education   320

SUMMARY   323

NOTES   325
SUGGESTED READINGS   327

10   Legal and Social Equality: The Struggle against Oppression and Bigotry   329

ISSUE BACKGROUND: THE IDEA OF EQUALITY   330

Equality under Law   330

Equality of Opportunity   334

Equality of Material Well-Being   337

The Civil Rights Movement and Equality   339

CONTEMPORARY POLICY: STRENGTHENING CONSTITUTIONAL GUARANTEES OF EQUALITY   339

The Erosion of the Fourteenth Amendment   339
Ending Segregation   340
Enforcing Integration   341
The Struggle for Racial Balance in Employment and Higher Education   343
Equality and the Women's Movement   347
Bias against Homosexuals, the Handicapped, and Native Americans   351

POLICY EVALUATION: THE DRIVE FOR PROPORTIONAL EQUALITY   355

Busing for Racial Balance   355
Retreat on Racial Preference Programs   357
Challenges to Racial Preference in Higher Education   361

FUTURE ALTERNATIVES: THE CHANGING CONCEPTION OF EQUALITY   363

The Debate over Affirmative Action   363
Race and Equality   369

SUMMARY   372

NOTES   373
SUGGESTED READINGS   375

11   Immigration Policy: The Barely Open Door   376

ISSUE BACKGROUND: FROM AN OPEN DOOR TO INCREASING LIMITS   376

The Open Door   376
Use of Quotas   377
Transition to a Preference System   380
Illegal Immigration   382

CONTEMPORARY POLICY: RESPONDING TO CHANGING IMMIGRATION DYNAMICS   383

POLICY EVALUATION: CONTRASTING PERCEPTIONS   388

Current Policy Concerns   388
Economic Concerns   388
Impact on Public Services   390
Quality of Life   392

FUTURE ALTERNATIVES: OPENNESS OR RESTRICTION?   394

SUMMARY   396

NOTES   397
SUGGESTED READINGS   399

**12   Foreign and Defense Policy: Security and Interests
in a Dangerous World   401**

ISSUE BACKGROUND: COMPETING APPROACHES TO FOREIGN
POLICY   401

   Realism or Classical Diplomacy   401
   The Balance of Power   404

THE AMERICAN STYLE IN FOREIGN POLICY: WILSONIAN
IDEALISM   405

   Universal Justice and the Nuremburg Principle   406
   Diplomacy, Force, and American Optimism   407
   Collective Security and Institutional Solutions to World Conflict   408

RECENT AND CONTEMPORARY POLICY: COLD WAR,
CONTAINMENT, AND AFTER   409

   The Failure of Containment in Vietnam   410
   The Search for a Comprehensive Peace in Palestine   412

POLICY EVALUATION: REALISM VERSUS IDEALISM
IN THE MIDDLE EAST   412

   Oil, U.S. Foreign Policy, and the Middle East   412
   Palestinian Nationalism as a Just and Achievable Cause   413
   American Options in the Region   416

FUTURE ALTERNATIVES: CONTROL OF TERRORISM   416

   Defining Terrorism   416
   Options for Confronting Terrorism   417

SUMMARY   419

NOTES   420
SUGGESTED READINGS   421

**13   Private Morality and Public Policy: Family Values, Social
Issues, and the Open Society   422**

THE IDEA OF THE OPEN SOCIETY   422

   The Emergence of Neo-Populism on the Right   422
   The Open Society and the Tolerance of Diverse Public Ideas   423

Community and Family Values versus the Open Society 424
The Role of the Court and the Presumption
   of Constitutionality 426

ABORTION, BIRTH CONTROL, AND THE LAW **427**
The Moral Issue 432

**THE FIRST AMENDMENT AND PUBLIC MORALITY:
SUPPRESSING OBSCENITY** **433**
Freedom of Speech 433
Protection against Insensitive Speech 436
Obscenity and the Law: The Roth Rule 439
The Conflict between Pornography and Public Morality 442

**CONFLICT OVER THE ROLE OF RELIGION
IN THE UNITED STATES** **448**
Freedom of and from Religion 449
The Establishment Clause 450
The Free Exercise Clause 454
Aid to Parochial Schools 457
Scientific Creationism and Secular Humanism 459

FAMILY VALUES AND FEMINISM **460**

SUMMARY **462**

NOTES **463**
SUGGESTED READINGS **464**

14 **The Continuing Policy Debates: A Conclusion** **466**
POLITICAL ACTORS **466**

IDEOLOGY, DEMOGRAPHY, AND POLICY STALEMATE **467**

PLURALISM **470**

THE LIMITS OF PUBLIC POLICY **471**

"PROBLEM" AND "SOLUTION" **472**

Index **474**

Preface

We have made a variety of changes for the seventh edition of *American Public Policy*. Having completed this edition in Spring 2002, we have tried to keep our text current by addressing the most prominent issues in the political debate without simply focusing on "current events." Some events, such as the American response to the terrorist attack of September 11, 2001, were not clear in their full effect at the time of this writing. We have restored a chapter on foreign policy from earlier editions to reflect the new prominence to international affairs at this time. In this edition, we address the economic policies that resulted from the end of the large budget deficits of the 1980s and 1990s, including the 2001 recession. The chapter on crime considers the continued decline in crime rates and the reasons for them. In 1996 the entire welfare system was reformed; we evaluate that reform in Chapter 7, as well as President Bush's "faith-based initiative" and Social Security reform proposals. Chapter 8 covers the major changes in health policy in the last five years. Education reform was a major theme in the early years of the Bush administration, so Chapter 9 details the results of these proposals. The events of September 11 made Americans more wary of immigration, a topic covered in Chapter 11. The final chapter provides a comprehensive summary.

American Public Policy is an introductory undergraduate text that focuses on the substantive issues of public policy. Most texts stress methods of policy analysis, models of policy, or the policymaking process. Although these topics are important, their dominance at the introductory level often makes the subject too abstract to engage students' imaginations. In our own teaching, we have found that an interest in more rigorous analysis grows most naturally out of a lively classroom discussion of specific, substantive policy issues—for example, welfare, abortion, tax reform, or crime control. We believe our book is unique in its emphasis on such issues, combining history and description with debate about alternative solutions.

This text is intended for a student's first undergraduate course in public policy, either a one-semester course or part of a two-semester sequence that includes both political institutions and public policy. We do not assume any prior knowledge of basic policy issues on the student's part, although we do presume an understanding of the basic structure of American government. Therefore, we present the policy material step by step, building a picture of existing policy that the student can use to evaluate alternatives.

Most chapters follow the same outline for easy access and comparison. The first section, "Issue Background," provides information the reader needs to know about the background of the particular topic, including descriptions of early policy actions. The second, "Contemporary Policy," outlines the evolution of present-day governmental policy. The section on "Policy Evaluation" presents an in-depth discussion of the principal successes and failures of policy relating to the particular issue under study. Finally, the "Future Alternatives" section evaluates possible alternatives to existing policy. Each chapter ends with a summary of its principal ideas and a list of helpful books and Web sites for further study. The book compares a wide range of perspectives—from conservative to liberal to radical—but does not take a single ideological position. Instead, this approach challenges students to develop their own evaluations of the alternatives proposed in contemporary controversies.

The book does not neglect the state and local dimensions of policy issues, although the focus is primarily on national policy and national policy debate. Cross-national comparisons of policies and their impacts are presented when relevant. Each chapter ends with a summary of important points and a list of resources for further study.

Chapter 1 introduces the study of substantive issues of public policy. Major policy concepts are defined, and the contexts in which contemporary public policy operates—institutional, economic, demographic, cultural, and ideological—are delineated. Each succeeding chapter examines an individual area. Chapter 2 focuses on the policies that link the levels of our federal system, policies such as revenue sharing and grants-in-aid. This chapter continues the structural introduction of Chapter 1.

Chapter 3 gives attention to questions of economic regulation, changes in the economy, and international competition, leaving an entire chapter (Chapter 4) for macroeconomic policy, including the federal budgets, taxes, and spending. Chapter 5 deals with both environmental and energy policy, which allows us to highlight the important interaction between these two policy areas.

In Chapter 6, the fluctuation in rates of crime is considered, including speculation about the causes of crime. The chapter evaluates the impacts of policies specifying an individual's constitutional rights: confessions and the right to counsel, the exclusionary rule and search and seizure, and capital punishment. It considers alternative methods of responding to crime, including gun control, capital punishment, and sentencing reform.

Chapter 7 looks at the double bind of income support and welfare dependence, beginning with a definition of poverty and an account of the creation of the welfare system. For greater clarity of presentation, the chapter now separates the discussion of Social Security and public assistance. Evaluation of the 1996 welfare reform law and proposals to "privatize" part of Social Security receive special attention.

Chapter 8 discusses the nation's health care as a different kind of double bind, one of unlimited needs but limited resources. Special attention is given to the prospects for reform in the future, with attention to proposed changes in Medicare and the effects of new research into the building blocks of life itself.

In Chapter 9, the tradition of free public education in the United States is shown to be in jeopardy. The chapter considers such problems as poor student achievement, teacher competence, inequities resulting from the system of local control, and the role of the federal government in education. The idea of equality, both legal and social, is discussed in Chapter 10. Programs of the 1960s and 1970s—those aimed at achieving equality in the schools and in employment—are now seriously questioned. An entire chapter is then devoted to the issue of immigration and the various responses that American government has made over time to its challenges. Chapter 12 describes the challenges to American foreign policy. Chapter 13 focuses on issues involving strong moral content—abortion, freedom of speech and censorship, the role of religion in society and politics, and feminism and family values.

American Public Policy may be used in a variety of ways. Instructors may choose to consider all of the policy areas presented or to select a group of them for special emphasis. Chapters 1 and 2 should be read first, but the rest of the chapters can be assigned in any sequence the instructor prefers. Supplementary readings focusing on particular issues may be conveniently added, or the text may be used in conjunction with other texts focusing on political institutions or the policy process.

Many people have read and commented on this edition, and we particularly wish to thank the following persons: Michael LeMay, Robert Keiser, John Hird, Patricia Freeland, Cecilia Rodriguez Castillo, Ed Miller, Christine Rossell, and Michael Mumper. We are grateful for their interest and suggestions. In addition, Lisa Sussman, Heidi Hood, and Marsha Polk Fried of Bedford/St. Martin's Press, Dianna Long of Wadsworth Publishing Company, and Emily Bush of Carlisle Publishing Services provided invaluable editorial assistance.

CHAPTER 1

Issues and Public Policy: An Introduction

Public policy in America affects each citizen in hundreds of ways, some of them familiar and some unsuspected. Citizens directly confront public policy when they are arrested for speeding, but they seldom remember that the advertising on the television shows they watch is regulated by the Federal Communications Commission and the Federal Trade Commission. Many citizens who complain loudly at tax time about government bureaucracy and overregulation have forgotten the fire and police protection or the paved streets those revenues provide. Indeed, public policy in America affects a vast range of activities, from nuclear warheads to bathroom plumbing, from arresting lawbreakers to providing medical care for the elderly. This book aims to clarify key dimensions of this ubiquitous influence on American life and to introduce the debates swirling around its major controversies. It takes an *issue-oriented approach* to the beginning study of public policy.

STUDYING PUBLIC POLICY

What Constitutes Public Policy?

Even though examples of public policy come readily to mind, defining public policy in clear and unambiguous terms is not easy. Political scientists have devoted considerable attention to the problem without reaching a consensus.[1] The term *public policy* always refers to the actions of government and the intentions that determine those actions. Making policy requires choosing among goals and alternatives, and making a choice always involves intention. The federal government, for example, chose to create Medicare in 1965 to help retirees with their medical needs. Policy is seldom a single action, but is most often a series of actions coordinated to achieve a goal. Thus, public policy is defined in this book as: *an intentional course of action followed by a government institution or official for resolving an issue of public concern.* Such a course of action must be manifested in laws, public statements, official regulations, or widely accepted and publicly visible patterns of behavior. Public policy is rooted in law and in the authority and coercion associated with law. (The terms *public policy* and *policy* will be used interchangeably.)

Two qualifications are necessary, however, for this definition of public policy. First, the idea of an intentional course of action includes decisions made *not* to take a certain action. For example, Congress voted in 1993 not to continue funding for the Superconducting Supercollider Project. Second, the requirement that official actions be sanctioned by law or accepted custom is necessary because public officials often take courses of action that step outside public policy—for example, they sometimes take bribes or exceed their legal authority. Such deeds should not be considered public policy—that is, unless they are openly tolerated in a particular political system. Of course, laws or official regulations should not be mistaken for the whole realm of policy. Lawmaking is not enough to establish a policy; implementation, interpretation, enforcement, and the impact of laws and regulations, discussed later, are also part of policy.

Why Study Public Policy?

Students of political science and public administration have several reasons for studying public policy. The first is *theoretical*: Political scientists seek to understand and explain the world of politics—that is, they attempt to develop and test explanatory generalizations about the political behavior of individuals and institutions. Because public policy is a part of politics, political scientists are concerned with how it is related to such things as political party structure, interest groups, interparty competition, electoral systems, and executive-legislative relations. Political scientists who seek explanation call for the discipline to develop and test "policy theory."[2] They often develop "models" of the policy process as a means to facilitate understanding of how policy is made across a number of areas. Such models can focus on interest group activity, powerful elites, institutional forces, or the choices made by voters and elected officials.[3]

A second reason for studying public policy is *practical*. Political scientists and students of policy apply scientific knowledge to solve practical problems. They are interested in how policymaking can be made more rational and effective, how the obstacles to implementing policy decisions can be removed, and how those policies affect the quality of individual and social life. The standard here, according to political scientist Lawrence Mead, is "effective governance"; that is, whether government action (or inaction) solves evident public problems.[4] As political scientists Duncan MacRae and James A. Wilde pointed out, the study of public policy requires "the use of reason and evidence to choose the best policy among a number of alternatives."[5]

A third reason for studying public policy, related to the second, is *political*. Debate and controversy over public policy in America is not new, but today the range of issues over which serious disagreement occurs is far greater than in the past. Constant bombardment with policy choices compels citizens to make choices. So many issues are placed before the public—health care and welfare reform, crime prevention, economic stability, and AIDS prevention at the national level; taxation and spending, teacher quality, and public utility regulation at the state level; zoning, mass transportation, and property taxation at the local level—that mental circuits begin to overload. As citizens, political scientists and college students hope the study of public policy will help them find their way through the tangle of complex issues and sophisticated policy proposals. They try to understand the arguments and ideological positions that define policy choices.

The emphasis of this book is on the second and third reasons for studying policy—the practical and political—but it draws on the first as well, for intelligent policy selection depends on the analysis and understanding developed by the theoretical findings of political science.

DEFINING MAJOR CONCEPTS

Policy Analysis

Policy analysis is principally concerned with describing and investigating how and why particular policies are proposed, adopted, and implemented. This is the theoretical side of policy studies. Policy analysis is not, however, "value neutral." Policy analysts want to discover which policy proposals best fulfill important public values.[6] Thus, policy analysis invokes such principles as freedom, equality, justice, decency, and peace. Indeed, politics often concerns debates about the very meaning of these terms.

Those who would sharply separate policy analysis from fundamental social values make a grave mistake. A policy option must be evaluated in the light of what policy analysis reveals about its chances of being adopted, the probable effectiveness of the option, and the difficulties of implementation. A proposal for increased spending for high school education, for example, would need to be tested against data on the impact of increased spending on student achievement levels. Advocates of fundamental restructuring of the health care system need to take into account the political inertia favoring only incremental reform. However, policy analysis without awareness of ethical perspectives is lame. This is particularly true when evaluating the impact of policy. Ethical principles must be brought to bear on the discovery of the good and bad effects of policy. Such principles not only measure success and failure; they also provide insight into consequences that otherwise would not be revealed.

Policy analysis, done by political scientists, can be distinguished from *policy advocacy* by politicians, partisans, or interest groups. Advocacy differs from analysis, because advocacy begins from a commitment to economic interests or to principles as interpreted by specific ideological systems, such as liberalism, conservatism, and environmentalism. Nevertheless, both advocacy and analysis draw upon similar principles and goals, and the two intertwine in the real world of politics. Although ideological commitments can bring important overlooked values to policy analysis, policy advocates are more concerned about advancing their ideology than understanding the policy process, which is the goal of policy analysis. The following chapters will discuss different ideological perspectives on policy at some length because the policy debates are often framed by ideology.

Categories of Public Policy

Thousands of different policies are under the responsibility of the American national government, and many thousands more are under state and local responsibility. Therefore, we need to classify policies into different types in order to discuss them clearly. Moreover, political scientists have found that political activity varies according to certain characteristics of policy. Classification of policies,

T/F

TABLE 1-1 ▪ Classifications of Policy

Purposes	*Types*	*Goods*
Security	Distributive	Collective
Membership	Regulatory	Private
Prosperity	Self-Regulatory	
Needs	Redistributive	

therefore, allows them to test which features of policy have the most influence on the politics of the policy process. There is no single classification suitable for all purposes. The following paragraphs summarize three common classifications (purposes, types, and goods) (see Table 1-1).

Because public policy is intentional; that is, attempts to fulfill certain purposes, we can group policies into classifications based on purpose. There are many different ways to classify, and political philosophers for centuries have debated the most fundamental purposes of government and the proper goals for it to pursue. The policies discussed in this book can be categorized under four headings. Government, first, exists to provide *security* from internal and external threats to the lives, liberties, and properties of its members. National defense and foreign policy (Chapter 12) are prime examples of this purpose. Another is crime policy, which intends to establish order and to protect citizens from each other through crime prevention and the punishment of criminals (Chapter 6). Government itself is often a threat to the security of residents; therefore, modern democratic nations enhance security by placing limits on government itself through constitutions and bills of rights. The chapters on equality (Chapter 10) and on morality policy (Chapter 13) discuss such rights as freedom of speech, religious freedom, and equal voting.

A second purpose of government is *membership*; that is, determining who is and who is not a member of society. Members of a political society are citizens, who enjoy certain rights and bear certain responsibilities denied to residents and visitors who are not citizens. The matter of citizenship has taken on considerable significance in recent decades with the large increase in immigration. The debate focuses on who may be allowed within the borders of the United States and who, once in, is eligible for citizenship. A second focus of membership debate in democratic nations such as the United States is equality. Democracies do not recognize first- and second-class citizenship. All citizens should be equal in fundamental rights and responsibilities. Yet racial and religious differences, gender, and other characteristics raise significant equality challenges and call into question the commitment to equal membership. Specific equality issues such as school integration and affirmative action involve the meaning of equality.

A third purpose of government is to help ensure the material well-being of its members. We may think of this as a *prosperity* goal. In democratic, capitalist nations government does not have the sole or even the primary role in providing the goods and services necessary for material prosperity. However, as we shall see in the two chapters devoted to economic policy, American citizens do expect the national government to help to manage the economy and to provide the legal and social infrastructure for economic growth. Environmental policy and energy policy (Chapter 5) might also be thought of as essential components of material well-being. State and local officials are often judged by their ability to attract employment and economic development to their cities or states.

Finally, government helps people to meet *needs*. As with the prosperity goal, the expectation is not that government has the main responsibility in all areas, but it takes a leading role in some, such as educating citizens. The extensive system of elementary, secondary, and higher education operated by state and local governments and funded in part by the federal government is ample testimony to the importance of government's role in meeting this need. In the case of other needs, government in the United States takes a supplemental role, stepping in when private efforts are not sufficient to meet citizens' minimum needs for health care or income support. Policies such as Medicare, Medicaid, Social Security, and food stamps are examples of this governmental purpose.

A second classification scheme emerges when political scientists try to determine whether certain kinds of policies affect the types of political activity involved in policymaking. One influential classification divides policies into distributive, regulatory, self-regulatory, and redistributive policies.[7] *Distributive* policies allocate benefits from government to certain segments of the population. The more widely the benefits are distributed, the more consensual the policies and the more popular the policy is likely to be. These benefits may be in the form of subsidies (agriculture price supports, for example) or contracts (for aircraft carriers). They can also come in the form of direct government provision of services (public schools) or direct payments to individuals (Social Security checks).

Regulatory policies impose constraints on individuals and groups. They reduce liberty of action. Some set up rules for the entire society, criminal justice laws, for example, or speed limits. Civil rights laws also regulate standards of employment, public accommodation, and housing for the entire society. Other regulations are far more particular, restricting who may enter the banking business (entrants must possess a certain amount of capital), or imposing limits on bank loans. Environmental laws restrict the kinds and quantities of pollutants businesses may generate. Regulatory policies may be highly conflictual, because those subject to the regulations may perceive themselves as losers in a battle with those favoring the restrictions. These conflicts are prominent in the chapters on morality policy, economic regulation, and energy and the environment.

Self-regulatory policies are similar to regulatory ones, except that the persons or groups being regulated are given considerable authority and discretion to formulate and police the regulations governing them. Attorneys, physicians, engineers, and other professions, for example, receive authority from government to license practitioners, thus determining who may and who may not practice the profession. Such groups often also develop and administer their own codes of ethics, enforce discipline, and help to govern the schools that produce the professionals. Farmers often develop and vote on various collective actions governed by state or federal law, such as pest control programs and crop marketing schemes. Self-regulatory politics often takes place outside of public scrutiny and can lead to charges of policies developed exclusively in the interest of the regulated, rather than in the public interest.

When the issue of *redistribution* takes the stage, politics becomes highly ide-ological and highly partisan. Redistribution involves not only the allocation of ben-efits or services to certain parts of the population, but the taxing of other parts of the population to generate the funds. Those who possess the funds, or the rights and powers reallocated, seldom give them up willingly. Moreover, liberals are gen-erally more favorable to redistributive measures than conservatives. Policies that help to meet needs or to guarantee equal membership are often classified as re-distributive. These involve taxing relatively more affluent members of society in order to provide income assistance, food, housing, or health insurance to the less affluent. The graduated income tax can also be considered redistributive, as can taxes on gasoline used to fund mass transit. The perception of winners and losers, as in regulatory politics, makes redistributive policymaking highly contentious. The benefits of a policy may be (or be perceived) as a *zero-sum game*, in which the benefits to some must be exactly balanced by losses to others. The redistribu-tion of scarce resources by government always generates intense opposition.

A third distinction often encountered in the study of public policy is that be-tween *collective* or *public goods* and *private goods*. Some policies involve the pro-vision of collective goods; that is, goods that cannot be divided. Thus, if the good is provided at all, it has to be provided to everyone. Examples are national de-fense, clean air, and traffic control. Of course, providing such goods may involve regulation or redistribution of funds, thus making the benefits of the policies seem divisible. The goods themselves, however, cannot be divided.

Private goods are the opposite. These are goods that can be divided and given to some persons, but not others. Most distribution and redistribution poli-cies fall into this classification. Some persons qualify for food stamps; others do not. Some students qualify for admission to a selective state university; others may be admitted to second-tier colleges or to junior colleges. Liberals, conservatives, and other ideological groups strongly disagree about the range of private goods that it is appropriate for government to distribute.

Models for Policy Analysis

Making public policy is extraordinarily complex. It involves public opinion, me-dia attitudes, expert ideas, active citizens, business and labor leaders, elected rep-resentatives, presidents and governors, judges, and bureaucrats. Policymaking calls on political resources, economic conditions, popular cultural attitudes, and international conditions. When political scientists do research attempting to un-derstand public policy, they try to reduce the complexity to a manageable degree by creating *models of policymaking* that summarize the primary forces at work. None of these models is complete; none captures all of the relationships that are important. No one model best describes the features of policymaking in every area. Although the chapters that follow do not adhere strictly to any of these mod-els, they draw upon the primary qualities of some political science models.

Features of the *institutional model* appear in the following description of the institutional context of public policy. This model stresses the opportunities and constraints on policy that are part of the very structure of the American con-stitutional order: judiciary, bureaucracy, executives, legislatures, separation of powers, federalism, and so forth. The *elite model* focuses on the influence over policy exercised by powerful individuals or groups. This model contrasts with the *pluralist model*, which stresses that many groups and individuals have an influence in the American democratic system. Each of these group's interests and ideas must be taken into account. The *group* or *subgovernment model* is similar to the pluralist model, but recognizes that different policy areas (for example, crime, health, transportation) are important to different actors. Legislators, bureaucrats, experts, and interest groups that are active in one area are often quite different from those active in a different policy arena.

A variety of political scientists model policy as a rational process. Policymakers in the *rational-comprehensive model* take account of all information about the policy problems and of all policy options, then select the options that best fulfill the policymaker's goals. The *public choice model* thinks of those active in policymaking as actors attempting to choose options that maximize their self-interest. They select policy options that help them realize their interests. *Game models* are a variation of this idea, focused on situations of policy choice with options that cannot be compromised.[8]

Stages of Policy Development

Political scientists often use a model of the policymaking process that focuses on the "stages" through which ideas and proposals move before becoming public policy. Some political scientists criticize these models as overly rigid and rational. That is, they argue that *politics* does not follow the clear lines and divisions of the stages model. Moreover, these models have not generated important theoretical insights into policymaking.[9] Despite the importance of these criticisms, the stages model is a good *heuristic* or suggestive tool; that is, it isolates various aspects of public policy and allows focusing attention on them. Certain of these aspects are widely recognized and need to be part of any introduction to public policy.[10] Different scholars label the stages differently and place different emphases on them, but the following terms are common (see Figure 1-1).

The development of a public policy begins with the public recognition that a problem exists. The three *prepolicy stages* are (1) problem definition or issues formation, (2) policy demands, and (3) agenda formation.

Before a policy issue is defined or adopted, a problem of public concern must be perceived. Ethical and ideological perspectives play an important role during this problem perception stage because different perspectives will "see" and define problems differently. For example, imagine how the same social phenomenon, the pornography industry, might be viewed by people of differing moral values. Some might view sexually explicit literature as a manifestation of a socially open and healthy attitude toward sexuality. Others might see it as a symptom of an unhealthy obsession with sex and a rejection of higher values. Due to the contrasting opinions of the two groups, different formulations of the issue will result. Thus, the issues formation stage leads to the next stage, policy demands: Now opposing demands are made for government action. For example, some people want the smut shops closed down and the owners thrown in jail. Others want the authorities to keep out of what they see as the private business of individual citizens (a

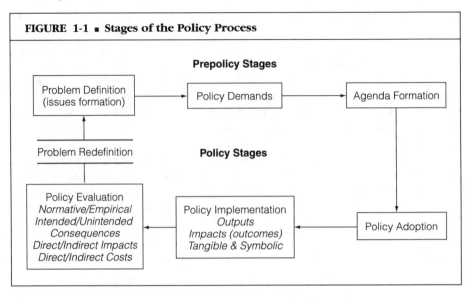

FIGURE 1-1 ■ Stages of the Policy Process

Prepolicy Stages

Problem Definition (issues formation) → Policy Demands → Agenda Formation

Problem Redefinition

Policy Stages

Policy Evaluation
*Normative/Empirical
Intended/Unintended
Consequences
Direct/Indirect Impacts
Direct/Indirect Costs*

Policy Implementation
*Outputs
Impacts (outcomes)
Tangible & Symbolic*

Policy Adoption

demand for government non-action). Gradually, this social give-and-take coalesces into a perception that policymakers must deal with this problem, and it competes with other problems for the attention of policymakers. Some problems fail to sustain attention in this competition; others rise to prominence. That is, some make it and some fail to make it onto the policy agenda. The various demands and perspectives create an agenda of alternative proposals for dealing with the issue. Some proposals and demands never make it to the agenda; others are put on the agenda in altered form.

Agenda-setting is always a political process; that is, groups struggle for power to control the agenda. Because all legislative and executive bodies are limited in the issues they can address at any given time, the power to have attention paid to "your" issue on the agenda is invaluable. Therefore, ideological and interest groups compete to broaden the agenda to include their issues or to narrow it by excluding issues that they do not want considered. Such groups may be elected officials, bureaucrats responsible for policy administration, public interest groups, or groups directly affected by particular policies. Pluralist, elite, issue-attention, and other political science theories attempt to explain the development of policy agendas. The following chapters call attention to groups active in the problem definition, policy demand, and agenda formation stages.

Following the prepolicy stages, the next major stage in the development of a public policy is deliberation and *policy adoption*. From the policy agenda, decision makers, with the input of interest groups, policy experts, and constituents, debate and bargain over alternative policy formulations, settling on an alternative or a combination of alternatives to respond to the problem. Decisions are made; policies are formulated; and policy statements are issued, taking such forms as orders, regulations, or laws. Clearly, the same kinds of considerations of power as in the policy agenda stage are relevant here. Also important is the constitutional and statutory structure of the institution making the policy decisions. Structure often determines which outcomes have a greater chance of success in the political struggle.

Policy statements and lawmaking are not the whole of policymaking. If they were, policy analysis would be easy. Rather, policy decisions must be implemented—that is, steps must be taken to put the policy statement into practice in order to achieve the policymaker's goals. *Policy implementation* means money spent, laws enforced, employees hired, and plans of action formulated. A law against theft would hardly be a policy if no public resources were devoted to preventing thefts and apprehending thieves. In implementation, "there's many a slip twixt cup and lip." Even programs involving little conflict can be difficult to implement if there are numerous participants with differing perspectives and if many particular decisions have to be made before the policy is fully implemented.[11] The more complex the implementation process, the more likely that the intent of the policy becomes distorted or lost. Successful achievement of the purposes of a public policy depend upon the "tractability" of the problem being addressed by the policy; that is, how possible it is to really make change. Implementation depends as well upon the clarity of the law, the talents and financial resources available to those administering it, and a variety of "political" factors, such as public support, media attention, socioeconomic conditions, and the attitudes and resources of groups affected by the policy.[12]

Policy implementation includes outputs and impacts. *Policy outputs* are the tangible manifestations of policies, the observable and measurable results of policy adoption and implementation. Stated another way, outputs are what governments in fact do in a particular policy area: The policy outputs of the food stamp program, for example, include money spent, stamps printed, poor persons served, employees hired, and regulations issued. All of these are tangible. Outputs may also be symbolic: Public statements of encouragement and hope are symbolic outputs of the government's response to the 9/11 terrorist attacks. Exercising defense policy includes making threats, posturing, and issuing conciliatory statements. Just as policy analysts can observe and measure money spent and employees hired, they can also record, classify, and count symbolic outputs, though doing so is more difficult.

Policy impacts (sometimes called outcomes) are the effects that policy outputs have on society. They are the policy's consequences in terms of the policy's stated goals as well as of the society's fundamental beliefs. For the food stamp program, major impacts would naturally include changes in recipients' diets. The impact of a defense policy includes military strength vis-à-vis other nations and some measure of national security, as well as various economic effects of defense spending. Evaluating a policy's impact requires taking into account its effects on the entire society, not only the target group toward which it is directed. Moreover, impacts include the policy's unintended as well as its intended consequences (see Aspects of Policy Evaluation).

Policy impact is a major component of an important focus of this text, the evaluation of public policy. *Policy evaluation* focuses principally on the impact of policy, because it is largely from the performance and consequences of policy that we assess its success or failure. Policy can be debated, problems defined, agendas built, and programs adopted and implemented; but what difference does all of this mean for improving the life of society as a whole or of its particular parts? This is the question of impact. Evaluation attempts to assess the outcomes of policies—their effects on society—in order to compare them with the policies' intended goals. It asks whether the goals have or have not been met, with what costs, and with what unintended consequences. It considers whether policy is equitable and efficient and whether it has satisfied the interests demanding action. For example, policy evaluation asks whether the welfare reforms legislated in 1996 did in fact reduce poverty, increase work, or improve the lives of the poor. Policy evaluation of antipoverty programs necessarily involves ideas about justice, the value of work, and the place of poverty in an affluent society. Thus, a policy can be evaluated only after it has been implemented. Moreover, evaluation leads back to issue formation and policy deliberation in a (nearly) endless loop. Evaluations of policy inevitably produce advocates for change and other advocates for maintaining the policy. The social problems that stimulate policy responses seldom can be completely fixed. "Policy is more like an endless game of Monopoly than a bicycle repair."[13]

Policies do not go on forever (though some appear to). Policies change over time; for example, Chapter 7 describes how welfare policy has changed in fundamental ways over the last half century. Policies also sometimes are terminated. Their reason for being passes, and legislatures end them. The processes involved in changing and terminating policies are the same as those involved in policymaking: problem definition, agenda setting, adoption, and evaluation.

Aspects of Policy Evaluation

Evaluating policy has both normative and empirical dimensions. The *normative dimension* refers to values, beliefs, and attitudes of society as a whole, of particular groups and individuals in society, and of the policy evaluators themselves. Persons of different values and ideologies use different normative concepts to evaluate policy. Evaluation, therefore, is always *political.* Liberals, conservatives, socialists, feminists, and anarchists differ fundamentally in their understanding of such concepts and in their ranking of them. Conservatives, for example, believe that free competition and protection of private property are the fundamental values to be pursued by economic policy. Socialists, however, see a just distribution of the social product as the principal value. Different policy evaluators and different political groups, then, will evaluate public policy differently. Normative perspectives come into play, not only in assessing the goals of policy, but also in analyzing how well policy accomplishes the desired goals.

Normative evaluation, however, is not enough. The *empirical dimension*— that is, understanding the facts—must precede judgment. Before praising or damning the Supreme Court's freedom-of-the-press decisions, one must examine the actual decisions and attempt to assess what difference, if any, they have made or are likely to make in the day-to-day operations of the press. And before criticizing "welfare fraud," one should obtain the most accurate statistics available on money lost through fraudulent claims. Policy evaluation without empirical analysis of policy content, output, and impact is like voting for a baseball all-star team without information on players' batting, earned-run, or fielding averages.

In evaluating a public policy, we distinguish between its intended and unintended consequences. *Intended consequences* are the stated goals of policy— that is, the effects that the policymakers want for the policy. Policy evaluation asks: How well have these goals been met? For example, the Federal Housing Administration (FHA) mortgage loan guarantee program intends to increase private home ownership. The intended goal has been substantially accomplished. The percentage of owner-occupied homes in America is the highest in the world. But policies also have *unintended consequences*, those not intended or foreseen by policymakers. FHA loans, more readily available for new homes, also encourage middle-class movement to the suburbs, unintentionally contributing to clogged highways and more spending on roads.

Moreover, policy evaluation distinguishes direct policy impact from indirect impact. The consequences of policy, both intended and unintended, on the policy's target population are its *direct impact*. The target population is the group of persons or institutions that the policy is principally designed to affect. For example, in the interstate highway construction program, the target population is the trucking industry and automobile drivers. Public policies, however, often have *indirect impacts* on third parties, which are referred to as spillover effects or externalities. The construction of good roads contributed to the decline of the passenger train and, to a lesser extent, of railroad freight business. Such spillovers are the indirect impact of the policy. Whether for good or ill, they can be substantial.

In a similar way, policy evaluation also involves what are known as direct and indirect costs. A policy's *direct costs* are the expenditures of time, energy, power, and money in the policy area itself. *Indirect costs* are no different except that they are incurred in areas indirectly affected by the policy—including the lost opportunities to do other things with the resources devoted to the policy in question. Spillover effects involve indirect costs.

Short-term and *long-term effects* must also be distinguished by policy evaluation. Policies cannot be fairly evaluated until their long-term effects can be reasonably assessed. It may take decades, for example, before the full effect of America's response to the terrorist attacks of September 11, 2001, can be known.

Finally, policy evaluation must assess both *symbolic* and *tangible impacts*, just as it must do with outputs. Many policies have as important a symbolic effect as they do a material one. This may be intended or unintended. The Vietnam War, for example, generated cynicism about many time-honored American beliefs, such as respect for the flag, America as a world peacekeeper, and the concept of national honor, all unintended (and negative) symbolic impacts. Public response to the September 11, 2001, attacks helped to restore many citizens' confidence in American abilities and dedication to such symbols as the flag.

Policy evaluation, then, is clearly a complex matter, requiring diverse skills, insights, and information. This book cannot even begin to make a complete evaluation of each of the policies and issues it covers. It does, however, describe the most important policies in each area, offer data on their most significant outputs and impacts, suggest the contending evaluation perspectives on each of the issues, and summarize the policy alternatives currently under discussion.

THE CONTEXTS OF CONTEMPORARY PUBLIC POLICY

The debate and shaping of public policy take place, of course, within the general social, political, and economic environment of the American nation. But they take place as well within contexts specific to each policy area. These specialized influences will be outlined in the substantive chapters, but it is important here to discuss some general factors that will influence policy in a variety of issue areas at the turn of the twenty-first century.

The Institutional Context

Obviously the unique features of the American political system, its basic structures—federalism, the party system, the power of the presidency, and the system of checks and balances—will continue to shape policy as they always have. Policy in the area of civil rights, for example, will continue to be shaped substantially by the federal courts because of the constitutional system of government and the courts' power of judicial review. The federal system will make national education policy difficult to formulate because education is primarily a responsibility of state governments. Indeed, the 1980s and 1990s saw the growth of state and local policy initiative as the federal government contracted its policy activity.

In addition to these lasting features of the American political system, however, a serious distrust of institutions, particularly political ones, surfaced in the last thirty years. This is not the simple distrust of government that is a constant in American history, but a deep cynicism and anger about government, politics, and politicians, even to the point of violence (most shockingly in the Oklahoma City Federal Building bombing in April, 1995). The statistics illustrate the American public's lackluster response to the political process: The percentage of the eligible population voting in presidential and congressional elections declined substantially after 1960, with only about half of voting-age Americans now voting for president, only one-third for Congress in nonpresidential years, and far fewer voting for state and local offices. Polls on confidence in leadership reveal substantial declines in the trust the public holds for leadership in all areas of life. The popularity of term limitations for elected officials and the popularity of politician-bashing on talk radio testify to the distrust of politics and politicians generally.

We need not go far to seek the sources for the decline in the trust of government.[14] The Vietnam War, the protests and social divisions it spawned, and its tragic impact on many veterans put American foreign policy leadership under a cloud from which it has only partially emerged. Findings of corruption and illegality at the highest levels of government have fed distrust. Such revelations have included the Watergate conspiracy during the Nixon administration, criminal investigations of major Reagan administration officials, and the revelation of corruption at the highest levels of the CIA and FBI in the Aldrich Ames and Robert Hanssen cases in the mid-1990s. "Monicagate" and the impeachment trial of President Clinton kept the scandal pot at the boiling point in the 1990s. Discovery of corruption and lawlessness in politics is nothing new, but the disclosures of the 1970s, 1980s, and 1990s were so serious and widespread, and occurred in such rapid sequence, that public trust in the ability and willingness of public officials to produce policy in the public interest has eroded.

At the same time that public distrust has grown, the presence of the federal government in economic, cultural, and social life has expanded as a product of modernization and technology. Federal regulations and federal spending increase each year. Suspicion that such growth is inevitable no matter which party is in power, that neither party has an interest in halting it, and that such growth produces no noticeable and dramatic improvement in the quality of life contributes to distrust in government. It also contributes to substantial resistance to new policy initiatives in health, education, and consumer protection, to cite only a few cases. High levels of distrust helped to defeat health care reform in 1994. Suspicion is growing among the public that the national government has been captured by corporate and other interest groups who use it for private benefit rather than for public good. In the technocratic age, leadership, responsibility, and accountability seem divorced from ordinary citizens. At the same time, as Americans (especially younger persons) become more cynical, they become less interested in and less informed about politics and policy.[15] Currently, there is much speculation about whether the antiterrorist campaign and revived patriotic fever will check the spread of government distrust and restore some measure of legitimacy to an active federal government.

The Economic Context

The 1980s added a new specter to the usual worries about unemployment, recession, and inflation—an enormous federal budget deficit that grew more rapidly during the Reagan presidency than at any time in history (see Chapter 4). Programs in many different policy areas, such as arts funding and health care reform, became hostage to the budget debate. The economy grew steadily in the 1990s, but wages stagnated for families in the middle and bottom of the distribution, and Americans had to work harder to keep pace. The economy turned down again, entering recession in 2001. Budget deficits were eliminated at the end of the 1990s, but returned again in the early 2000s. Corporate downsizing and the growth of temporary and part-time employment are simply the most dramatic symptoms of a rapidly changing economy. Economic uncertainties shape new policy initiatives and cause the reevaluation of old ones.

Confidence has waned that the economic pie is indefinitely expanding, and the question of how to manage scarce resources and to distribute them fairly occurs more frequently. The changing family income structure illustrates this concern. Median family income in inflation-adjusted terms, which increased steadily from the 1950s through the early 1970s, did not grow substantially in the 1980s or 1990s. The need to absorb millions of new workers, the decline in family size, trends in divorce, and the movement toward two-wage earner families all produced an economic squeeze on the lower and middle classes. Inflation-adjusted income declined for much of the 1980s and 1990s for the poorest 40 percent of families and expanded only modestly for the middle 40 percent, while growing substantially for the richest 20 percent. Young males and single females, young families, and older blue-collar workers face a highly uncertain economic future.

Later chapters more fully discuss these matters, especially economic policy (Chapters 3 and 4) and income maintenance (Chapter 7), but it is important to recognize here that these economic trends have an impact well beyond strictly economic issues. Major spending programs in education, income maintenance, and health, for example, have difficulty being enacted. Racial tensions also increase during hard economic times.

The Demographic Context

The generational, racial, and residential characteristics of a nation's population change constantly, reflecting new trends in birthrates, life expectancy, job opportunities, and migration patterns. Some of these trends directly affect policymaking.

The children born during the baby boom after World War II are nearing their sixties. The proportion of the population under twenty-five, which rose until the mid-1970s, declined until the mid-1990s, when it leveled off briefly. Such changes in the number of young people not only seriously affect education policy, but other areas as well. For example, persons between the ages of fourteen and twenty-five commit a highly disproportionate number of violent crimes (see Chapter 6). Economic policy will also be affected as increasing numbers of men and women in their thirties and forties compete for prestigious positions. Economic performance from 1960 to 1985 was substantially affected by the need to absorb millions of new, young workers.[16]

The proportion of the population sixty-five and older, now about 12 percent, is increasing at twice the national population rate and is likely to be 20 percent by 2030 (see Figure 1-2). The proportion of persons over eighty-five will reach 5 percent by 2050. Because only a small proportion of persons in this age group work full-time and because their health care requirements exceed those of the rest of the population, pressure on the Social Security system and on health care policy will be intense. Moreover, because the life expectancy for women is significantly higher than for men, many of those over sixty-five are widowed women, living alone or in some kind of institution, such as a nursing home or apartment complex for the elderly. It is possible that the working population will come to resent supporting such a large number of retired persons. However, because the elderly vote more regularly than the young do, the aged themselves have become a large and powerful political force for the protection of their own interests.

Immigration continues to change the shape of the American population and present challenges to both federal and local policy. The decade of the 1980s saw legal immigration approach the record of 9 million persons set in the decade from 1901 to 1910. Immigration accounted for one-third of U.S. population growth in the last two decades. These immigrants, primarily of Asian and Hispanic descent, present both opportunities for dynamic expansion of the economy and challenges for services in housing, schools, jobs, and health care. Moreover, the impact of immigration is not spread evenly across the country. About 70 percent of the new residents settle in Texas, California, Florida, New York, Illinois, and New Jersey, placing a critical assimilative burden on these states (see Chapter 11).

Public policy in a number of areas will also have to respond to changes in the racial mix of the population. Non-Hispanic whites made up 90 percent of the population in 1955. By the turn of the century the proportion had declined to 71 percent. Because of illegal immigration and the younger average age of the Spanish-surname population, the Hispanic proportion of the population nearly equals that of the African-American population. By 2000, Hispanic Americans accounted for 12 percent of the population; they comprised 6 percent in 1980. By the middle of the twenty-first century, one-quarter of Americans will be of Hispanic background (see Figure 1-3). Though they share many problems with African Americans, poverty and racism being the most important, Hispanics also bring with them a different language and culture. Historically, combinations of simultaneous racial change and economic

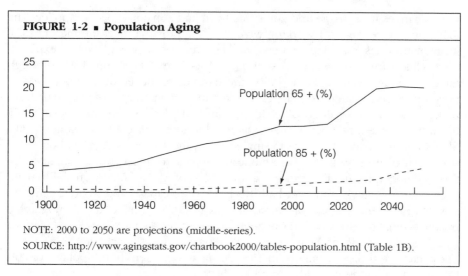

FIGURE 1-2 ▪ Population Aging

NOTE: 2000 to 2050 are projections (middle-series).

SOURCE: http://www.agingstats.gov/chartbook2000/tables-population.html (Table 1B).

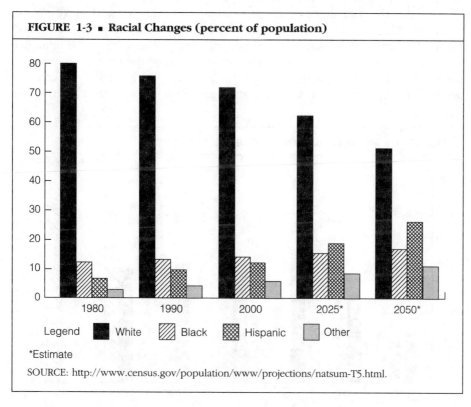

FIGURE 1-3 ▪ Racial Changes (percent of population)

Legend: White   Black   Hispanic   Other

*Estimate

SOURCE: http://www.census.gov/population/www/projections/natsum-T5.html.

uncertainty have been volatile. The passage of anti-immigration California Proposition 187 in 1994, as well as the polarization of voters (young and white male voters moving increasingly to the Republican Party, with older and African-American voters staying Democratic), were symptoms of this kind of volatility, as was the passage of federal immigration reform policy in 1996.

Changes in marriage and family life have had a major impact on policy. The increasing percentages of working wives, the high divorce rate, the high rates of illegitimate births, and single-parent families affect labor policy, welfare expenditures, child care, schools, and sexual equality policies (see Figure 1-4). Although the divorce rate declined in the 1990s, these trends produced the "feminization of poverty," closely linking women's issues with income maintenance and health care policies. Nearly 50 percent of all children born in the late 1970s experienced family breakup at some time prior to their sixteenth birthday. Currently, over one-quarter of children under eighteen live in single-parent, mostly female-headed homes for some part of each year. African-American families are most strongly affected by these demographic trends. Today over two-thirds of African-American children are born out of wedlock, and over half live in female-headed, single-parent families. Poverty, race, and changes in family life create an economic and demographic prison, a situation discussed in Chapter 7. Policy must also focus on child care for working parents and on health care and income support for children in poverty. These facts, and disagreements about their meaning, intensify the politics of culture and morality described later and in Chapter 13.

Finally, the declining population of such large urban centers as New York, Baltimore, Chicago, and Cleveland and the rising population of suburban, and small urban areas, especially in the South and Southwest, continues to influence a broad range of policies. Controversies rage over how the federal government should allocate its grant-in-aid money for urban rehabilitation, jobs, housing, education, unemployment assistance, water and sewer projects, and many other

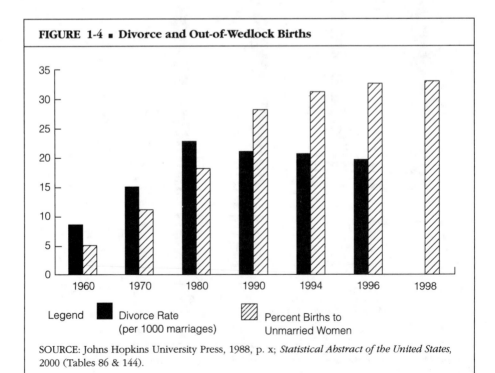

FIGURE 1-4 ▪ Divorce and Out-of-Wedlock Births

Legend ▪ Divorce Rate (per 1000 marriages)   ▨ Percent Births to Unmarried Women

SOURCE: Johns Hopkins University Press, 1988, p. x; *Statistical Abstract of the United States,* 2000 (Tables 86 & 144).

needs. Between 1980 and 2000, the North and Northeast lost, and the South and West gained, 40 congressional seats or nearly one-tenth of Congress.

The Ideological Context

Public policy is a field of debate over the meaning of basic values and principles. The definition of policy problems, according to political scientist Deborah Stone, is fundamentally about the conceptual and symbolic terms that we use to describe the problem. The numbers, symbols, and discussions of causality in the following chapters all appear in the context of ideological debate over their meaning and significance. Conservatives, feminists, liberals, and socialists fight over the very goals of public policy, such as equity, efficiency, security, and liberty.[17]

Perspectives on American public policy have always ranged along a broad spectrum of ideological beliefs—including extreme positions at either end, such as communists on the Left and militia groups on the Right. Historically, however, *conservatism* and *liberalism* have dominated policymaking and evaluation in America. The majority of Americans, including policymakers, are some variety of liberal or conservative, despite small and periodically powerful numbers of adherents to other ideologies. Although liberals and conservatives in America share a great many commitments to abstract ideals, such as freedom, democracy, the market system, and individualism, they also disagree on the principles to be used in making and evaluating policy. First, they disagree over the meaning of freedom and its limits: Conservatives tend to value civil and personal freedoms less and are more willing to limit them. They often favor censorship of sexually explicit materials, for example. Liberals are more ready to limit economic freedom, for example, by placing restrictions on advertisers. Liberals have a deeper commitment to equality than do conservatives. Conservatives are committed to tradition and authority, which is balanced by the liberals' commitment to change and individual choice in moral and social behavior. Liberals tend to have faith in the power of political action to make the world better; conservatives have a more pessimistic attitude toward the potential of politics. These disagreements affect policy debates in all areas, because the role of government itself and the extent to which market forces may be relied on for economic and social health are central issues today.

Traditional conservatism and liberalism have fragmented in recent years, with new ideological viewpoints surfacing from the two mainstream movements. *Neoconservatives* and the *New Right* have competed for influence within the Republican Party. In domestic policy, neoconservatives are critical of the government's regulation of business enterprise, and they are suspicious of government action to correct past injustices, such as affirmative action, when there is basic disagreement about the goals of such policies. They are not, however, as opposed to government economic action as traditional conservatives or libertarians, who also form part of the Right end of the ideological spectrum. The New Right, however, directs most of its attention to social issues. They oppose abortion, the extension of civil rights to homosexuals, feminism, pornography, and what they see as government interference in religious expression. Included in the New Right are the evangelical religious groups, such as the Christian Coalition, that became a prominent part of electoral politics in the early 1980s.

Movements on the Left of the spectrum are harder to define and classify, as they are more fragmented and less prominent than the Right in recent decades. *Communists* and *socialists* stress fundamental change in the social and economic system, government control of the basic means of production, and equal distribution of most income. Such groups have lost virtually all influence in American politics. Other groups on the Left that take a predominantly economic approach to policy stress democratic control of the means of production through worker self-management and local, direct democracy.

As the term "liberal" declines in popularity, many on the Left take the mantle of "progressive." Other groups often classified on the Left focus on social or environmental issues. Moreover, they contain within themselves more and less extreme varieties. The less extreme ones make up an important part of contemporary liberalism and of the Democratic Party politically. These are groups defined by feminism, environmental protection, or gay liberation. In these movements, public policy is viewed primarily through a particular lens. *Feminists* evaluate policy according to its impact on the role of women in society. "Liberal" feminists strive to make sure that men and women are treated equally and that women have the opportunity to achieve success in all areas of political, economic, and social life. More "radical" variants of feminism seek to challenge the traditional structures of society. Similarly, more liberal elements of the *gay and lesbian community* seek to integrate homosexual persons into the fabric of society by guaranteeing the same rights and responsibilities (job access and military service, for example) as heterosexuals. Some gay liberationists, however, wish to weave a very different fabric of society, by challenging, for example, the definition of marriage and sexuality. These splits within newer ideological movements and their uneasy relationship with more traditional liberals have made the Left and the Democratic Party highly fractious in recent decades.

Still other groups are more difficult to classify. Although *environmentalists* are most often counted as part of the liberal coalition, there are many traditional conservatives who value and participate in environmental groups that stress the conservation of natural resources and respect for the physical environment. This fact gives some environmental policy issues broad political support. *Libertarians* combine a conservative economic agenda with a liberal social agenda. Although usually classified on the Right, libertarians support abortion rights, oppose restrictions on sexually explicit speech, and favor keeping government out of the bedroom as well as out of the boardroom. Many college-educated young persons take a libertarian approach to public policy.

In the last few years, a movement known as "*communitarianism*" received national attention. Prominent communitarians, such as political scientist William Galston, have held important positions in the Clinton and Bush administrations. Communitarians focus on the interconnection between rights and responsibilities. Their policy attention concentrates on revitalizing local neighborhood and city institutions, on community policing, family restoration, character formation, and education reform.

Issue definition is not a neutral, apolitical process. The ideological perspectives just described affect the appearance of issues on the policy agenda. The definition of a policy problem is always a matter for disagreement among people of competing beliefs and principles. Poverty, for example, was not seen as a problem to be solved until the 1930s. Before that, it was held to be an inevitable social condition. Conservatives still tend to view it, at least partially, in this way. Radicals, however, view poverty as a requirement of capitalist society; from this standpoint, welfare policy becomes simply a device used by capitalism to maintain itself, not a response to a neutral problem. Even the statistics used to illustrate the dimensions of an issue will frequently vary depending on the perspective from which the issue is being defined. For example, as we shall see in Chapter 7, liberals and conservatives cite the same poverty statistics, but draw opposite conclusions from them. Care must be exercised in using and interpreting statistics—even those presented in this book!

We can expect that this decade will witness continued American preference for divided government, evidenced by the closeness and controversy over the 2000 presidential election. Voters suspect both Democrats and Republicans, and they do not trust most interest and ideological groups. Many citizens certainly *perceive* a failure in domestic policy programs, and this perception supports conservative politics. Yet, at the same time, Americans value the benefits that government programs bring them, their cities, and their employers. This commitment points toward more liberal policies. Moreover, as the previous examples illustrate, ideology is very much involved in the cultural changes sweeping American society. The meaning of our connections with each other, the definition of the family and its responsibilities, and the value and forms of sexual expression all create considerable turmoil within and among ideological groups, making it hard to achieve policy consensus.

The Cultural Context

During the 1980s, it became increasingly clear that many policy issues were caught up, not only in passionate ideological disputes, but also in a cultural conflict of increasing dimensions. Culture refers to the patterns of fundamental beliefs, principles, traditions, and social assumptions that characterize a society. There is frequently a dominant culture and one or more subcultures. During the last decade, political conflict challenged which fundamental values were to dominate American life.

The demographic changes previously discussed, particularly those affecting the family, directly affect culture. As family life changes, other parts of culture come into question. The family is one of the primary ways of passing on moral understandings, but clearly standards of morality with respect to sexuality, competition, money, material goods, and work, to name just a few, are hotly debated today.

Ideology is inextricably bound to attitudes toward culture. Among many, especially conservatives, there is a perception that something is wrong with the fabric of national life, starting with the family, but also reflected in crime, economic noncompetitiveness, and political and social corruption and greed. Communitarians also articulate these themes. According to conservatives, television and movies portray and advocate ways of life at odds with traditional American values. Abortion, pornography, and sexual promiscuity find prominent champions. Public schools do not permit prayer, and the educational system fails hundreds of thousands of young people. The role of women in the workplace and in public life also raises questions about the meaning of traditional cultural values, as does the recognition and acceptance of homosexual behavior.

Liberals, no less than conservatives, recognize fundamental changes in gender, sexual, and cultural roles of all kinds. Rather than fearing these changes, liberals tend to accept most. They support legislation protecting the right to abortion. They want fundamental political, social, and economic rights available to all persons, regardless of gender or sexual orientation. To the extent that traditional family life oppresses women and children, liberals accept necessary change in family structures.[18]

Cultural conflict thus runs through many of the policy issues that appear in the following chapters. Chapter 13 directly addresses this conflict. Cultural issues were significant in each of the presidential elections of the last two decades.

APPROACHES TAKEN BY THIS BOOK

This text covers areas that are of permanent major interest and controversy. Though other issues—for example, the use of silicone in breast implants—occasionally rise to prominence, the issues we discuss—welfare, health, education, economic regulation—are issues of long-range interest and controversy.

Chapter Plan

The chapters that follow present the major policy issues in American politics. Each chapter (except 13 and 14) follows a similar pattern. This pattern assumes that students need to know the history of policies and the most fundamental facts about them before evaluation is possible. Also vital is understanding of the ways the policies work (or don't work). It is then possible to speculate intelligently about possible modifications that the future will present.

Issue background.   Each chapter discusses the basic issue, problem, or dilemma toward which public policy is directed; that is, the general background. Policies do not arise in a vacuum, as we have already noted, but, rather, grow in response to developments that the public, or some part of it, perceives as requiring government action.

Contemporary policy.   Each chapter describes the evolution of present public policies in their areas of concern. They sketch in some detail the major features of substantive public policies, as adopted and implemented. The principal goals and target populations intended by the policymakers are also outlined. Although absolute neutrality and objectivity are impossible, we have tried to be as unbiased as possible.

Policy evaluation.   The third section of each chapter evaluates policy outputs and impacts empirically and normatively. Here our concern centers on the major successes and failures of policy in responding to the dilemmas specified. Our focus is on the ability of existing policies to reach their goals and to have the maximum beneficial effect, and we discuss the main differences of opinion on the good and bad effects of the policies.

Future alternatives.   Each chapter lists the major policy alternatives and their supporting arguments as specifically as possible. Here again, we present different values, different definitions of the issue, and different predictions for policy options. The authors do not put forth their own proposals but, rather, attempt to help the reader make sense of the welter of policy proposals, statistics, and competing values. The arguments of conservatives, radicals, and liberals, as well as a variety of interested parties, find their way into the following pages in order to illustrate the range of alternatives from which policy selections may be made.

Finally, each chapter ends with a summary of its major points, as well as a list of books and web sites to assist in study and reflection.

National Focus

Although the chapters on education and intergovernmental relations discuss state and local government activity extensively, our attention will be on the national arena, for the issues at stake on the state and local level, given the tremendous variation in their social, political, and economic climates, are less clear and less easily presented than those at the national level. Therefore, although state and local policies are obviously important, here they are discussed as they relate to national policies.

Comparative Information

Many chapters discuss comparable policies in other modern industrial nations. Noting international trends is essential to evaluate U.S. public policy properly.[19] To discuss American health care policies as though they were the only kind possible or practiced would be like discussing American wine as though France and Germany grew no grapes. Moreover, issues of crime, employment, economic stagnation, immigration, social welfare spending, and cultural change have begun to affect other advanced nations in ways similar to those occurring in the American context. Nonetheless, the focus of this book is on *American* public policy.

SUMMARY

Public policy is an intentional course of action followed by a government institution or official for resolving an issue of public concern. Policy is manifested in laws, public statements, and official regulations and in widely accepted and visible patterns of behavior. A course of action is understood to include the intentional choice *not* to take an action.

Public policy is studied for theoretical, practical, and political reasons. The emphasis of this book is on the second and third reasons, helping the reader to understand and respond to contemporary policy issues—that is, to become a better citizen and analyst of policy debates.

Classifying policies allows the testing of which features of policy have the most influence on the politics of the policy process. Three common classifications employ purposes (security, membership, needs, and prosperity), types (distributive, regulatory, self-regulatory, and redistributive), and goods (public or private).

Political scientists use a variety of models to explain how and why policies are made. Models such as the *institutional, elite, pluralist, interest group, rational, public choice,* and *game* are prominent.

Political scientists describe the development of a public policy as having a number of distinct stages. The prepolicy stages are issue formation (some sector of the public recognizes that an issue or problem exists), policy demands (people of differing ideological perspectives make demands for action—or nonaction—based on their divergent understanding of the issue), and agenda formation (government assimilates and legitimizes various conflicting demands and creates an agenda of alternative proposals for dealing with the issue). The next stages are deliberation and policy adoption (decision makers select a policy from the agenda and commit themselves publicly to that course) and policy implementation (concrete steps are taken to achieve the policymakers' goals).

Policy evaluation is concerned with assessing the success and failure of policy, especially by examining the policy's impact. We evaluate policy from two perspectives: normative dimensions, which comprise principles, beliefs, and attitudes; and empirical dimensions, which comprise the observation of the history and facts surrounding any given policy. Policy evaluation draws further distinctions based on whether a particular policy effect falls inside or outside its stated policy goals and target population (intended and unintended consequences, direct and indirect impact, direct and indirect cost), based on time (short-term and long-term effect) and the abstract as opposed to the concrete returns of a policy (symbolic and tangible impacts). Sometimes evaluation produces policy change or policy termination.

Various contexts influence each of the policy areas outlined in this book. These form the environment in which each policy area operates. Many of these influences change constantly, but there are five "policy contexts" that will remain more or less constant into the next century.

1. Distrust of American political and social institutions as a result of the Vietnam War, political scandals, and doubt about the performance of large national government may continue to dominate the institutional context of public policy, unless renewed post-September 11, 2001, patriotism produces greater government legitimacy.
2. Uncertainty will dominate the economic context. Employment instability, tight government budgets, trade imbalances, and an uncertain world economy influence economic policy as well as initiatives in other policy areas.
3. Public policy will be influenced by dramatic changes in the distribution of various age groups in the U.S. population: There is a lower proportion of young people and an increasing number of persons over sixty-five after 2000. The demographic context will also see dramatic growth in the proportion of racial and ethnic minorities and a movement of population from the large urban centers of the North and East to the sun belt of the South and Southwest. Changes in family life also strongly influence policy.
4. Policymaking will be affected by the changing balance of ideological forces in the future. The ideological context of the next decade will be fragmented and contentious.
5. Cultural conflict, focused on different visions of American society, will strongly influence issues of crime, education, social welfare, equality, and the meaning of fundamental freedoms.

Each issue area employs a similar, four-part format: (1) general background, (2) existing policies, (3) successes and failures, and (4) principal policy alternatives. Although the book focuses on national themes of public policy, most chapters compare American policy with the policies of other developed industrial nations. This is essential to gaining a better perspective on what otherwise might seem to be uniquely American problems.

NOTES

1. James E. Anderson, *Public Policymaking: An Introduction*, 2nd ed. (Boston: Houghton Mifflin, 1994), 4–8.
2. For example, Kim Quaille Hill, "In Search of Policy Theory," *Policy Currents*, 7 (April 1997): 1–9.
3. For a variety of such models, see Thomas R. Dye, *Understanding Public Policy*, 10th ed. (Upper Saddle River, NJ: Prentice-Hall, 2002), especially Chapter 2.
4. Lawrence M. Mead, "Public Policy: Vision, Potential, Limits," *Policy Currents*, 5 (February 1995): 1–4.
5. Duncan MacRae, Jr. and James A. Wilde, *Policy Analysis for Public Decisions* (North Scituate, MA: Duxbury Press, 1979), 4.
6. See Robert A. Heineman, et al., *The World of the Policy Analyst: Rationality, Values, and Politics* (Chatham, NJ: Chatham House, 1990); Deborah Stone, *Policy Paradox: The Art of Political Decision Making*, revised ed. (New York: Norton, 2002); and Henry J. Aaron, et al., eds., *Values and Public Policy* (Washington, DC: Brookings Institution, 1994).
7. This classification originated in Theodore J. Lowi, "American Business, Public Policy Case Studies, and Political Theory," *World Politics*, 16 (July 1964): 677–715. Many have adopted, adapted, and debated the original formulation. The discussion in the text draws upon Anderson, *Public Policymaking*, 11–18.
8. For a convenient summary of models and their development, see James P. Lester and Joseph Stewart, Jr., *Public Policy: An Evolutionary Approach*, 2nd ed. (Belmont, CA: Wadsworth, 2000), Chapters 4–9.
9. See Stone, *Policy Paradox*, especially pp. 5–14; and Paul A. Sabatier, "Toward Better Theories of the Policy Process," *PS: Political Science and Politics*, 24 (June 1991): 147–156.
10. More detailed discussion of these stages can be found in Anderson, *Public Policymaking*. See also Charles L. Cochran and Eloise F. Malone, *Public Policy: Perspectives and Choices* (New York: McGraw-Hill, 1995), 38–57.
11. See the pioneering study by Jeffrey L. Pressman and Aaron Wildavsky, *Implementation*, 3rd ed. (Berkeley and Los Angeles: University of California Press, 1984).
12. Paul A. Sabatier and Daniel Mazmanian, "The Implementation of Public Policy: A Framework for Analysis," in Stella Z. Theodoulou and Matthew A. Cahn, eds., *Public Policy: The Essential Readings* (Englewood Cliffs, NJ: Prentice-Hall, 1995): 153–173.
13. Stone, *Policy Paradox*, 261.
14. E. J. Dionne, Jr., *Why Americans Hate Politics* (New York: Simon & Schuster, 1991).
15. See Richard Morin, "They Only Know What They Don't Like," *Washington Post National Weekly Edition*, October 3–9, 1994, 37; and Richard Morin, "Tuned Out, Turned Off," *Washington Post National Weekly Edition*, February 5–11, 1996, 6–8.
16. John E. Schwarz, *America's Hidden Success: A Reassessment of Public Policy from Kennedy to Reagan*, revised ed. (New York: Norton, 1988), 116ff.
17. Stone, *Policy Paradox*.
18. For a broad discussion of cultural conflict and of the policy issues directly involved, see James Davison Hunter, *Culture Wars: The Struggle to Define America* (New York: Basic Books, 1991); and Raymond Tatalovich and Byron W. Daynes, eds., *Social Regulatory Policy: Moral Controversies in American Politics* (Boulder: Westview Press, 1988).
19. See Richard Rose, *Lesson-Drawing in Public Policy: A Guide to Learning across Time and Space* (Chatham, NJ: Chatham House, 1993); and Arnold J. Heidenheimer, Hugh Heclo, and Carolyn Teich Adams, *Comparative Public Policy*, 3rd ed. (New York: St. Martin's Press, 1990).

SUGGESTED READINGS

Books

Aaron, Henry J., Mann, Thomas E., and Taylor, Timothy, eds. *Values and Public Policy.* Washington DC: Brookings Institution, 1994.

Adolino, Jessica R., and Blake, Charles H. *Comparing Public Policies: Issues and Choices in Six Industrialized Countries.* Washington, DC: CQ Press, 2001.

Anderson, James E. *Public Policymaking: An Introduction,* 2nd ed. Boston: Houghton Mifflin, 1994.

Bardach, Eugene. *A Practical Guide for Policy Analysis: The Eightfold Path to More Effective Problem Solving.* New York: Chatham House, 2000.

Dye, Thomas R. *Understanding Public Policy,* 10th ed. Upper Saddle River, NJ: Prentice-Hall, 2002.

Ellis, Ralph D. *Just Results: Ethical Foundations for Policy Analysis.* Washington, DC: Georgetown University Press, 1998.

McCool, Daniel C. *Public Policy Theories, Models, and Concepts: An Anthology.* Englewood Cliffs, NJ: Prentice-Hall, 1995.

Pressman, Jeffrey L., and Wildavsky, Aaron. *Implementation,* 3rd ed. Berkeley and Los Angeles: University of California Press, 1984.

Robertson, David Brian, and Judd, Dennis R. *The Development of American Public Policy: The Structure of Policy Restraint.* Glenview, IL: Scott, Foresman, 1989.

Stone, Deborah. *Policy Paradox: The Art of Political Decision Making,* revised ed. New York: Norton, 2002.

Theodoulou, Stella Z., and Cahn, Matthew A., eds. *Public Policy: The Essential Readings.* Englewood Cliffs, NJ: Prentice-Hall, 1995.

Web Sites

Fedstats (Government statistics)   www.fedstats.gov/index.html

The New York Times   www.nytimes.com

Project Vote Smart   www.vote-smart.org/

Public Agenda   www.publicagenda.org/

Speakout.com   http://speakout.com

Statistical Abstract of the United States   www.census.gov/prod/www/statistical-abstract-us.html

The Washington Post   www.washingtonpost.com

CHAPTER 2

Intergovernmental Policies: A New Federalism?

The United States' political system is based in part on a separation of responsibilities among different units of government. Those problems that must be addressed by government, however, do not respect jurisdictional boundaries; therefore, intergovernmental actions are common in dealing with modern problems. Intergovernmental relations refer to the relationships among governmental jurisdictions. For our purposes, the term *intergovernmental relations* will mean the relationships between the national government, on one hand, and the states and local governments, on the other. The concept also includes interactions between and among states and local governments.

ISSUE BACKGROUND: THE FEDERAL SYSTEM

The federal system established by the U.S. Constitution ensured that there would be much flexibility in the way that governmental units interacted with one another, and the fact that a federal system was created ensured the need for interactions. As most American government textbooks point out, federalism is a middle ground between a unitary system of government and a confederation. In a unitary system, the central governmental unit controls the system's operation and the distribution of powers. Although the central government may delegate certain powers to local governments, the national level may change those powers or take them away without the consent of the local units. Great Britain is an example of a unitary system.

In a confederation, the local, or constituent, units control the fate of the government. Specifically, the constituent units have the final power to make and enforce laws over their own subjects, a concept called *sovereignty*. In such a system, the other governmental units create the central government. The local units define the powers of the central government. The United Nations is a confederation made up of nations. Our government under the Articles of Confederation was such a system, and the weaknesses of that experiment led to the creation of our federal system. With the dissolution of the Soviet Union, eleven former republics have formed a confederation called the Commonwealth of Independent States.

Issues in a Federal System

In a federal system, numerous issues arise concerning the proper role of the federation's respective units. Because the U.S. Constitution is not always clear on what exactly the division of responsibility should be, the issues become matters of public debate. Because no one office, division, agency, or branch of government has exclusive responsibility for intergovernmental relations, more confusion arises.

The principal issue in intergovernmental policies is what role each level of government should assume. The authors of the Constitution were wary of too strong a central government and cognizant of the problems of one too weak. They felt that it was necessary to have a national government that could reasonably coordinate the actions of the states, but they also wanted to give the states the autonomy to deal with their own concerns. In the evolution of relations among the states and the national government, there have been periods when the states were relatively stronger and periods in which the national government appeared to dominate. Generally, the states were relatively strong from the beginning of the Republic until the 1930s. After the 1930s, the national government assumed greater and greater responsibility until 1980. In 1980, the election of Ronald Reagan as president presaged an effort to reduce the influence of the national government, an effort that continues to this day.

The form of these intergovernmental interactions is also an issue. Should governmental units work together on common problems? Should the national government deal through the states to work with local units of government? Questions also arise as to whether the national government should only help other levels of government deal with their problems or whether it should also implement programs at the state and local levels.

Yet another concern is who should control program implementation. If the national government's money is used in programs, it is not surprising that the national government wants some control over how the money is spent. Without such control, the national government would take the blame for raising tax revenue but would have no say in how it is spent. Those responsible for raising money are not usually willing to give up that say. However, state and local officials wish to retain as much discretion as possible and do not want to be told by federal bureaucrats how to conduct their business, because they believe they can better address their own differing needs and situations.

Red tape is always an issue when intergovernmental relations are discussed. The controls and duplication of effort that often accompany programs developed at the national level but administered at state and local levels occasion much debate. Efficiency is thus an issue. Opponents of the national government efforts usually argue that state and local governments can deliver needed programs more efficiently on their own. However, many programs may be developed on the national level that would not get off the ground on the lower levels, programs that require tremendous capital and other resources available only to the national government or that require consistent application throughout the nation.

Many national government programs are created to stimulate states or local units to take action in areas in which they have been reluctant to do so. They also may be applied where there are great inequities among the states or localities. For example, intergovernmental programs may be created to eliminate inequity in education, health, or welfare programs. Other programs may stimulate states to improve transportation, the environment, or work safety when they would not be so inclined without federal government prodding. Of course, critics argue that federal programs reduce the initiative and creativity of local or state units. If left to themselves, without the carrot of federal monies, they might experiment more and develop innovative approaches to solving problems. Innovative approaches often have difficulty getting by the federal bureaucracy.

The form of funding also occasions differences of opinion. Most federal funding has been in the form of *categorical* grants in which money is provided for a specific project with stipulations on exactly how the money can be used. A grant to develop a program for gifted children is an example.

Advocates of fewer restrictions support *block grants*, which give money to state or local units for general purposes instead of a specific project. For example, instead of grants for a program for gifted students, a state may receive an education block grant. The state then determines how best to use the education funds.

General revenue sharing, which refers to the transfer of money from one level of government to another with little or no restriction on its use, was another popular form of national intergovernmental policy in the 1970s. A formula is used to determine how much money each jurisdiction is entitled to receive.

In recent years, *unfunded mandates* of the national government have become common and are the source of much complaint by state and local officials. Unfunded mandates are requirements imposed on state and local governments with no national government funding to implement them. For example, national government requirements on reducing air pollution or attaining a certain standard in drinking water system quality are mandates without funding that must be paid for by the state or local governments.

Participants in Intergovernmental Relations

Numerous groups or special interests affect intergovernmental policies. Congress is the main actor in that it passes the legislation that fosters intergovernmental activities. Congress also tends to want to impose conditions on programs it funds and is the focal point for broad national policy development, which often results in particular mandates on state and local government.

The executive branch, particularly the president, often takes the lead in pushing particular policy agendas. Many of those agendas have intergovernmental implications. In addition to the executive leadership, the bureaucracy is part of the executive branch and has the responsibility for implementing policies developed by Congress and the president. In the implementation process, the administrative agencies often impose their own restrictions and conditions, particularly regarding how the policy is to be administered. Much of the federal government red tape complained about is the result of agency action. Administrators who make their concerns about policies known also influence Congress and the president; thus, they also are involved in policymaking processes.

In recent years, the courts have become significant actors in intergovernmental relations as well.[1] Since the 1960s, activist courts have mandated state and local governments to take particular actions, especially in school desegregation, school funding, and management of corrections. In recent years, they even have required local governments to impose taxes. Some courts have assumed administrative responsibility for schools and prison systems. In the 1990s, the courts have sided more with the states, but their intrusion into state activities remains significant.[2]

The national government's actions are affected by the concerns of state and local governmental officials. The mayors and governors, through their conferences and organizations, make pronouncements on those national government policies that affect them. Within their own parties, they also attempt to influence the direction of national leaders on relevant issues.

RECIPIENTS   The recipients of services under intergovernmental programs often voice their feelings. For example, when aid to education is slated for change or reduction, teachers and school administrators are likely to make entreaties to Congress and the president. Similarly, changes in welfare programs bring reactions from welfare recipients. Other groups that might not benefit directly from a program may also participate in intergovernmental policy development; a program to develop a recreational lake is likely to stimulate environmental or chamber of commerce groups to take a stand on the issue. Of course, the taxpayer is another interested party, to whom political candidates often appeal in their efforts to reduce federal government spending. The main contention is that federal government involvement creates unnecessary administrative expenses that taxpayers have to absorb.

ACIR   A special interest is taken by the Advisory Council on Intergovernmental Relations (ACIR), which succeeded the Advisory Commission on Intergovernmental Relations created in 1959 and dissolved in 1996. The Advisory Council is a nonprofit organization that serves as a clearinghouse on federalism. It studies and reports on intergovernmental issues and recommends improvements in the relations among units.

Some forms of intergovernmental relations are referred to as *horizontal intergovernmental relations* because they involve relationships between or among units at the same level. Interstate compacts are examples of horizontal intergovernmental relations. States enter into formal agreements to deal with issues that cross state lines and cannot be dealt with effectively by individual states. The Education Commission of the States, the New York and New Jersey Port Authority, the Delaware River Basin Compact, and the Colorado River Authority are examples of interstate compacts that deal with specific issues of mutual concern. Local governments also often enter into agreements to deal with common concerns. Mass transit authorities in metropolitan areas are results of interlocal government agreements. Such agreements often also deal with air and water pollution, airports, community colleges, and public safety services. Compacts between states and tribal governments regarding casino gambling are examples of special intergovernmental compacts.

Another form of cooperative relationships involving all levels of government is emerging as political leaders attempt to integrate the variety of activities that are important to the resolution of problems. For example, forty states now have Rural Development Councils.[3] They involve collaborative efforts including federal agencies, state governments, local governments, tribal governments, and private sector organizations. These efforts recognize that many agencies and governments offer services and programs that have an impact on development activities. By collaborating, they hope to reduce duplication and conflicting policies and services.

With all the participants in the process, it is little wonder that there are conflicts over the direction that intergovernmental relations should take.

CONTEMPORARY POLICY: INTERGOVERNMENTAL REALITIES

During its first 150 years, the United States' federal system changed gradually. Because the nation was essentially rural and society was relatively uncomplicated, the responsibilities of the national government and the states were easy to define. Although there were major controversies, as illustrated by states' rights conflicts, for the most part the powers of the national government were interpreted to be rather narrowly defined. Citizens dealt primarily with state and local jurisdictions. Overriding the separation-of-powers concept was the general philosophy that government at all levels should be restricted in scope. With such an approach, there was not a great deal of intergovernmental interaction.

In the late nineteenth century, intergovernmental relationships began to develop more formally. In 1862, for example, the Morrill Act provided federal land grants for agricultural education programs; the land grant universities are the result of this program. Hatch Act grants beginning in 1887 were the first actual cash transfers from the national government to the states for specific program development. These grants were for establishing agricultural experiment stations. Still, the growth in intergovernmental activities was gradual until the 1930s. From the 1930s onward, however, changes occurred much more rapidly. It is now a settled issue that, by virtue of the supremacy clause in Article VI of the Constitution, the powers of the national government are not limited by any specific state powers. However, since 1992, the Supreme Court has been limiting national power relative to state autonomy, thus restricting the reach of the national government.

Modern Intergovernmental Relations

The term *intergovernmental relations* is sometimes used interchangeably with federalism, but the two really do not mean the same thing. Federalism refers to the formal, legal structure of the political system; intergovernmental relations refers to all the interactions of governmental units within the political system. Therefore, although not provided for specifically in the formal document establishing the political system, some intergovernmental activities occur anyway. The origin of the term intergovernmental relations is somewhat unclear, but political scientist Deil Wright believes that it originated in the New Deal of the 1930s.[4] Given that the New Deal really spawned a large part of what we now know as intergovernmental relations, it is appropriate that the term should have originated from those programs.

If the New Deal symbolizes the development of modern intergovernmental relations, then the Social Security Act of 1935 is the New Deal foundation of many intergovernmental relations activities.[5] This act, and the various amendments to it, such as Medicaid in 1965, created programs in social welfare that continue to underpin much of the nation's welfare policy today, although the programs' form and organization have changed (see Chapters 7 and 8). These programs began a trend toward federal financing of program activities. They had shared funding with the states and were administered through the state governments. Contacts with the local governments were minimal. But during the mid-1930s, some programs began to bypass the states and deal directly with the municipalities. The public housing program begun in 1937 is an example of such a program.[6] The New Deal programs introduced a new element into the relations between the national government and state and local units. Rules and regulations were developed to implement the federally funded programs. State and local governments permitted the national government to restrict their independence in order to acquire money for programs they had not yet developed, even though they had the authority to do so. Another important legacy was the categorical grant-in-aid, in which funds were provided for specific purposes, such as urban renewal, airport construction, and highways.

World War II preoccupied policymakers at all levels, and the development of intergovernmental programs diminished during that time. The immediate postwar activities included a gradual expansion of programs involving state, local, and national governments. Categorical grant-in-aid programs continued to dominate the system. The 1960s and 1970s brought dramatic growth in federal programs attempting to solve the problems of American society. During these years, society became highly urbanized, and much of the response to urban problems was to extend programs directly to the cities rather than channel them through the state governments, which were often unsympathetic to urban concerns. By the beginning of the Reagan administration in 1981, there were approximately 600 separate funding programs for state and local governments.[7] To the dismay of many state and local government administrators, these programs carried with them many detailed administrative regulations.

A major legacy of the 1960s and 1970s was the significant increase in the number of categorical grants, such as *Community Development Block Grants*, which required application for funds by the state and/or local government. The national government funding agency would then have to approve the grant. In doing so, the agency could pressure the jurisdiction receiving the money to structure the project or program as the agency wanted. Thus, the discretion of state and local units was further lessened. Of course, many entitlement grants continued to exist and expand. In those grants, the jurisdiction would be automatically eligible for funds according to some formula or criterion. Nonetheless, the emergence of the project grants requiring application increased the influence of the national government in programs at the state and local levels. Complicating the matter was that each program had its own application procedures and requirements.

Not surprisingly, state and local governments and many aspirants to national office criticized the federal grant-in-aid program. As a result of mounting pressures, efforts at the consolidation of programs took hold in the 1970s and *general revenue sharing* was created. Under general revenue sharing, state and local governments received an amount of federal tax dollars according to a formula. With minor exceptions, the money could be used for virtually any purpose the receiving jurisdiction chose. Instead of specific conditions and limitations on the use of the money, new general requirements such as equal employment opportunity and common accounting procedures had to be met by all programs.

By the late 1970s, pressures for reduction in federal government activities led to new approaches. The 1980 election of Ronald Reagan as president set the agenda for reduced federal spending and a limited role of the federal government in what were perceived to be the affairs of state and local governments. Spending cuts and other changes were directed at altering that intergovernmental relationship. Although other administrations had attempted to reverse some of the increases in federal government activity, they accepted the idea that the national government has responsibility for the social welfare system and worked basically to curtail federal control while retaining funding responsibilities. However, the Reagan administration perceived things quite differently and worked from a commitment to eliminate the national government's involvement in funding or managing such programs.[8] The Carter administration had in fact begun many of these reductions but progressed slowly; the significance of the Reagan approach was largely in its pace and the extent of restricting federal government influence.

Alice Rivlin suggests that the huge federal deficit created by tax cuts and large increases in defense spending under the Reagan administration were partially responsible for the pressure to devolve many programs back to the states.[9] Additionally, she notes that by the 1980s, reforms at the state level resulted in stronger governors, more representative legislatures, and more professional civil servants. At the same time, many began to perceive the federal government as unmanageable.

The changes of the 1980s remained strong in the 1990s. Aspirants to office at all levels seemed to be running against government. The elections since 1994 have focused on the evils of big government. It often is difficult to tell which party the candidates are from as they all seem to be running on platforms of reducing government and changing business as usual in Washington, D.C. President George W. Bush continues the philosophy of returning power to the state and local governments and decreasing national control. Current intergovernmental policy is a mixture of the recent emphasis on reducing national government prominence in public affairs and the historic development of national government responsibility in many areas of public concern. The terrorist attacks of September 11, 2001, seemed to produce increased support for a greater government role in some areas such as public safety and security, but there still is skepticism about too much national government involvement in other areas.

Other Forms of Intergovernmental Interaction

Because money provided by the national government is a major source of funding for intergovernmental activity, the emphasis in intergovernmental relations is often on fiscal relationships, but there are other forms of interaction as well. Intergovernmental relations include regulations and voluntary cooperative efforts.

In 1984, the ACIR identified four types of *regulations* that are part of intergovernmental relations: direct orders, cross-cutting requirements, crossover sanctions, and partial preemption.[10] *Direct orders* either prohibit or mandate state and local government actions. For example, equal employment opportunity legislation prohibits discrimination in employment by state and local government. The Safe Drinking Water Act requires water providers to reach and maintain certain standards in the drinking water they supply.

Cross-cutting requirements are those in which a condition on one grant is applied to all programs using federal funds. Thus, the Civil Rights Act of 1964 requires that jurisdictions cannot discriminate against people on the basis of race, color, national origin, sex, or handicapped status where federal funds are used. The Drug Free Workplace Act of 1988 and the Cash Management Improvement Act of 1990 are other examples.

(3) *Crossover sanctions* are sanctions applied to one area or activity for failure to comply with certain conditions in another area. For example, federal highway funds can be withheld from states that fail to enforce air quality standards.

(4) *Partial preemption* refers to situations in which the national government requires or permits states to administer policies as long as the states meet federal criteria for the program. If the states do not meet the federal criteria, the federal government may administer the program directly. Examples include the Clean Air Act Amendments of 1990 and Hazardous and Solid Waste Amendments of 1984.

These regulatory processes have engendered much criticism from state and local government officials. Generally, the policies reflected in these regulations are in response to a desire by some elements of society to further their vision of the public good. Congress often is supportive because, essentially, they represent good public policy. Imposing the requirements without having to provide funding for implementation allows Congress to satisfy strong interests without having to raise the revenue to fund them. Of course, state and local governments then have to find the revenue, thus raising the ire of officials at those levels. Ironically, state mandates in recent years have resulted in the same types of complaints from local governments, which feel that they have excessive costs imposed upon them by states. The complaints of local governments appear to have an impact; state mandates seem to be declining, at least in some states.[11] The national government, even with the efforts of the Reagan administration, continued to impose new mandates on state and local governments (see Table 2-1). The Unfunded Mandates Reform Act of 1995 requires federal funding for mandates costing more than $50 million and requires federal agencies to assess impacts of their new rules and regulations on state and local governments. In 1997, bills were introduced, but not passed, to require reimbursement by the national government of any direct cost to state and local governments resulting from federal mandates.

POLICY EVALUATION: CHANGING INTERGOVERNMENTAL RELATIONS

Complaints about the intergovernmental system usually have focused on the growth of the national government at the expense of state and local autonomy. The criticisms are there today just as they always have been. Regardless, it is clear that state and local governments have grown as the national government has expanded its involvement in domestic policy issues. The result has been more and more intergovernmental activities and a more complex web of relations. Of course, the intention of most advocates of system reform is to reverse that complexity and lighten the hand of the national government in the affairs of state and local governments.

Administrative Problems

One of the most common complaints about the federal government is that it imposes too much red tape on the state and local recipients of aid. State and local administrators complain about the amount of paperwork in applying for and administering grants. The paperwork increases the costs to the recipients and delays

**TABLE 2-1 ▪ Major Recent Enactments and Statutory Amendments
Regulating State and Local Governments**

Title	Regulatory Type*
Age Discrimination in Employment Act Amendments of 1986	DO
Americans with Disabilities Act of 1986	CC/DO
Asbestos Hazard Emergency Response Act of 1986	DO
Cash Management Improvement Act of 1990	CC
Child Abuse Amendments of 1984	CO
Civil Rights Restoration Act of 1987	CC
Clean Air Act Amendments of 1990	PP
Commercial Motor Vehicle Safety Act of 1986	CO
Consolidated Omnibus Budget Reconciliation Act of 1985	DO
Drug-Free Workplace Act of 1988	CC
Education of the Handicapped Act Amendments of 1990	CO
Emergency Planning and Community Right-to-Know Act of 1986	PP
Fair Housing Act Amendments of 1988	DO
Family and Medical Leave Act of 1993	DO
Handicapped Children's Protection Act of 1986	CO
Hazardous and Solid Waste Amendments of 1984	PP
Highway Safety Amendments of 1984	CO
Lead Contamination Control Act of 1988	DO
National Voter Registration Act of 1993	CC/DO
Ocean Dumping Ban Act of 1988	DO
Older Workers Benefit Protection Act of 1990	DO
Safe Drinking Water Act Amendments of 1986	DO/PP
Social Security Amendments of 1983	DO
Surface Transportation Assistance Act of 1982	DO
Voting Accessibility for the Elderly and Handicapped Act of 1984	DO
Water Quality Act of 1987	CC/DO/PP

*Key: CC = Cross-cutting Requirement; CO = Crossover Sanction; DO = Direct Order; PP = Partial Preemption

SOURCE: *Intergovernmental Perspective*, Vol. 18, No. 4 (Fall 1992): 8, provides the original concept and pre-1990 enactments. Newer enactments are added.

the project's completion. Much of the difficulty arises because the regional administrators of federal agencies cannot make the final decisions on most grants. Instead, they advise the central agency office, which in turn makes the final decision. Disputes in interpreting program criteria and rules and regulations take a long time to resolve, and conflicting rules and regulations and duplication of effort only compound the problem. Even more difficult for the state and local agencies is the need for clearance from numerous agencies from local officials on up to federal agency managers.

All of these requirements lead to inflexibility in the categorical programs. Local officials feel that their needs cannot be met; rather, the program requirements appear to be oriented more to the needs of the federal agency. Additionally, many of the categorical programs are so narrowly defined that it becomes difficult to fit them to the particular needs of the state and local governments.

Block grants and general revenue sharing were supposed to eliminate some of the administrative problems previously noted. Giving state and local officials more discretion in the structure of their programs would subject the money to fewer restrictions. Although block grants generally begin with such aspirations, state program administrators seem to recategorize them as part of their actual implementation. Conflicts develop within the state block-grant administrative agencies. Program specialists fight for funds for their programs, and the funds end up being allocated on a program basis. The result is that after they reach the state level, the block grants often begin to look again like categorical grants. Additionally, national government policy seems to reimpose conditions. For example, general revenue sharing was found to contain the compliance requirements of fifteen different federal agencies just four years after its adoption as federal aid without strings.[12]

Another effort to reduce the overlap in administrative rules was the Joint Funding and Simplification Act of 1974, which authorized one set of administrative rules for programs funded jointly by federal government agencies. The idea behind the act was to allow state and local governments to develop coordinated programs with funds from various grant programs to address local problems. However, there has been little success because there have been few joint funding programs. The program-specific detail of the federal agencies tends to ignore the more general problems faced by the state and local communities. As a result, the centralization inherent in most categorical grant programs often is another source of friction for state and local program administrators.

Monitoring

Related to administrative problems is monitoring by federal agencies. In granting money to other units of government, the national government tries to see that the money is used properly and for beneficial programs. To that end the federal government devised elaborate monitoring arrangements. Among the most important is the A-95 review process, which refers to Circular A-95 of the Office of Management and Budget. Although the Reagan administration abolished the A-95 review process as a requirement for receiving federal grants, the process persists because individual agencies use it, and many state and local governments recognize the need for coordination. This review procedure required that proposals be commented on by some unit other than the local government requesting funds. Typically, a regional council of governments or a regional planning commission is responsible for reviewing and commenting on grant applications. Additionally, the request usually had to be commented on by some statewide agency or office before going to the federal agency. The reason for these requirements was to reduce overlapping projects and to ensure that one project did not work at cross-purposes with other projects in the area. It also permitted the coordination of projects that would benefit an area. The end result should be cost savings to the taxpayer and more efficient use of grant monies, but there is no hard evidence that such objectives have been met.

There is no question that the review process has had many beneficial effects in generating greater cooperation among governments in a region. Nonetheless, the instrument has not been entirely successful. Because the regional councils of governments and the like are made up of representatives of the area's jurisdictions, they each pursue their own interests in making decisions. Coalitions of jurisdictions often work to the advantage of some and to the disadvantage of others. Typically, many small units of government may coalesce around issues and hamper the efforts of the one largest city in the region. It therefore is common for the largest city to withdraw from the regional association, thus closing the door on cooperative efforts. In instances in which representation on the regional association depends on the population of the constituent units, this may have the opposite effect. The larger jurisdictions may control and ignore the legitimate needs of the smaller units. But the A-95 review and its successors have been important to the intergovernmental grant system, despite these problems.

Monitoring occurs within agencies as well. The recipient of a grant normally has to be reviewed by the granting agency. Most federal agencies have so many programs and grants to monitor that it is impossible to do a complete job of monitoring, so recipient governments may find ways to get around or ignore compliance with impunity. And when an agency decides to take action against a unit, the affected government has many options at its command to lessen the agency's ability to do so. Because the agencies rely on congressional support to continue their activities, the affected government can turn to members of Congress to put pressure on the granting agency. The agency also depends on its clientele, the recipient units of government, to ensure support for its programs. Thus, agency administrators usually see the advantage of working things out with the state or local units rather than fighting with them.

Finances

Another feature of the intergovernmental system is the financial relationships between and among units. Because the national government increased the numbers of funded programs during the mid-twentieth century, intergovernmental transfers of funds became significant (see Figure 2-1). The problem with providing federal funds lies in who controls the use of those funds. With categorical grants, the national government clearly established criteria for using the money. With block grants and general revenue sharing, the expectation was that the national government would loosen its control. Of course, the main thrust of recent domestic policy was the loosening of restrictions coupled with major cuts in domestic spending. The Personal Responsibility and Work Opportunity Reconciliation Act of 1996, which reformed the welfare system (see Chapter 7), is a good example of devolving responsibility to the states and, in the process, providing less financial support for the program.[13]

With grants, the state and local levels are never certain what amount of money is going to be available from year to year. This uncertainty in the level of funding makes it more difficult for them to plan their own activities and budgets. Another irritating aspect of most federal grants for the recipient units is the maintenance of effort requirement, which means that state and local governments cannot use federal money to replace their own spending on the affected program. The receiving governments are locked into spending patterns if they wish to receive the grants with such requirements. For example, Community Development Block Grants could not be used to reduce the amount of money that the local government spent on redevelopment. Instead, the program requires a government to continue to spend at the level at which it had spent in the past, or it cannot continue to receive Community Development funds.

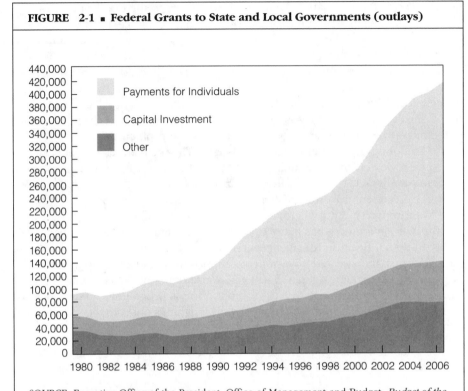

FIGURE 2-1 ▪ Federal Grants to State and Local Governments (outlays)

Payments for Individuals

Capital Investment

Other

SOURCE: Executive Office of the President, Office of Management and Budget, *Budget of the United States Government, FY 2002* (Washington, DC: U.S. Government Printing Office, 2001), Historical Tables, pp. 216–217.

Block grants and general revenue sharing, combined with the recent cuts in domestic spending, have had several effects on state and local governments. State and local units are faced with absorbing the costs of many programs if they are to continue to provide services, especially social and human services. Studies of the effects of block grants so far have indicated that the state replacement of lost federal funds has been relatively low.[14] The principal question is whether the state and local governments wish to continue programs and whether they have the resources to do so. The shift to block grants increased the internal competition for funds in state governments. Another feature of the funding shift has been to show the states how they can influence local units to a greater degree. The states themselves are now using the block grant approach to fund many programs.

Unfunded Mandates

Rivaling criticism over the current administration of grants is the objection to unfunded mandates. Unfunded mandates represent regulation of many activities traditionally left to state and local governments. State and local governments become especially upset with the fact that they are under pressure to operate with less revenue and, at the same time, the federal government develops policies requiring them to engage in new initiatives without providing money for those activities. States have even gone to court to attempt to reverse some of the mandates or to require the federal government to provide resources, but such efforts so far have been unsuccessful.

Structural Effects

The federal patchwork of grants affects the way state and local governments operate. One of the many criticisms of federal funding in the past has been that it distorts the priorities of state and local governments. The argument is that governments go after money where it is available. They are unlikely to spend money on programs or projects that are needed; rather, they pursue less-needed projects because they can get federal help with them. Because there are categorical grants for almost anything imaginable, it is less likely now than it was in the 1950s and 1960s that this criticism is accurate. However, federal priorities may become state and local priorities if the incentive is great enough.

Probably the greatest change in recent years is the emergence of the states as strong partners in the federal relationship. The evidence is clear that the states were beginning to gain influence during the 1970s as they instituted their own institutional reforms. President Reagan's emphasis on returning power to the states and eliminating many federal activities accelerated the trend toward more state participation and influence and probably ensured that it would not be reversed. The fact that block grants go through the states for distribution places state governments in a strong position to determine how the money will be used and what units of government will use it. Thus, the states won more independence from the national government at the same time that they increased their ability to control the distribution of money to the local units.[15]

Many policy analysts view the states as laboratories for experimenting with innovative approaches to problems. The critics of federal government dominance suggest that states ought to be given more discretion. Governors, in particular, press the Congress to provide funding, but to let them develop ways of using the money for social programs. For example, welfare reform (see Chapter 7) and other devolution of programs test the capacity of states to initiate and administer programs. Many critics question whether state and local officials will be up to the task.[16] Others note, however, that state leaders are now more active in these policy debates and are stronger than they have been in many years.[17] Innovative efforts of Oregon in health care reform, Massachusetts and Wisconsin in welfare reform, and over two-thirds of the states in the use of enterprise zones are examples of efforts that could be replicated elsewhere.

Another structural legacy of the Reagan administration is that the issue of intergovernmental relations has been raised as a prominent item on the national policy debate agenda. The relationship between the state and local governments and the national government became a major component of political discussion during the 1980s, and a serious consideration of altering that relationship resulted. The debate continues, and the Supreme Court has been redefining the relationship in recent decisions supporting state government autonomy.[18]

FUTURE ALTERNATIVES: CONTINUING ADAPTATION
OF THE INTERGOVERNMENTAL SYSTEM

Intergovernmental policies continue to evolve as differing demands are made on the political system. Political scientists Parris Glendening and Mavis Mann Reeves characterized the federal system as a pragmatic one, adapting to changing conditions and assuming new forms to accommodate political, economic, and social realities.[19] Thus, it is safe to say that there will be changes in intergovernmental policies, but the directions of those changes are at issue, and the proponents of alternative intergovernmental arrangements will attempt to shape the new intergovernmental policies.

The Reagan administration was the proponent of one type of intergovernmental redistribution of power. That policy perspective has been institutionalized in the current political context. As already noted in this chapter, proponents of this type would like to see the system change so that the national government reduces its influence in domestic affairs and leaves most government activities to state and local levels. Since the late 1970s, the status and influence of state governments increased and national government involvement in many activities diminished. The block grant programs developed in the 1980s were only a step to further withdrawal by the national government, with the hope that federal involvement in many of the block grant programs eventually would be eliminated. The pledge of the Republican majority elected to Congress in 1994, and reelected in 1996 and 2000, to return more authority to the states resulted in greater state and local influence and activity. The George W. Bush administration also supports this pledge.

The National Governors Association, the Conference of State Legislatures, and the Advisory Council on Intergovernmental Relations believe that the roles of the national government and states can be better defined. The problem is determining exactly which functions should be the responsibility of the national government and what should be the responsibility of state and local units. Commonly, suggestions are made that the national government assume all responsibility for health and income support programs and shift the responsibility for all other social programs to the states. Governors occasionally call upon the national government to assume all responsibility for funding welfare programs, in return for the states picking up other programs, such as education and transportation. Again, the primary emphasis is on turning over many functions to the state and local governments while reducing federal involvement, but there is little agreement on exactly how the division should be made. For example, in 1995 and 1996, many governors suggested devolving Medicaid more fully to the states, while others argued that there should be national standards governing the program.

The process of dividing responsibility suggests a view of intergovernmental relations in which functions can be neatly separated. But history has suggested that such neat divisions are unrealistic. Since most policy activities affect more states than one, it is unrealistic to leave such activities exclusively under the control of one or more states. That would leave the citizens of some states affected by policymaking activity by a governmental body in which they were not represented. This consideration was a primary factor in replacing the Articles of Confederation with the present Constitution, which provides for a national sovereignty. Therefore, it is improbable that any system could be devised that abolished sharing and cooperation. Nonetheless, proponents of this view expect that progress will be made toward their objectives. The success of the Reagan administration in redirecting the relationship in the 1990s suggests that some shift is possible. There has been continuing pressure for shifting the balance to the states. With governors and mayors putting pressure on the federal government and with a much more sympathetic Congress, shifts are certain to continue. The fact that Presidents Clinton and Bush were governors also led them to be sympathetic, thus fostering cooperative efforts with greater discretion for the states in such areas as health care, welfare, and economic development, as will be discussed in later chapters.

Opponents of the shift of responsibility to the states argue that states are not able to assume that responsibility. States are not likely to have the resources to fund the programs adequately. As previously noted, states may not always be inclined to continue such programs. Opponents of these proposals see the administrative complexity of fifty states administering programs as inefficient and burdensome as administration under the block grants. There are also concerns that some states will be less sensitive to issues such as equity, fairness, and civil rights in developing and implementing programs. Concerns also arise over which groups have access to decision makers, with many arguing that the poor and powerless bear the greatest burden of these reforms.

Those favoring the centralization of programs also are concerned about the complexity of the problems facing American society. They see problems as being so complex that only the national government can possibly marshal the resources to address them and provide a coordinated effort.

Some people advocate a radical change in the structure of the federal system that would greatly change intergovernmental policy.[20] They suggest that the states be eliminated and replaced by regional governments. The number of units would be reduced from fifty to about twelve; this smaller number would mean more efficiency, and interactions between the national and constituent governmental units would be less complex. Under the regional system, the national government would exercise more control over regional units than it currently does over the states.

The advocates of change are not likely to see their proposals realized completely, but some shuffles are certain. It appears certain that fiscal changes will continue: The trend toward fewer real dollars in grants is not likely to be reversed, especially with the renewed federal deficit pressures. As a result, there will be fewer dollars for state and local units to share. Competition for those dollars is bound to increase, and some analysts suggest that changes in political coalitions of public interest groups would result, as they now oppose one another, rather than work together, on grant requests.[21] With fewer dollars available, fiscal relationships are likely to give way to cooperative efforts in other ways and to the national government's attempts to regulate activities of states and local governments through general policy. Such general policy is likely to increase the costs of state and local government through unfunded mandates without providing federal monies to cover those costs.

It is hard to predict what will happen with the block grants. These programs appear to be popular with the general public and with state officials because they imply few strings. However, the general public is ineffective in pressuring Congress to sustain these programs. Categorical grants most likely will continue to be the most significant element of the fiscal relationship, because the interests affected by them often are strong and can influence Congress when cuts are contemplated. Even with the consolidation of programs into block grants, there has been little effect on the number of categorical grant programs. There were approximately 500 federal grant programs in 1978 and still over 400 in 1994. More significantly, categorical grants still account for more than 80 percent of grant funds.

SUMMARY

Intergovernmental policy is a natural outgrowth of the federal system, in which government responsibilities are loosely distributed between the national government and the states. The nation started with the states being relatively strong while the national government sought its proper role. Later intergovernmental interactions occurred through land grant programs and cooperative efforts to develop the economy. However, until the twentieth century, the national government was not closely involved in domestic policy, which was seen as the realm of state and local governments.

The twentieth century marked the era of escalating intergovernmental programs. During the 1930s, many national government programs were created to help the nation out of the Great Depression, and those programs signaled a strong national involvement in social and economic policy. Until the 1970s, the national government increased its involvement through many grant programs and took responsibility for the nation's general welfare. During the 1970s, however, national leaders began to question the propriety of the massive federal programs and began to return many of these responsibilities to the states. In the 1980s and 1990s, the trend toward reducing the influence of the national government and increasing the state governments' power accelerated; support for the trend continues in the early 2000s.

The issues in intergovernmental relations concern which level of government has the authority, inclination, and resources to engage in a particular activity. The national government entered many domestic program areas, such as social and educational programs, because states either did not have the resources or were not interested in providing some services. To ensure the equity of services, the national government offered grants to the states to encourage them to draw up particular programs. But with the grants came numerous restrictions and controls as well, which have prompted many state and local government officials to press for a different arrangement whereby they would have maximum flexibility in using federal funding. The 1980s brought those concerns to the forefront of the political debate. The 1990s began with a similar approach, although the major complaint now is that programs and mandates are passed on to state and local governments without money to fund them.

NOTES

1. Brady Baybeck and William Lowry, "Federalism Outcomes and Ideological Preferences: The U.S. Supreme Court and Preemption Cases," *Publius*, 30, No. 3, (Summer 2000): 73–97; "The Federal Courts: Intergovernmental Umpires or Regulators," *Intergovernmental Perspective*, 18 (Fall 1992): 12–15; Susan Mezey Gluck, "The U.S. Supreme Court's Federalism Jurisprudence: *Alden v. Maine* and the Enhancement of State Sovereignty," *Publius*, 30, Nos. 1&2 (Winter/Spring 2000): 31–38; David H.

Rosenbloom and Rosemary O'Leary, *Public Administration and the Law*, 2nd ed. (New York: Marcel Dekker, Inc., 1997), Chapter 1.

2. Baybeck and Lowry, "Federalism Outcomes and Ideological Preferences"; Gluck, "The U.S. Supreme Court's Federalism Jurisprudence"; Bert Waisanen, "Federalism: Watchdog for States," *State Government News*, 40, No. 2 (March 1997): 12–15; and Carol S. Weissert and Sanford F. Schram, "The State of American Federalism," *Publius*, 26, No. 3 (Summer 1996): 1–26.

3. Beryl Radin, *Intergovernmental Partnerships and Rural Development Councils: Profiles of Twenty-nine State Rural Development Councils* (Washington, DC: Government Printing Office, 1995); John DeWitt, Donald F. Kettl, Barbara Dyer, and W. Robert Lovan, "What Will New Governance Mean for the Federal Government?" *Public Administration Review*, 54 (March/April 1994): 170–175; and www.rudev.usda.gov/nrdp/what.html.

4. Deil S. Wright, *Understanding Intergovernmental Relations* (North Scituate, MA: Duxbury Press, 1978), 6–7.

5. Arnold M. Howitt, *Managing Federalism: Studies in Intergovernmental Relations* (Washington, DC: Congressional Quarterly Press, 1984). Much of this historical discussion draws on Howitt's account, 1–35. Also see David B. Walker, *The Rebirth of Federalism: Slouching Toward Washington* (Chatham, NJ: Chatham House Publishers, Inc., 1995), especially Chapter 4.

6. Howitt, *Managing Federalism*, 5–6.

7. Parris N. Glendening and Mavis Mann Reeves, *Pragmatic Federalism*, 2nd ed. (Pacific Palisades, CA: Palisades Publishers, 1984), 72.

8. See Samuel Beer, "Foreword," in John William Ellwood, ed., *Reductions in U.S. Domestic Spending* (New Brunswick, NJ: Transaction Books, 1982).

9. Alice M. Rivlin, *Reviving the American Dream: The Economy, the States and the Federal Government* (Washington, DC: Brookings Institution, 1992), Chapters 1 and 6.

10. U.S. Advisory Commission on Intergovernmental Relations, *Regulatory Federalism: Policy, Process, Impact, and Reform*, vol. 2 (Washington, DC: U.S. Government Printing Office, 1984).

11. Beverly A. Cigler, "State-Local Relations: A Need for Reinvention?" *Intergovernmental Perspective*, 20 (Spring 1994): 20–23; Susan A. McManus, "Mad About Mandates: The Issue of Who Should Pay for What Resurfaces," *Publius*, 21 (Summer 1991): 59–76; Joseph F. Zimmerman, "State Mandate Relief: A Quick Look," *Intergovernmental Perspective*, 20 (Spring 1994): 28–30; and David B. Walker, *The Rebirth of Federalism*, 264–267.

12. Lawrence D. Brown and Bernard Frieden, "Guidelines and Goals in the Model Cities Program," *Policy Sciences*, 7 (December 1976): 488; and Bruce A. Wallin, *From Revenue Sharing to Deficit Sharing: General Revenue Sharing and Cities* (Washington, DC: Georgetown University Press, 1998), Chapter 4.

13. Weissert and Schram, "The State of American Federalism." Also see Steven D. Gold, "Issues Raised by the New Federalism," *National Tax Journal*, xlix, No. 2 (June 1996): 213–287; Rosemary O'Leary and Paul Weiland, "Regulatory Reform in the 104th Congress: Revolution or Evolution?" *Publius*, 26, No. 3 (Summer 1996): 27–44; and John M. Quigley and Daniel L. Rubinfell, "Federalism and Reductions in the Federal Government," *National Tax Journal*, xlix, 2 (June 1996): 289–302.

14. John L. Palmer and Isabel V. Sawhill, *The Reagan Experiment* (Washington, DC: Urban Institute Press, 1982), Chapter 6; Richard P. Nathan and Fred C. Doolittle and Associates, *The Consequences of Cuts* (Princeton: Princeton University Urban and Regional Research Center, 1983); and Shana Gamkhar and Wallace Oates, "Asymmetries in the Response to Increases and Decreases in Intergovernmental Grants: Some Empirical Findings," *National Tax Journal*, xlix, No. 4 (December 1996): 501–511.

15. Timothy Conlan, *From Federalism to Devolution—Twenty-Five Years of Intergovernmental Reform* (Washington, DC: Brookings Institution, 1998); Nathan Glazer, "The Social Policy of the Reagan Administration: A Review," *Public Interest*, 75 (Spring 1984): 76–98.

16. Charles Babington, "Overloading the States," *The Washington Post National Weekly Edition*, October 23–29, 6–7; Bruce Feustel, "What Do We Do Now? Devolution and the Legislative Institutions," *State Legislatures*, 23, No. 6 (June 1997): 22–25; Rob Gurwitt, "Overload," *Governing*, 9, No. 1 (October 1995): 16–22; and Jonathan Walters, "Suiting Up for Devolution," *Governing*, 9, No. 2 (November 1995): 15.

17. Parris Glendening, "Pragmatic Federalism and State-Federal Partnerships," *Spectrum: The Journal of State Government*, 74, No. 3 (Summer 2001): 7–8; Rivlin, *Reviving the American Dream*;

Weissert and Schram, "The State of American Federalism"; Carol S. Weissert and Sanford F. Schram, "The State of U.S. Federalism, 1999–2000," *Publius*, 30, No. 2 (Winter-Spring): 1–9.

18. Baybeck and Lowry, "Federalism Outcomes"; Mezey Gluck, "The U.S. Supreme Court's Federalism Jurisprudence."

19. Glendening and Reeves, *Pragmatic Federalism.*

20. For example, Rexford G. Tugwell, *Model for a New Constitution* (Palo Alto, CA: James E. Freel and Associates, 1970).

21. George E. Hale and Marian Lief Palley, *The Politics of Federal Grants* (Washington, DC: Congressional Quarterly Press, 1981), 169–171.

SUGGESTED READINGS

Books and Articles

Barrales, Ruben. "Federalism in the Bush Administration." *Spectrum: The Journal of State Government*, 74, No. 3 (Summer 2001): 5–6.

Berman, David. *State and Local Politics*, 9th ed. Armonk, NY: M. E. Sharpe, 1999.

Conlan, Timothy. *From New Federalism to Devolution—Twenty-Five Years of Intergovernmental Reform.* Washington, DC: Brookings Institution, 1998.

Elazar, Daniel J. *Federal Systems of the World: A Handbook of Federal, Confederal and Autonomy Arrangements*, 2nd ed. New York: Stockton Press, 1994.

Fix, Michael, and Kenyon, Daphne A., eds. *Coping with Mandates.* Washington, DC: Urban Institute Press, 1990.

Glendening, Parris N., and Reeves, Mavis Mann. *Pragmatic Federalism: An Intergovernmental View of American Government*, 2nd ed. Pacific Palisades, CA: Palisades Publishers, 1984.

Kelly, Janet M. *State Mandates.* Washington, DC: National League of Cities, 1992.

Rivlin, Alice M. *Reviving the American Dream: The Economy, the States and the Federal Government.* Washington, DC: Brookings Institution, 1992.

Walker, David B. *The Rebirth of Federalism: Slouching Toward Washington.* Chatham, NJ: Chatham House Publishers, Inc., 1995.

Wallin, Bruce A. *From Revenue Sharing to Deficit Sharing: General Revenue Sharing and Cities.* Washington, DC: Georgetown University Press, 1998.

Weissert, Carol S., and Schram, Sanford F. "The State of U.S. Federalism, 1999–2000." *Publius*, 30, No. 2 (Winter-Spring 2000): 1–19.

Wright, Deil S. *Understanding Intergovernmental Relations*, 3rd ed. Pacific Grove, CA: Brooks/Cole, 1988.

Web Sites

Center for the Study of Federalism   www.Temple.edu/federalism/
Council of State Governments   www.csg.org
National Association of Counties   www.naco.org
National Association of Regional Councils   www.narc.org
National League of Cities   www.nlc.org/nlc_org/site
National Rural Development Partnership   www.rurdev.usda.gov/
United States Advisory Commission on Intergovernmental Relations
        www.library.unt.edu/gpo/ACIR/acir.html

CHAPTER 3

The Economy: Changing Government-Business Relationships

American government always has been preoccupied with economic activities. During its first century, the country's main concerns were with preserving the property of citizens. Although property rights still hold a high place in American ~~Property~~ values, other economic concerns—such as economic growth, level of employment, international competition, and the scarcity of natural resources—gradually replaced preservation of property rights as a major focus of government. Yet one factor has remained constant over the years: Government and economic activity are inextricably intertwined; therefore, activity in one sector automatically has major consequences for the other. At the same time, quality of life and the relationship of economic development to the environment and to social issues present current concerns for economic policy.

ISSUE BACKGROUND: KEY CONCEPTS IN ECONOMICS

Economic systems produce and distribute wealth among people in the form of goods and services. Different systems perform these functions in different ways. In theory, a market system operates according to the concept of supply and demand—that is, it responds to peoples' demands by supplying what they want, for a profit. The key to understanding the market system is that both prices and the allocation of goods and services are determined impersonally. That is, they are not set by any actor or institution according to some rational criterion, but rather are produced by the interaction of the impersonal forces of supply and demand. This simplified view of economic systems is predicated on the expectation that there will be a balance between supply and demand and that the economic actors have an essentially equal ability to bargain with one another. In reality, however, people vary in the economic power they have, and other factors affect the supply-demand relationship. As economist John Kenneth Galbraith noted, people band together in organizations to acquire power.[1] These organizations often serve their own economic self-interest, not that of society. Because some individuals and organizations have more money, property, or political access than others, imbalances in the distribution of wealth develop. Governments often intervene to protect the interests of those with power or to rebalance the system; economic policy deals with these governmental efforts.

43

The Free-Enterprise System

A variety of economic systems characterizes industrialized nations. They can, how-ever, be divided roughly between two extreme alternatives of economic organization: market capitalism, or free enterprise, and socialist, or public, ownership. Although each individual economy more closely approximates one of these two extremes, most combine elements of free-market enterprise and government control. One may actually conceptualize three types of economic systems. *Free-enterprise capitalism* implies both the market system and the private ownership of the major means of production, distribution, and exchange, with these means run for the profit of their owners. *Socialism* involves the public or governmental ownership and control of these major means of production, distribution, and exchange, presumably run for the public interest. In this system, government agents plan prices and the allocation of goods and services according to rational considerations. Between these polar op-posites is the system practiced in most industrial democracies, a type called *welfare-state capitalism.* In this system, the allocation of goods and services, and frequently prices, are to a large extent planned, but the major means of production are still in private hands and run for profit.

The major systems champion economic development and industrialization, but they favor different methods for achieving them. Proponents of free-market capitalism justify it on the grounds that the private ownership of firms provides incentives for production. They believe the state should refrain as much as pos-sible from interfering with the conduct of economic activity. In the socialist ap-proach, however, the political system plays a major role in the conduct of economic activity. Such a system is based on the assumption that economic wealth should be fairly equally distributed among the population and that such distribution improves social welfare. Socialists reject the assumptions that under-lie the market system. From the socialist perspective, a few wealthy owners and managers of private enterprise dominate capitalist societies. These are policy-makers neither chosen by nor responsible to the people as a whole. Proponents of capitalism see the same problems in a socialist economy, namely, that govern-ment officials concentrate economic power along with political and social power in their own hands, but capitalists view this as a threat to individual liberty.

In socialist economies, such as those in the pre-1989 Soviet Union and the formerly communist countries of Eastern Europe, government ownership pre-dominated. Thus, government controlled economic activity through its normal decision-making processes. Even within such societies, however, there were vari-ations, and some had more mixed economies than others. Eastern European na-tions, in particular, permitted private enterprise, particularly in agriculture, to coexist with the state-owned economic entities. East Germany, Yugoslavia, and Czechoslovakia diverged from total government ownership, often at the expense of incurring Soviet enmity and sometimes intervention. Relatively independent of Soviet dominance, Yugoslavia, for example, because of the decentralization of its productive mechanisms, had most of its prices determined by market forces. The Solidarity labor movement in Poland in the 1980s demonstrated that socialist gov-ernments could not maintain total control over economic activities.

With the failure of communism in 1989 and the dissolution of the Soviet Union and its control over Eastern Europe, the command economies collapsed.

As a result, the development of the free-market system accelerated. Although they face immense challenges, these countries are developing mixed economies reflecting elements of command and free-market systems.

In most industrialized nations—such as the United States, France, Germany, Italy, Sweden, and Japan—a capitalist approach dominates, but it is inevitably a mixture of private ownership and public control that characterizes such systems.[2] Government monopolies invariably run postal services and, in many nonsocialist nations, other economic activities, such as telephone and telegraph services and transportation. These activities (sometimes called natural monopolies) often are viewed as being so basic to the maintenance of society that government monopoly is justified.

What differentiates capitalist and socialist economies for purposes of government-economic interaction is that socialist states, as we have seen, have built-in controls through public ownership and operation of economic enterprise. Capitalist economies, however, utilize other kinds of intervention as a means of supporting, guiding, or controlling the activities of the private sector. Socialist states do not need the regulation or economic stimulation common in capitalist states as they exercise direct control; capitalist economies, however, use numerous methods to try to influence economic enterprise.

Among the industrial nations, the United States is one of the most purely capitalist in the way its economic activity is organized. The United States is especially distinguished by the extent to which it still relies on market forces. The majority of economic enterprise is privately operated, and few activities are totally publicly owned. Nonetheless, although economic activity is primarily privately owned, the United States does intervene in economic activity to a great extent. Thus, people in the United States, who pride themselves on having a nearly pure form of "free"-market capitalism, actually function within a regulated economy.

The economist Milton Friedman, probably the preeminent defender of the free-market system, suggested that a pure free-enterprise economy would be based on:

- A self-adjusting free market independent of any government intervention;
- Human beings seeking to maximize their own economic self-interest;
- Competition—stimulated by individual self-interest—that produces maximum benefits for all; and
- Private ownership of the means of production and distribution, which leads to competition, which results in the best quality of product at the lowest price.[3]

Critics of Friedman's position argue that the free-market approach is based on several assumptions that simply are not valid, at least as the so-called free market is known in the United States. Free-market theory rests on the imperfect assumptions that:

- Human beings are motivated essentially by economic wants;
- People have perfect information on which to make rational economic choices;
- Demand is elastic (adjusts to changing prices);

- Production and price are elastic (producers can respond easily to shifts in demand); and
- There is perfect competition.[4]

These assumptions are frequently not representative of real-life economics. The market often fails because human beings act on bases other than economic rationality. Producers, for example, often create demand through advertising—that is, they create artificial "needs" in people purely through the power of persuasive advertising and then fill these new "needs" at a profit to themselves.[5] Furthermore, people often do things because they enjoy doing them, even though there may be negative economic consequences. People do not have perfect information about goods and services and would probably not be able to assimilate and analyze all the information even if it were available. Time is limited, and choices must be made.

Nor is there perfect competition in the market. Instead, the economy is characterized by unevenness in resources among producers. Some students of economic systems suggest that our economy actually is made up of two different groups of economic entities.[6] On one side are the large, powerful firms that are few in number but have the resources to persist and to influence other actors in the economy. Then there are many very small firms that find it difficult to compete because they lack the resources to keep up with technological innovations. They often are absorbed by the large firms or are forced out of existence because they are not competitive. Consumers, by the same token, have little ability to influence the powerful producers. The result is that little effective competition takes place in the economy; therefore, prices do not follow the supply-and-demand curve. What happens is that those with resources end up dominating the market, taking advantage of their power to further their own interests.

Finally, consumers' choices within the market may be limited. Even though the cost of gasoline may be very high, some people have no other way to get to work than by automobile and thus are limited in how much they can reduce consumption. Similarly, regardless of cost, a sick or injured person needs medical assistance.

Because of the failure of the free-market system to operate perfectly, many governments intervene to guide and control the economic system. Much government policy is based on the intent to protect citizens and consumers against fraud and abuse, to control monopolies (and thus help make the market truly free), and to protect against inequities and inefficiencies. However, if those with economic power also have political power, as is often the case, government policy may be oriented toward protecting their interests. Still other goals of economic planners have been to keep the economy operating on a stable basis and to avoid constant sharp fluctuations between inflation with full employment and recession with unemployment. Such often-conflicting objectives have been difficult to pursue, and economic policy has been characterized by numerous unintended consequences and indirect impacts.

History of Government's Role

Many critics of government policies seem to mistakenly believe that the United States began with economic enterprise flourishing free from intervention by the political system. Actually, policies to influence economic activity always have been a part of the American political landscape. The American Revolution resulted, in part, from financial grievances of the colonists, who felt the British monarchy was unfairly impeding colonial development through its taxation policies. After the Revolution, policies affecting economic well-being continued to be a major concern. Witness the controversy surrounding the establishment of a national bank and its relationship to the national debt during George Washington's administration.

In its early history, the United States government stimulated the economy through public investment or attempts to create an environment in which the economy could prosper. The national government subsidized development through land grant programs to the railroad industry and to states to establish educational institutions that would, in turn, focus on supporting the agricultural economy. State governments set many precedents during this time in their attempts to spur economic growth. Roads and canals also were built with government subsidy, further illustrating government's efforts to stimulate development.

Although citizens became accustomed to government playing a supportive role in economic activity, they did not appear willing to accept government interference beyond that role. During the latter part of the nineteenth century, a very strong antigovernment sentiment developed. The national government had begun to develop regulatory policies aimed at curbing some of the abuses of large corporate enterprises. Industry, however, was politically influential and was successful in convincing the political leadership to take a laissez-faire approach to economic activities.[7] It was not until the 1930s that government returned to an interventionist approach. The severe economic depression following the market crash of 1929 led people to accept a greater government role, but even then there was a great deal of hesitation about permitting government to become too deeply involved in private enterprise.

When the Great Depression first hit, the immediate response of President Herbert Hoover's administration was to raise taxes and try to balance the budget. Unfortunately, these actions exacerbated the problem. The nation, in no mood for half-measures, sought a new leader in Franklin D. Roosevelt, who quickly took another approach. He convinced Congress to create several new agencies and programs to address the extraordinary problems of unemployment and the slump in production. This whirlwind of legislative action was unprecedented; within the first 100 days of Roosevelt's first term, Congress

- Passed the Emergency Banking Act, which was intended to put the banking industry back on a solid foundation;
- Created the Civilian Conservation Corps, a public works program to hire the unemployed directly by government;
- Funded state welfare programs through the Federal Emergency Relief Act;
- Passed the National Industrial Recovery Act to regulate wages, collective bargaining, and work hours and to permit business to organize combinations to eliminate waste and some forms of competition;
- Created the Agricultural Adjustment Administration to support agricultural production and prices; and
- Created the Securities and Exchange Commission to protect investors.

The preceding represent only a few of the new programs; an era had begun in which governmental intervention in economic matters would grow immensely. It is important to note, however, that these programs maintained the tradition of government support for economic prosperity and that intervention was limited to rebuilding the economy through aid to particular enterprises. Later came government efforts to influence the private sector to perform in a particular way, sometimes against its will. These programs helped in curing the ills of the Depression, but they did not lead to complete prosperity for the economic system.

During the late 1930s, many leaders, including Roosevelt, became convinced that the free-market system could not regulate itself satisfactorily. The Depression had shown that some of the assumptions of free-market theory, discussed earlier, were not valid. Now it was recognized that, for a variety of reasons, sometimes severe fluctuations in the market economy were inevitable without government intervention. Influenced by the ideas of John Maynard Keynes, whose *General Theory of Employment, Interest, and Money* suggested new approaches to the relationship between government and the economy, Roosevelt and his administration began to modify public policy.[8] Not until the economic impact of World War II became apparent, however, was the immense power of the political system in influencing the economy recognized. Active government intervention began in virtually every aspect of the economy.

The wartime economy, dictated in large part by the government, had clearly stimulated employment and economic growth. Recognition that government spending could create such dramatic effects created the foundation for sustained government action to influence desirable economic activity and to correct problems in the economy. It was, then, during the 1940s that maintenance of prosperity became a major public issue. Today this recognition remains one of the most, if not the most, important concerns of any national administration. The American people now expect the government to take action to resolve problems in the economy, but there are major differences of opinion on just what action will produce the desired results. The contrasts between the philosophies of Friedman and Galbraith outlined at the beginning of this chapter are examples of opposing perspectives on what the role of government should be.

Today, few argue that the government has no appropriate role in the economic sector. Instead, controversy exists over where government should intervene, and for whom. We already have reviewed most of the areas of responsibility. Traditionally, one purpose of government economic policy has been to stimulate economic growth. In the 1970s, however, many economic policies also had to address problems of scarcity, particularly in energy and food. Another purpose of economic programs is protecting and supporting the private enterprise system through promoting full employment, protecting the well-being of citizens, and controlling the pressures of inflation and/or recession. Ultimately, economic policies also result in redistributing resources among the various groups in society.

Inflation and Recession

Inflation is a rise in the price of goods and services, even though the actual value of those goods and services does not increase. Thus, although prices increase, production does not keep pace, resulting in a decline in the purchasing power of money—that is, each dollar purchases less than it did in the past.

Inflation may occur when the demand for goods and services grows at a faster rate than available supplies. Competing consumers drive up the prices for such goods. This type of inflation is known as *demand-pull inflation.* Another type, *cost-push inflation*, refers to an increase in the cost of a product, even though demand remains constant or drops. It occurs when prices are regulated in some way rather than impersonally set by supply and demand. The rise in oil prices, for example, is a form of cost-push inflation, as are rises in labor wage rates without a corresponding rise in productivity. Normally during periods of demand-pull inflation, employment goes up, although this may not be true during times of cost-push inflation. We shall see in Chapter 4 why different remedies are appropriate to these different inflation forms. The inflation of the 1970s and early 1980s seemed to result from a combination of demand-pull and cost-push factors. The demand-pull inflation was clearly initiated by the attempt to fight the Vietnam War without a tax increase. Military spending pumps many additional dollars into the economy without generating a corresponding increase in consumer goods and services those dollars can buy and is therefore the most inflationary kind of spending. Once this inflation is generated, the wage-price spiral of cost-push inflation perpetuates it.

Recessions are periods in which there is a decline in economic activity arising from a slump in effective demand for goods and services. An oversupply of goods and services may cause a drop in production, leading to increased unemployment. Unemployed people are able to purchase less, thus further nourishing the recession. Most recently, recessions hit the United States from 1981 to 1982, 1991, and in 2001 to 2002. Prolonged recessions are called *depressions.*

Microeconomic Approaches

Government concerns about the economy fall into two groups, microeconomic and macroeconomic policy. Generally, microeconomic policy refers to government activities regarding particular firms and businesses, and macroeconomic policy refers to the overall management of the economy. Examples of microeconomic policy are regulation and subsidy programs. Macroeconomic policy includes monetary and fiscal policies. Microeconomic approaches are the primary subject of the rest of this chapter; macroeconomic approaches are examined in the next chapter.

Government intervention now extends to almost every aspect of our lives in efforts to protect our health, safety, welfare, and environment, and to promote economic and social justice. The emphasis in this chapter, however, is on intervention, which directly affects economic activity. Other chapters address government activities as they relate to other substantive areas, such as the environment, health, education, and equality of opportunity.

As noted earlier, the U.S. government always has intervened in economic activities. Early on, those activities were supportive and eventually gave way to more of a regulatory approach. Today, we have a combination of the two. Regulation may be characterized as "old style" (economic) regulation or "new style" (social) regulation. Each has an impact on economic activity and the viability of economic enterprises.

Economic regulation.   Old style or economic regulation, in the form of early antitrust laws, began as a way of controlling concentrations of wealth and power in large private-sector economic enterprises; the purpose was to ensure that private economic gain did not hurt the public interest. Guarding the public interest generally meant protection against the economic abuse of citizens by prohibiting such practices as charging unreasonable prices, engaging in anticompetitive activities, or selling products hazardous to the health and safety of the public. Basically, the regulators are meant to be watchdogs for the public. In addition to protecting the public interest, economic regulation had the objective of preserving competition and controlling natural monopolies.

Regulatory agencies normally have a fair degree of independence from other governmental institutions. In establishing regulatory agencies, legislative bodies have delegated certain of their policymaking powers to them and have tried to protect them as much as possible against interference from the executive branch. A regulatory agency such as the Federal Trade Commission (FTC), for example, is created by legislative action. The mandate that Congress gave to the FTC is somewhat vague: to regulate in the interest of ensuring competition and to prevent deceptive advertising by industry. Five commissioners serve staggered seven-year terms on this commission, with the provision that no more than two may be from the same political party. The president designates one member as chairperson. Once appointed by the president and confirmed by the Senate, the president (except under unusual circumstances) may not remove a commissioner. Other regulatory agencies are similarly created and members similarly appointed, although the number of commissioners varies from agency to agency. Units within regular operating departments of the executive branch, which therefore are less independent of the president, also carry out much regulating. One example is the Food and Drug Administration in the Department of Health and Human Services.

Congress gave regulatory agencies relative independence from the president because it felt that partisan politics had no place in regulation, and it did not want to surrender its powers to the executive branch. Another reason why Congress delegated its powers was simply that it did not have the time, expertise, or other resources to carry out the specialized activities for which regulatory agencies were created. Ideally, the application of expertise and technical judgment is supposed to be free of politics. Though insulated from partisan political forces to the extent that board or commission members have fixed terms and ordinarily cannot be removed by the president, regulatory agencies have not escaped politics entirely. Rather, they are subject to many political pressures from interest groups, legislative committees, and the White House. Because Congress and the president have much to say about the budgets and, indeed, the very existence of regulatory agencies, the agencies pay attention to opinions from those sources.

In applying their expertise to problems, regulatory agencies give meaning to the general policies developed by the legislative bodies. To do so, regulatory agencies adopt rules and regulations that have the force of law. Unlike legislative policymakers, however, regulatory agencies also enforce and serve as judges regarding this policy. Thus, once they draw up a rule or regulation, they have the responsibility of seeing that the regulated party abides by the rules. They also decide whether a rule has been violated by an individual party and fashion a punishment appropriate for the violation.

Of course, a commission itself cannot do all the work of a regulatory agency and usually performs only the policymaking and judging functions. Its staff executes commission policy, although the staff also creates policy and does the major work in investigating and hearing evidence on cases in which violation of policy is charged. Once a hearing examiner has heard and evaluated the evidence, the examiner makes a recommendation on how the case should be decided. Normally, the commission accepts the examiner's recommendation, although the commission may make changes.

Social regulation. New style, or social, regulation attempts to correct problems in society through incentives or regulation to encourage or control various behaviors. Economic enterprises often are the vehicles for achieving social policy goals and thus are the objects of government intervention. Social regulation may be in the form of financial penalties, such as in emissions fees for emitting pollutants into the air. Presumably, private enterprise will reduce emissions to avoid the financial penalties. An alternative approach is to encourage action by providing financial support for conversion of plants or bonuses for early compliance. Another alternative is to allocate permits for a specific level of emissions. By reducing emissions below its permitted level, a company could sell portions of its permit to others. Presumably, such a system would serve as an incentive to modernize equipment and reduce pollution or at least stop the addition of more pollution. Policies that require contractors with the government to subcontract a certain portion of the contract with businesses owned by minorities or females represent another alternative for achieving a social goal.

Typically, social regulation occurs through already established executive departments, although there are exceptions as with the Equal Employment Opportunity Commission, which operates like the typical economic regulatory agency. Many of the social policies are implemented through contract compliance activities or through the departments of Labor and Commerce, although all departments have some role in such activities.

Regulation of economic activity is an attempt to stabilize the economy and protect the interests of the general public. We already have looked at the most common form of regulation in the United States, agencies that create specific rules and regulations to control the behavior of economic enterprises or that provide incentives or penalties to encourage particular actions. Control of activities also is accomplished in several other ways. These methods include government ownership and the creation of government corporations. Ownership of public lands by the Department of the Interior is intended to control how the land is used. The U.S. Postal Service and the Federal Deposit Insurance Corporation are government-owned corporations that regulate and control many postal and banking activities. In addition, there are many programs and policies to protect particular economic interests. In agriculture, for example, many of the programs and policies subsidize particular economic entities and interfere with the free market. The case studies which follow demonstrate the different types of government intervention to support economic enterprises.

CONTEMPORARY POLICY: CASE STUDIES
IN ECONOMIC INTERVENTION

In the following section we will examine how different forms of microeconomic intervention have been applied in influencing the economy through antitrust policy and subsidy of business activity, and old and new style regulation. Virtually every aspect of the economy is subject to some intervention by government, but to inventory them all here would be impossible. These case studies will illustrate pertinent approaches to today's economic policy.

The Federal Trade Commission: Traditional Economic Regulation

Around the close of the nineteenth century and the beginning of the twentieth, various energetic business entrepreneurs managed to acquire near monopolies on many American industries, including steel and the railroads. These concentrations of power in a few hands were accompanied by many abuses. Consumers were charged exorbitant prices, small companies were bullied into selling out or were ruined by the large firms, and local governments were pressured into making concessions. Ruthless employers exploited workers in such monopolies, with almost no bargaining power, at will. All of these factors led to the reaction, by the public and politicians alike, that concentration of economic power in a small number of enterprises was not in the public interest. A movement grew in the United States to regulate industry through antitrust policy (a trust is a combination of several companies, especially one that limits competition). See Table 3-1 for a glossary of terms. In time, a series of laws was enacted that forms the framework of today's government controls over such economic concentration. Policies evolved that went beyond antitrust to include other types of protection of the general public and also to support corporate entities as well.

Antitrust policy is aimed at preventing one or a small number of firms from directly dominating all or most of a particular market. It also attempts to prevent private firms from agreeing among themselves to restrict competition. Thus, antitrust policy prohibits monopolies, practices, and agreements that fix prices, divide markets, or collude on bidding. To control monopolies and to dissolve those that had already come into being, Congress passed the Sherman Antitrust Act in 1890. The Federal Trade Commission Act of 1914 went further by creating the FTC to stem the development of monopolies and prevent practices that would lead to unfair competition. Because these laws were only partially successful, the policy was strengthened in 1950 with the Anti-Merger Act, which gave enforcement powers to administrative agencies. As part of its activities, the FTC has the responsibility to control anticompetitive and unfair trade practices and to protect consumers from unfair advertising.

Taken together, the antitrust laws give government a number of enforcement tools. The Sherman Act, and subsequent legislation, makes illegal any action in restraint of interstate commerce. Government attorneys, currently the Antitrust Division of the Justice Department, can initiate criminal prosecution against companies charged with this violation. Additionally—and with greater effect—the Antitrust Division may initiate civil suits to obtain court orders requiring firms to cease practices that are found to be in restraint of trade. A similar proceeding may require a

---

TABLE 3-1 ▪ Glossary of Antitrust Terms

Antitrust policy: Policy aimed at preventing domination of a market by one or a small number of firms, or agreements to restrict competition.
Class action suit: Case in which one party sues on behalf of all people in a similar situation.
Horizontal merger: Combining of two or more firms which produce or sell the same or similar products.
Hostile takeover: Action in which the purchase of controlling interest by an outsider is opposed by the target firm's management.
Merger: Action in which two or more firms combine to form one firm.
Monopoly: Situation in which there is an absence of competition, blocked entry into the market, a single seller, or a few sellers who work together to limit competition.
Takeover: Action in which an outsider buys controlling interest in a firm.
Trust: Combination of several companies, especially one that limits competition.
Vertical merger: Action in which firms involved in different aspects or components of a product (e.g., manufacture and sales; computer hardware and software) combine to form one firm.

---

firm to break up into several units; the Standard Oil Corporation, for example, was divided into a number of companies in this way during the early part of the twentieth century. AT&T, which controlled 83 percent of the telephone market, was the object of antitrust litigation. Because the government's case was so strong, the company settled out of court in 1982 and agreed to dissolve, resulting in the current decentralized telephone service structure. Starting in 1995, the Antitrust Division charged Microsoft® with anticompetitive practices and, by 1997, sought orders to break up the company and to require the company to desist from some practices. While Microsoft® lost the initial round of the case, it has not been settled at this writing; thus, the Justice Department has not been entirely successful in its efforts.

The Antitrust Division also has the authority to approve or disapprove mergers. In the 1980s, the Justice Department essentially took a hands-off approach that led to virtually uncontrolled mergers. The Clinton administration approach was mixed in that it looked more carefully at mergers, but most of the effort was in adjusting terms of the mergers to assure market competition rather than disallowing them. The Bush administration seems to be following the same general approach.

Another weapon that can be used is a suit by an individual who has been hurt by an antitrust violation. Current law permits court awards of triple the amount of damages suffered. But relying on such suits is not a very effective method of enforcing regulations: Both lack of interest and the large amount of time required of the litigants and courts in such procedures discourage victims from suing. It is not an efficient method of controlling behavior unless all the parties affected join in a class action suit.

Class action suits are those in which an individual or individuals sue on behalf of all people who are in a similar situation. Thus, a female employee who has been discriminated against in pay and promotional opportunities may sue her employer for remedy and may include all other female employees who had worked for the employer during the same period of time. Those female employees would be part of the "class" on whose behalf litigation was being initiated. Because of the large number of people who may be affected in such cases, and because courts usually have required litigants to demonstrate personal injury in order to be a party to a court action, class action suits have been difficult to pursue. Also, courts often require the litigants to identify and notify all members of the class. This requirement can be difficult to meet because the people are hard to locate, and many may be too indifferent to respond. As a result, class action suits are not a major means of accomplishing regulation, although they are used on occasion.[9] In 2002, former employees of Enron, a Houston, Texas, energy company, initiated a class action suit against the company and its directors over the loss of their 401(k) pension investments after the company let most of its employees go as its stock value dropped precipitously.

FTC hearings. Until the late 1930s, antitrust legislation was not very effective because the Supreme Court was unsympathetic to such regulation. In particular, judges were hesitant to rule in favor of restrictions on the use of private property—owners were protected in their right to use their property as they saw fit. In its first decision regarding the Sherman Act, for example, the U.S. Supreme Court held that manufacturing was exempt from the act because it was not commerce.[10] Ironically, the Sherman Act became an ally of business because the court interpreted it to restrict labor unions as restraints of trade.[11] After 1937, however, the Supreme Court's receptivity to antitrust action grew, and the FTC became more active in pursuing antitrust violators. Cases have involved action against Exxon Oil Corporation, International Telephone and Telegraph, cereal companies, Heinz and Beech-Nut baby food companies, Kroger and Winn Dixie grocers, Coca-Cola and PepsiCo along with five other soft drink companies, and many others. The FTC, however, has not always been very successful in these cases. The ironies of antitrust policy were evident in 1997, when the FTC approved the merger of Boeing and McDonnell Douglas, resulting in a single aircraft manufacturer in the United States. Yet the FTC opposed the merger of Staples and Office Depot, office supply retailers, on the basis that the merger would lead to control of too much of the market, as Staples would be the only such retailer in some local markets.

The FTC, like most regulatory agencies, has a small staff and budget compared to the corporations it confronts in its work. The opportunities for the regulated parties to delay or buy time are many, including some which are the result of procedural protections required by the courts or the FTC's own rules. These requirements give FTC proceedings the aura of a courtroom process. The staff investigates complaints, and a formal hearing may ensue. The hearing requires notice to the parties involved, and each has the opportunity to present its case. Parties under investigation sometimes inundate the agency with volumes of testimonial material, considerably lengthening the time it takes for the investigation and hearing to be completed. Afterward, the hearing examiner, now called an administrative law judge, must evaluate the record before making a decision. With the record often comprising thousands of pages of very complex material, the examiner has a formidable task and needs time to reflect on the evidence.

Once the process is completed, a party to the case may appeal the decision of the administrative law judge. The full commission then hears the case as if it were a totally new proceeding. The same opportunity for delays exists here. After the commission makes its decision, the defendants in the case may appeal to the courts, and—given the high stakes in many cases—litigation can drag on for years, first through the appellate courts, then on to the Supreme Court. A case involving the makers of the diet supplement Geritol, for example, took thirteen years to resolve, although the FTC finally was successful in getting Geritol's ads—which claimed the product cured "tired blood" and "iron deficiency anemia"—removed from the air.[12] The amount of time and money expended caused many to question whether the whole process was worth it.

The FTC also is subject to political whims. Members of the commission are political appointees of the president and, of course, tend to reflect the president's political philosophy. Additionally, Congress controls the FTC's budget; thus, there is a tendency to be careful not to offend important members of Congress. During the 1960s, for example, Ralph Nader and his Center for the Study of Law in the Public Interest conducted a study of the FTC and castigated it for being timid and unresponsive to the consumer. A similarly critical report was issued by the American Bar Association in 1969. With the popularity of the consumer protection movement increasing in the 1960s and into the 1970s, members of Congress prodded the FTC to become aggressive in protecting the consumer. The agency responded and became active in pushing consumer rights.

By 1979, the commission had become so aggressive that many industries began to exert pressure on Congress to limit its activities. During 1979 and 1980, for example, the funeral industry, life insurance industry, and many professionals including doctors, dentists, and lawyers all brought pressure on Congress to limit the authority of the FTC to regulate their business practices. Many members of Congress agreed with their complaints, and it appeared that the powers of the FTC might be severely limited. Although Congress ultimately did not adopt this policy, the prospect of such restrictions does illustrate the tenuous position of the agency. Created to protect the consuming public, the FTC often finds itself the object of intense political pressures to conform to industry's position on regulation. The election of Ronald Reagan as president in 1980 led to a swing entirely in the opposite direction from the consumer protection focus of the 1970s. During the 1980s, the FTC became a protector of private enterprise, and budgets and staff were severely slashed. After 1989, with President Bush's appointment of Janet D. Steiner to the chair, the FTC developed a balanced stance, and Clinton and Bush II administration appointees have continued a balanced approach with a little more assertiveness on the commission's part through reviewing mergers carefully and pursuing price-fixing cases. The current position of the FTC appears to be that the free market can work, but that consumers have rights as well, and a balance between those interests is the best policy.

Mergers. The role of the Justice Department's Antitrust Division in the Reagan administration led to an era of almost uncontrolled mergers. The Antitrust Division stopped challenging mergers except in rare cases. As a result, some very large mergers, which probably would not have been approved in any previous administration, were completed. The $20.3 billion Kohlberg Kravis and Roberts Company deal to buy RJR Nabisco attracted a lot of attention in December, 1988, as the most expensive to that date. There were many implications, not the least of which was that approval by the Justice Department signaled that mergers were not of much concern to it. The Bush administration appeared to favor some regulation of mergers, and 1990 did witness a decline in the number and value of mergers (see Figure 3-1). There was an upswing in mergers again in the 1990s, despite a sharp decline in 1996. The causes may be economic as much as policy-based. In December of 2000, the FTC approved the merger of America Online, Inc. (AOL) and Time Warner Inc. in a deal worth $166 billion.

The courts have been less hostile to mergers as well in recent years. In the past, market share was a very important consideration in decisions on mergers. The FTC and the courts were likely to disallow any merger that increased market share of a corporation by even as much as 10 percent. In recent years, mergers have been allowed wherein market share was increased as much as 40 percent or, as in the case of Boeing and McDonnell Douglas, 100 percent of the domestic production. The courts have sanctioned such mergers even when the FTC has been opposed.

Weaknesses in U.S. antitrust policy are the result of many factors. One is a lack of clarity about goals. Given the responsibility to restore competition and prevent deceptive advertising, the FTC and the Justice Department would seem to have easily understood objectives. However, these are rather ambiguous goals in terms of the precise actions that might be taken to achieve them. Another factor also explains the sometimes erratic performance: The commission and the Justice Department have discretion as to which of these objectives they emphasize. As different presidents influence these regulators through their appointments, the perspectives of the agencies vary. Thus, uneven attention is given to enforcement of rules and regulations. Ambivalence about how strongly antitrust policy should be pursued also provides regulated industries with opportunities to articulate their positions. Industries have the resources and contacts to make their concerns known to regulators, who are often sympathetic in the first place. They are usually effective in mobilizing political forces to reduce the intensity of the enforcement efforts. With the increasingly

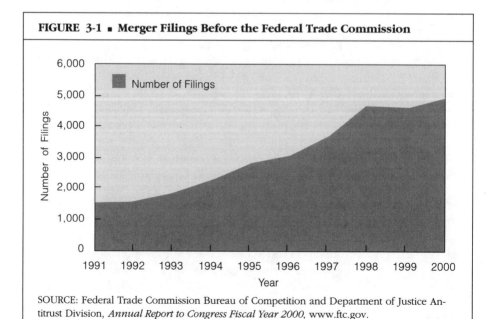

FIGURE 3-1 ▪ Merger Filings Before the Federal Trade Commission

SOURCE: Federal Trade Commission Bureau of Competition and Department of Justice Antitrust Division, *Annual Report to Congress Fiscal Year 2000*, www.ftc.gov.

global competitive environment, there also are pressures to be more flexible with domestic corporations so that they can compete with foreign corporations.

International approaches to antitrust. Industrialized nations generally favor some form of control over monopoly and restraint of trade, although some nations, such as Italy, have virtually no antitrust or antimonopoly laws. Reflecting a different perspective, most Western European nations identify their policies as competition policies as opposed to antitrust policies, as they are named in the United States. Although many of the Western European nations use approaches similar to that of the United States, there are variations. Some countries have weaker policies. For example, in Great Britain the approval of Parliament is required before the Monopolies Commission can prevent mergers. This provision opens regulation much more directly to political pressures and thus lessens its effectiveness. So long as mergers are not found to be contrary to the public interest, they are not prohibited. Very seldom does British government find them to be harmful.

Germany represents the opposite end of the spectrum. There, government approval is required before mergers of large corporations can occur. More significantly, the German Cartel Office also has the authority to dissolve a corporation brought about by merger. Most European nations employ an approach somewhere between these two extremes.

Japan appears less enthusiastic about controlling competition, believing that too much competition leads to inefficiencies. Nonetheless, after World War II, policy to break up monopolies was imposed upon Japan. Although enforcement has been weak, the law was strengthened in 1977, and efforts have been made to limit price fixing and protect consumers through communication about abuses.[13]

Community Revitalization Issues: Merging Social and Economic Concerns

Economic development has become a major concern of most levels of government, as the economy has had to adjust to rapidly changing conditions and technology. Economically depressed areas are fraught with many social problems, such as unemployment, crime, deteriorated housing, and limited tax bases among others. During the 1980s, the concept of enterprise zones was imported from Great Britain and implemented in many states.[14] The national government adopted the idea when the Clinton administration made enterprise zones a major part of its urban policy. Beginning with nine such zones nationwide, the number has grown to more than a thousand such designations by the national and state governments.[15] The designations carry various names including renewal communities, enterprise communities, and enterprise zones.

The zones target economic development geographically. They are partnerships in which government and the private and nonprofit sectors work together to attempt to stimulate economic development and to solve some of the social problems associated with economically depressed areas. The experiments are examples of how government supports business. The zones provide for such benefits as reduced taxes, tax credits, technical assistance, and reduction or elimination of regulations so that private sector entities can develop innovative economic activities.

In addition to the economic incentives and push for economic development, these zones focus intensive governmental agency attention to such social problems as crime, lack of good housing, and high unemployment in the zones. As economic development occurs, many of the social problems are expected to recede in severity, but not all can be cured by economic development alone. Thus, federal agencies, in cooperation with state and local units as well as private and nonprofit organizations, work together to apply resources to address the social problems.

The experience so far suggests that the zones can have beneficial effects, although it is difficult to measure just how much improvement can be attributed to the zones themselves. States usually provide income tax credits and some allow property tax abatements as well as waivers of sales taxes in the zone. Businesses building in some zones also receive discounts on utility bills. Encompassing broader purposes, some places have reinvested the tax revenues generated in the zones in the infrastructure of the zones to improve conditions even more. Job training programs have been developed for zone residents in some cases.

As an economic development tool, these initiatives represent a politically popular notion. Given the political climate supportive of less government and letting the private sector operate with fewer restrictions, the enterprise zone provides one avenue for doing so. Theoretically, innovative approaches will flow from the decreased taxation and regulation. Government is a facilitator and not the owner of the process. Business benefits and, in the process, so do residents of the zone as well as the general public, who presumably bear less expense resulting from crime and other social problems.

These efforts may cause dislocation of residents with the attendant breakdown of a sense of community. Finding new housing for displaced residents is not easy, either. Sometimes the social problems only move to a new area that becomes overpopulated with the press of residents who have been displaced. Critics of these approaches also note that economic development activity is attracted from other areas that might become economically depressed, thus just moving the problem. The loss in tax revenue caused by the tax abatements and waivers also concerns some people.

As noted earlier, government always has provided support to private enterprise, and these revitalization programs represent one facet of such support. Critics, however, often suggest that government goes too far in supporting economic enterprises. In the debate over government spending with the conservative Congress targeting welfare, liberals have issued a challenge to look at corporate welfare. They cite subsidies to corporations such as McDonald's, Campbell's Soup, and others to advertise abroad or billions in subsidies for agriculture that goes primarily to corporate farm organizations. Similarly, they note that mining companies gain title to land for much less than it is worth and then do not pay royalties on what they extract. Others note state and local government subsidies of professional sports teams through the building of facilities paid for by tax dollars. Obviously, the list of the various types of support provided to corporations is a long one and liberals challenge their conservative colleagues to look at those benefits as they try to find ways of reducing government spending and the deficit.

International Trade

International trade represents another aspect of the current economic environment. Most administrations in recent history have supported free trade in theory. In reality, the United States often fosters barriers like tariffs, import quotas, or subsidies to industries that give them advantages over others. Other nations do the same thing.

NAFTA. The North American Free Trade Act (NAFTA) agreed to by Congress in November, 1993, created a free trade area among the United States, Canada, and Mexico. Theoretically, NAFTA would result in the United States being better able to sell goods in the Mexican market and stimulate economic development in Mexico as well. Immigration pressures on the United States presumably would be lessened as better economic opportunities developed for Mexican citizens. Critics of the agreement fear the migration of U.S. jobs to Mexico and the lessening of health, safety, and environmental standards.[16] NAFTA built upon the United States–Canada Free Trade Agreement of 1988, which provided virtually free trade between the two countries.

The Omnibus Trade Act of 1988 provides for the United States to impose such restrictions as tariffs or import quotas on any trading partner that imposed barriers on American access to their markets. The trade act was a product of rising concern over the nation's growing trade deficit, particularly the trade imbalance with Japan. The act required the president to identify those nations with unfair trade practices and a large American trade surplus as targets for trade negotiations. If the negotiation process failed, American trade restrictions would follow as retaliation. It also created a training program for American workers adversely affected by international trade practices. Promotion of American exports and training for American industry to enhance the likelihood of success internationally also were parts of the act.

GATT. A major debate in Congress in 1994 involved ratification of agreements under the General Agreement on Tariffs and Trade (GATT). GATT was established after World War II and was designed to reduce national tariff barriers to international trade. It took almost a decade to negotiate the agreement, and it stirred emotions within the political establishment. The agreement reduces tariffs on manufactured goods an average of nearly 40 percent. Presumably, that would translate into lower prices for consumers. Opponents felt that reduced U.S. collection of tariffs would add to the federal deficit.

Supporters of GATT argued that it would lead to increased sales of U.S. products around the world, while opponents pointed to the increased sales of foreign goods in the United States, thus killing jobs and lowering wages for American workers. The agreement would provide more protection against piracy of software and other copyrighted works throughout the world. Advocates of the agreement also indicated that new markets would be opened for U.S. construction firms and architects and engineers.

Perhaps the most controversial part of the new GATT agreement was the creation of the World Trade Organization (WTO). WTO is the successor to GATT. It attempts to settle disputes and monitor and crack down on unfair trade practices. While advocates applaud the provision as bringing pressure on others to comply with fair trade practices, opponents suggest that it weakens health, safety, and labor laws in the United States. Further, they argue that it makes state and local governments conform to WTO policies and standards. Any suggestion of a world organization impinging on U.S. sovereignty is certain to arouse heated debate. While the political posturing during the 1994 election and after was intense, Congress did ratify the agreement in December of 1994. The United States joined 123 other nations in an effort to eliminate trade barriers on many items. Clearly, some industries that had been subsidized will have hard times, while others that have had to compete against subsidized firms will benefit. In 1996, the election of additional members of Congress who oppose the WTO resulted in weaker U.S. support of WTO. Another casualty of the new mood in Congress was the failure to renew the president's fast-track authority to negotiate trade agreements. *Fast-track* authority means that Congress has to vote an agreement up or down without amendment. It was renewed in 2002.

Many of the arguments used for and against the new GATT accord are ones used for and against NAFTA. Neither the grand promises of NAFTA's advocates nor the dire predictions of its detractors seem to have developed. There are initial indications of success, especially in the export of American goods to Mexico, although Mexico's monetary crisis and devaluation of the peso in 1995 slowed progress. NAFTA supporters point to improved economic conditions in Mexico as evidence that it is working. Opponents highlight the poverty and low wages in Mexico as evidence that NAFTA is not working and is hurting U.S. workers who command higher wages.

European Economic Community. Another issue related to trade and the economy is the move by the European Economic Community (EEC) to develop an integrated economy. In 1985, member nations of the EEC developed a detailed plan to achieve a unified economic system by the end of 1992, eliminating restrictions on trade, services, the flow of capital, and labor supply. The goal of this plan is to create an environment that stimulates economic growth in member nations. Although significant progress has been made, the goal of unification has not yet been achieved. Some nations, notably Sweden and Norway, so far have declined to join in the effort and others have been slow to implement some of the needed changes. A major stumbling block had been the effort to develop a unified currency, which finally occurred in 2002 with the substitution of the euro for national currencies in all but Great Britain, Norway, and Sweden.

Successful implementation of the EEC economic system has the potential to provide major economic competition for the United States in the global economy. The EEC represents a potential market of over 300 million consumers with a significant commercial and industrial base. The United States has yet to develop a comprehensive economic policy to address the impact of the change in Europe.

POLICY EVALUATION: ENCOURAGING COMPETITION OR DISCOURAGING INNOVATION?

Deregulation

A clear trend since the mid-1970s has been the deregulation of previously heavily regulated industries. The Carter administration began the process gradually by examining individual regulatory agencies and the industries they regulated. The Reagan and elder Bush administrations took a more sweeping approach to deregulation, reflecting strong commitment to a market economy free of governmental constraints. Ideologically, conservatives have been strong supporters of deregulation. The current political environment dictates a continued emphasis on reducing regulation.

With deregulation came many benefits to consumers and some parts of industry. Some businesses also suffered economic reversals. In the airline industry, for example, consumers benefited from increased competition as airfares declined. In the long run, airfares increased again, but competition has sustained many bargain fares. Service to smaller communities has suffered on occasion, and bunching of departure times around peak travel hours has led to complaints of inconvenience. However, the public seems to prefer the bargain fares to matters of scheduling and service inconvenience.

The relaxation of regulation has had broader implications. The Reagan and Bush administrations deemphasized implementation of such policies as antitrust, equal employment opportunity, and labor relations. The business sector found the administrators of these programs willing to interpret policies in ways more sympathetic to business. Thus, the National Labor Relations Board and the federal courts changed the direction of much of labor law. They permitted the use of bankruptcy laws, for example, to release corporations from contract obligations under collective bargaining agreements, as happened with Continental Airlines and the Manville Corporation. One effect is that labor unions found it necessary to accept bargaining agreements that scaled back their earnings and benefits. Corporations thus clearly have had a stronger hand in controlling their own destiny. While the Clinton administration generally was more supportive of labor and consumers, its tendency was cautious in reinstituting regulation, especially in light of the public complaints about the overregulated society. The new Bush administration emphasizes the interests of business in removing as much regulation as possible.

Similarly, antitrust policy under the Reagan administration was much more flexible. The Federal Trade Commission seemed less interested than ever before in prohibiting mergers based on the size of the market controlled. Merger mania began in the late 1970s and accelerated in the 1980s as the Reagan administration relaxed rules. Many of these mergers were "hostile" takeovers in which entrepreneurs took over undervalued corporations. The managers of the takeover targets usually are the most resistant to takeovers, although many stockholders also question the long-term wisdom of such actions. Mergers continue at a high rate with many high-profile mergers in the 1990s and early 2000s.

International Trade

Yet another aspect of the current business environment is the policy regarding international trade. Although the Reagan and Bush administrations strongly supported free trade as a stated policy, they did exert pressure on foreign competition. Other nations were pushed to agree to voluntary import quotas on such items as steel, textiles, and automobiles. The expectation was that import quotas would improve the prospects of domestic industry to sell its products. After the 1984 election, the administration lessened its efforts in maintaining voluntary quotas. Without the political pressures of an election, it was easier for the administration to act consistently with its free-trade stance. However, as the Reagan administration left office, it became involved in a trade war with members of the European

Economic Community, who banned U.S. beef that had been fed growth hormones. The administration retaliated with duties equal to 100 percent of the value of food imports from those nations. At the same time, a free-trade agreement was reached with Canada. The Bush administration signed a free-trade agreement with Mexico, but was less inclined to do so with Western Europe and others. In addition, the Bush administration entered into negotiations with Canada and Mexico and the member nations of the GATT. Eventually, NAFTA and the GATT agreement were negotiated and ratified in 1993 and 1994, respectively, under the auspices of the Clinton administration. In 1997, Congress refused to approve renewal of the president's fast-track authority in negotiating trade agreements, thus making agreements undoubtedly more difficult to reach. President Bush was successful in getting Congress to approve fast-track authority for him in 2002.

Assistance to Business

The efforts to support economic enterprise reflect some reaction to the increasing criticism of government intervention as a regulator of business activity. Thus, instead of being seen as an inhibitor of economic innovation, the effort is to support new approaches. Government provides the support and facilitation of efforts, but is not the controller of those activities. In the states that have used enterprise zones in the past, supporters usually point to impressive numbers, especially in job creation. However, critics note that many of those jobs would have been created in the absence of enterprise zones or other support. While the development and job creation may not have occurred in the particular locales, they probably would have happened in other places. Evaluation of the programs then needs to take into account program objectives other than just economic development. For example, do they actually help solve social problems?

The evidence on success of enterprise zones certainly is difficult to assess, partly because there are few formal studies of their impact. Those studies that have been done are inconsistent in their conclusions. A 1994 study in Indiana concluded that enterprise zones were very successful in achieving their goals while a similar 1996 study in New Jersey found "no evidence" that the program improved economic conditions.[17] Clearly, the Bush administration is convinced of their effectiveness as it is moving forward with identification of more project areas, as did the Clinton administration.

All of these elements of policy are sympathetic to the business community. The theoretical effects of government intervention in the economy were examined at the beginning of this chapter, but actual outcomes do not always match the expected results. Critics of regulation note that although much regulation is justified as a means of promoting competition, it often actually tends to stifle that competition. By making entry into a market very difficult, for example, regulation often restricts competition. Competition also is reduced by price controls, as was true in the airline industry until recently. Ironically, for this same reason many industries also defend regulation. Assured of a comfortable environment in which to do business, industry can count on a certain profit margin. Complete competition would make its situation less predictable. Consumers, or consumer advocates, object to this arrangement because it results in higher prices.

Effects of Regulation

One impact that industry often complains of is that government regulation interferes with its capacity to operate efficiently in a free society. According to this charge, regulatory agencies have become pervasive in all economic areas, and their red tape and complex regulations make compliance almost impossible. Many agencies make conflicting demands on industry, and paperwork has increased to the point that industry must employ people solely to deal with government regulation. Confusion abounds: Industries are firmly instructed not to consider race, sex, age, or religion in personnel decisions and, at the same time, are required to submit data on their work force according to the same taboo categories. Moreover, many critics wonder whether regulations are developed to benefit society or simply to keep the wheels spinning so the agency will have something to do.

Regulation also may have unintended consequences in terms of its effects on innovation. Generally, regulated industries appear to be less inclined to adopt new technology and improve their methods of doing business than are nonregulated industries.[18] As a result, regulated industry is likely to be outmoded and less efficient. This is especially true when regulation guarantees a profit. The losers are consumers.

Regulation also is criticized for contributing to the cost of doing business. In their proposals for deregulation, Reagan's staff members often suggested that the costs of regulation could exceed $100 billion a year. Putting that kind of money into nonproductive efforts diverts it from productive ones. However, critics—though usually agreeing that regulation has become excessive—are also anxious that deregulation not go too far, that is, to the point of eliminating legitimate controls.

A common complaint of consumer-oriented critics is that regulation is dominated by the regulated industries themselves, which have the money and other resources to keep abreast of policy. Consumers, especially individuals, find access to regulatory agencies difficult because they lack knowledge of procedures and because of the costs associated with input into decision making. Due to the fact that regulators constantly deal with people from the regulated industries, they develop strong rapport with them. It is only natural that the regulators should consider their interests when making decisions. After all, the regulators would have no one to regulate if they did not help promote their survival! This close relationship often results in strong industry influence and sometimes control over regulators. The interests of consumers may be ignored.

Closely related to the access issue is the complaint that regulatory agencies are outside normal political activities and therefore are not answerable to anyone but themselves and the industries they regulate. It is unreasonable to expect agencies to respond to the major concerns of society if they do not have to answer to the political leadership produced by that society. Of course, regulatory agencies were created to be independent of direct political pressure so that they could consider a wider "public interest." This criticism goes to the heart of the original reason for creating "independent" regulatory agencies in the first place. Independence has both benefits and costs.

It sometimes is argued that government is too involved in too many aspects of everyday life. Government seems to take the position that people need guidance in everything they do, and so virtually no activity is free of government intervention. Duplication of effort, red tape, and examples of bureaucratic bungling, constantly given coverage in the news media, reinforce negative images of regulation. Tax revolts and a rejection of governmental paternalism have led to serious questioning of regulatory efforts. As antigovernment feelings seem to grow, regulatory agencies face major challenges to their activities.

A new twist to these regulatory processes is the effort of the current Federal Trade Commission to keep state and local governments from interfering with competition in the marketplace. Most notable have been those cases in which the FTC has successfully sued municipalities to force deregulation of taxicab companies and their fares as a restraint of trade. This emphasis is a new use of antitrust law consistent with the pro-business, free-trade stance that national elections in the mid- and late 1990s and early 2000s seemed to support.

Deregulation is promoted as a consumer-oriented policy that will result in more competition and lower prices. In the rush to deregulate in the late 1970s and early 1980s, there was little consideration of the social benefits of regulation. But the experience of the airlines is causing some reevaluation. Passenger delays, safety concerns, the loss of service in many cities and regions, and the real cost increases in some fares have caused many to question the benefits of deregulating the airlines. The terrorist attacks of September 11, 2001, in which hijacked airplanes were intentionally crashed, caused even more support for regulations to improve safety. Similarly, there have been many calls for increased regulation of company-sponsored investment programs and of accounting firms after the collapse of Enron and accounting fraud in many corporations in 2002. The benefits of regulation in protecting consumers from capricious action, ensuring a reasonable distribution of important services at a fair cost, and protecting the health and safety of the community are now reemerging concerns as the effects of deregulation are assessed. As with any policy, deregulation has resulted in both positive and negative consequences.

Changes in Regulation

Changes in economic regulation have been many, and the effects have varied greatly. For example, the effects of de-emphasis of antitrust policy are very difficult to assess. While the business world generally applauds the reduction of control over its activities, consumers are not so sure of the benefits. The rash of mergers and leveraged buyouts creates impressive profits for many opportunists, but there are usually losers as well. Many employees, especially white-collar employees, lose their jobs and pensions as a result of the inevitable restructuring of the corporations that are merged. New and reorganized companies often pay lower wages and provide fewer benefits. For the consumer, of course, mergers can lead to less competition and eventually higher prices. Stockholders also are potential losers as total corporate debt increases, exceeding total corporate assets.

Much deregulation in the business sector reduced sensitivity to safety concerns that affect employees. Thus, the effect on employees has been negative. Similarly, the elimination of regulations on product safety can benefit producers in the short run and hurt consumers. In the long run, producers may also be hurt as lawsuits over liability for injury create major financial setbacks.

Mergers themselves do not always work out well. Many of them are undone through divestiture or spinning off parts of the acquired companies. For example, Mobil Oil Corporation bought Montgomery Ward and Company. After spending billions of dollars in attempting to shore up its acquisition, Mobil finally gave up and sold it off, after which Montgomery Ward finally closed entirely. There are numerous examples of similar experiences in which neither party to the merger benefited. In recent years, many of those companies that had diversified have begun divesting in order to narrow their focus and concentrate on what they do best. In this scenario, competition increases. Among those splitting up and paring down are RCA Corporation, ITT, Gulf and Western, and Textron. Supporters of deregulation claim that this trend also is a result of the greater flexibility allowed by deregulation.

An area of the economy that did not seem to benefit from the hands-off policies is agriculture. Farmers had several difficult years in which they have had to borrow heavily in hopes of good crops and prices. Many borrowed to expand their operations because their land values rose during the late 1970s and early 1980s and the market for their crops looked promising. Once land values and incomes dropped, farmers became unable to pay their loans or obtain more credit. Bankruptcy had reached epidemic proportions in the farm belt of the Midwest. In 1987 and 1988, land prices began to rise and the outlook was good. It came too late for many small farmers, however, because they had already gone under. Then the drought of the summer of 1988 brought more economic disaster as crops failed. Hopes were once again dashed. By 1991, farmers had not recovered very well although crops in the Midwest were good that year. The good yields pushed prices on corn and soybeans down. Winter wheat crops were hard hit by disease and profits dropped. In 1994, yields were so good on many crops that many farmers held grains off the market in hopes of raising prices. During the rest of the 1990s and early 2000s, farm income continued to go up and down. In 2002, the farm income is predicted to dip to $40.6 billion from $49.3 billion in 2001.[19] Stability in income continues to be an issue for farmers.

Many small farmers are still economically on the brink, with the cost of federal farm programs at an historic high. The Federal Agriculture Improvement and Reform Act of 1996 reduced the federal role in agriculture. The act eliminated many of the farm subsidies and replaced them with transition payments to assist farmers' movement to a free-market system. Eventually, these supports were to be eliminated. Farmers also were given more flexibility in crops to raise and in the amount of land they can use. Because of the farm difficulties in recent years, however, the new farm legislation passed in 2002 will reintroduce many of the supports eliminated in 1996.

Government economic intervention in the form of subsidies and supports for private enterprise raised serious questions as well. The federal government's efforts to stimulate and stabilize financial institutions through loans and loan guarantees, for example, have made them safe places for investors to place their money, but these supports have, at the same time, encouraged risky investments leading to bank and savings and loan failures. Similarly, the federal government provides loans and loan guarantees to homeowners, college students, farmers, and others; it guarantees other financial instruments, such as pensions. Currently, the "potential liability" of the federal government for all of these credit programs approaches $6 trillion. Careful regulation and oversight will be necessary to ensure that these potential liabilities do not turn into actual ones, as in the savings and loan collapse.

Even though there are questions about support for private enterprise, it always has been a part of American economic policy. New experiments utilizing the concept of enterprise zones are attempting to integrate economic and social issues in a comprehensive program focused on particular geographic areas. The experience of states that have developed enterprise zones is mixed. Many of the successes claimed in jobs created, industries enticed to open in the zones, and improvements in services in the area may have occurred without the enterprise zones. Nonetheless, the zones offer support in the form of subsidies, tax breaks, and technical assistance to business.

The globalization of the world economy and the emergence of the EEC in Europe have created a new environment for the private sector as well, resulting in efforts by the national government to negotiate trade agreements whose primary emphasis is reducing the barriers to free trade as in the NAFTA agreement. Produce farmers claim that they have been hurt by lower production costs in Mexico and thus lower prices for their produce. The movement of industry to Mexico to take advantage of cheap labor has not increased to the extent the opponents of NAFTA had claimed. GATT and WTO represent another effort to reduce trade barriers and some industries are certain to be hurt. The textile industry, in particular, has been hurt because of the inexpensive labor in those industries in many countries, while high-tech and construction industries benefit.

FUTURE ALTERNATIVES: REFORMING THE RELATIONSHIP OF GOVERNMENT AND THE ECONOMY

There are many suggestions for reform in government's relationship to the economy. As indicated earlier, many of the recommendations deal with eliminating government's intervention in economic activity. Thus, creation of a free-market economy independent of government influence is seen as a means to stimulate economic enterprise toward more productivity and to restore the economy to a strong position. However, given the long history of government involvement, it is highly unlikely that such action is possible. As critics of Milton Friedman's ideas (noted earlier) suggest, a true free market is likely to produce a situation in which those groups with power dominate the system. There would not be freedom for all participants to compete equally.

Perhaps the most drastic reform proposal is that regulatory agencies be abolished. Legislative bodies created regulatory agencies because of their own inability to regulate effectively. Regulatory agencies became little legislatures of their own, enjoying independence from normal political controls. Advocates of reform want a return to citizen control through elected political leaders and believe that redistributing control over economic activities among the three branches of government would permit the public to influence the regulators' activity more effectively. A variation on this theme is that because much regulatory activity ends up in the slow-moving courts, regulatory agencies could be abolished and the courts assigned the responsibility. Although courts usually are viewed as inappropriate for regulation because of their slowness and lack of expertise, the increasing slowness of regulatory agencies tends to undermine the argument. Nonetheless, courts may only respond to cases brought to them, and they lack the ability to constantly oversee a particular economic activity.

Abolition of the regulatory agencies may appeal to many, but given the tendency of Congress to create more and more regulatory policies and the agencies to enforce them, it is unlikely that such proposals will enjoy much success. First, there are too many interests that oppose abolition, including the regulatory agencies themselves, their clientele, and the beneficiaries of agency regulation. Consider, for example, the obstacles faced by the Reagan administration in its first year as it whittled away at various regulators' powers but failed to dismantle completely all but a few. Second, another factor in opposing abolition is that regulatory policy is likely to have less visibility if placed in a regular administrative department. A particular regulatory policy then may have to compete with other agency priorities and—especially if controversial—may be buried by the agency's politics. Robbed of its independent status, the regulatory unit is likely to be less effective. Hence, for both political and practical reasons, completely abolishing regulatory agencies seems improbable.

Deregulation. Deregulation, very popular among reformers, has enjoyed moderate success. We saw, for example, how the airline industry experienced a dramatic deregulation in pricing and, to a great extent, in the geographic areas its various companies could serve. But if some deregulation is good, does that automatically mean that total deregulation would be better? Again, consider the airline situation: Although some well-traveled markets prospered, other marginal areas suffered under partial deregulation. The failure of many airlines since deregulation raises concern, and concentration of the market in a few companies leads to decreasing competition. The question becomes one of weighing costs against social objectives, such as the need to serve communities that cannot support the service on a purely economic basis. Regulation can have several objectives, whereas deregulation proposals often focus on only the economic factor.

Some of the effects of deregulation have generated suggestions for again regulating some industries, for example, the airline and trucking industries. Representatives of America West Airlines (one of the airlines developed with deregulation) blamed chaotic market conditions for the company's financial troubles in the late 1990s and early 2000s and predicted disaster for the industry without some controls. Others are concerned that deregulation did not consider social costs and should do so.

Incentives. A number of new ideas come from industries that would like to put some controls on what they see as overregulation. One alternative proposed by some is that regulatory policy should focus on results rather than on punishment for violations. If the intent of a policy is to improve safety for employees, for example, the most effective method of accomplishing such an objective might be to reward industries for good safety records.

Another idea is that new rules and regulations should include assessing their economic impact. Congress already considers the economic impacts of its policies. Regulators now are required to make such assessments. Congress appears to be strongly in support of identifying the costs up front.

Sunset laws. Sunset legislation is yet another favored means of preventing excessive regulation. Sunset legislation requires that agencies and their programs be given specific periods of existence and be reviewed at the end of the time allotted. Thus, five years might be a common life span for an agency; at the end of that time it would have to justify its existence. The idea is that the regulatory agency would of necessity eliminate unneeded and nonconstructive activities in order to pass this five-year review. Similar state sunset laws are now in existence. This evaluation can lead to better performance and to a careful consideration by the legislature of whether to continue a regulatory activity. Most states now have such legislation, but the national level does not.

Nationalization. At the polar opposite of deregulation and regulatory abolition lies nationalization. Nationalization of industry—for example, steel production—would involve government bureaucracy in operating the economic enterprise directly. The criticisms often made of British railroads or the National Health Service—both nationalized institutions—generate serious opposition to this idea. Neither the American public nor its political leaders appear to feel that nationalization would lead to anything but more red tape and even less efficiency than regulation involves. Therefore, nationalization does not appear to be a viable alternative. With the move to get government out of business activities and the privatization of many government activities, the trend is clearly in the opposite direction. The opposition is reinforced by the fact that the current British government is committed to denationalizing some industry. One exception is the safety screening at airports. Since the September 11, 2001, terrorist attacks, support for nationalizing the security checkpoints increased dramatically, and the federal government took over their operation.

Consumer oversight. Another controversial suggestion is to create consumer committees to evaluate economic activities and then make suggestions for change. This is known as direct "consumer oversight." Industry tends to be hostile to this innovation, feeling that consumer groups often focus on one specific issue to the exclusion of the industry's general health. As a result, this proposal has not been accorded serious consideration.

Dramatic new economic proposals are often popular, but the realities of the political process must be faced. The parties with the resources to influence policy usually also have access to the regulatory and economic policymaking system. Thus, reform must confront them as well. The likelihood is that influential interests will prevail, and reform, if any, will continue to be gradual.

Community revitalization. The experiments with community revitalization such as enterprise zones will be watched carefully to determine whether they produce economic development. The enterprise and empowerment zones used in forty states probably are likely to be given credit for any success there is in economic development in the targeted areas. Assessing the evidence will be the difficult part. If they are viewed as helping to solve social problems, however, they are likely to spread.

Trade. The initiatives on free trade also will be important elements of future economic activities. Assuming that free trade does produce positive economic benefits for all nations involved, the administration will have been successful in creating a boon to private sector economic enterprises. National economic policy will have taken a dramatic step toward competition in the global economy. The successful negotiation and ratification of the NAFTA and GATT treaties took much effort on the administration's part. There will be many examples of businesses that cannot compete and have to fold, creating unemployment. They will provide the ammunition for those opposed to the agreements. At the same time, many that succeed probably will be hailed as evidence of their success. While these debates continue, the United States and South and Central America are attempting to reach agreements on widespread trade issues.

In the future, there will be increasingly international and domestic debate over economic "globalization." By the late 1990s, protests over the WTO's free-trade activities became more and more violent. Fearing that increased trade will harm domestic workers, exploit laborers in poor countries, and benefit only wealthy business owners, protestors now regularly appear at international trade meetings attempting to disrupt the international trade regime.

SUMMARY

Economic systems perform the function of distributing goods and services among people. Because of differing resources, some people or groups are able to exercise more influence than others over economic activities. Government policy may work to reinforce the unequal distribution, or it may attempt to re-distribute wealth.

Capitalist economies are based on the concept of a free-market system in which competition is open and everyone has an opportunity to participate. A socialist economy is one in which equal distribution of wealth is sought through government ownership and operation of the major means of production, distribution, and exchange. Most economic systems combine these two extremes.

The free-market system does not always operate smoothly because it rests on assumptions that are not completely valid. Thus, as instability in the free-market system develops, governments intervene. Intervention may be through monetary and fiscal policies or through regulation of specific sectors of the economy. Because monetary and fiscal policies are directed at stabilizing activity in the economy as a whole, they are referred to as macroeconomic policies.

Microeconomic policies deal with individual units of private enterprise. Regulation, the primary microeconomic tool, is accomplished in a number of different ways. Antitrust policies attempt to control the overconcentration of economic power in one or a few corporations. Other regulations license firms to perform economic activities, grant licenses to radio or television broadcasters, and award routes to airline, trucking, and bus companies. Microeconomic policies also include interventions to support industries. Thus, subsidies for crops and exports provide support for farm industries. Similarly, import quotas shore up domestic industries by shielding them from competition.

Government intervention in economic activities results in a number of major policy outcomes (or impacts), some positive and some negative: (1) an environment supportive of industry through an ensured return on investment and controlled competition; (2) consumer protection against unfair practices and defective goods; (3) increased costs of goods and services; (4) increased red tape and delay; (5) dampening of innovation; and (6) enhanced predictability in the provision of services.

The negative outcomes of regulation have resulted in proposals for reform, including suggestions for deregulation, government-industry cooperation, abolition of regulation, and a closer review of agencies through sunset legislation or citizen review committees.

Deregulation has been very popular during the past two decades. Economic policy of the 1980s attempted to soften the effect of regulation. Thus, greater flexibility in the implementation of policy allowed the market system to operate more freely. Efforts were made to get government off the back of business. The approach of the 1980s had numerous effects, both positive and negative. Industry found itself able to operate with many fewer restrictions and benefited therefrom. Consumers usually benefited as well in the short run from greater competition and lower costs in areas such as shipping and transportation. Nonetheless, the long-term effects have been reduced competition in many markets and increases in prices. Critics of deregulation also point to increasing concentration of economic power in many sectors of the economy as a long-term negative impact and are making proposals for reregulating some industry.

In addition to regulation, other forms of government intervention are constant themes of U.S. government economic policy. Government has provided tax breaks and subsidies to private enterprise since the birth of the nation. In contemporary policy, there are experiments to bring cooperative activities of federal agencies, state and local governments, and other organizations to focus on economic and social problems in particular geographic areas referred to as enterprise and/or empowerment zones. The zones expand the support of government for business to encompass work on the social problems that accompany economically depressed conditions.

The United States also has embarked on dramatic new initiatives in world trade. Negotiation and ratification of the NAFTA and GATT agreements lead the United States increasingly into a free-trade stance. This kind of globalization of economic activity generated increasingly violent reactions in the late 1990s.

There are inevitably conflicting goals in public policy, and intervention in the economy is no exception. Agencies have to be concerned with protecting the general public, but they also have to be concerned with the health of the economic sectors with which they work. Therefore, they often get caught in the middle between advocates of their industries and consumer advocates. It is left to the elected policymakers to mediate these conflicts and to determine what is best for everyone.

NOTES

1. John Kenneth Galbraith, *Economics and the Public Purpose* (New York: Signet, 1973), 3–4.

2. This discussion relies heavily on Richard L. Siegal and Leonard B. Weinbert, *Comparing Public Policies* (Homewood, Il: Dorsey Press, 1977), Chapter 4. Also see Richard Lehne, *Industry and Politics: United States in Comparative Perspective* (Englewood Cliffs, NJ: Prentice-Hall, 1992), especially Chapters 1 and 2; and Murray I. Weidenbaum, *Business and Government in the Global Marketplace*, 6th ed. (Upper Saddle River, NJ: Prentice-Hall, 1999).

3. Milton Friedman, *Capitalism and Freedom* (Chicago: University of Chicago Press, 1962).

4. For an excellent critique of Friedman's position, see Rick Tilman, "Ideology and Utopia in the Political Economy of Milton Friedman," *Polity*, 8 (Spring, 1996), 422–442.

5. John Kenneth Galbraith explores this and many of the following ideas in three of his books: *The Affluent Society* (Boston: Houghton Mifflin, 1958); *The New Industrial State* (Boston: Houghton Mifflin, 1968); and *Economics and the Public Purpose.*

6. The following position is taken by Robert Averitt in *The Dual Economy* (New York: W. W. Norton, 1968); and by Robert Seidman, "Contract Law, the Free Market, and State Intervention: A Jurisprudential Perspective," *Journal of Economic Issues*, 7 (December 1973): 553–575.

7. Seymour Martin Lipset, *The First New Nation* (New York: Basic Books, 1963), especially Chapters 1 and 2.

8. John Maynard Keynes, *General Theory of Employment, Interest, and Money* (New York: Harcourt Brace, 1936).

9. G. W. Roster, Jr., *The Status of Class Action Litigation*, American Bar Foundation, Research Contribution No. 4 (Chicago, 1974), examines the development of class action litigation in the United States. See also Deborah R. Hensler, *Class Action Dilemmas: Pursuing Public Goals for Private Gain* (Santa Monica, CA: Rand, 2000).

10. *U.S. v. E. C. Knight*, 156 U.S. 1 (1985).

11. *Loewe v. Lawler*, 208 U.S. 274 (1908).

12. John A. Jenkins, "How to End the Endless Delay at the FTC," *Washington Monthly* (June 1976): 42–50.

13. John O. Haley, *Antitrust in Germany and Japan: The First Fifty Years, 1947–1998* (Seattle: University of Washington Press, 2001); Richard Lehne, *Industry and Politics.*

14. Deborah K. Belasich, *Enterprise Zones: Policy Perspectives of Economic Development* (New York: Garland Publishing, Inc., 1993); Peter Hall, "Enterprise Zones: A Justification," *Journal of Urban and Regional Research*, 6 (1982): 417–421.

15. William Fulton and Morris Newman, "The Strange Career of Enterprise Zones," *Governing*, 7, No. 6 (March 1994): 32–36; Erik Huey, "Enterprise Zones: Introduction," www.bizsites.com; "Introduction to the rc/ez/ec initiative," www.bud.gov/offices/cpd/ezec/about/ezecinit.cfm.

16. Conrad Weiler, "GATT, NAFTA and State and Local Powers," *Intergovernmental Perspective*, 20 (Fall 1993–Winter 1994): 38–41.

17. Marlon G. Boarnet and William T. Bogart, "Enterprise Zones and Employment: Evidence from New Jersey," *Journal of Urban Economics*, 40 (September 1996): 198–215; and L. Papke, "Tax Policy and Urban Development: Evidence from the Indiana Enterprise Zone Program," *Journal of Public Economics*, 54 (1994): 37–49.

18. W. M. Capron and R. G. Noll, "Summary and Conclusion," in W. M. Capron, ed., *Technological Change in Regulated Industries* (Washington, DC: Brookings Institution, 1971), 221.

19. www.ers.usda.gov/briefing/farmincome/fore.htm.

SUGGESTED READINGS

Books

Ayres, Ian, and Braithwaite, John. *Responsive Regulation: Transcending the Deregulation Debate.* New York: Oxford University Press, 1992.

Belasich, Deborah K. *Enterprise Zones: Policy Perspectives of Economic Development.* New York: Garland Publishing, Inc., 1993.

Eisner, Marc Allen. *Regulatory Politics in Transition*, 2nd ed. Baltimore: Johns Hopkins University Press, 2000.

Evenett, Simon J., Lehman, Alexander, and Steil, Benn, eds. *Antitrust Goes Global: What Future for Transatlantic Cooperation?* Washington, DC: Brookings Institution, 2000.

Francis, John G. *The Politics of Regulation; A Comparative Perspective.* Cambridge, MA: Blackwell, 1993.

Hahn, Robert W., and Litan, Robert E. *Improving Regulatory Accountability.* Washington, DC: American Enterprise Institute and Brookings Institution, 1997.

Haley, John O. *Antitrust in Germany and Japan: The First Fifty Years, 1947–1998.* Seattle: University of Washington Press, 2000.

Harris, Richard A., and Milkis, Sidney M. *The Politics of Regulatory Change*, 2nd ed. New York: Oxford University Press, 1996.

Kerwin, Cornelius M. *Rulemaking: How Government Agencies Write Law and Make Policy.* Washington, DC: Congressional Quarterly Books, 1994.

Moss, Ambler H., Jr., ed. *Assessments of the North American Free Trade Agreement.* New Brunswick, NJ: Transaction Books, 1994.

Reich, Robert B. *The Work of Nations: Preparing Ourselves for the 21st Century Capitalism.* New York: Alfred A. Knopf, 1991.

Sparrow, Malcolm K. *The Regulatory Craft: Controlling Risks, Solving Problems, and Managing Compliance.* Washington, DC: Brookings Institution, 2000.

Web Sites

American Enterprise Institute   www.aei.org
Brookings Institution   www.brookings.edu
Federal Trade Commission   www.ftc.gov
Stanford University Jonsson Library of Government Documents (Depository for all World Trade Organization (WTO) and GATT publications) www.stanford.edu/group/Jonsson/wto.html
U.S. Department of Agriculture   www.usda.gov
U.S. Department of Justice Antitrust Division   www.usdoj.gov/atr

CHAPTER 4

Economic Issues: Taxing, Spending, and Budgeting

The federal government currently exercises a dramatically expanded role in economic policy compared to its relatively minor role 100 years ago. External pressures, such as World War I and World War II, created an environment in which increased government controls over wages, prices, and private-sector production levels were necessary in order to execute the war effort effectively. Internal pressures arising from the economic upheavals of the Great Depression of the 1930s contributed to public demands for an expanded governmental role in the American economy. The various economic programs implemented under the "New Deal" of President Roosevelt were products of internal pressures. The economic recovery experienced by the United States after the Depression demonstrated the effectiveness of governmental intervention and provided a foundation for continued economic intervention by the federal government.

These forces continue to be present as the United States maintains a global diplomatic and military posture with an economy dependent on international trade. Consequently, governmental involvement in economic policy continues to be an item on the policy agenda. Both liberals and conservatives accept the legitimacy of governmental involvement in economic policy, a marked change from the pre-Depression era. These ideological groups, however, disagree on the nature of appropriate governmental economic intervention. Liberals tend to favor a managed economy, where conservatives tend to favor only governmental utilization of monetary and fiscal policies to promote private-sector initiative.

ISSUE BACKGROUND: CONCEPTS AND ISSUES

The American economic system is a mixed economy in which the public expects government to take an active role to promote economic growth and maintain employment. The social and political values that guide government's role are dynamic and involve significant levels of conflict. Each value involves questions answerable only in the context of subjective preferences. These values establish the boundaries of government activity and provide policy direction for public officials.

One value relates to inflation and interest rates.[1] How much inflation is acceptable in order to sustain economic growth? Interest rates tend to mirror inflation and climb with inflation. What is an acceptable and desirable interest rate that will promote economic growth?

A second value relates to employment and unemployment. What is the desired employment rate? Total employment may not be possible to achieve. What,

then, is an acceptable unemployment rate? Economists and the two major political parties now tend to accept 5 percent unemployment as an appropriate definition of full employment.

Employment, inflation, and interest rates are also linked. One effective tool
to drive down the inflation rate is to raise interest rates. This acts to cut demand
(by increasing the cost of financing consumer goods) and exerts a downward pressure on prices. Unfortunately, a reduction in demand for goods also drives up unemployment as producers trim their work force in response to reduced demand.
What is an acceptable rate of inflation in order to maintain full employment? Which
presents the greater threat to the economic system: inflation or unemployment?

A third value relates to economic growth.[2] The gross domestic product
(GDP) represents the total value of all goods and services produced by the economy. What is the desired rate of growth of the GDP? What roles should government play in promoting GDP expansion? What level of growth (as measured by
GDP expansion) should the federal government actively pursue?[3]

A fourth value relates to equality. What should be the role of government in
promoting economic equality? Is equality of economic opportunity sufficient, or
should government actively pursue policies that seek redistribution of economic
benefits in order to achieve some specified level of economic equality either for
social groups or for geographic regions?

A fifth value relates to ideology.[4] What should be the nature and level of government involvement in economic policy? How much governmental involvement
is consistent with the free-enterprise economic system? At what level of involvement
does governmental action cease to be productive and become a counterproductive
restriction on the economic system? This value involves significant social and political conflict over the appropriate role of government in a free-enterprise system.

In the absence of universal agreement concerning these values, economic
policy becomes the product of political compromises.[5] Government formulates
and executes economic policy in this environment of political conflict and compromise. The necessity for compromise acts to limit ideological consistency within
economic policy. Economic policy in the United States is neither completely liberal nor conservative but contains a contradictory combination of values.

Economic Policy Obstacles

Economic policy is the product of compromise in a complex political environment. Consequently, a number of obstacles exist in developing an effective, consistent mix of economic policy options.

Fragmentation of governmental responsibility between the federal and state
governments is one major obstacle in developing economic policy. In the American federal system, state governments share a range of responsibilities with the national government, including economic policy options. Given the diversity of the
fifty states, they often pursue divergent economic policies. The economic interests
of agricultural states such as Iowa or Nebraska are not necessarily consistent with
those of heavily industrialized states, such as New York or Pennsylvania. The federal system is an environment in which state governments and the federal government often pursue conflicting economic goals.

Fragmentation of responsibility for economic policy also exists within the federal level. The president, representing a national constituency, shares responsibility with Congress for formulating economic policy options. This shared responsibility expands the number of actors who legitimately participate in establishing economic policy options. This means that every member of the U.S. Senate and the U.S. House of Representatives has a right to exercise a voice in economic policy. Members of Congress tend to represent the economic interests of their state or district with greater zeal than they do the economic interests of the nation as a whole. Conflict between the executive and legislative branches of government over economic policy is a legitimate characteristic of the American political system. The level of conflict between the president and Congress often becomes more intense when one party controls the White House and the opposition party controls Congress.

Fragmentation within the executive branch of government is an obstacle to developing economic policy. A number of cabinet-level departments share in this responsibility, notably the Commerce Department, the Treasury Department, and the Labor Department. This fragmentation of responsibility within the executive branch is extensive. Various agencies below cabinet level also exercise economic policy responsibility. The Office of Management and Budget (OMB), the Council of Economic Advisers, and the independent Federal Reserve Board are three of a larger number of agencies that exercise an extensive economic policy role.

On the negative side, this extensive structural fragmentation reduces centralized control and coordination over American economic policy. Ineffective policy responses to economic problems may be the product of a lack of policy coordination. On the positive side, fragmentation provides for significant private sector latitude in economic policy, which is consistent with the values of the free-enterprise system.

A second obstacle involves links between economic policy options. This is a problem because there is often significant conflict between economic goals. For example, the pursuit of full employment tends to fuel inflation. Policies designed to reduce inflation often produce higher unemployment. Similarly, a decision to expand domestic spending will exert budgetary pressures for a reduction in military spending levels. This means that economic policy goals often involve inherent conflicts resolvable only through the process of political compromise.

A third obstacle to effective economic policy involves uncertainty in predicting policy outcomes. Even when political consensus comes to adopt a specific economic strategy, no guarantee exists that the desired result will follow. For example, only after implementing a tax-rate change can analysts assess the actual impact of a tax-rate reduction on economic expansion and tax revenues. Economic forecasts rest on uncertain political and financial assumptions used in making the predictions. The conflict generated by this debate in an environment of uncertainty becomes an obstacle to the development of economic policy.

Macroeconomic Approaches

Traditionally, the free-market system was expected to be self-adjusting, ensuring that there would be no sharp swings in the business cycle. However, as we have seen in Chapter 3, because the free-market system failed in self-regulation, government intervention was necessary to reduce the impact of downward economic cycles. With the passage of the Employment Act of 1946, Congress formally assigned responsibility for maintaining economic stability to the federal government. This legislation stated that the federal government should "use all practicable means (to achieve) maximum employment, production, and purchasing power." The act did not specify the exact means the federal government should use to achieve full employment. Detailed strategies were for Congress to formulate. The act did create the Council of Economic Advisers (CEA) within the Executive Office of the President in order to provide the president with advice on making economic policy.

Government uses two primary instruments, monetary policy and fiscal policy, to accomplish macroeconomic goals and achieve stabilization of the economy.

Monetary policy. *Monetary policy* refers to the efforts of government to control the flow of money in the economy. Money includes not only cash, but also available credit and collateral used for credit or security. The major actor in monetary control is the Federal Reserve Board, commonly known as the Fed, which has powers that permit it to expand or contract the amount of money in circulation.

The Federal Reserve Act of 1913 created the Fed, which serves as the central bank of the United States. The Federal Reserve System sought to stabilize the banking industry through regulations developed and imposed by the seven-member board. The president, with Senate confirmation, appoints board members to fourteen-year terms. The chairperson of the Fed, also appointed by the president with Senate approval, serves a four-year term. Board members are removable only by impeachment resulting from the commission of a criminal act. They may *not* be removed over a disagreement about economic policy options with either the president or the Congress. The Fed is therefore a stable, independent, and powerful force in economic policy.

As an independent agency, the Fed is free to pursue monetary policies that may not find support either from the president or from Congress. The Fed has demonstrated a willingness to raise interest rates in order to "cool" the economy and reduce inflationary pressures even if the White House did not support this action.

A primary goal of the Fed is to regulate the economy through control of the *money supply.*[6] The currency in circulation today does not represent reserves of gold or silver held by the U.S. Treasury Department. The words "Federal Reserve Note" on paper currency reflect a departure from the reliance on these metals, a change from the "Silver Certificate" of years past. The supply and value of money in circulation is independent of gold and silver.

What determines the value of American currency is the supply in circulation and the level of confidence in the American economy by both citizens and international bankers and investors. The Fed has both the power and the responsibility to control the supply of money in circulation. Increasing the supply of money drives down interest rates and stimulates demand and economic expansion (with the risk of inflation). Decreasing the supply of money drives up interest rates, reduces demand, and cools the economy down (with the risk of higher unemployment rates).

Thus, when the economy is in recession, monetary policies usually aim at encouraging people to spend money. Lower interest rates and increased availability of money accomplish this goal. During inflationary periods, just the opposite is true: Government policy raises interest rates, making it less attractive for people to spend as it becomes more costly to borrow. This encourages savings by making it more profitable for people to save.

The Federal Reserve Board oversees the operation of banks participating in the Federal Reserve System and assists them by serving as a clearinghouse for banking transactions and by lending them money. Of particular impact on money supply is the power of the Federal Reserve Board to control the amount of money a bank must keep on reserve, the *reserve requirement.* As the amount required increases, banks have less to lend to customers; as the reserve decreases, banks have more to lend. Banks also borrow from the Federal Reserve System, and the rate of interest charged by the Fed on such loans, the *discount rate,* affects the ability of banks to lend money to others. Because the interest rates charged by the banks are directly affected by how much the money costs them, the Fed is able to exert control over interest rates charged to consumers. Lower discount rates stimulate consumer borrowing, and higher discount rates discourage such borrowing. The discount rate is a powerful tool available to the Fed for stimulating or cooling off the economy.

The Federal Reserve Board also has the power to buy up government bonds held by investors. These are *open market operations.* Purchasing such bonds places money directly in the hands of potential spenders. Selling bonds, in contrast, takes money out of circulation.

Monetary policy, though highly flexible, often proves difficult for the administration to control. Although the president may attempt to move in a particular direction, others, especially the Federal Reserve Board, are free to follow their own approaches.

Fiscal policy. *Fiscal policy*—which encompasses tax policy, government spending, and debt management—is the other major way in which government attempts to influence economic activity generally. Government can stimulate or discourage economic activity through its power to impose taxes. Tax incentives, for example, can encourage corporations to invest in plant expansion. Plant expansion ordinarily increases employment and stimulates economic expansion, because more people have more money to spend on goods and services. The same is true of a general tax cut: The demand for goods and services usually rises if taxes take less money from people. However, some of the money freed through tax reductions may be saved, instead of spent. Thus, when government changes tax rates for reasons of fiscal planning, it pays attention to what the recipients of tax benefits are likely to do with their money. During times of inflation, there is some reason for increasing taxes to reduce the amount of money in circulation.

Managing the national debt is another fiscal policy activity often subject to controversy. *Deficit spending* stimulates demand in times of recession and unemployment. Nevertheless, it may also add to the money supply without adding to production; hence, many critics of the national government suggest that increases in the national debt contribute to inflation.[7] Deficit spending causes inflation if the government artificially expands the supply of money by printing ever-higher quantities of paper currency to pay for government spending. This type of expanded money supply decreases the value of the dollar with a resultant rise in inflation.

Government borrowing makes it possible to practice deficit spending without fueling inflation, at least in the short run. Presidents Reagan, George H. Bush, and Clinton employed this strategy to finance budget deficits with minimal inflationary pressure. The price for this approach was a dramatic increase in the national debt with interest payments consuming a significant percentage of the federal budget. Currently, interest payments absorb about 13 percent of the federal budget.

These tools of monetary and fiscal policy are complex approaches to stabilizing the economy. There are those who think that government should act directly to increase the amount of money in the hands of consumers in hopes that they will spend it and thus stimulate economic activity. Others argue that government should make more money available to business in the hope that it will expand activities, increasing employment, and putting more money in the hands of employees, and therefore of consumers. The first approach, favored by liberals, is referred to as the *percolate-up theory*; the latter, championed by conservatives, is known as the *trickle-down theory.*

Other measures. Direct government action to set wage and price levels is also part of fiscal policy. Few economists currently advocate *wage and price controls* (as were imposed in 1972 to 1973 during the Nixon administration). Beyond discouraging production, wage and price controls are usually difficult to maintain: Everyone has a justification for exemption, and government agencies become inundated with such requests. Additionally, when controls end, prices and wages surge upward—as happened in the mid-1970s. In another approach, known as *jawboning*, the administration attempts to persuade businesses and unions to hold the line on increases voluntarily. This kind of approach is not always successful.

Wage and price control strategies are microeconomic techniques that are macroeconomic in purpose. These and other microeconomic policies (regulation, for example) have the potential for significant impact on the economy as a whole. Micro- and macroeconomic policies are not necessarily independent economic strategies.

CONTEMPORARY POLICY: APPROACHES TO MANAGING THE ECONOMY

Although there are still controversies concerning exactly how government should approach economic problems, the reality of government intervention has become widely accepted. The following section examines approaches to managing the economy, including monetary, fiscal, tax, and deficit policies as part of current macroeconomic policy.

With the exception of "supply-side economics," these fiscal and monetary policy tools reflect the *demand-side theory* of John Maynard Keynes. Keynesian economics holds that demand for goods and services drives the economy. A downward economic cycle occurs when business cuts production and downsizes its work force in response to reduced demand. This, in turn, reduces demand further, which results in more downsizing. Unless some action interrupts this cycle, a severe economic recession or depression results. Accordingly, the federal government has the obligation to create demand by purchasing goods and services through increased spending. Keynes argued that even government deficit spending (spending in excess of tax receipts) is appropriate in order to stimulate a sluggish economy and prevent recessions. During periods of prosperity, when inflation is a threat, government can reduce demand by increasing taxes, reducing spending, and balancing the budget. Keynesian economics is viable only if elected officials are willing to adopt politically unpopular measures such as eliminating budget deficits and raising taxes.

Supply-Side Economics

An alternative economic approach to Keynesian economics is supply-side economics. Supply-siders believe that the best method to achieve economic growth is to allow the market system to operate with minimal governmental interference. One basic tenet of the supply-side theory is that the relative price of any good, service, or activity determines how people will act toward it. Consequently, if the market operates freely, private demand forces will be sufficient to sustain the economy. Government interference in stimulating demand disrupts the system and has, at best, only a temporary effect on economic growth. Supply-siders believe that government taxes, regulation, and spending only interfere with natural economic activity and that if government concentrates on stimulating production, demand will follow naturally because of the production process itself.

Supply-side economic policy emphasizes low tax rates in order to stimulate production in the economy. Lowering tax rates, especially for businesses and individuals with higher income, leads to business investment, according to this view. Investment then leads to economic growth, with the bonus of higher levels of employment, a classic trickle-down argument. Supporters of supply-side economics believe that tax cuts pay for themselves through economic growth, because growth creates a greater number of prosperous taxpayers to replace the tax money eliminated in the tax cut. A fundamental tenet of supply-side economics is that the propensity to invest is a direct function of the tax rate on such risk-taking economic activity.

The American economy during the 1970s was sluggish. Inflation was high and productivity was below capacity. President Reagan was elected in 1980 with a major underlying pledge of implementing tax cuts consistent with supply-side economic theory.[8] Most supply-side tax cuts focus on upper-income levels, especially corporate profits and capital gains, which would constitute the most likely sources of significant investment. The theory is that as tax rates rise above a certain level, they so discourage economic activity that total tax revenue falls. Hence, a tax cut can raise revenue and reduce deficits by stimulating economic expansion.

The tax cuts resulting from the Reagan administration's supply-side policies were a 5 percent cut in personal income taxes in 1982 and 10 percent cuts in 1983 and 1984. They also added an indexing provision to the tax code so that taxpayers would not be hurt if inflation was the primary cause of increases in salaries and wages.

Enabling corporations to depreciate equipment more easily reduced corporate taxes. This depreciation reduced the overall tax burden on corporations and at the same time intended to encourage them to invest in new equipment because the write-offs increased corporate profits.

Impact. Though the tax reductions aimed at increasing the amount of money available for investment and thus for production, President Reagan viewed other aspects of economic policy as just as important to economic growth. For example, the Reagan administration perceived regulation as being burdensome to industry, so it accelerated the deregulation efforts of the Carter presidency. Conservatives and the business community consider regulations to be costly (see Chapter 3).[9] Reducing regulation means reducing expenses, thus allowing for investment of those funds.

Much of the Reagan administration's deregulation did not occur through changes in law or policy directives as such. Instead, appointments to boards and commissions led to significant shifts in policy interpretation and implementation. The Equal Employment Opportunity Commission, Civil Rights Commission, Federal Trade Commission, and National Labor Relations Board (NLRB) are examples of some of the agencies whose presidential appointees reinterpreted policy to fall in line with the perspectives of the administration. As a result, shifts in economic policy created a climate much more favorable to business.

Current advocates of supply-side economics argue that the economic expansion of the 1990s and the budget surplus created by the turn of the century were results of implementing supply-side tax cuts in the 1980s. This kind of argument drove the George W. Bush administration's successful push for major tax cuts in 2001, as well as its proposal for further cuts in 2002. Opponents of supply-side economics, however, point to the rapid growth in budget deficits in the 1980s and the strength of the economy in the 1990s during a more traditional Keynesian presidential administration.

Budget Deficits in the 1980s and 1990s

Supply-side economics did not initially reduce the budget deficit that President Reagan campaigned against in 1980. In fact, the budget deficits increased dramatically in the 1980s, as shown in Figure 4-1.

The annual budget deficit grew to $80 billion in 1981, $212 billion by 1985, and reached $290 billion in 1992, before beginning to decrease during the Clinton years. These deficits were the result of a combination of factors: the large tax cuts in 1981 to 1983; increased levels of defense spending during the 1980s; the Persian Gulf war of 1991; the savings and loan bailout; continued growth in federal spending for Medicare, Social Security, and other income support programs; and the recessions of 1981 to 1982 and 1991 to 1992, which lowered tax receipts and increased federal expenditures for welfare and unemployment. The annual budget deficits were an obstacle for federal spending on a variety of programs, such as crime, transportation, health care, education, and defense.

The data in Figure 4-1 indicate that the United States achieved a budget surplus beginning in 1998 of almost $70 billion. The dramatic shift from budget deficits to annual budget surplus is a function of several factors. First, the growth of government spending slowed since 1993 due to budget agreements between the president and Congress, particularly the Balanced Budget Act of 1997 (described in the Policy Evaluation section), which sealed the agreement between a Democratic president and a Republican Congress to set a realistic target for a balanced budget. The federal budget continues to grow, but at a slower rate than in the past. Second, the private sector experienced significant economic growth,

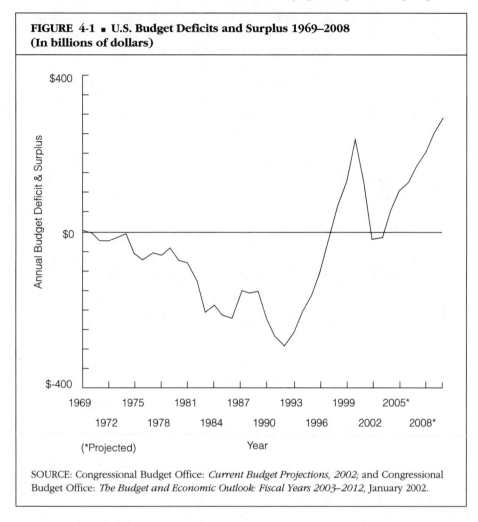

**FIGURE 4-1 ▪ U.S. Budget Deficits and Surplus 1969–2008
(In billions of dollars)**

SOURCE: Congressional Budget Office: *Current Budget Projections, 2002;* and Congressional Budget Office: *The Budget and Economic Outlook: Fiscal Years 2003–2012,* January 2002.

which produced higher annual revenues than originally projected by either the Congressional Budget Office (CBO) or the Office of Management and Budget. From 1992 to 1997, federal revenues increased at an average annual rate of 7.6 percent, while inflation remained under 3 percent, a fact that made the 1997 budget agreement possible. Third, the strengthened economy and low inflation rate reduced the rate of increase in spending for entitlement programs. Cost-of-living adjustments (COLA) for Social Security recipients were lower, and fewer individuals qualified for other entitlement programs due to low unemployment rates. (See Chapter 7 for a description of spending in Social Security and other income support programs.)

Whether Congress and the president will be able to maintain a disciplined approach to federal spending remains to be seen. Budget surpluses may be a temptation to increase spending or reduce taxes in future years by such a level that budget deficits may again reappear, as some analysts predict based on the 2001 tax cut described later.

Even with a balanced budget, interest on the national debt remains the third-largest federal budget item, behind Social Security payments and national defense spending. Since 1982, interest payments servicing a national debt of over $3 trillion consumed between 11 and 15 percent of the federal budget. By 2008, interest on the national debt will still consume about 7 percent of the federal budget, even after several years of annual budget surpluses (see Figure 4-2). If the CBO projections are inaccurate due to economic recession or increases in spending levels, this percentage will increase as the cumulative level of debt continues to increase. It is important to understand that interest payments of $170 billion in 2002 (interest payments are projected to remain in the $170 to $180 billion range through 2008 even with a balanced budget) did not pay for any public services in past years or the current year. This was simply a payment of interest on money borrowed during earlier years to pay for public services.

The impact of budget deficits on other parts of the economy is manifold. Budget deficits keep interest rates higher than they otherwise would be because of the increased demand for available money as the federal government competes with private-sector borrowers. Higher interest rates and increasing scarcity of cap-

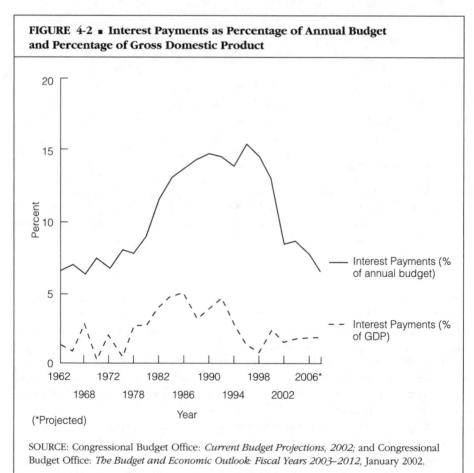

FIGURE 4-2 ▪ Interest Payments as Percentage of Annual Budget and Percentage of Gross Domestic Product

SOURCE: Congressional Budget Office: *Current Budget Projections, 2002;* and Congressional Budget Office: *The Budget and Economic Outlook: Fiscal Years 2003–2012,* January 2002.

ital may then discourage investment and weaken economic expansion. Higher interest rates mean less spending by consumers, who find loans too expensive, and so domestic purchasing declines. Interest rates for home mortgages and consumer loans were in the 3 to 4 percent range during the 1960s, a period of balanced federal budgets. During the 1980s, when budget deficits were at their highest, home mortgage rates rose to the 12 to 14 percent range. The federal budget deficit was a major cause of these high interest rates.

Additionally, high interest rates usually encourage foreign interests to convert their currencies to U.S. dollars, thus driving the value of the dollar upward relative to that of other currencies. The rise in the value of the dollar makes it difficult for U.S. firms to compete in world markets, leading to a trade imbalance.[10] The strength of the dollar is a measure of the ability of the dollar to purchase (or be purchased by) foreign currency in international money. A strong dollar translates into greater purchasing power for the American dollar on the international market, since a strong dollar will buy more foreign goods than a weak dollar. At the same time, the strong dollar decreases foreign purchasing power in the American market, since it requires more of their currency to buy American goods. American firms then find it more difficult to sell goods abroad. Interest rates partially determine the strength of the dollar.

Tax Reform

Tax reform efforts are an integral component on the economic policy agenda. Congress passed and President George W. Bush signed the Economic Growth and Tax Relief Reconciliation Act of 2001. Provisions of this act included the largest tax cuts since the Reagan administration in the early 1980s as well as the most extensive changes in the tax system since the Tax Reform Act of 1986.

Tax Reform Act of 1986. The Tax Reform Act of 1986 was an effort to establish a federal tax system that was fairer, simpler, and more efficient than the previous federal income tax structure.[11] Many of the act's provisions intended to create greater *fairness* in the federal tax system. The act retained most of the major deductions previously used in itemizing: home mortgage interest, charitable contributions, medical expenses, certain other taxes, and business expense deductions. By lowering the maximum tax rate for individuals from 50 percent to 28 percent, Congress sought to increase taxpayer confidence in the system and to reduce attempts to avoid tax liability. The act also sought to broaden the tax base of the federal government by eliminating certain deductions, such as interest on consumer loans, and by placing restrictions on the number of home mortgages that a person could claim. The act did provide some aid to low- and middle-income families by increasing the standard deduction, and it did provide limited tax relief to the elderly.

The act also sought to simplify the tax structure by reducing the paperwork and computations involved in preparing and filing a tax return. After other tax code changes, five individual tax brackets remained (15, 28, 31, 36, and 39.6 percent).

Efficiency was probably the most significant component of the 1986 Tax Reform Act. The act sought to reduce potential interference with business and investment programs by the tax structure. Under past tax structures, unprofitable investments could reduce tax liability. The reformers argued that such a structure encouraged waste and inefficiency because taxpayers did not make investment decisions on their economic merits, but on their impact on tax liability. The tax reform sought to diminish the importance of tax laws in business decision making. Tax reform served as an economic policy instrument to expand the federal tax base and to change investment patterns.

Economic Growth and Tax Relief Reconciliation Act of 2001 (EGTRRA). The EGTRRA act followed the policy direction established by the 1986 act. EGTRRA cut income tax rates, created new tax incentives, and repealed the estate tax. *Fairness* was sought through implementation of lower tax rates. The legislation immediately implemented a new minimum tax rate of 10 percent. By 2006, the federal tax rates will be reduced to the following levels: 10 percent, 15 percent, 25 percent, 28 percent, 33 percent, and 35 percent. Child tax credits increased and the marriage tax penalty (where married couples pay higher rates than do single individuals filing separately) will gradually decrease. Taxpayers with incomes under $130,000 can receive new education subsidies. The law will gradually reduce the estate tax and then repeal it in 2010. Over the ten-year life of the EGTRRA, tax reductions will total some $1.35 trillion.

An intriguing element of EGTRRA is the fact that all of the changes included in the bill will sunset in 2010. This means that, unless Congress reapproves the legislation, all of the changes produced by the 2001 act will terminate, and tax policy will revert to pre-EGTRRA policy. The sunset provision is in the legislation to limit its budget surplus and deficit effect. In 2002, President Bush appealed to Congress to make the tax reductions permanent, but Congress resisted that call in light of the return of recession and new deficit projections following the September 11, 2001, terrorist attacks.

POLICY EVALUATION: SUCCESS OR FAILURE?

In any policy evaluation effort, the perspective of the analyst has an impact on the conclusions. Critics of governmental monetary and fiscal policies claim that such policies tend to favor those who have economic resources. Economist John K. Galbraith, for instance, argued that the economic planning system, well-developed and representing the people with money, does not help those who need help the most.[12] He sees business and financial interests as having captured monetary and fiscal policy; therefore, consumers, workers, and the poor do not receive sufficient consideration. Milton Friedman,[13] who suggests that government controls stifle economic activity because they make business too costly to operate profitably, takes the opposite stance. Regardless of perspective, many critics of economic policies agree that these "solutions" tend to distort economic development and lead to the maldistribution of resources in the society. How that maldistribution is explained depends on the critic's point of view.

Social Orders

To explain preferences for governmental activity in economic policy, the concept of "social orders" as discussed by Aaron Wildavsky is useful.[14] Economic and budgetary policies reflect the values of three social orders that have emerged since the founding of the republic. One social order reflects a commitment to the preservation of a *social hierarchy* as the standard by which to judge government activity. A second emphasizes the operation of *market forces* as the most appropriate standard for evaluating public policy. The third places an emphasis on *egalitarian values* as the prime standard for public policy. This concept of social orders is consistent with the traditional liberal-conservative classification, but it may be more useful in understanding policy preferences than a simple liberal-conservative dichotomy, because it provides additional insights into basic economic and political values.

The order favoring the preservation of a social hierarchy supports an active role for the central government in maintaining the status quo in the distribution of wealth. Social hierarchists hold that a natural order divides society into strata based on ability. The distribution of wealth reflects this natural ordering. Government should therefore pursue economic policies to preserve this uneven distribution pattern and avoid policies that would artificially erase these natural distinctions. Promoting equality of economic opportunity is not an appropriate sphere of government activity because individuals are primarily responsible for their own economic status. By extension, this order favors low taxation, vigorously opposes redistributive economic policies, favors low levels of domestic spending, and supports higher levels of defense spending to protect the security of the existing economic system.

The market-oriented social order places emphasis on the allocation of social goods through the values of a free-market framework. Individual competition is valued and encouraged. Therefore, government ought to avoid excessive entanglement in economic policy. Government should pursue policies that promote equality of economic opportunity only when such policies enhance market operations. Accordingly, this order favors a limited role for government in economic policy, opposes adoption of redistributive economic policies, favors low levels of domestic spending, and supports higher levels of defense spending.

The egalitarian social order places an emphasis on social and political equality. This order views government as an appropriate mechanism to regulate the distribution of economic benefits to promote individual equality. The emphasis on equality directly affects economic policy preferences. Simple equality of economic opportunity, as advocated by the market approach, is an overly limited goal, for it does not entail actual achievement of equality. Egalitarians emphasize redistributive policies to achieve a degree of economic equality. They also favor higher levels of taxes, support higher domestic spending, place reduced emphasis on defense spending, and favor a generally stronger role for government in economic policy.

Historically, American economic policy has been a function of the equilibrium between these three social orders and a shared commitment to a balanced budget with a minimal national debt.

Inflation

Individuals drawn from the market and social hierarchy orders dominated the Reagan administration. This helps to explain that administration's emphasis on inflation as a greater economic problem than unemployment. Inflation threatened

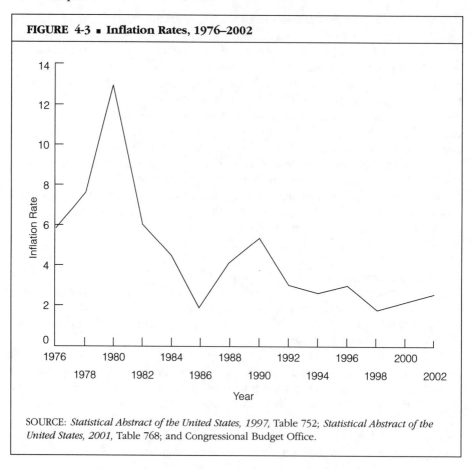

FIGURE 4-3 ▪ **Inflation Rates, 1976–2002**

SOURCE: *Statistical Abstract of the United States, 1997,* Table 752; *Statistical Abstract of the United States, 2001,* Table 768; and Congressional Budget Office.

the smooth operation of the market and eroded the wealth of the upper income strata. The decision to finance federal spending with a massive program of debt proved to be an effective strategy against inflation, though it helped to produce the massive deficits of the 1980s and 1990s. The inflation rate dropped from 13 percent in 1980 to a low of 1.9 percent during 1986 and is currently around 2.4 percent, as reflected in Figure 4-3.

Since the 1990s, economic growth in the United States has remained about 5 percent of GDP, as reflected in Figure 4-4. A long period of economic expansion followed the planned recession of 1982 and its negative GDP growth rate. The economic policies of the 1980s and 1990s are associated with this domestic economic growth.

Fiscal Policy

The Reagan and George H. Bush administrations took pride in the fiscal and monetary policies that they claimed fueled the economic recovery of the 1980s, which persisted through 2001, longer than any other recent period of recovery. The tax

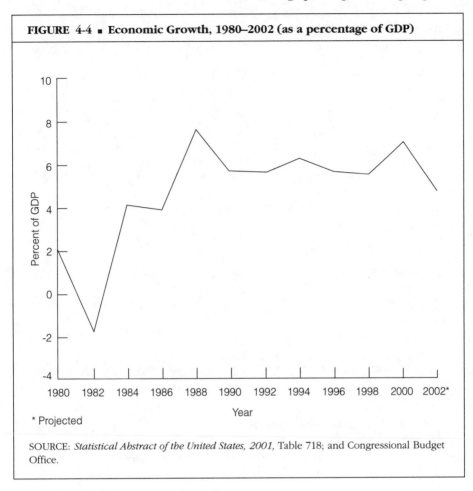

FIGURE 4-4 ■ Economic Growth, 1980–2002 (as a percentage of GDP)

* Projected

SOURCE: *Statistical Abstract of the United States, 2001,* Table 718; and Congressional Budget Office.

reductions pumped more money into the economy, aiding in an industrial investment boom.

Critics of these tax and spending policies focused on two issues. The first is the "fairness issue" related to the equity of tax and spending reductions. A constant theme of opponents to tax cuts was that those policies favored the rich and hurt the poor, that the impact of domestic budget cuts would increase the real income of those in the highest income categories, and that the majority of taxpayers would experience either no increase in income or a decline.

The second issue raised by critics was that these policies fueled the explosion of the national debt and the budget deficit, whose long-range consequences are severe.

Figure 4-5 shows the growth of the national debt. The national debt peaked in 1999 to 2000 and then decreased only slightly with the advent of budget surpluses (Figure 4-1). The United States economy now carries over $3 trillion in debt. The deficit spending of the 1980s and 1990s created two policy problems. First was a habit of annual deficit spending that proved difficult to break. Second, and probably more severe, was the size of the national debt.

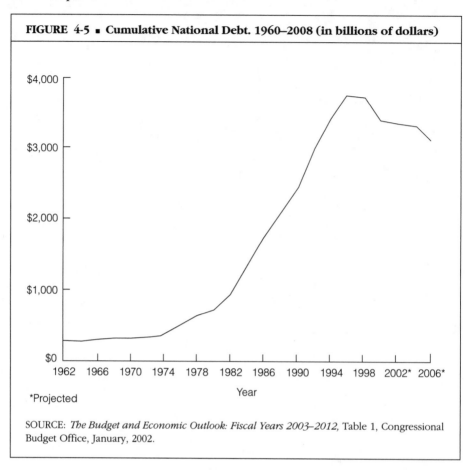

FIGURE 4-5 ▪ Cumulative National Debt. 1960–2008 (in billions of dollars)

*Projected

Year

SOURCE: *The Budget and Economic Outlook: Fiscal Years 2003–2012,* Table 1, Congressional Budget Office, January, 2002.

The size of the debt presents long-term costs to the wealth of the nation. Even with the elimination of the annual deficit, interest payments will continue to consume a significant percentage of the federal budget. Stated another way, interest payments in 2002 absorb over $170 billion of federal spending per year, spending diverted from productive uses.

Historic Budget Deficit Control Efforts. In its first attempt to reduce the deficit and stop growth of the national debt by imposing spending limitations, Congress passed the Balanced Budget and Emergency Deficit Control Act of 1985, otherwise known as the *Gramm-Rudman Act.* This act resulted in two significant changes in the federal budget process. First, the act specified target deficit levels for fiscal years 1986 through 1991 that both Congress and the president were required to follow. As originally enacted, the measure called for a maximum federal deficit of $72 billion for 1989, $36 billion for 1990, and a balanced budget by 1991.

The second provision of the act required imposing automatic spending cuts across the board if spending exceeded the targeted budget deficit levels. This process of "sequestration" would come into play if Congress and the president were unable to agree on spending priorities that would reduce the deficit.

The Gramm-Rudman process was amended in 1987 to establish new budget deficit goals with deficit targets of $100 billion for 1990, $64 billion for 1991, $28 billion for 1992, and a balanced budget for 1993. In the event of sequestration, half of the spending cuts would come from defense spending, with the other half falling on domestic spending.

Failure of Gramm-Rudman. These deficit reductions were not achieved. In fact, the 1992 budget had a record deficit of $362 billion. Gramm-Rudman proved ineffective in reducing the federal budget deficit. One reason for its ineffectiveness is that Gramm-Rudman deficit targets had to be met at the beginning of a fiscal year based on revenue and spending projections. It was therefore possible to achieve compliance only on paper. The actual deficit at the end of the fiscal year continued to be higher than the target deficit level because of differences between projections and actual revenue receipts.

Congress and the president further weakened Gramm-Rudman in 1990. These changes were to remain in effect until 1995 with new budget rules that avoided sequestration if spending were the result of events "beyond the control" of the president and Congress. This allowed the deficit to exceed the Gramm-Rudman limits and avoid the draconian cuts associated with sequestration. The provisions of Gramm-Rudman were effectively suspended. The experience with Gramm-Rudman demonstrated that the strategy of imposing legal mandates on Congress and the president would be ultimately unsuccessful. Economic expansion would prove to be the factor that ultimately would eliminate annual federal deficits.

Federal Revenues and Spending

In order to understand the possibilities and limits of fiscal policy, and the obstacles to deficit reduction faced by Congress and presidents in the 1980s and 1990s, one must grasp the patterns of federal income and expenditures. Figures 4-6 and 4-7 provide a visual display of the facts. Individual income taxes and social insurance taxes account for 84 percent of federal revenues. Corporate income taxes cover less than 8 percent of federal revenues. A significant point is that federal borrowing dropped from over 12 percent of revenues in 1995 to a minor level by 2002. Borrowing is no longer important as a source of federal revenue.

Eliminating the budget deficit reduced the pressure of interest payments on the federal budget. During the late 1990s, interest payments went from the third- to fifth-highest spending category in the federal budget. They now consume some 10 percent of federal spending, down from 15 percent in 1997. Following the election of George W. Bush to the presidency in 2000 and the "war on terror," defense spending reversed its course and now receives a growing share of the federal budget.

Fiscal Policy Evaluation

In 1992, the deficit was projected to rise to the $400 billion range by 1994 and to continue increasing through the decade. These projections were inaccurate, and the federal budget deficit disappeared by 1998. What were the policy changes that produced this change?

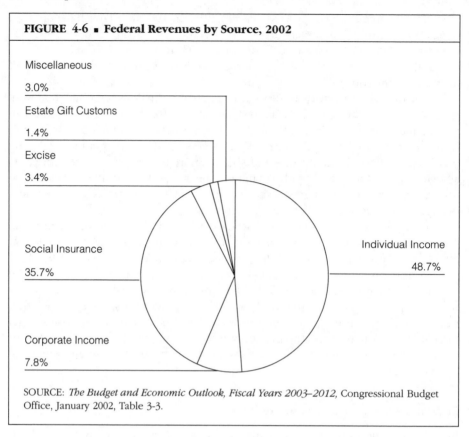

FIGURE 4-6 ▪ Federal Revenues by Source, 2002

Miscellaneous
3.0%

Estate Gift Customs
1.4%

Excise
3.4%

Social Insurance
35.7%

Corporate Income
7.8%

Individual Income
48.7%

SOURCE: *The Budget and Economic Outlook, Fiscal Years 2003–2012,* Congressional Budget Office, January 2002, Table 3-3.

1990 and 1993 Budget Compromises. First, the Omnibus Budget Reconciliation Act of 1990 (OBRA-90) contained tax increases and spending cuts designed to reduce the deficit by almost $500 billion between 1991 and 1995. The tax increases generated $158 billion in new revenues for the federal government. These tax measures raised individual income tax rates for high-income taxpayers and included a 5 cents per gallon tax on motor fuels. Federal excise and other taxes also increased slightly. A variety of entitlement programs received mandatory spending cuts. Some $57 billion came from Medicare and other federal health programs. This legislation also placed spending restrictions on national defense.

OBRA-90 also imposed spending caps on discretionary categories for the 1991 to 1995 period and established spending ceilings for defense, domestic, and international categories. A companion Budget Enforcement Act (BEA) provided a sequestration process if spending in the three areas exceeded the established caps. The act also introduced a "pay-as-you-go" (PAYGO) provision for entitlement programs. Current programs could be maintained, but spending for any new program would have to be matched by a corresponding tax increase or cuts in other programs.

The provisions of OBRA-90 and the BEA did not reduce the deficit to the levels promised in 1990. The deficit remained at high levels, but some deficit reduction did happen. Through 1992, the spending caps held, and the PAYGO pro-

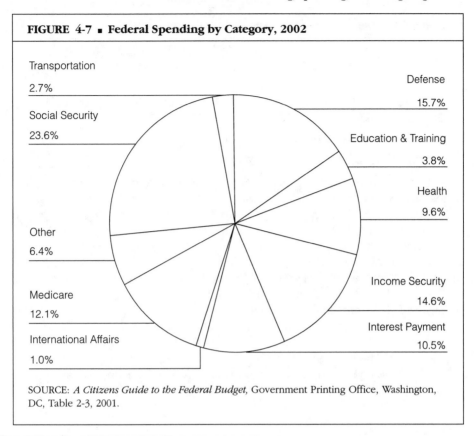

FIGURE 4-7 ▪ Federal Spending by Category, 2002

Transportation
2.7%

Social Security
23.6%

Other
6.4%

Medicare
12.1%

International Affairs
1.0%

Defense
15.7%

Education & Training
3.8%

Health
9.6%

Income Security
14.6%

Interest Payment
10.5%

SOURCE: *A Citizens Guide to the Federal Budget,* Government Printing Office, Washington, DC, Table 2-3, 2001.

visions acted to discourage both tax cuts and major spending increases in entitlement programs.

In 1993, Congress enacted OBRA-93, extending the provisions of the BEA, including spending caps and PAYGO, through 1998. OBRA-93 also included income tax increases and increased taxes on motor fuels. Medicare spending was targeted for a reduction of $77 billion. Collectively, OBRA-93 sought to generate an additional $240 billion in new revenues and a reduction in the growth of federal programs by $200 billion.

The Balanced Budget Act of 1997. Strong economic growth, producing higher tax revenues and lower expenditures, facilitated the Balanced Budget Act of 1997 (BBA). In this act, the president and Congress achieved compromises on spending and taxes, and proposals from the president, the House, and the Senate were reconciled in August, 1997. A combination of spending reductions, some new programs, and tax changes, the BBA projected a declining deficit and a modest surplus by fiscal year 2002. By early 1998, it became clear that a surplus would occur as early as that year. This set in motion political maneuvering over whether to use the surplus to (1) reduce the national debt, (2) finance new programs or expand old ones, or (3) finance tax cuts.

The healthy economy allowed the BBA to support modest new spending programs, some of which are described in other chapters. These budget actions

TABLE 4-1 ■ Defense Spending, 1996–2006 (in billions of dollars)							
	1996	*1997*	*1998*	*1999*	*2000*	*2002*	*2004** *2006**

	1996	1997	1998	1999	2000	2002	2004*	2006*
Dollars	244	255	268	271	295	325	343	363
Percent of Budget	15.0	15.0	14.5	14.7	16.0	17.6	18.6	19.7

*Projections
SOURCE: Congressional Budget Office.

plus steady economic growth reduced the annual federal budget deficit and ultimately eliminated it. Budget deficits may return if Congress is unable or unwilling to comply with BBA provisions. In 1999 and 2000 Congress enacted
legislation relaxing BBA reductions in health care programs (see Chapter 8), created numerous "emergency" spending bills exempt from the provisions of BBA,
and eliminated PAYGO provisions for fiscal years 2001 and 2002. The presence
of significant budget surpluses began to erode Congressional budget discipline.

Level of Debt. Some analysts argue that the deficit is a relatively minor economic issue. The annual budget deficit remains at less than 2 percent of GDP. This
low percentage places only minor pressure on the nation's economy. Other analysts argue just the opposite. They emphasize the size of the total debt, not the
annual deficit. The difference is that the total debt is approximately 50 percent of
GDP. The issue concerning how much debt the American economy can support
remains unresolved.

Defense Spending

Defense spending increases will place additional pressure on projected surpluses.
As indicated in Table 4-1, the Congressional Budget Office projects defense spending to increase from $244 billion in 1996 to $363 billion in 2006. This spending projection rests, in large part, on the assumption that the United States does not face a
major global threat from the former Soviet Union. These spending levels also assume
a relatively minor role for the American military in localized conflicts around the
globe. However, they also reflect the impact of American involvement in Afghanistan
and in other areas of the world in response to terrorism. They have the potential to
dramatically increase the defense spending and significantly alter budgetary policy.

The new patterns of defense spending have potentially significant impacts on
military preparedness, as indicated in Table 4-2. The reduction in strategic forces
is due in large part to the ratification of the Strategic Arms Reduction Treaty. The
drop in conventional forces is a function both of the breakup of the Soviet Union
and the perceived reduction in the need for conventional forces and of budget
pressures from the annual deficit in the early to mid-1990s. The current force structure is almost too small for unilateral military action by the United States, except
on a small scale. Deployment of the American military now requires cooperation
and extensive support from allies if any type of theater-wide action is anticipated.
This force projection, however, was developed prior to the "War on Terror," which
will require a different foreign policy and a new force alignment (see Chapter 12).

TABLE 4-2 ■ **U.S. Military Forces, 1990 and 2001**

Military Forces	1990	2001
Strategic Forces		
Land-Based ICBMs	1,000	550
Strategic Bombers	277	154
Submarine-Launched Missiles	584	432
Conventional Forces		
Army		
Divisions	18	10
Reserve Divisions	10	8
Navy		
Battleforce Ships	546	317
Aircraft Carriers	15	12
Air Wings	13	10
Marine Corps Divisions	4	4
Air Force		
Tactical Fighter Wings	24	21
Reserve Wings	12	4
Airlift Aircraft	860	722

SOURCE: U.S. Department of Defense Annual Report to the President and Congress, 2001.

FUTURE ALTERNATIVES: SPENDING, TAXES, AND THE DEFICIT

Conflict marks debate over economic policy. The issue of governmental involvement in the economy is complex and reflects basic ideological values. During the 1980s, desire to reduce the role of government in the economy guided policymaking departments of the executive branch of government. Others outside the executive branch argued that more, not less, government intervention is necessary to stabilize the economy. The liberal wing of the Democratic Party appears to be most committed to this approach, with its egalitarian values. Its partisans want policies that increase the power of those who have little opportunity to participate in the economic system. Their proposals include such items as industrial policy, plant closure warnings, and an increase in the national minimum wage. Such policies would intensify coordination and centralization of economic policy. In fiscal and monetary policy, liberals favor attention to unemployment and other symptoms of economic stagnation. They prefer stimulus of the economy even at the cost of some inflation and deficit spending. Conservatives tend to be stronger advocates of balanced budgets and believe that inflation is more dangerous than rising unemployment.

Taxes

Legislators regularly propose tax reforms. Tax cuts are often confused with tax reform, though the two are not the same. *Tax reforms* change the basic type and incidence (who pays) of taxation, and *tax cuts* merely reduce the rate of taxation. The tax reform achieved in 1986 acted to shift tax incidence. Critics of the tax reform claimed that deductions and exemptions favor high-income brackets and hurt middle-income people and the poor. Middle- and upper-income taxpayers bear the largest burden of national income taxes. State and local taxes, however, fall somewhat harder on lower-income groups. Pressure to alter and modify the 1986 tax reforms resulted in the tax increases for wealthier taxpayers in 1990 and again in 1993. In 2001, Congress adopted Bush administration proposals to reduce tax rates for all income levels, but especially for upper-income brackets. Efforts to influence tax incidence continue as economic agenda items.

An item on the economic agenda for this decade centers on tax policy appropriate to an era of budget surpluses. Conservatives continue to propose a reduction in capital gains taxes (somewhat achieved in 1997), but congressional Democrats favor some combination of middle-income tax cuts and tax increases on the wealthy. Any form of tax cut will reduce the surplus or increase the deficit unless accompanied by a corresponding cut in spending or by significant economic growth that produces higher tax revenues.

Alternatives include the *flat-tax proposal.* The flat-tax approach would eliminate many deductions and reduce the number of tax brackets.[15] Additionally, the proposals call for lowering the maximum rate that everyone would pay. Although a true flat tax is unlikely because of the many special interests supporting deductions and other advantages, it is almost certain that there will be additional changes. The major conflict is how and where to generate additional tax revenues.

Another tax reform proposal is a *value-added tax* (VAT) to supplement income taxes. The value-added tax is like a national sales tax on goods as they pass through each phase of the economic system. As economic activity adds value to each natural resource or good, a tax is paid on the increase in value. European nations frequently employ a VAT. Members of the Brookings Institution have proposed yet another approach, a *cash-flow tax* based on a household's gross income minus savings. Thus, all income would be included in figuring the tax. This proposal would encourage saving, as savings would be subtracted from total income for tax purposes. It would make a similar reform in corporate taxes. Again, this proposal is appealing in that it is simple and arguably fair. Moreover, higher rates of savings would stimulate economic investment and growth. Political reality, however, suggests that those with a stake in the current complex tax system would work hard to retain their special position. The value-added tax does have the advantage of being a less-visible tax than the income tax, which may be a factor in its consideration.

Other Future Issues

Budget Surplus.   Concern for maintaining budget surpluses in economic and budgetary policy has replaced concern for deficits. The passage of OBRA-90 and OBRA-93, along with the Balanced Budget Act of 1997, provided some restraint in the growth of spending. The economic expansion of the late 1990s gave the government significant new revenues that eliminated the annual budget deficit.

Defense spending will grow slowly with the size of the American military falling. Systems once targeted for production (such as the F-22 combat aircraft) will be purchased in very limited quantities. The American military presence in

Europe and other areas is being reduced, except for peacekeeping missions in various areas of the world.

Yet the aging of the population (Chapters 7 and 8), concern for crime and education (Chapters 6 and 9), environmental protection (Chapter 5), transportation needs, and many other priorities will press themselves upon policymakers and place strain on the budget from the spending side. These tend to be liberal priorities. Conservatives will place pressure on the budget from the revenue side by pressing for extension of the 2001 tax cuts. These twin pressures will make it difficult to sustain budget surpluses in the coming decade.

Monetary policy. A widely accepted view is that changes in monetary policy do not have long-term impacts on prices and interest rates. If the Fed restricts the supply of money, this will only defer demand, not eliminate it. When it lifts restrictions, demand will surge forward. Interest rates and economic activity tend to respond in only a short-term manner to changes in monetary policy. There is less agreement about the impact of long-term monetary policy changes on the GDP. The CBO has used two econometric models, the Washington University Macroeconomic Model and the Data Resources, Inc. model, to predict the impact of monetary policy on GDP. The CBO found that a gradual increase in the supply of money is necessary to support economic growth in order to avoid deficits without adversely affecting the economy by reducing growth of the GDP. Accordingly, actions by the Fed to tighten the supply of money may be counterproductive.

Balanced budget amendment. In the late 1980s and early 1990s a popular conservative proposal to address deficits involved amending the Constitution to mandate a balanced federal budget. This was one provision of the Republican "Contract with America" of 1994. A significant weakness with this approach was that the policy actions and enforcement mechanism necessary to balance the budget were not (and probably cannot) be specified in the amendment. Experience with Gramm–Rudman demonstrated that even when enforcement mechanisms exist, political strategy can negate their effectiveness. The experience of the late 1990s, especially passage of the Balanced Budget Act in 1997, demonstrates that genuine deficit avoidance comes only when the president and Congress together have the political will and support to make difficult choices about specific spending and tax programs.

A balanced budget amendment also could create a number of problems. First, there is an absence of consensus concerning the composition of the federal budget. Defense spending, entitlement spending, spending for health care, and other programs compete for limited fiscal resources. This competition would encourage Congress and the president to achieve compliance "on paper" by using such budgetary gimmicks as overly optimistic economic forecasts, moving some agencies and programs to an off-budget status, and transferring financial responsibility for programs to state and local governments. Second, such an amendment restricts the ability of the government to deal with emergencies like military actions, economic recessions, and natural disasters that require an immediate federal response.

Line-item veto. Most recent presidents have argued that they should have the line-item veto, the power to veto specific budget items. Proponents of the line-item veto claim that the president would use it to eliminate unnecessary federal spending, known as pork-barrel projects, due to his national perspective. Supporters note that forty-three of the fifty governors possess the line-item veto and that state governments operate with balanced budgets.

Critics of granting this power to the president argue that it represents a major shift in power between the three branches of government and concentrates too much power in the hands of the president. Others observe that the line-item veto would probably not have a significant impact on the deficit, because it applies only to discretionary and not mandatory federal spending. Discretionary spending accounts for only 25 percent of the federal budget. Presidents would be tempted to use the line-item veto to support their spending programs rather than to reduce overall spending and reduce the deficit. Detractors also argue that this power will simply replace Congressional budget priorities with those of the president, not reduce federal spending.

Congress granted this power to the president in 1996, and President Clinton used it for the first time on August 11, 1997. Some members of Congress, however, challenged the constitutionality of the line-item veto, and the U.S. Supreme Court ruled that the law was unconstitutional as written.

Caps on mandatory spending.   Outlays for mandatory spending, often called entitlements (for example, Social Security, Medicare, Medicaid, food stamps, and farm price supports), consume over half of the federal budget. Congress cannot easily impose caps on these programs. Social Security checks and medical benefits cannot be stopped when a spending ceiling limit is reached without imposing severe hardships on millions of Americans. In order to limit spending in programs, Congress must adopt policy options that would modify the programs, restrict benefits, or transfer them to discretionary status. Chapters 7 and 8 consider the difficulty of limiting spending in such programs.

Energy costs.   The price of oil has fluctuated since 1973 (see Chapter 5) with significant economic consequences. The drop in oil prices has had a direct economic impact by exerting a downward pressure on inflation. Oil prices have remained relatively low (in the $13 to $20 per barrel range). If OPEC member nations are able to achieve tighter control over oil production and increase the market price for oil, this will exert inflationary pressures on the American economy.

Homeland security.   Following the terrorist attacks of September 11, 2001, the United States began an extensive program to strengthen homeland security. Congress has approved over $17 billion in spending for homeland security, and that figure will increase in the coming years. Given the open nature of American society, efforts to protect government institutions and the population from terrorist activities are expensive undertakings. There will be a continued emphasis on this type of spending. However, its total impact on the nation's economy is uncertain.

SUMMARY

The role of the federal government in the area of economic policy has expanded significantly during the twentieth century in response to both internal and external pressures. These pressures persist and form the foundation for continued intervention in the economic arena.

The role of the government in regulating the economy calls upon a number of values, which have differing policy implications and divergent goals. These values include questions surrounding inflation, unemployment, level of economic growth, and equality.

Obstacles exist in developing economic policy. The separation of powers at the national level, fragmentation of responsibility within the executive branch, and the division of power between state and federal government act to hinder the development of a coordinated national economic policy.

Monetary policy refers to regulating the flow of money in the economy and involves control over interest rates and the reserves that banks must maintain to cover their deposits.

Fiscal policy concerns such things as tax policies, wage and price controls, and government spending. Government employs changes in these policies to combat inflation or recession. Inflation occurs when prices are increasing and the output of goods and services is not. In a recession, there is a drop in demand for goods and services, and there is little or no growth in the economy.

Supply-side economics characterized the policy of the Reagan administration. This policy flowed from the premise that, if taxes were reduced, the economy would be stimulated. The resulting economic expansion would provide increased tax revenues, even with significantly lower tax rates. The promise of supply-side economics was not realized in the 1980s. Tax rates were cut, but tax revenues did not initially increase as supply-siders had predicted. The national debt increased dramatically, and interest payments on it now consume 10 percent of the annual federal budget.

The Gramm-Rudman mechanism to reduce the deficit proved only marginally effective. Budget agreements between the president and Congress in 1990 and again in 1993 effectively removed the threat of sequestration until fiscal 1999. Attempts to reduce the federal budget deficit were successful only in the late 1990s, largely due to unanticipated economic growth that produced significant increases in tax revenues.

Tax rates and tax reforms are popular issues for political debate. Reduction in tax revenues without similar reductions in government spending led to record deficits in the 1980s, thus sparking continuing debate over appropriate government policy. Because of the elimination of the federal deficit, the issue of tax policy will be high on the economic agenda for the early twenty-first century.

Elimination of the budget deficit depends on economic growth. Any economic downturn or recession will eliminate the viability of a balanced budget and return the issue of budget deficits to the policy agenda. In this regard, the costs of responding to terrorism and of supporting a new military strategy for a post-Cold War world are uncertain.

NOTES

1. See Timothy Cogley, "What Is the Optimal Rate of Inflation?" *Federal Reserve Bank of San Francisco Economic Letter* (September 19, 1997), No. 97–27, for a discussion of the factors the Federal Reserve System can use to determine an optimal rate of inflation.

2. Herbert Stein, "Should Growth Be a Priority of National Policy?" *Challenge* (March/April, 1986): 1–17. Late in 1991, the Commerce Department changed its economic measure from Gross National Product (GNP) to Gross Domestic Product (GDP). Figures in this book are GDP unless otherwise indicated.

3. See Mary C. Daly, "Assessing the Benefits of Economic Growth," *Federal Reserve Bank of San Francisco Economic Letter* (October 17, 1997), No. 97–30, for a discussion of various approaches to assess benefits of economic growth.

4. Anthony Solomon, "Economic Ideology and Public Policy," *Challenge* (July/August, 1986): 11–17.

5. Edward R. Tufte, *Political Control of the Economy* (Princeton, NJ: Princeton University Press, 1978).

6. See Brian Motley, "Should Monetary Policy Focus on 'Core' Inflation?" *Federal Reserve Bank of San Francisco Economic Letter* (April 18, 1997), No. 97–11, for a discussion of some of these issues.

7. Thomas J. Cunningham, "The Long-Run Outcome of a Permanent Deficit," *Economic Review* (May, 1986): 25–33.

8. Arthur Laffer, "Supply Side Economics," *Financial Analysts Journal* (September/October, 1981): 29–43.

9. Marc Levinson, "The Verdict on Deregulation," *Dun's Business Monthly* (November, 1986): 30–34. See also Christopher Douglass, Michael Orlando, and Melinda Warren, *Regulatory Changes and Trends: An Analysis of the 1998 Budget of the U.S. Government* (St. Louis, MO: Center for the Study of American Business, August, 1997).

10. C. Fred Bergsten, "The Second Debt Crisis Is Coming," *Challenge* (May/June, 1985): 14–21.

11. "Tax Reform—At Last," *Business Week* (September 1, 1986): 54–58.

12. John K. Galbraith, *Economics and the Public Purpose* (Boston: Houghton Mifflin, 1978).

13. Rick Tilman, "Ideology and Utopia in the Political Economy of Milton Friedman," *Polity*, 8 (Spring, 1976): 422–442.

14. Aaron Wildavsky, "Budgets as Compromises Among Social Orders," *The Federal Budget: Economics and Politics* (New Brunswick, NJ: Transaction Books, 1982).

15. Robert Hall and Alvin Rabushka, *Low Tax, Simple Tax, Flat Tax* (New York: McGraw-Hill, 1984).

SUGGESTED READINGS

Books

Baily, Martin N., Burtless, Gary, and Litan, Robert E. *Growth with Equity: Economic Policymaking for the Next Century*. Washington, DC: Brookings Institution, 1993.

Bingham, Richard D. *Industrial Policy American Style*. Armonk, NY: M. E. Sharpe, 1997.

Brace, Paul. *State Government and Economic Performance*. Baltimore, MD: Johns Hopkins University Press, 1994.

Collender, Stanley E. *The Guide to the Federal Budget*. Lanham, MD: Rowan and Littlefield, 1997.

Friedman, Benjamin. *Day of Reckoning: The Consequences of American Economic Policy*. New York: Vintage Books, 1990.

Friedman, Milton. *Capitalism and Freedom*. Chicago: University of Chicago Press, 1981.

Hartley, Keith. *The Economics of Defense Policy*. London: Brassey's, 1991.

Peretz, Paul, ed. *The Politics of American Economic Policy Making,* 2nd ed. Armonk, NY: M. E. Sharpe, 1996.

Plotkin, Sidney, and Scheuerman, William E. *Private Interests, Public Spending: Balanced-Budget Conservatism and the Fiscal Crisis*. Boston: South End Press, 1994.

Sahu, Kanandi P., and Tracy, Ronald L. *The Economic Legacy of the Reagan Years: Euphoria or Chaos?* Westport, CT: Praeger, 1991.

Schick, Allen. *The Federal Budget: Politics, Policy, Process*. Washington, DC: Brookings Institution, 1993.

Stabile, Donald R., and Cantor, Jeffrey A. *The Public Debt of the United States: An Historical Perspective, 1775–1990*. Westport, CT: Praeger, 1991.

Sundquist, James L., ed. *Beyond Gridlock? Prospects for Governance in the Clinton Years and After*. Washington, DC: Brookings Institution, 1994.

Thurow, Lester. *The Zero-Sum Society: Distribution and the Possibilities for Economic Change*. New York: Penguin, 1981.

Tomkin, Shelly. *Inside OMB: Politics and Process in the President's Budget Office*. Armonk, NY: M. E. Sharpe, 1998.

Wildavsky, Aaron. *The New Politics of the Budgetary Process,* 2nd ed. New York: HarperCollins, 1992.

Web Sites

American Enterprise Institute for Public Policy Research: www.aei.org
Brookings Institution, Washington, DC: www.brookings.edu
Cato Institute: www.cato.org
The Century Foundation (formerly the Twentieth Century Fund)   www.tcf.org
Congressional Budget Office: www.cbo.gov
Ewing Marion Kauffman Foundation   www.emkf.org
The Heritage Foundation: www.heritage.org
Office of Management and Budget: www.whitehouse. gov/omb/
Office of Tax Policy, United States Treasury   www.ustreas.gov/taxpolicy/
Organization for Economic Cooperation and Development (OECD)   www.oecd.org
U.S. Federal Reserve System   www.federalreserve.gov
The Urban Institute: www.urban.org

CHAPTER 5

Energy and Environmental Policies: Policy Complacency

Complacency best describes the attitude of the American public toward the development of a national energy policy and environmental protection strategies until the 1970s. An abundant supply of cheap energy minimized public concern over energy policy. The availability of inexpensive energy combined with an absence of policies designed to protect the environment were major factors in the economic prosperity of the United States. The dominant public policy value was that, because the United States had vast natural resources available, regulatory and protective environmental policies were unnecessary.

ENERGY POLICY ISSUE BACKGROUND: COMPLACENCY AND CRISIS

In 1973 U.S. energy history changed when the Arab oil embargo triggered the emergence of a new era in energy policy. Consequently, energy policy in the United States falls into two periods, with the 1973 Arab oil embargo serving as the dividing line. The period before 1973 was the traditional period; the years following the embargo were a period of crisis, uncertainty, and finally renewed complacency.

Traditional Energy Policy

Before 1973, the belief that the private sector could provide the nation with an unlimited supply of inexpensive energy governed policy. America benefited from an abundance of fossil fuels: coal, oil, and natural gas, all developed and provided by the private sector. The limited government regulations that did exist were designed to maintain stable prices in order to protect the economic security of the energy producers with little concern for energy conservation. Energy policy was a patchwork of state and federal actions designed to encourage consumption with little emphasis on efficiency or national independence in energy production. U.S. energy policy was unprepared for the events of 1973 in the Middle East that threatened the nation's energy supply and moved the politics of energy into the public agenda.

Policy values. Several values guided energy policy during this early period. The Mineral Leasing Act of 1920 reflected an acceptance of the federal government's role in regulating and protecting mineral resources on public lands. The act designed government leases to encourage energy exploration and production. Energy producers paid royalties to both states and the federal government under this system. When conflict arose between coastal states and the federal government concerning leasing powers for offshore oil and gas exploration during the 1940s, President Truman attempted to bring all offshore land under federal jurisdiction. Texas, Louisiana, and California signed their own leases for offshore exploration with oil and gas companies. This dispute was resolved in 1953 when the states obtained leasing responsibility for lands within their traditional boundaries (three to ten miles offshore), with the federal government retaining control over all other offshore lands.

Taxation. Federal tax policy for energy producers remained relatively unchanged from World War I until 1973. The primary value guiding energy tax policy involved granting tax deductions and other tax breaks to energy producers in order to encourage exploration and production. This policy did result in increased production, which initially led to calls for prorationing.

Prorationing involves using governmental regulations to impose production quotas on private companies in order to reduce supply. The nation faced an oversupply of oil until the 1940s and continues to face an oversupply of coal. This strategy was an effort to achieve market stability in order to protect producers from unlimited cutthroat competition. Prorationing became an accepted policy position for both federal and state governments.

Antitrust policy. The federal energy policy of prorationing conflicted with antitrust policies. In 1911, the federal government abolished the Standard Oil Trust in order to increase competition. During World War II, the government dropped its limited antitrust efforts targeting the oil and gas industry. By the 1950s antitrust actions targeting oil companies tended to be viewed as counterproductive to the effort to secure an increasing supply of oil.

Decentralization. Traditional energy policy reflected a commitment to private sector initiative through market operations. In order to allow the private sector the freedom necessary to provide energy, regulatory and other energy policy powers remained fragmented and decentralized. No single regulatory body or level of government had responsibility for establishing energy policy options. Decentralization of policy responsibility was consistent with an emphasis on market operations.

Coal. Before the late 1920s, coal was a primary source of energy, supplying almost 75 percent of the nation's consumption. The abundant coal supply provided cheap energy but also acted to depress prices, which resulted in low profits for companies and low wages for miners. By the early 1920s, a combination of federal and state policies served to protect the coal industry from oversupply and unlimited competition. These policies also provided a degree of wage stability for miners. However, the late 1920s marked a shift from coal to oil as the fuel of choice for homes and industry. As the demand for coal decreased, the industry began a long and gradual slide into depression.

The oversupply of coal was so extensive, and competition so severe, that by 1932 over 4,000 coal companies had failed and only 300 of the 1,864 companies still in operation reported a profit.[1] Efforts by the United Mine Workers (UMW) and coal operators resulted in Congressional enactment of the Bituminous Coal Acts of 1935 and 1937. These acts attempted to impose production quotas and stabilize profits and wages. The success of these efforts was limited, and after World War II, the industry again slid back into depression due to the shift to oil as the preferred energy source.

Oil. Basic to the long history of oil policy was government protection for the industry. Much of the early regulation involved attempts by the states and the federal government to limit production and create a balance between supply and demand through prorationing. Since most American oil came from Texas, the policy decisions of the Texas Railroad Commission (which regulates oil production in Texas) tended to define national oil policy. Production limits set by Texas influenced other oil-rich states to adopt similar policies concerning production and distribution of their lucrative resource. Federal controls applied only to the interstate transportation of oil.

The adoption of the oil depletion allowance by the federal government in 1926 exemplifies the protective nature of these policies. At the end of World War I, the U.S. Geological Survey (USGS) predicted that the nation's known oil reserves would be depleted within ten years. The oil industry used the USGS prediction and argued that just as machinery wore out and buildings deteriorated, oil wells also lost their value over time as the underground reservoir emptied. Congress responded with depletion legislation that allowed oil companies to deduct 27.5 percent of their gross income from taxable income, if the total amount deducted did not exceed 50 percent of the company's net income. The USGS prediction proved inaccurate as oil exploration efforts led to the addition of vast reserves in Oklahoma and East Texas by the 1930s. The industry, however, continued to argue successfully that the oil depletion allowance should continue because it protected the producer's profit margin, which encouraged continued exploration across the United States and around the world as the tax savings were plowed back into new oil drilling expeditions.

Natural gas. Natural gas also has a long history of regulation. Natural gas production is not labor-intensive, because it requires very little refining before commercial use. Natural gas production involves three major activities: production in the field, distribution through pipelines, and a specialized distribution network to consumers at the end of the pipeline. The bulk of effort involves building and maintaining pipelines.

Early federal regulation of natural gas centered on interstate transportation (pipelines), while state governments focused on production and final consumption. The 1938 Natural Gas Act assigned regulatory authority at the federal level to the Federal Power Commission (FPC). The FPC regulated the price of natural gas in the interstate market and approved pipeline construction and deactivation. The primary policy impact of these regulatory powers was to maintain an orderly supply of low-cost energy.

FPC regulations maintained an artificially low rate for interstate natural gas consumers. Interstate rates for natural gas were significantly less than the unregulated intrastate rates. Gas selling for $2.50 per thousand cubic feet in the intrastate market could be sold for only $1.00 in the interstate market. An unintended consequence was waste, since the low price structure did not encourage efficiency or conservation. Reduced profits due to regulation also discouraged exploration for new gas supplies, which lowered production of natural gas while increasing demand.

Nuclear power. During the 1950s and 1960s, citizens and government alike viewed nuclear power as a potential major source of energy for both the United States and Western Europe. Congress established the Atomic Energy Commission (AEC) to promote and to control the development of this new source of power, with development of nuclear reactors for commercial generation of electricity assigned to the private sector.

Western Vulnerability: OPEC and the Arab Oil Embargo

Americans were comfortable with what appeared to be an inexhaustible supply of energy combined with the ability to control foreign energy resources. The most important of these were the oil fields of the Middle East and North Africa. Before the 1973 Arab oil embargo, the oil-producing countries did not control the oil industry within their own borders. Major American and European oil companies exercised nearly complete control over the production of oil, its selling price, and the profit levels they chose to share with producing countries.

The power of Western oil companies. How did Western private enterprise consolidate this near stranglehold on the oil resources of the nations that would emerge as the Organization of Petroleum Exporting Countries (OPEC)? As the oil industry developed in the 1930s, seven major companies dominated oil production and distribution: Standard Oil of California (Chevron), the Texas Company (Texaco), Socony-Vacuum (now Mobil), Gulf Oil, Standard Oil of New Jersey (Exxon), Royal Dutch Shell, and British Petroleum. These industry giants found cooperative arrangements in their best interests for international oil exploration. The result was a reduction in competition in the international oil market. Competition further eroded when the Arabian American Oil Company (Aramco) was organized by four companies (Standard Oil of New Jersey, Standard Oil of California, Socony-Vacuum, and The Texas Company) in 1947 to develop the enormous oil reserves of Saudi Arabia. This and other cooperative efforts were so successful that, by 1952, the seven oil giants controlled over 90 percent of the total crude oil production outside North America and the communist nations.

This control was so effective that the companies were able to resist governmental actions taken by producing nations. When Iran attempted to nationalize the Anglo-Iranian Oil Company between 1951 and 1953, the combined resistance of the major companies eliminated the market for Iranian crude oil. They simply increased production in the fields of other countries to offset the boycott of Iranian oil. A similar situation occurred when Iraq nationalized its oil fields in 1961.[2]

The origins of OPEC. This climate of exploitation fostered the oil-producing states' creation of an organization with the aim of achieving equitable price and production levels for its members. OPEC began in 1960 with the membership of seven Arab nations—Algeria, Iraq, Kuwait, Libya, Qatar, Saudi Arabia, and the United Arab Emirates—and six non-Arab nations—Ecuador, Gabon, Indonesia, Iran, Nigeria, and Venezuela. Several factors acted to limit the strength of the new organization in the 1960s. First, the United States was nearly self-sufficient in the production of oil, with relatively little need for imports. Second, the cooperative agreements among the major oil companies created an international oil cartel with near-monopolistic powers. Oil companies could meet belligerent actions by a producing nation, as in the cases of Iran and Iraq, with a boycott of that nation's crude oil. Third, the production of crude oil exceeded international demand, which produced a buyer's market and limited the power of suppliers. The low price of oil restricted producing nations from generating sufficient oil tax revenues for economic development. Only by acting in concert could the producing nations achieve a measure of control over the production and price of their oil reserves.

The 1973 Arab oil embargo. October 6, 1973, marked the opening date of the Yom Kippur War between Israel and the Arab states. This event provided the catalyst for Arab unity and demonstrated the power of collective action available to all OPEC members.[3] On October 17, the Arab oil ministers met in Kuwait and resolved to use oil as a weapon in the struggle against Israel. Accordingly, they imposed a 5 percent monthly reduction in exports to nations supporting Israel. Nations supporting the Arab cause were exempt from the embargo. The embargo had limited impact on oil imports by the United States, as non-Arab sources, primarily Venezuela and Iran, were readily available. The Arab nations lifted the embargo against the United States in March 1974, following the Egyptian-Israeli cease-fire. Yet, the embargo did achieve some of its original political objectives, as support for Israel in Western Europe and Japan softened. The real value of the 1973 Arab oil embargo was the dramatic example of power through unified policy that it gave to OPEC nations. OPEC ministers realized that if action were taken in concert by all thirteen member states, their demands would be impossible to resist. This period marked the beginning of a rapid escalation in the price for OPEC oil and of systematic controls on production levels. Figure 5-1 shows the price paid for light crude oil between 1965 and 2001.

The rapid increase in oil prices depicted in Figure 5-1 coincides with the 1973 embargo. Within its first three months, the price of Arabian oil had increased

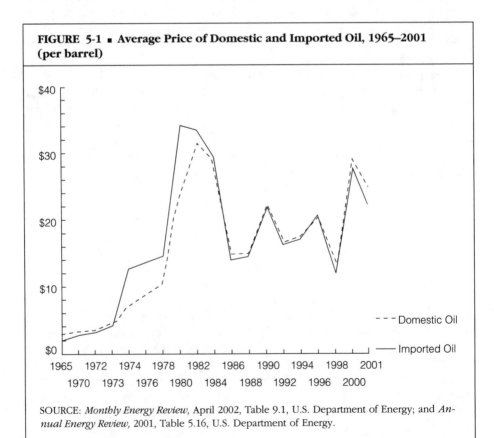

FIGURE 5-1 ■ Average Price of Domestic and Imported Oil, 1965–2001 (per barrel)

SOURCE: *Monthly Energy Review,* April 2002, Table 9.1, U.S. Department of Energy; and *Annual Energy Review,* 2001, Table 5.16, U.S. Department of Energy.

dramatically from $3.00 per barrel to $11.65 per barrel. Oil-exporting nations began to recognize that collective action was a mechanism to demand higher prices for their oil exports.

The increasing cost of oil exerted inflationary pressure on the economies of the oil-consuming West. These inflationary pressures and a need by OPEC nations to generate revenues to fund economic development acted to fuel an upward spiral in oil prices. During the late 1970s, OPEC could not agree on a fixed price for oil, so a price increase by one nation stimulated similar increases by other producers as well.[4] The reality of oil selling at $50 or even $100 per barrel seemed imminent. By 1982 to 1984 a combination of forces, including a reduction in demand, discovery of reserves outside OPEC, overproduction, and OPEC disunity, brought about a drop in global crude oil prices which has stabilized in the $19 per barrel range.

CONTEMPORARY POLICY: FROM CRISIS TO COMPLACENCY

Energy Problems Emerge

The Arab oil embargo coincided with the end of American energy self-sufficiency. Before World War II, the United States was an exporter of oil, but by 1947 the nation had to import oil for domestic use. However, the amount was minimal, less than one-half of 1 percent of total oil consumption. By the mid-1950s, foreign imports accounted for 10 percent of America's oil consumption, in part because of the lower cost of imported oil, typically about half that of domestic oil. A refinery might pay $3.00 per barrel for American oil, but could obtain imported oil of the same quality for $1.50 per barrel.[5]

In order to protect the domestic oil industry, President Eisenhower recommended in 1954, and then imposed in 1959, an import quota equivalent to 12 percent of domestic production. By 1973, American oil consumption reached nearly 17 million barrels per day, while domestic production levels were slightly less than 11 million barrels per day. This gap between domestic supply and demand prompted President Nixon to remove all import quotas on oil in the spring of 1973, which allowed imported oil to rise and reach the current figure of about 60 percent of total American oil consumption (see Figure 5-2).

Natural gas is not as abundant as domestic oil. Domestic natural gas production reached a peak of 24.7 trillion cubic feet in 1975 and then began a gradual decline. Currently, annual consumption levels are exceeding additions to known reserves. In order to meet demand, it is necessary to import increasing amounts of natural gas. Nuclear power did not develop into a source of unlimited energy because of problems with the safety of the technology. The major accident in 1979 at the Three Mile Island nuclear plant in Pennsylvania and less-serious incidents at other nuclear-power facilities acted to shift American policy priorities away from this energy option in the 1980s. Coal furnishes a large percentage of energy consumption, but serious environmental problems exist with this energy source. Gases produced by the burning of coal contribute to acid rain, and strip-mining activities degrade the environment. Other sources of renewable energy such as solar power, wind power, and geothermal technologies have yet to develop sufficiently to take up the slack left by the depletion of oil

FIGURE 5-2 ■ U.S. Dependence on Oil Imports, 1973–2001 Persian Gulf to
Non-Persian Gulf (in percentages of total U.S. oil consumption)

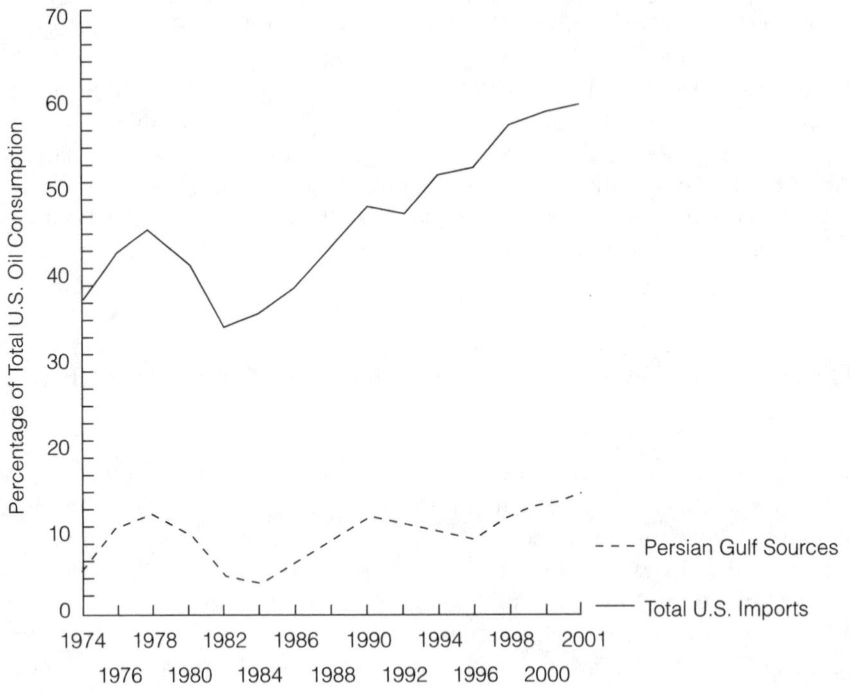

SOURCE: *Monthly Energy Review,* U.S. Department of Energy, online database, 2002.

and natural gas. The United States continues to depend on fossil fuels as its primary source of energy. This reality means continued reliance on oil imports.

Global Dependence on Fossil Fuels

Dependence on oil as the primary energy source continues to be a worldwide
pattern. Figure 5-3 reflects the importance of oil and natural gas as primary energy sources. The proportion of energy provided by these two sources is now approximately 63 percent of total global energy consumption, an increase from
around 36 percent in 1950. When energy consumption is examined on a regional
basis, the importance of oil and natural gas to the industrialized world becomes
even more evident. Coal has declined as a primary source of fuel in Western Europe from slightly over 85 percent to less than 19 percent of total energy consumption in 2000. The same pattern holds true for Japan, as reliance on coal
dropped from over 86 percent to less than 19 percent of total energy consumption. Oil and natural gas are now the world's primary energy sources, except in
Communist Asia, where coal remains the primary energy source, even though oil
and natural gas are becoming increasingly important as fuels.

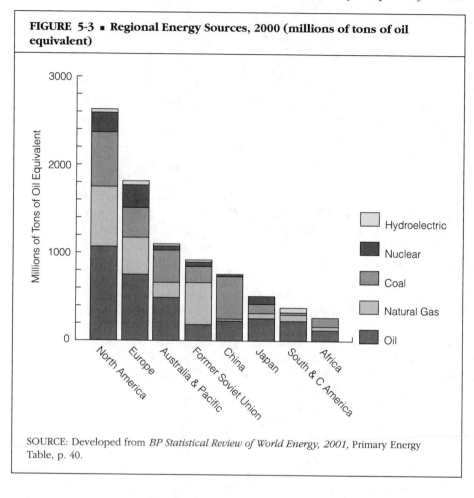

FIGURE 5-3 ▪ **Regional Energy Sources, 2000 (millions of tons of oil equivalent)**

SOURCE: Developed from *BP Statistical Review of World Energy, 2001,* Primary Energy Table, p. 40.

Dependence on imported oil is especially significant for the industrialized democracies of the free world.[6] As of 2000, the United States imported almost 60 percent of its oil from foreign sources. The figure is substantially higher for Europe and Japan, with oil imports accounting for 74 percent of European oil consumption and 99 percent of Japanese oil consumption. An important source of oil for Western Europe and Japan is the Middle East and North Africa. Approximately 59 percent of the oil that Japan imports originates in the Islamic world. The United States has established a pattern since the mid-1970s of obtaining between 10 and 12 percent of its imports from Islamic nations. This means that the West's economic stability depends upon the uninterrupted flow of oil from the Islamic world and, therefore, upon political stability in the Middle East.

Energy Policy after 1973

The disruption of oil supply and the economic consequences of the rapid increase in the cost of oil created by the 1973 oil embargo produced an environment in which the role of the federal government in energy policy expanded dramatically.[7] President Nixon announced "Project Independence" in 1973 as a strategy to achieve energy self-sufficiency by 1980. The basic elements of the plan were: (1) imposition of a national speed limit; (2) adoption of daylight saving time on a year-round basis; (3) increased federal funding for energy research and development; (4) standby authority for gasoline rationing; (5) relaxation of environmental standards to increase the use of coal; (6) deregulation of natural gas; (7) construction of the Trans-Alaska pipeline; and (8) the creation of a federal Department of Energy.

American energy policy failed to develop a unity of purpose and a clear strategy. Policies tended to emphasize administrative reorganization; they also created a number of energy "czars" theoretically charged with formulating energy policy. Political and technological constraints made self-sufficiency by 1980 an unrealistic goal. With the lifting of the Arab oil embargo in the summer of 1974, the crisis atmosphere surrounding energy began to evaporate. Energy policy floundered as debate over the direction it should take continued and agreement on a unified energy policy proved elusive.

During this period, Congress acted to authorize construction of the Trans-Alaska pipeline over the objections of environmental groups. It adopted a national fifty-five-mile-per-hour speed limit in December 1974. Two new governmental agencies were created in 1974, the Federal Energy Administration (FEA) and the Energy Research and Development Administration (ERDA). These agencies had the responsibility to develop and coordinate new federal energy policies. The emphasis on an increased federal role peaked with the creation of the Department of Energy in 1977 under the Carter administration.

Legislation. The National Energy Act of 1978, enacted in response to President Carter's extensive energy proposals, provided an energy policy framework. The act sought to encourage increased energy efficiency, reduce consumption, and change energy use patterns. First, it deregulated natural gas as federal price controls were ended in an effort to encourage increased exploration. Second, the act contained provisions aimed at reducing consumption of oil and natural gas to encourage conversion to coal as a major fuel source in generating electricity. Third, the act mandated changes in utility rate structures to represent the real cost of supplying electric service to customers. "Declining block rates," in which the unit cost of electricity decreased as the level of consumption increased, could continue only if the reduced rate actually represented the costs of providing the electricity. These increases in the cost of electricity were designed to reduce oil and natural gas consumption by reducing the demand for electric power produced through the burning of both fuels.

The act relied on a mixture of taxes and tax credits to encourage a reduction in energy consumption and development of "renewable," nonfossil energy sources. Homeowners received an income tax credit for a percentage of the expenses spent on insulation or other energy-conserving improvements. The tax credit also applied to the installation of solar, wind, or geothermal energy equipment in homes. An important provision of the act included a tax, paid by the manufacturer, on "gas-guzzling" cars. The tax initially ranged from $200 to $500 for the 1980 model year and gradually increased to a range of $500 to $3,850 by the 1986 model year. The Corporate Average Fuel Economy (CAFE) standard required that the automobile industry produce a mix of cars with an average fuel efficiency of 27.5 miles per gallon by 1985.

The tax and CAFE standard contributed to a change in the size and fuel efficiency of automobiles, which reduced oil consumption by American drivers. Chrysler Corporation achieved total compliance with the new standards. When faced with the prospect of imposing severe tax penalties on General Motors in 1986 (the fleet of GM cars did not meet the new standards), Congress balked and reduced the CAFE standard to 26.0 mpg for the 1986 model year. The auto manufacturer was given more time to achieve compliance in order to protect the jobs of GM workers. Neither Ford nor General Motors reached the 27.5 mpg fleet standard for the 1989 model year. In October 1988, the Department of Transportation adjusted the CAFE standard to 26.5 mpg in order to allow compliance by both General Motors and Ford.

The National Energy Act of 1978 did have an impact on energy consumption patterns, but it clearly did not move the nation toward the long-range goal of U.S. energy independence. The act encouraged increased efficiency and conservation, but did not contain provisions to develop major alternative energy sources. Therefore, American dependence on foreign oil supplies continued.

Decontrol and the windmill profits tax. Federal regulation of domestic oil prices began under the Nixon administration in 1971 as one mechanism to control inflation. As American consumption of oil continued to increase in the 1970s, proponents of decontrol argued that the removal of price controls would reduce oil consumption by up to 100 million barrels of oil per year, because the increased cost would reduce consumer demand. A second impact would be the stimulation of domestic production as increased profits encouraged additional exploration efforts. Critics of decontrol argued that, although consumption might decline and domestic production increase, significant social and economic problems would also emerge because the poor and elderly would face additional financial burdens during winter months and because increased energy costs would add inflationary pressure to the economy.

Under the provisions of the Energy Policy and Conservation Act of 1975, all price controls on domestic oil would be eliminated by 1981. In order to reduce the opposition to decontrol, Congress devised a "windfall profits" tax on the likely new oil company profits. The Crude Oil Windfall Profit Tax Act of 1980 stipulated that a tax rate in the 30 percent range (with a host of exemptions) would be levied until $227 billion in revenues were reached, with the tax being phased out by 1993. These revenues would go toward (among other things) helping the poor and elderly cope with energy costs.

Energy policy thus moved in two conflicting directions. Decontrol intended to provide economic incentives to spur domestic production and exploration. At the same time, taxes reduced the magnitude of the economic incentives provided by decontrol. Following decontrol there was a huge increase, followed by a decline, in the level of oil and gas exploration in the United States (see Figure 5-4). By 1998, exploration levels had dropped lower than in 1973. It was not until the election of President George W. Bush in 2000 that exploration efforts increased.

Energy Policy after 1980

The basic assumptions guiding energy policy changed dramatically following the election of President Reagan in 1980. His administration firmly rejected the concept

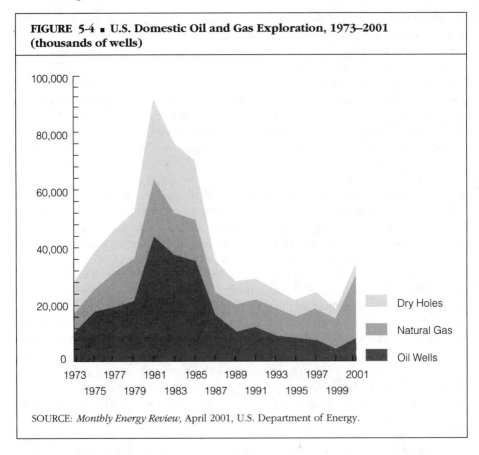

FIGURE 5-4 ▪ **U.S. Domestic Oil and Gas Exploration, 1973–2001 (thousands of wells)**

SOURCE: *Monthly Energy Review*, April 2001, U.S. Department of Energy.

of dwindling energy supplies, arguing that the United States had massive undiscovered oil and gas reserves and that energy policy of the 1970s had discouraged domestic exploration and production. Reagan's energy policy emphasized private sector responsibility and a reduced role of government. His policies emphasized the decontrol of oil, opposition to the windfall profits tax, and increased offshore exploration for oil and gas. His administration favored opening federal lands to oil and gas exploration, opposed government mandates designed to achieve a shift from oil to coal in American industry, and opposed strict environmental standards that restricted exploration activities.

Reagan-inspired policy values. The energy policy of President Reagan reflected three values. First was a belief that the United States had an abundance of energy supplies.[8] This resulted in the rejection of energy conservation and regulation strategies. Policy efforts focused on increasing production and consumption. Second, Reagan's policy rejected clean energy as a policy value. Accordingly, the environment should not take precedence over energy policy, and environmental standards for clean air and water should be relaxed. The operation of the market economy would create optimal environmental standards with a balance between energy for growth and a clean environment. Third, market operation, not government action, could best secure an abundant energy supply for the United

States. Import quotas, conservation measures, and allocation systems were inappropriate and counterproductive. The private sector could rise to the occasion and provide a secure energy supply for the future needs of the United States.

Energy policy in the 1990s. These values resulted in a significant change of direction in energy policy. Solar energy developmental support declined by 70 percent by 1982. Conservation programs were reduced on the assumption that market forces are the most appropriate means of regulating energy consumption. The one link to the past was a continued interest in nuclear energy in the form of federal research and development funding. However, federal support for research and development of synthetic fuels was curtailed in favor of private investments (which have not been forthcoming). The Energy Department assumed a reduced role in oil and gas regulation, distribution, and production.

Since 1980, energy policy has generally sought to reduce the role of government and rely on incentives to the private sector through the operation of market forces. It should be noted that the United States has never followed a program of unrestricted competition in energy policy. The federal government and the state governments imposed regulations only after industry demanded protection from unlimited competition—that is, from threats to their profits. The cries for deregulation today are motivated not only by an ideological commitment to the free-enterprise system, but also by a desire to shift the costs to consumers as a vehicle for maintaining industry profits.[9]

POLICY EVALUATION: CONTINUED FOSSIL FUEL DEPENDENCE

Energy consumption patterns have changed significantly with the decrease in oil and natural gas consumption balanced by a rise in the use of coal, nuclear, and hydroelectric power. Imposition of reduced speed limits, the automotive fuel economy standards, energy tax credits, and other programs had an impact on energy usage. Some analysts argue that changes in consumption patterns have been the result of economic conditions, not energy policy or technological changes in energy. Figures 5-5 and 5-6 indicate U.S. energy production and consumption patterns since 1973.

Alternatives to Fossil Fuels

Research and development. The energy crisis of the 1970s increased the political popularity of alternative sources of energy such as solar, wind, and geothermal power. Before the rapid rise in the cost of fossil fuels, these alternatives were too expensive to utilize as major energy sources; that fact largely explained the paucity of investment in developing the relevant technology. With the drop in the price of oil to less than $17 per barrel by 1992, the economic incentives for continued research and development of alternative energy sources were again minimal. Federal funding for energy research and development activities is no longer a national priority.

Solar energy. An element of President Carter's energy program was the proposed national goal that, by the year 2000, the United States should meet 20 percent

FIGURE 5-5 ■ U.S. Domestic Energy Production, 1973–2001 (in quadrillion BTUs)

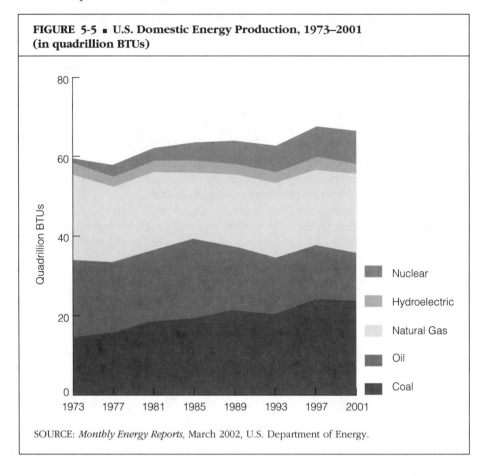

SOURCE: *Monthly Energy Reports,* March 2002, U.S. Department of Energy.

of its energy needs by solar power. Congress did not adopt this goal; solar power experienced relatively little development in the United States. The major piece of legislation so far has been the Solar Heating and Cooling Demonstration Act of 1975. This act created a limited solar demonstration program and clearinghouse. To date, the president, the Congress, and private-sector energy companies have not yet established solar power as a major source of energy for the near future.

Coal liquefaction. The liquefaction of coal into a crude-oil substitute provides the ability to convert coal into a relatively clean-burning fuel. The 1980 Energy Security Act, which created the Synthetic Fuels Corporation, provided authority for federal funding for research and development of this technology. The drop in the market price of crude oil that began in 1986, combined with an abundant global oil supply, has limited the economic viability of coal liquefaction. This energy source remains undeveloped.

Geothermal energy. Tapping the heat deep within the earth to convert water to steam for electricity generation is the goal of proponents of geothermal energy. Geothermal energy development would be most promising in scenic geologically active areas such as Yellowstone National Park and Hawaii Volcanoes National Park. Concern over potential damage to "Old Faithful" led to Congres-

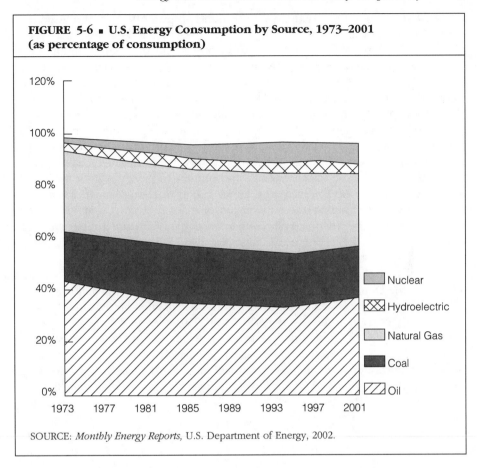

FIGURE 5-6 ■ **U.S. Energy Consumption by Source, 1973–2001 (as percentage of consumption)**

SOURCE: *Monthly Energy Reports,* U.S. Department of Energy, 2002.

sional restrictions on geothermal developments in the Yellowstone area in 1994. The Geysers, located in California, produce limited geothermal electricity. Iceland and New Zealand make significant use of geothermal energy. Expanding geothermal energy in the United States is no longer a policy priority.

Nuclear Power

Nuclear power is the only nonfossil energy source to experience significant growth and important policy development in recent decades. The growth of the nuclear energy industry and the emphasis on nuclear technology as a source of energy were products of the government's desire to use nuclear energy for peacetime purposes. There are two different nuclear processes, fission and fusion. Fission is splitting atoms; fusion produces energy by fusing atoms. To date, fusion technology is still in the early stages of development. Nuclear–fission technologies grew out of the nuclear submarine program of the U.S. Navy, in which light-water reactors (LWR) used uranium 235, a relatively scarce substance, to produce heat for steam generation of electricity. Fusion technologies use the more-abundant uranium 238, converting it into plutonium 239.

Although nuclear power plants do account for nearly 10 percent of America's energy consumption, nuclear energy remains questionable because it has yet to overcome three problems: safety, waste disposal, and decommissioning strategies.[10] Initial research indicated that nuclear safety would not be a problem. The 1975 Rasmussen Report issued by the Nuclear Regulatory Commission (NRC) concluded that nuclear accidents would probably never occur and provided a foundation for expanding nuclear power. The March 1979 accident at Three Mile Island in Pennsylvania dramatically demonstrated the inaccuracy of the Rasmussen Report. Then, in 1981, investigators discovered that the earthquake protection system at the Diablo Canyon, California, nuclear power plant was installed backwards.

Safety.   The issue of nuclear safety continues to have a significant impact on energy policy in the United States. Flaws in construction plagued the nuclear industry. Adequate training and supervision of plant personnel remains a major issue for the industry. Adequate planning in the event of a major accident has also been difficult to achieve. Nuclear plants may also be at risk from attacks by international terrorists.

The experience of the Department of Energy (DOE) with nuclear reactors utilized by the Department of Defense to produce material for the nation's atomic arsenal illustrates the potential problems with nuclear safety. Most of these facilities were constructed in the late 1940s and the 1950s; they now approach the end of their useful life. Construction standards in place at the time were less stringent than today's. In late 1988, an investigation revealed that these nuclear facilities created significant environmental contamination and had major safety defects. Inspection revealed cracks in reactor vessels, deficiencies in emergency cooling systems, defective fire-protection systems, obsolete and deteriorated equipment, and routine maintenance unperformed.

Waste.   Nuclear waste disposal has also proved to be a problem without a solution. Initially, experts assumed that spent nuclear fuel could be reprocessed into new fuel. This technology did not develop. Given the failure of the reprocessing option, the problem of long-term disposal of nuclear wastes remains unsolved. However, nuclear waste will not reach the levels projected during the 1970s. This is primarily because utility companies have not ordered any new reactors for over ten years. While the volume of waste generated has not reached projected levels, the costs associated with nuclear waste management have skyrocketed dramatically. In 1983, DOE estimates for nuclear waste management were $23 billion. By 1988, this had almost doubled to $40 billion. These costs continue to escalate given the technological difficulties of managing nuclear waste.

Another difficulty with nuclear waste management involves the identification of old, inactive sites that pose a threat to health and the environment. Authorities have identified some 1,200 inactive waste sites, and DOE officials expect to identify over 1,700 sites as the process continues. The majority of these sites do not provide adequate containment of radioactive waste, and analysts cannot estimate accurately the costs associated with providing adequate storage until thorough and systematic evaluation of each site is completed.

Nuclear plant age and decommissioning.   The nation's nuclear generating plants operate under forty-year licenses issued by the NRC. These licenses began to expire in 2000 for the oldest plants, and by 2020 the licenses of over half of the current 111 nuclear power plants will expire. The potential loss of these plants represents a serious energy problem since they generate 10 percent of the nation's electricity. One potential solution is to extend their operating license by an additional ten to twenty years.

License extensions are a source of intense controversy. Opponents argue that it is unwise to extend to fifty or sixty years the operating life of nuclear plants designed and manufactured for a forty-year life cycle. Neither the NRC nor the nuclear industry has data on the structural integrity of materials continuously exposed to radiation in a nuclear reactor. Supporters argue that proper maintenance and repairs can easily extend the life cycle. In 1992, the NRC adopted procedures for extending the license of existing nuclear power plants on a case-by-case basis. One controversial component of the policy involves the decision to use the plant's current license requirements as a basis for extension. Critics argue that the more-rigid safety standards based on today's knowledge should guide license extension, not standards in place when a plant was first licensed some twenty to thirty years ago.

Decommissioning a nuclear power plant means shutting down and deactivating the plant to the extent that the site poses no environmental threat. To date, the NRC has not specified the guidelines and standards that will apply to future decommissioning activity. There are three options: dismantlement, mothballing, and entombment. Dismantlement presents problems of storage, because the fuel rods, containment buildings, and the reactor vessel will be radioactive for several thousand years. Some estimates indicate that up to 800 tons of radioactive material will require permanent storage from each nuclear unit dismantled. Mothballing simply means locking the facility behind a security perimeter and waiting several thousand years until the radioactive material decays on its own. This approach has been entitled SAFSTOR, or safe storage, by the NRC. Entombment takes mothballing a step further by constructing a large concrete structure around the facility. Both options present problems of protecting people and the environment from dangerous material for up to 80 thousand years.

The actual costs for decommissioning a nuclear power plant are subject to debate. In 1978, the NRC estimated that costs would range between $43 million and $58 million, but the Rand Corporation published information that these costs might be in the $500 million range. The actual costs to achieve a partial decommission at Three Mile Island exceeded $1 billion. By 1987, the NRC had increased its estimates to between $100 and $135 million to decommission a 1,100-megawatt reactor. Most experts agree that the NRC estimates are excessively low. In February 1992, the NRC approved its first decommissioning of a major nuclear power plant for the Shoreham Nuclear Power Station of the Long Island Lighting Company (LILCO). The Shoreham facility is not as radioactive as other nuclear reactors since it never became fully operational due to flaws in construction and other licensing issues. LILCO is spending over $1 billion to decommission Shoreham. Consumers will probably pay the costs associated with decommissioning a nuclear power plant over an extended number of years. For example, its owners shut down the Maine Yankee nuclear facility in 1991, and customers of the utility have continued to pay for the decommissioning process through rate increases for electricity. State agencies and the Federal Energy Regulatory Commission (FERC) granted the utility rate increases to cover these costs. The costs of decommissioning a nuclear facility will fall on future customers over ten to twenty years after the plant has closed.

A national policy to apportion the costs of decommissioning a nuclear power plant has yet to be developed. Some plans call for the states to be involved and the federal government to assume all costs. The financial liability of the utility company that constructed and operated the plant has yet to be determined, and the impact on consumers served by utility companies operating nuclear power plants is unknown.

An unresolved policy issue is how to keep future generations informed (for 10 to 80 thousand years) concerning the location and lethal nature of radioactive wastes. If such a mechanism had been in place since 1940, policymakers would know the location, nature, and the threat posed by nuclear wastes to the public and the environment today. No mechanism exists either for short-term (50–100 years) or long-term (thousands of years) transmittal of knowledge. Policy adopted by the Department of Energy in 1980 states, "Although this generation bears the responsibility for protecting future societies from the waste it creates, future societies must assume the responsibility for any risks which arise from deliberate and informed acts which they choose to perform."

The future. The United States is moving away from nuclear technology as an energy option. Power plant construction has ceased, projects have been canceled, and the licensing procedure has been stiffened. Since 1978, the utility industry has placed no new orders for nuclear power plant construction. Nuclear power will not expand as a major source of energy in the near future in the United States. Plant construction was virtually complete by 1990 (see Table 5-1).

This pattern does not hold true for other nations. Currently there are 438 nuclear power plants in operation outside the United States, with more facilities under construction and still more in the planning phase. Table 5-2 depicts the status of global nuclear power plants. On a global scale, nuclear power continues to be a major source of energy. Only two European countries are reducing their dependence on nuclear power. Austria has deactivated its only nuclear power plant, and Sweden has announced plans to eliminate nuclear power plants by the year 2010.

Global emphasis on nuclear power traces to two factors. First, construction of nuclear power plants represents an investment of billions of dollars. The size of this investment exerts economic pressure to maintain the nuclear power plants in order to obtain a return on the massive construction expenditures. Second, many countries simply have no other currently available viable source of electricity. As of 1988, approximately 15 percent of global electricity was the product of nuclear power. By 1990, this figure had increased to over 20 percent. Even a major nuclear accident such as that at Cher-

---

TABLE 5-1 ■ Operating Nuclear Power Plants in the United States 1975–2002

Year	Number of Operating Plants
1975	54
1978	70
1987	95
1997	110
2002	104

SOURCE: U.S. Department of Energy.

TABLE 5-2 ▪ Operating Nuclear Power Plants, by Country, 2002

Country	Reactors	Country	Reactors
Argentina	2	Mexico	2
Belgium	7	Netherlands	2
Brazil	2	Pakistan	2
Bulgaria	6	Russia	29
Canada	14	Slovak Rep	6
China	3	Romania	1
Czech Republic	5	South Africa	2
Finland	4	South Korea	16
France	59	Spain	9
Germany	19	Sweden	11
Hungary	4	Switzerland	5
India	14	Taiwan	6
Italy	3	Ukraine	13
Japan	53	United Kingdom	35
Lithuania	2	United States	104
		Yugoslavia (former)	1

SOURCE: U.S. Department of Energy.

nobyl in the former Soviet Union has not deterred emphasis on nuclear power plants on the international scene.

Political Impact of Continued Oil Dependence

There are two central political consequences of the free world's dependence on oil imports. The first is the uncertainty of supply. Interruptions or threats to the supply of oil can severely weaken the West's economic, political, and military power. Truly, the West's Achilles' heel is its dependence on imported oil. Interrupt the oil flow, and the West faces economic collapse. Yet, the oil reserves the West must have to survive are mainly in the highly volatile Middle East. Consequently, the Western world has been drawn into increased military and political involvement in the Persian Gulf region, with a primary goal of promoting internal stability in order to maintain an adequate oil supply.[11] Western involvement ranges from military sales and assistance to air and naval bases in the Middle East. Currently, the United States has either an established presence or arrangements for military bases in Oman, Egypt, and Saudi Arabia. In response to the war between Iran and Iraq, Western navies assigned warships to patrol the Persian Gulf. The United States military presence expanded dramatically in 1990–1991 with Operation Desert Storm in response to the Iraqi invasion of Kuwait.

The dissolution of the Soviet Union is a source of concern for stability in the Middle East. Some of the newly independent republics have a predominantly Islamic population, and the known oil reserves in what was the Soviet Union are unevenly distributed among the new republics. The foreign policy values and orientations of these new nations are not at this point clear, and the political, military, and economic consequences for stability in the Middle East and Central Asia remain uncertain.

Hidden costs. A consequence of dependence on imported oil is the impact on military and defense spending. In order to maintain economic stability within the United States it is necessary to protect America's sources of oil from disruption. This involves a significant military commitment in the Persian Gulf region. The cost of this military presence is not included in the price of imported oil. One mechanism to include this cost would involve implementation of a surcharge or tax on imported oil as a mechanism to pay for the military activities necessary to protect the industry and maintain an uninterrupted flow of oil. Imported oil adds significantly to military spending of the United States.

American reliance on imported oil has the potential to contribute a structural element to the trade deficit. As oil imports rise, the trade deficit of the United States increases. Oil imports account for approximately 50 percent of the U.S. trade deficit. This means that the United States must achieve ever-higher trade surpluses with trading partners who do not export oil to offset a continuing energy trade deficit. The cost of imported oil saddles the American economy with an additional international trade burden.

Organization of Petroleum Exporting Countries (OPEC). An additional consequence of Western dependence on imported oil has been an inability to control the price of oil. When OPEC acted from a position of strength, the oil-consuming West demonstrated a marked inability to limit price increases. This was a major problem in the late 1970s, when an upward spiral in oil prices placed increased inflationary pressure on Western economies. Erosion of OPEC unity was a major factor in the dramatic drop in global oil prices. OPEC disunity is a function of disagreement over oil prices, production levels, and political conflicts. In 1981, Western oil consumption was still high, and OPEC oil was selling for $32 per barrel. Some members called for a price increase to $41 per barrel. However, Saudi Arabia, the largest oil exporter, opposed the increase and refused to raise the price of its oil, effectively thwarting the proposed price increase.

Disagreement over production levels also reduced OPEC unity. As the West began to become more energy efficient, demand for oil also began to decrease slightly. The most appropriate strategy to maintain price when demand drops is to reduce supply. OPEC has not been able to establish an allocation formula for reducing production levels. Member states, in need of revenues, have continued to produce at levels higher than global demand, which has acted to keep oil prices under control.

Political disunity also is a factor. The prolonged war between Iraq and Iran during the 1980s contributed to higher production levels as each nation sought revenues to fund the war effort. In the aftermath of the Persian Gulf War of 1991, Iraqi production was at minimal levels and the oil fields in Kuwait were inoperable until the fires were extinguished in late 1991. By 1993, production from the Kuwaiti fields was restored. The potential for military and political conflict in the Persian Gulf contributes to the uncertainty over oil production levels.

Conflict between Israel and the Arab nations has the potential to strengthen unity with OPEC. In 1973, the Arab members of OPEC found that oil was a common weapon to weaken support for Israel around the world. The possibility of an Arab-Israeli conflict may provide a force for OPEC unity again in the future.

OPEC was unsuccessful in its attempt to establish and apportion production quotas among member countries, and oil prices continue at about $19 per barrel.

Although OPEC is in disarray, it would be a mistake to assume that the organization will have little impact in the future. Internal events in the member nations can disrupt production, and external events can provide OPEC unity, as demonstrated during the mid- to late 1970s.

FUTURE ALTERNATIVES: ENERGY POLICY COMPLACENCY

The "energy crisis" of the early 1970s evaporated, and the public concern that stimulated energy policy activity diminished. Lower energy prices and an adequate supply of oil mark the most recent period. These factors contribute to an attitude of complacency toward energy policy. Is the current attitude of complacency justified? Was the extent of the energy crisis overestimated, or did energy policy responses act to solve the problem of energy scarcity?

One factor that contributed to the energy shortfall of the early 1970s was a product of faulty demand projections by the energy companies and governments. During the 1950s and 1960s, experts always underestimated the demand for oil. Ten-year projections were off by as much as 25 or 30 percent.[12] A gap of five to ten years exists between the decision to seek additional oil and gas reserves and actual production from those new sources. Before the 1970s, the routine underestimation of demand failed to stimulate sufficient exploratory efforts to maintain a balance between supply and demand. By the early 1970s, energy consumption patterns, which were the cornerstone of forecasting, produced projections of dramatic increases in energy demand for the decade of the 1980s and beyond. The OPEC unity achieved in 1973, which provided a framework for price increases and limited production quotas, added credibility to the projections of a continuing future gap between supply and demand. Between 1973 and 1978, the growth in the demand for oil did exceed the growth in the oil supply, with several consequences. First, decisions were made to increase the oil supply by exploring the North Slope in Alaska, to increase exploration in the North Sea, and to intensify exploration efforts in other regions of the world as well as across the United States.

Second, the increase in the cost of energy produced slow but continuous changes in consumption patterns. Homeowners now insulated their homes better. The efficiency of residential and commercial heating units increased. Fuel efficiency became an important value in the transportation industry as new trucks and aircraft were designed and manufactured. Changes in manufacturing techniques also provided increased energy efficiency. These changes acted to decrease the rate at which energy demand grew. A gradual change to more energy-efficient automobiles took place. However, during the late 1990s consumer preference for less fuel-efficient vehicles began to increase with the popularity of trucks and sport utility vehicles. This shift in consumer purchasing preferences is another indication of complacency toward energy supply.

Third, OPEC economies were becoming increasingly dependent on the oil consumption patterns of the West. Modernization and development programs created an ever-increasing demand for oil revenues within OPEC nations. The need to market oil and maintain production became a driving force within OPEC nations.

Gradually, demand fell to levels lower than global supply. Between 1974 and 1988, non-OPEC oil production increased by over 80 percent, from 17 million to over 31 million barrels per day. This increase in production, combined with the improvement in energy efficiency and other conservation measures, acted to create an imbalance in which supply exceeded demand by 1988.

The condition of adequate energy supply and lowered prices has had a major impact on the United States. Complacency replaced public concern, as oil remained a primary energy source. This complacency may not be justified. Contrary to public perceptions, the energy system is considerably more volatile and dynamic now than in the past. Before 1973, the actions of the international oil companies largely controlled the supply and price of energy. During the 1970s, the OPEC oil cartel acted to control oil supply and prices. The power of these two systems of control has evaporated as oil supply, production, and cost respond to international market forces and competing international interests.

This has at least two policy implications for the United States. First, continued dependence ties American economic strength to access to foreign energy sources. Any disruption in oil supply will have potentially profound economic consequences. Second, low international prices act to reduce domestic oil production in the United States. Forecasts indicate that the cost of oil will not increase dramatically and that global supply will continue to exceed demand. In order for OPEC to eventually achieve higher prices for its oil it must (1) maintain high production and low prices to discourage the development of alternative energy sources, (2) minimize expansion of non-OPEC oil sources, and (3) increase dependence on OPEC as a primary source of energy. Thus, complacency may create a future in which the United States will find itself vulnerable to a situation similar to what it experienced in 1973.

Moreover, the insatiable American appetite for energy places energy companies in strong political positions, as the early years of the George W. Bush presidency demonstrate. Worry about foreign imports and about sufficiency of energy supply impact the environment. In 2002, the Bush administration pushed hard for opening the Arctic National Wildlife Refuge to oil drilling. The energy crisis in California in 2000 and the collapse of energy giant Enron in 2001 signalled instability and uncertainty in energy markets to which government must respond.

ENVIRONMENTAL POLICY

Public concern over environmental policy was minimal until the end of the nineteenth century. As the United States expanded westward, the horizon seemed to present an unlimited supply of land, water, mineral deposits, and timber. Farming techniques reflected little concern for soil depletion. Settlers and loggers cleared forests without concern for reforestation or the devastation of soil erosion. Minerals were mined and metals smelted without concern for their effects on freshwater supplies; when contamination did result, it seemed a minor problem, because alternative sources of water seemed endless.

Once the nation began to reach the limit of its geographic expansion, to industrialize, and to experience rapid population growth, the problem of environmental preservation and protection could no longer be easily avoided. From the 1870s through the 1930s, conservation was the dominant theme of environmental policy. Examples include the establishment of Yellowstone Park as the first national park in 1872 and the 1897 legislation that created an extensive national forest system. Although the conservation standard provided a general policy focus, there was significant disagreement over specific strategies. To some, conservation meant resource management for effective utilization, such as scientific forestry; others viewed conservation primarily as wilderness preservation. This conflict over strategy remains present today as a major policy issue.

Despite a history of conservation policies, fundamental concerns with environmental protection were still absent from the policy agenda as late as the 1950s. The publication of *Silent Spring* in 1962 drew attention to the dangers of pesticides, such as DDT, in the food chain.[13] This book acted as a catalyst to mobilize a heightened environmental consciousness. The sense of social responsibility that emerged in the 1960s also moved environmental policy from the background to the forefront of the policy agenda.

ISSUE BACKGROUND: A LEGACY OF ENVIRONMENTAL ABUSE

Indifference and neglect have left their mark on the physical environment of the United States. The environmental problems the nation now faces are the product of the historic lack of public concern with the unintended but harmful consequences of the economic growth and development of an industrialized society. Air pollution, water pollution, solid-waste pollution, toxic- and hazardous-waste pollution, acid rain, and changing land-use patterns all pose important problems.

Air Pollution

Air pollutants can be categorized in two groups: particles and gases. Particulate matter includes such material as ashes, soot, and lead (a noncombustible gasoline additive). Though particulate pollution is a problem, the dangers presented by the release of gases into the air are just as real but probably less well understood by the public. The major air pollutants sort into the following five categories:

Carbon monoxide (CO). Carbon monoxide is a colorless by-product of the incomplete combustion of carbon fuels. Gasoline engines are its primary source.

Sulfur dioxide (SO_2). The combustion of fuels containing sulfur produces sulfur dioxide. When combined with water vapor, it can form sulfuric acid and fall as "acid rain."

Hydrocarbons (HC). Hydrocarbons, consisting of various combinations of hydrogen and carbon, are the unburned fuel resulting from incomplete combustion. The compounds have a major impact in the production of photochemical smog in urban areas.

Nitrogen oxide (NO). Nitrogen oxide is a by-product of fossil fuel combustion at high temperature levels. It combines with hydrocarbons to produce smog.

Particulate matter. Particulates include liquids or solids released into the atmosphere.

In 1980, the EPA estimated substantial increases in air pollution by the year 2000, with total emissions of particulate matter projected to double by that year.[14] The agency projected generation of sulfur dioxide to increase at a rate of 4 to 6 percent annually. Emissions of nitrogen oxides would grow dramatically as coal continued to be an important fuel source. By the year 2000, nitrogen oxide emissions

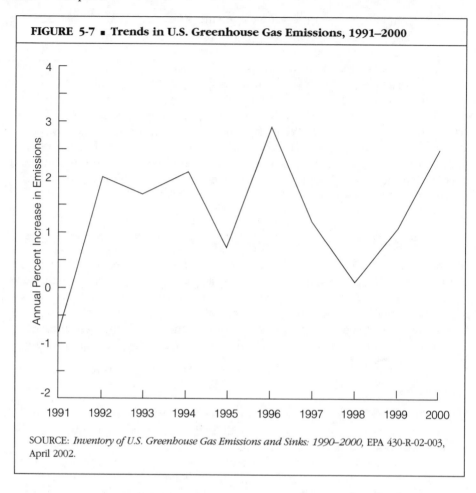

FIGURE 5-7 ▪ Trends in U.S. Greenhouse Gas Emissions, 1991–2000

SOURCE: *Inventory of U.S. Greenhouse Gas Emissions and Sinks: 1990–2000*, EPA 430-R-02-003, April 2002.

could be 90 percent higher than in the late 1970s. Hydrocarbon emissions were estimated to remain at a constant level or to increase slightly by the year 2000. Emissions of carbon monoxide also were expected to rise.

As indicated in Figure 5-7, the emission of greenhouse gases has increased but at a lower rate than projected by the EPA, even though an upward trend in emissions exists and there is no indication that a reduction in emission levels is probable. Total greenhouse gas emissions over the last decade increased by almost 14 percent.

The focus on measuring the raw amount of individual pollutants produced can be a deceptive approach to the problem, because serious health problems can result from either short-term exposure to high levels of these compounds or long-term exposure to relatively low levels. There is also evidence that these pollutants act synergistically on animal and plant life. This means that exposure to the compounds together produces more harmful impacts than would result from exposure to them separately.

Not all emissions are easily categorized as either harmless or polluting. Such is the case with carbon dioxide (CO_2) (see Figure 5-8). So far, policy has not

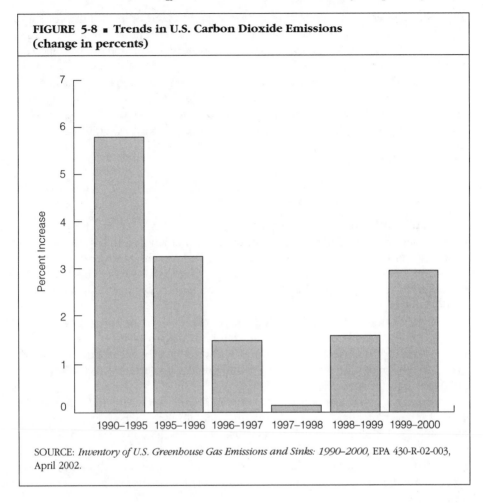

FIGURE 5-8 ▪ **Trends in U.S. Carbon Dioxide Emissions (change in percents)**

SOURCE: *Inventory of U.S. Greenhouse Gas Emissions and Sinks: 1990–2000,* EPA 430-R-02-003, April 2002.

clearly identified CO_2 as a major pollutant, and there are no regulations governing its emission in the United States. However, scientists are increasingly concerned that high levels of CO_2 in the atmosphere may warm the earth and result in major climatic changes, the "greenhouse effect." Increased atmospheric levels of CO_2 trap the earth's heat by reducing the escape of infrared radiation from the surface into space. There is debate within the scientific community over the seriousness of the greenhouse effect. Debate also focuses on the origins of the rising levels of atmospheric CO_2. Some experts attribute high CO_2 levels to the use of fossil fuels; others believe that the rapid deforestation in Africa, South America, and Asia is the primary cause.[15]

Ozone layer. A thin layer of ozone some thirty miles above the surface protects the earth from excessive ultraviolet rays. The production and continued use of chlorofluorocarbons (CFCs) now threaten the integrity of that protective layer. Scientists have discovered a hole in the ozone layer over Antarctica roughly the size of the United States. Scientists also have documented a thinning of the ozone layer above North America and Europe. Depletion of the protective ozone layer would result in a higher incidence of skin cancer, cataracts, and other health problems. This is primarily due to the harmful nature of ultraviolet-B radiation from the sun.

Chlorofluorocarbons are the primary cause of ozone depletion. Air-conditioning and refrigeration units employed CFCs extensively. In 1987 the European Economic Community (EEC), the United States, and twenty-nine other nations initially approved the Montreal Protocol on Substances that Deplete the Ozone Layer, a group that represented 82 percent of the world's consumption of CFCs. A number of other nations have since signed the protocol, with the result that CFC emissions significantly declined during the 1990s.

Water and Solid-Waste Pollution

Water pollution. Neglect of the nation's waterways has been a major environmental problem. Perhaps the most dramatic incident illustrating the seriousness of water pollution occurred in the 1960s: The Cuyahoga River in Cleveland caught fire because of the extensive discharge of flammable wastes into the river. Although this is not a typical event, virtually all surface waterways have experienced some type of pollution.

Even though water pollution is a well-documented nationwide problem, its severity varies considerably among the different regions of the country. Waterways of the industrialized Northeast and Midwest have been especially abused. Even though sources of water pollution vary greatly, it is possible to classify most pollutants into four categories.[16]

Industrial wastes contain a wide range of organic and inorganic compounds, including heavy metals such as mercury and zinc. A relatively new water-pollution phenomenon is thermal pollution; the cause is the discharge of heated water into rivers and lakes after cooling certain equipment used primarily in electric power plants. Thermal pollution heightens the toxicity of some other pollutants and, by accelerating the decomposition of organic matter, lowers the oxygen level in surface waters.

Domestic and municipal wastes include human wastes and other compounds disposed of by people in their day-to-day lives.

Agricultural wastes include animal waste and other compounds that may pose health risks, such as fertilizers and pesticides that run off into waterways and enter the food chain. One of the greatest threats posed by agricultural wastes is the excess nutrients that enter lakes, rivers, and streams. These nutrients foster rapid growth of algae and other microorganisms that deplete the oxygen supply for fish and other organisms. One such organism, *pfiesteria piscicida,* killed millions of fish in the late 1990s in the mid-Atlantic states of Maryland, Virginia, and North Carolina. It may pose a threat to human health as well. The Centers for Disease Control (CDC) notes that *pfiesteria* outbreaks occur in watersheds that drain large concentrations of chicken, hog, and other livestock operations.

Miscellaneous pollutants may be "natural" and include silt and sedimentation entering surface waters following rains. Also included are more serious pollutants, such as those from accidental oil spills. While offshore oil spills from supertankers and drilling accidents receive publicity due to their magnitude, the hundreds of other smaller spills that occur each year receive relatively little attention. Mining activity also adds to water pollution. Strip mining exposes sulfur compounds in the soil, which react with rain to form sulfuric acid, which then runs off into surface waters. Already a major pollutant in Appalachian mining regions, it is now also a problem in Western states where coal mining has been on the increase.

One approach to reducing water pollution involves aggressive wastewater treatment by cities and industry to eliminate most of the contaminants before they enter surface waters. There are three levels of waste treatment. Primary treatment uses settling chambers to remove solid contaminants before the water returns to streams and rivers. Secondary treatment filters the remaining wastes through beds of rock and sand to remove organic contaminants, with the addition of chlorinates to kill bacteria. Tertiary systems use additional filtration (such as activated charcoal) to remove inorganic compounds and heavy metals.

There is no lack of waste-treatment technologies available to municipalities and industry to minimize the discharge of contaminants. The major obstacle has been cost. Construction and operation of a tri-level treatment system is beyond the financial means of many cities and industries. Such a system can cost three to four times as much as a bi-level treatment system. The reality of immediate economic costs has historically acted to shift policy options away from a completely aggressive waste-treatment strategy.

Solid-waste pollution. Solid-waste pollution correlates directly to the level of economic activity. The United States produces over 6 billion tons of solid wastes each year. This includes agricultural solid wastes (2.5 billion tons annually), residential and commercial solid wastes (220 million tons), industrial solid wastes (1.5 billion tons), and mineral solid wastes (1.8 billion tons of slag and mill tailings).

The traditional approach has been simply to bury the waste in landfills, an option that is less than satisfactory given the projections of rapid growth in annual solid-waste production. Despite this veritable landslide of solid waste, recycling is not a major priority in the United States.

As indicated in Figure 5-9, solid waste from municipal areas has more than doubled since 1960. Recycling is now at approximately 30 percent of municipal waste generated. The slow growth in recycling owes to the fact that it is economically expedient, in the short run, to discard processed materials and utilize new raw materials in the production process. For example, it is cheaper to use pulp timber than to recycle paper. Government action, which would itself be costly, could institute mandatory recycling, as is already done in some localities, but that does not seem likely at the national level within the next decade. Perhaps only when society depletes the supply of raw materials will the economic basis of the "throwaway" society change.

Toxic and Hazardous Waste

Hazardous wastes are those wastes that pose a significant threat to either health or the environment due to their "quantity, concentration, physical, chemical, or infectious characteristics."[17] The EPA estimates that the United States produces between 38 million and 60 million tons of hazardous wastes each year. Seldom are hazardous wastes disposed of in a completely safe manner. In fact, some estimates indicate that less than 10 percent of toxic wastes are disposed of safely.

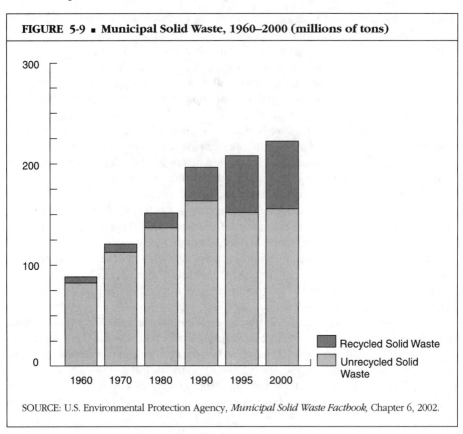

FIGURE 5-9 ▪ Municipal Solid Waste, 1960–2000 (millions of tons)

SOURCE: U.S. Environmental Protection Agency, *Municipal Solid Waste Factbook,* Chapter 6, 2002.

The impact of improper toxic-waste disposal may emerge only decades later, as illustrated by the events at Love Canal in Niagara Falls, New York. The Hooker Chemical Company buried more than 20 thousand tons of chemical wastes containing over 300 different chemicals at Love Canal in the 1950s. Two decades later, in the 1970s, residents in the Love Canal area were experiencing mounting incidences of health problems directly attributed to the buried toxic wastes. It took over $30 million to clean up the site and relocate residents.

Toxic wastes can threaten communities far removed from toxic-waste sites and the chemical industry. The case of Times Beach, Missouri, illustrates this point. Times Beach was located on Interstate 44, about twenty-five miles southwest of St. Louis. This small rural community appeared safe from the threat of toxic wastes; yet, events were to prove otherwise. Road crews spread oil contaminated with dioxin over the asphalt streets of the town at levels high enough to make the whole city a health risk. Eventually, the entire city was purchased by the federal government, all homes and businesses were demolished, the contaminated waste was burned in an incinerator, and residents were relocated to surrounding communities. Times Beach no longer exists.

One type of increasingly important—and controversial—hazardous waste is radioactive waste. The two main sources of radioactive waste are the nuclear weapons program and nuclear power plants used to generate electricity. Some of these high-level wastes are so toxic that they must be stored for 500,000 years. Low-level wastes also pose a major problem. The United States produces over 3 million cubic feet of this waste, which requires safe storage for hundreds of years. Nuclear waste-management policy is an area marked by controversy and uncertainty.

Safe disposal of radioactive wastes has proved to be an elusive goal. As the United States began to develop nuclear technology during World War II, there was minimal concern for finding safe disposal techniques. Radioactive wastes were typically burned, buried in shallow pits, or simply dumped into the existing sewage system. The governing philosophy was that safe disposal involved simply the dilution of radioactive wastes, which facilitated dispersal of the wastes in the environment. During the late 1940s and the 1950s, government and industry produced ever-higher quantities of radioactive wastes. The high volume of waste required developing a new disposal system: ocean dumping. This technology involved using containers (primarily 55–gallon drums) to hold radioactive wastes. These containers were then filled with concrete and dumped off the coast of the United States.

Between 1945 and 1967, the United States dumped almost one hundred thousand of these containers into the waters off the Atlantic and Pacific coasts. This practice was terminated by 1970 because of the long-term threats posed to the environment. Gradually, the containers corrode and the wastes become exposed to ocean currents and enter the food chain. Currently, ocean dumping of radioactive waste is not a formal policy of any nation.

With the elimination of ocean dumping, land disposal is now the method of choice. The only problem is that a viable technology for long-term disposal does not yet exist. Current surface facilities are rapidly reaching or exceeding capacity. A safe, technologically feasible storage system is not in existence, and the level of radioactive waste continues to accumulate.

One policy obstacle to solving the problem of toxic-waste dumps, nuclear and otherwise, is that many sites are not yet identified. The EPA has located over 17 thousand potentially dangerous sites, but possibly thousands more still await discovery. Virtually every state in the union contains at least one hazardous toxic dump. Congress has not provided the EPA with the budget and the personnel to complete this critical first step.

Acid Rain

An environmental problem of growing concern is the phenomenon of acid rain. This is produced when sunlight chemically converts air pollutants, primarily sulfur dioxide, nitrogen oxides, and hydrocarbons, into sulfates, nitrates, and other acidic compounds, which are returned to earth by rain and snow and gradually change the acidic balance in both water and soil.

Acidity is measured in pH units on a scale ranging from 0 to 14, with the pH value of 7 representing neutrality. Values greater than 7 represent alkalinity, and values less than 7 represent acidity. The logarithmic nature of the scale means that a pH level of 5 is ten times more acidic than pH 6 and that pH 4 is one hundred times more acidic than pH 6. For example, a lake that increases in acidity from Ph 4.5 to Ph 4.2 has doubled its level of acidity. A lack of understanding of Ph levels has minimized public concern with the potential threat posed by acid rain.

When acidity in a body of water exceeds the level of Ph 5, the water loses the ability to support fish and plant life. Given that over 20 million tons of sulfur dioxides and 20 million tons of nitrogen oxides enter the atmosphere each year, the United States faces a potential problem of enormous magnitude. Data from the EPA indicate that the acidic level for rain and snow is below the level of Ph 5 for the entire eastern half of the nation. This means that increased levels of acidity threaten virtually all rivers and lakes in the affected region. There are geologic differences, however, that can reduce the impact on bodies of water in this region. For example, the limestone floors of some lakes in New England neutralize some of the acidity. The problem is that often more acidity enters a lake or stream than it can neutralize naturally.

Acid rain also harms agriculture and forestry. The U.S. Office of Technology Assessment (OTA) has estimated that acid rain reduced agricultural production in the United States by 6 to 7 percent and that up to 20 percent of the land in the eastern United States is seriously threatened.[18]

The Environmental Legacy

The absence of an aggressive environmental-protection strategy has produced potentially severe air, water, and toxic-waste problems. Other environmental issues also pose problems for the nation. Both conventional and strip-mining activities continue to have significant impacts. Without extensive reclamation efforts after strip mining, the land is permanently unusable for productive or recreational purposes. The tailings from conventional mining activity also present problems as wind and rain transport contaminants into the ecosystem. This is a significant problem for uranium mining, because it leaves radioactive debris in the open in mammoth sand piles. Land-use patterns are also an issue of concern. Topsoil erosion, the loss of wetlands, and forestry practices remain areas of policy conflict. An area of increasing concern is indoor air pollution. The traditional view presumed that pollution was only an "outdoor" problem: People could escape the problem by remaining inside. However, such is not the case; studies have documented serious indoor health hazards such as formaldehyde foam (used in building insulation), asbestos, and other toxic substances.

As with energy, the environmental policy legacy has been one of historical neglect of environmental protection, which allowed environmental abuse to develop into a significant public policy problem.

CONTEMPORARY ENVIRONMENTAL POLICY

Although there are unquestionably severe environmental problems facing the United States, government has undertaken efforts to address them. This section will look at these major policy responses, including the historical background of some environmental legislation, and will outline the most important features and goals of the evolving public policies.

Water-Pollution Policy

The federal government gradually and partially assumed leadership in this policy area. The origins of the federal role go back to the Refuse Act of 1899, which sought to limit the blockage of navigable rivers by municipal and industrial debris. Although largely ignored, the act did indicate the necessity for action by the federal government to respond to a problem that extends beyond state borders.

Congress gradually expanded this federal role. The Water Pollution Act of 1948 provided federal funds for sewage-plant construction, leaving standards and enforcement largely to the states. In 1956, Congress amended the act to authorize federal funds to sponsor conferences on water pollution and to assign the Public Health Service (PHS) a permanent role in monitoring water quality standards in municipalities across the nation. The 1961 Water Pollution Control Act and the 1965 Water Quality Act continued to provide federal funds for sewage-plant construction and to assign primary responsibility for water standards and enforcement to the states.

The underlying assumption of the emphasis on state responsibility held that states would be vigilant in protecting their own water resources, but this was not typically the case. State governments proved unwilling to enact strict standards for fear of driving industry into other states with less-stringent standards. The result? Most adopted very weak water-quality standards.

The Clean Waters Restoration Act of 1966 signaled the beginning of the transfer of water-quality enforcement responsibility from the states to the federal government as it assumed the power to initiate court action to force municipal and industrial compliance with water-quality standards. The Water Pollution Control Act Amendments of 1972 continued this trend of increased federal responsibility. The unrealized goal of this act was to end the discharge of pollutants into waterways by 1985 by mandating that industry and municipalities adopt the "best available" sewage-treatment technology. The 1974 Safe Drinking Water Act continued the emphasis on federal action by assigning the EPA responsibility for establishing minimum standards for drinking water.

Air-Pollution Policy

Attempts to control and improve air quality in the United States followed a similar pattern of gradually expanding the federal role. The first action taken by Congress, the Air Pollution Control Act of 1955, did little more than fund research on air quality. The federal role was gradually increased as the Clean Air Act of 1963 provided funds for state air-quality programs, and the Motor Vehicle Air Pollution Control Act of 1965 empowered the former Department of Health, Education and Welfare (HEW) to set automobile-emission standards. This was the first federal program to regulate emissions directly. The National Emissions Standards Act of 1967 expanded the program.

The 1970 Clean Air Act Amendments signaled a major change in air pollution policy in the United States. These amendments sought to reduce, by 1975, all air pollutants that constituted a health threat. Congress delegated primary responsibility for establishing and enforcing standards to the EPA. Initially, these standards reflected a primary emphasis on the protection of public health and welfare, with a secondary emphasis on economic issues. The 1977 Clean Air Act Amendments, in which the federal government responded to the energy crisis and to protests from industry, relaxed the high standards. Emission standards were also relaxed, and lax compliance deadlines were established.

Congress enacted another series of amendments to the Clean Air Act in November 1990. These amendments aimed to move air quality toward the standards originally targeted for 1975. One specific provision includes reducing SO_2 emissions in order to reduce the threat of acid rain. The amendments also allow tailoring some air-quality standards to the degree of pollution in individual communities, as opposed to setting uniform nationwide standards for all emissions. Critics of these amendments argue that they do not contain sufficiently stringent nationwide air-quality standards. Supporters hold that these amendments do embody a move in the direction of the standards in the original Clean Air Act.

The National Environmental Policy Act (NEPA)

The National Environmental Policy Act, signed into law on January 1, 1970, reflected a major change in environmental policy by the federal government.[19] The act placed greater emphasis on federal leadership in formulating national environmental policy through the creation of the Council on Environmental Quality (CEQ), within the Executive Office of the President, to provide advice on environmental policy issues. Although the CEQ was largely an advisory body with no direct power to stop pollution violations, its existence within the Executive Office provided the framework for a strengthened federal role under the leadership of the president. The legislation also mandated that the president submit an annual "environmental quality report" to Congress and that federal agencies submit "environmental impact statements" on any action that would affect the environment.

The impact statements are filed with the CEQ and are open for public inspection. The act sought to force public agencies to undertake a deliberate and thorough analysis of the potential environmental consequences of any projects under their control, and to investigate the feasibility of using alternatives to achieve the same goals if the proposed activity would have a significantly adverse effect on the environment.

The *Environmental Protection Agency (EPA)* was part of a reorganization of the federal bureaucracy. The EPA combined some fifteen offices and agencies into a single agency assigned responsibility for (1) water pollution, (2) air pollution, (3) solid-waste management, (4) radiation control, and (5) pesticide and toxic-substance control. The legislation intended that the new agency centralize federal power in environmental policy by eliminating the previous pattern of fragmentation and decentralization.

Unlike the advisory Council on Environmental Quality, the EPA is a regulatory agency with power to establish and enforce policy. The actual impact of the EPA on environmental issues is a function of the values and assumptions of the president and of the administrator that he selects to guide the agency in interpreting and enforcing environmental rules and statutes. Political values and arrangements influence the agency. Critics periodically charge the EPA with making "sweetheart deals" with major industrial polluters and with scheduling EPA cleanup projects based on political considerations instead of environmental concerns.

The hazardous waste Superfund. One program that continues to be long on controversy and short on actual delivery is the Superfund, created during the Carter administration by the 1980 Comprehensive Environmental Response Act. The Superfund provided the EPA with the authority and the funds to assist in cleanup operations at toxic- and hazardous-waste sites across the country. The creation of the fund intended to allow an active role for the EPA in dealing with emergencies and with abandoned toxic-waste sites. By 1984, the EPA had identified over 17 thousand disposal sites, with estimates that an additional 5 thousand sites exist. EPA estimates indicated in 1984 that the cleanup operations at the 2 thousand most dangerous sites would cost between $8 billion and $16 billion, roughly five to ten times the size of the original level of the Superfund.

The provisions of the Superfund act have generated relatively few site cleanups. In fact, a number of the sites have been cleaned, not by disposal, but by simply transferring the wastes to another toxic-waste site. This transfer of wastes from one location to another does not indicate progress in a cleanup program. The program failed to have a significant impact due to the lack of financial support as well as problems with administration of the program.

POLICY EVALUATION: SEARCHING FOR DIRECTION

Current Policy Direction and Values

The 1960s and 1970s were decades in which extensive environmental legislation was enacted and regulatory policies and agencies were created. The trend toward increased regulation and federal leadership changed, as new values became the source of environmental policy during the 1980s. The favored policy position during this period was to relax standards and to reduce federal regulatory activity.[20]

In addition, the "bubble concept" was developed. It applied clean-air standards to a plant as a whole, rather than to the specific parts of the plant causing emissions. This meant that increased levels of pollution at one source within a plant were acceptable if the overall levels of contaminants for the particular plant remained within EPA guidelines. Although this concept makes emissions enforcement easier, it reduces pollution less rapidly than shutting down specific pollution points. Proponents advocated cost-benefit analysis and market forces as the most appropriate mechanisms for guiding environmental policy. They valued environmental protection less than economic growth. Advocates saw market values as an appropriate mechanism for determining environmental policy. Environmental protection policies were to be avoided if the associated costs to society were higher than the monetary benefits. Finally, this approach gave a stronger role to state governments, as opposed to federal government regulation, in environmental legislation.

Environmental activists greeted the election of Bill Clinton and Al Gore with enthusiasm in 1992. Al Gore's book *Earth in the Balance*[21] reflected a major concern with environmental problems and with the need for governmental action to remedy those problems. Clinton and Gore seemed to represent the opportunity for a more active and aggressive federal role in environmental protection. The new administration disappointed these expectations. Immediately after the election, President Clinton called for "peaceful coexistence" between environmentalists and the business community. His policy actions indicated an environmental policy that varied in style but not substance from those of his predecessors. In 1995, he signed a logging exemption bill that expanded timber industry access to national forests. When signing the legislation President Clinton stated, "I've done more for logging than anyone else in the country."[22]

A significant shift in the federal role did not occur for two reasons. First, there was a growing concern that environmental policy had been based on popular opinion, instead of on scientific evidence. According to former EPA Administrator Walter Reilly, environmental policies have been "based on responding to the nightly news. What we have had in the United States is environmental agenda-setting by episodic panic."[23] Second, concern for reducing the federal deficit and achieving a balanced budget provided a basis for questioning the validity of environmental spending programs. Given the competition for increasingly scarce federal monies and strong reaction to "unfunded mandates" imposed by the federal government on state and local governments (see Chapter 2), environmental spending programs must increasingly provide more benefits than they cost.

The current Bush administration clearly has pursued this course. He is far less likely than President Clinton to use Executive Orders to set aside wilderness areas to protect them from economic activity. He has reduced a number of environmental standards, and his administration strongly favors energy exploration, even in environmentally sensitive areas such as the Arctic National Wildlife Refuge. Finally, he has moved toward selecting Yucca Mountain, Nevada, as the final repository for nuclear wastes.

Reduced Public Concern

The beginning of the twenty-first century witnessed a marked reduction in the intensity of public opinion supporting aggressive environmental policies. Conflicting scientific reports concerning causal relationships in environmental policy weakened public confidence in environmental research findings. Costs associated with environmental protection efforts have escalated, dampening public enthusiasm. Lifestyle values are in conflict with pro-environmental policies. The popularity of large, gas-guzzling sport utility vehicles (SUVs) in urban areas is one indication of a willingness to sacrifice environmental concerns with energy conservation and emissions reductions for personal lifestyle preferences. The public verbalizes a concern for the environment, but since the 1980s has shifted away from supporting comprehensive environmental policies and programs. Some analysts would observe that public support for environmental protections may be compared to early descriptions of the Platt River in the Westward expansion, "a mile wide, but an inch deep."

The Politics of Regulation

The regulatory process itself is subject to political pressures from competing interests, which can influence the formulation of an effective environmental policy.

One political factor that affects regulation is the pressure on administrators and elected officials to emphasize short-term economic benefits as opposed to long-term consequences of environmental damage. A second factor involves emphasis on the primacy of economic growth as a basic value in the political system. Economic growth carries an almost universal environmental cost, and the American system has historically concentrated on the desirability of growth. A third factor that directly affects the regulatory process is the value placed on compromise in our political system. The Constitution itself is a product of compromise, and the American system places a great deal of importance on seeking the middle ground. Although compromise is a politically expedient technique for making policy, it is not necessarily the best approach in establishing an effective environmental policy. Compromise becomes a factor in the delay and weakening of environmental-protection policies.

Given the nature of the political system, regulatory policy tends to be a product of political pressures, a fact that hinders development of effective policy choices. Even if lawmakers could formulate policy without these factors, problems with enforcement would remain.

Enforcement Problems

Effective enforcement of environmental policy is difficult to achieve for a variety of reasons. A major obstacle is the climate in which the EPA must operate. The EPA had the mandate to provide scientific evidence to support the environmental standards established by Congress. The procedure of establishing a solid scientific base for its regulations required financial and personnel resources beyond what the EPA had available. Increasingly, the courts placed the burden of proof on the EPA to defend the standards it proposed to enforce. Gathering and documenting this evidence is a time- and resource-consuming activity. From the late 1980s onward, the EPA received less political and budgetary support. This decline in support eroded the ability of the agency to aggressively pursue a policy of strict enforcement.

FUTURE ALTERNATIVES: UNRESOLVED POLICY ISSUES

International Treaties

The role of international agreements and treaties remains unresolved concerning environmental policy in the United States. There has been increasing interest in the international arena concerning the need for a coordinated international approach concerning threats to the global climate. The United Nations has been active in this area through the activities of the Framework Convention on Climate Change (FCCC). One product of U.N. activity is the Kyoto Protocol of 1997. This protocol is the result of negotiations dating back to 1995. The basic provision of the Protocol involves a global reduction in the emission of greenhouse gases to a level 5 percent below 1990 levels. This reduction is to happen between 2008 and 2012. Under the protocol, the European Union would reduce emissions by 8 percent, the United States by 7 percent, and Japan by 6 percent.

The protocol would have had the force of law if ratified, and it could have had a significant impact on both environmental policy and economic activity. An unanswered question involves the appropriate role of international agreements in defining American environmental policy. Opponents to these types of international agreements argue that such agreements restrict national sovereignty, will have a detrimental impact on the American economy, and rest on unverified scientific research.[24] President George W. Bush announced soon after assuming the presidency that the United States would not agree to the Kyoto global warming provisions, thus signaling the United States' commitment to forge its own environmental policy path.

Environmental Justice

Some groups have charged that race and economic status heavily influence the location of hazardous waste sites. Typical of the evidence cited by these groups is the location of America's largest commercial hazardous waste landfill in Emelle, Alabama. African Americans comprise almost 90 percent of Emelle's population. Other hazardous waste sites have been located on lands occupied by Native Americans. The EPA and others have investigated this concern. The EPA's Environmental Equity Workgroup found that while there is a lack of data concerning the actual impact of hazardous waste sites on racial groups, there did appear to be some type of correlation between race, socioeconomic status, and exposure to environmental pollutants.[25] Other studies indicate that no evidence exists that minorities or low-income people are overrepresented near a majority of the nation's hazardous or nonhazardous municipal landfills.[26] Critics of "environmental racism" argue that the claim that proximity to hazardous waste facilities adversely affects minorities rests on flawed studies.[27] Studies supporting the existence of environmental racism have ignored population density as a variable. When population density is controlled, the major factor that emerges involves locating sites in less densely populated areas. The response of government and the private sector will depend on the nature and strength of evidence presented to support charges that racism is a factor in the location of hazardous waste sites.

Self-Regulation of the Market

Should government take an active role in planning and regulating activities that affect the environment? Alternatively, can this issue best be solved by a minimal governmental role, with the primary responsibility shifted to the operation of the free market system?[28]

Conservatives, who advocate reduced environmental regulation and increased reliance on the market, point to the negative consequences of environmental regulations. Regulations mean higher costs to business and so contribute to inflationary pressures on the economy.[29] These critics also contend that regulations interfere with national business planning, are difficult to comply with, are often arbitrary, and lack a scientific consensus. They point to the once-stringent clean-air standards, which they contend are a good example of arbitrary and unrealistic standards forced to bend to more practical needs.[30]

Market-oriented individuals argue that the market economy would not produce rampant environmental spoilage. Rather, the free market would produce conditions that make it profitable for the private sector to recycle waste products and to develop technologies to reduce pollution at the source. The level of pollution that did exist would be a product of the relationship between the costs and benefits to society.

Liberals, however, strenuously disagree.[31] They point out that consumers tend to purchase the least expensive item when quality is similar. Industry would never voluntarily install pollution-control equipment that would drive up the prices of its goods and put them at a competitive disadvantage. Thus, the market could not provide a basis for making intelligent environmental policy choices. Therefore, liberals argue, without governmental regulation, the environment will continue to deteriorate. Pollution is an externality, an indirect impact of market activity, which will continue to have costly social and economic effects without the policy hand of government to minimize them.

Taxes and Legal Action

There are several alternatives to the current administrative enforcement mechanisms for achieving environmental goals and compliance with environmental regulation.[32] First, taxes or fees for the discharge of pollutants might replace the system of rules, regulations, guidelines, and air- and water-quality standards. Such a system represents a modified market approach popular with many neoconservatives. It would, they argue, reduce the administrative costs associated with regulation and allow industries to calculate the costs and benefits of environmental damage themselves. Critics of this alternative point out that some level of government would have to monitor discharges precisely in order to compute the tax; taxes would have to be set and adjusted continuously for particular pollutants; and companies in noncompetitive sectors of the economy could simply continue to pollute and pass the cost of the tax to consumers.

A second alternative, employed in some situations today, is the use of injunctions to halt pollution. This means obtaining a court order requiring that pollution be eliminated or reduced by a specified time or the polluter will be forced to cease operation. This strategy has the advantages of clarity and finality, but it is available only on a case-by-case basis.

A third alternative rewards enterprises that reduce pollution by awarding them tax subsidies or underwriting the cost of pollution-control equipment. This approach provides economic incentives to cease pollution activities and has a parallel in the tax credits already given industries that install energy-conservation equipment. Yet, tax subsidies ultimately transfer the cost of environmental protection from the polluter to the public.

Stiff fines and jail sentences are a fourth approach to the problem. They would impose a strong negative incentive to cease polluting. Nevertheless, enforcement problems remain. Even when prosecutors obtain a conviction, perpetrators almost never receive jail terms in these types of white-collar crimes, and fines—considering the resources of big industry—may be absorbed as routine business expenses.

Other alternatives to enforcing environmental compliance have been debated and sometimes used, but, like those discussed here, they have met with limited success, and no consensus has been reached. An effective strategy to achieve compliance with pollution standards remains elusive.

The Role of State Governments

The issue of state responsibility for environmental enforcement remains unresolved. Early regulatory efforts concentrated authority in the hands of state government, with limited success. There is evidence that a reduction of the role of the federal government and transfer of responsibility for environmental policy to the states will result in a general weakening of standards.

One reason is that the governing coalitions within state governments have a relatively narrow political base. In other words, compared with the national level, the proportion of the population concerned with political events at the state level is relatively small. Public-opinion polls indicate that less than 30 percent of the electorate regularly follows state government actively. Consequently, it is relatively easy for a special-interest group to gain considerable power in state government.

State governments also face severe staffing problems. Job vacancies reach levels as high as 20 percent in the regulatory agencies of some states, and the turnover of trained, qualified personnel is a problem. Limited fiscal resources are a primary source of this problem.

A third problem emerges when federal agencies, primarily the EPA, fail to issue regulations in a timely manner. The result is a negative impact on state enforcement procedures. Inconsistency, confusion, and delay follow as states operate without federal leadership.

A fourth problem grows from a perception that federal regulations fail to appreciate the states' unique needs, producing inflexible program requirements. The states view the inflexibility as a barrier to state initiative, as states must implement rigid programs that may not meet their needs.

A fifth problem stems from the perception that federal EPA officials may not be interested in establishing meaningful communication with the states. A lack of responsiveness by the EPA builds perceptions at the state level that the "feds" do not understand and do not care about the problems and issues faced by state officials.

A sixth problem is conflicting interests among the states themselves. The same environmental pollutants do not threaten all states to the same degree. Acid rain is unevenly distributed across the nation and is not an issue in certain areas of the country. States vary with respect to their economic base. Strict environmental policies have differing levels of economic impact across the nation. Given the differences among the states, dissatisfaction with environmental policies adopted at the federal level will occur at the state level, and interstate conflict may lead to policy deadlocks in Congress and the EPA.

These six problems relate to the issue of dividing leadership responsibility between the federal government and the fifty states. Leadership requires the expenditure of financial resources. The states have not been overly eager to assume the leadership role in enforcement policy.

Public Attitudes

A marked trend within the public is declining concern about environmental issues, as indicated in Figure 5-10. As the public becomes more complacent about environmental issues, public policy will mirror that complacency. As the figure indicates, there has been a marked decrease in the percentage of people who consider themselves environmentalists and a corresponding drop in the percentage of individuals who believe in the necessity of drastic action to protect the environment. Yet, even conservative, pro-market, and pro-energy presidents such as George W. Bush try to portray themselves as environmentalists. Public opinion data seem to suggest that politicians can lose votes by appearing uncaring about the environment, even though they cannot gain many votes by taking dramatic steps.

Energy and the Environment

Regulatory policies designed to protect the environment often conflict with policies intended to increase the supply of energy available to the nation. The onset of the energy crisis and the emphasis on economic growth created pressures to

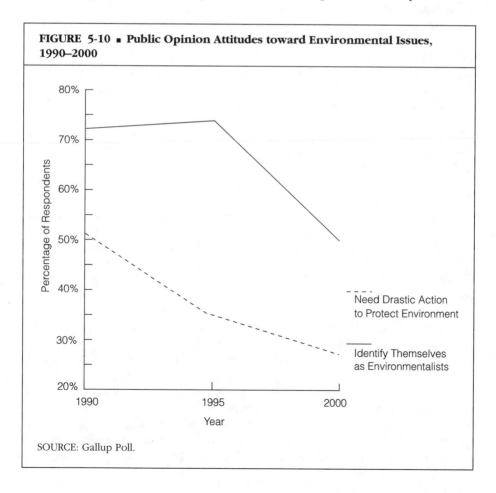

FIGURE 5-10 ▪ Public Opinion Attitudes toward Environmental Issues, 1990–2000

SOURCE: Gallup Poll.

postpone compliance deadlines and to relax environmental standards and rules. This linkage between energy policy, economic expansion, and environmental policy is a source of conflict, as was graphically demonstrated on March 23, 1989, when the Exxon Valdez ran aground in Prince William Sound and spilled between 10 and 12.5 million barrels of oil in the coastal waters of Alaska. The impact on fish and wildlife was extensive.

This spill, the largest in American history, illustrates a basic public policy conflict: the desire for a pristine environment and a commitment to produce energy to maintain economic stability. Continued economic growth seems to necessitate energy production and consumption patterns that threaten the environment. Continued reliance on fossil fuels results in massive emissions of carbon dioxide, which may generate a greenhouse effect in which the earth's atmosphere warms excessively. At the very least, continued reliance on fossil fuels will increase the incidence of acid rain.

Emphasis on the development of coal as a major fuel source intensifies several environmental problems. Increased utilization of coal will generate higher levels of CO_2, because coal contains higher levels of carbon than either oil or natural gas. This strategy would also result in higher emissions of sulfur dioxides, a major factor in the acid-rain phenomenon.

The process of energy resource development also poses significant environmental threats. Strip mining for coal denigrates the environment, because it removes the ground surface to reach the underlying coal beds. Shaft-mining techniques for coal and uranium present problems, because an effective policy for handling the tailings from the mines has yet to be developed and implemented. Offshore oil drilling efforts present significant environmental threats as well. Oil spills, leaks, and seepage threaten both water quality and wildlife.

The process of developing synthetic fuels from nontraditional fossil fuel sources (obtaining crude oil from oil shale or from the process of coal liquefaction) also presents significant environmental risks. These include surface and subsurface water contamination, air pollution, and disposal of the tailings and other solid waste from the associated mining activities.

Nuclear energy exploitation also presents significant environmental threats. Miners are exposed to carcinogenic radon gas, and the mine tailings contain low-level radioactive materials that are scattered beyond the immediate mining area by the process of wind and water erosion. The wastes from nuclear plants present an environmental risk apart from the potential damage from a nuclear accident, such as the disaster at the Chernobyl facility in the former Soviet Union.

Given the close relationship between energy-use patterns and the environment, basic values within society come into conflict. The American public has a long history of valuing nature, and the history of environmental legislation reflects this. One example is the creation and expansion of the national park system. At the same time, the American public has come to expect continued economic growth and personal prosperity. The result is a willingness to accept potential risks to the environment to guarantee a ready supply of energy. The guiding assumption is that any environmental damage produced will have little impact on environmental quality. Given its traditional confidence in science and technology, the American public finds it plausible to believe in an optimal "scientific" mix for energy and environmental issues.

The integral bonds between energy and environmental policies are the political, social, and economic issues and the conflicts they produce. The task for political institutions and actors is to resolve or minimize the conflicts and develop policies that promote growth in the energy supply and the economy while protecting the environment.

SUMMARY

The United States has grown accustomed to an abundant supply of cheap energy, and the consumption patterns that have developed place primacy on economic growth. Today, despite the addition of new domestic fossil fuel reserves, domestic supply has failed to outdistance demand. The result is an increased dependence on imported oil supplies.

International events in 1973 temporarily combined to provide the Organization of Petroleum Exporting Countries (OPEC) with the power to control global oil prices, which resulted in dramatic price increases during the 1970s. Disunity within OPEC, combined with increased exploration and conservation measures by Western consuming nations, contributed to the significant drop in oil prices between 1986 and 1988.

Attempts to establish a policy leading to energy independence in the United States have been unsuccessful. Congress did not enact the comprehensive proposals of Presidents Nixon and Carter. The goal of American energy independence seems an elusive, if not impossible, goal.

The development of alternative energy sources has moved at a slow pace because the technology is both complex and expensive. The lack of profit potential for business has caused corporate policymakers to withhold their support, thus retarding development. Current federal policy has reduced financial assistance for research and development in this area.

The political values that mold energy and environmental policies have changed significantly during this decade. Market forces gradually replaced the expanded role of the federal government in formulating energy policy. In a major policy reversal, the leadership role of the federal government has been reduced in favor of uncoordinated efforts by the private sector in response to market forces.

During the twentieth century, the federal government's role in environmental policy has grown tremendously. This is true for air pollution, water pollution, and most other areas of concern. The 1960s and 1970s saw the passage of such pivotal legislation as the Water Pollution Control Act, the Clean Air Act, and the National Environmental Policy Act, among others.

Given the nature of the American political system and the necessity for compromise, even environmental policy strong on intent may be weak in enforcing regulations. For a variety of reasons—the climate of legal challenge in which the EPA must operate, fuzzy lines of responsibility with state governments, the difficulty in gathering scientifically based information on which to base regulations— regulation as it does exist is not always enforced to its fullest.

The role of government itself has become a major policy issue. There is opposition to government regulation and the financial burden that this regulation imposes. Recent administrations have turned more toward market forces as the most appropriate mechanism for determining policy options.

Environmental policy and energy policy are inextricably linked. With the onset of the energy crisis, efforts to increase coal production and use and to develop synthetic fuels became aggressive. Yet, the production of these energy sources has a substantial negative impact on the quality of the environment. At the same time, environmental regulations add to the already high cost of energy production and consumption. The energy crisis and an emphasis on economic expansion have tipped the energy-environment balance toward relaxation of some environmental standards and regulations. Issues of international treaties and demands for "environmental justice" complicate policymaking.

NOTES

1. For a complete discussion of the status of the coal industry, see Richard H. Vietor, *Energy Policy in America Since 1945* (New York: Cambridge University Press, 1984).

2. Raymond Vernon, ed., *The Oil Crisis* (New York: W. W. Norton, 1976).

3. Melvin A. Conant and Fern R. Gold, *The Geopolitics of Energy* (Boulder: Westview, 1978).

4. David Davis, *Energy Politics,* 2nd ed. (New York: St. Martin's Press, 1978).

5. See Seymour Warkov, *Energy Policy in the United States* (New York: Macmillan, 1978).

6. Douglas Evans, *Western Energy Policy* (New York: MacMillan, 1978).

7. Marc H. Ross and Robert Williams, *Our Energy Future: Regaining Control* (New York: McGraw-Hill, 1981).

8. Don Kash and Robert Rycroft, *U.S. Energy Policy* (Norman: University of Oklahoma Press, 1984).

9. For a complete discussion of cost allocation, see Lester Thurow, *The Zero-Sum Society* (New York: Penguin, 1980).

10. See Nicholas Lenssen and Christopher Flavin, "Meltdown," *World Watch,* (May–June, 1966), 23–31, for an early discussion of some of the major problems facing the nuclear industry around the globe.

11. Hanns Maull, *Europe and World Energy* (London: Butterworth, 1980).

12. Peter Schwartz, "What Happened to the Energy Crisis? The Dilemma of an Energy Decision Maker in a Dynamic World," in Jack M. Hollander, Harvey Brooks, and David Sternlight, eds., *Annual Review of Energy* (Palo Alto, CA: Annual Reviews, 1987).

13. Rachel Carson, *Silent Spring* (Boston: Houghton Mifflin, 1962).

14. *Environmental Outlook, 1980* (Washington, DC: U.S. Environmental Protection Agency, 1980).

15. See Shawna Vogel, "Has Global Warming Begun?" *Earth* (December, 1995), 24–35; and Mark Dowie, "A Sky Full of Holes," *The Nation* (July 8, 1996), 11–12, for a discussion of this issue in greater depth. For a skeptical look at claims of global warming and other environmental disasters, see Bjorn Lomborg, *The Skeptical Environmentalist: Measuring the Real State of the World* (New York: Cambridge University Press, 2001).

16. For example, see Environmental Protection Agency, *Quality Criteria for Water* (Washington, DC: Government Printing Office, 1976), and "Water Pollutants," *Environmental Outlook, 1980,* Chapter 6.

17. The Resource Conservation and Recovery Act, PL 94–580, Section 4001 (1976).

18. Office of Technology Assessment, *Acid Rain and Transported Air Pollutants: Implications for Public Policy* (Washington, DC: Office of Technology Assessment, 1985).

19. National Environmental Policy Act, PL 91–190, January 1, 1970.

20. George C. Eads and Michael Fix, eds., *The Reagan Regulatory Strategy: An Assessment* (Washington, DC: Urban Institute Press, 1984).

21. Al Gore, *Earth in the Balance* (New York: Houghton Mifflin, 1992).

22. Alexander Cockburn and Jeffrey St. Clair, "Slime Green," *The Progressive* (May 18, 1996), 18–21.

23. Keith Schneider, "New View Calls Environmental Policy Misguided," *New York Times* (March 21, 1993), 1.

24. See Frederick H. Rueter, *Framing a Coherent Climate Change Policy* (St. Louis, MO: Center for the Study of American Business, Washington University), October, 1997; and William H. Lash, *Green Showdown at the WTO* (St. Louis, MO: Center for the Study of American Business, Washington University), March, 1997, for a discussion of some these issues.

25. *EPA Journal,* 18, No. 1, 1992.

26. General Accounting Office, *Hazardous and Nonhazardous Waste: Demographics of People Living Near Waste Facilities* (Washington, DC: U.S. Government Printing Office, 1995).

27. Christopher Boerner and Thomas Lambert, *Environmental Justice?* (St. Louis: Washington University-Center for the Study of American Business, 1994).

28. See Guy Benveniste, *Regulation and Planning* (San Francisco: Boyd and Fraser, 1981), and Thurow, *Zero-Sum Society.*

29. Murray Weidenbaum, Christopher Douglas, and Michael Orlando, *Toward a Healthier Environment and a Stronger Economy: How to Achieve Common Ground* (St. Louis: Washington University-Center for the Study of American Business, 1997).

30. Stephen Huebner and Kenneth Chilton, *EPA's Case for Ozone and Particulate Standards: Would Americans Get Their Money's Worth?* (St. Louis: Washington University-Center for the Study of American Business, 1997).

31. See Benveniste, *Regulation and Planning,* Chapter 9.

32. Stuart S. Nagel, "Incentives for Compliance with Environmental Law," in Lester W. Milbrath and Frederick R. Inscho, eds., *The Politics of Environmental Policy* (Beverly Hills, CA: Sage Publications, 1975).

SUGGESTED READINGS

Books

Brenton, Tony. *The Greening of Machiavelli: The Evolution of International Environmental Politics.* Washington, DC: Brookings Institution, 1994.

Cahn, Matthew A., and O'Brien, Rory. *Thinking about the Environment.* New York: M. E. Sharpe, 1996.

Feldman, David L. *The Energy Crisis.* Baltimore, MD: Johns Hopkins University Press, 1996.

Foreman, Christopher H. *The Promise and Peril of Environmental Justice.* Washington, DC: Brookings Institution, 2000.

Gore, Al. *Earth in the Balance.* Boston: Houghton Mifflin, 1992.

Hird, John A. *Superfund: The Political Economy of Environmental Risk.* Baltimore, MD: Johns Hopkins University Press, 1994.

Layzer, Judith A. *The Environmental Case: Translating Values into Policy.* Washington, DC: Congressional Quarterly Press, 2002.

Lomborg, Bjorn. *The Skeptical Environmentalist: Measuring the Real State of the World.* New York: Cambridge University Press, 2001.

Mitchell, John V., and Selley, Norman. *The New Economy of Oil.* Washington, DC: Brookings Institution, 2001.

Pirages, Dennis C. *Building Sustainable Societies.* New York: M. E. Sharpe, 1996.

Portney, Kent E. *Controversial Issues in Environmental Policy.* Newbury Park, CA: Sage Publications, 1992.

Rosenbaum, Walter A. *Environmental Politics and Policy,* 5th ed. Washington, DC: Congressional Quarterly Press, 2002.

Rothenberg, Lawrence S. *Environmental Choices.* Washington, DC, Congressional Quarterly Press, 2002.

Scriven, Tal. *Wrongness, Wisdom and Wilderness: Toward a Libertarian Theory of Ethics and the Environment.* Ithaca, NY: State University of New York Press, 1996.

Switzer, Jacqueline V. *Environmental Politics.* New York: St. Martin's Press, 1994.

Vannijnatten, Debora; Laurier, Winfrid, and Boardman, Robert, eds. *Canadian Environmental Policy.* New York: Oxford, 2001.

Vig, Norman J., and Kraft, Michael E. *Environmental Policy: New Directions for the 21st Century.* Washington, DC: Congressional Quarterly Press, 2002.

Zimmerman, Michael E. *Contesting Earth's Future.* Berkeley: University of California Press, 1994.

Web Sites

Energy Policy Related Web sites

American Petroleum Institute   www.api.org/
International Atomic Energy Agency   www.iaea.org/worldatom/
Nuclear Energy Institute   www.nei.org/
Nuclear Regulatory Commission   www.nrc.gov
Organization of Petroleum Exporting Countries (OPEC)   www.opec.org
Public Citizen: National Nonprofit Public Interest Organization   www.citizen.org
U.S. Department of Energy   www.energy.gov
U.S. Energy Information Administration   www.eia.doe.gov
White House Energy Policy   www.whitehouse.gov/energy/

Environmental Policy Related Web sites

American Lung Association: Air Quality   www.lungusa.org/air/
Audubon Society   www.audubon.org
European Topic Center on Air and Climate Change   http://etc-acc.eionet.eu.int/
The Heritage Society   www.heritage.org
Institute for European Environmental Policy   www.ieep.org.uk/
National Park Service   www.nps.gov
U.S. Department of Energy, Office of Environmental Policy and Guidance
      www.tis.eh.doe.gov/oepa/
U.S. Environmental Protection Agency   www.epa.gov
U.S. Environmental Protection Agency Hazardous Waste Data   www.epa.gov/epaoswer/
      hazwaste/data/
World Wildlife Fund   www.panda.org

CHAPTER 6

Crime and Criminal Justice: Dilemmas of Social Control

The public, throughout the late twentieth century until about 1990, perceived crime as having reached intolerable levels. In America's major cities, crime was not only intolerable with respect to the incidence of criminal acts, but also with respect to the exponentially rising monetary costs to society. Each of the first six editions of this book reported the gloomy consensus that crime appeared to be out of control. This perception has created a widespread demand that government do something to attack the problem. In the 1992 presidential campaign, the eventual winner, Bill Clinton, promised major legislation to attack the crime problem in America. The result of this pledge, the 1994 Crime Bill, will be discussed later.

However, the 1990s saw a dramatic reversal of this twentieth-century trend. The data released by the FBI showed that violent crime, the kinds of crime that Americans fear the most and that most affect American life, declined in 1999 for the eighth consecutive year. The Uniform Crime Report issued yearly by the FBI indicates a drop in all seven major categories of violent and property crimes. The one category in which there was a crime increase from 1999 to 2000 was motor vehicle theft, which rose 1.2 percent. Among violent crimes, arrests for murders were down 7.5 percent, and arrests for forcible rape decreased by 3.6 percent. There were 10,208,334 violent crimes in 1999. The figure for 2000 dropped to 10,181,462, a reduction of 0.3 percent. The estimated number of persons murdered in the United States in 2000 was 15,517, virtually unchanged from the 1999 figure of 15,522. However, this rate is down sharply from five years earlier (21 percent), and it is 37.2 percent below the figure of a decade earlier.[1] It should be noted, however, that even this lower homicide rate (5.5 murders per 100,000 population, down 25.6 percent from the 1996 figure and slightly over half of the 1993 figure of 9.3 per 100,000) still places the United States significantly higher in this category than any other Western democracy, as Table 6-16 (later in this chapter) shows. Actually, it is the homicide rate that makes America appear to many as a crime-plagued nation. Moreover, unlike other categories of crime, the homicide rate increased sharply in many large American cities in 2001 over the figures of the previous year. Boston and Phoenix led the rise with over 60 percent increases over the year 2000. Homicides also jumped 22 percent in St. Louis, 15 percent in San Antonio, 12 percent in Atlanta, 9 percent in Los Angeles, and 5.2 percent in Chicago.[2] The major exception to this rise was New York City, which had a 5 percent drop for the period through December 16, 2001, compared to the same period of 2000.[3]

The United States is not particularly higher than other nations in its rates of other categories of crime. Property crimes (an estimated 10.2 million offenses) also declined slightly (0.3 percent) from the 1999 figures. In 2000 there were 3,618 reported property crimes per 100,000 population. This figure is 18.7 percent below those of five years prior and 29.6 percent below those of the decade before.[4] Thus, where this chapter in the first five editions primarily focused on explaining the burgeoning crime rates of post-war America, the last two editions try to explain the clear and significant reversal of that trend. Moreover, this edition will try to explain why crime rates in the 1990s seem to have leveled off. Can the good news of declining crime rates be attributed to public policies that are at last "working" or is the trend due to impersonal forces beyond the control of government and, if so, why have these dramatic reductions leveled off in the past couple of years?

This chapter will describe policies developed to deal with crime, analyze the impact of these policies, and suggest alternatives presently available. The chapter will focus on one widely assumed strategy for the prevention of crime, *deterrence*. Deterrence refers to discouraging criminal acts by imposing prohibitive costs on criminals. In general, this means severe punishment. Research shows, however, that a high probability of punishment and the swift execution of punishment are more conducive to deterrence than is increasing the severity of punishment. The chapter will examine the factors that may impede such punishment and those that keep the perpetrators of crime out of jail. In addition, this chapter will investigate those factors that allow criminals to escape with punishments less severe than those allowed by law or demanded by a widespread sense of justice.

Evaluating the impact of public policy on crime depends on knowing the nature and extent of crime. It is therefore necessary to assess the extent to which the incidence of crime has actually changed one way or the other in recent years. It is important to note that crime is not an undifferentiated phenomenon. There are different types of crime with different rates of occurrence and different causes, and they require different policies to reduce their incidence. Policies designed to reduce one kind of crime may have no effect on, or may even increase, other types of crime. The unintended consequences, or *spillover effects,* of public policy are crucial to the evaluation of crime policies.

Too often, politicians generalize about one type of crime—for example, "crime in the streets"—as if that type of crime encompassed the universe of the crime problem. Actually, crime is any behavior that some duly constituted legislative body chooses to make illegal. These behaviors include crimes against property (robbery and auto theft), crimes against persons (assault, murder, and rape), white-collar crimes (stock fraud and price-fixing), "victimless" crimes against a dominant moral code (sodomy, fornication, adultery, and the sale of pornography), and political crimes (illegal campaign contributions and bribery). These are distinct types of activities, the causes and prevention of which differ. Even within these categories, many distinctions may be discerned. Carefully planned murders, spontaneous killing in anger or in a fight, and violent rape born out of a general hatred of women—all crimes against persons—will not respond to the same remedies. Because the concept of crime covers too diverse a category of actions to be analytically useful, this chapter will distinguish various types of illegal activities with respect to their causes and means of prevention.

ISSUE BACKGROUND: THE GROWTH
AND DECLINE OF CRIME

The Extent of Crime

It is not difficult to find factual support for the perception that crime increased at an alarming rate in the first four decades after World War II. The crime rate, as defined by the FBI's *Uniform Crime Report,* rose dramatically for the two decades after the current method of tabulating the FBI index went into effect, until 1981. This crime index refers to the number of crimes per 100,000 population for seven categories of crime: (1) murder and manslaughter, (2) forcible rape, (3) robbery, (4) aggravated assault, (5) burglary, (6) larceny and theft, and (7) auto theft. The rise in index crimes of violence from 1967 to 1978 was 192 percent, and the rise in index crimes against property was 168 percent.[5] Clearly, these statistics represent significant increases, whatever the definitional problems. Significant increases also were recorded in the four years from 1988 to 1992 in those categories that generate the most fear among the population: violent crime, murder, aggravated assault, and forcible rape, with increases of 19 percent, 11 percent, 19 percent, and 14 percent, respectively. These are the kind of figures that cause a public perception of crime as a public safety crisis. However, from 1992 to 2000 the crime rate reversed to a downward trend in all categories. Moreover, this downward trend was especially strong in those aforementioned categories that generate the greatest fear among the population, as shown in Table 6-1. However, as previously mentioned, the trend in the homicide rate has leveled off in the years from 1999 to 2001.

The crime rate grew a spectacular *355 percent* over the three decades from 1960 to 1990 with respect to violent crimes per capita, the kind of crimes that generate the most fear and have a consequently severe impact on urban life. This increase included a rise in violent crime against random victims (crime unrelated to the identity or behavior of the victim), thus exacerbating a widespread fear of crime. This fear and the perception of victimization are illustrated by the fact that, according to the February 9, 1992, edition of the *New York Times,* sales of home alarm systems increased from 1986 to 1992 by 80 percent.

Crime then took a sharp downward turn as we have shown, especially pronounced in those categories that generate fear of crime. The violent crime rate decreased 7.4 percent from 1995 to 1996, while the clearance rate for such crime increased from 45 to 47 percent in that same one year span.[6] While the decreases

---

TABLE 6-1 ■ Crime Rates 1991–2001 (percentages)

Type of Crime	Crime Rate Drop 1996–2001	Crime Rate Drop 1991–2001
Total Crime	18.9	30.1
Property Crime	13.8	21.4
Total Violent Crime	15.6	25.5
Forcible Rape	6.3	15.4
Homicide	21.0	37.2

SOURCE: Federal Bureau of Investigation, *Uniform Crime Report,* 2001.

TABLE 6-2 ■ **Public Attitudes toward Crime—Percentage of Sample Naming Crime and Violence as "Most Important Problem"**

1982	1994	1998	2000	Jan. 2001
3	37	20	13	9

SOURCE: Federal Bureau of Investigation, *Sourcebook for Criminal Justice Statistics,* 2001, p. 1000.

TABLE 6-3 ■ **Homicides by Year in the United States**

1970	16,000
1975	20,510
1980	23,040
1985	18,980
1990	23,440
1993	24,540
1995	21,606
1996	19,645
1999	15,522
2000	15,517

SOURCE: *Newsweek,* August 14, 1994, p. 25, updated from Federal Bureau of Investigation, *Uniform Crime Report,* 2000, p. 15.

in the homicide rates have been less pronounced in the two year span from 2000 to 2001 than they were through the mid-1990s, the homicide figure for 2000 was below that of 1970 (see Table 6-3). After a brief lag, public perceptions of the threat of crime are beginning to catch up to the data. The change in these perceptions is shown in Table 6-2.

There is varied speculation but no consensus among social scientists trying to explain the drop in crime in the 1990s. Many refer to the demographic factor of the aging baby boom generation. Crime is most prevalent among males from their early teens to their mid-twenties. Accordingly, when large numbers of baby boomers were in that age category, crime rates went up. However, as they moved beyond that age category, the rates went down. A more controversial theory has been advanced by two University of Chicago economists, Steven Levitt and John Donahue, who link the drop in crime rates in the 1990s to the facilitation of abortions a couple of decades earlier. Levitt and Donahue argue that the increase in abortions occurred disproportionately in the demographic groups whose children had a greater statistical chance of committing crime. This work, posted on the Social Science Research Network on the Web, has generated much peer criticism. Critics argue that it is an unwarranted inference from aggregate data to individual behavior (what scholars call the "ecological fallacy"). Other scholars refer to aggressive police tactics instituted in that period. These strategies are discussed later.

White-collar crime. Problems of the definition and interpretation of crime statistics abound, however. The crime index does not exhaust the universe of illegal activities. For example, the index does not include most white-collar crimes, which cost the American public more in lost dollar value than the total of all the index crimes.[7] The scandals associated with the collapse of energy giant Enron Corporation in early 2001 cost employees and investors billions of dollars including, in many cases with employees, their entire life savings and retirement plans. The alleged fraud involved the upper management and their accountants covering up the financial state of the company, partly by hiding company losses in numerous covert "partnerships," and encouraging employees and investors to tie up their money in company stock, thereby inflating the price of that stock, just prior to management unloading their own stock at billions in profits. Enron chairman Ken Lay reaped $37,683,887 in stock sales between May 2000 and August 2001. In the past four years, Lay made $205 million in stock option profits.[8] Other Enron executives made similar profits while their employees lost everything. Meanwhile, at one point, management actually "locked down" the 401(K) retirement packages, preventing employees from selling them. Shortly thereafter, the company's bankruptcy rendered the stock virtually worthless as it plunged from $90 a share to 26 cents.

FBI figures estimate that for 1988 the total loss to victims of street crime was $16.6 billion, if one adds in less-direct costs, such as pain, suffering, and the risk of death. The U.S. Chamber of Commerce has estimated that embezzlement, fraud, commercial theft, and "business-related arson" cost the public over $40 billion per year in the late 1970s, ten times the value of the property lost through street crime. Antitrust violations may cost another $160 billion per year.[9] In late 1988, the securities firm of Drexel Burnham Lambert pleaded guilty to felony counts involving mail, wire, and securities fraud, and paid a fine of $650 million.

An even bigger scandal involved the financial collapse of a large number of savings and loan institutions in the 1980s, forcing the government to cover billions of dollars in insured deposits, a total sum of close to $550 billion. It became apparent that these institutions had been engaged in making large risky loans to speculators, especially in real estate, and substantial investments in the junk-bond market. They were able to escape the scrutiny of government oversight and regulation with the assistance of several United States senators to whom the savings and loan executives had made large campaign contributions. A similar charge has been levied with respect to the Enron scandal. The appearance of malfeasance in high places at the public's expense was exacerbated in the savings and loan scandal by the revelation that President George Bush's son, Neil, was among the executives involved in that scandal. Such scandals erode the perception that market competition is "fair" and thus erode the legitimacy of unequal market-based outcomes. The scandal surrounding President Bill Clinton's involvement in the Whitewater resort investment scheme when he was Governor of Arkansas also undermined trust. The scandal involved allegations that then-Governor Clinton used his position to ease state regulation of a savings and loan association that was financing property in which the Clintons were heavily invested.

The public officials elected to uphold and implement the law can prove to be among the more flagrant white-collar criminals and add to the atmosphere of disrespect for the law. Public officials may betray their trust in various other ways. President Clinton's lack of candor about his sexual relationship with his intern and the apparent similar lack of candor in late 2001 by Congressman Gary Condit with regard to a similar relationship with one of his interns (who subsequently was found murdered) have contributed to the growing lack of trust by Americans of their public officials. Such casual disregard for the rules on the part of people who may act as role models for many young Americans may make others regard with respect those who successfully break the law. This example of malfeasance in high places further erodes the declining trust that Americans have in their political system, a trend that was substantially exacerbated by the Watergate scandal of the Nixon presidency. A critical difference remains, however, between these political crimes of recent years and the seminal Watergate affair to which all political crimes are compared. Assuming all of the worst allegations are true about the Whitewater affair, these were acts designed to enrich their perpetrators. In contrast, Watergate refers to a series of acts to abuse powerful but supposedly neutral administrative institutions and powers of government to punish and suppress political opposition and thereby subvert the political process itself. Watergate, therefore, refers to a subcategory of white-collar crimes we call *political crimes,* illegal acts intended to impact or even subvert the political process itself. Such actions came into focus in 1997 with widespread charges of illegal solicitation of campaign funds by President Clinton and Vice President Gore. The charges were that such solicitations were from the White House itself, in government offices, in violation of the Pendleton Act that is designed to prevent government officials from using their power to coerce money from their clientele. It was also charged that such contributions came from foreign sources which is proscribed in order to protect the integrity of our foreign policy process. Clinton's defense was that both parties engaged in such practices.

Street crime. Although white-collar crime may cost American society in the aggregate more money than street crime does, James Q. Wilson persuasively argued that what is called crime in the streets has a more negative impact on America's sense of community.[10] Even for those who are not actually victims of crime, the fear of street crime alters one's lifestyle and patterns of interaction. People may no longer feel free to walk the streets and in effect become prisoners in their own homes. In many cities, downtown businesses have failed to prosper because people no longer feel safe in those areas, and such failures can be considered to be an indirect cost or spillover effect of street crime, a cost that does not enter into the crime statistics themselves. Moreover, the perception that there is a relationship between street crime and violence adds to fear and makes even the prospect of such crime more traumatic than that of white-collar crime, regardless of the dollar value lost. Furthermore, the perception that there is a relationship between potentially violent street crime and race or ethnicity exacerbates the problem of prejudice against and distrust of America's minorities.

The rising costs of crime. The dollar value lost to society because of crime has risen so sharply in the past three decades that it cannot be ignored. According to estimates by the Justice Department, insurance companies, and academic researchers, the overall costs to society of street crime by the mid-1990s ranged in the neighborhood of $163 billion, up from $43 billion [adjusted for inflation] in 1965—an almost four-fold increase. The value of stolen property alone for all reported index crimes in 2000 was $16.4 billion. Other factors contributed to the remaining costs of crime. The following example serves to illustrate the expense incurred by each crime. When eighteen-year-old James Hunter was murdered in Washington, D.C., on June 7, 1994, police officers, detectives, and forensic experts came to the scene, costing the city $4,626. An emergency vehicle rushed Hunter to the hospital, costing another $1,310. The autopsy cost $1,046. Thus, even while police pursued his killer, the murder of one person cost that city around $7,000. The costs of the prosecutorial resources if a suspect is apprehended and the over $22,000 per year to keep someone in the District prison in the event of a conviction must also be added in. This not-atypical crime was one of over 200 in the first three quarters of 1994 in the District of Columbia alone.

Reported crime. The FBI index includes only reported crimes. Sample surveys, however, report that two to three times more crimes are committed than are reported. This rate of underreporting, such "victimization surveys" indicate, varies according to geographical area. The crime rate as indicated by the index therefore depends on what proportion of actual crimes is reported and becomes a statistic. A greater proportion of crimes being reported would lead to an increase in the crime rate in the index even if the actual crime rate did not increase. Such a reporting increase has occurred.

There are two reasons why the proportion of crime that is reported and recorded in the crime index increased in modern times. The first reason is that the development of computers and other data-processing equipment has facilitated the accuracy and completeness of collecting and tabulating crime data. The second reason is that more stolen property is now insured, and in order for the benefits of such a policy to be claimed, a police report must normally be filed. In past years, the likelihood that the perpetrator of a crime would be apprehended or that stolen property would be recovered was always low; therefore, there was little incentive outside insurance considerations to report crimes. This generates a rise in the crime index even if the number of actual crimes committed remains constant. Some types of crime (for example, murder) are more likely to be reported than others (robbery). Rape had been seriously underreported, in part because of the kind of treatment rape victims once received in court. With court reforms easing the potential embarrassment of victims in pressing charges, the rate of reporting rape may be going up significantly, in turn affecting the statistics for that crime. Thus, while crime rates in general decreased in the past year, forcible rape, whose rate had steadily decreased from 1991 to 2000, increased slightly less than a percentage point in 2001. (Forcible rape involves violence or the threat of violence against the victim, as opposed to statutory rape which refers to an adult having sex with an underage partner. Forcible rape constitutes 89.5 percent of all rapes.)

Reasons for Crime

It is important to keep in mind that a "crime" is an activity that some legislative body decides to make illegal. This activity may be one that harms persons or property, it may be an activity that offends some ethical principle adhered to by the segment of society that dominates the lawmaking process, or it may be some silly or innocent activity the illegal status of which is inexplicable. Old laws are seldom repealed, whereas new ones are continually being passed as each generation seeks to ban something that it finds odious. The number of proscribed activities has expanded over time. Clearly, the more things that are declared illegal, the greater the crime rate will be, even if behavior patterns remain constant. A statistical increase in crime does not necessarily reflect changes in behavior patterns.

"Victimless" crimes. Acts among willing adults that violate some moral principle supported by the dominant forces in society constitute a substantial fraction of crimes. Although some such acts may in fact inflict genuine harm—for example, drug use that leads to crimes to pay for the habit, or prostitution that spreads disease—they are called "victimless crimes" because participation in such activity is presumed to be voluntary. Obviously reasonable people differ with respect to the identification of victims. Thus, pro-life forces would regard an aborted fetus as a victim, while pro-choice forces regard abortion as a "victimless" activity. Estimates vary with the definition of the term and the range of activities proscribed, but in many estimates arrests for victimless crimes account for over half the total number of arrests. Such laws often attempt to ban conduct that is widely practiced. Consequently, they are often ineffective in altering the actual behavior of people strongly disposed to engage in the proscribed conduct. Thus, the impact of these laws is not to prevent the conduct in question, but rather to criminalize large segments of the American population. Many Americans at some time in their lives violate some of the laws regulating sexual behavior. These laws include bans on sodomy, fornication, and adultery. Sodomy refers to unnatural or abnormal sex. Because what is natural or normal in sexual behavior is a subjective judgment over which reasonable people disagree, many respectable citizens violate vaguely drawn sodomy statutes. Such statutes often prohibit any form of oral-genital sex, even among married partners, with prison penalties of up to thirty years. Georgia, for instance, forbids "carnal knowledge and connection against the law of nature." Yet not only has the existence of morals legislation failed to prevent the conduct being banned, but there are indications that with the growing secularization of our society and with the "sexual revolution," the rate of such conduct actually increased. Despite all efforts to punish prostitution, it continues. The increase in such sexual conduct has apparently abated in recent years, primarily due to the fear of HIV/AIDS, not in response to the threat of criminal prosecution or moral considerations. Whatever the causes of homosexuality, it is apparently a deep-seated predilection undeterred by the threat of legal punishment. Recent data indicates that with the crackdown on cocaine, heroin is once again becoming the drug of choice among the young on the streets. Because the behaviors or services proscribed by such legislation are strongly demanded by certain segments of the population, an illegal network has been created to take the risks of supplying them. Thus, the development and maintenance of organized crime is a spillover effect of banning strongly desired behaviors for moral purposes.

Drugs. Drug abuse may constitute a special category among victimless crimes. When a non-addicted youth is seduced into drug use by a "pusher," the concept of voluntary behavior is stretched quite thin. Because many mind-altering drugs are physically or psychologically addicting—or both—the demand for them by the addicted is largely unaffected by costs, including potential punishments for their use. Consequently, the disposition to use such drugs is unlikely to be deterred by the threat of punishment. The legislative control of drug use in the United States is far from a recent phenomenon; however, this legislation has failed to stem a sharp rise in the use of mind-altering drugs in recent decades.

Drug users in search of money to finance their expensive habits have brought higher rates of property crime along with the drug epidemic. In the mid-

1970s, the Drug Enforcement Administration estimated that an average heroin habit cost $57.50 per day, or $21,000 annually, to support.[11] This cost is beyond the financial capability of typical upper-middle-class people, not to mention addicts who have a diminished capacity to pursue middle-class careers. Consequently, addicts have little choice but to turn to crime to support their habit. Given the rigid demand, the successful interception of the drug supply would only make the drugs more scarce and more expensive. This would produce the spillover effect of increasing the crime rate even further. The strong relationship between criminality and drug abuse is shown in the data in Table 6-4.

Heroin was the drug of choice in the post-Vietnam War period. Cocaine, which was even more expensive, was primarily used by middle- and upper-class addicts. However, in the 1980s, a cheaper version of cocaine called "crack" made that drug easier to obtain on the streets and less expensive than heroin. Hence, crack has become the drug of choice on the streets. The extent of the steady and substantial rise in drug addiction is indicated by the data in Table 6-5, which reports the rate of arrests for drug violations. Rates of drug usage, as measured by the percentage of a sample reporting use in the previous twelve months, has declined modestly since 1985 and declined sharply in the case of cocaine. This reflects that recreational drug usage among middle-class people, which largely involved cocaine and which peaked in the late 1970s, has declined substantially while usage of illegal drugs increased among teenagers and the lower-class. The percentage of teens ages twelve to seventeen using illegal drugs increased from 9 percent to 11.4 percent from 1996 to 1997 compared to the all-time low figure of 5.3 percent in 1992.[12] Although the rate of other crimes has sharply declined in recent years and although the reported rate of over-all

TABLE 6-4 ▪ Percentage of National Sample Reporting Drug and Alcohol Usage in Past Twelve Months

Substance	1985	2000
Marijuana	41.7	34.0
Cocaine	17.3	4.8
Crack Cocaine	n/a	0.9
Heroin	0.2	0.5
Alcohol	92.0	83.2

SOURCE: Federal Bureau of Investigation, *Sourcebook for Criminal Justice Statistics*, 2001, p. 259.

TABLE 6-5 ▪ Arrests for Drug Use

Drug arrests for all drugs from 1991–2000	up	49.4%
Drug arrests for all drugs from 1995–1996	up	35.55%
Drug arrests for all drugs from 1980–1995	up	153.5%
Drug arrests for heroin and cocaine from 1990–1996	up	5.7%
Drug arrests for heroin and cocaine from 1980–1995	up	741.5%

SOURCE: Federal Bureau of Investigation, *Uniform Crime Report*, 1996, p. 280; *Ibid.*, 2000, p. 19.

drug usage has not significantly increased, the rate of arrests for drug violations has continued to climb as shown in Table 6-5. This is apparently related to "get tough" policies with regard to drug abuse.

Enormous increases in both total sales and possession of drugs between 1980 and 1990 are found, despite the fact that marijuana use decreased significantly in that period. The arrests for the sale of the two most-addictive drugs went up over seven times in that period while arrests for possession increased slightly less than that. Clearly, increases of this magnitude must necessarily lead to significant increases in the rate of crime committed to sustain such addictions. Moreover, the spread of crack cocaine in America's inner cities was accompanied in recent years by the formation of rival youth gangs seeking to control the inner city for the sale of crack. These gangs engaged in an armed struggle of unprecedented violence among themselves for control of that turf. This violence not only claimed the lives of rival gang members, but of innocent bystanders as well, frequently children, who were caught in crossfire. However, Table 6-4 suggests that crack usage has gone down recently with less than 1 percent of respondents reporting usage in 2000.

Although drug usage declined in the early 1990s, possibly contributing to the beginnings of a decline in violent crime rates, drug arrests are up sharply in 2000–2001. Arrests for all forms of drug usage (including marijuana) are up more sharply, however, than arrests for the more definitively addictive heroin and cocaine. Moreover, the arrest rates for usage of these latter two drugs have risen more slowly recently than they did in the previous decade (see Table 6-5).

Demographic change.   Other categories in the crime statistics increase with the influence of demographic trends, such as the urbanization of America. Cities offer a greater crime potential than do smaller towns and rural areas. The high concentrations of people in America's urban population centers mean more interaction among people, more opportunities for crime, and less chance of being apprehended. There is normally a greater selection of valuable, concealable, and transportable goods in cities than in rural areas. Furthermore, the anonymity of a city makes it easier for the perpetrator of a crime to escape detection or capture. Until recently, crime has been a distinctly urban phenomenon, and the fact that a greater proportion of the population lived in urban areas has meant more crime. In recent years, however, crime in small towns and suburban settings has been increasing faster than crime in urban areas, and the gap between the two types of settings has disappeared (see Table 6-6). Thus, in 2000, cities outside metropolitan areas had a crime rate of 4,485 offenses per 100,000 population, while metropolitan areas had a rate of 4,428. The reasons for this may be that with urban sprawl, previously isolated smaller towns are being absorbed as suburban parts of a metropolis. The rate for rural areas was 1,864 offenses.

Another demographic trend that contributed to the increased incidence of crime in past decades is that those categories of people statistically more likely to commit crimes have grown as a proportion of the total population. Lower-class people in general, and lower-class African Americans and Hispanics in particular, tend to have higher birthrates and higher crime rates than do middle-class whites, but the percentage of African Americans has stabilized in recent years. Youth is also an important crime indicator. 55.8 percent of offenders in 2001 were between fifteen and twenty-five years of age, and only 13.2 percent were between forty and fifty years old. Until recently, there was a growing proportion of the popula-

TABLE 6-6 ■ **Urban-Rural Definition of Crime, 2000: Offenses Known to Police (rates per 100,000)**

Crime Area	Offenses
Metropolitan Statistical Area*	4,428
Other Cities	4,485
Rural Areas	1,864

*Central city or urbanized area of at least 50,000 people.

SOURCE: U.S. Department of Justice, *Sourcebook of Criminal Justice Statistics,* 2001.

tion under twenty-five, due in part to the post-war baby boom, and crime has statistically been a young man's phenomenon. However, this trend has ended with the aging of the "baby boom" generation. With increasing longevity, the proportion of the older population is beginning to rise. This fact could account for the aforementioned downturn in crime rate statistics after 1982.

The fact that crime is very much a young man's activity—especially with respect to "street crimes"—further weakens the deterrent impact of the criminal justice system. Much of the most vicious crime is committed by juveniles, and the most active part of a career criminal's life is over by around the age of twenty-five or thirty. By one set of data, slightly over 35 percent of those arrested in one year for index crimes were juveniles. Marvin Wolfgang and his associates, however, find that a small number of delinquents—juveniles who have had five or more recorded contacts with police—are responsible for a majority of all crimes and two-thirds of all violent crimes.[13]

Yet the criminal justice system does not fully accept the responsibility of minors for their actions. Sentences usually are lighter, alternatives to actual incarceration are preferred, and the police records of minors are erased and they are released from the custody of the juvenile detention system when they become twenty-one years old. For example, a Rhode Island civil rights officer filed a brief in the state supreme court in July 1994 for the unconditional release of one Craig Price on his twenty-first birthday in October, despite the fact that he stabbed a thirty-nine-year-old widow and her ten-year-old daughter to death (the latter stabbed sixty-two times) and stabbed another twenty-seven-year-old woman fifty-eight times, all before his fifteenth birthday. Long-term imprisonment was generally not a likely possibility until an adult record was well established, and, as we have seen, this is usually after the most active part of the criminal career is over. Hence, the prison system functions more as a source of room and board for semi-retired criminals than as a means of removing from our midst those who present the greatest current and future danger to society. However, in recent years more juveniles have been tried as adults.

For many juveniles in lower-class neighborhoods, a brush with the law is not the mark of shame among one's peers that it would be to middle-class youths. Rather, it is often a source of pride and status for having stood up to the system. The kinds of light punishments at stake in the juvenile justice system do not present credible deterrents to the growing army of teenage recidivist criminals who grow to understand that they can continue to flout the law with impunity as long as they are minors.

Ethnicity. A cultural factor that may have contributed to the crime increase in the 1960s and 1970s is the heightened awareness by different ethnic or racial groups of their distinct identities and interests; that is, a growing sense of identification with particular interests that may not be compatible with the interests of the community as a whole. This phenomenon has created a sense of particularistic rights and entitlements that seems to be rising faster than the capacity of the political system to satisfy these new demands. In other words, the cumulative total of what these groups have perceived as their just desserts exceeds the finite resources that society has to distribute. This inability to satisfy demands leads to a widespread perception of justice impeded, which in turn generates frustration. A well-developed literature in social psychology and political science links frustration with violence.[14]

The major identity-conscious ethnic group with a rising sense of having experienced egregious injustice is the African-American population. In 2000, with African Americans making up less than 13 percent of the national population, 28 percent of the persons arrested for serious crimes were African American, a figure that is down from its level of 33.8 percent in 1978, but virtually unchanged from its figure of 28.9 percent in 1996. For example, vagrancy and prostitution constitute harassment kinds of arrest involving a high degree of police discretion (middle-class people exhibiting the same behavior are rarely arrested for these crimes). African Americans accounted for 43 percent of the 32,542 year 2000 arrests for vagrancy and 39 percent of the 87,620 arrests for prostitution. African Americans also accounted for 34.5 percent of the 1,579,566 arrests for drug abuse. These data, which some could argue support suspicions that there is some racial bias in the dispensing of justice, are summarized in Table 6-7. The disproportionate percentage of African Americans who are jail inmates in the United States, given that they are about 13 percent of the population, is shown in Table 6-9.

A related issue with regard to race and crime and the disproportionate percentage of African Americans incarcerated is racial profiling. This refers to the disposition on the part of numerous police personnel to regard the fact of being African American in and of itself as grounds for suspicion of past or prospective criminal activity. African Americans, without showing any other indications of criminality, are more likely than comparable whites to be stopped by police, interrogated, searched, and arrested for minor infractions. This undercuts the perception by African Americans that the system is fair. The lower level of trust in the criminal justice system, on the part of African Americans as compared to whites in the year 2000, a fact that threatens the overall legitimacy of the system, is sum-

TABLE 6-7 ▪ Arrests by Race, 2000

	Entire Population	African-American Population	Percentage of African Americans to Total
Total All Arrests	9,068,977	2,528,368	28
Total Vagrancy	21,967	9,524	43
Total Prostitution	61,347	24,222	39
Drug Abuse	1,039,086	358,571	34

SOURCE: Federal Bureau of Investigation, *Sourcebook for Criminal Justice Statistics,* 2000, p. 36.

TABLE 6-8 ■ Confidence in the Criminal Justice System, 2000

	A Great Deal	Some	Very Little	None
White	25	42	29	2
African American	18	43	28	9

SOURCE: U.S. Department of Justice, Federal Bureau of Investigation, *Sourcebook of Criminal Justice Statistics*, 2000, p. 108.

TABLE 6-9 ■ Jail Inmates by Race

	1999	1998	1997	1990
Total	665,943	592,462	657,079	405,320
White	249,900	244,900	230,300	169,600
African American	251,800	244,000	237,900	172,300
Hispanic	93,800	91,800	88,900	58,100
Other	10,400	11,800	10,000	5,400

SOURCE: U.S. Bureau of the Census, *Statistical Abstract of the United States, 2000*, p. 220.

marized in Table 6-8. Police respond that since there is a significantly higher probability of criminal behavior among African Americans, such profiling is a useful tool for clearing or preventing criminal acts.

It is true that the problem of a high African-American crime rate is not a recent one. African Americans have long been statistically more likely than whites to possess the various attributes associated with criminality: living in urban areas, having a large youth population under twenty-five, coming from broken homes, and living in poverty. But according to political scientist Edward Banfield, during the early 1960s African-American crime rates began to exceed those of whites even when these foregoing crime-inducing attributes were statistically controlled.[15] In other words, Banfield suggested that African Americans have become statistically more likely than whites to engage in criminal behavior even if they do not differ from whites in social class, level of urbanization, average age, and so forth. Actually, African-American crime rates exploded in the 1960s, the decade of great successes in the Civil Rights Revolution and a decade in which African-American income rose significantly.[16] This disproportionate crime rate among African Americans has continued in more recent years. In 1995, although comprising about 12.5 percent of the population, African Americans comprised some 56 percent of persons arrested for murder, 60 percent of those arrested for robbery, 42 percent of those arrested for rape, and 40 percent of those arrested for aggravated assault.[17] Thus, there clearly are data and literature to support this claim; however, others hold that in comparable circumstances African-American and white crime rates would not significantly differ. There appears to be an even greater tendency for African Americans to constitute a disproportionate fraction of the prison inmates, a category in which African Americans make up just under half. These data are summarized in Table 6-9. It is possible that the greater racial imbalance among prison inmates compared to persons arrested may indicate a greater disposition to convict African Americans and to incarcerate them compared to whites. Prominent scholars such as Professor Charles Ogletree of Harvard Law School in effect charge that many of the young black males in prison are in fact innocents caught up in a racist system.[18] Therefore, with regard to the question of whether African Americans are more crime-prone than whites even when all other attributes are controlled, the evidence is inconclusive. Although African Americans are more likely to commit crime than whites are, it should be noted that most African-American crime is directed at African-American victims. Thus, in 1995, 85 percent of the murders committed by African Americans were on African-American victims, and African Americans in that year were victims of other violent crime at a rate one-third higher than the rate for whites. Murder has become the leading killer of young African-American males.

If African Americans are found to remain more crime-prone than whites are when individual attributes are controlled, the difference may be due to a heightened sense of injustice. This rising African-American perception of justice denied may in turn be partially attributed to the very success of the early phases of the Civil Rights Movement, a success that many feel generated premature expectations of basic social change. This would explain the otherwise-puzzling nexus between the legislative success of the Civil Rights Movement and the rise of African-American income. The perception of justice denied is periodically renewed and exacerbated when the violent treatment of African Americans is apparently not prosecuted and punished with the same vigor as would be the comparable treatment of whites. In late 1980, the acquittal of three Miami policemen after they had beaten an African-American suspect to death and the acquittal of several Nazi party members and Ku Klux Klansmen of killing some North Carolina radicals pressing for African-American advancement, as well as the 1991 videotaped beating by Los Angeles policemen of an African American, Rodney King, illustrate the kinds of events that generate a perception of injustice.

This perception may have lent some legitimacy to African-American crime and violence. Many of those committing arson, looting, and assault during the 1992 Los Angeles riots certainly saw their action as somehow justified by the acquittal of the four police officers charged with Rodney King's beating. The African-American defendants who were videotaped beating white truck driver Reginald Denny during those riots based their defense on the claim that they were psychologically caught up in the anger and frustrations of the riots and the King case. A young African American, Lemerick Nelson, who was in possession of the knife (stained with the victim's blood) used to stab Yankel Rosenbaum to death in the Crown Heights riots in New York in 1991 and who bragged about committing the deed, was nevertheless acquitted because African Americans on the jury said they could never vote to convict a fellow African American in such a racially biased system. This verdict epitomizes the lack of legitimacy that the rules of our society have for some African Americans. (Nelson was convicted by a federal jury for violating Rosenbaum's civil rights. His conviction was overturned by a federal court of appeals in 2000 because of an inadequate effort to select African Americans for the jury.) The racial divide over the verdict in the case of O. J. Simpson, a former football star who was acquitted by a mostly African-American jury on the charge of killing his former wife and her friend despite an overwhelming body of incriminating evidence, illustrates the African-American distrust of our criminal justice system. The rendering of such a verdict in the face of an overwhelming body of evidence to the contrary is known as "jury nullification," a technique formerly used by southern white juries to protect whites who had killed or assaulted African Americans. Paul Butler, a professor at George Washington University Law School, argued in a law review that "it is the moral responsibility of black jurors to emancipate some guilty black outlaws."[19] Perceptions of a racist criminal justice system may increase the propensity to crime. Looters would rather see themselves as "urban guerrillas" attacking white racism than as scavengers of kitchen appliances. The aura of political legitimacy surrounding otherwise criminal behavior is further encouraged by those whites who attribute looting in predominantly African-American neighborhoods to political motivations rather than greed. This view of African-American crime as a reaction to racism would attribute part of the increase in crime to a growing awareness of social and economic disabilities faced by those most likely to commit crime.

Ideology. Certain types of crime are clearly related to poverty and unemployment, a fact that accounts for much of the apparent correlation between crime and race or ethnicity. The philosophical question is to what extent persons, regardless of their individual circumstances, remain free to choose between criminal and law-abiding behavior and hence are responsible for their actions. To the extent that criminality is a choice made under conditions of free will, one cannot posit socioeconomic conditions as a cause of certain types of criminality. Conservatives tend to emphasize free will and individual responsibility for criminal behavior, whereas liberals are more likely to attribute such behavior to sociological circumstances, such as poverty and racism, which they claim "cause" the individual to act in aberrant ways. Of course, sociological conditions are more amenable to public policy solutions than are defects in individual character, and liberals tend to be more optimistic than conservatives are about the prospect of reducing crime by improving the environment in which people live.

Whatever conclusions one wishes to draw about this question, the fact remains that people in certain socioeconomic circumstances are statistically more likely to engage in criminal behavior. Accordingly, whether such circumstances are a cause of crime or a rationalization for it, a reduction in such circumstances may subsequently reduce the rate of certain types of crime.

CONTEMPORARY POLICY: CONSTITUTIONAL RIGHTS AND THE DETERRENCE OF CRIME

Common sense tells us that criminal behavior can be prevented by confronting the prospective perpetrator with the threat of punishment. Accordingly, the conventional idea is that severe treatment of criminals will deter subsequent criminality and that lenient treatment will encourage it.

This conventional outlook has attributed the problem of rising crime in large part to a significant expansion in the rights of persons accused of crime, an expansion that was associated with the Supreme Court under the Chief Justiceship of Earl Warren (1953–1969). This expansion, however, was largely halted with the appointment of several Supreme Court justices under the Reagan and Bush administrations who were thought to be politically conservative and less sympathetic to an expansive view of individual rights implicitly protected by the Constitution. This Court, headed by Chief Justice Rehnquist and buttressed by the addition of Justices O'Connor, Scalia, Kennedy, Souter, and Thomas, had a more conservative majority. The addition of two justices expected to be moderates or centrists, Ruth Bader Ginsberg and Stephen Beyer, by Democratic President Clinton leaves the nature of the court majority unclear at this writing. The solid conservatives remaining from the Reagan-Bush Court makes it unlikely that procedural rights will be significantly expanded in the near future. We will see later that some modifications and qualifications have occurred, however. Moreover, the respect that legal scholars in the Anglo-American common law system have for the force of precedent will probably limit the extent to which the Court can undo the revolution in procedural rights.

Because the accused is presumed innocent until proven otherwise in our system, the rights of the accused are the rights of the innocent. These rights require the judicial system to proceed according to the rules of evidence, rules that prevent people from being punished on the basis of hearsay, rumor, emotional prejudice, or other factors that do not objectively establish guilt. Given the choice of punishing all of the guilty, even if some innocent are also caught in the net, or taking care not to punish the innocent, even if some guilty people thereby escape punishment, Western society has opted for the latter alternative. It must be remembered that each of these procedural rights or "legal technicalities" came into being in response to a particular abuse of government power. As Justice Felix Frankfurter once said, "The history of liberty has largely been the history of procedural safeguards."

This expansion of rights has come about in two ways. First, it has involved an expanded meaning of the U.S. Constitution's Fourteenth Amendment to incorporate progressively more of the guarantees in the federal Bill of Rights. The Bill of Rights limits the national government's criminal law and trial procedures only in federal courts. Most crimes, however, are violations of state law, and most criminal trials are resolved at that level. It is only through that ambiguous phrase of the Fourteenth Amendment that "no State shall deny any person life, liberty or property without due process of law . . ." that the U.S. Constitution imposes any restriction on state criminal procedure. Reasonable people on the Supreme Court and elsewhere can and do disagree on which of the specific provisions of the Bill of Rights applicable to criminal justice are or should be implied by that "due process" clause. Although the Court has always formally subscribed to the standard that only those rights that are "fundamental" or part of "the essence of ordered liberty" should be incorporated, the Court in practice has now incorporated most of the listed rights of the Second through Eighth Amendments in addition to several inferred or unlisted ones, called "penumbra rights," such as the right to privacy.

The second mode of expansion of the rights of the accused has been through a broadened interpretation of existing rights. With each of these rights, the question was not whether it existed but rather what it meant or implied. The expansion of the rights of the accused has generated the most controversy in three areas:

1. The right to counsel and the admissibility of confessions.
2. The exclusionary rule and the admissibility of illegally obtained evidence.
3. Constraints on the use of capital punishment.

Confessions and the Right to Counsel

It was decided quite early that the right to counsel applied to state criminal proceedings. What this right entails, however, has changed over the years. To the Founding Fathers, it was understood by its common-law meaning: the right to hire an attorney. The concept that the state had any obligation to pay for one's attorney is a modern extrapolation from this earlier concept. The practice of providing defense counsel in federal criminal trials had long been standard procedure but not a constitutional requirement. The first expansion of the right to counsel occurred in 1932 when the Supreme Court held in the infamous *Scottsboro* case that the accused had in capital cases (cases in which the death penalty is a legal possibility) the right to be provided with effective counsel.[20] The *Scottsboro* opinion noted that even intelligent laypersons lack "skill in the science of the law." Clearly, the prosecution is legally trained and, in an adversary proceeding, has a distinct advantage in knowing how to manipulate the rules of evidence and procedure. The logic of this argument prevailed as the Court extended the right to counsel at state expense to all felony trials in the *Gideon v. Wainwright* case of 1963.[21]

Even this expansion of the meaning of the due process clause did not satisfy all the needs of defendants for counsel in state criminal processes. Most convictions in fact have been obtained from confessions, often through plea bargaining, before the cases ever come to trial. *Plea bargaining* is a frequently used process involving an agreement between the prosecution and the defendant by which the latter is allowed to plead guilty to a lesser crime than he or she is charged with. In return, the prosecution drops the more serious charge. The prosecution in this way avoids the necessity of satisfying the burden of proof for the more serious charge, the crowded court docket is relieved of another time-consuming case, and the defendant is freed from the threat of the more serious punishment.[22] This "bargain" is generally offered to a defendant with either the implicit or explicit threat that if the deal is rejected, successful prosecution under a more serious charge will be the outcome. Even innocent people may in such circumstances be persuaded to "cop a plea" in order to escape the threat of dire punishment. Furthermore, prosecutors sometimes overcharge in order to allow themselves room to bargain. At the same time, plea bargainers who have committed serious crimes may get by with more lenient punishment and early release from detention. The pressure from overcrowded court dockets on harried, overworked prosecutors to dispose of cases in this short-cut fashion can thus frustrate the goal of physically removing dangerous criminals from society for long periods of time and detract from whatever deterrent effect serious punishment may exercise on subsequent crime. Potential criminals thus have good reason to assume that they can obtain leniency by plea bargaining.

Thus, for a period of time, many cases were being settled in the pretrial stage, when defendants did not have a guaranteed recourse to counsel. The *Escobedo*[23] and *Miranda*[24] cases extended the right to state-provided counsel effectively to the point of arrest. Culminating in the famous "Miranda rule," this right now includes: (1) the right to remain silent, (2) the right to know that anything said could and would be used against the accused in court, and (3) the right to be represented at that time by counsel, at state expense if necessary. Before any confession or damaging statement can be entered as evidence, all of the above rights must be consciously waived. Of course, the first thing that an attorney is likely to do is advise his or her client to say nothing, thereby placing the burden of proof on the police or prosecution to prove their case. This would seem on the surface likely to reduce the rate of convictions, because so many are obtained by confession. Furthermore, the decision seemed to mean freeing, on a legal technicality, a person who had voluntarily confessed to a heinous crime. For many, it epitomized a dangerous precedent for freeing other criminals on similar technicalities. This decision was widely perceived as symbolic of a trend toward an obsessive concern for the rights of the accused at the expense of the swift and severe punishment of criminals, and it was therefore roundly criticized by many as an excellent example of misguided liberalism interfering with the maintenance of law and order.

The Exclusionary Rule and Search and Seizure

The *exclusionary rule* is the principle that evidence obtained in an illegal search and/or seizure may not be admitted in a court of law. The Fourth Amendment merely proscribes "unreasonable searches and seizures"; the Constitution is altogether silent on the admissibility of any evidence gathered. The core of the argument that the Fourth Amendment ought not to be construed as excluding illegally obtained evidence is that such a principle would protect only the guilty, whereas constitutional rights are designed to protect the innocent. Furthermore, if one is not guilty of a crime, an unreasonable search and seizure will not yield any incriminating evidence. The secondary argument against the exclusionary rule is that other remedies are available to deter police from illegal searches; namely, police can be sued or arrested for such behavior.

Despite these arguments, the Supreme Court held in the famous *Mapp* decision that the due process clause of the Fourteenth Amendment requires the exclusion from court of illegally obtained evidence.[25] In *Mapp v. Ohio* (1961), the Court rejected the argument that the exclusionary rule protects only the guilty. The Court found that other remedies were ineffective; hence, the exclusionary rule was a necessary means to enforce the admittedly fundamental right to be free from such illegal searches. The rule protects more than the guilty, because if illegally obtained evidence is inadmissible, there is no motive for police to make illegal searches of the guilty or the innocent. Police are less likely to undertake illegal searches if they know that they cannot use any incriminating evidence they find through such searches. The Court in *Mapp* cited evidence that alternative procedures to deter illegal searches have been ineffective; therefore, the exclusionary rule is a necessary deterrent to illegal searches. Moreover, the Court noted that an increasing number of states have voluntarily adopted the exclusionary rule, a fact that weakens the argument that the exclusionary rule goes against custom and practice in the United States. The exclusionary rule came into headlines in the murder trial of ex-football star O. J. Simpson in summer, 1994, when a key piece of evidence in the prosecution's case was challenged by the defense team. However, the judge ruled that the warrantless search was not illegal due to the perceived emergency situation at the time.

The Supreme Court in 1984, driven by then-Chief Justice Burger's avowed hostility to the exclusionary rule, chipped away at the rule without specifically overturning it. The Court announced a decision in the case of *Nix v. Williams*

(1984) that held that illegally obtained evidence would be admissible if the Court found that the police would have discovered the evidence sooner or later by legal means. This pleased conservatives, who argued that it would render clearly guilty people less likely to be released on a mere "technicality." But liberals feared that this dampening effect on the disposition of the police to engage in illegal searches may be seriously weakened by this case. Subsequently, the Court made another inroad on the exclusionary rule in the case of *U.S. v. Leon* (1984), in which it held that if the police acted in "good faith" that the search was legal, the fact that the search turned out to be technically illegal would not be grounds for suppressing any evidence found.[26] These exceptions might have been claimed by the prosecution in the Simpson case if the search had been technically illegal.

Capital Punishment

The third area in which the expansion of the rights of the accused has provoked the most controversy is that of capital punishment. The relevant constitutional provision is the Eighth Amendment protection against "cruel and unusual punishment," which opponents of the death penalty have variously held either prohibits the imposition of capital punishment itself or, failing that, at least limits the mode and circumstances of its imposition. Given the ambiguity of the words "cruel and unusual punishment," their implications for the practice of capital punishment are something on which reasonable and informed legal scholars can and do disagree. The controversy is exacerbated by serious disagreement over the importance of capital punishment as a deterrent to capital crime.

The Supreme Court has affirmed that there are two legitimate social purposes that may be served by the death penalty: deterrence and retribution. Most of the published arguments supporting the retention and use of capital punishment have focused on its putative value as a deterrent to future crime; the essentially normative, retributive argument is apparently distasteful to many scholars. Yet for the person in the street, retribution is also a real consideration. Clearly, there are some crimes for which mere imprisonment seems an inadequate punishment. Many people's intuitive sense of justice is deeply offended when a brutal mass murderer, such as John Wayne Gacy, (the murderer and sodomizer of twenty-eight young boys) or Jeffrey Dahmer (convicted in 1992 of not only killing and sodomizing but also of cannibalizing his victims) is allowed to live on in prison. (After years on death row, Gacy was finally put to death in May 1994. Dahmer was murdered in prison in 1994.) The issue of retributive justice was raised in 1997 in the case of the alleged perpetrators of the bombing of the federal building in Oklahoma City that killed 168 people. For this worst act of terrorism in U.S. history prior to the September 11, 2001, disaster, convicted perpetrator Timothy McVeigh was sentenced to death but co-conspirator Terry Nichols was not. As an ethical argument, the issue of retributive justice cannot be resolved; yet it may more easily withstand scrutiny than the more frequently relied-upon deterrence argument.[27]

Although the retributive argument regards capital punishment as an end in itself, the deterrent argument regards capital punishment as a means to the end of preventing serious crimes. Accordingly, the question of whether capital punishment is in fact an efficient means is in principle an empirical question, a question resolvable by observable data.

Deterrence? If, on the basis of common sense, it seems clear that punishment deters proscribed acts, it follows that death should deter such acts more effectively than less-severe punishment will. As the British Royal Commission on capital punishment stated in 1953, *"Prima facie,* the penalty of death is likely to have a stronger effect as a deterrent to normal human beings than any other form of punishment. . . ."* There is in fact evidence that punishment in general does deter crime. However, another body of research indicates that it is the swiftness and certainty of punishment rather than its severity that most effectively operates as a crime deterrent. Yet, the death penalty, in the American context, can neither be swift nor certain. It is hedged by automatic appeals and the right of almost any judge to personally stay an execution based on any question about the manner of arrest or conviction. It is limited also by the reluctance of judges and juries to impose the death sentence and the even greater reluctance of states to carry it out. Sociologist Thorsten Sellin has reported that, historically, the risk of suffering the death penalty in the United States if caught and convicted of capital murder *during a period of widespread executions* (1933–1950) was only 3.67 percent. For instance, between 1961 and 1968 in Chicago, only 0.7 percent of the persons charged with capital murder and 1.5 percent of persons convicted of that crime were even sentenced to death, let alone actually executed.[28] A person sentenced to die can usually find a judge to stay the execution on some grounds, delaying the implementation of the death penalty for lengthy periods. There is less than a 1 percent probability that a convicted murderer will be executed; but, more important in terms of the deterrent effect of "swift and certain" punishment, there is virtually no chance that a murderer will be executed within two years of conviction. The relative frequency of people sentenced to death and the frequency of people actually being executed in recent years are indicated in Table 6-10. At the 1999 rate of ninety-eight executions per year, it would take nearly thirty-six years to dispatch everyone currently under a sentence of death, assuming no one else is so sentenced in that period.

There is very little doubt that if every person convicted of murder were to be immediately dispatched, other murders would be deterred. However, the foregoing data suggest that there is very little likelihood of such a policy being implemented. First, the system seeks through appeals and rehearings to resolve all uncertainty before carrying out an execution. Second, America's more secularized society is uncertain about judging who deserves to live and die. Finally, there ap-

TABLE 6-10 ▪ Death Sentences and Executions

Year	Under Sentence of Death	Executed
1996	3,219	45
1997	3,335	74
1998	3,485	68
1999	3,527	98

SOURCE: U.S. Department of Justice, *Sourcebook of Criminal Justice Statistics,* 2000, p. 549.

pears to be a cultural strengthening of the sanctity of life itself under way in the nation. Consequently, to execute promptly all or even most people convicted of murder is politically unthinkable. Failing that extreme approach, it is hard to see how capital punishment can have a greater deterrent effect than do other forms of punishment. Despite these aforestated reservations about the deterrent effect of capital punishment, belief in that deterrent effect continues to be a widespread, although by 2001 a minority, opinion. Specifically, 42 percent of a national sample believed that the death penalty deters crime, and 52 percent said it did not, with 7 percent unsure.[29] Thus, supporters of the death penalty may be playing to public opinion rather than social scientific knowledge.

There are some data on the actual deterrent effect of the death penalty, but they are inconclusive.[30] For example, studies have compared homicide rates of states that administer the death penalty with states that have abolished it. If the administration of executions were in fact a deterrent to capital crime, the murder rates in death penalty states should be significantly lower than those in the abolitionist states. Table 6-11 presents such a comparison among selected states from two geographic regions (ensuring that variations between the states in homicide rates cannot be attributed to regional cultural differences).

Contrary to expectations, the death penalty states in fact had slightly higher mean homicide rates than did the abolitionist state. These differences are not, however, statistically significant except for the atypical cases of Texas and Louisiana; they could easily have occurred by chance if we assume that the categories (abolitionist and death penalty states) do not explain any of the variation in homicide rates. Moreover, the state that used the death penalty the most is Texas. From the time the death penalty was reinstated in the *Gregg* case in 1976 to January 1998, Texas executed 104 people. Florida had the second-highest number of executions at 36. Yet, the murder rate for Texas in 1998 was 9.68 per 100,000 people, near the national figure of 9.9. Overall, death penalty states have had a higher homicide rate than abolitionist states, data that clearly do not support the claim that the availability or exercise of capital punishment acts as a deterrent to the perpetration of capital murder.

This failure to find a significant impact of the death penalty on capital crime may be attributable in part to the fact that murder, the major capital offense, is, relative to property crimes, one of intense passion. Whether much rational calculation goes on in the mind of a murderer about the probable costs (punishment) of the act is a doubtful question to many. It seems fair to conclude, then, that the

---

TABLE 6-11 ▪ Homicide Rates per 100,000 Population, 1998

State	Murder Rates	Death Penalty Status	Executions 1977–1999
Rhode Island	2.4	abolitionist	0
Massachusetts	2.0	death	0
Connecticut	4.1	death	6
Texas	6.8	death	199
Louisiana	25.0	death	25

SOURCE: *Statistical Abstract of the United States* (Washington, DC: U.S. Government Printing Office, 2000), pp. 204, 223.

death penalty as it may conceivably be practiced in the United States would not have a significant deterrent effect on the crime of murder. Therefore, *the justification* of capital punishment would have to rely on the retributive argument (an issue that will be discussed shortly).

Capital punishment and the law. The legal status of capital punishment itself has always been accepted by a majority of the Supreme Court. As recently as June 1999, the Supreme Court upheld the federal death penalty under the 1994 Federal Death Penalty Act, a law which expanded the range of federal crimes subject to the death penalty. The Eighth Amendment prohibition of cruel and unusual punishment, however, does constrain the *manner of execution*. Reasonable people differ on what forms constitute cruelty. It is safe to presume that practices of medieval torture, such as the use of the rack or the screw, burning victims alive at the stake, drawing and quartering, or crucifixion, would violate the amendment, but beyond such obvious cases, states have been given wide latitude. Recent years have witnessed a trend in favor of adopting the method of lethal injection as the presumptively least painful one over other forms of execution. Florida, one of the few remaining states using the electric chair, switched to lethal injection in January 2000. The variety of still-legal means for dispatching people convicted of capital crimes is shown in Table 6-12.

Although practice and precedent in our common-law system support the legality of the death penalty itself, such common-law principles should also reflect evolving community standards. Public opposition to the imposition of the death penalty was strong in the decades before 1970, but opinion has now moved in the opposite direction. Legal principles responsive to community standards have become more restrictive on the manner and circumstances of imposing the death penalty, and it is in this area that constitutional challenges to the death penalty have been based.

First, death has not been regularly assigned to those convicted of murder. As noted, only a minority of those prosecuted for murder are even charged with capital murder. Capital murder is homicide for which the death penalty may be assessed. It is limited to premeditated murder and, since *Gregg v. Georgia* (1976), limited to certain types of premeditated murder, such as multiple killings, homicide committed in the course of another felony, or killing a police officer in the line of duty. Moreover, even conviction for capital murder in a death penalty jurisdiction far from guarantees that the death penalty will actually be assigned. In California in the period from 1950 to 1975, only 104 of the 2,111 persons convicted of capital murder were sentenced to die.[31] This raises the question of whether there are consistent criteria for determining why one murderer is sentenced to die and another

---

TABLE 6-12 ▪ Methods of Executions in the United States, 2000

Lethal Injection	Electrocution	Gas	Hanging	Firing Squad
35* **	10	4	3	3**

*Six of these offer an alternative method.

**Utah offers a choice between these two methods.

SOURCE: Federal Bureau of Investigation, *Sourcebook for Criminal Justice Statistics,* 2000, p. 561.

is not, criteria based on the nature of the act itself. The likelihood of facing death when one commits murder remains remote. Recall that there were 98 executions in 1999 while there were 15,522 homicides, or one execution for every 156.4 murders. As the rising execution rate in some states converges on a declining homicide rate to reduce that figure from the 1995 figure of one execution for every 385 murders, the probability of facing execution for a given homicide is still small.

Research shows that, rather than the nature of the act, factors such as the defendant's race, socioeconomic status, or gender have proved to be better predictors of whether the death penalty will be assigned. African Americans have been executed in disproportionate numbers in American history, especially in southern states. For instance, a study of executions in North Carolina from 1933 to 1937 showed eighty-one African Americans but only forty-five whites being executed. A study of capital cases in Texas from 1924 to 1968 produced a higher percentage of convicted African Americans being executed than convicted whites, and the difference was statistically significant.[32] From 1930 to 1997, while African Americans made up only 12.5 percent of the population, they comprised 52 percent of those executed. This figure, however, may be viewed in the context of the fact that African Americans are even more disproportionately likely to be convicted of murder; some 58 percent of those currently serving prison time for murder are African Americans. Thus, white defendants convicted of murder were, in one study cited by the Thernstroms, 80 percent more likely to be sentenced to death than similarly convicted African Americans.[33] Furthermore, socioeconomic status has been an important determinant of suffering or avoiding the death penalty, because such status is related to the ability of one's lawyer. The disproportionate tendency for African Americans to suffer executions is shown in Table 6-13.

Such data on the impact of race constituted the bases of several challenges to the constitutionality of the death penalty. The Supreme Court under Chief Justice Rehnquist, however, does not appear to be receptive to such challenges. Most notably, in 1987's *McCleskey v. Kemp* case, the Court rejected the argument that the Georgia death penalty statute should be invalidated because the death penalty was more likely to be assigned when the victims of capital murder were white than when the victims were African American, as well as more likely when the perpetrators were African American than when they were white. Julian Epstein, an aide to Michigan Representative John Conyers, reported a study of thirty-two states that revealed that killers of whites have an 11.1 percent chance of reaching death row, whereas the killers of African Americans have only a 4.5 percent chance. In some states, the discrepancy is even greater. For example, in Maryland, the killer of a

TABLE 6-13 ▪ Executions by Race in the United States

	Total	White	African American
1930–1997	4,291	2,016	2,228
1994	31	20	11
1995	56	33	22

SOURCE: Bureau of Justice Statistics, *Sourcebook for Criminal Justice Statistics,* 2001 (Albany, NY: SUNY Hindelang Criminal Justice Research Center), p. 560.

white person is eight times more likely to receive the death penalty than the killer of an African American.[34] The Court appears to be backing away from inferring racial bias from the fact that race is a good predictor of who actually is sentenced to death. The racial discrepancy in who gets executed generated one of the major issues surrounding the 1994 Omnibus Crime Bill. The Congressional Black Caucus insisted that a provision be inserted in the bill providing that such statistical disproportionality be grounds for a legal challenge that the execution of any particular African American is based upon racial bias, what was called "the racial justice amendment." The opposition of the Black Caucus combined with the opposition of conservative opponents of the assault weapons ban in the bill to initially block the passage of the whole bill. However, intense lobbying by the president achieved passage of the bill a week later without the social justice amendment.

Gender, though not widely discussed in this context, is perhaps an even better predictor than race is. Women are far less likely to be assigned the death penalty than men are. From 1930 to 1967, of the 3,334 persons executed for murder in the United States, only thirty, or 0.8 percent, were women. Of course, such data should be seen in relation to a comparison of capital crime convictions of men with those of women. Unfortunately, such convictions are not broken down by sex in the available data. However, statistics do provide clues: in 1978, there were 12,736 arrests of men for murder and nonnegligent manslaughter (the index category that includes capital murder) and 2,234 such arrests of women. Because women, who accounted for about 17.5 percent of capital murder arrests, accounted for less than 1 percent of the executions in earlier years, the conclusion that women are significantly less likely than men to be assigned the death penalty appears to be reasonable. Of the 3,122 prisoners under sentence of death in 1966, only 1.6 percent were women. In 1998, Texas, the state that has accounted for a third of the nation's executions since 1977, executed a woman, Karla Faye Tucker, for the first time in 135 years. Tucker claimed she derived sexual pleasure with each blow of an ax on her two victims. This reprises the issue raised two years earlier by Guinevere Garcia in Illinois, who implored the review board considering whether to commute her death sentence, "Do not consider this petition on the basis that I am a woman." The issue is whether to spare women the punishment much more frequently meted out to men for crimes that were not any more heinous is degrading and in effect a denial of equality to women. Ultimately, death penalty opponents got Garcia's sentence commuted to life in prison.

Furman v. Georgia. It was the importance of such determinants on who receives the death penalty—rather than the nature of the criminal act—that the Court found objectionable in the landmark case of *Furman v. Georgia* (1972), in which the Court laid down the first major explicit constitutional restraints on the practice of capital punishment in the United States.[35] Although a majority clearly rejected the notion that capital punishment is inherently cruel and unusual, five justices agreed that it was cruel and unusual as it was then practiced in this country. There is no single pattern of reasoning to be discerned in these five diverse opinions, but one concept is that the imposition of capital punishment shall not be arbitrary. That is, its imposition must be on consistent criteria grounded in the nature of the criminal act.

POLICY EVALUATION: FLAWS IN THE CRIMINAL JUSTICE SYSTEM

In the preceding section, the evolution of contemporary policy in the area of constitutional rights and the deterrence of crime was studied with an emphasis on the two reasons for the expansion of such rights: (1) the expanded meaning of the U.S. Constitution's Fourteenth Amendment to incorporate more of the federal Bill of Rights' guarantees, and (2) the broadened interpretation of existing rights. It is this second category that has generated the most controversy in three areas:

1. The right to counsel and the admissibility of confession.
2. The exclusionary rule and the admissibility of illegally obtained evidence.
3. Constraints on the use of capital punishment.

Confessions and the Right to Counsel

As already seen, *Miranda v. Arizona* pointed up the legal ramifications of not informing a suspect of his or her rights before entering any confession or damaging statement as evidence. Many feared that the rights of the accused would be excessively protected at the expense of obtaining otherwise-valid confessions and swift punishment. But the available evidence does not support this fear.[36]

However, *Miranda* may have lowered the rate at which confessions are obtained in the first place. One study found that in Pittsburgh, in 1964, the police obtained confessions in 54.5 percent of the cases before *Miranda* procedures were implemented and in only 37.5 percent of the cases after the procedure was implemented.[37] Moreover, studies of the frequency of suppressing confessions on *Miranda* grounds do not take into account cases dismissed in preliminary stages or arrests not made because of the requirement of the *Miranda* rule.[38]

The impact of *Miranda* on reducing the number of confessions may be ameliorated by the fact that a large number of arrestees, having been informed of their *Miranda* rights, still decline to exercise them. In one study, a third of eighty-five defendants processed did not choose even to avail themselves of the services of a lawyer on hand in the police station for that purpose, 75 percent of the defendants did not exercise their option for counsel other than the station house counsel, and 40 percent chose to make incriminating statements after having waived their *Miranda* rights.[39] These somewhat startling data become explicable in the light of the findings in the same study that 15 percent of the eighty-five defendants failed to understand their right to remain silent, 18 percent did not understand their right to the presence of counsel at that time, and 24 percent failed to understand that the state would appoint counsel at its expense.

A related question is the extent to which confessions are necessary to dispose of cases. The *Miranda* case illustrates this point. The victim's bloodstained effects were found in Miranda's car, Miranda could not account for his whereabouts at the time the crime occurred, and he was identified by the victim. Hence, Miranda confessed when confronted with an overwhelming case against him. When the Supreme Court quashed the conviction on the admissibility of the confession, it did not acquit Miranda. Rather, when the Court nullifies a conviction on constitutional grounds, it is saying that there is a problem with the manner in which the conviction was obtained, but the Court is not determining guilt or innocence. The case is remanded back to the prosecution, which may then choose to retry the accused in a manner consistent with the Supreme Court ruling. Miranda was in fact convicted on other evidence.

The point is that if the only ground for conviction is a confession obtained from an uninformed suspect under the psychological stress of an intense interrogation, the possibility exists that the suspect may in fact be innocent. If the accused is guilty, there should be a good chance that physical evidence or witnesses can be found to implicate him or her in the crime without a pressured confession. Moreover, when it is easy to pressure a confession from any plausible suspect, police may be tempted to use that technique to avoid the difficulty of seeking evidence to find out who really committed the crime.

The expanded right to counsel at state expense may reduce the enormous advantage of wealth for people accused of crime, an advantage highlighted by O. J. Simpson's ability to have a multimillion dollar defense team in his 1995 murder trial. These high-priced legal talents won an acquittal despite a mountain of incriminating evidence.

The Burger Court and *Miranda*. The Burger Court made some decisions that had the effect of narrowing the impact of *Miranda* without actually overruling it. Chief among such decisions is *Harris v. New York* (1971), which held that statements made by a defendant without *Miranda* warnings could be used to impeach his or her credibility. *Oregon v. Haas* (1975) extended the *Harris* principle to a defendant whose request for an attorney had been ignored. However, that same year, in *Brown v. Illinois,* the Court held that a confession is inadmissible, even though voluntarily made, if the arrest that preceded the confession was invalid (that is, made without warrant or probable cause).[40]

A 1981 Court ruling extended the *Miranda* principle to hold that the testimony of psychiatrists who have examined a defendant cannot be used to justify the imposition of capital punishment if the defendant was not accorded *Miranda* warnings before the psychiatric examination. The Court that year also extended the *Escobedo* and *Miranda* principles on the right to counsel, holding that once an accused requests counsel, interrogation of the accused alone must cease even if the accused is willing to continue talking. These unanimous decisions suggest that even the conservative Burger Court did not abandon the controversial *Miranda* principle.

The Exclusionary Rule and Search and Seizure

We have already discussed the immediate importance of *Mapp v. Ohio;* that is, that the due process clause of the Fourteenth Amendment requires the exclusion from court of *illegally obtained evidence.* In effect, the Court rejected the argument that the exclusionary rule only protects the guilty; instead, it felt that if illegally obtained evidence is inadmissible, there is no motive for police to make illegal searches of the guilty or the innocent.

However, Chief Justice Burger disagreed. In his attack on the exclusionary rule, he made two claims: that it has a negative effect on successful prosecutions and that there is no evidence that it has a countervailing effect of deterring illegal police behavior. But according to data cited by Stephen Wasby, Burger was wrong on both counts. With regard to Burger's fears that *Mapp* will allow guilty people to "get away with it," Wasby did note a substantial decrease of some 41 percent in the number of suspects actually reaching trial in New York in 1961, immediately following *Mapp*. However, he found that the rate of successful prosecutions rose again the following year, suggesting that police were becoming adjusted to the new constraints on their behavior. Political scientist Stuart Nagel also found increased police adherence to the rules on legal searches and seizures.[41]

The states, however, have varied in the strictness with which they have applied the *Mapp* ruling. The dictates of the Supreme Court are not self-enforcing; the mere handing down of a ruling does not automatically alter behavior. That is why there is a growing body of research on the compliance with and the impact of such rulings.

Beyond the exclusionary rule, the other major question on illegally obtained evidence that the courts have had to deal with is what constitutes an unreasonable search and seizure. The issue here is under what conditions it is permissible to search for and seize evidence without first obtaining a search warrant. Issued by a judge, a search warrant authorizes a public official to search private property without the consent of the property owner and specifies what is being sought.

The rules on what constitutes a legal warrantless search emerge from a complex array of cases and appear to be formulated with the goal of protecting police from the danger of hidden weapons. At the same time, these rules must protect the expanding concept of privacy immune from government intrusion. In a lawful arrest in which a warrant has not first been obtained, the following forms of search may be made: (1) the person and pockets of the arrestee and (2) the arrestee's car or the room in which he or she was arrested ("the area under his possession"), but not the entire house.[42] A person merely stopped for questioning may be subjected to a pat down or frisk for weapons, but his or her pockets may not be searched.[43] The very complexity of these rules illustrates the difficulty that the courts have in trying to balance two important conflicting values: the right of individuals to be free from governmental oppression or harassment and the control of crime and punishment of criminals. The expansion of limits on search and seizure to include electronic surveillance illustrates this growing concept of the right of privacy and at the same time illustrates the problem of constraining police use of an important law enforcement tool.[44]

Capital Punishment

After *Furman* outlawed capital punishment as practiced but invited new statutes to conform to the standard of not being arbitrary, many states passed new statutes listing specific mitigating and aggravating circumstances as guides to be considered in deciding whether to assign the death penalty in a particular case, rather than making the imposition of the penalty mandatory for an entire category of crimes.[45] The legality of capital punishment has in this way been explicitly reaffirmed by the Court. Liberals have expressed the fear that this would bring about a flood of executions. The rate has increased, especially in the southern states (Texas and Louisiana alone accounted for 224 of the 598 post-*Furman* executions carried out from 1977 to 1999, including that of a North Carolina grandmother, one of only two women executed in the post-*Furman* era). By 1999, 3,527 persons were under a sentence of death.

Debating capital punishment.   The capital punishment issue epitomizes the widespread confusion with regard to the purposes of punishment. Although capital punishment is usually defended in terms of its deterrent effect, it is clear from the discussion earlier that capital punishment, as it can conceivably be practiced in the United States, is unlikely to have any significant deterrent effect on crime. It is possible, however, that many of those who defend capital punishment on deterrence grounds are really concerned about maintaining its role in retribution. The Court has explicitly said that retribution is a constitutionally valid purpose of punishment, stating in *Gregg v. Georgia* (1976) that

> . . . capital punishment is an expression of the society's moral outrage at particularly offensive conduct. This function may be unappealing to many, but it is essential in an ordered society that asks its citizens to rely on legal processes rather than self-help to vindicate their wrongs. . . . Retribution is no longer the dominant objective of the criminal law but neither is it a forbidden objective.

Many claim that the Eighth Amendment ought to be interpreted as banning capital punishment *per se,* but much of this argument is framed in ethical terms. Justices Brennan and Marshall, in making this argument, repeatedly evoked "the evolving standards of decency that mark the progress of a maturing society" to argue that a penalty that was permissible at one point in our history is no longer permissible today.[46] The precise content, however, of such "evolving standards of decency" is a subjective judgment on which reasonable people may disagree; the issue of whether the Eighth Amendment does or should prohibit capital punishment becomes instead the refining issue of how morally abhorrent capital punishment has become.

Execution of minors.   The constitutionality of applying the death penalty to capital crimes committed while the perpetrator was a minor has been a hotly debated issue in the 1980s. Opponents characterize the practice as "killing our children" and point out that the United States is virtually the only remaining Western nation that executes teenagers. The presumption of such opponents is that minors are not fully aware of the nature and consequences of their actions; therefore, they should not be held as fully responsible for their actions as are adults.

Those who support the application of the death penalty in these cases argue that violent and even vicious crimes increasingly are committed by teenagers. The growing problem of gang warfare in our large urban centers, a phenomenon discussed elsewhere in this chapter, only highlights the violence and mayhem that can be committed by teens. As noted earlier in this chapter, crime is to a large extent a young person's phenomenon; therefore, the policy of protecting the very sector of the population most likely to commit serious crimes from serious punishment weakens whatever deterrent effect that punishment might have.

Opponents argue that evolving standards of decency in the Western world are violated by the execution of "children." They say that the rarity of such executions supports the claim of an evolving consensus that they violate the Eighth Amendment ban on cruel and unusual punishment. (In the twentieth century, there have been twenty executions for crimes committed by persons under sixteen years old; none of these has taken place since the death penalty was revived by *Gregg v. Georgia.*)

The Court addressed the question of teenagers on death row in the 1988 case of *Thompson v. Oklahoma.*[47] William Thompson, a fifteen-year-old with a record of three convictions for violent assaults with deadly weapons, murdered his brother-in-law by savagely beating him, shooting him, and then cutting his carcass up with a knife, a crime for which he received the death sentence. The Court overturned the death sentence on a five-to-four vote; however, only four justices held that the death sentence for crimes committed by people under sixteen years old is necessarily cruel and unusual. The fifth justice, Sandra Day O'Connor, voted with the majority on narrower grounds. This leaves the possibility of executing teenagers open; however, the case indicates that a growing segment of the population is very uncomfortable with the idea of putting minors to death, and it is likely that states will remain reluctant to do so.

Limits on the death penalty. Although there remains significant public support for the retention of the death penalty, the Court continues the general trend of increasingly circumscribing its application without invalidating the penalty itself. In *Sumner v. Shuman* (1987)[48] the Court struck down the Nevada statute that made the death sentence mandatory for murder perpetrated by a prisoner who was serving a life sentence without the possibility of parole at the time of the crime. Justice Blackmun, writing for the Court, argued that the mandatory nature of the sentence did not allow consideration of mitigating circumstances or factors and therefore did not allow the punishment to be clearly related to the individual or unique nature of the crime.

This case, together with the aforementioned *Thompson* case and the case of *Maynard v. Cartwright* (1988),[49] appear to indicate that even this putatively conservative Court will continue to insist upon circumscribing the imposition of the death penalty with a set of carefully drawn and precise mitigating and aggravating factors as a guide to tie the penalty to the nature of the individual act. In the *Maynard* case, the Court struck down an Oklahoma death-penalty statute on the grounds that the state's phrasing of aggravating circumstances as crimes that are "especially heinous, atrocious or cruel" was unconstitutionally vague.

In the 1990s, the Court began to limit death penalty case appeals from state to federal courts in an effort to shorten the seemingly interminable amount of time that elapses between a death sentence and the imposition of that sentence.

The disposition of the Court to circumscribe the means and conditions under which the death penalty could be assigned and to insist further that the decision to assign the death penalty be a function of the particular circumstances of the crime had earlier been manifested in the victim impact cases *Booth v. Maryland* (1987) and *South Carolina v. Gathers* (1989), which ruled that evidence about the impact of the crime on the victim or the victim's family must be excluded from consideration in assigning punishment.[50] A new disposition of the more conservative Court of the 1990s to pull back from its previous defendant's rights emphasis, perhaps informed by the public's demand for a greater stress on victim's rights, was manifested in a series of decisions in 1991. This began with *McCleskey v. Zant* (1991), which overruled *Booth* and allowed the victim's impact statements to be read with regard to sentencing decisions.[51] The *McCleskey* decision permitted statements read by the families of a murder victim testifying as to the devastating impact of their loss on their lives, statements that were followed by a death sentence to McCleskey. The liberal defense position continued to be that such statements constitute an emotional appeal that is extraneous to the hard facts of the case and therefore ought not to be salient in the assignment of appropriate punishment.

However, information about difficulties and deprivations in the background of the convicted perpetrator have long been admissible in sentencing decisions.

The expansion of the range of crimes subject to the death penalty under federal law by the Death Penalty Act of 1994 was challenged in 1999. The Supreme Court upheld that statute, indicating a reluctance by the Court to circumscribe the application of the death penalty by judicial fiat.

The reservations about the death penalty have been reinforced in recent years with the introduction of DNA evidence into the criminal trial process. This genetic material often enables one to resolve questions of guilt or innocence definitively. The use of DNA evidence has overturned several death penalty convictions by proving that the condemned persons were innocent of the crime for which they were convicted. Renewed awareness of the reality of mistakes in the criminal process causes a reluctance to impose so final a punishment as death.

Conclusion: Crime and Criminal Procedure

These issues surrounding capital punishment apply in large part to the broader question of the impact of expanded rights of defendants on the crime rate. Any rights that affect only the severity of punishment are unlikely to have an adverse impact. Rather, it is the rights that actually diminish the likelihood or swiftness of punishment that could lessen the deterrent effect and thus "encourage" more crime. The principal question in deterrence, therefore, is the perceived probability that the person who commits a crime will in the foreseeable future have to face some serious punishment.

Have expanded defendants' rights indeed served to hobble the deterrent effects of punishment? Before answering such a question, it is important to keep in mind that the theoretical route from criminal act to punishment is marked by numerous exit points, only one of which is an overturned conviction due to the expansion of defendants' rights (see Figure 6-1).

First, the rights of the accused can only come into play *after* a suspect is arrested. However, it is unlikely that any given criminal act will ever actually lead to an arrest. One scholar estimates about twelve arrests for every one hundred crimes in the United States.[52] James Q. Wilson claims that the odds are fourteen to one that the perpetrator of any given felony will not be caught.[53] In any event, the chances that a given criminal act will never lead to an encounter with the criminal justice process are extremely high, probably over 90 percent; therefore, the nature and content of that process remain largely irrelevant to crime deterrence (see Table 6-14). Recall that data show there are *at least* twice as many crimes as are reported: hence, a 20 percent clearance rate in the FBI report indicates a clearance rate of less than half that for actual crime. Moreover, the clearance rate has decreased from the 21.7 percent figure for 1996.

A second factor detracting from the deterrent effect of punishment is the bail system together with the delay of trial. In those cases coming to trial, everyone except those accused of the most heinous capital crimes is accorded the option of posting bail and remaining free until the trial. For a large percentage of the accused who can afford the cost of bail, punishment is postponed until after the trial—and sometimes until after a series of appeals. Given the slowness with which our overburdened judicial system operates, punishment could and often

FIGURE 6-1 ■ Exit Points in the Criminal Justice System

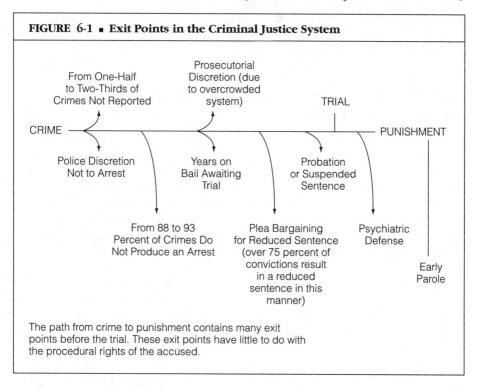

The path from crime to punishment contains many exit points before the trial. These exit points have little to do with the procedural rights of the accused.

TABLE 6-14 ■ Crimes Cleared by Arrest, 2000 (index crimes only; does not include unreported crimes)

Type of Crime	Percentage Cleared
Murder	63.1
Aggravated Assault	56.9
Forcible Rape	46.9
Property Crimes	16.7
Total Serious Crime	20.5

SOURCE: Compiled from Federal Bureau of Investigation, *Uniform Crime Report,* 2000.

does take years. Yet it is the swiftness and certainty of punishment that most deter crime. Studies show that from 30 percent to 70 percent of robbery suspects out on bail are rearrested for the commission of other crimes.[54]

Finally, because of the overcrowded nature of the judicial system, over three-quarters of convictions are obtained through plea bargaining, as previously noted. This fact also gives potential criminals reason to believe that they can escape serious punishment even if they are caught.

Thus, the expansion of defendants' rights has played a very small role in impeding or postponing the punishment of those who commit serious crimes. However, these rights do help protect the innocent and enhance the perception of the system as a just one, thereby contributing to the legitimacy of the system. It can be concluded that the restriction of defendants' rights does not offer a cost-efficient method for controlling crime. However, alternative policy options do exist, and these will be explored in the following section.

FUTURE ALTERNATIVES: POLICY OPTIONS FOR REDUCING CRIME

One obvious goal of public policy aimed at reducing crime is to increase the cost of illegal activity to the criminal, a result that a classic economic model predicts should reduce the quantity of crime.[55] These costs include material costs, time costs, and psychic costs as well as the familiar costs of expected punishment.

For example, encouraging or even requiring increased security devices in homes and businesses can add both to the time and the materials needed to commit a crime. Logically, it may be surmised that if the perceived opportunities for earning a better return by noncriminal means exceed the opportunities for the return from crime (breaking into the now-electronically secure business has become too much trouble), assuming an equal expenditure of time and effort, the potential criminal would find it rational to opt for noncriminal pursuits and crime would be reduced. (This kind of analysis points to an oft-cited conclusion: Programs to reduce unemployment and to provide jobs for the most crime-prone segments of the population would cut crime.)

The logic of this argument presumes that criminals are rational, economically motivated beings. This assumption is only imperfectly valid. It would most likely apply to property crimes, but crimes against persons are frequently acts of passion or anger that have nothing to do with the rational pursuit of economic rewards. Even in the case of some property crimes the economic assumption remains imperfectly valid, most notably in crimes to support drug addiction.

Drug-Related Crimes

Estimates vary on what proportion of street crime (for example, mugging, robbery, and auto theft) is committed to support an addiction to illegal drugs; however, such estimates uniformly place the figure at over half and sometimes as high as three-quarters. As explained earlier, the high cost of addictive drugs on the illegal market combined with an inflexible and economically inelastic demand for such drugs almost requires the addict to commit crimes to support the addiction. Clearly, a reduction in the extent of drug addiction should lead to a reduction in crimes against property. Moreover, since intravenous drug users now constitute the primary source of new AIDS cases, reducing drug addiction would affect the spread of that disease.

Attacking supply. The first strategy to reduce drug addiction—and perhaps the most popular to the public—is to try to intercept the supply. President Nixon, for example, initiated the much-heralded "Project Intercept." This strategy was reemphasized in the Reagan and Bush administrations. Though the heroic efforts of federal agents to catch drug smugglers, punish them, and confiscate their wares make sensational newspaper headlines, such efforts do not have a positive impact on the extent of drug addiction. The supply may be temporarily diminished, an unintended consequence of which raises the price of the remaining available drugs. The demand for drugs, however, is not sensitive to price. Therefore, the higher price probably has the effect of driving addicts to commit more crime in order to afford the higher prices.

Efforts to intercept the drug supply can never be completely successful. The nation's borders are too extensive, and the many ways of concealing smuggled illegal drugs make thorough searches impractical. For example, smugglers now swallow balloons full of pure cocaine and retrieve them when they have passed through their alimentary canal after clearing customs. Because most drugs, such as cocaine and heroin, are highly diluted for street sale, a valuable quantity of pure, uncut white powder occupies very little space. Furthermore, the stakes are so high and the potential profits so great that there will always be someone willing to take virtually any risk or go to any lengths to supply the drugs.

Attacking demand. A second strategy in dealing with the drug problem is to attempt to rehabilitate the addict. This means assigning criminal addicts to a hospital-type facility rather than a prison. Here the addict could receive psychological counseling in conjunction with medically supervised withdrawal. Yet records indicate the failure rate of such programs to be well over 90 percent.[56] Smaller community rehabilitation efforts have had a somewhat better record, but they process too few addicts to resolve the drug problem. Moreover, addicts frequently return to heroin use even years after withdrawal. Apparently, the anxieties that produce the heroin hungers still exist for such people, even though the physical addiction may be over.

A third strategy is maintaining the addict on a heroin substitute, usually methadone (a synthetic narcotic developed by the Germans in World War II). Methadone maintenance programs have achieved some success in stabilizing known addicts and removing them from the drug subculture, which leads to a life of crime and other antisocial behavior. One study of one thousand patients in such a program reported a 92 percent reduction in arrest records over a four-year period. This study also reported a substantial increase in the rate of employment, from 26 to 61 percent at the end of one year.[57] Methadone is, however, an addictive drug itself, and a black market has grown up around the legal dispensing of methadone. Moreover, methadone has proved to be less than a totally satisfactory substitute for heroin from the addict's point of view, in that methadone can only relieve the agonies of heroin withdrawal—it cannot duplicate the euphoric "highs" that heroin offers to new addicts. Therefore, a market for expensive heroin continues to exist, and pushers still have the economic incentive to find new addicts.

The drug epidemic in the United States was exacerbated in the late 1980s with the introduction of crack, which is apparently more highly addictive than ordinary cocaine and even more so than heroin. Moreover, its misuse can easily result in death. The spectacular death of basketball star Len Bias in 1987 from cocaine highlighted the less-publicized but equally tragic deaths of thousands of young people from the misuse of this highly lethal substance. Crack has fast replaced heroin as the drug of choice in the inner-city slums.

We have already alluded to the growth of gang warfare associated with the crack epidemic. Gangs frequently possess sophisticated weapons, especially semiautomatic assault rifles, such as the Israeli-made Uzi and the Chinese-made AK-47. Eruptions of gang violence often involve drive-by shootings in which innocent bystanders are killed. This caused geometric increases in the murder rates in some areas.

A public outcry to control the widespread ownership of these weapons, stimulated by the random shootings of schoolchildren, motivated the previously anti-gun control President George H. Bush to impose a ban on the importation of assault rifles. This did not address the sale or manufacture of these weapons domestically. President Clinton's crime bill, passed with modifications in August, 1994, includes a ban on stipulated models of assault weapons. Despite vigorous lobbying efforts by the National Rifle Association (NRA), this provision was left in the final bill.

Other proposals to address this phenomenon include committing federal resources to the task of policing Washington, D.C. In 1991, with its counterintelligence functions rendered largely moot by the end of the Cold War, the FBI announced that it was diverting many of its resources to a program of cooperation with the Washington, D.C., police department to curb the soaring crime rate and in particular to combat the growing problem of gang violence in that city.

Violence against Women

The crime of rape and other forms of violence against women have come into increasing focus in recent years, due in part to the rising prominence of the feminist movement. Technically, rape consists of using force or the threat of force to obtain sexual interaction with a woman against her will. Rape has come to be widely perceived not merely as a means of obtaining sexual gratification but rather as an extreme manner of expressing hostility to women. This broader definition of the term is related to the heightened awareness that far more often than not sexual aggression occurs within the context of courtship or friendship relationships (called "acquaintance rape" or "date rape") or even that of marriage. Although serious discussion of acquaintance rape has arisen only recently, Laurie Bechofer and Andrea Parrot trace it back to the biblical book of Samuel.[58] Susan Brownmiller, in *Against Our Will*, calls rape "nothing more than a conscious process of intimidation by which all men keep all women in a state of fear"; and Andrea Dworkin goes further, arguing that heterosexual coupling is a form of dominance in a context of unequal roles and that what appears as consent on the woman's part is simply a form of collaboration obtained by the man in the inevitable war between the sexes.[59] This orientation, critics charge, blurs the distinction between a rape that involves the explicit use of physical force and threat of imminent bodily harm and seduction involving an aggressive effort to persuade a reluctant partner to submit to sexual activity.

The ongoing problem of classically defined rape is shown in the fact that while crime rates in general, and the rate of violent crime in particular, have been declining in the United States, the number of forcible rapes rose slightly from 89,411 in 1999 to 90,186 in 2000, an increase of less than 1 percent, although, due to a growing population, the rate per 100,000 declined slightly from 32.8 to 32.0 in that same time span. Moreover, the 2000 rate of rape represents a decrease of 11.3 percent from that of 1996. Still, forcible rape (which accounts for 89.5 percent of all rapes as opposed to statutory rape) remains a very serious problem in the United States, as shown by the stark fact that in 2000, 62.7 of every 100,000 women were raped. There were noticeable regional variations in that 38 percent of all rapes occurred in the south.

The problem of male power over women also arises in the matter of sexual harassment, here defined as the behavior (including speech) of a man who, holding some form of dominance over a woman, attempts to initiate a sexual relationship (broadly defined) with her. This relationship may take the form of conversation or subtle pressure that makes the woman in question feel uncomfortable, offended, or embarrassed. Conservatives criticize this expanded meaning of sexual harassment with the observation that it is difficult to reconcile a right to not be offended with the freedom of expression implied by the First Amendment. (This issue is developed in Chapter 13.) The essential elements in sexual harassment are expressed or implied male power in an asymmetrical relationship and some form of sexual content. If a man were to require his secretary to pick up his laundry, it would be harassment, but not sexual harassment. This form of sexual intimidation came most acutely to public attention in October 1991, when Supreme Court nominee Clarence Thomas was accused of such harassment by law professor Anita Hill, a former employee. In 1994 to 1995 Senator Robert Packwood was accused of sexual harassment by numerous women formerly employed by him, charges that ultimately forced him out of the Senate.

The murder of the wife of former football star O. J. Simpson and the revelation that he had a record as a wife beater brought the issue of violence against women to the forefront of national consciousness. There can be no disagreement that men, who are typically stronger than women, all too frequently beat their wives and girlfriends. The issue revolved around the question of the actual extent of violence perpetrated against women by the husbands and boyfriends. At the high end of the estimates, some have publicly alleged that as many as 4 million women are regularly beaten by their male partners. Others, including some feminists, dispute that estimate. Two sociologists who specialize in domestic violence, Murray Strauss and Richard Gelles, conducted a survey in which they found that less than 5 percent of the families surveyed experience what they call "extreme violence," which would include punching and kicking.[60] While some allege as many as 4 thousand women are killed by spousal abuse each year, Justice Department figures show that in the high-risk category of eighteen to thirty-four years of age there were 702 fatalities. Moreover, some data suggests that domestic violence is not all one way. Justice Department data shows that in 1992 some 38 percent of white spousal murder victims were men, and 47 percent of black spousal murder victims were men. However, in the longer run, it is twice as likely that a husband will kill his wife than she will kill him. Still, in St. Paul, Minnesota, one can find the only shelter in America for battered men. In fact, Strauss and Gelles claim that in domestic violence, men and women are equally likely to be the aggressor. However, it is likely that many women who murder their spouses do so in response to being abused. Whatever the truth behind these conflicting claims, the public is now more aware that domestic violence is a serious public issue and not the private family matter that police all too frequently regarded as none of their business.

Despite their vicious and exploitive nature, the crime of rape and the related civil wrong of sexual harassment present unique problems for the criminal justice system, which is, after all, dedicated to providing due process for those accused of even the most heinous acts. With an expanded definition of rape, rape and sexual harassment confound a *sine qua non* of criminal law: that the behavior being proscribed be precisely defined. For sexual activity to be rape, it must occur against the will of the victim. Prosecutions for rape have always been weakened by problems of evidence and especially by the ages-old myth of implied consent; that is, the assumption or the assertion that although the woman said no, she must really have meant yes. Moreover, even expressed consent is frequently held by some to be implicitly coerced by the asymmetrical power relationship between men and women, a position reported by law professor Susan Estrich, who indicates, "Many feminists would argue that so long as women are powerless relative to men, viewing yes as a sign of true consent is misguided."[61] Estrich's presumption that women are necessarily "powerless relative to men" and that they are incapable of rejecting or, of their own free will, accepting the sexual advances of a man regards women as victims and thus conflicts with the equality wing of the feminist movement discussed in Chapter 10.

The recognition that the forms of coercion used by men over women can go beyond direct and overt use of force brings legal theory closer to reality. However, some scholars fear that the expanding conceptualization of rape and the imprecise definition of sexual harassment serve to blur the distinction between this kind of vicious behavior and other widespread forms of interaction between the sexes, especially between the expanded conceptualization of rape and male-initiated seduction. These problems in defining behavior can exacerbate the difficulty in obtaining rape convictions from male jurors who may perceive an uncomfortable similarity between some of their own past actions and those of a defendant in such cases.

These difficulties in the definition of date rape versus seduction were epitomized in a case that attained notoriety in Great Britain in 1993, which involved thirty-seven-year-old Angus Diggle and a twenty-five-year-old female attorney. After a night of drinking, the woman invited Diggle to spend the night in her room. When she undressed and laid down on her couch, he disrobed and climbed on top of her. She screamed and pushed him off before he could go any further. He was convicted of attempted rape and sentenced to three years in prison.

Clearly, there is heightened sensitivity to the problems of rape and sexual harassment that will lead to accelerated efforts in legal and legislative policy formation. Reflecting this heightened sensitivity is the $1.6 billion in the 1994 Crime Bill to fund the Violence against Women Act. The challenge is to fight rape and harassment in all their forms while protecting the rights of women and men.

Crimes of Violence and Gun Control

Drug-related crimes are primarily crimes against property; that is, theft in order to support expensive addictions. Of course, violence is frequently involved in such crimes as a means of obtaining the economic benefit. When the violence becomes the end in itself, the causes and the means of combating such crime are quite different from those in the case of crimes against property.

When the goal of the crime is material gain, a certain amount of rational calculation—cost-benefit analysis—may indeed go into the decision to commit the crime. Even drug-related crimes, with the addict's inelastic demand, can be curbed by removing the pusher's economic incentive and the addict's economic need. When the goal of the criminal act is violence to another person, however, the element of rational calculation diminishes. Although there may be certain psychic benefits that accrue to the perpetrator of a crime of violence, it is doubtful whether much rational calculation is involved. Rape, for instance, is now thought by most psychologists to be an act of violence (an act of woman hating) rather than an act motivated by sexual passion or need. Rapists have been known to commit their crime within hours of experiencing consensual sexual relations.

The point is that in such crimes the traditional theory of deterrence breaks down. Because the benefits are emotional, the decision to commit the crime is, by definition, nonrational. This is why the data fail to show that the death penalty deters capital crimes of rape or murder. One policy option on crimes against persons is to contain the proliferation of the instruments of violence. In practical terms, this means gun control.

Guns and violence. In the United States, the proliferation of firearms far exceeds that in any other civilized nation. Estimates of the number of privately owned firearms in the United States range from 50 to 200 million guns in the possession of some 40 million individuals. (Though, according to Table 6-15, a smaller percentage of homes now report owning a firearm.) Firearms have been used to shoot over 200,000 people per year, some 20,000 of whom die. In 1996, the United States had a homicide rate of 7.4 per 100,000 population, down from the 1995 rate of 8.2 but still the highest among industrialized nations. The U.S. rate was more than three times as high as the second-highest nation (see Table 6-16). Even Northern Ireland, until 1994 in the grip of a virtual undeclared civil war, had a substantially lower homicide rate of 4.3. In 1996, there were 19,645 murders known to police, of which 67.8 percent were committed by firearms. Indeed, more people in America were

TABLE 6-15 ▪ Firearms in the Home (Percentage of national sample acknowledging ownership of at least one firearm)

1959	1980	1990	1997	2000
49	45	47	42	42

SOURCE: U.S. Department of Justice, Bureau of Justice Statistics, *Sourcebook on Criminal Justice Statistics,* 2000 (Albany: SUNY at Albany, Hindelang Criminal Justice Research Center), p. 49.

TABLE 6-16 ▪ Homicide Rates of Selected Advanced Industrial Democracies (latest available year)

Nation	Number of Homicides	Rate per 100,000	Year
Canada	498	1.7	1994
United States	25,653	9.9	1993
Austria	84	1.0	1995
France	649	1.1	1994
Germany	954	1.2	1994
Italy	1,275	2.2	1992
Sweden	113	1.3	1993
Israel	119	2.2	1994
Ireland	23	0.6	1992
Australia	323	1.8	1994
Netherlands	171	1.1	1994

SOURCE: United Nations, *Demographic Yearbook,* 1995, pp. 486–507.

killed by handguns during the years of the Vietnam War than American soldiers were killed in Vietnam. Firearm violence extends beyond criminal activity to suicide and accidents.

Estimates indicate that some 20,000 to 22,000 people are killed by handguns each year, if approximately 12,000 annual suicides using these weapons are included. Experts estimate that only one person in ten who attempts suicide really intends to die. Many stage the attempt to draw sympathy or get attention. However, the presence of a gun renders many of these suicides successful, whereas someone swallowing pills or standing on a window ledge may be saved.

Moreover, the proliferation of guns means that many of them inevitably fall into the hands of children, who are less likely to use them responsibly. In 1987, an average of one child under the age of fifteen died in the United States each day from a handgun accident, and ten others were injured, according to the Center to Prevent Handgun Violence. Moreover, from 1987 to 1989, there was a 34 percent increase in the number of children under fifteen killed by guns, according to the Coalition to Stop Gun Violence. Since only about 10 percent of the murder victims in the year 2000 were under eighteen years of age, many of the youthful victims of firearms are shot accidentally. Many of these tragedies occur because gun owners leave their weapons where children can find them. Accordingly, a number of state and local governments have either adopted or considered legislation holding gun owners responsible under both civil and criminal laws for any harm caused by leaving weapons accessible to children. Not surprisingly, the powerful National Rifle Association (NRA) opposes such legislation insofar as it covers young people fourteen years of age or older, claiming that fourteen-year-olds are capable of making their own decisions about guns. The NRA legislative counsel further opposes legislation that mandates criteria for storing weapons. As we shall see again later, this powerful lobbying group for gun owners has consistently opposed any effort to regulate firearms possession and use and is in part responsible for the extraordinarily permissive policies in this country compared to those in other industrialized nations.

As we have seen, the growing phenomenon of gang violence in the underclass neighborhoods of our large cities thrives on easily obtainable weapons. Police forces are increasingly seeking to counter the firepower of street gangs with more powerful and more sophisticated weapons of their own, creating a kind of domestic arms race.

There is no question that the proliferation of firearms contributes to their use in shooting people. Despite the cliché of the opponents of firearm regulation that "Guns don't kill people; people kill people," the correlations are far too strong to be dismissed as coincidental. Nations that restrict firearms have far fewer people shot. Japan, with half as many people as we have, had forty-six handgun deaths in 1985; Great Britain had only eight handgun murders that year among its 54.5 million people; whereas Houston, Texas, had approximately 150 such murders among only 1.5 million people in 1986 (based on a reported rate of 22.9 murders per 100,000).

Opposition to gun control. Despite these data, there are two rationales for the opposition to gun control. The first is the belief that gun control would not correct the crime problem. The second is that it would violate the rights of gun owners.

A key assumption of the first rationale is that guns are not the only available deadly weapon. Knives and blunt instruments can and do serve as instruments of violence, yet no one seriously advocates restricting the private ownership of such items. Opponents of gun control hold that if guns were not available, potential perpetrators of crime would simply resort to other means.

It is further argued that persons determined to commit crimes would find illegal ways of acquiring firearms even if laws banned them. Prohibition did not prevent the use of alcoholic beverages, nor do laws eliminate prostitution, pornography, or illegal drugs. Therefore, gun control would by definition take guns away from law-abiding citizens only and leave them in the hands of criminals.

Neither of these arguments invalidates the utility of gun-control legislation in reducing the number of people who are shot each year. First, it is both physically and psychologically easier to kill someone with a gun than with a blunt instrument or with a knife. It takes a greater degree of strength, passion, commitment, and insensitivity to bash in a head with an andiron or to plunge a knife between someone's ribs than it does to stand across a room and pull a trigger. Furthermore, the possibilities of resistance are much greater in a knife or club attack, means requiring physical proximity, than when one is shot from a distance. The proliferation of firearms, the data show, not only correlates with the number of people who are shot, but also with the total number of people who are murdered. Guns in general, and handguns in particular, account for a preponderant proportion of homicides in this country. Nationwide, two-thirds of all murders are committed with firearms, half with handguns. This far outstrips other methods of committing homicide, as shown in Table 6-17. In 1998, Rhode Island, with strict gun-control laws, had 2.4 total murders per 100,000 population; Texas, with a high incidence of gun ownership, had 6.8 murders per 100,000 population.

The ease of taking lives with firearms as opposed to alternative methods is clearly shown in the figures for suicides by firearms in Table 6-18. It should be noted that despite the availability of numerous other means to commit suicide, firearms were used in over half the cases in the 1970s. Through the 1990s firearms accounted for almost two-thirds of all suicides. Taking one's own life is frequently an essentially irrational or impulsive act, and one that might not have taken place had the victim been forced to cool off in the light of day or to use some other,

TABLE 6-17 ■ Murders in the United States by Weapons (percentage)

	1995	1996	2000
Guns (all)	68.2	67.8	65.6
Handguns	55.8	n/a	51.7
Knives	12.8	13.5	13.5
Blunt Objects	4.5	4.6	4.7
Hands, feet, etc.	5.9	5.9	7.0
Strangulation	1.9	1.5	n/a
Fire	0.8	1.0	n/a
Poison	n/a	0.9	n/a
Explosion	n/a	0.1	n/a
Asphyxiation	n/a	0.6	n/a
Other	6.1	4.7	n/a

SOURCE: *Statistical Abstract of the United States*, 1997, p. 204; *Uniform Crime Reports*, 2000, p. 18.

TABLE 6-18 ▪ Suicides by Method in the United States, 1994	
Drugs	2,044
Gases and Vapors	4,745
Hanging and Suffocation	302
Handguns	15,059
Other Unspecified Gun	2,359

SOURCE: Federal Bureau of Investigation, *Uniform Crime Report*, 1996, p. 18.

possibly unsuccessful, means. Moreover, guns are a more efficient means of killing oneself; shooting yourself in the brain is almost always fatal.

The third corollary, that banned firearms would still be available by illegal means, presumes a determined criminal who plans his or her use of the gun in advance. In fact, the majority of homicides are not premeditated, but are crimes of passion committed on the spur of the moment. The argument that would end with a punch when a gun is not available may end with someone dead if a gun is available. Many shootings occur in domestic quarrels or in drunken arguments in bars. If the combatants had to go out the following day and seek a firearm from illegal sources, surely some of their passion would have cooled off in the sober light of day.

Unquestionably, some determined criminals would still seek out firearms by illegal means and use them. But, equally undeniable, other potential killers would cool off and not pursue a weapon. The claim is not that gun control would totally prevent murder, but rather that gun control would save many lives. The issue is, then, how much a human life is worth against the convenience of a law-abiding gun enthusiast's unrestricted access to firearms.

The second rationale against gun control is its alleged infringement on the right of law-abiding citizens to keep and own firearms, supposedly a constitutional right based on the Second Amendment, which reads:

> A well regulated militia, being necessary to the security of a free State, the right of the people to keep and bear arms, shall not be infringed.

It is important to note that there are two parts to this sentence. Presumably the opening gerund phrase, if it is not redundant, modifies the main clause. Therefore, it is reasonable to conclude that the purpose of the amendment was to prevent the national government from disarming the state militias. The Constitution therefore does not unambiguously prevent Congress from choosing to regulate private ownership of firearms. It is essentially a political rather than a constitutional question.

Regulation of guns. Even on the assumption that Congress could regulate firearms if it chose to do so, it is argued that Congress ought not to do so because such regulation would interfere with the rights of two groups of people who require firearms. The first group consists of those who hunt game for recreation. A large part of this difficulty could be dealt with by distinguishing among kinds of firearms. Most hunting is done with rifles, whereas most crime is committed with concealable handguns; thus, the fairest solution would be to prohibit the handguns that kill people and not ban rifles. Allowing hunting rifles would not eliminate the occasional crime committed with one, and handgun control might inconvenience the adventurous soul who chooses to hunt wild boar with a snub-nosed .38. However, the overall impact would be unimpeded hunting recreation for the sportsperson and a significant reduction in homicides. In addition, guns could be distinguished by barrel length and/or melting point, criteria that would distinguish the cheap, small handguns used in much crime from rifles and longer-range handguns occasionally used in hunting.

The second group consists of people who genuinely need a gun for protection. This would include those who work in high-crime neighborhoods, those who must travel late at night, and those whose safety has been threatened.

The needs of this second group constitute another important argument against gun-control legislation. The argument is that law-enforcement institutions and the justice process are unable to protect citizens from being victims of serious crime; therefore, such people have the right and the obligation to seek protection for themselves and their families. The argument states that if potential criminals believed that most people kept guns in their homes and knew how to use them, the number of break-ins would decrease dramatically. Consistent with the logic of this argument several states, most notably Texas and Florida, have passed laws giving people the right, subject to a permit, to carry concealed weapons. To qualify for such a permit, the applicant has to have a record free from any felony conviction or mental illness and must take a course on firearm use and safety. In Texas, between January 1, 1996, when their law went into effect, and January 1, 1998, the state issued 163,096 licenses to carry these weapons. Supporters of this law argue that it will lead to a decrease in street crime because potential perpetrators will be aware that their potential victim may be hiding the means to blow them away. Some initial studies support that argument. Street crime was significantly down in Florida in the first year after the concealed weapons law went into effect. Opponents of the law, especially groups and individuals actively working for firearms control in general, argue that many of the holders of these permits use their guns to commit crimes. In the first twenty-one months the Texas law was in effect, 946 permit holders were arrested, 263 for felonies, including six charges of murder or attempted murder. It should be noted that the felony arrests are less than two-tenths of 1 percent of the permit holders.[62]

FBI statistics do not support the argument that private ownership of firearms is an effective means of self-defense, however. Their data show that a handgun used for "self-defense" is *one hundred times* more likely to kill or injure its owner than it is to stop a potential criminal. The owner will tend to be less ruthless than the criminal in shooting another human being or may be less adept than the criminal in handling the gun. Another way of putting this may be found in a recent study from the prestigious *New England Journal of Medicine* in which a research team led by Emory University Professor Arthur Kellerman found that homes in which guns are kept are three times more likely to experience a homicide than homes without guns. In 1992, 26 women used handguns to kill in self-defense while in that same year 1,908 women were killed by handguns. Thus, data do not support the widely held perception that in this crime-ridden society, ordinary people are somehow safer when they have a gun for protection. Permits can be issued on an individual basis to anyone who makes a case for a genuine need for a gun and who does not appear to present a high risk of using that gun for undesirable purposes.

Therefore, gun control does not have to ban guns from the entire population. It may be confined to the requirement that prospective purchasers of weapons be identified and the records checked to see whether they fall into one of the high-risk categories before they are allowed to actually possess the weapon.

Such regulation might even be confined to small handguns. It is perhaps not too much to ask that a gun seller not be permitted to sell an arsenal to someone recently released from prison or from an institution for the criminally psychotic.

The requirement that prospective purchasers of handguns undergo background checks is the essence of the Brady Bill, whose passage in 1994 was one of the first major legislative defeats for the powerful National Rifle Association, the nation's largest and most strident opponent of nearly all forms of firearms regulation. The bill was named after presidential aide James Brady, who was critically wounded in John Hinckley's attempt to kill President Reagan in 1981, and after Sarah Brady, his wife, who has become one of the leading activists for handgun control. The bill mandates background checks for prospective purchasers of handguns to determine if they are part of a high-risk group (a convicted felon, a former mental patient, and such). These checks take a day or two and purchasers have to wait five days before taking possession of guns, a period of time that also serves as a "cooling-off period." Opponents of this bill, led by the NRA, argue that criminals will get their guns by illegal means anyhow. Meanwhile, they argue, this bill creates unnecessary regulations adding to the costs of doing business for purveyors of guns and making for unnecessary inconvenience for prospective purchasers of guns. Supporters of the Brady Bill note that in the four years after its passage over 100,000 applications to buy guns were denied because the applicants were in the proscribed high-risk categories: having a record of felony convictions or mental illness. If just 1 percent of these were prevented from killing someone, that is 1,000 lives saved. Obviously, supporters of the bill argued, the denial of so many applications constitutes evidence that some people who might misuse firearms do try to purchase them legally and may lack the resources to obtain them by other means. The Supreme Court in 1997 struck down that part of the Brady Bill that requires state officials to do the background checks on prospective purchasers of guns on federalism grounds. Many people believed that this takes the heart out of the Brady Bill by removing the means of implementation. However, some states still do the checks, and the federal government is now in the business of doing background checks. A major loophole in Brady is that it only applies to licensed gun dealers; hence, one can purchase firearms at a gun show without either the waiting period or the background check. Gun-control advocates have concentrated efforts in 2000 to 2002 to close that loophole. These efforts have thus far been unsuccessful.

Semi-Automatic Weapons and the Crime Bill of 1994. The debate on the control of semi-automatic weapons, which hold many rounds of ammunition and allow many more rounds to be fired in less time, was activated by several mass killings, including the murder of five children and the wounding of some thirty others in a Stockton, California, elementary school in 1989 by a deranged man with a semi-automatic assault rifle. In the wake of that killing, the Bush administration banned the import of assault rifles, such as the Israeli-made Uzi, but refused to extend the ban to the domestic manufacture of such weapons, even though three-fourths of the country's weapons are produced domestically. This debate continued when a Glock 17 was used by another deranged gunman, George Hennard, to kill twenty-two people and wound many others in a Killeen, Texas, cafeteria in October 1991. The Glock has the advantage of being semi-automatic with a large seventeen-round magazine like an assault rifle, which renders it efficient in killing large numbers of people. It is a 7.4-inch-long, 21.8-ounce pistol that, unlike an assault rifle, is concealable. The significance of large ammunition magazines was highlighted in a random mass shooting on the Long Island Railway, a commuter train into New York City, by an African-American man angry at whites in general. It was only after emptying his magazine that the assailant was subdued by bystanders while reloading; hence, the number of people shot in such incidents may well be approximately equal to the number of rounds in the first magazine. A provision in the Omnibus Crime Bill of 1994 bans the domestic manufacture and sale of nineteen types of these semi-automatic weapons and limits the size of ammunition magazines. Although this provision would not have outlawed the Glock, it would have prevented the legal sale of the seventeen-round magazine able to kill so many so quickly. In addition to banning some weapons by name, the bill stipulates certain attributes of other weapons that would render them illegal. The opposition to the Crime Bill of 1994 was eventually overcome in the face of widespread public perception that crime was one of the nation's most important problems. However, the passage of the bill spawned an industry of producing "copycat" weapons that were not specifically named or that lacked one or more of the stipulated criteria. For instance, if a gun lacked a folding stock or a special muzzle, it could still be a legal clone of an AK-47 or Uzi, grenade launcher and all. Although the Colt AR-15 assault rifle was banned by the bill, Olympic Arms Company began manufacturing a nearly identical weapon, the PCR-1 (initials stand for politically correct rifle). The only difference between the PCR-1 and the AR-15 is that the former lacked a flash suppressor and a bayonet mount.[63]

Other provisions in the bill provided federal money to hire more policemen and to build more prisons. Since the local governments would have to match these federal grants, it was not clear that as many new policemen would be hired as promised by the bill's supporters. Moreover, it appears that the bill assumes that after three years the local community will pick up the tab for the new policemen, and many communities will be financially unable to do so. Hence, some of these policemen will be temporary. It also appears that many of the communities getting grants for additional policemen are very small towns with little or no crime problem.[64] The bill also provided funds for programs for inner-city youths in the name of crime prevention, programs such as midnight basketball leagues to keep potential gang members off the streets. Conservatives in Congress strongly objected to the idea of fighting crime with spending on social programs. These conservatives also provided key opposition to the Crime Bill of 1994 and forced a reallocation of funds from such programs to funding more jail space.

The polls have shown for some time that a substantial majority of Americans support some form of gun regulation (see Table 6-19).

TABLE 6-19 ■ **Attitudes toward Gun Control (percent of respondents)**

	Protect Right to Own Gun	For Gun Control	Don't Know
1993	34	57	9
1999	30	65	5
2000	38	57	5

SOURCE: U.S. Department of Justice, Bureau of Justice Statistics, *Sourcebook for Criminal Justice Statistics,* 2000 (Hindelang Criminal Justice Research Center at SUNY Albany), p. 151.

Moreover, an impressive 81 percent of all respondents to a 1993 national poll favored registration of all handguns, up from 66 percent in 1982.[65] Why, then, has this policy not been adopted on a national level?

The answer lies in the intense regard that a substantial minority of Americans still have for the guns as part of our frontier heritage and in the efforts of one of the wealthiest and most powerful interest groups in the nation, the NRA, whose zealous and intense efforts to oppose almost any form of firearm regulation epitomize the ability of a passionate minority to overcome a passive majority. The NRA supports or opposes politicians on the single-issue "litmus test" of their position on gun control, and the group's vociferous opposition to politicians who support gun control has been a major factor in defeating some candidates. The passage of the Brady Bill and the retention of the assault weapons ban in the 1994 Crime Bill diminished the NRA's image of invulnerability. However, they nearly succeeded in removing the assault weapons provision from the Crime Bill, showing that they are still a powerful if not irresistible force.

Decriminalization and Deterrence

Recall that the swiftness and certainty of punishment are thought to be the major ingredients in deterring crime. There are two factors at work in the criminal justice system that greatly slow down the meting out of that punishment. One is the long wait that criminals spend free between arraignment and trial, and the other is the enormous case load of "victimless crime" defendants.

A substantial portion of the total justice system case load is processing the so-called victimless crimes. The people who are arrested for such things as prostitution, public intoxication, or drug abuse take up a very large portion of the court time in any large city, time that might otherwise be used to prosecute more swiftly the perpetrators of crimes against persons or property. In addition to the court time spent on victimless crime, the use of such resources as prosecutorial forces, court-appointed defense attorneys, and police time must be added. Such laws often demean law enforcement officers, who must consort with prostitutes, addicts, and gamblers in order to catch them. Police are pressured to apprehend such people, not because of any threat they pose to public safety, but solely because they offend the dominant morality. Having to assume undercover roles that themselves violate accepted morality detracts from the public image and self-image of the police. These laws are also selectively enforced against social undesirables. Police arrest streetwalkers but rarely arrest expensive call girls. Lower-class people are arrested for public intoxication on the street, but middle-class people are rarely bothered for intoxication except when driving. These laws also encourage organized crime, which provides criminalized services. Finally, these laws fail to prevent the conduct they proscribe; they may not even substantially reduce such conduct. *Decriminalization,* the legalization of such conduct, is a policy option that would permit a reallocation of criminal justice resources to crimes against persons and property.

Opponents protest, however, that the legalization of such "immoral" conduct would in effect constitute a legitimization of it, an official stamp of approval that would result in its expansion. Laws against murder do not prevent the crime from occurring, but they reduce its incidence and place society squarely in the position of saying that murder is not tolerable. It is argued that there are principles of ethical conduct that define the essence of society as a community and that society's officially sanctioned code of conduct must embody these principles.[66]

Others argue that there is a basic difference between laws proscribing crimes against persons and property and laws proscribing conduct that a dominant group finds immoral. With the former case, there is a widespread consensus on the wrongful nature of acts such as murder, robbery, and rape. With the latter, there is no such consensus on the immorality of such conduct as getting intoxicated, sexual "swinging," or homosexuality. The legislation of morality is thus an attempt to impose a moral unity in a society in which ethical pluralism is a fact of life. In fact, the toleration of such pluralism has long been held as a hallmark of an open society. Moral and philosophical homogeneity can be imposed only at the cost of considerable resources of coercion and legitimacy. If such resources are scarce and finite, the criminalization of what dominant groups consider to be immoral may have the effect of reducing society's ability to control crimes against persons and property. Therefore, one effective method to reverse the situation— to free up the criminal justice system's resources to deal with priority crimes—is to decriminalize the kinds of victimless offenses discussed in this section.

Strengthening the Police

Providing for more police or enhancing their technical law-enforcement capabilities would seem to be an effective means of deterring crime. It is not clear, however, what effective actions specifically can be taken to secure this end. Some of the most obvious innovations have been tried and shown not to be effective, as previously indicated in the discussion of the addition of police personnel as a result of the 1994 Crime Bill.

For instance, an experiment has been conducted on the effect of increasing the numbers of police in a given geographical area. Political scientist Robert Lineberry reported on an experiment in Kansas City that reduced the police presence in one section of the city, greatly increased the police presence in a second section, and left a third section unchanged with respect to police presence. The experiment failed to reveal significant differences in crime rates among the three neighborhoods.[67] The report did not deal with arrest rates, however, and the experiment was in place only a short period of time. Obviously, one study is inconclusive, and increasing the police in one area may simply displace crime to other areas. These data caution us from expecting great reductions in crime from the provisions in the Crime Bill of 1994 to fund the placing of thousands of additional police on the streets even if the doubts, previously discussed, about how many new policemen will actually be hired are resolved. It is not clear that police forces use the personnel they have in the most effective way for battling crime. For example, a large portion of police personnel's time is devoted to the enforcement of minor traffic violations, although a 1994 study shows that writing significantly fewer tickets had no effect on traffic safety. However, placing more patrolmen walking the beat in a neighborhood, one tactic instituted by former New York Mayor Rudy Giuliani, has been credited with having some impact on the sharply reduced crime rates in that city in recent years.

Increased physical paraphernalia, such as riot control vehicles, or higher police salaries and sophisticated recruitment practices have also not been shown to have a significant impact on police effectiveness. Although increasing the resources allocated to police may give the psychological satisfaction of supporting the forces of law and order, it does not hold out much promise of contributing to the goal of deterring crime.

Penal Reform, Sentencing, and Recidivism

Criticisms of the disposition of our criminal justice system to impose insufficiently harsh penalties are frequently directed at the discretion available to judges to impose sentences. The issue over whether the maximization of jail time served will in fact reduce the crime rate involves assumptions about the impact prison time served has on the criminal. It is widely assumed that discretionary sentencing has resulted in excessive leniency for serious criminals, as well as resulting in unjustly harsh sentences that depended on which judge was presiding in a given case. It is assumed, in other words, that society cannot trust judges to mete out punishments suitable to the circumstances and nature of each particular crime. These assumptions have led to a demand for a standardization in sentencing.

Mandatory sentencing at the state level may mean limiting the alternatives to jail time served, or it may mean imposing a minimum of time served before parole eligibility. However, the impact of such laws would be undercut by plea bargaining and the greater disposition to enter such bargains in the face of a mandatory sentencing law. At the federal level, an elaborate and comprehensive set of guidelines for the standardization of sentencing was enacted into law in 1987 and subsequently upheld by the courts. Of course, such federal laws have no impact on the vast preponderance of crime that involves state law, except insofar as the federal policy serves as a model for the criminal justice systems of several states.

The fact that most career criminals will serve prison time at some point in their lives renders the recidivism rate one of the more important facts about criminality. *Recidivism* is the rate at which crime is committed by people who have been convicted of previous crimes. A high recidivism rate indicates that people who have been punished for committing at least one crime have a higher probability of committing subsequent crimes than do people who have never been so punished.

One authority has estimated that as many as 80 percent of all felonies are committed by people previously convicted of other felonies; others place the rate as low as one-third.[68] Widely accepted estimates suggest that recidivists account for around 60 percent of all felonies. One study of 18,000 people arrested in 1963 found that within three years, 55 percent had been arrested again, and another study of persons arrested for robbery found that only 38 percent went back to jail within two years. Problems of definition and data gathering account for the wide variation among these statistics.

The serious implication of the high recidivism rate is that rather than deterring individuals from committing additional crimes, punishment and incarceration appear to make it more likely that they will engage in criminal behavior again. The recidivism rate attests to the failure of our prison system. Its importance be-

TABLE 6-20 ■ **Incarceration Rate per 100,000**

1985	313
1990	458
1995	601
2000	699

SOURCE: U.S. Department of Justice, Bureau of Justice Statistics, *Sourcebook for Criminal Justice Statistics,* 2000 (Hindelang Criminal Justice Research Center at SUNY Albany), p. 568.

comes even more obvious in light of the more than 800,000 people incarcerated in American prisons, and the rate at which the United States imprisons its population is increasing (see Table 6-20). We imprison citizens at rates far higher than other developed, democratic nations. The desire to curb this relentless relapse into criminality has inspired an increasing concern for the reform of the prison system.

Many charge that the prison system increases the inmates' tendency toward criminality. First, the system is seriously overcrowded. This fact in turn results in the bitterness and dehumanization that occur when people must spend years in substandard conditions. The 1994 Crime Bill allocated billions of new dollars for prison space. The new space, however, would immediately be filled by new inmates, as will similar spaces built in state prisons. Second, prisons are understaffed with respect to trained personnel who could help rehabilitate inmates. Third, improper supervision by staff and a lack of standards for choosing them results in such brutalizing experiences as beatings by guards, homosexual rape, and interracial violence.

Yet it is dangerous to characterize the prison system as if it were an undifferentiated whole. Although clearly some prisons have been notoriously brutalizing places—city jails such as the Cook County Jail in Chicago and the Tombs in New York City are frequently cited in this regard—other places are well-staffed, modern facilities that resemble college campuses as much as institutions for punishment.

Another characteristic of the prison system alluded to by its critics is a failure to prepare inmates to lead productive lives upon their release. Little is done to impart the skills needed to make the inmates more employable than when they turned to crime. There is little call in today's economy for laundry workers or license plate manufacturers.

Drugs are easily available within many prisons, and under the pressures of prison life, addicts are sometimes created. This addiction, of course, almost guarantees the subsequent criminal activity of such inmates.

Among the suggested strategies in prison reform are better vocational training and improved psychological counseling, rehabilitative services aimed at changing the circumstances in which the individual became a criminal in the first place. (This argument assumes, however, that "environment" breeds criminality, an assumption not universally accepted.) Overcrowded conditions can be addressed by building more facilities, by shorter sentences, by probated or suspended sentences, by work release programs, and by early paroles. Work release programs offer the added benefit of additional vocational training. More rigorous standards and better training for supervisory personnel and even "conjugal visits" from the mates of prisoners, which permit them to maintain a normal heterosexual life, have been suggested as means of mitigating the dehumanizing nature of the prison experience.

The controversial nature of these proposals is due in large part to confusion and ambivalence over the goals of the prison system. Liberals and many social scientists assume that the main purpose of the prison system is rehabilitative and correctional. Prisons are in fact frequently called "correctional facilities." Others stress the deterrent effect of punishment. Still others see prisons as places to house and isolate crime-prone individuals from society, thus physically preventing them from inflicting any further harm.

The kind of malevolent conditions that would seem best to fulfill the function of punishment are different from the more benevolent prison conditions frequently held to encourage rehabilitation. Therefore, those who seek to use the prisons for punishment charge that they are "schools of crime" because convicts are treated too kindly.[69] Yet many believe that by making prisons more brutal in order to punish criminals effectively, we make prisons less able to rehabilitate criminals into law-abiding citizens. The recidivism estimates previously cited are used as evidence for this interpretation. The main impediment to serious prison reform is financial. As it stands, the nation already spends over $24 billion per year on its prison system. Prison reform would almost certainly require substantial tax increases. More and more such increases are mandated by federal court decisions requiring states to end overcrowding.

Zero tolerance for petty street crime. A number of policies instituted by former New York Mayor Rudy Giuliani have been given partial credit for the sharply reduced crime rate in New York City during his administration, which ended in 2001. One of these was a policy on cracking down on vandals and graffiti artists who deface a neighborhood. Once a neighborhood became so defaced, its demographic character may change and people may take less pride in the neighborhood. Moreover, the perpetrators of such petty crimes perceive that they can and do get away with flouting the laws and standards of society. New York claims success for this zero-tolerance option.

Limiting the Alternatives to Punishment

The deterrent effect of prospective punishment is further reduced by the various mechanisms for circumventing the full weight of the law even when a person is convicted. The widespread availability of such mechanisms gives criminals reason to believe that the chances are remote that they will ever suffer the maximum punishment provided by law. These mechanisms include the defense of insanity, indeterminate sentencing with the widespread use of parole, probated or suspended sentences, and the separation of juvenile offenders from the regular criminal justice system. All of these mechanisms except the insanity defense reflect the problem of our overcrowded criminal justice system. They promote the release of inmates short of the maximum penalty provided by law, thereby freeing prison facilities for the continued influx of new inmates. *Indeterminate sentencing* means that the judge specifies a range of time for incarceration, say, two to ten years. The inmate then becomes eligible for parole any time after the minimum period is served. There is a movement to specify mandatory sentences of determinate length for certain types of crimes. Indeterminate sentencing is still the norm, however, because penologists feel that it offers the needed flexibility to fit the punishment to the unique circumstances of each case.

Parole is a process by which a convicted inmate is released from prison before serving the full extent of the sentence; a parole board decides whether an inmate can and probably will lead a socially constructive existence. Such a parolee must report for the duration of his or her sentence to a supervisory official known as a parole or probation officer. A judge may, at his or her discretion, *suspend* the sentence, in effect waiving all incarceration for the convicted criminal. The only thing the convicted criminal suffers is the onus of having the conviction on his or her record. A *probated sentence* means that incarceration is not imposed, but the judge imposes a requirement that the convicted criminal must report to a probation officer at specified intervals. Judges and juries have the discretion to hand down suspended or probated sentences for a wide range of crimes. Although this discretion clearly lowers the deterrent impact of legally possible punishment, the mandatory incarceration of all convicted felons, especially for the length of their maximum sentences, would necessitate a substantial increase in available jail space. Neoconservatives tend to favor reducing these alternatives in favor of more determinate but shorter sentences. Their motive is both for the deterrent effect (every conviction means jail) and for the retributive effect (determinate sentencing as punishment).

The question of the insanity defense came anew into prominence in 1998 when "Unabomber" suspect Ted Kaczynski was put on trial for killing and maiming numerous people with mail bombs over a seventeen-year period in protest of the perceived evils of modern technology. Kaczynski, a brilliant former mathematics professor, had dropped out and was living in the Montana wilderness in a wooden shack without plumbing. He objected to his lawyers claiming that he was innocent by reason of insanity. The legal definition is the McNaughten Rule, that the accused could not tell that the act was wrong. It was argued by some that anyone living like an animal and sending lethal bombs to strangers through the mail should be considered insane. However, others argued that he must have known his acts were "wrong" because he had to work to evade capture for seventeen years. The case showed that the finding of insanity (a legal concept) or of psychosis (a medical concept) is a very subjective enterprise; equally eminent psychologists can disagree with respect to a given case. Conservative scholars like criminal justice expert James Q. Wilson argue that too often perpetrators perceive that they can escape responsibility for their acts by claiming that they were victims of some imprecisely conceptualized pathology, especially legal insanity.[70]

Earlier we alluded to the fact that juveniles commit much of the violent crime in this country. Yet because we do not hold juveniles fully responsible for their actions, they are immune from the regular punishments of the criminal justice system. Moreover, their juvenile record does not carry over beyond their minority; they begin adulthood with a clean slate, regardless of the number or nature of their criminal acts as minors. Whatever deterrent effect the punishments of the criminal justice system may provide, it does not apply to teenagers, the age group most likely to commit crimes against persons and property.

The idea that children cannot be held responsible for their actions in the same ways as adults can appeals to our sense of fairness. After all, little children cannot be expected to possess the powers of judgment to discern right from wrong. But it is not clear that this inability to discern right from wrong also applies to people in their middle to late teens, the time of greatest criminality. Therefore, there are those who suggest that for violent and serious crimes, the laws of the regular criminal process ought to apply at a younger age. Obviously, we would not want to imprison a five-year-old, regardless of what act was perpetrated. But few would have problems with incarcerating a seventeen-year-old murderer, rapist, or mugger. It is this gray area in between where the lack of consensus exists. At what age do we draw the line? Alternatively, it has been suggested that juvenile records be carried into adulthood to establish recidivist patterns immediately upon coming of age.

Among conservatives the preferred strategy toward the crime problem is to lock up those individuals who are a threat to society and to keep them locked up. Specifically, this would involve *preventive detention* and *selective incapacitation*. The former strategy would authorize judges to deny bail to accused persons that they consider likely to commit additional crimes. The latter would target chronic offenders for long-term incarceration. Related to this is the proposal to notify communities when former sex offenders are released in their midst. Similarly, the 1994 Crime Bill contains provisions for life imprisonment for persons convicted of three federal felonies—the so-called "three strikes and you're out" principle. Versions of this principle exist in various states. Critics argue that such measures flood the prisons with aged inmates and persons convicted of nonviolent felonies. Samuel Walker argues that such strategies would fail significantly to reduce crime because of two factors: the prediction problem and the costs of incarceration.[71] The prediction problem means that we cannot really identify who is dangerous and likely to commit more crimes, and we cannot predict which criminals would likely commit violent crimes. Therefore, we would not incarcerate some who would actually commit the crimes we are trying to prevent, while we would incarcerate many people who are not really dangerous. The cost problem is that these policies would significantly increase the population of our already overcrowded prison facilities. The estimated cost for new facilities is between $45,000 and $70,000 per inmate. Costs of keeping an inmate in prison vary from $8,000 to $50,000 per inmate. Using the lower estimates, Walker calculates that the cost of implementing preventive detention and selective incapacitation over the next five years would be around $120 billion, an astronomical sum in an era of budget deficits.

SUMMARY

Rather than being a single undifferentiated phenomenon, crime comprises a variety of manifestations, each with its distinct "causes" and its own possible "cures." The causes discussed in this chapter include the following:

1. The increasing number of acts designated as crime, including the vast category of crimes against a dominant moral standard rather than against persons or property.
2. The increasing abuse of addictive drugs that in turn leads to more property crime and violent crime to support the habit.

3. The urbanization of America, the increasing percentage of the population included in the most crime-prone groups, and poverty and a pervasive sense of injustice among subordinate groups.

The most commonly prescribed cure for the problem of crime is the deterrent effect of severely punishing criminals. In this regard, many conservatives feel that the expansion of the rights of the accused by the U.S. Supreme Court has prevented the punishment of many guilty people, thereby encouraging more crime.

These rights have been expanded by the increasing incorporation of the Bill of Rights into the meaning of the Fourteenth Amendment—thereby applying them to state criminal processes—and by the broadened interpretation of the rights themselves. The most controversial expansion of the rights of the accused occurred in three areas: the right to counsel, the exclusionary rule, and capital punishment.

The expanded *right to counsel* makes it mandatory that one be informed at the point of arrest of the right to remain silent and to be provided with a lawyer by the state. The *exclusionary rule* is an interpretation of the Fourth Amendment right to be secure against unreasonable searches and seizures; it holds that illegally obtained evidence cannot be admitted in a court of law. *Capital punishment* must now be imposed according to consistent standards related to the nature of the act being punished and not in an arbitrary or capricious manner.

Most scholars believe that the swiftness and certainty of punishment, more than its severity, deter crime. Factors other than the rights of the accused have most often impeded this swiftness and certainty of punishment. The one exception to this is the right of juveniles not to be held fully responsible for their acts and therefore not to be tried and punished as adults. These factors include the low probability that the perpetrator of any given crime will be arrested; the overcrowded criminal justice system that requires plea bargaining, light sentences, early parole, and probated and suspended sentences; diversion of the police and prosecutors to the enforcement of "victimless crimes"; and the principle fundamental to the criminal justice system, granting the benefit of the doubt to the accused. There is little evidence to support the proposition that crime has been encouraged by the expansion of the rights of the accused.

Yet crime remains a serious problem calling for some effective remedies from the makers of public policy. Several policy options and their potential effectiveness have been presented. Among those with the most promise are the expansion of both our judicial and prison systems, combined with the decriminalization of truly consensual behavior among adults to cope with the impact of overcrowded court and jail systems; and some constraints on who may own certain types of firearms. Unfortunately, these are, for political and cultural reasons, among the options most difficult to implement. Other choices, such as buying more hardware for law enforcement or employing more police officers, have shown little impact on the crime problem. These choices, being simpler and less costly, have great appeal, although they are less effective. Reforming the juvenile justice system, harsher sentences, and federal criminal laws made up the centerpiece of crime-control debates. The public itself will have to face these choices and decide whether it wants to pay the ideological and economic costs of confronting the crime problem in the 1990s.

NOTES

1. Federal Bureau of Investigation, *Uniform Crime Reports, 2000.*

2. These figures are from *The New York Times,* on the Internet, December 21, 2001.

3. *The Lubbock Avalanche Journal,* December 21, 2001, p. 14A. The article speculates that an increased police presence in Manhattan in the wake of September 11th events may have contributed to the lower crime rates in that borough.

4. FBI, *Uniform Crime Reports,* 39.

5. U.S. Bureau of the Census, *Statistical Abstract of the United States,* 100th ed. (Washington, DC: U.S. Government Printing Office, 1978), 177.

6. Federal Bureau of Investigation, *Uniform Crime Reports, 1996* (Washington, DC: U.S. Government Printing Office), 204.

7. Mark Green, Beverly Moore, and Bruce Wasserstein, "Criminal Law and Corporate Disorder," in Jerome Skolnick and Elliot Currie, eds., *Crisis in American Institutions,* 4th ed. (Boston: Little Brown, 1979), 527–547.

8. The figures for the Enron scandal are drawn from *Newsweek,* January 21, 2002, 19–25.

9. Cited in Michael Parenti, *Democracy for the Few,* 2nd ed. (New York: St. Martin's Press, 1980), 122. See David Hellman, *The Economics of Crime* (New York: St. Martin's Press, 1980), Table 2–1, 23.

10. James Q. Wilson, *Thinking about Crime,* rev. ed. (New York: Basic Books, 1983), especially Chapter 2.

11. Hellman, *Economics of Crime,* 147.

12. CQ Researcher, *Issues for Debate in American Public Policy* (Washington, DC: CQ Press, 1999), 205.

13. Cited in Samuel Walker, *Sense and Nonsense about Crime,* 2nd ed. (Pacific Grove, Calif.: Brooks-Cole, 1989), 38 and 55.

14. For example, see John Dollard, et al., *Frustration and Aggression* (New Haven, CT: Yale University Press, 1939); and Ivo K. and Rosalind Feierabend, "Systemic Conditions of Political Aggression: An Application of the Frustration-Aggression Theory," in Ivo Feierabend, Rosalind Feierabend, and Ted Gurr, eds., *Anger, Violence and Politics* (Englewood Cliffs: Prentice-Hall, 1972), 136–183.

15. Edward Banfield, *The Unheavenly City* (Boston: Little Brown, 1970), 172; Earl Moses, "Differentials in Crime Rates between Negroes and Whites based on Comparisons of Four Economically Equated Areas," *American Sociological Revue,* 12 (August, 1974): 411–420.

16. Stephen and Abigail Thernstrom, *America in Black and White, One Nation Indivisible: Race in Modern America* (New York: Simon & Schuster, 1997), 280.

17. Thernstrom and Thernstrom, *America in Black and White,* 263–264.

18. Cited in Thernstrom and Thernstrom, *America in Black and White,* 268.

19. Paul Butler, "Racially based Jury Nullification: Black Power in the Criminal Justice System," *Yale Law Journal,* 105 (December, 1995), 677.

20. *Powell v. Alabama,* 287 U.S. 45 (1932).

21. *Gideon v. Wainwright,* 372 U.S. 335 (1963).

22. The Court has ruled that once a guilty plea has been entered under such a plea bargain, the prosecution's side of the bargain must be kept. Failure by the prosecution to keep its bargain will cause the conviction to be vacated. *Santobello v. New York,* 404 U.S. 257 (1971).

23. *Escobedo v. Illinois,* 378 U.S. 478 (1964).

24. *Miranda v. Arizona,* 384 U.S. 436 (1966).

25. *Mapp v. Ohio,* 367 U.S. 643 (1961).

26. *Nix v. Williams,* 104 S. Ct. 2501 (1984); *U.S. v. Leon,* 104 S. Ct. 3430 (1984).

27. See the argument that the criminal justice system must be perceived as "just" in James Q. Wilson and Richard Herrnstein, *Crime and Human Nature* (New York: Simon & Schuster, 1985), 506–507.

28. Thorsten Sellin, *The Penalty of Death* (Beverly Hills: Sage Publications, 1980), 80–81.

29. U.S. Department of Justice, Federal Bureau of Investigation, *Sourcebook on Criminal Justice Statistics, 2000,* 147.

30. Isaac Ehrlich, "The Deterrent Effect of Capital Punishment: A Question of Life and Death," *American Economic Review,* 65 (June, 1975), 398; Peter Passell and John Taylor, "The Deterrence Controversy: A Reconsideration of the Time Series Evidence," in Chester Pierce and Hugo Bedau, eds., *Capital Punishment in the United States* (New York: AMS Press, 1976), 359; Sellin, *Penalty of Death,* Chapter 10.

31. These data are from Sellin, *Penalty of Death*, 52.

32. Guy Johnson, "The Negro and Crime," *Annals of the American Academy of Political and Social Science*, 217 (1941), 100. Cited in *Furman v. Georgia*, 408 U.S. 32 (1972).

33. Cited in Thernstrom and Thernstrom, *America in Black and White*, 275.

34. Cited in *Dallas Time Herald*, November 17, 1985; *McCleskey v. Kemp*, 107 S. Ct. 1756 (1987).

35. 408 U.S. 32 (1972).

36. James Ridella, "Miranda: One Year Later—The Effects," *Public Management*, 49 (July, 1967), 183–190. This author found that in data drawn from St. Louis less than 1 percent of those arrested have been freed on *Miranda* grounds.

37. Richard Seeburger and Stanley Wetlick, "Miranda in Pittsburgh: A Statistical Study," in Theodore Becker and Malcolm Freely, eds., *The Impact of Supreme Court Decisions*, 2nd ed. (New York: Oxford University Press, 1973), 154.

38. Stephen Wasby, *The Impact of the United States Supreme Court: Some Perspectives* (Homewood, IL: Dorsey Press, 1970), 156.

39. Richard Medalie, Leonard Zeits, and Paul Alexander, "Custodial Police Interrogation in Our Nation's Capital: The Attempt to Implement Miranda," *Michigan Law Revue*, 66 (May, 1968), 1347–1422.

40. *Harris v. New York*, 401 U.S. 222 (1971); *Oregon v. Haas*, 420 U.S. 714; *Brown v. Illinois*, 422 U.S. 590.

41. Wasby, *Impact*, 162; Stuart Nagel, *The Legal Process from a Behavioral Perspective* (Homewood, IL: Dorsey Press, 1969), 314.

42. *Chimel v. California*, 394 U.S. 752 (1969).

43. *Terry v. Ohio*, 392 U.S. 1 (1968); *Sibron v. New York*, 392 U.S. 40 (1968).

44. *Katz v. United States*, 389 U.S. 347 (1967). Wiretaps can be used under a warrant requested by the Justice Department or when the president makes a demonstrable finding that national security is at stake. Such a finding is, however, subject to judicial scrutiny.

45. *Proffit v. Florida*, 49 L. Ed. 2nd. 913 (1976); *Gregg v. Georgia*, 428 U.S. 153 (1976); *Jurek v. Texas*, 49 L. Ed. 2nd. 929 (1976).

46. Justice Marshall in *Furman*, 408 U.S. 238, at 329; Brennan at 269.

47. *Thompson v. Oklahoma*, 108 S. Ct. 2687 (1988).

48. 107 S. Ct. 2716 (1987).

49. 108 S. Ct. 1453 (1988).

50. *Booth v. Maryland*, 107 S. Ct. 2529 (1987); *Payne v. Tennessee*, 59 LW 4814 (1991).

51. *McCleskey v. Zant*, 59 LW 4288 (1991); *Coleman v. Thompson*, 59 LW 4789 (1991); *Yost v. Nunnemaker*, 59 LW 4809 (1991).

52. Attributed to Norval Morris as reported in Norton Long, "The City as Reservation," *Public Interest*, 25 (Fall, 1971), 31.

53. Wilson, *Thinking about Crime*, 118.

54. Wayne H. Thomas, *Bail Reform in America* (Berkeley: University of California Press, 1976).

55. Hellman, *Economics of Crime*, 49.

56. Alexander Smith and Harriet Pollach, *Some Sins Are Not Crimes* (New York: New Viewpoints, 1975), 100.

57. Cited in Smith and Pollach, *Some Sins*, 104.

58. Andrea Parrot and Laurie Bechofer, *Acquaintance Rape: The Hidden Crime* (New York: John Wiley, 1991), 15.

59. Susan Brownmiller, *Against Our Will: Men, Women, and Rape* (New York: Simon & Schuster, 1975), 15; Andrea Dworkin, *Intercourse* (New York: Free Press, 1980), 125–126.

60. Murray Strauss and Richard Gelles, *Intimate Violence: The Causes and Consequences of Abuse in the U.S. Family* (New York: Simon & Schuster, 1989).

61. Susan Estrich, *Real Rape: How the Legal System Victimizes Women Who Say No* (Cambridge, MA: Harvard University Press, 1987), 102.

62. Figures are from a study from the Violence Policy Center, cited in the *Lubbock Avalanche-Journal*, January 14, 1998, A1.

63. This discussion of the weakness of the crime bill is drawn from Stephen Glass, "The Anatomy of a Policy Fraud," *The New Republic* (November 17, 1987): 22–25.

64. Glass, "Anatomy."

65. Source in Table 6-19.

66. For this kind of argument, see, e.g., Clarke Cochran, "Authority and Community," *American Political Science Review*, 71 (June, 1977): 546–558.

67. Robert Lineberry, *American Public Policy* (New York: Harper & Row, 1977), 189.

68. Daniel Glaser, "The Effectiveness of a Prison Parole System," cited in Vergil Williams, *Dictionary of American Penology* (Westbrook, CT: Greenwood Press, 1979), 217–219.

69. For example, Clark, *Crime,* Chapter 13; Lockard, *Perverted Priorities,* 306.

70. James Q. Wilson, *Moral Judgment: Does the Abuse Excuse Threaten Our Legal System?* (New York: Basic Books, 1997). See also Charles Sykes, *A Nation of Victims* (New York: St. Martin's Press, 1992).

71. Walker, *Sense and Nonsense,* 79.

SUGGESTED READINGS

Books and Articles

Banner, Stuart. *The Death Penalty: An American History*. Cambridge: Harvard University Press, 2002.

Berns, Walter. *For Capital Punishment: Crime and Morality of the Death Penalty*. New York: Basic Books, 1979.

Cole, George. *Criminal Justice: Law and Politics,* 4th ed. Pacific Grove, CA: Brooks-Cole, 1984.

Gelles, Murray, and Strauss, Richard. *Intimate Violence: The Causes and Consequences of Abuse in the American Family*. New York: Simon & Schuster, 1989.

Hellman, David. *The Economics of Crime*. New York: St. Martin's Press, 1980.

Jacob, Herbert. *The Frustration of Policy: Responses to Crime by American Cities*. Boston: Little, Brown, 1984.

Jenkins, Phillip. *Crime and Justice, Issues and Ideas*. Pacific Grove, CA: Brooks-Cole, 1984.

Schur, Edwin. *Crime Without Victims*. Englewood Cliffs, NJ: Prentice-Hall, 1965.

Sellin, Thorsten. *The Penalty of Death*. Beverly Hills, CA: Sage Publications, 1980.

Smith, Alexander, and Polloch, Harriet. *Some Sins Are Not Crimes*. New York: New Viewpoints, 1975.

Sutherland, Edward. *White Collar Crime*. New York: Holt, Rinehart & Winston, 1949.

Sykes, Charles. *A Nation of Victims*. New York: St. Martin's Press, 1992.

Tullock, Gordon. "Does Punishment Deter Crime?" *Public Interest,* 36 (Summer 1974): 103–111.

Van Den Haag, Ernest, and Conrad, John B. *The Death Penalty: A Debate*. New York: Plenum, 1984.

Walker, Samuel. *Sense and Nonsense about Crime,* 2nd ed. Pacific Grove, CA: Brooks-Cole, 1989.

Wilson, James Q. *Moral Judgment: Does the Abuse Excuse Threaten Our Legal System?* New York: Basic Books, 1997.

Wilson, James Q. *Thinking about Crime,* 2nd ed. New York: Basic Books, 1984.

Web Sites

American Civil Liberties Union   www.aclu.org

Federal Bureau of Investigation Uniform Crime Report   www.fbi.gov/ucr/00cius.htm

Handgun Control   www.bradycampaign.org

Moratorium Campaign (Death Penalty)   www.moratorium2000.org

National Rifle Association   www.nra.org

Pro-death Penalty.com   www.prodeathpenalty.com

Public Agenda   www.publicagenda.org

Restorative Justice Online   www.restorativejustice.org

CHAPTER 7

Income Support: Security, Work, or Dependence?

Social welfare programs cover a broad range of activities, including Social Security, public assistance, job training, public health, unemployment compensation, and education. This chapter discusses the following: *social insurance programs,* which provide for the aged, disabled, widowed and orphaned, and unemployed; *public assistance programs,* which aim to alleviate poverty for those not covered by social insurance; and *work/employment programs,* designed to provide jobs, job training, or other assistance to those needing help to lift themselves out of poverty. Collectively, these programs are *income maintenance* or *income support programs.* The following two chapters cover other social programs. The policies discussed here and the health policies discussed in the next chapter constitute over half of all federal spending.

ISSUE BACKGROUND: RESPONDING TO POVERTY

Income support programs intend to provide security for persons unable to support themselves because of old age, disability, or temporary unemployment. They attempt to alleviate poverty where possible and to assure an income sufficient for a decent standard of living. They assume that most persons are able and willing to work to support themselves. Yet these programs also reflect the fear of having to support people who do not want to work and anxieties about making people dependent upon government. The goals of income support are in conflict. A decent standard of living guaranteed by government can promote dependency, but something lower than such a standard leaves many citizens mired in poverty.

Defining Poverty

Poverty may be defined in absolute or relative terms. An absolute definition specifies a minimal level of well-being in nutrition, shelter, clothing, health, and so on and then determines what income is sufficient to maintain this level, taking into account family size and perhaps other factors, such as ages of family members and location of the family residence. This minimum level fluctuates with inflation and the general standard of living. Though always tied to the cost of material goods, this minimum income level also implies psychic consequences for those living below its standards:

> Poverty should be defined psychologically in terms of those whose place in the society is such that they are internal exiles who, almost inevitably, develop attitudes of defeat and pessimism and who are therefore excluded from taking advantage of new opportunities.[1]

Feelings of helplessness and powerlessness in the face of overwhelming political, economic, and social forces and personal tragedies help keep such persons mired in poverty.

Relative definitions of poverty do not specify a particular level of material well-being, but compare the poor to other members of society. In this definition a family is poor if its resources place it well below the average standard of living. Most relative definitions define poverty as any family income below one-half the nation's median family income.

The type of definition chosen makes a big difference in evaluating policy. Under most absolute definitions, poverty has varied in the last thirty-five years, but under relative definitions, the proportion of poor Americans has remained constant, with the gap between the wealthy and the poor widening.

Absolute definitions. The most widely used measure of poverty is the Social Security Administration (SSA) figure. This figure is calculated each year from an early 1960s formula based on multiplying the Department of Agriculture's Economy Food Plan by three (the "multiplier"), on the assumption that a poor family of four at that time spent one-third of its income for food. This figure is updated each year and is calculated for different family sizes. Thus, the poverty guideline for a family of four in 2002 was $18,100. (The poverty guidelines in 2001 ranged from $8,860 for a one-person family to $30,420 for an eight-person family.) The SSA figure is compared with the income levels of the population as reported by the Bureau of the Census, and the number and percentage of persons below the poverty level are calculated (see Table 7-1).

Although the SSA standard is the most widely cited and is the official definition for all government statistics on poverty, its value has been severely criticized by liberal and radical students of poverty. Their basic argument can be condensed into four points. First, the food budget central to the calculation allots (in 2001) only about $4 per person per day for food. This food budget, they argue, is inadequate for long-term good nutrition and health. Second, the SSA standard does not take account of regional variations in cost of living. Third, the SSA standard is adjusted annually according to the Consumer Price Index rather than to the actual cost of food. Finally, the multiplier is artificially low; poor people today actually spend about a quarter of their income on food, sometimes needing to spend up to half on shelter. For all these reasons, liberals argue, the official poverty figure is too low, substantially underestimating the number of poor in America and the government effort needed to eliminate poverty.

There are other ways of computing the poverty line.[2] For example, the same multipliers as the SSA standards applied to a more generous food plan would set the poverty line approximately 25 percent higher than the SSA, meaning that poverty for a family of four in 2002 would have been approximately $22,500. Because SSA estimates are very low, a sound case can be made for this approach.

TABLE 7-1 ▪ **Number and Percentage of Persons below the SSA Poverty Standard**

	Non-Hispanic White (millions)	African American (millions)	Spanish Origin (millions)	Total (millions)	Percent of Population
1960	n/a	9.9	n/a	39.8	22.2
1965	n/a	8.9	n/a	33.2	17.3
1970	n/a	7.5	n/a	25.4	12.6
1975	14.9	7.5	3.0	25.9	12.3
1980	16.4	8.6	3.5	29.3	13.0
1985	17.8	8.9	5.2	33.1	14.0
1990	16.6	9.8	6.0	33.6	13.5
1995	16.3	9.9	8.6	36.4	13.8
2000	14.6	7.9	7.2	31.1	11.3

SOURCE: U.S. Bureau of the Census, *Current Population Reports,* Series P-60, No. 214: *Poverty in the United States, 2000* (Washington, DC: U.S. Government Printing Office, 2001), Table A-1 (see www.census.gov/hhes/www/poverty.html).

Using this standard, 44 million persons, or 16 percent of the population, were considered poor in 1998.[3]

Relative definitions. Many policy analysts favor relative definitions of poverty because they focus on the inequality of income and wealth. A family is poor, many argue, if its income is insufficient to bring it close to the current median standard of living in society. In the last forty years, a constant one-fifth of the population has been in poverty; that is, about 20 percent of families earn less than half the median income. In 2000, median family income was $50,891, and about 23 percent of families earned less than half that sum. As Table 7-2 indicates, the lowest fifth of the population consistently receives under 5 percent of the national income. The distribution of wealth is even more unequal, with the wealthiest 20 percent consistently controlling over 90 percent of corporate stock and 70 percent of total wealth. Moreover, after a long period of stability, wealth inequality began to rise in the 1980s. The richest 1 percent currently holds 25 percent of wealth.[4] The measure of income concentration has shown no significant change, and the United States has the largest gap between rich and poor of any modern democracy. Indeed, the most recent years witnessed a growing inequality of income distribution. From 1950 to 1980, the lower income groups remained stable or increased their share of national income; from 1985 to 2000, however, every group's share shrank except for the richest (see Table 7-2 and Figure 7-1). In 1973, the typical thirty-year-old man could make payments on a median-priced home with 21 percent of his salary. By 1984, these payments would have taken 44 percent. Between 1979 and 1997, the average after-tax income of the poorest 20 percent of the population *declined* from $10,900 annually to $10,800 (in constant 1997 dollars). The average income of the wealthiest 20 percent *rose* 53 percent (from $79,100 to $121,000). The three middle quintiles saw modest gains during this period of 6, 10, and 17 percent, respectively.[5]

The United States is now in a situation of rising economic inequality, complicated by changing demography. For example, if two wage earners making

TABLE 7-2 ▪ Share of Aggregate Family Income (unrelated individuals excluded)

	Poorest 20 Percent	Second 20 Percent	Third 20 Percent	Fourth 20 Percent	Richest 20 Percent	Richest 5 Percent
1947	5.0	11.9	17.0	23.1	43.0	17.5
1950	4.5	12.0	17.4	23.4	42.7	17.3
1955	4.8	12.3	17.8	23.7	41.3	16.4
1960	4.8	12.2	17.8	24.0	41.3	15.9
1965	5.2	12.2	17.8	23.9	40.9	15.5
1970	5.4	12.2	17.6	23.8	40.9	15.6
1975	5.6	11.9	17.7	24.2	40.7	14.9
1980	5.3	11.6	17.6	24.4	41.1	14.6
1985	4.8	11.0	16.9	24.3	43.1	16.1
1990	4.6	10.8	16.6	23.8	44.3	17.4
1995	4.4	10.1	15.8	23.2	46.5	20.0
2000	4.3	9.8	15.5	22.8	47.4	20.8

SOURCE: U.S. Census Bureau, *Current Population Reports,* P60-213 (www.census.gov/hhes/income/histinc/f02.html; accessed 1/4/02).

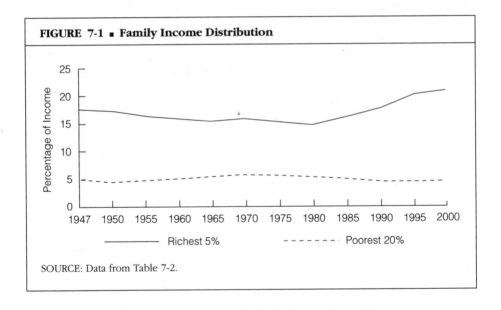

FIGURE 7-1 ▪ Family Income Distribution

SOURCE: Data from Table 7-2.

$40,000 each marry, they create one well-to-do family out of two middle-income families. If divorce occurs in a family earning the median income, it creates two families—one likely to be poor—out of one.

The ideological context is important here. Use of a relative measure of poverty, conservatives and neoconservatives point out, has certain disadvantages. First, welfare benefits, only partly counted as income, encourage single-parent families to set up independent households, biasing the figures toward the low end. Second, concentrating on percentages and on the low end of the scale falsi-

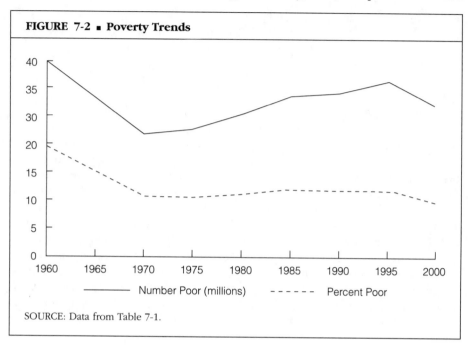

FIGURE 7-2 ▪ Poverty Trends

Number Poor (millions) ————— Percent Poor - - - - -

SOURCE: Data from Table 7-1.

fies the income picture. Opponents of the relative approach to poverty argue that the facts cited are misleading and that poverty should not be confused with inequality. Many families in the top 20 percent are not *rich,* having incomes in the $92,000 to $110,000 range. (In 2000 the income range for the top 20 percent began at $91,700. The top 5 percent began at $160,250.)

How Many Poor?

Debates over the definition of poverty link with disagreements about the cause of poverty and the number of poor persons in America. In the income support arena, problem definition is robustly disputed. As can be seen from Figure 7-2, SSA-defined poverty declined sharply between 1959 and 1970, from 40 million poor (22 percent of the population) to 25 million poor (13 percent); since that time, however, the poverty rate remained relatively constant at 13 to 14 percent, until the most recent years. In 2001, 32 million persons (11.7 percent of the population) fell below the poverty threshold.

Disagreements about poverty definitions in the early 1990s led Congress to appoint a panel from the National Academy of Sciences to study the problems and to propose a new definition. When the panel reported its findings in April 1995, it recommended a poverty index based on disposable income, the amount of money left after a family pays taxes and essential expenses. Under this proposed definition, government cash benefits and such noncash benefits as food stamps, housing subsidies, and school lunches would be counted as income. However, poverty calculations would deduct from cash income such necessary expenses as taxes, child care, medical payments, and work costs. The panel also recommended adjusting the poverty threshold for geographic differences in housing

costs. Adoption of its recommendations would produce a poverty rate approximately 2 percent higher than the SSA definition. Congress rejected these recommendations, and the old guidelines are still in use.

The Census Bureau data used in Figure 7-2 disguise a basic reality generally
accepted by both conservative and liberal economists. These data reflect pretax
cash income, including government transfer payments. That is, social insurance
and public assistance cash benefits are counted as family income. Thus, if by
"poverty" one refers to income earned without government help, removing cash
payments from the measure reveals that nearly 20 percent of the population is
poor, even at the very low SSA definition of poverty. Thus, one quarter of the entire American population is unable to avoid poverty without government help.
Radicals use this figure to indict the American economic system. However, the official poverty figures do not take account of the income value of in-kind benefits,
such as medical care and food stamps, or employer-provided health care or other
benefits, nor are they adjusted for the tendency of people to underreport income.
Adjusting for these factors leaves about 8 to 10 percent of the population as poor,
a figure cited in support of the enormous success of income maintenance and job
programs. Thus, although official statistics disguise the number of persons highly
dependent on government aid, they also hide the success of federal programs in
reducing poverty. (Data on the effect of different ways of counting appear in
Table 7-3.)

Who Are the Poor?

The incidence of poverty does not fall evenly across the nation; particular areas,
groups, and classes bear a far higher incidence of poverty than others. Although a
majority of the poor are white, the incidence of poverty is higher among racial minorities, reflecting racial prejudice, low job skills, and poor education. Although only
7.5 percent of non-Hispanic whites are poor, 21 percent of Hispanics and 22 percent of African Americans are poor. Poverty among Native Americans is even higher.

Age is also associated with poverty. The poverty statistics include a substantial number of elderly widows attempting to live on meager Social Security,
pension, and public assistance checks. Although government cash (chiefly Social

TABLE 7-3 ▪ Effects of Taxes and Government Transfers on Poverty

	Persons in Poverty (millions)	Percent of Persons in Poverty
1. Current definition	31.1	11.3
2. Current without government transfers	51.3	18.6
3. Definition 2 with EITC and payroll taxes	48.3	17.5
4. Definition 3 with means-tested cash transfers	27.9	10.1
5. Definition 4 with means-tested in-kind transfers	23.9	8.7

SOURCE: U.S. Census Bureau, *Historical Poverty Tables,* Table 5 (www.census.gov/hhes/
poverty/poverty00/table5.html; accessed 1/4/02).

Security) and in-kind benefits reduced poverty among the elderly to 10 percent, youth poverty is alarming. Benefits to the elderly, principally Social Security, are generally indexed to keep pace with inflation. Benefits for others are not indexed and therefore decline over time in terms of real purchasing power. Almost 40 percent of the poor are under eighteen. Over 16 percent of children under age eighteen live in poverty. Some analysts estimate that half of American children under age three are at risk of abuse, poverty, or lack of care.

There is increasing reason to refer to the "feminization of poverty." The majority of the poor now live in female-headed families, and the number of such families is growing, with 25 percent (versus 5 percent of two-parent families) classified as poor (including one-third of African-American and Hispanic female-headed families). About half of poor families are now headed by women, compared with 26 percent in 1960.

The feminization of poverty reflects the demographic trends discussed in Chapter 1. High rates of divorce and illegitimacy place more women with small children in poverty. Lacking adequate child care facilities and so unable to work full-time and care for their children, they fall below the poverty line. Sometimes these women do work full-time, but at jobs that do not pay enough to support their families.[6] For most of these female-headed households, poverty is a painful but temporary phenomenon that lasts until marriage or remarriage places them in a two-earner situation. Yet for many it is a more or less permanent condition. Single parenthood has dire consequences for future generations with respect to education, illegitimacy, and welfare dependency.[7] Figures 7-3 and 7-4 present some of the disturbing statistics on families and poverty.

Poverty also correlates with education and residence. Persons lacking a high school diploma are disproportionately poor, as are those who live in the core of large metropolitan cities and in rural areas. The rural poor are more chronically poor than the urban poor, more dispersed, and less likely to use public assistance.

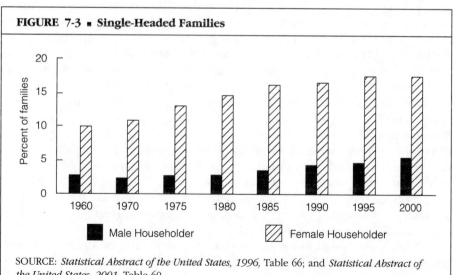

FIGURE 7-3 ▪ Single-Headed Families

SOURCE: *Statistical Abstract of the United States, 1996,* Table 66; and *Statistical Abstract of the United States, 2001,* Table 60.

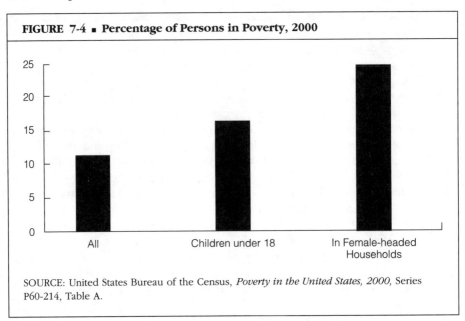

FIGURE 7-4 ▪ Percentage of Persons in Poverty, 2000

SOURCE: United States Bureau of the Census, *Poverty in the United States, 2000,* Series P60-214, Table A.

Poverty is also regional. The states with the highest rates of poverty (greater than 20 percent) lie largely in the South: Mississippi, Louisiana, New Mexico, Kentucky, Alabama, and the District of Columbia.

Despite stereotypes, very few of the poor are lazy, work-avoiding, welfare dependents. Except for mothers staying at home to care for small children, most of the poor work either full- or part-time or have become unemployed because of technological changes. Many workers in low-skill jobs are in or near poverty because of low wages, seasonal work, and frequent layoffs. For example, a person working full-time for fifty-two weeks at the 2002 federal minimum wage of $5.15 an hour would have an income of $10,712. This is nearly $7,500 below poverty level for a family of four persons. Such people also lack opportunities for advancement. Thus, despite very low unemployment in the late 1990s, food banks nationally reported increasing hunger and requests for food. For the working poor, wages do not support families without recourse to public and private charity. Nearly half of low-income families (below 200 percent of poverty) report difficulty affording food; about one-third report an inability to pay rent or mortgage during at least one month per year; both rates are far higher than for those with higher incomes. As we shall see in the following chapter, low-income working families tend to lack health insurance, and they have higher levels of anxiety and depression. Older workers who lose their jobs through recession or technological change are unlikely to find new employment at the same pay. Accompanying this dismal employment picture are feelings of rejection, defeat, and powerlessness. Mental illness has a higher incidence among the poor.

The persistence of poverty reflects a complex conjunction of factors. First, demographic trends swell the ranks of the elderly, of female-headed households, and of young adults. These groups tend to be at the low end of employability. Similarly, declining blue-collar manufacturing jobs, expanding part-time and temporary employment, and growing income inequality contribute to poverty. However, the larger number of two-income families helps to offset these trends. Finally, government programs of income support, especially programs targeted at the elderly, push poverty rates down. The result of these countervailing forces is a poverty rate varying between 11 and 13 percent.

Particularly in large cities there is a small but growing "underclass" barely touched by income support policies. Members of this class are unskilled, uneducated residents of the most dismal slums. For most poor persons poverty is temporary; the population fluctuates as some climb out of poverty, and some briefly fall into it. But the underclass lives year in and year out in a culture of poverty, presenting the greatest challenge to social welfare policy.

The Causes of Poverty

Conservative views. Conservatives argue that there is little involuntary poverty in the United States. Those who wish to work and to achieve a decent standard of living can do so by taking advantage of the free-enterprise system's opportunities. For those unable to work, because of age, physical handicap, or other disability, sufficient resources exist from social insurance programs and private philanthropy. The poor who are adult and healthy are, in this view, poor because they lack the self-discipline to work hard, save, and to delay immediate pleasures for a better future—that is, the poor choose not to pursue the educational and employment opportunities available to everyone. Conservatives also attribute these supposed qualities of the poor to a "culture of poverty." Individual poor persons learn these attitudes from the culture around them, which teaches satisfaction with a life of casual social relationships, irresponsibility, immediate gratification, and sexual license. The religious right cites the decline of moral standards leading to family breakup, drug use, unwed pregnancy, and other social disorders.

Conservatives and neoconservatives argue that traditional government welfare programs cannot prevent or cure poverty because they do nothing to change the basic attitudinal causes of poverty. In fact, these persons contend, government programs have the unintended consequence of encouraging persons to remain in poverty by guaranteeing support for this way of life. These programs encourage families to break up; reward sexual license by increasing benefits for additional, often illegitimate, children; and make only very weak work demands on recipients. Cheating and fraud are rampant in public assistance programs in the view of many conservatives.

Liberal views. Liberals and progressives dispute the notion that the attitudes of the poor make them responsible for their poverty. They argue, instead, that the poor are no different from the nonpoor; they simply lack the opportunities for education, employment, job training, and decent housing. If they had such opportunities, they would take advantage of them. There is no firm evidence, they argue, that government programs decrease work effort, increase illegitimacy, or promote family breakup.

Liberals emphasize that the opportunities offered to the poor must be real. Job-training programs must provide salable skills, not temporary, menial work with no future. The basic liberal premise is that lack of genuine opportunity is the root cause of poverty. Sometimes liberals accept a variation of the conservative "culture of poverty" argument. They insist, however, that the source of this culture lies in a realistic assessment by the poor of their chances for success in a society and economy structured against them. Changing that structure could break the cycle of poverty.

According to liberal theory, racial discrimination against African Americans, Hispanics, and other minority groups and sexual discrimination against women are important causes of poverty among these groups. Discrimination affects progress in school, employment choices, job advancement, wages, and housing conditions. Racial minorities and women have high poverty rates because of the pervasive discrimination they still suffer.

Liberals also see poverty as a result of the harmful side effects, the indirect costs, of a capitalist, free-enterprise economy. Economic progress makes job skills obsolete, swelling the ranks of the unemployed. The pay for less-skilled jobs falls so low that even some full-time workers do not make a wage high enough to keep their families out of poverty.

Radical views. Marxists and socialists agree with much of the liberal analysis of the causes of poverty, but they see the roots of its family strife, unemployment, and discrimination lying deep within the American socioeconomic system itself. Capitalism, such radicals argue, necessitates a large proportion of poor persons, because it exists to create wealth for a small group of property owners. Poverty is necessary in a capitalist society because it provides a large pool of surplus labor to do menial and dirty tasks and to keep general wages low. Fear of the hardship and shame of poverty keeps the middle class hardworking and subservient to the attitudes and desires of the upper class. The culture of poverty is also useful to the middle and upper classes, as it offers them such outlets as gambling, prostitution, and charity work. Moreover, the violence, crime, and immorality of the poor provide a convenient focus for moral indignation, neatly deflecting attention from the corruption, injustice, and crass materialism of capitalist culture.

Welfare is publicly distributed in ways that keep it demeaning and despised, whereas handouts for the rich are dignified in hidden tax loopholes, investment credits, loans and loan guarantees, and government grants and contracts, especially for military purposes. Radicals scoff at the potential of government programs to create jobs and economic expansion. Such tactics will not work because poverty is built into the structure of the economy itself; only radical economic change can attack poverty.

Recent changes in the causes of poverty. Whatever the differences of opinion among ideological groups concerning the fundamental causes of poverty, it is clear that certain changes in the last two decades contributed to the persistence of poverty at relatively high levels.

First, the real earnings of high school graduates and high school dropouts declined significantly beginning in the late 1970s. At the same time, the real wages of college graduates rose rapidly. This fact contributed to the growing gap between the wealthy and the poor. It also means that jobs with low educational qualifications are less able to keep families above the poverty or near-poverty level.

Second, despite steady economic growth for most of the 1990s, corporate downsizing and the decline of semi-skilled, relatively high-wage jobs produced stagnant income levels in the middle class and persistent unemployment in the lower class. The recession of 2001 to 2002 wiped out some gains from the long economic expansion of the 1990s. Families go into poverty when the primary breadwinner loses employment or when one working parent in a two-worker family loses a job.

Finally, handicapping conditions discussed in other chapters, such as violent crime, drug addiction, poor schools, unplanned pregnancy, and poor health, produce high obstacles to gainful employment. It is difficult even in booming economic times to escape these handicaps.

Dozens of federal programs provide social insurance, public assistance, and employment assistance to Americans. These are the *outputs* of income support policy. They range from huge programs, such as Old Age, Survivors, and Disability Insurance (Social Security) to relatively small programs, such as the Women, Infants and Children nutrition program. Expenditures total over $600 billion per year, and administration is complex and confusing. Many programs are joint federal-state ventures, requiring fifty different sets of regulations and bureaucracies. At the federal level alone, jurisdiction is divided among numerous committees in the House of Representatives and the Senate and among various executive departments and agencies. The majority of federal aid recipients benefit from two or more programs, with most receiving aid from three.

The Welfare State

The United States is not a welfare state in the way that term is normally understood, despite the extensive welfare programs just described. It is important to understand the difference in approach to social welfare between the United States and Western Europe. With the exception of public education, government social services in the United States, including cash assistance, social insurance, nutrition, health care, and housing, focus on the concept of the deserving poor and therefore employ minimum-income criteria (means-tests) or the recipient's previous self-contributions (as in Social Security). Although the means-test does exist in Great Britain, Sweden, France, the Netherlands, and other welfare states, it plays a far smaller role than in the United States. The essential feature of the European welfare state is that it aims to guarantee a generous minimum standard of life through social services, education, public assistance, social insurance, and employment programs to all citizens as a political right, not as charity.[8] In Western Europe, subsidized housing, health services, child care, employment, and other benefits are available not only to the poor, as in the United States, but to all or most citizens.

The basic programs of social insurance—retirement, disability, and unemployment compensation—are similar across nations. Public assistance to the aged, blind, disabled, and children is universal, as are job training and retraining and job creation programs.[9]

There are, however, significant divergences between American policy and policy in other countries. Nations such as Sweden and Germany, among others, have more extensive programs of sick leave and maternity benefits, and all have programs of family or children's allowances, which, in effect, provide assistance to poor families without the stigma of public assistance. Subsidized housing and child care for extensive segments of the population are available in Europe, providing decent low-cost housing for the poor and freeing mothers to work. Pressures in the European welfare system are building, however. Housing shortages are increasingly common, and there is a constant demand for expansion of child care facilities as more women enter the labor force. Chronic high unemployment, rising income support expenditures, and budget crises have forced many European countries to look toward reduction of "welfare state" spending or reorganization of programs.

The United States has been consistently last in establishing welfare and income support programs, and its funding of them remains at a level well below that of most other developed nations. Rates of participation among those eligible for public assistance are higher in Europe than in the United States. Case workers actively seek to enroll eligible people, but in the United States there is a widespread attitude that public assistance should be difficult to obtain, even for those who qualify. The United States may be more properly described as an "opportunity-insurance state,"[10] in which the focus is on making opportunities for success available to the vast majority of citizens and on rewarding those who succeed. Minimal public assistance programs partially cushion those who fail.

This difference in approaches to public programs to assist the poor, combined with lower wage rates for full-time workers in the United States, produce higher levels of poverty than most other economically prosperous nations. Although cross-national comparisons of absolute and relative poverty are difficult, it does appear that despite its greater economic prosperity than the nations of Europe, Japan, and Australia, poverty in the United States is from 50 percent to nearly 100 percent higher than the average in such nations, depending on the measure used.[11]

Income support in both the United States and Europe extends far beyond the "needy poor" definition of programs discussed in this chapter. The modern state supports the income and the standard of living of the wealthy and the middle class to an even greater extent than it does the poor. Government grants, loans, loan guarantees, and subsidies to farmers, transportation companies, small businesses, large corporations, trade associations, and thousands of other interests help to prop up the incomes of workers, managers, and owners. Income support is a way of life throughout modern nations, accounting for a good deal of the political support and legitimacy of modern governments. The policies considered in this chapter are only a part of these endeavors. The following pages first consider programs of social insurance, their successes and failures, and reform proposals. It then considers programs of public assistance.

CONTEMPORARY POLICY: SOCIAL INSURANCE PROGRAMS

During the 1930s the widespread poverty, hardship, and unemployment of the Great Depression stimulated the first large-scale federal income support programs. President Franklin D. Roosevelt proposed, and Congress enacted, the Social Security Act of 1935 as the centerpiece of federal efforts. The act's social insurance provisions are the parents of today's Old Age, Survivors, and Disability Insurance (OASDI), popularly known as "Social Security."

Social insurance programs are based on contributions (by both employees and employers) to a trust fund. The only persons eligible to receive benefits are those persons, or their dependents, who have contributed to the program. Benefits are paid out of contributions on the basis of contribution amount and need. Social insurance programs are not, strictly speaking, antipoverty programs, because benefits go to contributors who in many cases are quite well-to-do. They are, however, antipoverty programs in one sense, because their primary goal is to prevent individuals and families from falling into poverty in the event of old age, disability, temporary unemployment, or the death of a family's breadwinner. The Social Security law requires workers to purchase insurance against these possibilities.

Social Security

Originally a retirement program only, Social Security added survivors' benefits in 1939 and disability insurance in 1956. Health insurance (Medicare, covered in Chapter 8) was added in 1965. Today Social Security constitutes the largest single item of federal spending. It covers over 90 percent of the working population, including the self-employed. Over 15 percent of the population (about 45 million persons) currently receive benefits; expenditures are about 25 percent of federal spending; and Social Security taxes account for about one-quarter of all federal revenues. In addition to the Social Security program covering most workers, the federal government also administers special retirement programs for federal workers, railroad employees, and veterans. These programs constitute the vast bulk of government *entitlement* spending; that is, benefits to which persons have a legal right because they meet program criteria. This chapter describes only Social Security; the other pension programs, however, offer similar challenges.

The program is administered by the Social Security Administration, an independent federal agency, headed by a Commissioner and Deputy Commissioner, advised by a seven-member, bipartisan advisory board. This status and independence signify political support for Social Security and the political power of its growing number of aged recipients.

OASDI is financed by a payroll tax, in theory paid in equal shares by employer and employee. Most economists, however, believe that the burden of the employer's share is nearly always passed on to the employee in the form of lower wages. The bulk of the tax goes to two trust funds, Old Age and Survivors' Insurance, and Disability Insurance, which finance the benefits paid out of these programs. Originally set quite low, both the payroll tax rate and the wage base on which it is applied have steadily risen, from the original 1 percent each for employer and employee on the first $3,000 of wages to 6.20 percent each on a wage base of $84,900 in 2002. (In addition, Medicare imposes a tax of 1.45 percent on *all* wages, without an upper limit. This portion goes to a Hospital Insurance Trust Fund, discussed in Chapter 8.) The most rapid increases have come in the last twenty-five years.

Benefits under OASDI follow a complicated formula using the worker's previous average monthly earnings and a schedule that pays higher percentages of average earnings for lower income brackets. Thus, the highest-paid workers receive higher benefit amounts up to the maximum amount, but lower-paid workers receive higher percentages of their average wages in

TABLE 7-4 ▪ Monthly Benefits and Beneficiaries under OASDI

	OAS Recipients (in thousands)	Monthly OAS Benefits (in $ millions)	Average Benefit (retired worker)	Disability Recipients (in thousands)	Monthly Disability Benefits Paid (in $ millions)	Average Benefit (disabled worker)
1940	223	4	$ 23	n/a	n/a	n/a
1950	3,477	127	44	n/a	n/a	n/a
1960	14,157	888	74	688	48	$ 89
1970	23,567	2,386	118	2,665	242	131
1980	30,936	9,432	341	4,682	1,262	371
1985	33,151	14,442	479	3,907	1,460	484
1990	35,566	19,717	603	4,257	1,970	587
1995	37,530	24,993	720	5,858	3,155	682
2001	38,889	30,772	848	6,780	4,427	789

SOURCE: *Social Security Bulletin,* 59 (Winter 1996), Tables 1.B.1 and 1.B.2; and OASDI Fact Sheet, June 30, 2001 (www.ssa.gov/OACT/FACTS/fs2001_06.html).

monthly benefits. In 2001 the average benefit for a retired worker was $848 per month (with a maximum of $1,536 per month). Disability benefits are calculated in a similar way. A divorced spouse (male or female) can receive benefits on a former husband's or wife's Social Security record if the marriage lasted at least ten years. The divorced spouse must be at least sixty-two and unmarried and must wait until two years after the divorce to receive benefits for the first time.

Benefits and expenditures have risen rapidly with growth in the number of aged recipients, their longer life span, and liberalized definitions of disability (see Table 7-4 and Figure 7-5). Inflation is also an important factor, because benefit levels have been indexed since 1972 to increases in the cost of living through cost-of-living adjustments (COLAs). Total OASDI expenditures were about $430 billion in 2001. It is important to note that Social Security benefits are not the only source of income for retired workers and their dependents, particularly those who have earned high wages. Private retirement plans have proliferated in recent decades, and Congress acted in 1974 to ensure retirees' rights to benefits and the financial integrity of such plans.

Unemployment Insurance

Unemployment compensation is the other principal form of social insurance. Its purpose is to maintain the income of workers in periods of involuntary unemployment. About 90 percent of all employed persons are covered. The program provides a federal tax incentive for each state to establish and administer its own program. Thus, unlike OASDI, unemployment insurance is financed and administered at the state level, under general federal guidelines. Taxes are paid by employers based on their payrolls and prior experience with unemployment. Thus,

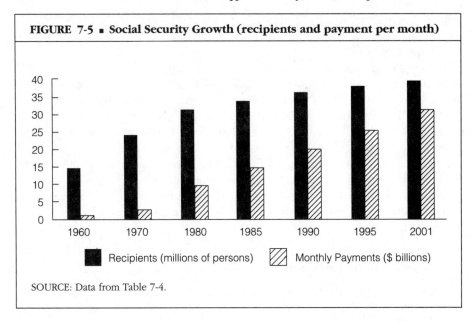

FIGURE 7-5 ■ Social Security Growth (recipients and payment per month)

■ Recipients (millions of persons)   ▨ Monthly Payments ($ billions)

SOURCE: Data from Table 7-4.

tax rates and benefit levels vary from state to state, as does the duration of eligibility for benefits. Persons receiving aid are required to accept a "suitable" job if one is offered, and states must have job counseling and job placement programs. An average of 2.2 million persons per week received benefits in 1999. Congress frequently extends the duration of unemployment insurance benefits and adds special supplements to meet emergency needs during recessionary periods. The cost of unemployment compensation was $21 billion in 1999. State-administered Workers' Compensation programs also help ensure against the loss of income. In 1998, Workers' Compensation medical benefit payments were $15.9 billion; wage loss compensation totaled $25.8 billion.

POLICY EVALUATION: DOES SOCIAL SECURITY STILL WORK?

Social Security Successes

Although social insurance spending greatly exceeds spending for public assistance programs, until the late 1970s it generated comparatively little controversy. First, these programs, particularly OASDI, have a good record of accomplishing their goals. Moreover, because benefits are related to the self-contribution mechanism under the insurance aspect of OASDI and unemployment compensation, they are compatible with American value systems. Most see benefits as returns on an investment, albeit a mandatory one, rather than a handout.[12]

OASDI and unemployment insurance have done a good job of keeping recipients out of poverty, particularly when combined with tax breaks, private pensions, and other benefits, such as SSI, Medicare, Medicaid, and food stamps, for which beneficiaries may also be eligible. Social Security helps to keep the elderly poverty rate lower than the national average. Social Security gives retirees, survivors, and the disabled a fair return on their investment, as most can expect to receive more in benefits than their taxes. Current retirees, especially those with lower incomes, will likely recoup their payroll tax contributions rapidly.[13]

Despite fears of many younger workers that the Social Security system will be bankrupt by the time they retire, Congress regularly acts to ensure its financial stability. In 1983, for example, Congress raised the tax rate and the wage base for Social Security contributions and mandated a gradual increase in the retirement age from sixty-five to sixty-six by 2009 and to sixty-seven by 2027. At the same time, it subjected to federal taxation half of the Social Security benefits of high-income retirees (retired individuals with incomes over $30,000 in 2001). These provisions will keep the program solvent until the late 2020s. In the next decade, Social Security will require further adjustments to maintain solvency. The Future Alternatives section describes proposed program changes.

The Social Security Dilemma

Despite the generally acknowledged success of social insurance programs in meeting the goals intended, there are serious issues and controversies, particularly with respect to long-term financing. Social Security has become a major public issue. OASDI is financed, unlike private insurance programs, on a pay-as-you-go basis. Taxes paid into the system go into trust funds, but these funds do not have large enough reserves to cover benefits. As a result, taxes collected each year are expended for benefits in that same year. The taxes of those currently working pay the benefits of the retired. This situation caused no problem so long as benefits were low and the ratio of active workers to beneficiaries was high. The crisis developed when benefits began to expand rapidly because of inflation and a high wage-replacement rate, and it has deepened as the number of retirees has grown and their life spans increased. The financial crisis has been exacerbated by a rapid rise in disability claims as definitions of disability expanded, allowing, for example, substantial claims for psychological incapacity to work. Moreover, the majority of persons now retire with partial Social Security benefits between age sixty-two and sixty-five.

The pay-as-you-go nature of Social Security means that it is a compact between generations. The present generation in effect agrees to pay for its predecessor's retirement if the following generation will agree to pay for the present generation's retirement. The problem is that economic fluctuations within a particular time period can affect the relative well-being of the generations and the ability of the present generation to tax itself to pay benefits. Moreover, in the long run, the fact that the generations are of different sizes has enormous implications. As birthrates remain low and life spans lengthen, the number of workers will shrink relative to the number of retirees, straining their ability to pay the taxes necessary to support the system. Although there are three workers today for every beneficiary, in thirty years there will be only two, or possibly fewer. It must be noted, however, that because of women's entry into the labor force, a larger proportion of the population will be working in the future than at present, and there will be proportionally fewer children for workers to support. Therefore, total dependency on workers will not change appreciably in the future.

Indexation of benefits to the cost of living and high wage-replacement rates encourage early retirement and less work after retirement. This reduces economic output in the economy as a whole. Finally, the large sums absorbed by Social Security reduce private savings and thus the level of capital available for economic investment. The political clout of the elderly helps to maintain benefit levels. These problems are endemic to the social security systems of all developed nations.[14] The crisis in Social Security, then, is as much political as it is economic. It is a crisis of confidence and trust in the system's ability to continue paying benefits through the economic and demographic changes of the coming decades. It also challenges the ability of Congress and the president to fashion policy changes in the midst of strong and conflicting political pressures. They must choose to reduce the growth of benefits, to increase Social Security taxes, or to make major structural changes in a popular program.

Is Social Security Fair?

The fairness issue stems from a basic disagreement over the goals of OASDI: whether policy should aim at the equity of taxes and benefits or at the adequacy of benefits to cover retirement needs. Equity means that benefits should be proportioned to taxes paid into OASDI: the more a person pays, the more he or she should receive on retirement. Conservatives, who stress equity as the most important element of OASDI, argue that the program should be placed on an insurance basis and that benefits paid out should reflect taxes paid in. Moreover, recent increases in the wage base have made for serious equity problems. Higher-income persons, who are paying considerably more in Social Security taxes, may not receive in benefits as much as they contribute. Some conservatives go so far as to argue that, because the system may not in the future give upper income retirees a fair return on their contributions, they should be allowed to opt out and to have the Social Security contributions placed in individual retirement accounts. Liberals and radicals stress the adequacy of benefits. Adequacy means that benefits should be sufficient to keep recipients out of poverty; that is, they should be linked to current need rather than past contributions. Lower-income workers should receive proportionately higher benefits upon their death, disability, or retirement—in other words, more than they had contributed. Liberal supporters of adequacy are not satisfied with benefits either, because OASDI for the poorest workers must often be supplemented by public assistance programs and because 60 percent of all OASDI benefits go to those already above the poverty line. OASDI embodied these contradictory goals from its beginning, but there was little friction until recently because, as long as financing was no problem, both goals could be met.

In addition to the recent financial problems, the growing gap between financially secure and poor elderly persons exacerbates the equity-adequacy problem. The income of most of the elderly has improved substantially in recent years, especially for those with pensions and savings in addition to Social Security benefits. But those whose retirement depends entirely or largely on Social Security exist at or below the poverty line. A two-class system among the elderly is increasingly a reality, particularly among elderly women, who have lower Social

Security incomes because of their generally lower wages than men and because they typically work fewer years than men, taking time off to raise children.

Unemployment Compensation

Unemployment insurance benefits and wage replacement rates vary from state to state, but are generally sufficient to support the temporary unemployment they were designed for, particularly when combined with the benefits available from some unions and from public assistance. Long-term unemployment is a more serious problem, but the unemployment insurance system was never intended to handle it.

However, fewer than half of the unemployed (currently about 38 percent) receive unemployment compensation because of eligibility restrictions and limited benefit periods. Unemployment insurance is of most help to those with stable work histories and good prospects for finding a new position rapidly. Those with weak job skills and erratic work experience frequently find themselves ineligible for benefits. Low benefit levels and complex eligibility requirements also discourage many low-income workers from applying when they become unemployed.

These problems of unemployment compensation have become increasingly evident as the American economy goes through fundamental restructuring. Many unemployed persons are not readily qualified for jobs that require new skills or higher education. Moreover, part-time and temporary workers are not eligible for unemployment benefits, and the numbers of these persons losing their jobs has jumped. Longer-term proposals for reform in unemployment compensation call for increasing the wage base for the unemployment tax in order to build up sufficient funds to cover more persons for longer periods of job searching.[15]

FUTURE ALTERNATIVES: THE DIFFICULTY OF SOCIAL SECURITY REFORM

The Future of Social Security

Perhaps the most pressing Social Security issue is the relationship between the Trust Funds and the federal budget. Because of the 1983 Social Security reforms, the OASDI and Disability Trust Funds build up surpluses each year. By 2001, the surpluses were in excess of $150 billion per year. These surpluses will occur until approximately 2020, totaling an estimated $3.5 trillion by that year. That enormous sum of money will help pay the Social Security benefits of the baby-boom generation, but these payments will exhaust Trust Fund balances by the year 2040, at which time taxes would have to be raised to generate funds to pay full benefits.

All of this seems a long way off. What is the immediate problem? Simply this: The Social Security surplus counts against the surplus or deficit generated by current spending and taxing. Thus, if the OASDI Trust Fund surplus were not counted, the 2001 budget, for example, would have a $33 billion deficit, instead of a $160 billion surplus. Moreover, the Trust Funds are invested in the government securities that fund the national debt. That is, we borrowed from the Trust Funds, especially Social Security, to support deficit spending in the 1980s and 1990s. When surpluses appeared in the late 1990s and early 2000s, it appeared that they could be used to reduce the federal debt, taking pressure off the Trust Funds. But the reappearance of deficits in 2002 makes that very difficult. The borrowed funds will eventually have to be paid back (ultimately to the tune of over $3 trillion) when the Trust Funds have to be used to pay retirees. That will require an enormous tax hike or other borrowing from the general public. Having said this, it is important to recognize that the economy will not remain static over the next few decades. If the productivity and output of the economy grow by as much as 1 percent per year on the average, Social Security and other taxes could be raised enough to cover requirements and still leave the average family with more disposable income than at present. But all projections of future economic performance, demographic trends, and Trust Fund expenditures are highly uncertain, especially those forty to seventy-five years in the future.

There are four different directions for significant changes to meet Social Security's equity, adequacy, and long-term financing issues. The first two do not require fundamental changes; the second two would alter Social Security's basic structure. A sharply divided Advisory Council on Social Security that reported to President Clinton in 1997 considered most of these.[16] President Bush appointed a new Social Security reform commission intended to produce a report favoring the fourth option (privatization). The commission supported that option in a late 2001 report.

Quick Fixes

Two strategies can be worked singly or in combination. The *first* is to increase tax revenues to keep the system solvent. Raising the payroll tax on employer and employee from the present 6.2 percent each to a little over 7 percent each would provide enough additional revenue to keep the system solvent for another seventy-five years. However, it would require the politically difficult step of raising taxes and would be challenged particularly by younger workers, who would pay far more in Social Security taxes over their working lives. Additional funds could also be raised by keeping the tax rate the same, but increasing the salary cap from the current $84,900 per year. This would go against the interests of upper-income earners, unless their benefits were substantially increased upon retirement. Therefore, this alternative has little political support.

Second, minor changes in Social Security could stretch out the available funds. Such changes include raising the Social Security and Medicare retirement age from the current sixty-five to age seventy for persons currently under age twenty-eight, or to accelerate the age sixty-seven retirement policy. (Retirement age is scheduled to begin rising gradually to sixty-seven. By 2027, full retirement age will be sixty-seven for persons born after 1959.) Other proposals place heavier penalties on early retirement at age sixty-two or increase taxes on benefits to middle- and upper-income retirees, thus introducing additional means-testing into Social Security. Additional minor change options are gradual reduction in benefits by 1 percent per year or changing the COLA to inflation minus 1 percent in order to reduce the upward adjustment in benefits over time. Each of these options makes sense in terms of the long life spans of the elderly today, in terms of the way that current measures overstate actual inflation, and in terms of the value of sharing widely the pain of achieving solvency. Each, however, also generates considerable opposition from current retirees and those close to retirement. All of these options implicitly reduce benefits for future retirees.

Two other minor changes could be combined with either of the previous options or with the options that follow; both are widely recognized as important: increasing the minimum benefit for lower-income workers and providing greater protection for divorced spouses and surviving spouses. Both measures have wide political support, but would increase program expenditures if enacted.

Diversifying Social Security Investment

The *third* reform proposal is major: Change the program's structure by building up a genuine reserve fund through investing part of the Social Security Trust Fund in the private stock and bond market. The argument here is that real reserves must be built up now to avoid a huge bill coming due in the next forty years. Private securities historically earn a higher rate of return than government bonds. Proponents of this option also argue that high rates of return in the stock market would allow Social Security in the future to raise everyone's benefit checks substantially, thereby increasing both equity for high-income earners and adequacy for lower income earners. Federal, state, and local governments currently invest large retirement funds for government employees without significant negative effects. The chief drawback of this proposal is its risk. Government trust funds, though low in return, are guaranteed. Private stocks and bonds are not. Their fluctuations over time could mean that some retirees do far better than others, simply based on the fortunes of the market at the time they retire. Moreover, this plan would involve Social Security employees investing huge sums of public money in private securities markets, running the risk of losses and distortions in the stock market.

Privatizing Social Security

In the most recent period, political momentum points to a *fourth* alternative. Demographic trends, flat wages, the growing influence of conservative principles, and the dire projections of Social Security's collapse combined to increase support for elements of choice and competition in Social Security that would partially replace the present system with a combination of mandatory private pensions and increased public assistance. The least radical of these proposals would take 1 to 2 percent of the current 6.2 percent payroll deduction, and allow individuals to open retirement accounts to be managed by each worker and retiree under some government guidelines. The promise of this strategy is higher returns for all and the accumulation of a "nest egg" that can be passed on to one's survivors, unlike current Social Security. It also encourages individual responsibility for retirement and expands popular access to financial markets. Banks, financial institutions, and stock brokers strongly support this idea, seeing an opportunity for managing a major influx of capital. The stock market slump of 2001–2002 weakened support for this option.

Yet privatizing any portion of the program draws significant objections. One focuses on the risk of poor management and hence lost retirement funds if individuals are left free to make their own investment decisions. If there are too many program rules to reduce risk, however, then government would in effect be doing the investing. There is also a major issue of transition costs. The most common estimate is $1 trillion. If the 1 to 2 percent were subtracted to be invested now for current workers, what would replace those funds to pay for the benefits of current retirees? The answer once was: the budget surplus, but that has become a deficit for the next few years, and surplus projections for the next ten years are quite modest. The administrative costs of private accounts are also substantially higher than the current collective management of Social Security. Finally, if retirees miscalculate and withdraw too much money from their accounts in their early retirement years, they could live long enough to exhaust their investment funds. What happens then?

A more radical proposal is to abolish Social Security altogether. Abolition would replace the entire system with individual retirement accounts. This option means even more substantial transitional costs over a long period of time. The more radical option also would reduce the "we're all in this together" political support for Social Security, perhaps leading to greater distrust and fragmentation over time.

Three facts must be kept in mind with respect to any of these four options. First, Social Security does not exist alone and is not only a retirement program. Underneath Social Security is the Supplemental Security Income program, food stamps, and other programs supporting low-income persons. Any change in Social Security will effect these programs as well. Second, retired workers and their spouses are only 70 percent of beneficiaries; the others are surviving spouses and their children, and disabled workers and their dependents. Changes to make Social Security better for retirees should not adversely affect other parts of the program. Third, the massive size of Social Security has effects on the entire economy and the national savings rate (see Chapter 4). Any proposed changes must evaluate positive and negative economic consequences. The very size of the Social Security program in revenues, expenditures, and number of participants means that any basic change would be a major disruption of political, economic, and social systems, and of the lives and expectations of millions of persons. Thus, the larger the changes proposed, the more politically unlikely they become.

Pensions

As noted in the Evaluation section, private pensions have become a major part of the resources of the elderly, in many cases outweighing Social Security. In 1974, Congress created the Employee Retirement Income Security Act (ERISA) as a federal guarantee for many private pension funds. ERISA intended to ensure that pension funds would indeed be available at retirement time for those counting on them. This legislation, however, insures only about one of every eight pension plans covering about half of all workers. Other workers have little or no insurance for their pension funds.

Two problems loom on the horizon.[17] First, the long trend toward growing numbers of workers covered by pensions reversed itself in the late 1980s. Currently, only about 44 percent of the work force has a pension plan. About 50 million workers have no pension coverage whatsoever. This is especially a problem for small businesses, with only 25 percent coverage. Moreover, for those now receiving pensions (about 40 percent of Americans sixty-five and older), the average benefit is less than $10,000 per year. Additionally, current pension plans are increasingly "defined contribution," or 401(k) plans. Poor investment decisions or overinvestment in particular stocks, as in the Enron debacle, can devastate the value of these plans. Moreover, since workers can withdraw money early, there is a danger that in the future more and more workers will retire without adequate private pensions. About one-third of such funds are withdrawn early for education, cars, vacations, and medical expenses. At the present time, Social Security plus traditional employer pensions produce a retirement income equal to 65 percent of preretirement pay for the typical worker; but Social Security plus 401(k) savings produce less than 50 percent of preretirement pay. If these trends continue, more workers will depend primarily on Social Security in the future.

Second, the pension industry has significant financial troubles. The United States has almost 700,000 private pension plans, with assets of nearly $7 trillion, covering 95 million persons. In some cases, adequate funds have not been placed into the pensions, or funds have been siphoned off by administrators to cover business losses or to pay other business expenses. Other plans fail when a company goes bankrupt. When a guaranteed pension plan fails, it becomes the responsibility of the federal Pension Benefit Guaranty Corporation to bail it out. The federal government itself, however, has seriously underfunded its own pension plans, just as its obligations to retirees are expanding.

CONTEMPORARY POLICY: PUBLIC ASSISTANCE PROGRAMS

Public assistance, generally thought of as *welfare,* intends to help certain categories of persons whose circumstances place them in poverty. Its goal is to assist families temporarily unable to support themselves and persons ineligible for social insurance, but needing help because of age or disability. Much thinking about the poor in Anglo-American history reflects the assumption that public assistance should go only to people who deserve it; that is, those not responsible for their own poverty. Thus, public assistance has traditionally been available to children and to adults who are aged, blind, disabled, or to guardians of small children. Adults who are none of these are assumed to be undeserving and are seldom eligible for assistance.

Federal programs to assist the poor have their origins as far back as the Social Security Act of 1935. There is little coordination among these programs, and gaps in coverage are substantial. General tax revenues pay for public assistance programs, and any person who is a member of an eligibility category may receive benefits. The use of eligibility categories generates the term *categorical programs.* Benefits are related not to previous earnings but to present need. In the jargon, they are *means-tested.* Examples of public assistance programs are Supplemental Security Income (SSI), food stamps, and Temporary Assistance to Needy Families (TANF).

Public assistance programs come in two forms, *cash assistance* and *in-kind assistance.* Cash assistance is simply a transfer of money from a government agency to an individual—a Supplemental Security Income check, for example. In-kind assistance refers to programs in which a tangible benefit, but not cash, is given to the recipient. Food stamps, for example, are convertible into food but not into money, and Medicaid provides direct health care. Assistance to the poor also comes in the form of services. Examples are marital counseling, literacy training, job training, family planning, and foster care.

Cash Assistance Programs

The four main categorical, means-tested cash assistance programs available to the general public are: Temporary Assistance to Needy Families (TANF), Supplemental Security Income (SSI), the Earned Income Tax Credit (EITC), and General assistance.[18]

Welfare reform. Cash assistance programs changed radically with 1996's welfare reform legislation. TANF, the program most persons have in mind when they speak of welfare, is jointly funded by the states and the federal government and administered by state or local welfare departments under federal regulations. It replaced the former Aid to Families with Dependent Children (AFDC). Although federal law guaranteed recipients some minimum income under AFDC, each state agency set its own standard of need for food, clothing, and shelter, and AFDC payments were calculated on this formula. Families with countable incomes below that standard were eligible for aid, but states were not required to pay benefits at 100 percent of need, and few did. For example, the median state's *standard of need* in 1993 was $867 per month, which was 87 percent of the poverty line for a family of three. Because of the joint federal-state structure and provisions of the funding formula, benefit levels and eligibility varied widely from state to state. Families generally could receive benefits for as long as their income level made them eligible.

Some states began to take a more aggressive stance regarding public assistance in the late 1980s. They experimented with a variety of incentives and punishments to encourage AFDC recipients to find jobs and leave welfare. Wisconsin had the most visible profile, instituting a "Learnfare" program. Learnfare required children thirteen to nineteen from welfare families to attend school regularly. Benefits could be cut up to $100 per month if children were truant. The "Wisconsin Works" plan included strong work requirements and sanctions on those who did not work. Other states adopted regulations that required teenage mothers on public assistance to live with a parent or guardian and to attend school, on penalty of benefit reduction. Others increased benefits for public assistance parents who married or for women who accepted long-term birth control implants, as an incentive to break the cycle of single-parent families. In 1991 New Jersey adopted regulations denying benefits to children born while the family received public assistance.

The national political pressures to reform public assistance became intense during the 1990s. The election of a Republican Congress in 1994, combined with a Democratic president already disposed to reform from his experience as Governor of Arkansas, produced fundamental reform in August of 1996. The "Personal Responsibility and Work Opportunity Reconciliation Act" (PRWOR) eliminated the AFDC program and modified other pieces of the public assistance framework. This legislation, fully implemented during 1997, turned responsibility for cash assistance for families and children to the states. PRWOR replaced AFDC with TANF, a totally new system of block grants enabling states to design their own cash assistance programs. PRWOR ended the federal *entitlement* to assistance and imposed new work requirements and time limits on recipients.[19]

The goals of PRWOR were very ambitious: (1) to assist needy families so that children can be cared for in their own or in relatives' homes; (2) to end welfare dependency by promoting work and marriage; (3) to reduce unwed pregnancy; and (4) to promote two-parent families.

TANF provisions.   Instead of reimbursing the states for expenditures linked to eligible individuals, TANF is a *block grant* to the states of approximately $16 billion per year through FY 2001. Each state's part of the $16 billion depends on its previous AFDC spending. States have wide discretion in determining who is eligible for assistance under TANF and in setting various requirements for recipients. In addition, there are incentive grants to help states reduce out-of-wedlock births, to help states with fast-growing populations or high unemployment, and to reward states successful in moving welfare recipients to work.

Some federal requirements remain. States must appropriate from their own taxes at least 75 percent of the funds that they previously spent on AFDC. Adults (with few exceptions) receiving TANF must begin working within two years of receiving assistance. Single parents must work at least thirty hours per week. The states must have at least 50 percent of their former caseloads engaged in work. States missing these targets have their block grants reduced. Jobs taken as part of the work requirement provisions must pay at least minimum wage and carry the normal benefits that the employer gives to other employees.

Time limits are a major TANF provision. States may not use federal TANF funds for adults who have received welfare for more than a cumulative total of five years in their lifetime or for adults who do not work after two years of assistance. States may impose shorter time limits and may exempt up to 20 percent of their caseload from the five-year time limit (reflecting the reality that many adults are so limited in their abilities as to be nearly impossible to employ). States also may deny assistance to unwed mothers under eighteen and to children born to TANF recipients. Recognizing the importance of health insurance coverage for the working poor, PRWOR requires the states to continue to offer Medicaid coverage for one year to TANF recipients who lose cash assistance because of increased earnings from work.

TANF marks a fundamental change in public assistance. No longer is the *federal* government directly responsible for the support of poor families. Rather, a new federalism devolves this responsibility to the states. Moreover, TANF is not an *entitlement*. If state and federal money appropriated to fund the program runs out before the end of the fiscal year or before all persons receive their benefits, those eligible have no guarantee of support. Moreover, states are free under TANF to divert some funds from income support to pregnancy prevention, job training, or other services. There is also no guarantee that devolution of responsibility must stop at the state level. States can transfer financial responsibility to county or city governments. Some states have contracted with private businesses to perform eligibility and other functions formerly done by state employees.

Child care assistance is vital for public assistance recipients seeking to find and keep employment. PRWOR folds all major federal child care programs into the existing Child Care and Development block grant. Federal funding rose to nearly $3 billion by 2002. States must use at least 70 percent of the funds to help welfare recipients seeking work or those at risk of needing welfare.

PRWOR included a special provision that encourages states to contract with private not-for-profit groups, including religious organizations, to provide child care, work training, and other social services for TANF recipients. This was called "Charitable Choice," and it formed the foundation for President Bush's proposal in early 2001 to reform the basis of many social assistance programs. He wished to make it easier for federal agencies and for state agencies implementing federal public assistance laws to form partnerships with religious and other private organizations with the same goals—helping those in need. Bush's *Faith-Based and Community Initiative* encountered strong resistance based on different ideas of church-state relations. Congress debated it in highly diluted form in 2002.

The strong economy of the late 1990s made it possible for many former welfare recipients to find work. The economy, plus TANF provisions, produced a dramatic decline in public assistance enrollment (see Figure 7-6). PRWOR expires after six years, so it must be either re-authorized or changed before the end of 2002. The following sections evaluate this new program of public assistance and its likely future.

Supplemental Security Income. The SSI program began in 1974. SSI replaced the jumble of state and federal programs for the aged, blind, and disabled with a single, centrally administered program. It is the only guaranteed minimum-income program in the United States funded from general revenues. The Social Security Administration sets benefit levels, adjusting them annually for cost-of-living increases. In 2000, a couple with no other income received a maximum of $769 per month, though the average benefit per couple is under $400. An individual without other income received $512 per month.

Despite the expectation of one simplified, consolidated program, SSI has turned out to be quite complicated. First, the benefits have been insufficient, with

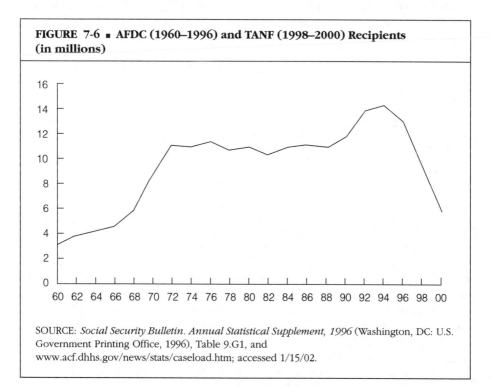

FIGURE 7-6 ▪ **AFDC (1960–1996) and TANF (1998–2000) Recipients (in millions)**

SOURCE: *Social Security Bulletin. Annual Statistical Supplement, 1996* (Washington, DC: U.S. Government Printing Office, 1996), Table 9.G1, and www.acf.dhhs.gov/news/stats/caseload.htm; accessed 1/15/02.

benefit levels low enough that most states supplement SSI with their own funds. Second, the federal government is not the only administrator; most states administer their supplemental programs directly. Third, SSI supplements OASDI when its payments are below SSI standards. In fact, over 70 percent of all aged recipients and nearly 30 percent of all blind and disabled recipients use SSI to supplement Social Security. Federal and state SSI expenditures totaled $31 billion in 1999 for 6.6 million recipients.

Earned Income Tax Credit. Another major form of federal cash assistance is the EITC, which is important to low-income working families. Under the EITC the taxpayer receives a tax credit from the government for each dollar earned up to a certain point; the credits gradually phase out as income rises. This credit is refunded to eligible taxpayers who claim it on their income tax forms. The EITC provides a benefit of anywhere from a few hundred dollars to a maximum of $4,000, as of 2001. This program is a very important part of antipoverty efforts, because it rewards persons who work, a strong emphasis for both Democrats and Republicans. EITC is now the largest federal, means-tested cash benefit program, and sixteen states have adopted a state EITC linked to federal benefits.

In 2000, for families with two or more children, a worker's earnings up to $32,131 generated minimal credit, with the largest credits going to those earning under $15,000. That year approximately 20 million tax filers received credits amounting to $31 billion dollars (an increase from $11.4 billion for 14 million filers in 1991).

General assistance. General assistance refers to wholly state-funded and administered programs that help individuals, usually on an emergency basis, not eligible for other types of cash aid. Virtually all states have such programs, but expenditures are quite modest, amounting to less than $3 billion for about 1 million persons.

In-Kind Benefits

Public assistance in the form of in-kind benefits now constitutes a higher proportion of public assistance than cash benefits. *Medicaid* is the largest in-kind public assistance program. It is described in Chapter 8.

Food stamps. Food stamps are the most significant in-kind benefit available to the poor. Families below certain income levels receive coupons redeemable in grocery stores (for food items only). The fact that cash does not go directly to recipients reveals basic assumptions about welfare and poverty in America, rooted in the desire to see the poor adequately fed but also in a distrust of their spending habits.

The program is administered by the Department of Agriculture, which pays the entire cost of the coupons and almost two-thirds of the state's administrative costs. Benefits follow the price of food, the cost of a decent diet, family size, and income. Most recipients between the ages of eighteen and fifty now must work an average of twenty hours per week in order to receive food stamps. PRWOR requires states to terminate food stamp benefits after three months in any thirty-six-month period for any such recipients not working or participating in employment programs, although states may exempt 15 percent of such recipients. States also have the discretion to align food stamps with TANF and other parts of public assistance, creating a uniform set of eligibility and work requirements. They may also convert food stamp benefits to wage subsidies for employers who hire recipients, partly explaining the recent decrease in persons receiving food stamps.

Because eligibility guidelines differ from the income levels in cash assistance programs, many persons ineligible for the latter are eligible for food stamps. Because TANF and SSI income are counted in determining eligibility, persons in states with high TANF and SSI benefits receive fewer food coupons, and vice versa. This feature of the program tends to narrow the interstate disparities of cash assistance. The food stamp program is very sensitive to changes in the economy; in times of recession and unemployment the program expands rapidly. Federal expenditures for food stamps totaled approximately $18 billion in 2001 (see Figure 7-7). The average number of recipients was about 17 million, a reduction of 10 million from the program's peak in 1994. Still, 40 percent of those eligible by virtue of low incomes do not receive benefits, many because they are unaware of their eligibility. The federal government also operates other, smaller nutrition programs, such as the Women, Infants, and Children (WIC) program and the school lunch and breakfast programs.

Housing. Millions of Americans live in substandard, dilapidated, and overcrowded dwellings. Various programs of housing assistance stretch as far back as 1937. Examples are public housing, rural farm labor housing, rent and mortgage subsidies, the Community Development Program, and neighborhood rehabilitation. All attempt, in one way or another, to restore urban and rural housing and to provide decent shelter for low-income persons. Yet federal housing aid makes only a small contribution toward this goal.

Although the Farmers Home Administration operates some rural programs, most housing programs come under the authority of the Department of Housing

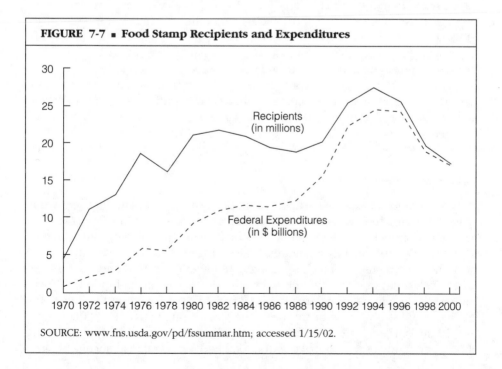

FIGURE 7-7 ▪ Food Stamp Recipients and Expenditures

SOURCE: www.fns.usda.gov/pd/fssummar.htm; accessed 1/15/02.

and Urban Development (HUD). Important HUD programs include public housing, in which the federal government provides funding to local housing authorities to build and maintain subsidized public housing units for qualified low-income individuals and families. Public housing accounts for about $4 billion covering 1.3 million housing units. Far larger is the Section 8 rental assistance program (about $16 billion), which assists families in nearly 3 million units with rental certificates, rental vouchers, and moderate rehabilitation assistance.

Spending for housing programs totaled about $30 billion in 1998. Yet, only one-fourth of those eligible for federal housing assistance receive it, and nearly two-fifths of the nation's low-income households pay more than half of their income for rent. Such families live close to the edge of homelessness (see Future Alternatives). Federal policy, through the deductibility of mortgage interest payments and home loan guarantee programs, provides more housing assistance to middle- and upper-income than to poor families. Indeed, federal tax expenditures provide a wide array of benefits for the non-poor.[20]

Work/Employment Programs

The primary purpose of *job-training programs* is to help nonworkers attain marketable skills. These programs provide funds for training welfare recipients and others in job skills. They offer grants to state and local governments for skills training, counseling, remedial education, subsidized employment, and job creation in areas with high unemployment. They also fund the Job Corps, summer youth employment, and the Young Adult Conservation Corps. Since the mid-1980s job training was redirected toward the private sector. The Job Training Partnership Act placed most job-training programs in the hands of local Private Industry Councils, constituted by business persons, educators, labor officials, and other community representatives. PRWOR directed major attention to job readiness and job training for public assistance recipients. Expenditures for federal employment programs *declined* from $17 billion in 1980 to $6 billion in 1990, and remain under $4 billion today.

Other in-kind programs represent far smaller dollar figures than food stamps, housing, and employment assistance. Examples are nutrition programs for infants and the elderly, social services, and assistance with home weatherization and other energy costs.

Public Assistance Spending

Public assistance programs are highly unpopular in America, and their growth in spending during the 1970s and 1980s ultimately led to PRWOR in 1996. One reason for that growth was demographic. As divorce and illegitimacy rates climbed, so did public assistance expenditures. These programs also grew because of the high unemployment generally prevailing until the mid-1990s. Programs designed for the working poor and the unemployed grow rapidly in such periods. These causes of expenditure growth reflect social and economic patterns external to the income support programs themselves. The size of public assistance draws outraged criticisms; yet mistaken impressions about such means-tested spending abound. In terms of their impact on the total budget, social insurance programs, which account for 75 percent of income support expenditures, dwarf public assistance. Moreover, all federal expenditures for public assistance, other than medical care and education, amount to less than 9 percent of the federal budget and under 2 percent of GDP. Widespread dislike of and dissatisfaction with these programs may focus on their cost, but their inequities and inefficiencies are a far more appropriate target for controversy.

POLICY EVALUATION: PUBLIC ASSISTANCE

Because there are so many public assistance policies and because all aim at the general problem of poverty and its manifestations in poor health, nutrition, and housing, each program cannot be evaluated separately. Rather, the following pages consider the overall success of public assistance and its principal failures and problems as a whole.

Because of the radical differences in their perspectives on poverty and its causes, critics of various ideological stripes have different evaluations of income support, with little agreement on their *impacts* or *outcomes*. Conservatives, given their belief that poverty is the fault of the poor and of misguided welfare spending, generally evaluate public programs negatively, especially prior to 1996. Liberals, believing that poverty is involuntary and related to a lack of opportunity, have a generally favorable evaluation of welfare and income support programs, although they advocate expanding programs to all eligible persons. Radicals see poverty programs only as bandages on a wound, neither intended to, nor able to, accomplish prevention or cure. It is the economic system itself, not government programs, that causes persistent poverty.

Accomplishments of Public Assistance

Americans are highly ambivalent about public assistance programs. Most believe that government programs are ineffective in relieving poverty and that most recipients do not deserve help. Yet a majority also are highly compassionate, believing that government should spend *more* money, not less, on helping poor persons with food, housing, medical care, and income.[21]

Despite these highly critical public attitudes, the welfare system has accomplished many intended goals. First, public assistance, through its combination of cash and in-kind aid, moves many Americans out of poverty. For many unfortunate enough to suffer from poverty, it will be a transitory experience ending in economic health. Each public assistance program, examined in isolation, has important shortcomings and inequities, but taken together, they balance and provide for many of the poor a basic minimum living standard. This combination effect is the reason many liberals oppose cutting what appears to be excessive spending in particular programs.

The EITC has been the most effective mover of persons out of poverty, each year raising approximately 5 million from below to above the poverty line.[22] It is also highly effective in reaching its target: persons who work hard, but whose earned income alone cannot support a family. Recent studies show that the EITC encourages single parents to enter the work force and to work more hours. At the same time, it enables some married couples to have one parent spend more time at home with the children. Moreover, the EITC is not costly to administer, as it uses the existing tax structure. However, the EITC has very high error rates, as it is difficult for many persons to determine whether their family situation qualifies them for EITC or not. Moreover, its attractiveness lures fraudulent tax claims. On the whole, however, the EITC retains strong liberal, conservative, and popular support, although liberals are inclined to expand its benefits.

The food stamp program contributes to improved nutrition among the poor. More than half of all recipients are children, who would have severe nutrition problems in the program's absence. Moreover, the near-poor can maintain decent living standards when economic hard times place severe restrictions on income. Food stamps are more than an antihunger program; they are now an essential part of the network of benefits supporting a minimum income. Housing assistance and other in-kind programs also supply many basic needs. America's great wealth makes its residual poverty shocking; even more shocking would be the extent of poverty if no public assistance programs were available. Without government programs 51 million would be poor; with them, the number drops to 24 million (see Table 7-3). Public assistance is more successful than usually acknowledged in alleviating poverty, hunger, ill health, and inadequate housing.[23]

The use of public assistance by most American families conforms to the policy's intention, to provide temporary help until jobs are found, health is regained, or the divorced or widowed are remarried. Going on welfare is primarily an economic decision influenced by the unavailability of jobs and by prevailing wage rates. Despite widely held opinion, fraud and corruption are no more or less of a problem than in most other government programs or in private business, for that matter. Moreover, social science research consistently shows that public assistance does not produce an increase in illegitimacy or additional children as a means of receiving more money.[24]

Liberal critics obscured these successes by shifting the issue from poverty to income inequality. During the 1960s, liberal action focused on remedying absolute poverty. During the 1970s, that focus implicitly changed to an attack on relative inequality. Although public assistance made strides in minimizing the former, it did little about the latter.[25] Public assistance's primary goal is not reduction of inequality, but reduction of economic insecurity. Liberals retreated from traditional welfare programs because they recognized the accuracy of some conservative critiques. Yet liberal loyalty to the welfare idea remains strong. Indeed, liberals tend to confuse their strong sense of justice and compassion for the poor with the ability of public assistance to solve the poverty problem.

Conservatives, however, often fail to see the successes of welfare because they are ideologically predisposed to oppose it. Yet public assistance has protected American private enterprise from its own shortcomings. The very successes of welfare in reducing poverty smothers demands for a more radical reform of the American political and economic system, as radicals lament.

Has Welfare Reform Worked?

Public assistance does have numerous serious shortcomings. Seven main problems identified prior to PRWOR in 1996 were (1) cost, (2) administrative complexity, (3) inadequate benefits, (4) punitive features, (5) unfairness, (6) the plight of poor children, and (7) work disincentives. Conservatives tended to stress the first and second; liberals and radicals the third, fourth, and fifth. All recognized the sixth and seventh. Has the switch to TANF been successful in addressing these problems?

1. Cost. The total cost of all federal nonhealth public assistance is less than 10 percent of the federal budget. Nevertheless, total dollars spent are quite large, and the proportion of expenditures for administration is high, evidence of inefficiency in getting funds to the target populations. Moreover, because most public assistance programs are jointly funded and administered by federal and state governments and because many states supplement federal funds, program growth puts a severe financial strain on some state and local governments, particularly in times of economic recession when tax revenue falls.

Because TANF is a block grant, rather than an entitlement, after the initial change from AFDC to TANF in 1997, program expenditures neither fell nor rose. The legislation targets a set amount of federal funding to the states regardless of the number of TANF recipients. The states have spent all that money on a variety of programs, although less than half was expended for basic cash assistance. Other amounts went for child care, transportation, work activities, and administrative costs (about 10 percent). Indeed, some states, through "creative" accounting practices, moved some TANF dollars into roads, education, and other state services.[26]

2. Administration. The problem of administrative complexity is a serious dilemma for public assistance programs of all modern nations and an important reason for high administrative costs. Confusion and complexity are inherent in categorical and means-tested programs because hundreds of questions, forms, and regulations are needed to define categories and levels of need and to establish whether particular persons are needy and fit the defined categories. Multiply this by the determination process for other programs, add periodic rechecking of eligibility to reduce fraud and waste, and the administrative burden of these programs becomes staggering. On top of all this is the complexity of having separate rules and regulations at each level of administration: federal, state, and local. The system is so confusing that substantial sums are often mistakenly overpaid, for the caseworkers are sometimes as bewildered as the clients.

Paradoxically, antifraud regulations contribute to high error rates. As regulations to close loopholes pile up, the complexity of the program increases (an unintended consequence). As this happens, program employees are more prone to mistakes; caseworker turnover increases, and new workers—having had less time on the job—are even more prone to mistakes. A double bind operates. Public assistance can be either lower in administrative costs and higher in fraud, or higher in administrative costs and lower in fraud. Low overhead and low fraud rates cannot be achieved simultaneously. The shift to TANF did not change this equation.

3. Adequacy. Another major problem is inadequate benefits. Poverty rates in the United States remain higher than in comparable nations. TANF, food stamps, SSI, and other benefits barely maintain any kind of decent living standard. Moreover, there are substantial gaps in public assistance coverage, particularly for single individuals and childless couples under sixty-five. Pegged as they are to the "deserving" poor, public assistance programs contribute little to relieving the poverty of these persons. Few of the programs provide assistance solely on the basis of need; most exclude certain categories of persons. The prosperous economy of TANF's first five years masked the seriousness of the adequacy problem. Moreover, only in 2001 and 2002 did many persons begin to exceed the two-year and five-year limits for receipt of benefits. Without basic cash assistance, food stamps, housing, and other programs cannot support families who remain poor after exhausting their TANF eligibility. In short, the change to TANF likely makes the adequacy problem worse for many families, particularly during recessionary economic times.

4. Punitive features. Means-tested public assistance carries with it a degree of degradation for the recipient. Determination of eligibility requires embarrassing personal questions, long waits in crowded offices, and possibly home inspections. Denials of benefits often happen for trivial reasons in order to keep the rolls low. Given American attitudes toward welfare recipients, TANF and food stamps brand one as lazy and probably immoral. TANF reinforces these punitive features by instituting strict time limits for most families: two years of continuous receipt, five years over a lifetime. Moreover, the states may institute stricter time limits, and many have done so.

5. Unfairness. Inequity, in two senses, is a problem in public assistance. Horizontal inequity refers to the fact that poor persons with the same degree of need frequently do not receive the same degree of aid. Vertical inequity refers to a twofold imbalance: the most needy often do not receive aid, and the system sometimes offers high benefits to some of the poor, while providing none for the near poor.

These inequities have two main sources: benefit level variation from state to state and the categorical nature of the programs. Because each state sets eligibility and benefit levels for TANF, a poor family receives different income depending on where it lives. A family with an income of $6,000 in California receives higher benefits (even adjusting for differences in the cost of living) than a family in similar circumstances with the same income in Alabama. It seems unfair that families with identical needs are treated differently simply because of where they live. Additionally, families with an earned income slightly above these guidelines receive no support, where others without such income are eligible for a variety of programs, the combined benefit of which makes them better off than the working family.

Food stamps, EITC, and other in-kind programs available to the working poor reduce some of these inequities, but substantial ones remain. Because many in-kind programs are funded at a low level, their benefits are not available to all those technically eligible. Only a fraction of those who could qualify receive housing assistance, for example. Those who receive it are better off than those, equally needy, who do not. If TANF proves successful in moving people from welfare to work, then it will reduce vertical unfairness.

6. Children and public assistance. The growing number of children spending years in poverty, living in squalid conditions, dependent on public assistance, and learning few job skills became one of the most striking indictments of public assistance. Public assistance was designed many years ago as a temporary support for children and their mothers. For many, it serves that purpose. For others, however, it became a way of life linked to many social pathologies: illegitimacy, drug abuse, crime, poor housing, homelessness, and chronic unemployment. PRWOR's change from the old system of public assistance primarily aimed to correct the growing number of children growing up in poverty and to address work disincentives. If successful in these aims, it would indirectly improve matters for problems one through five.

7. Work disincentives.   The most universally recognized problem of public assistance prior to the 1996 welfare reform was that, despite work requirements, there were discouragements to work built into program structures, particularly given the effect of multiple programs. There is little empirical evidence of large effects, but some were real. Work disincentives keep recipients dependent even when work is available to them, which is obviously an unintended and undesirable effect. These disincentives come into play because in many programs benefits are phased out as earned income increases. The rate at which this phase-out occurs is called the *marginal tax rate.* The graduated benefit reductions that accompany rising income aimed to encourage welfare recipients to work and to be fair to workers not receiving benefits; as a family is able to support itself, its dependence on government should decrease. The problem was that the marginal tax rate of all the programs combined reached or exceeded 100 percent in some circumstances, so that for every dollar earned, the welfare recipient lost a dollar or more in benefits. In addition to marginal tax rate problems were so-called *notch problems.* A notch is the point in the benefit scale at which an additional dollar of earnings does not simply reduce benefits but rather makes the person totally ineligible for benefits. The loss of Medicaid for families with health problems was a strong work disincentive.

TANF, Children, and Work: Evaluation and Re-authorization

Congress had to re-authorize TANF by October 1, 2002. In order to do so, it had to determine the accomplishments and shortcomings of the program. Social scientists invested considerable energy in program evaluation during the last five years, and some results are clear.[27] Yet most states did not implement TANF fully until 1998, and the most recent data for evaluation comes from late 2000 or early 2001. Therefore, the research base is rather slim. The most obvious effect of TANF is the steep reduction in welfare rolls (see Figure 7-6). Other effects are less clear, and the role of TANF itself in producing caseload reduction is difficult to separate from the economic expansion of the 1990s, the growth of EITC, changes in other public assistance programs, and larger cultural changes in marriage and family.

Children, marriage, and family.   One important goal of welfare reform was to reduce the appallingly high number of children growing up in poverty, as well as to reduce out-of-wedlock births and to strengthen family life. Fewer children live below the poverty line, as the child poverty rate fell 6 percent between 1994 and 2000. The teen birth rate continued to fall and is now at the level of the mid-1970s (though this trend began in the late 1980s), more children are in child care and after-school programs, and there is some evidence of higher rates of marriage and lower rates of single-parenthood among welfare recipients. Child support enforcement on absent fathers substantially raised the percentage of support judgments and collections, though these rates remain stubbornly low.

It is difficult, however, to attribute most or all of these changes to TANF's effects. In fact, the states have devoted very little attention to implementing the child and family provisions of TANF, instead focusing on increasing employment and reducing welfare rolls. Moreover, although there is some evidence that low-income young children are doing better in school, more behavior problems are reported in adolescents from families in which the mother is now working instead of staying at home and receiving welfare. Finally, welfare rolls declined far more rapidly than child poverty rates, signifying that a family's leaving welfare only sometimes lifts it out of poverty. There is little information on those parents (about 40 percent) who left TANF rolls, but are not working. President Bush's proposals for TANF reauthorization placed renewed financial emphasis on programs to encourage marriage for present and potential TANF recipients. Democrats in Congress preferred to see the money go to maintaining cash assistance funding levels.

Work, earnings, and poverty rates. Have those leaving welfare found gainful employment? The states placed most of their resources into "jobs first" efforts to move persons rapidly from welfare to work, and these efforts seem to have succeeded with the help of a robust economy eager for workers and with the assistance of a more generous EITC that makes work at low wages more rewarding. The typical state's welfare caseload declined 50 percent from its 1994 peak, and the states have considerable TANF block grant money to help those who remain to acquire jobs and job skills. The economic recession that began in 2001, however, will make job retention and new job placement far more difficult. It is clear the economic changes will mar the rosy picture of the period from 1997 to 2001, but how significantly is far from evident.

About 75 percent of mothers leaving welfare have been employed at some time, though only about 60 percent have consistently been employed. These mothers typically work for low wages (about $6.75 per hour on average), and seldom work a full forty-hour week. Yet the earnings of the lowest income groups have increased, though modestly. The lowest 20 percent of mothers had a net increase of $900 per year since 1993, and the second-lowest 20 percent had a net increase of $3,000 per year. Yet the poorest of the poor (the bottom 10 percent income) seem to have a net loss of income after reduced welfare benefits and increased earnings. Studies of consumption patterns, however, seem to indicate modest increases in family spending, even though income is stagnant, which shows either the availability of unreported income or credit card spending. The simple truth is that work plus EITC often is not enough to bring a family out of poverty, if its wage earners have little education or job skills. The poverty rate among working single-mother families (after government benefits and taxes) in 1999 remained stuck at its 1995 rate of 19 percent. Local food pantries report an increase in long-term need for food assistance, especially among working families, with the decline in food stamps and government cash assistance.[28]

Re-authorization. At the time of this writing, Congress had completed little work on the renewal of TANF that must occur by late 2002. The re-authorization debate takes place during a recession, in which budget pressures have driven many states to reduce public assistance spending, even as the number of persons needing assistance grows. Seven issues dominate the re-authorization debate, issues that likely will continue after 2002 as defining questions in the American approach to income support.[29]

Assuming that for the foreseeable future welfare will come in the form of block grants instead of entitlements, debate will focus on *funding levels*. Conservatives wish to reduce funding when welfare rolls shrink; liberals focus on the more severe needs of those who remain and argue to sustain current levels of federal support for state programs. They also want bonus funding for states that successfully reduce poverty rates. The Bush administration supports current funding levels, but not a shift to program evaluation based on poverty reduction. *Time limits, sanctions, and exemptions* are a fundamental part of PRWOR, but has the experience of protracted poverty among some groups shown the need for more flexibility in granting exemptions from work requirements or in extending time limits on welfare for those having difficulty finding steady employment? Liberals answer yes; conservatives, no. The argument for flexibility recognizes that the poor are not an undifferentiated group. There are, first of all, the elderly and disabled, for whom direct income assistance is the most appropriate form of aid. Indeed, it is this group that has been most assisted out of poverty in the last two decades, particularly by Social Security increases. A second group of the poor is single mothers with young children. To move out of poverty, they need child care, child support from absent fathers, health insurance, and assistance in finding jobs. Another group is the working poor, who are underemployed or employed only part-time or at minimum wage. Their primary need is a solid EITC, job training for higher-wage skills, remedial education, health insurance, and unemployment insurance when jobs run out. Finally, there is the urban "underclass," to be discussed later. No single, simple program can address all the needs of these diverse groups.

Food stamp and Medicaid rolls fell faster than TANF rolls and poverty rates. Therefore, many persons eligible for these programs are not being served. Debate here focuses on how active public assistance workers should be in promoting enrollment. The *family and marriage* goals of PRWOR have been the least enthusiastically pursued by state governments, as most bureaucrats and most Americans remain ambivalent about government responsibility to interfere in private choices about marriage and family. Liberals support this reluctance and wish to minimize attention to these aspects of welfare reform; conservatives advocate strongly for attention to these.

The goals of *child care and child support* are central to welfare reform. When work is required of adult guardians of children, where will good quality child care be found? Conservatives argue that existing child care funding is adequate and that strong efforts at requiring absent fathers to pay child support are needed. Liberals argue for increased child care funding, contending that good quality, affordable child care remains difficult to find. The fact of the matter is that it is cheaper to pay welfare recipients to stay at home and take care of their children than it is to pay for job training and placement and to pay the child care expenses of persons in low-skill jobs with minimum wages. There are also substantial issues of quality and the well-being of children following rapid growth in the low-cost child care industry. Unless the child care available to now-working, former AFDC/TANF mothers is of relatively high quality, PRWOR may produce higher rates of crime, poor education, and addiction as unintended consequences, the legacy of child neglect and lack of quality supervision.

Finally, *job training and job advancement* are critical if former public assistance recipients are to remain off the rolls and out of poverty. Liberals contend that too much of the current PRWOR effort has been on having the recipients land their "first job." After that, they are on their own. Liberals argue that enrollment in job training should not count against the welfare time limits and that the states should continue to support former recipients with social services until they have achieved a steady and an improving work history. Conservatives wish to strengthen work requirements, to require more hours of work, and to focus welfare reform on work itself, instead of getting ready for work.

FUTURE ALTERNATIVES IN PUBLIC ASSISTANCE: CHILDREN, UNDERCLASS, HOMELESSNESS, AND WORK

As TANF and other parts of PRWOR develop over time, it will be very difficult to design effective program evaluation measures because of the many different state approaches, because of the many program provisions, and because of the various behavioral changes expected of recipients. It will be quite difficult to sort out which provisions of the reform are affecting which results. The primary considerations are, first, how the individual states respond to the increased freedom and changed fiscal responsibilities they now have. What role will the private sector play? Who will be eligible? Which programs will be effective, for whom, and at what cost? Second, what will be the consequences of reform on the well-being of children and families? What will happen to the lives of the disabled, immigrants, teen mothers, and children? Will the lot of the working poor improve? The first round of PRWOR focused on reducing public assistance rolls and getting recipients into work. Long-term reduction of poverty and its causes is a far more difficult goal.

Public assistance in the future must address four intractable welfare reform dilemmas: (1) the large number of children spending all or part of their childhood in poverty, (2) the "underclass," (3) the large numbers of homeless persons in our country, and (4) the availability of jobs that lift people out of poverty.

Children and Poverty

As reported in the first section of this chapter, children are disproportionately poor. Although rates of child poverty declined during the 1990s, still one of every seven lives below the official poverty line at any given time, and many more live in poverty for at least part of their childhood. Moreover, children are increasingly living in single-parent families. Twenty-five percent of all children under eighteen live in such households, and about half of all children will live in such a household at some time. Many go for years without seeing their fathers, even for short visits. A growing proportion of TANF benefits are "child only," meaning that the children receive aid while their parents do not, either because the parents have exceeded their time on TANF, because the child lives with grandparents or other relatives, or because the parents are ineligible for benefits because of their immigration status.

The problems associated with child poverty and family breakup include poor education, teenage pregnancy, child abuse, suicide, drug addiction, and high crime rates. Moreover, poorly educated, addicted, abused, or imprisoned children cannot grow up to be productive citizens.

Despite these problems, government spending on children has become less effective in recent years, when compared with spending on the elderly. In 1965, government spending on the elderly was 21 percent of all income maintenance and other social welfare spending, while 37 percent went to children. By the late

1980s, spending on children was 24 percent and spending for the elderly reached 33 percent. These expenditures lifted out of poverty 82 percent of the elderly who would have been poor without government programs. Only 32 percent of children escaped poverty through such spending.[30]

Other wealthy, democratic nations have far more generous programs for children, without slighting the elderly. Most, for example, have a universal children's allowance, amounting to 5 to 10 percent of the median wage. They also provide cash benefits to parents at the time of childbirth, as well as allowances that support a parent for taking time away from work in the first months of the child's life. Other nations also generously support preschool and child care programs.

Children's advocates advance many proposals to attack the problem of child poverty and associated social problems. Reducing the tax burden on families with children finds support among both liberals and conservatives, and the 1997 tax changes in the Balanced Budget Agreement and in the 2001 tax legislation went some distance in this direction by creating a $500 per child tax credit, providing various tax credits and deductions for college expenses, and reducing the tax burden on married families. But these will do little for poor children unless their parents find and keep jobs with reasonable income and benefits.

Other proposals include increased funding for Head Start and other preschool programs, extending Medicaid coverage to larger numbers of poor children, and expansion of the food stamp and WIC programs to ensure adequate early childhood nutrition. The conservative mood of the late 1990s in Congress made all of these impossible, except for expanded children's health care (see Chapter 8). Increased focus on the educational attainments of poor children might pay off handsomely, as the future productivity of such persons is far more related to their education and that of their mothers, than to whether their families receive public assistance.[31] Educational reform, however, is complicated and costly, as Chapter 9 discusses.

One measure that has been widely adopted and has been in place for some time is strengthened enforcement of court-ordered child support payments by absent fathers. Thousands of absent parents are in arrears on these payments, which is one of the reasons why single-parent families have a high poverty rate. States, in cooperation with the federal government, have developed extensive networks for locating absent fathers and for enforcing child support payments with the garnishment of paychecks and threats of imprisonment. Welfare reform included national goals for child-support payment, requirements for computerized tracking of absent parents, forced deductions of court-ordered payments from wages and other income, and incentives to establish paternity of all children at birth, but collection rates are still low.[32] Moreover, most absent fathers of poor children themselves have low incomes, limiting their ability to support their children.

The causes of illegitimacy are complex. The debate over children and poverty is really part of a larger debate over how to deal with teen childbearing and the decline of the two-parent family. Such debate may also include measures to reform divorce law to place the well-being of children first and to make divorce more difficult, as well as measures to reform the tax code to reward intact families. (See Chapter 13 on morality policy in American politics.) Within public assistance programs, options are limited to create incentives for marriage, apart from removing marriage penalties in existing laws and developing jobs programs that focus on the kinds of rewarding employment for young men that would make them both more inclined to family stability and more attractive marriage partners. It is not clear what such programs would be, so the best TANF can do is to fund a variety of state-based experiments to determine what, if anything, works.

The Underclass

Definitions and estimates of the underclass vary, and some policy analysts reject the term itself. However defined, the problem is serious. The underclass are those persistent poor, who also have serious educational, family, attitudinal, job-skill, or emotional-psychological problems. They also tend to live in areas in which such problems are endemic to a large proportion of the population.[33] The underclass, then, refers not simply to the persistently poor, but to the long-term poor living in desperately run-down neighborhoods, who are deeply involved in teen pregnancy, drugs, crime, and poor education and job skills. Most estimates of the urban underclass population are about 2 to 3 million persons, or about 7 to 10 percent of the poverty population.

Disagreements about the causes of underclass poverty and its growth during the last two decades are rooted in two different explanations, associated with the liberal and conservative explanations of poverty discussed in the first section of this chapter. Liberal structural explanations focus on racial discrimination and the disappearance of entry-level manual labor jobs in the urban marketplace, combined with the flight of the African-American and white middle classes to the suburbs. This leaves a sizable population of unemployed and unemployable persons behind, concentrated in the inner cities of major metropolitan areas. The conservative explanation focuses on a culture of poverty, dependency, and antisocial behavior passed from generation to generation in ghetto areas. Many researchers are now coming to accept that both explanations contain part of the truth.

The underclass presents a special challenge to income support policy. It is particularly hard to reach with traditional programs to alleviate or cure poverty. This class seems immune to periods of economic improvement and to traditional compensatory social programs. Because there are multiple dimensions to underclass poverty, multiple approaches are needed to attack it. Simply increasing public assistance spending will not work. Job skills must be cultivated and transportation to job sites provided so that underclass persons can compete for skilled-labor positions.

But job skills also depend on qualities of law-abidingness, marriage before childbirth, going to work every day, literacy, and many other factors that the middle class takes for granted. Programs to change attitudes, provide rehabilitation from drug and alcohol addiction, and improve education and the health of children must all be brought to bear over a long period, not just on a hit-or-miss basis. Child support programs also appeal to students of the underclass. What is needed is an intensive effort to enable children to arrive at adulthood properly educated, healthy, and prepared for jobs. To do so takes commitment to the underclass and the money and creativity to support that commitment. It is not clear at this time whether the new state politics of welfare or the structures developed under TANF will motivate such a commitment. There is very little in PRWOR directed specifically at the underclass.

Housing Programs and Homelessness

President Clinton targeted federal housing programs for major reform during his administration's first term (1992 to 1996). The changes focused on making public housing safe and attractive by allowing police more latitude in sweeping them for guns and drugs. More significant, however, were efforts to break up concentrations of public housing by allowing tenants to purchase their own apartments, by tearing down some units, and by replacing such housing as much as possible with rent vouchers that recipients can use for housing on the private market. The hope is that these changes will disperse the public housing population and the associated concentrations of crime, violence, and urban decay. Yet federal spending on low-income housing remains stagnant in the face of increasing need. By 1995 HUD reported more than 5.3 million households spending more than 50 percent of their income on rent or living in "severely substandard" housing. Two million heads of these households worked, and over one million were elderly.

Housing subsidies for the well-to-do however (chiefly mortgage interest deductions, but also FHA and VA insurance) continue to increase. Mortgage interest deductions alone were worth $61 billion in foregone federal taxes in 2001, with over half going to the top one-third of incomes. Home ownership is increasingly difficult for the lower-middle class, and housing for the poor is even scarcer and more expensive.

The problem is not simply lack of housing stock. In many cities there are significant vacancy rates. Rather, the problem is lack of affordable low-cost housing. Much of this housing was demolished in recent decades to make room for office buildings and upper-income condominiums. More strict enforcement of housing codes, designed to rehabilitate or to prevent deterioration of neighborhoods, had the unintended consequence of reducing the availability of single-room-occupancy apartments that formerly housed many of today's homeless. Public housing units have not been built to replace them, nor have housing allowances or subsidies been sufficient to stimulate building or rehabilitating low-cost units.

At the same time, jobs became more scarce for the unskilled, and great numbers of mental patients were released from hospitals and residential programs. All of these factors contributed to the large number of homeless in the United States. Estimates range from 300,000 in the 2000 Census to 3 million, but the best estimates seem to be about 500 to 600 thousand persons.[34] This figure, of course, estimates the number homeless on a given night; many thousands more experience temporary spells of homelessness. Urban shelters reported an upswing in demand during the economic downturn of late 2001.

The long-term homeless are predominantly male, single, disproportionately nonwhite, and have little attachment to the labor force. Single male homelessness is in a sense the flip-side of the feminization of poverty. The same trends that devastate mothers and their children also set many single men adrift. A considerable number, though not a majority of the homeless, have spent time in mental hospitals, and a fairly large number are alcoholics or drug addicts. The *new* homeless tend to be women, parents, and married persons with little history of mental illness or alcoholism. Rather, lack of stable family connections and low incomes forced them from their last housing. For many of the new and old homeless, living on the streets or in shelters is a recurring rather than a permanent phenomenon, but for a substantial number it is a permanent condition. Sympathy for the homeless is waning in many cities, where such tough measures as street sweeps, vagrancy law enforcement, and legislation against "aggressive panhandling" replaced efforts to find housing.

The major federal policies are the 1987 McKinney Homeless Assistance Act and the Cranston-Gonzalez National Affordable Housing Act of 1990. These provide Emergency Shelter grants to state, city, and county governments from HUD, as well as the Supportive Housing Demonstration Program, which provides funds to local governments for projects helping the homeless toward independent living. These laws also support rental housing assistance in connection with services for homeless people with disabilities, particularly persons who are seriously mentally ill, having chronic alcohol or drug problems, or having AIDS and related diseases. Finally, the McKinney Act requires the federal government to identify all surplus federal property that could be used to shelter the homeless. Total federal spending on programs for the homeless is around $2 billion.

The problem of homelessness is really three problems, and each requires a different set of actions. The first group consists of down-on-their-luck individuals and families, especially children. Loss of affordable housing and marginal job skills affect this group. Many low-income persons are just one paycheck away from homelessness. Loss of the job or serious medical problems push them over the brink. Attacking their lack of housing requires not simply assistance with shelter, but also remedial education, vocational training, health insurance and employment counseling.

Another large group of the homeless are the seriously mentally ill, especially those suffering from schizophrenia. Their homelessness at least in part results from dismantling of the system of mental health care in the United States. Inadequate community mental health services and lack of a comprehensive system of tracking and supporting the non-institutionalized mentally ill means that many are left to their own meager resources. Attacking homelessness requires a coherent system of treatment, housing, and rehabilitation.

Finally, alcoholism and drug addiction cause many persons' homelessness. As with the mentally ill, rehabilitation and vocational programs are needed for them as much as the provision of food and shelter.

Employment Issues

Many state public assistance programs focused first on those recipients most "job-ready" because of their education, former employment history, and motivation. These were easiest to place and take credit for. Recipients who are more difficult to place because of long-term dependency, low intelligence, drug or alcohol abuse, criminal record, histories of being sexually abused, or having low education are far more difficult (and far more costly) to work with. This is doubly so because, under current federal law, all persons required to work must receive a minimum wage and be covered by employment rights, such as health and safety regulations. Moreover, the children of public assistance recipients often have health or behavior problems that make it very difficult for their mothers to obtain and hold full-time work. Expenditures for training, educating, and placing such persons, when it is done well, are more costly than traditional welfare. PRWOR, however, does not directly appropriate additional funds for job training and placement. Thus, some states will likely use their own funds to establish creative job programs, but others will place the most responsibility on recipients themselves, sanctioning those who fail the challenge, thus saving the state's money.

Job training alone is insufficient to ensure work for all. In poor neighborhoods there are multiple applicants for the few jobs that come open. All the quality training in the world will not obtain a job when no jobs are available. Job creation strategies must accompany work requirements for welfare reform to be effective. Yet there is little consensus and less experience in making more employment available in areas suffering high rates of poverty and economic decline, as well as high rates of addiction and other pathologies.

Liberal and conservative welfare reformers agree that work is the best and most permanent path out of poverty. It is not clear, however, how to make that path available. Proposals run from the most extreme, cold-turkey approach on the libertarian side (abolition of all public assistance with each individual responsible for finding work in the private sector) to proposals to imitate the German system of apprenticeship in which schools and businesses combine for three-year education and job-training programs.

Proposals in the middle of these extremes look to reform the current system of required education and job training for able-bodied public assistance recipients. Such proposals include boot-camp type, residential school and work training for youth; intensive one-on-one job counseling; public service work experience; and public-private partnerships, such as the Job Training Partnership Act and JOBS. There are numerous variations. All, however, run into difficult problems.

First, job-training programs are most successful with the marginally poor. Persons with reasonable intelligence, stable life situations, and good motivation can benefit from job training and placement. The underclass and those with long-term unemployment histories are far more difficult to reach and programs for them are very costly.

Second, many of the hard-core unemployed have longstanding substance abuse problems, criminal histories, or mental instability that make employment difficult. Work requirements or job-training requirements that do not tackle these problems are unlikely to be successful. Yet addressing these problems is very difficult and costly.

Third, the jobs available to the poor are likely to be low paying, without such benefits as health care, and without decent possibilities of advancement. Even successful workfare programs have only marginally improved the lives of participants. Welfare mothers can sometimes obtain jobs paying $6 to $7 an hour, but without housing, health care, and occasional food assistance, they cannot support a family. Jobs at the bottom of the labor market generally pay little, have little chance for advancement, may not be permanent, and generally carry few retirement or health benefits. Thus, neither the new workers nor the present working poor can fully escape dependence. What happens when they lose their jobs, become sick or injured, or grow old? If PRWOR leads Americans to think that work and dependence are mutually exclusive alternatives, they will be sadly surprised.

Finally, if private employment is not sufficient to place all recipients required to work, will the states and local governments be willing to create and fund public service employment, or will those recipients who cannot find private employment simply be written off as failures?

CONCLUSIONS

Current income maintenance programs, whether social insurance or public assistance, combine features in tension with each other. Sympathy for the plight of the elderly, widows, and children drives policy in a liberal direction; that is, toward the notion that all members of society deserve an income and sufficient economic dignity to support a decent life in a liberal, democratic society. However, commitment to the free market and suspicion that government programs encourage dependency drive policy in a conservative direction. It may well be that recent changes, particularly in public assistance, signal not so much liberal-conservative tension as movement toward a more communitarian political ideology. Here the focus is on opportunity and responsibility, where government programs should provide opportunities and support to persons so that they can succeed if possible on their own; at the same time, every person has a responsibility to use his or her talents to make the most of the opportunities furnished by government and the market.[35] The primary challenge is to discover what combination of public policies best enacts opportunity and responsibility.

SUMMARY

Poverty may be defined in absolute or relative terms. Absolute definitions vary, but the most widely used is the Social Security Administration's definition. Relative poverty usually is defined as half the median family income.

The extent of poverty in the United States depends on the definition used. The SSA standard estimates poverty at 11 percent of the population; other definitions produce a proportion closer to 18 percent. Counting in-kind benefits, making other adjustments, and using the SSA standard indicates approximately 8 percent in dire poverty.

Although poverty declined during the 1990s, the incidence of poverty remains high among racial minorities, children, female-headed families, rural dwellers, central-city residents, and persons with minimal education. The semi-permanent poverty "underclass" is a growing problem in many cities.

The causes of poverty are subject to heated ideological debate. Conservatives and neoconservatives largely blame the poor themselves and government programs that encourage dependency. Liberals see discrimination, technological change, and lack of opportunity as the principal causes of poverty. Radicals point to the structural flaws of the capitalist economic and political system.

This chapter examined the national income support system: social insurance (requiring contributions as a condition of benefits), public assistance (financed categorically from general revenues), and employment and job-training efforts. Forms of assistance are cash or in-kind benefits.

European income support programs are similar, but are available to a wider spectrum of the population and are less stigmatizing. America lags in expenditures, benefit levels, and family allowances. Despite the claims of some, the United States is not a welfare state.

Social insurance programs began with the Social Security Act of 1935. Old Age, Survivors, and Disability Insurance (OASDI) is financed by payroll taxes on employers and employees; expenditures increased rapidly in the last decade. Unemployment insurance is financed by taxes on an employer's payroll, and payments are made to workers involuntarily jobless for temporary periods.

Social Security and unemployment insurance have been highly successful, with relatively high public approval. Serious questions have emerged, however, concerning the long-term financial soundness of these programs. Debate focuses on how these programs should be financed, how long-term population trends will affect payroll taxes and benefits, the appropriate retirement age, whether equity or adequacy of benefits should be more strongly emphasized, and, in the case of unemployment insurance, the declining percentage of the unemployed who are supported.

The most important future issue in Social Security, aside from traditional debates over payroll taxes and benefit levels, is how to reform Social Security so that it will be available for the retirement years of the "baby boom" generation, beginning in 2011. The Trust Fund surplus will be exhausted unless measures are taken to reduce benefits or increase revenues coming into Social Security. Proposals for significant changes involve investing part of the Trust Fund in the private stock market and allowing individuals to invest all or part of their own Social Security contributions.

Public assistance programs help certain categories of persons whose circumstances place them in poverty. Principal cash assistance programs are TANF, SSI, EITC, and General assistance. Food stamps, Medicaid, housing assistance, nutrition, and work programs constitute the bulk of in-kind aid.

Public assistance has had substantial success in alleviating the worst effects of poverty, ill health, poor nutrition, and inadequate housing. The EITC is very effective in moving low-income families out of poverty. Despite stereotypes of "welfare cheaters," most recipients use public assistance as intended: for temporary emergency relief. The primary failings of public assistance are high total program cost, inadequacy of benefits, unfairness, work disincentives, excessive complexity and inefficiency in administration, punitive features in some programs, and their impact on children.

With respect to public assistance programs, the most significant future issues are those following the substantial reforms of 1996, which abolished AFDC and created Temporary Assistance to Needy Families (TANF). 2002 saw the debate over re-authorization of PRWOR. The most important issues in that debate were: funding levels, time limits, food stamps, encouraging marriage, child care, and job training for former public assistance recipients. The enormous problems of children in poverty, the urban underclass, and the homeless are other issues that challenge income support policy.

NOTES

1. Michael Harrington, *The Other America: Poverty in the United States* (Baltimore: Penguin, 1963), 175.

2. For excellent, brief discussions, see Robert Havenman, "Changing the Poverty Measure: Pitfalls and Potential Gains," *Focus,* 14 (Winter 1992–1993): 24–29; and Joint Center for Poverty Research, "Measuring Poverty—A New Approach" (www.jcpr.org/policybriefs/vol1_num6.html).

3. Data on the number of persons below 125 percent of the SSA poverty figure are from the U.S. Bureau of the Census, *Statistical Abstract of the United States, 2001* (Washington, DC: 2002), Table 679.

4. Edward N. Wolff, "The Distribution of Household Wealth," in Lars Osberg, ed., *Economic Inequality and Poverty: International Perspectives* (Armonk, NY: Sharpe, 1991), 92–133; see also Sheldon H. Danziger and Peter Gottschalk, eds., *Uneven Tides: Rising Inequality in America* (New York: Russell Sage, 1993).

5. Isaac Shapiro, Robert Greenstein, and Wendell Primus, "Pathbreaking CBO Study Shows Dramatic Increases in Income Disparities in 1980s and 1990s: An Analysis of CBO Data" (Washington, DC: Center for Public and Policy Priorities, 2001).

6. Indeed, recent research by Kathryn Edin and Laura Lein shows that, because public assistance benefit levels are well below poverty standards in most states, virtually all women receiving welfare benefits supplement their income with off-the-books work and sporadic contributions from friends and relatives. *Making Ends Meet: How Single Mothers Survive Welfare and Low-Wage Work* (New York: Russell Sage Foundation, 1997).

7. Sara McLanahan, "The Consequences of Single Parenthood for Subsequent Generations," *Focus,* 11 (Fall 1988):16–21. The dire consequences and the extent of *teen* pregnancy, however, may be somewhat overstated. See "Negative Consequences of Teen Childbearing Less Than Commonly Believed," *Poverty Research News,* 1 (Winter 1997): 6–8.

8. See Norman Furniss and Timothy Tilton, *The Case for the Welfare State* (Bloomington: Indiana University Press, 1977); and Alfred J. Kahn and Sheila B. Kamerman, *Not for the Poor Alone: European Social Services* (New York: Harper Colophon Books, 1977). See also Robert Havenman, Barbara Wolfe, and Victor Halberstadt, "The European Welfare State in Transition," in John L. Palmer, ed., *Perspectives on the Reagan Years* (Washington, DC: Urban Institute, 1986), 147–173.

9. This section draws heavily on Heidenheimer et al., *Comparative Public Policy,* Chapter 7; Richard L. Siegel and Leonard B. Weinberg, *Comparing Public Policies* (Homewood, IL: Dorsey Press, 1977), Chapter 6; and Kahn and Kamerman, *Not for the Poor Alone.*

10. Theodore R. Marmor et al., *America's Misunderstood Welfare State: Persistent Myths, Enduring Realities* (New York: Basic Books, 1990), 31ff.

11. Timothy Smeeding, Lee Rainwater, and Gary Burtless, "United States Poverty in a Cross-National Context," *Focus,* 21 (Spring 2001): 50–54.

12. An excellent orientation to Social Security and the issues discussed in this and the next section is Congressional Budget Office, *Social Security: A Primer* (Washington, DC: U.S. Government Printing Office, 2001).

13. Martha Derthick, *Policymaking for Social Security* (Washington, DC: Brookings Institution, 1979), especially 215. See also Charles W. Meyer and Nancy L. Wolff, "Intercohort and Intracohort Redistribution under Social Security," in Charles W. Meyer, ed., *Social Security* (Lexington, MA: Heath, 1987), 49–68.

14. Jean-Jacques Rosa, ed., *World Crisis in Social Security* (San Francisco: Institute for Contemporary Studies, 1982); Heidenheimer et al., *Comparative Public Policy,* 248–265.

15. A recent evaluation of unemployment insurance is Jeffrey B. Wenger, "Divided We Fall," Briefing Paper from the Economic Policy Institute, August 2001; available at http://epinet.org.

16. Brief discussions of many of these options may be found in Congressional Budget Office, *Social Security: A Primer,* Chapter 4; and in Robert Kuttner, "Rampant Bull," *The American Prospect,* No. 39 (July–August 1998): 30–36 (http://epn.org/prospect/39/39kuttner.html).

17. See Spencer Rich, "Not Even a Gold Watch," *Washington Post National Weekly Edition,* December 9–15, 1996: 17.

18. For an excellent summary of the development of public assistance programs, see Paul E. Peterson and Mark C. Rom, *Welfare Magnets: The Case for a New National Standard* (Washington, DC: Brookings Institution, 1990), especially Chapter 4; and Anne Marie Cammisa, *From Rhetoric to Reform: Welfare Policy in American Politics* (Boulder, CO: Westview Press, 1998).

19. Detailed accounts of the history of welfare reform are Cammisa, *From Rhetoric to Reform;* and R. Kent Weaver, *Ending Welfare as We Know It* (Washington, DC: Brookings Institution, 2000).

20. See *Statistical Abstract, 2000,* Table 539, for a list.

21. A recent survey of attitudes is Richard Morin, "A Welfare Tug of War," *Washington Post National Weekly Edition,* March 14–20, 2001: 34.

22. Recent studies are summarized in Joint Center for Poverty Research, *Poverty Research News,* Vol. II, No. 3 (1998) and Vol. 5, No. 3 (2001).

23. John E. Schwarz, *America's Hidden Success,* revised edition (New York: Norton, 1988), Chapter 2. For a recent assessment, Susan E. Mayer, "Has America's Antipoverty Effort Failed?" (Institute for Policy Research; Northwestern University; www.library.nwu.edu/publications/nupr/mayer.html; accessed May 29, 1997).

24. See Ellen K. Coughlin, "Experts Add Their Voices to Welfare-Reform Debate," *Chronicle of Higher Education* (August 3, 1994): A6–7.

25. Government tax and transfer payments have little effect on redistributing income among groups or in reducing inequality. See Patricia Ruggles, "The Impact of Government Tax and Expenditure Programs on the Distribution of Income in the United States," in Osberg, ed., *Economic Inequality and Poverty,* 220–245.

26. "How are TANF Funds Being Used? The Story in FY 2000" (www.clasp.org/pubs/TANF/FY00; accessed 1/14/02); and "Acrobatic Accounting: Federal Welfare Funds Replace State Spending," *Lubbock Avalanche-Journal,* June 3, 2001: 9A.

27. This evaluation of TANF draws primarily upon the following sources: Ron Haskins, Isabel Sawhill, and Ken Weaver, "Welfare Reform: An Overview of Effects to Date," Policy Brief No. 1, January 2001 (Welfare Reform & Beyond Project, Brookings Institution); Lawrence Mead, "Welfare Reform: Meaning and Effects," *Policy Currents,* 11 (Summer 2001): 7–13; and Mark Greenberg and Steve Savner, "Comments to the U.S. Department of Health and Human Services Regarding the Reauthorization of the Temporary Assistance to Needy Families (TANF) Block Grant" (Center for Law and Social Policy, November 30, 2001). See also "Reauthorizing TANF," *Focus,* 22 (Special Issue 2002). As of the final editing of this text in August 2002, Congress had not yet completed its TANF reauthorization.

28. "The Private Food Assistance Network," *Focus,* 21 (Spring 2001): 12–15.

29. See Rebecca M. Blank and Ron Haskins, eds., *The New World of Welfare* (Washington, DC: Brookings Institution, 2001); and Joint Center for Poverty Research, *Poverty Research News,* November–December 2001.

30. Paul Taylor, "Like Taking Money from a Baby," *The Washington Post National Weekly Edition* (March 4–10, 1991): 31.

31. Peter Brandon, "Trends over Time in the Educational Attainments of Single Mothers," *Focus,* 15 (Summer and Fall 1993): 26–34. See also Charles F. Manski, "Income and Higher Education," *Focus,* 14 (Winter 1992–1993): 14–19.

32. For discussion of the evolution and mixed goals of child support policy, see Jyl Josephson, *Gender, Families, and the State: Child Support Policy in the United States* (Lanham, MD: Rowman & Littlefield, 1997); see also *Focus,* 21 (Spring 2000).

33. Christopher Jencks and Paul E. Peterson, eds., *The Urban Underclass* (Washington, DC: Brookings Institution, 1991); and Christopher Jencks, *Rethinking Social Policy: Race, Poverty, and the Underclass* (New York: HarperCollins, 1992), Chapter 5.

34. Christopher Jencks, *The Homeless* (Cambridge: Harvard University Press, 1994); and Gordon Berlin and William McAllister, "Homelessness," in Henry J. Aaron and Charles L. Schultze, eds., *Setting Domestic Priorities: What Can Government Do?* (Washington, DC: Brookings Institution, 1992), 63–99.

35. See Mark Rom, "From Welfare State to Opportunity and Responsibility (OAR) Inc.," *Policy Currents,* 11 (Summer 2001): 2–7.

SUGGESTED READINGS

Books

Aaron, Henry J., and Reischauer, Robert D. *Countdown to Reform: The Great Social Security Debate.* New York: Twentieth Century Foundation Press, 2001.

Bane, Mary Jo, and Ellwood, David T. *Welfare Realities: From Rhetoric to Reform.* Cambridge: Harvard University Press, 1994.

Blahous, Charles P. III. *Reforming Social Security: For Ourselves and Our Posterity.* Westport, CT: Praeger, 2000.

Cammisa, Anne Marie. *From Rhetoric to Reform: Welfare Policy in American Politics.* Boulder, CO: Westview Press, 1998.

Edin, Kathryn, and Lein, Laura. *Making Ends Meet: How Single Mothers Survive Welfare and Low-Wage Work.* New York: Russell Sage Foundation, 1997.

Ehrenreich, Barbara. *Nickel and Dimed: On (Not) Getting By in America.* New York: Metropolitan Books, 2001.

Jencks, Christopher. *The Homeless.* Cambridge: Harvard University Press, 1994.

Jencks, Christopher, and Peterson, Paul E., eds. *The Urban Underclass*. Washington, DC: Brookings Institution, 1991.

Levitan, Sar A., Mangum, Garth L., and Mangum, Stephen L. *Programs in Aid of the Poor*, 7th ed. Baltimore, MD: Johns Hopkins University Press, 1998.

Rodgers, Harrell R., Jr. *American Poverty in a New Era of Reform*. Armonk, NY: M. E. Sharpe, 2000.

Shaviro, Daniel. *Making Sense of Social Security Reform*. Chicago: University of Chicago Press, 2000.

Weaver, R. Kent. *Ending Welfare as We Know It*. Washington, DC: Brookings Institution, 2000.

White, Joseph. *False Alarm: Why the Greatest Threat to Social Security and Medicare Is the Campaign to "Save" Them*. Baltimore, MD: Johns Hopkins University Press, 2001.

Web Sites

Institute for Research on Poverty   www.ssc.wisc.edu/irp/

Research Forum on Children, Families, and the New Federalism   http://www.researchforum. org/

Social Security Administration   http://www.ssa.gov/SSA_Home.html

Social Security Network   www.socsec.org

Speakout.com   http://speakout.com

Welfare Reform and Beyond (Brookings Institution)   www.brookings.edu/dybdocroot/ es/wrb/wrb_hp.htm

CHAPTER 8

Health Care: Unlimited Needs, Limited Resources

The same perplexing logic and inherent goal conflicts that characterize the policies of public income support studied in the last chapter plague health care policy. Indeed, an intimate connection between the two areas makes it essential to consider them together. First, the high cost of health care is a primary contributor to poverty for many Americans. Second, the poor and the aged are more likely than the rest of the population to suffer illness and to wrestle with high medical bills. Goals and priorities, moreover, are in conflict—pursuit of one goal (greater access to medical care for the poor, for example) seems to preclude pursuit of others equally desirable (long-term care insurance for the elderly, for example). The potential need for health care is unlimited; yet, individual and social resources are limited.

Health and medicine are basic concerns of American citizens. Annual expenditures from public and private sources for health care amount to one of every seven dollars of the Gross Domestic Product. Americans each year spend more on health care than on national defense, and more per capita for health care than for automobiles and gasoline combined. Malpractice cases and medical-ethical questions, such as euthanasia, abortion, and experimentation with new forms of life, claim an increasing share of popular attention. Conditions once handled by the moral, religious, or criminal systems, such as alcoholism, gambling, anxiety, overwork, and family conflict, now tend to be classified as sicknesses treated by mental- or physical-health professionals. Jogging, health food, body building, and other physical fitness activities signal a growing concern for health.

How a society deals with pain, as well as the meaning and value assigned to it, reveals its fundamental beliefs and commitments. Pain and death are basic concerns of medicine, but they are also experiences that address the meaning of life, the value of the body, and the significance of the human spirit. Health care policy is basic because the resources and attention given to medicine, the institutions that deliver it, and the way it is received affect all social relations.

ISSUE BACKGROUND: THE HEALTH CARE SYSTEM AND ITS PROBLEMS

The Structure of American Health Care

The traditional American health care system combines public and private institutions without central planning or coordination. At the highest level of the health care profession—among physicians, dentists, psychiatrists, and psychologists—solo, *fee-for-service* (FFS) practice was the rule until recent decades. That is, the professional provider of health services established his or her own office (with perhaps one or two others sharing the same specialty), saw only his or her own patients, and charged a separate fee for each individual service performed. If a patient saw more than one provider, the patient would receive a separate bill for each service from each provider; for example, a bill might have charges for injections, blood work, urinalysis, an office visit, and so forth. Institutions like hospitals, clinics, and laboratories operated primarily on the same FFS basis. This traditional system changed in fundamental ways during the last two decades, moving away from FFS toward *managed care* systems. Nevertheless, a substantial part of the system is still FFS (especially Medicare) or discounted FFS reimbursement systems.

Changes under way in American health care delivery are producing effects not yet well understood. As advances in medicine reduce admissions and length of stay, hospitals are closing or redirecting their missions. Outpatient surgeries and freestanding surgical units, as well as minor care clinics ("Doc in a Box"), direct care away from traditional hospital inpatient care and physician offices. In 1976, hospital employment accounted for two-thirds of all health care employment; it is now about half. In recent years a more competitive hospital environment produced a wave of hospital mergers and the emergence of major hospital systems, many organized by for-profit corporations, instead of the charitable institutions that formerly dominated hospital management. Hospitals are also developing partnerships with (in some cases even ownership of) physician practices that use their facilities. They are also joining with nursing homes, home health agencies, pharmacies, and medical supply companies in partnerships or vertically integrated corporations to deliver a full range of care and to control their costs.

Advocates of this new business approach to health care argue that greater attention to the financial bottom line helps to control costs, provide services more efficiently, and introduce a customer service orientation to health care. Opponents note that these practices are unproven in their financial benefits and that they carry the danger of an entrepreneurial-driven health care system that might sacrifice access and quality to corporate profits. Much of the debate focuses on the movement of the American health care system toward *managed care.*

Managed care. In managed care the federal government, employers, and private insurers attempt to hold down costs by using *selective* contracting; that is, requiring patients to see only certain providers, either through a *health maintenance organization* (HMO), a *preferred provider organization* (PPO), or an *independent practice association* (IPA).[1] The HMO is a form of prepaid group practice. A sponsoring organization—a public, private, professional, business, or consumer group—employs doctors and other health professionals on salary to provide comprehensive health services. An HMO also may contract with independent physicians (IPA) to treat subscribers at discounted fees or on a capitation basis. Subscribers pay a set fee each month, and all medical needs are covered without additional costs. Incentives to control costs are built into HMOs. Because the premiums are prepaid and providers are salaried or working for reduced fees, unnecessary or questionable services produce no additional income, only additional costs. Hospital care is not used unless clearly necessary. Physicians, who may be given bonuses if costs are kept low, have an incentive to offer preventive care and early diagnosis and treatment. The more common PPO is an association of independent physicians who agree to contract with particular insurers to serve their customers at reduced rates (discounted FFS). Managed care insurance plans also restrict patient choice of providers in significant ways, providing significantly more generous benefits for use of hospitals, pharmacies, and other providers in the managed care network, which have agreed to discounted fee schedules. Managed care networks also stress simplified administration and reduced paperwork as cost-saving measures.

In addition to these new structures of health care delivery, managed care employs other devices to hold down costs. One uses *gatekeepers,* primary care physicians who must see patients first and whose permission is needed for patients to see specialists. The idea here is to utilize costly specialists only when clearly medically necessary. Sometimes, managed care networks also use nurses and physician assistants for initial patient contact and simple procedures. *Utilization review* is another key managed care practice; this requires some combination of second opinions before surgery or hospitalization, prior approval before a major procedure, and case management teams to coordinate all aspects of major and lengthy treatments. Similar items are *drug formularies* and *treatment protocols* requiring physicians to prescribe only certain lower-cost effective drugs or to use proven low-cost treatments before attempting more expensive and newer treatments.

Managed care has come to dominate the health care delivery system in just a few years. HMO enrollments doubled between 1980 and 1990. By 1999, over 90 percent of all insured employees were enrolled in one form or another of managed care. Market-driven forces and managed care practices reduced both patient and physician freedom of choice and independent decision making in favor of cost-conscious management of health care delivery.

Paying for Health Care

Medical bills are paid through complicated arrangements among government agencies, individuals, and private insurers. Federal, state, and local governments provide a number of health-related services directly (for example, inoculations, health inspections, vector control, veterans' care, and epidemic control). They also reimburse private medical providers through direct payments for services. Individuals pay for a variety of services directly, but they also pay indirectly by purchasing health insurance from private insurance companies and Blue Cross-Blue Shield plans. These companies then reimburse providers for covered services, which vary widely according to the terms of particular policies. Most private insurance is purchased through employers, with the employers passing their share of premiums to employees in the form of lower wages.

The U.S. health care system absorbs a massive proportion of national resources. Total spending from all sources was $1.3 trillion in 2000, a sum that amounted to 13.2 percent of the GDP for that year and an average of $4,637 spent for every man, woman, and child in the nation. That share of the GDP has been growing: In 1965, medical expenditures were only 6.2 percent of the GDP; from

1965 to 1993, they grew between 5 and 16 percent every year. Public sources paid 45 percent of the total bill, individuals paid 15 percent directly, and private insurance picked up 36 percent of the tab.[2] These percentages, however, vary greatly with the type of service. For example, direct out-of-pocket payment by individuals for hospitalization represents less than 10 percent of the total, but direct payment for dental care represents over two-thirds.

Other Nations

The United States is unique among industrial nations in its mix of private insurance, public financing, and direct patient spending.[3] In other nations, compensation by salary or by *capitation* (a fixed payment for each patient on a physician's register) is more common. Where FFS practices do exist, fee schedules established in negotiations between the government and providers restrain private fees.

There are two main types of health care systems: The central government either (1) operates a national health service, as in Great Britain and the former Soviet Union, or (2) mandates universal insurance coverage through employer or other private policies plus government insurance for the population unable to obtain private insurance, as in Germany, Sweden, France, and Italy. The systems with national health services may properly be called *socialized medicine,* for in them health care institutions are government owned and operated. Physicians and other providers work for the government, and private practice is minimal. *Universal health insurance* systems, however, vary widely in the amount of government control and are not socialized medicine. For example, in Sweden the central and local governments do not actually operate all health care programs, but they do exercise considerable influence over them; compare this with Germany, where government control is minimal.

The health care systems of the industrial world (excluding the United States) have other important features in common (notwithstanding wide differences in organization). In these nations virtually the entire population is covered by mandatory insurance for all or the major part of its health needs. The only exceptions in some nations are the wealthy, who may opt out of the mandatory system and seek private health care. In the United States, however, government-guaranteed insurance covers only the elderly and some of the poor, although tax subsidies encourage it for others. Thus, gaps in U.S. health care coverage are far more substantial than elsewhere, with millions of persons lacking appropriate access to needed health care.

Coverage in other nations is generally broader than coverage by public or private insurance in America. Coverage for nursing home care, medicines, eyeglasses, and dental services is the norm rather than the exception. These systems often cover home health care, as in England where health workers regularly visit new mothers and children. In Sweden and the Netherlands, social service agencies visit the elderly regularly to care for their health and other needs. In the case of children, these visits provide low-cost preventive services; in the case of the aged, they limit the need for expensive nursing home care.

Although some systems, such as those in France, New Zealand, and Sweden, employ relatively high deductible and coinsurance requirements, generally third-party payments cover a higher percentage of medical bills than in the United States. These international patients have fewer out-of-pocket expenses than Amer-

TABLE 8-1 ▪ Total Health Expenditures as Percentage of GDP (selected years)

	1963	1985	1998	Average Annual Growth Rate, 1960–1998
Australia	5.0	7.7	8.5	3.7%
Belgium	3.5	7.4	8.8	5.3
Canada	5.5	8.4	9.5	3.6
Denmark	3.6	6.3	8.3	4.7
France	4.2	8.5	9.6	4.5
Germany	4.8	8.5	10.6	4.3
Great Britain	3.9	5.9	6.7	3.4
Japan	3.0	6.7	7.6	6.9
The Netherlands	3.9	7.9	8.6	4.6
Sweden	4.7	9.0	8.4	3.4
United States	5.2	10.7	13.6	4.4

SOURCE: Edward Cody, "Lessons from Abroad: Is the U.S. Ready for National Health Insurance?" *Washington Post National Weekly Edition,* May 1–7, 1989, p. 38; George J. Schieber, et al., "Health Systems Performance in OECD Countries, 1980–1992," *Health Affairs,* 13 (Fall 1994), p. 101; and Gerard Andersen and Peter Sotir Hussey, "Comparing Health System Performance in OECD Countries," *Health Affairs,* 20 (May/June 2001), Exhibit 5.

icans do, and in none of these countries do medical bills place a catastrophic financial burden on families.

Despite more extensive coverage than the United States, costs in other nations are lower (see Table 8-1). There seems to be no correlation between the type of health care system and the amount of money, public and private, spent on health care. Nor is there any correlation with general levels of citizen health. All nations seek ways to hold down costs; most succeed better than the United States.

Because other nations stress physicians in general practice, strict controls on hospital utilization, and comprehensive coverage, they avoid most of America's major problems. The numbers of specialists and primary care physicians are in rough balance, financial burdens from medical care are absent, and, because programs are comprehensive, access is universal.

Yet there are disadvantages and problems in these systems as well. Virtually all are facing cost escalation. Even in systems that serve all, regardless of financial status, there are inequities in access to care and in the health of different classes that remain. In England, for example, there is still a strong correlation between mortality and morbidity rates and social class. Nations such as Great Britain and Germany have introduced some elements of managed care and provided financial incentives to control costs.

How Healthy Is America?

Expenditures for medical care cannot be translated directly into better health or longer life. Medical technology, however, certainly keeps many persons alive and

TABLE 8-2 ▪ Comparison of Infant Mortality and Life Expectancy, 1995 or nearest year (1991 for age 80 life expectancy)

	Infant Mortality (deaths per 1,000 live births)	Life Expectancy at Birth (males)	Life Expectancy at Birth (females)	Life Expectancy at Age 80 (males)	Life Expectancy at Age 80 (females)
Australia	5.7	75.0	80.9	7.0	8.8
Belgium	7.6	73.0	79.8	6.1	7.9
Canada	6.3	75.3	81.3	6.3	9.3
Denmark	5.5	72.5	77.8	6.4	8.0
France	5.8	73.9	81.9	6.8	8.6
Germany	5.3	73.0	79.5	6.2	7.8
Great Britain	6.2	74.3	79.7	7.1	8.3
Japan	4.3	76.4	82.8	6.9	8.8
The Netherlands	5.5	74.6	80.4	6.2	8.1
Sweden	4.0	76.2	81.5	6.6	8.4
United States	8.0	72.5	79.2	7.2	9.1

SOURCE: George J. Schieber, et al., "Health Systems Performance in OECD Countries, 1980–1992," *Health Affairs,* 13 (Fall 1994), p. 108; and *OECD in Figures—1997 Edition,* pp. 50–51.

in good physical condition. Intensive care units, coronary bypass surgery, and hemodialysis, as well as immunizations, fillings of dental cavities, and penicillin, lessen pain and prolong life for millions.

The most widely used statistics on health are encouraging. By 2000 life expectancy at birth in the United States averaged seventy-seven years, and the death rate for infants during the first year of life had fallen to 6.9 per 1,000 live births, the lowest rate ever. These figures represent considerable improvements over previous decades, but they are more than matched by other nations (see Table 8-2). Even though American medical technology is the most advanced in the world, the United States ranks equal to or behind such countries as Sweden, Japan, the Netherlands, Denmark, Canada, France, England, and others in life expectancy and infant mortality. Life expectancy for the very aged, however, is slightly above the median in the United States, reflecting an emphasis on the elderly in American health care policy. Obviously, many factors other than medical care influence infant mortality and life expectancy—nutrition, genetics, environment, levels of violent crime, and risk-taking, for example. Yet these figures indicate that there is substantial room for improvement in American health. Other phenomena point to major problems in the U.S. health care system.

The perception is widespread among professionals and public alike that, despite improvements in health statistics and advances in medical knowledge and technology, Americans are only marginally healthier now than in previous decades. Despite massive increases in health care expenditures and numbers of medical professionals, it is not clear that the additional benefits have outweighed the additional costs. Most Americans, although satisfied with their individual care, believe that there is a crisis in the system as a whole.[4]

If the basic ills of the American health care system are looked at generally, an overall pattern is clear: The health care system emphasizes some kinds of care at the expense of others. In particular, cure of acute medical conditions, those lasting less than three months and requiring medical attention or restricted activity, takes priority over care for chronic conditions, those debilitating illnesses lasting over three months. Expensive, high-technology, curative hospital care receives more attention than disease prevention, health education, rehabilitation services, low-cost chronic care, or neighborhood health centers.

The main problems of U.S. health care can be grouped into three categories: access, cost, and quality. The politics of health care is so perplexing because solutions to these three problems are widely regarded, perhaps mistakenly, as being in conflict. Guaranteeing access to health care for all Americans could increase costs and could reduce quality. Some health policy scholars, however, believe that cost control and universal access can only happen together. The following paragraphs describe the three problems. The Contemporary Policy and Evaluation sections describe and evaluate federal policies designed to affect them. The Future Alternatives section discusses reforms proposed to fulfill the seemingly contradictory goals of broadened access, cost reduction, and high quality of care. That section also discusses ethical questions in medical policy and the problem of providing long-term care, especially for the elderly.

Inequities in Access to Health Care

The uninsured. The percentage of the population having health insurance coverage has declined since 1980. Currently, about 40 million persons (16 percent of the population under age sixty-five) lack public or private health insurance coverage and have serious difficulty obtaining health care services. This figure counts those persons who do not have health insurance at a given point in time. In truth, however, uninsurance is a dynamic condition, with people moving into and out of uninsured status constantly. For some the status is brief, but for about 10 million persons it lasts more than a year, and an estimated 60 million persons go without insurance for at least one month out of the year.[5] About 25 percent of working-age adults making less than $25,000 per year are uninsured and another 10 to 20 percent have experienced a spell of uninsurance during the preceding two years. Medicaid, the federal health care program for the poor, covers only about half of the poor and near-poverty population, leaving millions of such persons without insurance. Even those living close to health care facilities, if they lack insurance, are likely to be "dumped;" that is, transferred to an overcrowded and understaffed public hospital. Most of those without insurance work full-time or live in families with at least one full-time worker, but that worker's employer may not provide insurance, or the worker cannot afford the premiums.

Of course, health insurance is not health care, and health care is not health itself. Health *practices* such as fitness, adequate rest, avoidance of smoking, and so forth contribute more to life and well-being than health *care*. Yet, when illness or injury strike, medical care becomes vital to a person's health. Health *insurance* is the ticket to medical care in the United States.

Many Americans believe that persons without insurance can receive care in a public hospital with state-of-the-art medical facilities if they are truly sick. Although this is true, the care received is often too little and too late. Emergency care received when a condition has progressed beyond the initial stages is far more expensive than the basic care that could have alleviated the condition earlier. Moreover, persons treated in this fashion remain ill longer, have more disability, and face more obstacles to productive work. In addition, recent data indicate that uninsured persons, even when admitted to hospitals, receive less care, as well as fewer tests and other procedures, and are dismissed earlier than insured persons with the same conditions; their death rates are also substantially higher. The quality of care received by the uninsured, even when they can see medical professionals, is significantly inferior to that received by those with insurance. Moreover, the "safety net" of public hospitals, clinics, and charity care has become highly frayed in the last decade. Competition, mergers, and financial belt-tightening have reduced the number of beds in safety net hospitals for the poor and have made it more difficult for clinics providing free or reduced-cost care to remain open. Physicians and other health professionals have likewise reduced their levels of charity care.

The problem of lack of access has a number of dimensions not apparent from the previous bare statistics. Loss of insurance means difficulty in getting health care. Since health insurance is so closely tied to employment, many persons experience "job lock"; that is, they are tied to jobs that they may wish to change but fear changing because a new employer may not provide insurance. Similarly, unemployed persons with health problems find difficulty securing employment, because prospective employers cannot afford to carry them on their health insurance policies. These problems are now beginning substantially to affect the middle class, and they are growing worse. Rates of uninsurance rise in periods of economic slowdown as employers, particularly small businesses, drop insurance because of high costs. Employment is falling in the traditionally well-insured manufacturing sector, and growing in the service and part-time sectors, which have high rates of uninsurance.[6] These factors have other indirect effects, placing more of a burden on taxpayers, public hospitals, and employers who continue to offer insurance benefits.

Maldistribution of resources.   Medical care is maldistributed; that is, the areas and persons with the greatest needs for health care are not the areas and persons with the greatest access to care. Hospitals, nursing homes, clinics, doctors, dentists, and other health care professionals disproportionately locate in well-to-do urban and suburban areas because the highest incomes can be generated there. The residents of these areas have better access to care than do the poor and residents of rural areas. This phenomenon is particularly true for access to specialized institutions and personnel, but it is also true, to a lesser extent, for general practitioners and basic care institutions. Ability to pay rather than need determines who receives medical care.

This limited-access pattern contributes to the poor health and shorter life expectancy of those who are poor or live in rural communities. African-American infant and maternal mortality rates are nearly twice those of whites and comparable to many countries in the Third World. The average life expectancy for African Americans is seven years lower than for whites. One-third of Hispanics

and one-quarter of African Americans are uninsured, compared to about 13 percent of whites. Sixteen percent of African Americans and 10 percent of Hispanics
rely on emergency rooms for their primary care, compared to 5 percent of whites.
Poor children tend to be inadequately immunized and to suffer more than other
children do from chronic and acute conditions, such as vision problems, low he-
moglobin, upper respiratory ailments, and elevated blood lead levels; a quarter
have severe dental problems. Substantial racial gaps exist in incidences of heart
attack and stroke, kidney disease, meningitis, and pneumonia. African Americans
are less likely than whites (even at the same income levels) to receive coronary
bypass and kidney transplant surgery. The poor suffer as well from significantly
higher rates of mental illness, and they have many more days of restricted activity, bed disability, and lost work than those who are not poor.[7] Thousands of communities have no health care professionals at all. Half of all hospital closures since
1983 have been in rural areas, and one-quarter of all existing rural hospitals are
in danger of closing. The number of medical doctors per 100,000 rural population
is half that in metropolitan areas. However, life expectancy is lower, infant mortality higher, and the incidence of accidents and chronic illness greater in rural areas than in metropolitan areas.

High Cost

Cost escalation in the medical field has been constant. Table 8-3 and Figure 8-1
illustrate this trend. Although the rate of health care inflation slowed in the mid-
1990s, it remained well above the rate of inflation in the economy generally, and
the slowdown was caused in part by the rising numbers of the uninsured going
without health care. Very high health care inflation reappeared in the late 1990s.

**TABLE 8-3 ■ Aggregate and Per Capita National Health Expenditures
(selected years)**

	Aggregate ($ billions)	*$ Per Capita*	*Percent of GDP (GNP before 1965)*
1940	4.0	$ 30	4.0
1950	12.7	82	4.4
1960	26.9	146	5.3
1965	41.1	202	5.7
1970	73.2	341	7.1
1975	130.7	582	8.0
1980	247.2	1,052	8.9
1985	428.2	1,733	10.2
1990	697.5	2,683	12.1
1995	988.5	3,621	13.6
2000	1,299.5	4,637	13.2

SOURCE: "National Health Expenditures, 1986–2000," *Health Care Financing Review*, 8 (Summer 1987), Table 12; *1997 Data Compendium* (Baltimore, MD: Health Care Financing Administration, March 1997), p. 18; and Katharine Levit, et al., "Inflation Spurs Health Spending in
2000," *Health Affairs*, 21 (January/February, 2002), 172–181.

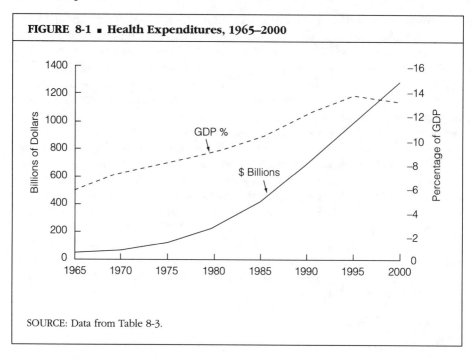

FIGURE 8-1 ▪ Health Expenditures, 1965–2000

SOURCE: Data from Table 8-3.

There is no universal agreement among students of the problem on all the reasons for cost increases or on their order of priority. Some factors, however, are commonly accepted as important.[8] Certainly general inflationary trends have contributed to the rise in medical costs. Because medicine's share of the GDP has been increasing, however, reasons more particular to health care must be sought to explain the growth in costs.

Third-party payments. The most important contributor to rising cost in the 1960s and 1970s was the growth in third-party payments for medical care. Third-party payers are not health care providers (hospitals, doctors, and the like) or patients, but are those who pay the charges to providers on behalf of the patients. The primary third-party payers are governments (particularly through Medicare and Medicaid), the Blue Cross-Blue Shield plans, and private health insurance companies. Formerly, patients paid most health costs directly from their own resources. Now most are paid indirectly, through privately purchased or employer-provided health insurance or through public programs. Patients, not seeing the direct cost, ask for the best in service. Until the mid-1980s, public and private insurers did little to hold down costs, preferring the easier route of passing them on to consumers in the form of higher insurance premiums and taxes. In general, third-party payment does not currently contribute to health care cost increases, except for prescription drugs (explained later).

Technology. Modern medical technology contributes substantially to increased health care spending. Diagnostic and treatment procedures—such as Magnetic Resonance Imaging (MRI) for exact images of internal tissues and organs, renal dialysis, Neonatal Intensive Care Units, chemotherapy, coronary bypass surgery, and fiberoptic surgery—are tremendously expensive, because of both the equipment and materials themselves and the specialized personnel needed to operate them. Yet there has been little scientific assessment of the effectiveness of most new treatments in extending life or improving well-being.[9] Some argue that they have not contributed importantly to an increased life expectancy and that they carry their own dangers of harm to the patient from risky diagnostic procedures, unnecessary surgery, and drug side effects. Others contend that such criticisms are exaggerated and that many persons have benefited from the new procedures through longer life and freedom from pain and disability.

Some new technologies reduce costs. New drugs can treat conditions formerly requiring surgery. MRI scanners can look inside the body to make diagnoses that formerly required exploratory surgery. Such cost reductions apply, however, to the cost of individual procedures. Because they are noninvasive, doctors now perform such procedures more often than the old ones they replaced, adding to the total cost of the health care system. This is an example of technological change producing increased *service intensity*. Patients tend to receive more procedures today than they did before. New procedures do not necessarily replace old ones. Of course, the FFS system was also an incentive to service intensity. Service intensity may, indeed, be the most important cause of higher health care costs, because it interacts with all of the other cost increase factors.[10]

There are also serious cost problems associated with medical technology that derive from status competition among hospitals and doctors. Helicopter ambulances, open-heart surgery units, and chemotherapy units have become items of high prestige, and often hospitals in the same area will have duplicate versions of the same technology, irrespective of the actual need for them. The result is high acquisition costs, underutilization of equipment and staff, and the danger that medical skills will become rusty. Each patient entering the hospital helps subsidize the equipment.

Labor costs. Medical care remains a highly labor-intensive field, despite its high technology. The fact that medicine is the only major industry that is both labor and technology intensive is a primary contributor to its high costs. In 1972 American hospitals employed 221 persons for every 100 patients. By 1992 the number employed had more than doubled to 525 per 100 patients. American hospitals employ a higher ratio of staff to patients than any other nation. Because it has become more difficult to find registered nurses and some other medical professionals, salaries and bonuses are rising rapidly, an additional cost pressure. Interestingly enough, although there has been a dramatic rise in the number of workers per patient, there has also been a sharp increase in complaints from patients about a lack of attention and care. Job responsibilities become fragmented among various levels of nurses, aides, therapists, and orderlies, so that effective supervision is difficult to achieve.

Prescription drugs. Although still making up less than 10 percent of all health care spending, prescription drugs claim an increasing share of the national health budget. Drug costs increased by 18 percent in 1999 and 14 percent in 2000, helping to fuel the latest round of health care cost inflation. Four factors drive prescription cost inflation: managed care organizations now provide more generous drug coverage; physicians write more prescriptions per patient; new and expensive drugs exist, which entered the market in greater numbers in the late 1990s; and drug companies raise the price of existing drugs. Aggressive marketing of new drugs to the public and to doctors reinforces these tendencies. Drug cost inflation highlighted

Medicare's lack of prescription coverage and stimulated Congressional debate over adding such coverage. With more and more medicines in the research and development pipeline and with no slowing of physician or public interest in the latest "miracle drugs," pharmaceuticals will remain a major contributor to cost increases.

Age.   The aging of the population also drives health cost increases. Life expectancies at ages sixty and eighty-five began to increase significantly in 1950. By 1995, male life expectancy at age sixty-five had increased to an additional 15.3 years; for females, the increase was an additional 19.1 years. This means that the average sixty-five-year-old female will live to age eighty-four (see Figure 8-2.). Presently, there are about 15 million Americans over age seventy-five; in thirty years, there will be 25 million. The aged have more severe health care problems than working adults or children. They also have more instances of disability and of the inability to perform the ordinary activities of daily living. The elderly require substantially more acute care, more chronic care, and more assisted living care than persons of other ages.

Public expectations.   The public's exaggerated expectations of medical science, coupled with its unprecedented fear of illness, old age, and death, also contribute to the cost problems. Americans treat these as abnormal conditions, rather than as part of human life. Thus, the sick and aged increasingly use medical specialists, hospitals, and nursing homes. As the population ages, the demand for these services increases dramatically. Medical science discovers more and more "risk factors" for disease and at earlier ages, thus placing more and more people under medical care.

The public's exaggerated expectations of the health care system also account for the rise in costs, when they spend billions of dollars each year on visits to the doctor for colds, flu, and other self-limiting illnesses and for undifferentiated pains

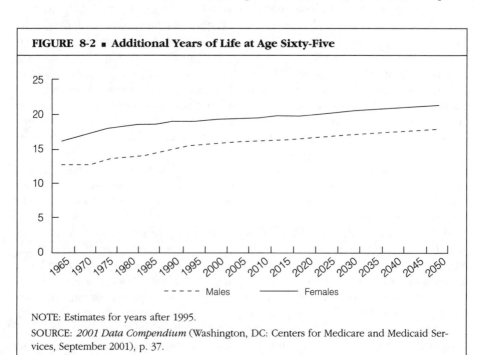

FIGURE 8-2 ▪ Additional Years of Life at Age Sixty-Five

NOTE: Estimates for years after 1995.

SOURCE: *2001 Data Compendium* (Washington, DC: Centers for Medicare and Medicaid Services, September 2001), p. 37.

and anxieties. As a result, primary care physicians and many specialists spend most of their time providing psychological reassurance, rather than physical "curing." The increasing tendency of public and private insurance to cover treatment for mental illness, drug addiction, and other addictions means that more persons use the health care system for such conditions, also adding to the total cost.

Other causes. Contributions from employers to employee health insurance are nontaxable. Moreover, individuals may deduct all medical expenses over 7.5 percent of income. Thus, the federal tax system encourages employees to take additional income in the form of insurance benefits and to use deductible medical services. These tax policies cost the treasury approximately $81 billion in 2000. Most of these benefits go to middle- and upper-class persons. When health insurance and treatment were made tax deductible in the early 1950s, it was to make sure that Americans obtained health insurance; now it has the unintended consequence of driving up health care costs.

A small proportion of health cost increases is due to medical malpractice suits filed by injured or disgruntled patients. Malpractice insurance companies raise their premiums to providers, who in turn raise their fees to consumers to cover the additional costs. Moreover, doctors have begun to practice "defensive medicine" by ordering more extensive tests and procedures than strictly necessary, in order to guard themselves against possible lawsuits. Malpractice, however, has been exaggerated as a reason for the high cost of health care, contributing recently to less than 10 percent of health care inflation. Physicians and the public often attribute to "defensive medicine" tests and procedures that would have been performed anyway because of the desire for absolute certainty in diagnosis and because of "service intensity."

Quality of Health Care

Health statistics are improving, and most Americans are satisfied with their health care. Moreover, American medical technology and health care innovation are the best in the world. Yet, fear of high health costs, impersonality, and increased size in the health care field leave Americans feeling uneasy. In addition, there are significant concerns that efforts to hold down costs through managed care may adversely affect the quality of care that most Americans receive. Some aspects of the current system do raise serious quality issues.[11]

First is the severe and growing problem of uninsured Americans and unequal access to care, previously discussed. It is difficult for Americans to claim to possess the highest quality of care in the world when such a high proportion of the population lacks access to it and suffers unnecessary disability, pain, and death.

Second is the focus of the American system on sickness, not health. Although we do very well in curing life-threatening conditions and treating trauma, we do not do well in providing basic prevention and wellness services. These failures produce lower quality of life and health.

A third quality problem, linked to the first two, is overspecialization among physicians. Primary care physicians, that is, family doctors and general practitioners, now constitute a small proportion of American physicians. Cardiologists, neurosurgeons, urologists, and other specialists dominate the medical profession. In 1950, two-thirds of all physicians were general practitioners; today, fewer than one-fourth are. In other nations, the percentages are significantly higher; for example, 35 percent in Sweden and 50 percent in England.

Serious consequences flow from the predominance of specialists. It may help account for the rather poor performance on measures of infant mortality and life expectancy relative to those of other developed nations, because these measures are more sensitive to high-quality routine care than to sophisticated, exceptional procedures. Overspecialization also contributes to the high cost of medical care, because specialists charge more and use hospitals more than do general practitioners. Supply-and-demand economics did not work to reduce prices when specialized fields became overcrowded. At a median income of $160,000 per year, American physicians are by far the most well-compensated in the world. The growth of managed care and legislative reactions to overspecialization have produced a surging demand for primary care physicians and a corresponding decrease in specialization in medical schools, but these measures will take decades to produce a substantial reduction in the proportion of specialists.

American medicine's focus on developing and applying new technologies in drugs, diagnostic tests, and surgical procedures produces a "service intensity" (higher numbers of procedures per patient) that not only increases cost, but also produces a greater likelihood of medical errors that harm patients. Even though the *percentage* of errors is low, the large number of procedures per patient produces a high *number* of errors. In 1999, the Institute of Medicine shocked the nation with an estimate of up to 100,000 deaths per year resulting from medical errors. The Institute followed up in 2001 with another report recommending substantial changes in American medicine to reduce unacceptable quality problems.[12] Even if, as some experts allege, the number and magnitude of medical errors has been exaggerated, such indicators point to serious concerns. Moreover, there is no single federal agency responsible for monitoring the quality of American health care. Responsibility is divided among a wide variety of federal, state, and private actors.

CONTEMPORARY POLICY: HEALTH CARE FOR THE POOR AND AGED

Until the mid-1960s, government was a relatively small part of the health care picture. Typically at that time, state and local governments provided garbage and sewer services, furnished safe drinking water, and kept rabies, disease-bearing insects, and epidemic diseases under control. The importance of these measures should not be overlooked, as they contributed the principal element to increased life expectancy in the twentieth century. State and local governments did support some health care services, providing free clinics and immunizations for the poor and supporting charity wards in county hospitals. The federal government has a fairly long history of monitoring the quality and safety of consumer goods that could represent adverse health risks. The Department of Agriculture inspects and grades meat and poultry products. The Food and Drug Administration reviews, tests, and licenses drugs. Chapter 5 described the federal government's programs for monitoring air and water purity.

In addition, the federal government has long provided direct medical care to active duty military personnel and veterans. Beginning with the establishment of the National Institutes of Health (NIH) in 1937, the federal government supported biomedical research. In addition to NIH, the National Science Foundation, the Department of Health and Human Services, and the Department of Agriculture also fund research. Between 1950 and 2000 federal expenditures for health research and development increased dramatically from $160 million to nearly $18 billion, accounting for almost half of the nation's health research spending.

It was not until the mid-1960s that the volume and complexity of federal health legislation increased dramatically, and expenditures exploded.[13] Medicare and Medicaid, the most important programs, were enacted in 1965 after years of debate. Many legislators had long disputed any federal responsibility in this area, and others had advocated a program of national health care along European lines. A compromise was reached in which social insurance would be extended to cover the serious health needs of the aged; this was the birth of Medicare. Almost as an afterthought, Medicaid was added to help the states pay the medical expenses of welfare recipients.[14]

Medicare

Congress designed Medicare as a supplement to Social Security for elderly persons, who have more extensive medical needs and expenses than the general population. Medicare intends to protect this population against the risks of medical disaster. Approximately 40 million persons benefit from Medicare coverage, which consists of two parts: Hospital Insurance, known as Part A, and Supplementary Medical Insurance, or Part B. *Hospital Insurance* covers a broad range of hospital and posthospital services, subject to some deductibles and coinsurance. (A *deductible* is a set dollar amount that a patient must pay directly before insurance benefits begin. *Coinsurance* is a percentage of the bill that a patient must pay directly after meeting the deductible.) For a given benefit period, beneficiaries pay a deductible for hospital care set at the approximate cost of one day of hospital care, $812 in 2002. Medicare pays the entire cost of the first sixty days in the hospital; patients pay coinsurance of $203 per day for days sixty-one to ninety, and $406 per day for stays beyond ninety days. To encourage early discharge from expensive hospital care, Medicare covers certain types of posthospital care, such as skilled nursing facilities and home health service. Beneficiaries pay $102 per day from 21 to 100 days in a skilled nursing facility. Thereafter, benefits cease. Medicare does not pay for ordinary nursing home or routine home care, but it does pay the reasonable cost of hospice care for terminally ill patients.

A special payroll tax finances Part A of Medicare. Both employer and employee pay a tax of 1.45 percent of the employee's total wage. In addition to the aged, Hospital Insurance since 1974 covers persons with end-stage renal (kidney) disease and disabled persons, if they have been entitled to Social Security disability payments for at least two consecutive years.

Supplementary Medical Insurance (Part B) is a voluntary insurance program for persons age sixty-five and older. Monthly premiums were $54 in 2002. These premiums cover 25 percent of the cost of Part B; general tax revenues pay for the remaining 75 percent of expenditures. The premium is so low that 98 percent of the elderly elect to buy coverage. Part B covers physicians' services, outpatient hospital services, home health, and other medical services. After a yearly deductible of $100, Medicare pays 80 percent of allowed charges (the maximum fees that the government specifies) for covered services. Physicians who accept Medicare fees and bill the program directly receive more rapid payment, and patients are responsible only for the 20 percent coinsurance. Physicians not accepting assignment may charge higher fees, but no more than 115 percent of the Medicare-approved fees, and they must collect directly from patients, who then claim Medicare reimbursement themselves. Medicare managed care options combine both Parts A and B into one contract with a managed care agency for all covered services, plus other services that such agencies may cover. The Medicare + Choice program created by the Balanced Budget Act of 1997 requires seniors to choose between traditional Medicare and a variety of Medicare managed care options when they enroll.

Many of the elderly retain private insurance coverage from their previous employers or choose to purchase private health insurance to cover those parts of their care not covered by Medicare Part A or B. These private choices are referred to as "medigap" policies. Federal law regulates coverage and rules for such policies. Elderly persons whose low income makes them eligible for Medicaid are automatically covered by Medicare in most states, which have elected to "buy in" to the program by paying the recipient's premiums, deductibles, and coinsurance. Persons with both Medicare and Medicaid are "dual eligibles."

Medicare costs.   The costs of Medicare have been prime contributors to health cost inflation. Medicare costs were $242 billion in 2001. Figure 8-3 shows the increases in costs and numbers of recipients since the program's beginning. The reasons for this growth are clear. Growth in hospital costs, physician's fees, drug prices, and technology previously discussed are the prime causes. Moreover, because the proportion of the elderly is growing and they are living longer, the increase in beneficiaries and years covered contribute substantially to cost increases.

Congress took action in the 1980s to change the way Medicare pays hospitals and physicians. These policy changes slowed Medicare's rate of growth, but

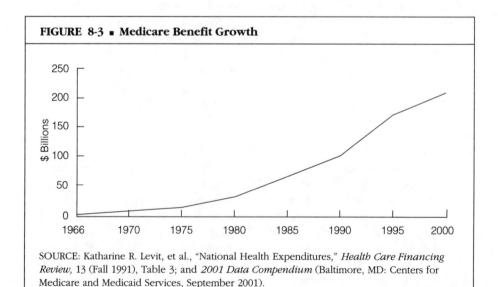

FIGURE 8-3 ▪ Medicare Benefit Growth

SOURCE: Katharine R. Levit, et al., "National Health Expenditures," *Health Care Financing Review,* 13 (Fall 1991), Table 3; and *2001 Data Compendium* (Baltimore, MD: Centers for Medicare and Medicaid Services, September 2001).

not its overall tendency. Medicare first replaced its system of reimbursements to hospitals with a system of prospective payments. Instead of reimbursing hospitals for their claimed "reasonable costs" for patient care, as in the past, the prospective payment system (PPS) utilizes a fixed scale for treating nearly 500 different conditions (Diagnosis Related Groups, or DRGs). The hospitals have incentives for cutting costs and making sure that only necessary services are given to patients, for if their costs are higher than the set fee for their treatments, they must still accept the DRG-established fee as payment in full and may not charge the patient the difference. However, if their costs are below the PPS payment, they keep the difference as profit.

Hospitals responded to these changes by moving many procedures from an inpatient to an outpatient basis and developing satellite clinics, skilled nursing facilities, and home health agencies to perform many procedures formerly covered in the hospital. This change is partly a reflection of new technology, but also a response to the fact that outpatient procedures were not subject to PPS. When spending for these forms of care grew in the 1990s, Congress responded by directing the federal agency responsible for administering Medicare (and Medicaid), the Centers for Medicare and Medicaid Services (CMS), to develop and implement prospective payment systems for outpatient, skilled nursing, rehabilitative, and home health treatments, which phased in between 1999 and 2002.

Medicaid and private insurers have now implemented prospective payment systems. Yet they have important limits. Hospitals faced with declining revenues place subtle and not-so-subtle pressures on physicians to discharge patients early, the so-called quicker and sicker alternative. Additionally, the expansion of DRGs forced some hospitals to close unprofitable departments or to "dump" patients to other hospitals when costs cannot be shifted to non-Medicare patients. Private insurers now work increasingly hard to cut their costs and have clamped down on hospitals' ability to "cost shift" Medicare losses to private patients. In turn, this forced hospitals into rapid restructuring and, in some cases, into severe financial difficulty.

Congress also acted to reform the way in which Medicare reimburses physicians. There is now an annual cap on Medicare physician payments, and a new scale of reimbursement called the "resource-based relative value scale" (RBRVS) is in effect.[15] Over time, the primary care specialties, such as family practice and internal medicine, saw reimbursement rates increase, while surgeons, anesthesiologists, and ophthalmologists saw their rates rise more slowly or, in some cases, even decrease. The intended effect is to encourage more use of lower-cost primary care and less of high-cost specializations, as well as to provide incentives for physicians to enter the primary care fields. The phase-in of RBRVS produced considerable political conflict within the medical profession, as procedure-oriented specialists lobbied against primary care physicians over the figures to be used to create the RBRVS payment lists. Growth in Medicare physician payments slowed considerably by the mid-1990s.

Medicaid

Medicaid is a public assistance program funded out of general revenues. Like TANF (reviewed in Chapter 7), it is a federal-state program with benefits varying among the states. States must cover SSI beneficiaries, those who would have been qualified for AFDC under pre-TANF rules, and certain other poor persons, particularly young children and pregnant women. The states must cover all children in families with incomes below the poverty line. In addition, they may choose to cover children in families with incomes up to 185 percent of poverty and other "medically needy" persons as defined by state law. Because of state variations in definitions of eligibility and difficulties in enrolling eligible persons, the proportion of the poor covered varies by state. Nationally, fewer than half of the poor and near-poor receive Medicaid coverage.

To receive Medicaid funds, states must offer certain basic medical services without cost to the patient. Depending on the state's per capita income, the federal government reimburses 50 to 80 percent of the costs for these services, which include inpatient and outpatient hospital services; physician's services; prenatal care; laboratory and X-ray services; home health services; skilled nursing; early screening, diagnosis, nursing home care, and treatment of physical and mental defects in those under twenty-one; and family planning services and supplies. Additionally, states may include other services for which the federal government will reimburse a proportion of costs. Optional services include clinical services, dental care, physical therapy, drugs, dentures, and eyeglasses. All states offer some optional services.

The states can "buy in" to Medicare for elderly Medicaid recipients by paying SMI premiums. The reverse is also true, as many poor Medicare recipients also are eligible for Medicaid, particularly for nursing home care and other services not covered by Medicare. About one-fourth of all Medicaid recipients are supplementing Medicare, and Medicaid costs reflect this, with over 40 percent going for nursing home and intermediate care. Medicaid supplies 85 percent of all third-party payments to nursing homes and nearly half of all nursing home revenues. Although the aged, blind, and disabled are only 25 percent of Medicaid recipients, their care accounts for two-thirds of the program's cost. Only one-third is expended on children, their mothers, and other non-aged, nondisabled recipients.

Just as with Medicare, the costs of Medicaid exploded far beyond original estimates, growing 200 percent between 1980 and 1993, accounting for two-thirds of all public assistance spending by the mid-1990s. This explosive growth severely strained state budgets. Combined federal and state expenditures were $228 billion in 2001 for over 42 million recipients. Figure 8-4 shows the program's growth in federal and state costs. The number of recipients increased rapidly in the late 1980s, because of legislatively mandated eligibility. This legislation also expanded Medicaid subsidies to help the poor elderly with home health care costs and with the cost of Part B premiums. Medical inflation in general and the high costs of nursing home care for the impoverished elderly and disabled account for most increases. In recent years, the large number of persons without medical insurance strained local public hospital budgets, for state law often mandates that they provide indigent health care on an emergency basis. Local governments faced with these bills pressured state governments to make more persons eligible for Medicaid, thus passing part of the costs on to the federal government.

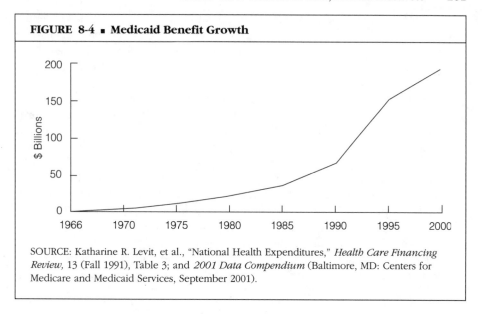

FIGURE 8-4 ■ Medicaid Benefit Growth

SOURCE: Katharine R. Levit, et al., "National Health Expenditures," *Health Care Financing Review*, 13 (Fall 1991), Table 3; and *2001 Data Compendium* (Baltimore, MD: Centers for Medicare and Medicaid Services, September 2001).

State Children's Health Insurance Program (SCHIP)

Children are the one group of uninsured for which it is easiest for legislators of both parties and all ideological stances to show sympathy. The Balanced Budget Act of 1997 (BBA) (see Chapter 4 for a summary of the whole bill) established a federal block grant to the states totaling $20.3 billion from FY1998 to FY2002. States may use these funds to expand Medicaid to children not presently eligible, or they may use it to establish a separate child health insurance program.[16] Under either option states must expend some of their own funds as a condition for receiving the block grant money. State plans must meet minimum federal standards and receive approval from the Department of Health and Human Services. (See Chapter 2 for a discussion of block grants and their conditions.)

Although many states were slow to create their SCHIP programs, enrollment expanded rapidly in the last three years. This law intends to cover as many as half of the estimated 10 million children who were without insurance in 1997. By December 2001, 3.5 million children were enrolled. States have begun to create seamless application forms for Medicaid and SCHIP and to undertake extensive programs of outreach through schools, churches, health fairs, shopping centers, and the mass media. These efforts intend to help parents to know about the availability of these federal programs for their children and to make it easier and less bureaucratic to enroll them.

Other Federal Programs

Though Medicare, Medicaid, and SCHIP account for most public health expenditures and for nearly one-fifth of the entire federal budget, there are other important federal health programs. Many were developed in the late 1960s and early 1970s to attack the problems of access and escalating health care costs.

Thousands of Federally Qualified Health Centers and other federally funded systems of rural and migrant clinics serve over 10 million low-income and uninsured persons each year. Community Health Centers are funded by a Primary Care Block Grant, now standing at approximately $1 billion per year. Other clinics receive funding from different federal block grants and from state and local funds. In addition to the system of public hospitals, they are the central "safety net" health care institutions for the uninsured. The federal government also funds three other health-related block grants to the states: Maternal and Child Health Services; Alcohol, Drug Abuse, and Mental Health; and Preventive Health Services. Through its spending on medical research and education, the federal government helps to support the medical and allied health schools that train physicians, nurses, and other medical care providers. Medicare and Medicaid provide nearly $10 billion per year in direct and indirect Graduate Medical Education funds to train resident physicians. In addition, there are special programs aimed at training providers for rural and other underserved areas, particularly the National Health Service Corps, the Disadvantaged Minority Health Improvement Act of 1990, and the Health Careers Opportunity Training Program.

POLICY EVALUATION: HEALTH CARE AT THE CROSSROADS

When policy analysts evaluate health care policy in terms of its intended goals, a mixed picture emerges. Federal programs have helped to train thousands of health care providers and to fund path-breaking research. U.S. health care, for acute life-threatening conditions and injuries, is the best in the world. Medicare and Medicaid have reduced the financial burden of health care for the elderly and poor and addressed inequitable distribution of care by lowering financial barriers to medical care. Yet burdens remain for much of the population, and serious problems of access persist. Moreover, unintended consequences are a major concern, as health policy contributes to the overspecialization of physicians, and Medicare and Medicaid contributed substantially to the cost escalation in health care.

Health statistics have improved during the last twenty years, and government support of medical research, federal training programs for health workers, and public financing of medical care for the aged and poor have assisted this advance. Infant mortality, for example, has declined over 50 percent in the last twenty-five years. Deaths from heart attack, high blood pressure, and stroke are down substantially, and deaths from most major diseases are decreasing in the forty-five to sixty-four age group, meaning longer and healthier life. Medical research developed chemotherapies for cancer treatment, artificial joints and internal organs, computer-aided imaging, and electronic fetal monitoring. Medical professionals and the public know far more today about the hazards of drugs, smoking, environmental pollution, and poor diet. Yet the American health care system is far more successful in delaying the onset of death from acute illness than it is in relieving the effects of chronic conditions such as diabetes and arthritis or in providing preventive services. Moreover, we are no nearer solving problems of access, rising cost, and quality than we were three decades ago. Indeed, access and cost problems now seem more intractable.

Medicare and Medicaid

Successes.   Medicare and Medicaid are responsible for some of the most dramatic gains in health.[17] Most people see physicians regularly, though gaps between poor and nonpoor still persist. Approximately 42 million persons each year benefit from Medicaid and 40 million from Medicare. These two programs pay for about 16 million hospital stays per year, and about 50 million persons receive physician services. Five million receive home health services.

Measures of health also show improvement for the poor and aged. Data are not available on death rates by social class, but data by race show that age-adjusted rates fell 10 percent for whites and 13 percent for African Americans and others between 1965 and 1974, the years immediately following the implementation of Medicare and Medicaid. Infant mortality declined in this period by 38 percent for nonwhites and 31 percent for whites. The 1980s and 1990s continued declines in death rates from diseases, particularly those afflicting the elderly. Medicare and Medicaid achieve these results with extremely low administrative costs, less than 2 percent of benefits paid for Medicare and less than 5 percent of expenditures for Medicaid, a result far better than private health insurance carriers.

Problems.   Medicare and Medicaid, however, have failed to do all their sponsors hoped and have led to increasingly high costs. Both programs have, moreover, some structural flaws that inhibit their ability to deal most effectively with the major problems in health care. Access to health care remains a problem along geographical, racial, and income lines. Large differences in death rates, life expectancy, and infant mortality persist. There is also some evidence of high rates of unnecessary surgery under Medicare and Medicaid. Because of state variations in eligibility definitions, half of the poor are not covered by Medicaid. Burdensome qualification procedures keep millions of persons from receiving benefits for which they are otherwise qualified. Rural residents still find it difficult to see doctors, dentists, and other providers. Because of state variations in coverage, the amount spent per recipient varies widely. Some states, because of cost increases in Medicaid, have placed limits on levels of coverage that amount to very high coinsurance requirements.

Gaps in coverage exist within the Medicare program. It has no dedicated long-term care component; therefore, it is highly restrictive on nursing home and home care. Those aged who need this care indefinitely, unless they are well-to-do, must "spend down" their financial resources until they are poor enough to qualify for Medicaid. The lack of a prescription drug benefit in Medicare has become a very significant problem as more and more drugs come onto the market, and their cost rises. Medicare pays for drugs only as part of inpatient care. Many of the aged, especially those with major prescription needs, continue to have high out-of-pocket expenditures because of deductibles and coinsurance, averaging $2,200 per year, an enormous burden for those near poverty. Numerous seniors do not take all the drugs prescribed for them, because they cannot afford to fill the prescriptions. (Medicaid does have a drug benefit, but most states severely limit the number of prescriptions per month that it will pay for.) Medicare pays only about 45 percent of the health costs of the aged. The rest must come from Medicaid, out-of-pocket spending, or privately purchased "medigap" insurance.

State governments have been reeling under the burden of the rapidly increasing Medicaid costs, which rose from 11 percent of state budgets in 1988 to

17 percent in 1992. By 1992 New Hampshire spent over one-third of its budget on Medicaid; Wisconsin spent 21 percent, as did Texas and Missouri. This fact puts tremendous pressure on the ability of states to fund public and higher education, roads, and public safety.[18] These costs and problems in state health care for the indigent led many states to work toward reform of their Medicaid programs as described in the Future Alternatives section. Federal government spending for health care concentrates on the elderly, to the neglect of children and others. To some extent this concentration is necessary. The elderly need more health care. Yet the consequences of poor prenatal and postnatal care for mothers and their children are serious and long term. They produce weakened general health, decreased learning ability and poor performance in school, and decreased motor skills, resulting in poorer employability.

Structural problems also inhibit the effectiveness of Medicare and Medicaid, preventing them from accomplishing all their goals. Because they were not designed to alter the health care delivery system but merely to pay a portion of its bills, they contributed to cost escalation in health care by underwriting the most expensive forms of care. Medicare regulations allow its most generous payments for acute hospitalization; Medicaid pays nearly half of all nursing home costs and has largely financed the expansion of that industry. Medicare costs remain very high and are projected to increase over 10 percent in 2002, placing severe pressure on both the Hospital Insurance Trust Fund and the federal budget. The Trust Fund is projected to be safe for the next twenty years, but the retirement of the "baby boom" generation beginning in 2011 will put very hard pressure on Part A. Medicaid costs also continue to grow, and Medicaid eligibility creates important "notch" problems in the public assistance programs described in the previous chapter.

An additional structural problem in Medicaid is that many physicians and dentists refuse to accept Medicaid patients because they must then legally accept the Medicaid fee schedule as full payment. The Medicaid fee structure is about two-thirds less than Medicare (which itself is significantly lower than private insurance fee levels) for the same procedures. The result is a barrier to care or a financial burden on the poor. Fraud and corruption on the part of providers is a serious problem, though difficult to document precisely. Some dramatic instances of Medicare and Medicaid "mills" have been revealed; here, patients are treated for nonexistent conditions or overtreated for illnesses, with the "clinics" making a tidy profit.

Questioning the Structures of Health Care

From the political left come charges that the health care system discriminates against rural residents, the poor, and racial minorities. According to this view, persons in these groups are less healthy than others because they are powerless, unable to control or to gain equal access to quality health care. Medicare, Medicaid, and other programs have alleviated conditions only marginally. They point out that one of the most important trends of the last decade has been the entry of for-profit corporations into the health care industry, especially managed care organizations, for-profit hospitals, and nursing homes. The growth of for-profit hospitals, the decline of public hospitals, and the new emphasis on cost cutting have the potential to reverse the gains made in health care for the poor. Hospitals are beginning to compete for paying patients through advertising and special services. The medically indigent patient, even when covered by Medicaid, is not a source of profit for the hospital, and such patients may be turned away to overcrowded, declining public hospitals, or to no hospital at all, if a public one is not locally available. These trends produce severe financial pressure on the "safety net" of public hospitals and clinics, placing their survival in doubt. For these reasons adherents of the political left believe that the primary impact of public programs has been to aid the wealthy providers of health care. Liberals, therefore, stress greater federal regulation of the health care system and removal of financial barriers to access by enacting a form of comprehensive national health insurance.

Conservatives and neoconservatives find no hope in regulation. The medical market, they argue, although not truly competitive now, could be made much more so. The political right charges that the regulated system penalizes both professionals and the productive public. Excessive government intervention leads to lower medical standards and higher costs. Medical decisions should be left in the hands of the professionals qualified to make them. If government were to cease regulating the medical market and subsidizing third-party payments, they believe, consumers' freedom of choice coupled with the availability of alternative types of health insurance would make the market more competitive and less costly. Let the current market-driven changes have a chance to work, they argue.

Another group of critics contends that the principal problems of health care are the fault of an overemphasis on medical care. More funding, they argue, should go toward the environmental causes of ill health. The great advances in health and life expectancy made early in the twentieth century came through immunizations, inoculations, and public health measures creating a more sanitary environment. Comparable gains likely will not come through cancer and heart research and treatment, through preventive medicine, or through increased spending on doctor, hospital, and nursing home care. Rather, progress will come from attending to cancer- and other disease-causing agents in the workplace, air, and water. Society knows what many of these are and should devote its resources to removing them and preventing their entry into the environment. Those who take this position argue that these environmentally induced cancers, lung diseases, kidney diseases, and other ailments are already costing billions of dollars for health care and lost work time. Expenditures to reduce their causes would be prudent investments in health and economic productivity.

Accompanying environmental concerns is the notion of preventive self-measures for personal health. The greatest potential for improving health and extending life may lie within the control of the individual, who can add years to life by following basic health habits, such as regular exercise, moderate alcohol consumption, not smoking, and regular sleeping and eating patterns. Individual control also appeals to those who distrust the medical establishment and turn to "alternative medicine" practices, such as herbal remedies, acupuncture, and massage therapy. Patients often find in these practices the individual, holistic concern that often seems missing in conventional medicine.

Liberals who emphasize these ideas also strongly support government programs of occupational safety and health, strict controls on disease-causing chemicals, efforts to clean up the environment, and antismoking campaigns. Government's responsibility for public health cannot be avoided, as the anthrax attacks in 2001 demonstrated. Without strong public health measures and good individual health practices, the cost of health care based on acute, curative medicine will be unafford-able in the future.[19] Conservatives point to individual responsibility, arguing that the choice of whether to practice good health habits is essentially outside government influence and that personal risk-taking is not an appropriate area for strong govern-ment action. But society even now ends up paying for individual decisions adversely affecting health through Medicare, Medicaid, public hospitals, and increased health insurance premiums. Surprisingly, however, preventive medicine itself does not seem clearly to lead to reduced medical costs, and preventive measures can have serious externalities. Lifestyle factors may be used to deny or raise insurance premiums; health screening may be used to deny or terminate employment or promotions.[20]

Managed Care Backlash

Some health care reformers once saw greater use of managed care as a means of controlling runaway costs. Greater use of managed care was, in fact, at the heart of *managed competition* proposals for health care reform, such as President Clin-ton's failed plan in 1993 to 1994, and the BBA's creation of Medicare+Choice in 1997. Managed care is a quasi-market device for introducing economic incentives to control cost into provider's decision making. There is some evidence that for a few years in the mid-1990s, managed care did help to take some inflation pres-sure out of the system. Other analysts, however, believe that the free market has never worked and could never work in health care. Therefore, managed care needs regulation to protect both patients and providers.

Those who take this position also argue that managed care's limitations on consumer choice and provider judgment interfere with health care quality. Physi-cians cannot exercise their own professional expertise in treating patients, but are subject to approval or second-guessing by nonphysician administrators of insur-ance plans. Most physicians, in fact, moved into managed care plans only reluc-tantly, when faced with a lack of alternatives. Moreover, managed care and other market-driven changes in health care cannot solve the access problem. They could, in fact, make it worse. Attention to the financial bottom line tends to make sick persons a tremendous drain on profits. The incentive is to avoid selling in-surance to such persons. New forms of health care delivery have changed the face of American medicine, but it is not clear whether this change will control costs or whether the new recognition of economic incentives will have an adverse effect on quality of care.

Doubters of managed care seem more influential than believers at the pres-ent time. During the late 1990s many states enacted patient and provider "bills-of-rights" to address alleged abuses. Such legislation mandates access to emergency room treatment whenever a "prudent layperson" would believe it necessary, min-imum lengths of stay for such procedures as childbirth and mastectomy, prohibi-tion of "gag clauses" limiting information that doctors may communicate to patients, and other patient rights to information about the terms of managed care contracts with doctors and hospitals. The federal government enacted some of these measures in the late 1990s, but Congress and Presidents Clinton and Bush debated without resolution a comprehensive federal "Patients' Bill of Rights" from 1999 through 2002. The most difficult issues were whether to cover all insured persons or only those in federally regulated insurance plans, whether patients would be allowed to sue their managed care plans for denials of care or bad outcomes (instead of being limited to suits against physicians), and what limits if any to place on the monetary value of any lawsuits allowed. Indeed, developments in the insurance industry following public, employer, physician, and government resistance to limiting health care choices produced substantial weakening of the gatekeeping, utilization review, and other restrictive features of managed care. The health care system by the early years of the twenty-first century seemed to be moving back toward fee-for-service and toward greater freedom for both patients and physicians, with managed care companies loosening a variety of restrictions and becoming less concerned with controlling expenditures.[21]

FUTURE ALTERNATIVES: HEALTH CARE REFORM, ETHICS, AND LONG-TERM CARE

The principal current issues in health care policy may be grouped into three categories: reforming health care to address the problems of cost, access, and quality; ethical controversies such as embryonic stem cell research; and financing long-term care for an increasingly aging population. Each of these contains strong ethical components. Because pain and death affect perceptions of the meaning of life and the value of the body, medical issues necessarily evoke philosophical, religious, and moral beliefs.

The most comprehensive ethical issue associated with health care reform is whether there is or should be a right to health care. Closely tied to a right to health care is the question of whether the right, if it exists, is an equal right. Those who argue that there is a right to health care and that it is an equal right support the most extensive proposals for expansion of health policies to cover all citizens fully, such as President Clinton's proposals in 1993 to 1994.

Advocates base the right to health care on the principle of justice that health is a requirement for a decent life, equally as important as food, clothing, shelter, and political and civil freedom. Because law and policy guard these aspects of life, they should guard health. Those who need health care because of injury or illness deserve to get it. Government has the responsibility to see that all persons, insofar as humanly possible, have access to the care needed to preserve health. Justice demands that government act to secure the right to health care for all citizens. Those who oppose this position contend that the Anglo-American constitutional tradition recognizes such political and civil rights as freedom of speech and the right to a trial by jury, but it has never recognized rights to the public distribution of economic goods, such as food, health care, and shelter. Government may, indeed, provide these for citizens, but not as rights to which all have a claim. They are given as charity or as services.

Among those who recognize a right to health care there is considerable disagreement over whether it is a right to a basic minimum of care or a right to equal care.[22] Proponents of an equal right point out that health is one of the fundamental goods a person can possess. It affects job, income, education, social status, and sense of worth. Therefore, to distribute health care unequally on the basis of income or residence or age is to commit a grave injustice. All must have an equal right to the most extensive health services available. It would be wrong to allow the wealthy to extend their lives by buying access to chemotherapy while consigning the poor to early deaths from cancer.

However, many believe that providing equal access to the most expensive services available would drive up the demand for them, imposing an enormous burden on society. Also, they argue, visits for minor and imagined illnesses would impose heavy demands on doctors' time. (There is, however, no evidence of such a phenomenon in nations recognizing an equal right to health care.) Those who take this position contend that all have a right to a basic minimum of care necessary for good health, but beyond that minimum, individuals' ability to buy services may be used to allocate resources. Would it be just, they may ask, to demand country club memberships for all because the rich can afford the health-enhancing benefits of golf, tennis, and sauna?

The Failure of Universal Health Care and Future Prospects

The right to health care was at the heart of the health care reform debates during the 103rd Congress (1993 and 1994). President Clinton's reform proposal, the *American Health Security Act,* proposed to guarantee health care insurance and, thereby, health care access to all citizens. The ultimate failure of the Clinton plan and all other health care reform in 1994 doomed comprehensive health care reform for a decade (at least).

Proposals for major reform of the American health care system have emerged approximately every twenty years, starting in the early 1920s. Since the passage of Medicare and Medicaid in 1965, major legislative debate focused on the issue of whether the United States should follow the European lead and develop a comprehensive federal insurance scheme covering the major health needs of the entire population. By the early 1990s, the issue of national health care was important once again. The decline of employer-based coverage during the 1980s, the growth of managed care, the increased cost of premiums and of medical treatment, and the fragmentation of health care interest groups opened a window of opportunity for reform toward universal coverage.[23] During the presidential campaign, candidate Bill Clinton made guaranteed security of access a fundamental part of his platform.

The Clinton plan. President Clinton's reform plan was a variant of the idea of *managed competition.* The basic idea of managed competition is that pure competition in the health care market will not work to extend access and control costs. In a purely competitive market insurers have incentives not to insure sick persons, and physicians and other providers have many incentives to overtreat, thus driving up costs. However, a carefully designed system of government regulations, in the view of supporters, can provide a fair structure within which market competition can work to extend access and control costs.

Plans called *health insurance purchasing cooperatives* (HIPC) would be used to structure competition. The plans would contract with providers, such as hospitals and doctors, to provide care; then insurance companies would bid to furnish a *standard benefit package* of covered services. The HIPC would guarantee that all plans met certain conditions, and they would make it possible for small employers to pool their employees together into larger groups for more purchasing power and lower rates. Many managed competition plans, including the Clinton plan, incorporated government *subsidies to small businesses* in order to make it possible to afford insurance coverage for their workers.

If employer-based insurance is to be the foundation of health reform, as it is in *managed competition,* then the only way to reach full coverage is an *employer mandate;* that is, a requirement that every employer provide insurance coverage for all employees. The self-employed and others would also be required to purchase insurance. The unemployed and the poor would be covered by a new federal system to replace Medicaid. Medicare would remain.

Managed competition proposals had the advantage of building on the current system and of universal access and significant cost control measures. However, there was doubt among some liberals that medical markets would work at all and, from conservatives, that *managed* markets can work. The Clinton plan also seemed heavily bureaucratic, cumbersome, and relied on unproven cost savings from managed care mechanisms, such as HMOs.

Health insurance vouchers. Reliance on relatively unregulated markets was the reform of choice for conservatives in 1993 and remains so today. Such recommendations often take the form of *health insurance vouchers* or *medical savings accounts* (MSA). They propose using the income tax system to provide health insurance vouchers in the form of refundable tax credits or tax deductions to low-income persons who purchase health insurance policies. Medical savings accounts would be individual tax-free savings plans that could be used to cover medical expenses. Persons without insurance would receive government subsidies of a few thousand dollars per family per year to purchase insurance. The system of private health insurance companies would remain in place. Employers would not be required to provide or purchase insurance for workers, but they could join in *voluntary* HIPCs if they choose. Consumers would make choices of insurance among the most cost-effective plans.

The disadvantages of this proposal, however, are very substantial. It does nothing significant to reduce costs, because it leaves virtually unchanged the incentives that have made the American health care system the most expensive in the world. Second, it assumes that low-income and other uninsured persons will in fact be intelligent, cost-conscious health insurance consumers and that cost-effective individual or group policies will be available to them. Finally, and most significantly, this proposal would encourage many small employers to drop their insurance coverage, forcing their employees to resort to the tax-credit financed individual policies. This would shift more of the cost of health insurance from the private to the public sector.

Single-payer. In light of the complexities and disadvantages of the proposals previously described, a comprehensive restructuring of the health care system may be in order. At least this is the argument of many liberals inside and outside the health care system. This restructuring, known as the *single-payer plan,* would provide public health insurance to every person as a right of citizenship. Health providers would still be private; government would not take over private hospitals or physicians' practices. However, such a program would eliminate all private insurance, as well as Medicaid, in favor of a national or state-administered single health insurance program.

The failure of health care reform. All of these proposals miscarried during 1994. There is no single cause for their failure. The Health Security Act, when finally delivered, was too large and cumbersome to explain clearly to Congress, the public, or opinion leaders. Finally, the political weakness of Clinton's electoral mandate (43 percent of the popular vote) and the ineptness of his administration in selling the plan meant that he could not put together a winning coalition.

Interest group activity also helps to explain the failure. Small businesses, the health insurance industry, and for-profit hospitals and other providers mounted very effective lobbying campaigns against the Clinton proposal, while failing to support any of the alternatives. PAC spending and campaign financing directed against reform hit record levels in 1994.

Members of Congress, both Democrats and Republicans, also share the responsibility. Those congressional leaders who favored reform would not compromise their own positions to find common ground. The Democrats divided over requiring employers to provide insurance (employer mandates) and rejected bipartisan alternatives until too late. Congressional deficit-reduction rules also furnished a roadblock, since any proposal estimated to raise the deficit in even one future year needed a three-fifths majority vote. A number of the major proposals ran afoul of this so-called "Paygo" provision. The combination of all of these factors produced stalemate in late 1994 and the abandonment of reform efforts.

Current prospects for significant health care reform toward universal coverage are dim. Failed attempts at reform deplete energy for new efforts. It is highly unlikely, then, that significant health care reform efforts to expand access and to control costs will emerge again in the near future. The Bush Administration and Republicans in Congress, although favorable toward voucher or medical savings alternatives, do not see their interest in passing major health legislation. Democrats in any event probably possess enough strength to block proposals that fail to go very far toward universal health insurance coverage.

The Promise of Incremental Reform

Legislation passed in 1996 is typical of the kinds of small, incremental steps that remain the only realistic possibility for expanding access to those without health insurance. The Health Insurance Portability and Accountability Act (HIPAA) removed a few obstacles to obtaining health insurance. One obstacle is pre-existing conditions that make many persons unable to obtain insurance at reasonable rates. HIPAA prohibits insurance companies from denying coverage to a group or refusing coverage to a particular person in the group because of that person's health status. It also requires that coverage of pre-existing conditions can be excluded from policies only for one twelve-month period in a person's life. This makes insurance more portable; that is, it makes it easier for persons to change jobs without the fear of losing insurance or of being denied coverage for a certain illness that they already have. HIPAA also required insurance companies to sell individual policies to persons with employer-based coverage, if they leave that job for another that does not offer insurance. The new law also made a few other changes in insurance law designed to enhance coverage, including a limited experiment with *Medical Savings Accounts* (MSA).

HIPAA made it easier for some of the currently uninsured to purchase coverage; however, few persons can take advantage of its provisions. Insurance companies charge very high premiums for HIPAA-mandated policies and employ other tactics to discourage the sale of policies to sick persons trying to take advantage of its provisions. Moreover, HIPAA could have the unintended consequence of *increasing* the number of uninsured. This is so because those who would be helped by these measures are sicker on the average than others. Hence, insurance companies would raise their rates to cover the additional costs. As this happens, some individuals and small businesses will drop their coverage because of the new higher rates. This incremental reform, in other words, does nothing to limit health care cost inflation and has only minor effects on the growing problem of the uninsured.

The State Children's Health Insurance Program (SCHIP) described in the second section of this chapter represented another incremental step after the failure of comprehensive reform. It focused attention on children in near-poverty families, children being perennially a sympathetic target for politicians. From time to time advocates of universal coverage float other proposals to develop coverage for other groups in order to reduce the number of uninsured. Most commonly mentioned are extending Medicaid and SCHIP to the parents of eligible children; temporary (six to twelve months) insurance for unemployed persons while they look for work; and making Medicare available for purchase by the "near-elderly," persons aged fifty-five to sixty-four, who lack insurance. Following the economic decline linked to the terrorist attacks on the World Trade Center and the Pentagon in 2001, there were proposals for federal subsidies to the recently unemployed to help them retain their former employment-based insurance under so-called COBRA provisions.

During 2002, the Bush administration remained wedded to proposals for market-based methods to expand insurance coverage: Medical Savings Accounts and tax credits for persons without access to employer-based insurance to purchase individual health insurance policies. Democrats oppose such measures as insufficient to make much of a dent in the uninsurance problem; most remain committed to Medicaid and SCHIP expansion. After news of another 2 million persons losing health insurance in 2001, a diverse coalition of twelve labor, business, civic, and health care interest groups emerged under the umbrella of *Covering the Uninsured*. This coalition aims to keep pressure on both political parties to create measures to reduce substantially the 40+ million persons currently without insurance.

States and Health Care Reform

Most states experimented in the early 1990s with control of Medicaid costs by requiring all or most recipients to enroll in managed care plans. The BBA of 1997 and subsequent laws facilitated this movement. Managed care plans claim to save money. The savings could be used to extend Medicaid to uninsured persons and to reduce expensive uses of emergency rooms and other inappropriate use of resources. The results of such reforms are too sketchy to evaluate at this time. Early accounts suggest that some states have done this effectively, but in others there is strong resistance from physicians and from patients to the requirement to be part of a managed care plan. Since these plans must often be created from scratch, there have been difficulties in getting them running, in persuading existing plans to enroll Medicaid recipients, and in reimbursement to providers. Even more far-reaching than these Medicaid reforms are proposals by some governors that the federal government simply grant states the funds necessary to run Medicaid without substantial federal oversight, a proposal unlikely to muster majority support among the states or in Congress.

Insurance market reform. Some states enacted insurance market reforms similar to those enacted federally by the 1996 HIPAA previously described (portability and pre-existing conditions). State-facilitated HIPCs help small employers pool their risks in order to obtain insurance and to create risk-pools for the hard-to-insure. Some states, most notably New York, have moved to a more radical insurance reform, the replacement of experience rating of insurance premiums with community rating.[24] *Experience rating,* now used by most commercial insurance companies, sets higher premiums (or even denial of coverage) for groups with older or sicker members, thus making it more likely that they will lose coverage from the inability to pay. *Community rating* charges the same (or nearly the same) premium for all groups, spreading the costs of older and sicker members among all the insured. Community rating would make it possible for some of the uninsured to afford coverage, but would raise rates for all groups, thereby driving others out of the market, as has been the experience in New York. Although community rating is a fairer system, it cannot work to extend access or control costs without a requirement on individuals or employers that all persons have health insurance (individual or employer mandates). Such a requirement will not come from the Congress, and it is unlikely that many states will adopt it.

Mandated coverage. Some states began experiments in the late 1980s and early 1990s that aimed at universal access through changes in Medicaid and through employer mandates. The fullest development of such changes is in Hawaii, which requires all employers to provide insurance for their workers.

Washington, Oregon, Vermont, Massachusetts, and Minnesota passed one form or another of employer mandates to be phased in over a number of years, at the end of which all workers and their dependents would be covered by health insurance. Republican state electoral gains in 1994 and after doomed these laws. Republican legislators (and sometimes governors) in Oregon, Washington, Minnesota, and Florida repealed most of this legislation. Moreover, ERISA (the federal Employee Retirement Income Security Act of 1974) forbids states from regulating self-insured health care programs and from mandating a standard benefit package. Courts have interpreted ERISA to forbid states to enact employer mandates on self-insured firms. In a desire to escape regulation, more and more employers (especially large companies) have turned to self-insurance. Therefore, states cannot enact significant reform.

This combination of factors, plus the high cost to state budgets if they were to subsidize purchases of insurance by the uninsured, means that the states are unlikely to play a significant role in expanding access to health care, particularly to the millions of working adults who lack it. The harsh reality is that the states lack the financial flexibility to lead the drive to cover the uninsured. The recession of 2001 underscored this truth, as one state after another imposed either enrollment limits or sliced provider reimbursements in Medicaid and SCHIP in order to rein in accelerating health care spending.

In short, solving the uninsurance problem has reached a political stalemate. The political system has never found the money or the political will to require insurance coverage for all Americans. Fundamental health insurance reform faces very high political obstacles. Yet incremental reform falters as well on the inability of the states to lead the way and on the basic disagreements on strategy between liberals and conservatives, between Democrats and Republicans evenly balanced in power in Washington.

Medicare Reform

As described in the Evaluation section, the Medicare program faces significant challenges over the upcoming decades, especially in how to finance Medicare when the baby boom generation begins reaching age sixty-five in 2011. In 1997 Congress and the president, in the Balanced Budget Act (BBA), attempted to solve short-term financing problems and began addressing Medicare's future.

The BBA made a series of structural changes in Medicare. Home health expenditures were shifted from Part A to Part B, and Part B premiums were scheduled for substantial increases (rising to an estimated $105 per month by 2007). Signaling a potentially more far-reaching change in Medicare structure, the separate payment advisory commissions for Part A and B were combined into one—the Medicare Payment Advisory Commission (MedPAC).

The BBA's combination of reductions on payment increases to hospitals and physicians; its shifting of Medicare home health, skilled nursing, rehabilitation, and outpatient treatment to a prospective payment system; and intensive investigations of Medicare provider fraud and abuse resulted in significant slowing of Medicare's expenditure growth, especially in 1998 and 1999. The restrictions were so substantial on Medicare spending that hospitals and insurance companies successfully lobbied in 1999 and 2000 for a rollback of some of the BBA's provisions in order to prevent severe financial crises in these industries. The BBA's success, however, was merely temporary. New financial pressures emerged by the turn of the century.

Medicare prescription drug coverage. With the rising importance and expense of pharmaceuticals since the mid-1990s, Medicare's lack of a prescription drug benefit has become a major political issue.[25] Many seniors depend heavily on prescriptions to maintain their health. The number and cost of prescriptions naturally place strong pressure on retiree budgets. Often Medicare recipients do not fill prescriptions or take smaller doses than prescribed, because they cannot afford everything the doctor orders. Some Medicare recipients do have drug coverage through Medicare HMOs or through Medigap policies, but the HMOs are cutting back on coverage, and the premiums for Medigap policies that cover prescriptions are beyond the means of low-income seniors.

During the 2000 election campaign, candidates of both political parties promised Medicare prescription coverage, and Congress in early 2001 looked poised to add some form of outpatient drug coverage. A number of factors prevented this action. First, Democrats and Republicans could not agree on the shape of the benefit. Although both parties favored making a Medicare prescription benefit voluntary instead of mandatory, Democrats favored placing its administration under the federal government, and they wanted a somewhat more generous level of benefits than the Republicans, who favored letting private insurance companies market a variety of subsidized prescription plans to seniors. Pharmaceutical companies, fearing price regulation, favored the Republican plan, but many advocacy groups for the elderly favored the Democratic plan. Second, the estimated cost of a prescription benefit increased steadily as drug inflation continued unabated. Leaders in both parties became more worried about adding a benefit as its price tag rose. Third, the budget surplus that elected officials depended upon to finance the new benefit disappeared by the end of 2001, a result of the major federal tax cut enacted in the middle of the year, the economic slowdown, and the terrorist attacks of September 11th. Thus, the prospects of a new Medicare prescription benefit, which looked highly likely in January 2001, became very uncertain in 2002. Although President Bush advocated subsidies for states to provide Medicare prescription coverage, Democrats in Congress and many interest groups were highly suspicious of that strategy in the short or the long term.

Yet the need for prescription coverage for the elderly and the demand by seniors and their interest groups for Medicare coverage will not disappear. Adding such a benefit in some form remains prominent on the short-term Medicare reform agenda.

Long-range prospects for Medicare. The BBA includes two measures with potential long-range impact. The first measure is the gradual phasing in of a new approach to Medicare termed "Medicare+Choice." The idea is to give Medicare recipients greater choices in their coverage, thereby encouraging recipients to choose more cost-effective forms of coverage, especially encouraging them to move to greater use of managed care. Skeptics, however, argue that greater market choice in health care does not produce the same kinds of savings and efficiencies as in other sectors of the economy, a point developed earlier in this chapter.

"Medicare+Choice" became fully operational in 2002. Medicare recipients must choose among a variety of coverages: traditional Medicare fee-for-service in which recipients visit physicians and other providers they select; Medicare HMOs which provide a fuller range of services but with reduced choice among providers; newly created "Provider-Sponsored Organizations" operated directly by groups of providers such as doctors and hospitals; and Medicare MSAs. The early results of the Medicare+Choice experiment, however, are not encouraging. Designed to encourage more managed care companies to enter the Medicare business and to encourage Medicare recipients to enroll in managed care, its results have been largely the opposite. In 1998 346 HMOs held Medicare contracts; by 2002 that number had shrunk to 157. Enrollment in Medicare managed care plans declined from 6 million persons in 1998 to 5.7 million in 2001. Many former managed care recipients found themselves with reduced coverage and higher costs when their HMO withdrew from Medicare managed care.[26]

The BBA created a seventeen-member Bipartisan Commission on the Future of Medicare. This commission had the task of studying how to preserve Medicare and adequately finance it for the next forty to fifty years. The hope was that it could duplicate the success of a similar commission that successfully proposed long-range changes in Social Security in 1983. Having members of both parties on the commission, including influential members of Congress, carried the promise of nonpartisan but politically feasible changes. The Medicare Commission, however, failed to achieve consensus on reform recommendations and went out of existence in 1999. By early 2002, policy debate coalesced around the following options.

First, Medicare could preserve its present structure, but continue to squeeze payments to physicians, hospitals, and other providers. This measure may become *part* of any long-term reform plan, but by itself it will not generate savings sufficient to pay for the millions of newly eligible persons beginning in 2011.

Second, Medicare could keep its present structure, but payroll taxes could be raised on present workers to fund the Hospital Insurance Trust Fund. In addition, Part B premiums could be increased, especially on higher-income Medicare recipients. In principle, such tax and premium increases *could* fund Medicare indefinitely if they were set high enough. Doing so, however, would be politically impossible, given the opposition by current workers and by senior citizen lobby groups. Small increases, however, might accompany the more fundamental Medicare restructuring options that follow.

Third, the age for becoming eligible for Medicare could be increased from sixty-five to sixty-seven (or even higher). This would parallel increases in Social Security eligibility. Such a measure makes a good deal of sense for that reason, but without guaranteed health insurance coverage for all Americans, an age increase would produce a higher number and percentage of uninsured persons than the present unacceptable levels.

Fourth, Medicare could be changed from the present "defined benefit plan," in which Medicare promises to pay whatever it costs to fund a defined list of medical services for all recipients, to a "defined contribution plan" (or a similar plan called "premium support"), in which Medicare promises a fixed yearly payment to all beneficiaries, which they in turn use (in combination with their own funds) to purchase the health insurance plans that they choose. "Medicare+Choice" begins to move Medicare in this direction. The Medicare fee-for-service option could be phased out and all newly eligible persons required to choose a managed care plan, much as employed persons now must do. A defined-contribution plan allows government to control its costs far better than a defined-benefit plan. In essence, Congress and the president could agree on exactly how much the country can afford for health care for its senior citizens and then appropriate only that much. The disadvantage of such a plan is that, unless underlying health care costs can be controlled, each year's defined contribution would buy less and less medical care. In this case, Medicare recipients too poor to afford additional coverage out of their own funds would be left with inadequate health care insurance in their most feeble years.

Fifth, there are more radical changes that some scholars and policy advocates have proposed, but these make such fundamental changes in Medicare or are so costly that they are highly unlikely to be adopted by Congress. These options include privatizing Medicare by funding it wholly by individual savings accounts built up by workers or expanding Medicare by adding long-term care insurance.

Political forces in Congress are now so evenly balanced, and Medicare is so politically volatile, that none of the previous strategies is likely to emerge in the next few years. Because Medicare is such an important part of the American health care system and because it faces such important short- and long-term financial challenges, vital debate about program changes will occupy the beginning of the twenty-first century.

Ethical Issues

Rationing. No matter how the reform debates at the national and state levels are resolved, health policy must confront the question of how to allocate limited resources to different kinds of need. The health needs of the young and old differ substantially. Is it enough to invest enormous sums under Medicare and Medicaid in high-cost acute care technologies for seriously ill old persons or in expensive long-term nursing home care, or should these sums go to support the basic medical, dental, and psychological care needed by the young whose lives are just beginning? Similarly, policy advocates debate whether research and treatment should focus on the major fatal diseases, such as heart disease and cancer, as they do now, or on the long-term chronic, crippling diseases, such as mental disorders, arthritis, and senility. These are moral, rather than medical or scientific, questions, because they involve the values that determine how society should allocate scarce resources among its different segments.

The truth is that all health systems ration care. Many deny that rationing exists in the United States, yet any health care reform will only alter the *type,* not the *fact* of rationing. At present, American health care is rationed by insurance status, place of employment, income and wealth, insurance policy coverage limitations, willingness to wait in line, and other factors. Extending coverage to more persons would change the dimensions of some factors, but it would neither create nor eliminate rationing. Similarly, measures to control costs raise issues of whether it is ethical to ration care according to the age of patients, according to the imminence of their death, according to the quality of their life, or other considerations.

By the late 1980s, a debate had opened up regarding the ethics of rationing health care access by age. The principal question is whether certain expensive procedures should be available to all persons or whether they should be denied to persons beyond a certain age, since at that point they are unlikely to significantly prolong the quality or length of life. Examples of such procedures are kidney dialysis, heart transplants, and chemotherapy.[27] These are serious questions that raise significant ethical debates. Refusal to address them will not keep rationing from happening; it will merely permit the present rationing structures to remain and allow others to emerge without conscious decision. Ultimately, the rising cost of health care may focus the rationing question on how aggressively to pursue life-saving and technological innovation when other desirable goods become unaffordable.

Euthanasia and assisted suicide. The subjects of birth and death raise major policy questions. Abortion, discussed in Chapter 13 in a different context, is such a question. In the realm of health care, debate centers on the Hyde amendment, upheld by the Supreme Court in 1980, which bans federal Medicaid funding for most abortions. Some argue that this denial discriminates against the poor; others, that it saves the lives of thousands of unborn infants. At the other end of life, debate focuses on whether society should fund or encourage the use of sophisticated medical technology to keep alive those, particularly the aged, with terminal illnesses. Should government discontinue funding such treatments in order to use the resources elsewhere? Similar issues were raised by the "Baby Jane Doe" case and others, which asked whether physicians and parents may withhold life-saving care from severely handicapped newborns.

State "living will" laws allow persons to refuse extraordinary technologies should they become terminally ill. Federal law now requires hospitals to give patients the opportunity to complete living wills or durable powers of attorney on admission, even for minor surgery. Some ethicists go farther, arguing in favor of active euthanasia; that is, allowing terminally ill persons to request and receive an injection or other means to end their lives. Dramatic examples of physician-assisted suicide raised the issue to national prominence during the 1990s, and Oregon voters approved a measure making it legal for physicians to assist terminally ill persons to commit suicide. Physicians have assisted more than forty persons to die under the authorization of this law. Some proponents of assisted death challenged state laws forbidding assisted suicide, but the U.S. Supreme Court ruled in 1997 that there is no constitutional right to assistance in committing suicide. It did not declare a constitutional prohibition on such a method of death, if state laws such as Oregon's permit it. Many oppose these measures on the ground that they cheapen life, making it a matter of economic calculation. They also believe that such policies diminish the religious value of suffering for the human spirit and that they "play God" by allowing the state, physicians, or individuals to determine the time and manner of death.

The Moral Dilemmas of Research and Technological Development

As medicine moves into the realm of genetics, new moral dilemmas emerge. As difficult as these will be, however, their inherent difficulty will merge with the already-existing dilemmas of access and cost to create significant challenges for policymakers in the next decade.

American medicine is high-tech medicine, depending fundamentally on research and development of new drugs and medical techniques. The new research frontier is the human genome itself. To unlock its secrets, it seems, is to unlock the secret to curing many devastating diseases. The debate in 2001 over federal funding for research on human embryonic stem cells illustrates the moral dilemmas. Within the human embryo in its first weeks of development are stem cells that during the course of growth toward birth differentiate into all the cells of the human body. Many scientists believe that such cells could be used to cure conditions in adults; for example, stem cells could be grown to form heart tissue to repair heart damage or to form kidney cells to repair those damaged by diabetes, and so forth. Yet harvesting embryonic stem cells destroys the embryo itself; that is, it ends nascent human life. Government must decide whether the promise of healing, assisted by federal funding through the National Institutes of Health, justifies destruction of the embryo. And what about creating embryos specifically for research purposes? Scientists, religious groups, and ordinary citizens are divided on these questions. Yet Congress and the president must make policy decisions to fund or not to fund. President Bush in late summer 2001 decided, as he interpreted current law, that research on existing stem cell lines could receive federal funding, but that stem cells derived from future destruction of embryos could not be funded, a decision that occasioned sharp disagreement from both proponents and opponents of embryonic stem cell research.

The issue of whether it is permissible to clone human beings for therapeutic or reproductive purposes presents similar moral and political issues to policymakers. Therapeutic cloning involves the same embryo destruction as previously described, and reproductive cloning (creating a genetic double of a child or adult) raises substantial questions of the meaning of human identity. Even farther down the road, as the secrets of the human genome become known, is the prospect of genetic engineering; that is, operating directly on the cellular makeup of a person to cure a disease (Parkinson's, for example) or to enhance performance (increase height or intelligence, for example). Germ line engineering would apply these techniques in such a way as to reproduce them in all of a person's descendents. Many citizens believe that such techniques not only are morally permissible, but hold great promise of curing disease, reducing suffering, and extending life. Others equally strongly believe that permitting such things tampers with human life itself, setting the present generation as the arbiter of the lives of all future generations. Such techniques would, in their view, lead to genetic discrimination, eugenics programs, and swollen human pride.

Yet government must decide. In general, it has four options for any new medical research or technique (really the same options as for any controversial social development). First, it may *encourage* the technique by funding it. Second, it may *permit,* but not fund, the technique. This is equivalent to leaving it to the free market to develop or not develop. Third, government may permit the technique, but *regulate* its development or implementation through laws that restrict what the market may do. Fourth, government may *forbid* the activity, as the House of Representatives voted to do with human cloning in summer 2001.

The issues raised by human cloning, embryo research, and genetic engineering are not limited to those previously mentioned. Medical treatments resulting from them will contribute to the high cost of American health care. Remember that technology already is the principal driver of health care inflation. These techniques, at least initially and perhaps indefinitely, will be very expensive. Covering them through public or private insurance will help to keep American health care the most costly in the world. Not to cover them will leave them to the wealthy to afford, exacerbating already existing health care injustices. Moreover, the higher cost of health care will make it less affordable for ordinary citizens, thereby increasing the number of uninsured and making access more and more difficult. These are some of the policy issues that legislators must face in the coming decades.[28]

Long-Term Care

A major issue for the future is how to finance long-term care for the elderly. Expenditures on long-term care have risen dramatically in recent decades, along with the increase in the number of aged persons (see Figure 8-5). When the baby boom generation begins to retire, the problem will intensify. Medicare, as previously mentioned, does not pay for ordinary nursing home care, although Medicaid does. Therefore, Medicare recipients who need such care must first exhaust all of their resources so that they become poor enough to be eligible for Medicaid. On any given day about 5 percent of those over sixty-five and 20 percent of those over eighty-five are in nursing homes. Moreover, about 20 percent of the elderly have some disabling condition, and nearly one-third of all American health care expenditures benefit the aged.[29]

Policymakers must pay attention to finding ways to fund less-expensive care provided at home and to develop continuity of care for the many different health-

FIGURE 8-5 ▪ Growth in Long-Term Care Spending ($ billions)

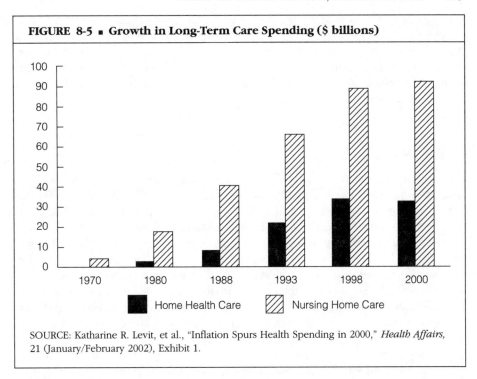

SOURCE: Katharine R. Levit, et al., "Inflation Spurs Health Spending in 2000," *Health Affairs*, 21 (January/February 2002), Exhibit 1.

related needs of the aged. The current set of programs is highly fragmented, with responsibility for establishing a continuum of care falling largely to the elderly themselves or their children, who often lack the ability to navigate a complex set of regulations and agencies to put together a coherent system of care. Nevertheless, any solution will be costly, and little alternative exists to Medicare and Medicaid. HIPAA contains tax incentives to encourage individuals to purchase their own long-term care insurance policies. However, private insurance for long-term care is unlikely to grow. First, it is prohibitively expensive if purchased after sixty-five; yet (without large government subsidies) the young hesitate to invest scarce dollars in policies designed to cover possible nursing home care many years in the future. Policy can continue inadequately to finance long-term care through the means-tested welfare solution of Medicaid, or it can reform Medicare. If the latter option is selected, then the question of financing will prove a major political battleground. Should Medicare recipients finance long-term care themselves, or should it be provided by the working population through payroll or income taxes?

Health care politics. The cost, access, long-term care, and ethical dilemmas of health care make health care politics highly contentious, involving the politics of distribution, redistribution, and regulation (Chapter 1). Any major reform proposal has potential far-reaching consequences for all citizens, for employers, and for one-seventh of the entire national economy. Substantial structural changes in the health care system affect everyone as a consumer of health care, but also affect powerful interests that have conflicting purposes. Building a political coalition for such change is extraordinarily difficult. The costs of health care fall widely among the population, but the financial benefits are concentrated.

Change, therefore, is strongly resisted. Finally, the growing numbers of the elderly and new technology place demands on the system that no reform can
change. Health is a basic value in all cultures, and the resources Americans devote to health care indicate its high priority. Whether these resources are as effective as possible in advancing the goal of good health is the central issue in
health care policy.

SUMMARY

The health care system changed quickly in the last two decades toward "managed
care," and this new form of health care delivery presented important challenges
of regulation to assure access and quality. The most important features of managed care are selective contracting, gatekeepers, and utilization review.

The American health care system is a mixture of private individual behavior, private corporate endeavors, and government policy. Lack of coordination characterizes
the provision of and payment for services. Other nations have more comprehensive
systems of health care that guarantee access to good quality health care at lower cost
than the United States. American health care lags behind the rest of the world on basic measures of health, and it suffers serious problems of access, cost, and quality.
About 14 percent of the population lacks insurance, and American health care costs
are the highest and most rapidly rising in the world, absorbing 14 percent of GDP.

The most important problem in health care, shared by many nations, is its
soaring cost to society. The chief causes of cost escalation in the United States are
growing numbers of elderly, overspecialization, modern medical technology,
"service intensity," and the public's exaggerated expectations of medical science.
But the United States also has serious problems of access to health care and growing doubts about the quality of care delivered.

U.S. health policy prior to 1965 largely concerned public health: regulating
and licensing drugs and food, supporting health research, funding hospital construction, and minor efforts aimed at improving the health of the poor.

Passage of Medicare and Medicaid in 1965 revolutionized this situation.
Medicare provides hospital insurance and voluntary medical insurance for those
sixty-five and older. Medicaid is a cooperative state-federal program offering
health care services to the poor. Funded from general revenues, it supports a variety of such services, varying from state to state. The costs and number of recipients is increasing rapidly in each program.

Other federal health care programs include the State Children's Health Insurance Program (SCHIP), support for professional training, community health
centers, and health-related block grants.

Federal health care policy, particularly Medicare and Medicaid, has been
successful in reducing the financial burden of medical care on the aged and the
poor, and it has improved both their access to care and their general health. Some
of the health gaps between African Americans and whites and aged and non-aged
have been narrowed.

There are substantial problems with federal health care policy, however.
Many differences in quality and access to care still remain among various groups.
Medicare and Medicaid have contributed to health care's inflated costs and have

not challenged structural problems in its delivery. Both have important gaps in coverage. Neither regulatory policies nor the fundamental structural change toward "managed care" have had the success hoped for in introducing rational coordination, increased access, or cost control.

Ideological disagreement pervades the evaluation of health care policy. The political left charges that the health care system is biased against the poor, rural residents, and minorities. The political right stresses the failures of market regulation and advocates less government intervention and more competition in the health insurance sector. Liberals stress the failure of the medical marketplace and the need for government regulation and insurance for all citizens. Other groups see individual responsibility for good health habits as the direction for substantial improvement in health.

Substantial criticism of managed care, led by hospitals and physicians, generated a public policy backlash in the middle to late 1990s. States developed managed care regulations, and the federal government debated a national "patients bill of rights."

Ethical issues are important to health care policy today. Whether there is a right to health care and, if there is, whether it is a right to basic minimum care or to full care for all are central questions, as are abortion, euthanasia, and embryonic stem cell research.

Access to health care remains a fundamental problem, and policy initiatives in the 2000s will have to address three of its most difficult dimensions: finding ways to provide coverage for the millions of persons below the poverty line not now covered by Medicaid, providing health insurance for millions of workers without employer-provided insurance, and financing long-term health care for the elderly.

Major reforms are unlikely in the near future after the failure of all major health care reform bills in 1994, but minor reforms were enacted in 1996 and 1997. Proposals for incremental expansion of health insurance include subsidies for the working poor to purchase individual policies, subsidies to laid-off workers to purchase COBRA insurance coverage, and expansion of Medicaid and SCHIP to cover the parents of children enrolled in these programs. Although a number of states also developed strategies for expanded coverage, prospects for success are limited.

The Balanced Budget Act of 1997 and a good economy ensured the short-term future of Medicare and initiated potential long-range changes. These include adding prescription drug coverage, changing benefit and financing terms in order to save money, and changing Medicare from a "defined benefit" to a "defined contribution" plan.

Health and medicine present a number of significant moral dilemmas: euthanasia or assisted-suicide of terminally ill persons, abortion, research on nascent life in the form of embryonic stem cells, enhancement of human traits through genetic engineering, and cloning. Because the public is so deeply involved in research on these new developments and in funding and regulating medical care, it cannot avoid the ethical dilemmas and moral choices that will come increasingly frequently in the future, including the choice of encouraging, permitting, regulating, or forbidding morally controversial practices.

Finally, the aging of the population and the imminent retirement of the baby boom generation demands the development of policies to provide for the long-term care needs of this population.

NOTES

1. For a summary of changes toward managed care and an explanation of managed care terminology, see Jonathan P. Weiner and Gregory de Lissovoy, "Razing a Tower of Babel: A Taxonomy for Managed Care and Health Insurance Plans," *Journal of Health Politics, Policy, and Law,* 18 (Spring 1993): 75–103; also R. A. Dudley and H. S. Luft, "Managed Care in Transition," *New England Journal of Medicine,* 334 (April 5, 2001): 1087–1092.

2. Other private funds accounted for 4 percent of the total. See Katharine Levit, et al., "Inflation Spurs Health Spending in 2000," *Health Affairs,* 21 (January/February 2002): 172–181.

3. The comparative material in this section is based upon Arnold J. Heidenheimer, Hugh Heclo, and Carolyn Teich Adams, *Comparative Public Policy,* 3rd ed. (New York: St. Martin's Press, 1990); Victor G. Rodwin, "Comparative Health Systems," in Anthony R. Kovner, ed., *Health Care Delivery in the United States,* 4th ed. (New York: Springer, 1990), Chapter 17; and Joseph White, *Competing Solutions: American Health Care Proposals and International Experience* (Washington, DC: Brookings Institution, 1995), Chapter 2. See also Lynn Payer, *Medicine and Culture: Varieties of Treatment in the United States, England, West Germany, and France* (New York: Penguin Books, 1988).

4. Karen Donelan, et al., "The Cost of Health System Change: Public Discontent in Five Nations," *Health Affairs,* 18 (May/June, 1999): 206–216.

5. Katherine Swartz, "Dynamics of People without Health Insurance: Don't Let the Numbers Fool You," *Journal of the American Medical Association,* 271 (January 5, 1994): 64–66. For later data see Jonathan Gardner, "No Plans to Boost Coverage," *Modern Healthcare* (December 15, 1997): 24.

6. Victor R. Fuchs, "National Health Insurance Revisited," in, John K. Iglehart, ed., *Debating Health Care Reform: A Primer from HEALTH AFFAIRS* (Bethesda, MD: Project HOPE, 1993): 80–91; Deborah Chollet, "Employer-Based Health Insurance in a Changing Workforce," *Health Affairs,* 13 (Spring I, 1994): 315–326.

7. See, for example, David McBride, "Black America: From Community Health Care to Crisis Medicine," *Journal of Health Politics, Policy, and Law,* 18 (Summer 1993): 319–337; and Gregory Pappas, et al., "The Increasing Disparity in Mortality between Socioeconomic Groups in the United States, 1960 and 1986," *New England Journal of Medicine,* 392 (July 8, 1993): 103–109.

8. Katharine Levit, et al., "Inflation Spurs Health Spending in 2000," *Health Affairs,* 21 (January/February, 2002): 172–181; and Ernst R. Berndt, "The U.S. Pharmaceutical Industry: Why Major Growth in Times of Cost Containment?" *Health Affairs,* 20 (March/April, 2001): 100–114.

9. Bryan R. Luce, "Medical Technology and its Assessment," in Stephen J. Williams and Paul R. Torrens, eds., *Introduction to Health Services,* 4th ed. (Albany, NY: Delmar, 1993), Chapter 9; H. David Banta, "Technology Assessment in Health Care," in Anthony R. Kovner, ed., *Health Care Delivery in the United States,* 4th ed. (New York: Springer Publishing Company, 1990), Chapter 15.

10. See Kenneth E. Thorpe, "Health Care Cost Containment," in Kovner, ed., *Health Care Delivery,* Chapter 11; and Henry J. Aaron, *Serious and Unstable Condition: Financing America's Health Care* (Washington, DC: Brookings Institution, 1993), Chapter 3.

11. Barbara Starfield, "Is U.S. Health Really the Best in the World?" *Journal of the American Medical Association,* 284 (July 26, 2000): 483–485. See also John M. Eisenberg and Elaine J. Power, "Transforming Insurance Coverage into Quality Health Care," *Journal of the American Medical Association,* 284 (October 25, 2000): 2100–2107.

12. Ed Lovern, "IOM Strikes Again," *Modern Healthcare,* March 5, 2001: 4–6.

13. For a chronology of federal health care legislation, see Theodore J. Litman, "Appendix," in Theodore J. Litman and Leonard S. Robins, eds., *Health Policy and Politics,* 3rd ed. (Albany, NY: Delmar, 1997): 445–471.

14. Good summaries of the development and impact of Medicare and Medicaid are Theodore R. Marmor, *The Politics of Medicare,* 2nd ed. (New York: Aldine de Gruyter, 2000); Paul Starr, *The Social Transformation of American Medicine* (New York: Basic Books, 1982), Chapter 3; and Rashi Fein, *Medical Care, Medical Costs* (Cambridge: Harvard University Press, 1986), Chapters 5–6.

15. For a description of RBRVS, see William C. Hsiao et al., "Resource-Based Values: An Overview," *Journal of the American Medical Association,* 260 (October 28, 1988): 2347–2353.

16. Kaiser Commission on Medicaid and the Uninsured, "CHIP Program Enrollment: December 2000" (Kaiser Family Foundation, 2001).

17. Information on these gains comes primarily from Karen Davis and Cathy Schoen, *Health and the War on Poverty,* (Washington, DC: Brookings, 1978), Chapters 2–4; and Stephen M. Davidson and

Theodore R. Marmor, *The Cost of Living Longer: National Health Insurance and the Elderly* (Lexington, MA: Heath, 1980). Utilization figures come from *2001 HCFA Statistics* (Washington, DC: U.S. Department of Health and Human Services, 2001).

18. See *Frustrated Federalism: Rx for State and Local Health Care Reform* (Albany, NY: Nelson A. Rockefeller Institute of Government, 1993), Chapter 3.

19. Daniel Callahan, *False Hopes: Overcoming the Obstacles to a Sustainable, Affordable Medicine* (New Brunswick, NJ: Rutgers University Press, 1998).

20. Louise B. Russell, *Is Prevention Better than Cure?* (Washington, DC: Brookings Institution, 1986); Jack A. Meyer and Marion Ein Lewin, eds., *Charting the Future of Health Care* (Washington, DC: American Enterprise Institute, 1987), Part III; Deborah A. Stone, "The Resistible Rise of Preventive Medicine," in Lawrence D. Brown, ed., *Health Policy in Transition* (Durham, NC: Duke University Press, 1987): 103–128.

21. James C. Robinson, "The End of Managed Care," *Journal of the American Medicine Association,* May 23/30, 2001: 2622–2628.

22. See, for example, Norman Daniels, *Just Health Care* (New York: Cambridge University Press, 1985). For a comprehensive review of this issue and of a variety of ethical issues in health care, see John M. Freeman and Kevin McDonnell, eds., *Tough Decisions: Cases in Medical Ethics,* 2nd ed. (New York: Oxford University Press, 2001); and Joseph H. Howell and William Frederick Sale, eds., *Life Choices: A Hastings Center Introduction to Bioethics,* 2nd ed. (Washington, DC: Georgetown University Press, 2000).

23. Accounts of the events of 1993 to 1994 include Henry J. Aaron, ed., *The Problem that Won't Go Away: Reforming U.S. Health Care Financing* (Washington, DC: Brookings Institution, 1996); Litman and Robins, eds., *Health Policy and Politics;* and Theda Skocpol, *Boomerang: Clinton's Health Security Effort and the Turn against Government in U.S. Politics* (New York: W. W. Norton & Company, 1996).

24. For an outstanding discussion of the meaning of these terms, the complexity of insurance rating, and the ethical issues involved, see Deborah A. Stone, "The Struggle for the Soul of Health Insurance," *Journal of Health Politics, Policy, and Law,* 18 (Summer 1993): 287–317.

25. John K. Iglehart, "Medicare and Prescription Drugs," *New England Journal of Medicine,* 334 (March 29, 2001): 1010–1015.

26. Marsha Gold, "Medicare+Choice: An Interim Report Card," *Health Affairs,* 20 (July/August 2001): 120–138.

27. For an introduction to the debate, see Daniel Callahan, *Setting Limits: Medical Goals in an Aging Society* (New York: Simon & Schuster, 1987); and Timothy M. Smeeding, ed., *Should Medical Care Be Rationed by Age?* (Totowa, NJ: Rowman & Littlefield, 1987).

28. See especially Callahan, *False Hopes.*

29. See William P. Brandon and Dana Burr Bradley, "The Elderly and Health Politics: The 'Coming of Age' of Aging," in Litman and Robins, eds., *Health Politics and Policy,* 323–351; and Judith Feder, Harriet L. Komisar, and Marlene Niefeld, "Long-Term Care in the United States: An Overview," *Health Affairs,* 19 (May/June, 2000): 40–56.

SUGGESTED READINGS

Books

Callahan, Daniel. *False Hopes: Overcoming the Obstacles to a Sustainable, Affordable Medicine.* New Brunswick, NJ: Rutgers University Press, 1998.

Hackey, Robert B., and Rochefort, David A., eds. *The New Politics of State Health Policy.* Lawrence: University Press of Kansas, 2001.

Howell, Joseph H., and Sale, William Frederick, eds. *Life Choices: A Hastings Center Introduction to Bioethics,* 2nd ed. Washington, DC: Georgetown University Press, 2000.

Litman, Theodore J., and Robins, Leonard S., eds. *Health Politics and Policy,* 3rd ed. Albany, NY: Delmar, 1997.

Mann, Thomas E., and Ornstein, Norman J., eds. *Intensive Care: How Congress Shapes Health Policy.* Washington, DC: American Enterprise Institute and Brookings Institution, 1995.

Marmor, Theodore R. *The Politics of Medicare,* 2nd ed. New York: Aldine de Gruyter, 2000.

Patel, Kant, and Rushefsky, Mark E. *Health Care Politics and Policy in America,* 2nd ed. Armonk, NY: M. E. Sharpe, 1999.

Payer, Lynn. *Medicine and Culture: Varieties of Treatment in the United States, England, West Germany, and France.* New York: Penguin Books, 1988.

Skocpol, Theda. *Boomerang: Clinton's Health Security Effort and the Turn against Government in U.S. Politics.* New York: Norton, 1996.

Starr, Paul. *The Social Transformation of American Medicine: The Rise of a Sovereign Profession and the Making of a Vast Industry.* New York: Basic Books, 1982.

Weissert, Carol S., and Weissert, William G. *Governing Health: The Politics of Health Policy.* Baltimore, MD: Johns Hopkins University Press, 1996.

White, Joseph. *Competing Solutions: America's Health Care Proposals and International Experience.* Washington, DC: Brookings Institution, 1995.

White, Joseph. *False Alarm: Why the Greatest Threat to Social Security and Medicare is the Campaign to "Save" Them.* Baltimore, MD: Johns Hopkins University Press, 2001.

Web Sites

Centers for Medicare and Medicaid Services (CMS)   www.cms.gov

Electronic Policy Network (health policy) www.movingideas.org/ideas/subjects/health-l.html

The Hastings Center   www.thehastingscenter.org

Health Affairs   www.healthaffairs.org

Health Policy Cyberexchange   www.hpolicy.duke.edu/cyberexchange/

Henry Kaiser Family Foundation   www.kff.org/

CHAPTER 9

Education: Conflict in Policy Direction

Education policy decisions deeply touch the life of the American family. Because of this profound impact, conflict becomes an integral part of policymaking. Since the United States is a pluralistic society, there is often deep disagreement over the basic values that guide education policy. Frequent changes in education policy act to create conflict and controversy. Much of this conflict can be traced to two opposing traditions within education theory: conservative and liberal thought.

Conservative thought ties personal development to an emphasis on individual initiative and responsibility. Conservatives tend to view variability in initiative and ability between people as natural. These variations place the burden on each individual for educational achievement, and they justify resulting economic and social inequalities. The rewards of society are accumulated through competition. This emphasis on the individual places traditional conservative thought in general opposition to an expansion of federal involvement in education policy. Conservatives emphasize the responsibility of the family, state government, local school boards, and private institutions (such as the church) as the appropriate structures for molding education policy.

Liberal thought reflects a conviction that government has an obligation to compensate for individual deprivation resulting from social inequities. Liberals emphasize individual rights in programs designed to eliminate the effects of privilege and discrimination. The concern of liberalism is to create an educational system that promotes an equality of opportunity. This concern with equality leads liberals to advocate an expanded role for the federal government in education policy. Liberal thought underscores the federal government's positive contributions in promoting equality in other policy areas, such as civil rights. These contributions provide a framework for advocating an expansion of the federal role in education policy as a means to remedy past policies by local school boards and state governments, which have, as in the case of segregation, produced unequal educational opportunities.

These two traditions have generated cross-pressures and conflicting goals in American educational policy. Schools have received the multiple and sometimes conflicting tasks of teaching students the basic skills necessary for a productive life, establishing a positive self-image, offering a system of values by which they may direct their lives, laying the groundwork for an integrated society through contacts with individuals from different racial and ethnic backgrounds, providing the nation with an adequate supply of highly trained citizens for scientific and technical enterprise, and creating a sense of loyalty to American values.

285

ISSUE BACKGROUND: HISTORICAL PERSPECTIVES AND THE ONSET OF FEDERAL INVOLVEMENT IN EDUCATION

Two principles are the basis for education policy in the United States: first, education should be free and universal, and second, control over education should be centered on the local level.

The Tradition of Free Public Education

Thomas Jefferson held that a system of free public education for all citizens is a basic requirement for democracy. He wrote in 1816, "If a nation expects to be ignorant and free, in a state of civilization, it expects what never was and never will be."[1] Jeffersonian thought embodied three educational goals: first, to provide mass literacy training; second, to expand access to education to all children without regard to social background and to open positions of leadership to those with high levels of educational achievement; and third, to provide for an educational system in which leaders could be trained in the United States rather than in Europe. The free public education system of the United States reflects these values. During the early decades of the United States, education was seen as the means to enable the public to make choices consistent with democratic values and maintain stability of the republic. Free education was a strong force for maintaining the existing social order.[2]

The shift from a private, largely church-based education system to free public education was due to a variety of factors. Education was a tool for political socialization and a key element in the "melting pot" approach to nation building. Immigrants to America brought a variety of religions, languages, customs, and political values to the new nation. Immigrants arriving from countries without democratic institutions needed to develop an understanding of democracy and a new identification as Americans. A free public education system best achieved this integration into the American social and political system, according to its advocates. Education became the instrument for increasing a sense of nationalism and the promotion of national unity, and a tradition of free public education became entrenched in American thought.

The Tradition of Local Control

There is no direct provision in the U.S. Constitution for federal involvement in, or control over, the educational system. The American educational system grew out of an English heritage in which the church and home took responsibility for education. This heritage evolved into the early district school in America. Residents of each independent district decided policy issues relating to education such as tax rate, appointment and removal of teachers, school calendar, and selection of classroom materials. Community control is a basic tenet of American education manifested in the local school district of today. Federal control over education was viewed as an inappropriate exercise of national power in the early years of the nation.

An Emerging Role for State Governments

State governments gradually assumed an increasingly important role in education policy. State government creates local school districts, which can exercise only those powers specifically granted to them by the state. As state funding for local schools increased, states exercised greater influence over education policy. State education departments now determine education policy guidelines for local districts. State government specifies curriculum models and teacher certification standards and establishes guidelines for virtually all education programs, including the provision of special education services.

State governments also establish the framework for financing education programs. Local districts are free to tax and spend only within guidelines established by the state. State governments have primary responsibility for establishing minimum expenditure levels for local districts. The increasing power and influence exercised by state governments conflicts with the tradition of local control.

Federal Involvement in Education

In the last half of the twentieth century, the role of the federal government in education policy emerged as a major issue. Historically, the fear of a strong central government drove the states to guard their authority from intrusions by the national government, yet the federal government played some role in education from the earliest years of the republic. A partial history of major federal education programs appears in Box 9-1.

Note, however, that the various programs described do not represent a major federal financial role in education. Federal aid to education remains limited in scope and indirect in nature. Supporters justify these programs on the grounds that they represent limited solutions to specific problems. Given this orientation, most Americans accept a limited federal role in education.

The Elementary and Secondary Education Act of 1965: Expanding the Federal Policy Role

The "baby boom" at the end of World War II produced a dramatic increase in school enrollment beginning in the 1950s. During the Great Depression, capital expenditures for education had been reduced. During World War II, they were almost completely suspended. Thus, after the war, the nation's schools found it difficult to accommodate dramatically increased enrollments.

Even though public opinion supported expanded federal financial aid to education, Federal aid legislation failed to pass because it had become entangled in two broad areas of social conflict: public education versus private sectarian education (the problem of separation of church and state) and integrated versus segregated schools (the problem of racial discrimination).

Interest groups also divided along national- versus local-control lines and took positions favoring or opposing federal aid. Liberals tended to support increased federal aid and viewed the infusion of federal dollars as a means of improving education quality and as a solution to the problem of inequality in

---

BOX 9-1
Federal Education Programs

1787 Northwest Ordinance: Required one section of land in each township of the Northwest Territory to be reserved for the support of education.

1862 Morrill Land Grant Act: Provided public land for colleges that would specialize in agricultural and mechanical arts.

1867 Office of Education Act: Created the U.S. Office of Education.

1917 Smith-Hughes Act: Provided limited federal funds for vocational education.

1920 Smith-Bankhead Act: Provided for vocational rehabilitation grants to the states.

1935 Social Security Act: Provided for vocational rehabilitation of the handicapped.

1941 Amendment of the 1940 Lanham Act: Provided federal funding for construction of schools in areas with extensive federal tax-exempt property.

1944 Servicemen's Readjustment Act (GI Bill):   Provided financial assistance to veterans in education programs; these benefits were extended to Korean conflict-era veterans in 1952 and to Vietnam-era veterans in 1966.

1946 National School Lunch Act: Provided students nutrition subsidies through school lunch programs.

1950 Federal Impacted Areas Aid Program: Authorized federal funds for aid to school districts in which large numbers of federal employees and tax-exempt federal property contributed to high school enrollment and a reduced local tax base, such as school districts serving military institutions.

1950 National Science Foundation (NSF):   Created with the goal of promoting scientific research and improving the quality of teaching in the areas of science, mathematics, and engineering.

---

educational spending. The infusion of federal dollars would equalize per-pupil spending across geographical regions and eliminate this source of inequality. Groups opposing federal aid tended to be conservative. Given the tradition of local control, many conservatives felt that federal funding would mean federal encroachment in education policy, an event to be resisted at all costs. Transfer of responsibility for education policy to the federal level was in basic conflict with their commitment to limited government.

Even more controversial than the issue of federal control were the issues of race and religion. Minority groups, such as the National Association for the Advancement of Colored People (NAACP), and many liberal groups opposed federal aid to segregated schools on moral grounds. For this reason many liberals wished to prevent the enactment of such legislation until segregation had been abolished, as mandated by the Supreme Court in its landmark decision in *Brown v. Board of Education* (1954), which outlawed "separate but equal" educational facilities.

In 1964, President Johnson abandoned the strategy of enacting a general program of federal aid and adopted an approach that emphasized a broad range

---

BOX 9-1   *(continued)*

1958 National Defense Education Act: Provided federal financial support to strengthen the areas of science, mathematics, and foreign language instruction, and to establish a system of direct loans to college students.

1964 Economic Opportunity Act: Provided federal work study grants to students from low-income families.

1965 Elementary and Secondary Education Act (ESEA):   Provided limited financial assistance to local schools for textbooks, libraries, and other instructional materials.

1968 Elementary and Secondary Education Act Amendments: Provided financial assistance for educating handicapped children.

1974 Educational Amendments: Consolidated some federal programs and established the National Center for Educational Statistics.

1978 Career Educational Incentive Act: Provided for the creation of career education programs in elementary and secondary schools.

1979 Department of Education Organization Act: Created the cabinet-level Department of Education by consolidating education programs from other federal departments.

1985 Montgomery GI Bill: Provided education benefits to veterans entering active duty after 1985 (extended in 1991).

1994 Goals 2000: Educate America Act: Created the National Education Standards and Improvement Council to develop voluntary national skills standards for local districts.

1997 Taxpayer Relief Act of 1997:   Created the Hope Scholarship Program for college students.

1998 Charter School Expansion Act: Provided for expansion of charter schools.

---

of categorical assistance programs designed to remedy specific problems, especially the educational needs of disadvantaged children. The Elementary and Secondary Education Act (ESEA), passed in April 1965, provided federal funding to local public schools. Under the concept that ESEA gave aid to children but not to schools, the law authorized funds to parochial schools for the purchase of nonreligious textbooks and library materials, but excluded teachers' salaries.

Intergovernmental conflict on ESEA.   Despite the passage of ESEA, the role of the federal government in providing financial aid remains relatively minor, although federal regulations increase in number and scope. Figure 9-1 indicates that the federal government today still accounts for only 7 percent of funding for public schools, with about 93 percent of education revenue provided by state and local sources. ESEA had the effect of legitimizing an expanded federal regulatory role over states and local school districts in education policy without a corresponding requirement for the infusion of significant federal dollars. Congressional re-authorizations of ESEA in 1994 and again in 2002 contain provisions that require states to comply with additional federal regulations without providing a significant increase in federal funding dollars.

FIGURE 9-1 ▪ U.S. Education Expenditures by Source, 2001

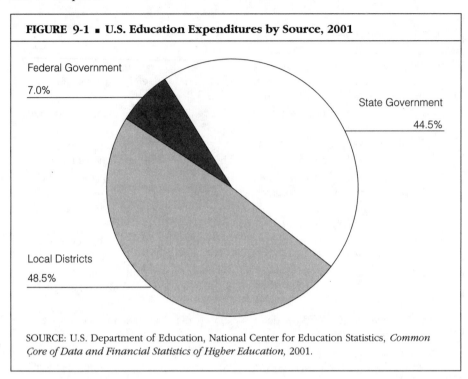

Federal Government

7.0%

State Government

44.5%

Local Districts

48.5%

SOURCE: U.S. Department of Education, National Center for Education Statistics, *Common Core of Data and Financial Statistics of Higher Education,* 2001.

State government revenues have increased in importance as a source of revenue for local districts. State governments now supply nearly 45 percent of the revenues to local districts, a far higher proportion than a few decades ago. The increase in state funding has translated into increased power over education policy. For example, curriculum content and structure as well as minimum competency standards for students and teachers are now the domain of state governments. The tradition of local control continues to weaken as the role of state government in financing schools expands.

Problems also have surfaced with the federal government's expanding role. Federal officials continue to impose policies and mandates on state and local authorities, often without the funding necessary for implementation, an issue discussed in Chapter 2. State and local officials lament this federal policy intrusion and the accompanying financial burden. One dimension of the conflict between local and federal officials can be traced to conservative and liberal assumptions held at the two levels of government. Since the 1960s, federal education programs and guidelines have tended to reflect a liberal bias, demonstrated in the concern for equality of opportunity with an accompanying acceptance of expanded federal regulations.

These conflicting philosophical positions add to the conflict over education policy. Many state and local officials fear that the federal government will increasingly control policy through a strategy of withholding financial aid without adequately considering the values of local residents.

The Federal Role in Higher Education

Tax-supported public institutions dominate higher education in the United States today. Before the 1940s, private colleges and universities were dominant. The southern states began the tradition of establishing public colleges. The enactment of the Morrill Act in 1862 resulted in the rapid and extensive development of public higher education. The agricultural and mechanical colleges fostered by the Morrill Act had a practical orientation that increased public support for universities. Today almost 80 percent of the nation's college students attend public institutions of higher education. Increasing numbers of people have decided to attend college. In the words of a former Office of Education official, "In a democratic society there is really no choice but to accommodate the educational demands of the people."[3] This demand for access to higher education presents the problem of maintaining a quality education while allowing almost unrestrained public access to higher education.

State institutions of higher learning rely primarily on state funds and tuition payments for operation, but a variety of limited federal funding programs exist. Work study programs and the GI Bill have provided financial assistance to university students. Federal aid in the form of grants for research also subsidizes higher education. Universities have utilized this additional money to support research activities and create faculty positions. These federal research dollars have increased the ability of the federal government to exercise influence over the educational policies of recipient institutions. Universities now find it necessary to comply with federally mandated policies in order to receive research grants and contracts. Figure 9-2 provides an indication of the level of federal funding for education.

CONTEMPORARY POLICY: REMEDYING SOCIAL INEQUALITY THROUGH EDUCATION

Disagreement on the objectives of education remains a source of policy conflict. Education can serve as an equalizing and leveling institution, or it can be a selection mechanism to maintain an existing stratification system. The concept that education is to function as an equalizer was not widely accepted at the time of Washington and Jefferson. Attempts to use education for such purposes only served, in the opinion of many, to "pull down what is above, never raise what is below." This conservative orientation toward protecting established elites conflicts with a more liberal concern for the creation of an egalitarian education system.

Leveling is central to achieving the socioeconomic goals of education and is directly related to educational equality. Equalization of educational opportunity provides students with the potential for social and economic advancement. Yet, *Plessey v. Ferguson* (1896) legitimized inequality for much of American education. In this ruling, the Supreme Court established the doctrine of "separate but equal" regarding race in American life. One result was the establishment of a dual education system in the South based on race. This segregated system was unequal, both in physical facilities and in the quality of education provided. Education policy served as a mechanism for restricting opportunity. Even though the Supreme

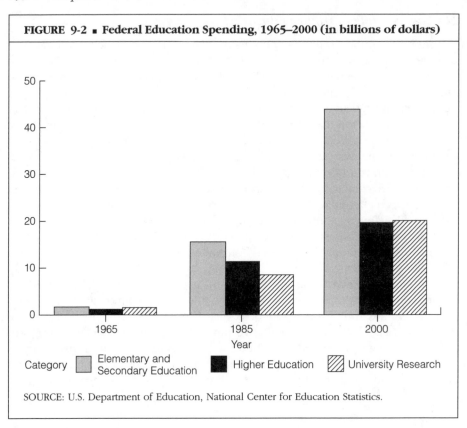

FIGURE 9-2 ▪ Federal Education Spending, 1965–2000 (in billions of dollars)

SOURCE: U.S. Department of Education, National Center for Education Statistics.

Court recognized the effects of separate educational systems and rejected the "separate but equal" doctrine in 1954, it was not until the administration of President Johnson (1963 to 1968) that equalizing educational opportunities for all Americans became a national education policy priority.

The Issue of Unequal Financial Resources

Because of the uniquely American tradition of local control, local sources, primarily the property tax, generate about 48 percent of elementary and secondary school revenues. The result is a system in which local school district funds are limited by the value of taxable property, which varies widely from district to district within a state. This unequal distribution of resources works to the disadvantage of residents of poor districts. Revenue is a product of the tax rate multiplied by the value of taxable property (the tax base).

 Districts with extensive property wealth can generate a large amount of revenue with a relatively low tax rate. A less-wealthy district must tax at a higher rate to generate the same amount of revenue. The result is a disparity in per-pupil expenditures. In many cases the districts with low levels of spending are taxing at a relatively high rate, yet they lack the financial base to support spending at higher levels. This situation exists at the state and regional levels as well. The national per-pupil spending average for 2000 was $7,146. Utah spent $4,282, the lowest of the fifty states.[4] Education spending is a function of wealth (tax base) and willingness to tax (tax rate).

One potential mechanism to equalize per-pupil spending across the nation would involve the massive infusion of federal dollars. This approach is not feasible for two reasons. First, state governments and local districts desire to retain primary responsibility for education policy. Second, competing demands on the federal budget act to prevent such a course of action. Today, emphasis is on state assistance to local districts, but surplus state revenues are shrinking. The federal government has not played a leadership role in encouraging financial reform, nor has it attempted to provide assistance to states that are wrestling with the problem.

There are often high levels of financial inequality among districts within a given state. Financial disparities within a state can be profound. State court challenges to finance formulas cited significant gaps (for example, $9,333 to $2,223 in Texas).[5] Financial inequality is a problem in many states, with a ratio of unequal spending of two or even three or four to one being common. Urban school districts in large cities tend to face the problem of low fiscal resources to a greater extent than suburban and rural districts. Federal aid has not been a factor as a remedy for fiscal inequities.

Efforts to reform financial disparities. Attempts were made at the state level to force school finance reform in the direction of greater equality. The California Supreme Court ruled in *Serrano v. Priest* (1971) that under the provisions of the California constitution, education is a fundamental right that cannot be a condition of the wealth of a child's parents or neighbors.[6] This doctrine of "fiscal neutrality" found that reliance on the property tax resulted in excessive financial disparities among school districts. Following the *Serrano* decision, lawsuits were filed in about thirty states in an attempt to spread the California reform.

The U.S. Supreme Court in 1973 declared the issue of school finance reform off-limits to lower federal courts. In the case of *San Antonio Independent School District v. Rodriguez,* the Court refused to equate inequities in property values and the resultant differences in educational expenditures with violation of the equal protection clause of the Fourteenth Amendment.[7] The Court reasoned that the United States Constitution did not explicitly or implicitly guarantee the "right" to an education. Furthermore, differences in spending levels could not be equated with "interference with fundamental rights." The Court supported the continued use of the property tax in Texas by stating that there was no evidence that the arrangement deprived Texans of "an adequate minimum educational offering." Because many state constitutions do guarantee the right to an education, litigation concerning school finance reform was restricted to state court systems.

During the 1990s, various state supreme courts heard some twenty-one cases with school finance reform. About half of these cases required the affected state to engage in some type of funding change. Lawsuits attempting to change the existing approach to funding education have met with some success, as supreme courts in states such as Montana, Kentucky, and Tennessee ruled that school funding practices violated provisions of their state constitutions. The record is one of mixed success in developing and implementing funding formulas that achieve a degree of equality in per-pupil spending. Although the state court system acts as a lever to stimulate change, state legislators have demonstrated a hesitancy to redistribute money from wealthy districts to poor districts.

Conflict over school finance reform.   The reform movement embodies policy conflict.[8] Conservatives often see finance reform as one more attempt to solve a problem by simply spending more money. Accordingly, they argue that reform efforts should focus on education philosophy, not education finance. Education finance has been traditionally distributive in nature, with little emphasis placed on a redistribution of financial resources. The redistributive nature of school finance reform is in conflict with conservative thought. Redistributive policies are often liberal in inspiration. The politics of redistribution are far more conflictual than distributive policy (see Chapter 1). Increased power and control over education exercised by state governments also concerns proponents of local control. This type of financial reform is therefore viewed as a threat to a basic tradition in the American educational system.

The controversy over financial equalization reflects the conviction that expenditures affect the quality of education.[9] The relationship between expenditures and educational achievement, however, is less than clear. Conventional wisdom holds that the "life chances," or future opportunities, of students attending poor districts are restricted when compared with the life chances of others. Consequently, it is assumed that such deprived students will achieve less in life, have lower incomes, find it more difficult to advance economically and socially, and contribute less to making America more economically competitive than will students from wealthier schools. Studies in this area have not resolved the question because of conflicting results and differing interpretations.[10]

There is little doubt, however, that expenditures do affect the educational environment. Wealthy districts do spend differently than poor districts.[11] Poor districts tend to (1) have a higher student-teacher ratio, (2) spend more on core instructional programming and less on college preparatory electives, (3) spend less on capital projects (building construction and maintenance), and (4) have lower teacher salaries than wealthier districts.

Because the research is ambiguous, it is not unequivocally clear that students attending districts with high expenditure levels will have higher levels of achievement than those attending districts with lower expenditure levels. However, it is clear that the educational options available to students in poor districts are not as extensive as those attending wealthier schools. Part of the problem with building a strong case for school finance reform is the lack of unambiguous evidence that dollars make a difference in educational achievement. If such data existed, the reform movement would be strengthened.[12]

What we do not know relative to school district spending for specific education purposes complicates the issue of financial equity. First, it is possible to assess total per-pupil spending between districts, yet information relative to the costs of elementary education as compared to secondary education within a district are less easily understood. Understanding the relationship between the cost of providing instruction across subjects (for example, high school chemistry as compared to high school social studies) and student achievement is also less than clear. Related issues involve the issue of per-pupil spending within a district. "Should per-pupil spending be the same for all schools, for all grade levels, and for all subject areas within a district?" remains an unanswered question in the debate surrounding financial equity.

A second factor involves differences surrounding cost-of-living issues for various regions within a state. Schools in higher cost-of-living areas face higher costs (teacher salaries, land acquisition costs, student transportation costs, labor costs for support staff) in the delivery of equivalent education programs than do other schools within the same state. A mechanism for adjusting these differences remains elusive.

A third factor involves establishing accountability measures for school districts in student achievement when a program of financial reform provides additional funding. With the contention that increased spending will result in higher student achievement, what specific student outcomes should be expected to be produced (higher graduation rates, reduced absenteeism and truancy, higher standardized test scores) in districts benefiting from additional state dollars?

It appears that state court cases are tending to focus more on disparities in student achievement than on disparities in per-pupil spending when dealing with finance reform cases. Debate increasingly centers on defining "adequate" spending and the appropriate mix of state and local funding necessary to achieve that spending level.[13] This emphasis on "adequacy" is a significant shift in thinking about school finance reform, since it does not require equal per-pupil spending.

Adequacy implies a sufficient minimum level of funding that will promote student achievement, an outcome of the education system. Reform efforts focusing on equality of spending reflect a concern with inputs of the education system. Historically, adequacy was simply assumed and defined in terms of available tax revenues raised by a local district. This approach was modified over time as states adopted "foundation formulas" that provided a mechanism for distribution of additional state dollars to local districts designed to guarantee a minimum spending level across the state. These spending levels were never equal, and the school finance reform movement challenged them.

Increasingly, adequacy is now defined in terms of goals related to student achievement. This means that the school finance reform movement may increasingly emphasize student performance gaps as the foundation for changing funding patterns, rather than claims based solely on differences in per-pupil spending.

Equality in Education

All, regardless of race or class or economic status, are entitled to a fair chance and to the tools for developing their individual powers of mind and spirit to the utmost. This promise means that all children by virtue of their own efforts, competently guided, can hope to attain the mature and informed judgment needed to secure gainful employment, and to manage their own lives, thereby serving not only their own interests, but also the progress of society itself.[14]

The concept of equality is a central tenet of the American ideological system. Yet, when asked to define equality, most Americans find it difficult to arrive at an explanation free of contradictions. We have discussed the role of education in supplying the individual with the tools necessary for a productive life. The definition of equality in education has slowly changed over time.[15] Initially, conflict centered on the appropriate role of government in guaranteeing equal opportunity. Gradually the more liberal position prevailed, and education as a means of achieving equal life chances became public policy.

The notion of equality of opportunity implies that the rules for success and failure are fair. Although there is disagreement on the definition of what is "fair," most Americans endorse the basic principle of fair competition. As the nation recognized that equality and fair competition did not exist for all groups, public leaders turned to the education system as a technique for eliminating the inequality of opportunity and for achieving a degree of social justice for the poor.

The concept of educational equality varies along a liberal-conservative continuum. The conservative orientation holds that individuals possess differing levels of ability. Accordingly, efforts to guarantee an equal education are an exercise in futility. Intelligence rather than equal opportunity determines the individual's life chances. This conflicts with the orientation of classic liberalism, which emphasizes equality of opportunity. All external barriers should be removed to allow complete development of individual potential. Social and background characteristics should not determine individual opportunity. Government would use its power to assure each child an equal education. The emphasis lies on the inputs of education; that is, on the expansion of special programs designed to give graduates equal standing for competition in a free-enterprise system.

This concern for equality of opportunity gradually gives way to a concern for "representative equality" as manifested in affirmative action policies. The focus shifted from the inputs to the outputs of education policy; that is, to the occupational outcomes of education. Increasingly, education policy is assessed by the degree to which employment patterns reflect population demographics. (In the perfect model, for example, the same percentage of African Americans as in the total U.S. population would be found employed in, say, engineering careers.) Effectiveness then would depend on the advancement experienced by previously disadvantaged groups. This shift of concern from the inputs to the outputs of education policy has widened the gaps between conservatism and liberalism.

Equality and busing. After three decades of busing to achieve educational integration approaches, the nation is moving away from that social experiment. The nation's oldest busing program in Charlotte, North Carolina, ends in 2002, as have similar programs in other cities and school districts across the country. The U.S. Supreme Court has slowly withdrawn its support for extending federally mandated busing programs as a mechanism to achieve racial balance in the schools.

Academic support for busing traces to the publication of *Inequality: A Reassessment of the Effect of Family and Schooling in America* in 1972. Christopher Jencks, then director of the Harvard Center for Educational Policy Research, and a group of seven other scholars identified key assumptions that supported the move toward equalization of educational opportunity.[16] The main reason that children cannot escape the hold of poverty is a lack of cognitive skills: the ability to read, write, and function effectively in a complex society. Minority children, these scholars argued, could attain the needed cognitive skills by attending schools with middle-class children and through the extension of special programs designed to compensate for past inequities.

This thinking was an outgrowth of James Coleman's *Equality of Educational Opportunity* (1966).[17] According to Coleman's research, the primary factor that affected student learning was family background, both the individual student's and that of his or her classmates. The Coleman report did not make specific policy recommendations, but the federal government utilized it as a basis for educational change.[18] Reanalysis of his data indicated that educational achievement scores were higher for African-American students attending predominantly white schools than for African-American students attending predominantly African-American schools. Analysts noted that achievement levels of white students were not affected by the presence of small proportions of African-American students.

The Civil Rights Commission utilized these analyses to support its advocacy of an end to segregation and racial imbalance in the schools. The commission challenged the institution of the neighborhood school, which often had led to segregated schools, and advocated busing as an alternative to improve the quality of education available to minority Americans. This perspective influenced the Supreme Court when, in 1971, it approved of busing as a viable method to achieve racial balance in the nation's schools.

Educational Inequality Outside the United States

Equality as an issue in education is not limited to the United States. There has been concern in Western Europe with the relationship between educational opportunity and life chances available to citizens. Various surveys and studies indicate the existence of a general lack of equality of educational opportunity. Following World War II, although the GI Bill greatly expanded education opportunities in America, only 2 to 5 percent of the same age group in Western Europe enrolled in higher education.

In Europe, education tends to select individuals based on test scores and early tracking of students, devices that tend to reflect society's class structure. In post-war Sweden, over 60 percent of university students came from the upper and upper-middle classes. Only 6 to 7 percent had origins in the lower socioeconomic strata (which made up about 55 percent of the population). The same was true for all of Western Europe. Studies in Germany, England, and France revealed similar patterns: only a small percentage of university students were drawn from the lower and lower-middle classes. European reform efforts in recent decades have moved to change these patterns.

Equality of educational opportunity is also restricted in the former communist countries. Although the data are not so readily available, some pertinent observations exist. The vast majority of students attending universities come from the upper socioeconomic levels. Even though the United States is not alone in the struggle to increase educational equality, it has made greater efforts than has Western Europe to achieve equality of opportunity.

POLICY EVALUATION: EDUCATIONAL QUALITY IN THE UNITED STATES

Concern with the educational system in the United States has led to a variety of efforts to evaluate the quality of education provided to students. A variety of "quality" measures have been employed, and there remains considerable debate about how best to measure educational quality. In the following section, attention will be given to some of the common measures of the various dimensions of quality: SAT test scores, minimum competency tests (MCTs), teacher competency, master teachers, bilingual education, and multiculturalism.

TABLE 9-1 ■ SAT Scores (average), 1967–2000

	1967	1975	1980	1984	1988	1992	1996*	1996**	2000***
Verbal	466	434	424	426	428	423	427	505	505
Math	492	472	466	471	476	476	484	508	514

* 1996 scores on original scale

**1996 recentered scale scores

***2000 scores based on recentered scale

SOURCE: College Board, National Report, 2001; and U.S. Department of Education.

Concern over Poor Student Achievement

During the 1960s and 1970s, many school districts adopted "innovative" programs that reduced the emphasis on the traditional "three Rs" and instead focused on a student's emotional growth, self-direction, and individualism. Because these changes coincided with a decline in student achievement, the public came to believe that these curriculum reforms were not academically adequate. Performance levels of students on such standardized tests as the SAT have declined since 1967, as indicated in Table 9-1.

In 1996 this pattern of declining SAT scores artificially appeared to be reversed because the test was "recentered" to provide an average score of 500 for both the verbal and math scales. In the words of the College Board, "Setting the average verbal and math scores at 500 means that most students' scores will be higher."[19] On the new recentered scale, a verbal score of 500 would have been a score of 422 on the original scale, and a math score of 500 would have been a score of 474 on the original SAT scale. "Recentering" means that interpreting SAT scores must now be based on a contemporary rather than an historical reference group. Critics of education policy and curriculum are in a position to argue that "recentering" SAT scores to a higher level is indicative of a loss of overall rigor and quality in the nation's schools.[20]

Although there is little debate on the fact that the average performance on standardized tests declined over an extended number of years, there remains disagreement concerning the causes of the decline. Many analysts cite parental attitudes and societal changes as the major factors contributing to low levels of performance. However, many parents and taxpayer groups believe that the departure from education basics—reading, writing, and arithmetic—fostered the decline in student achievement.

Investigators of the decline in the SAT mean scores have attributed it to several factors.[21] More students are taking the test now than in any previous period. Specifically, there has been a marked increase in the number of students from families that have not traditionally attended college. Low scores by this group tend to lower the mean score on the test (see Figure 9-3). Accordingly, the SAT average scores cannot be an accurate barometer of student achievement in society as a whole. Television viewing and family instability have lowered the motivation of students to excel. The findings of these studies have not been conclusive, and research into factors that might explain the decline has remained problematic.[22]

FIGURE 9-3 ▪ **Average SAT Scores by Level of Parental Education, 2001**

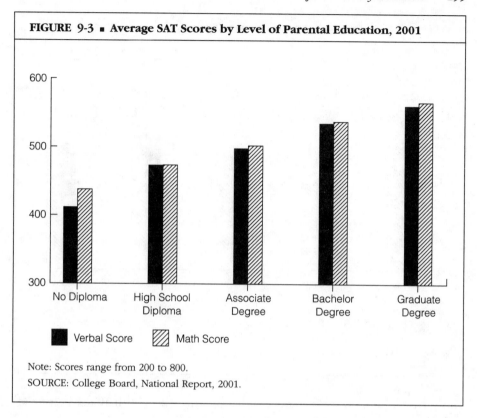

Note: Scores range from 200 to 800.

SOURCE: College Board, National Report, 2001.

Figure 9-4 indicates the variation in average scores between demographic groups on the SAT. White students had higher average verbal and mathematical scores than did all other demographic groups, with one exception: the Asian-American math score. This pattern has persisted over time and has contributed to the issue of cultural bias in standardized tests.

The SAT is constructed in such a manner as to be "blind" to high school curriculum. Consequently, if a curriculum declines in rigor, a pattern of declining SAT scores could result.

The College Board, which administers the SAT, has indicated that the decline in SAT scores indicates a "disturbing pattern of educational disparity" in the nation's schools. There is concern that the nation's schools may be producing two categories of students: a small group of well-educated students and a larger group of ill-educated students.

Family background characteristics clearly affect student SAT performance, as indicated in Figure 9-3. The higher the level of parental education, the higher the average SAT score earned by the child. Children of parents with a graduate degree had average verbal and math scores of 559 and 567, respectively. Children of parents without a high school diploma had average verbal and math scores of 411 and 438, a difference of 148 points on the verbal scale and 129 points on the math scale! Since level of education is one indicator of socioeconomic status, a positive relationship between socioeconomic status and student performance appears to exist.

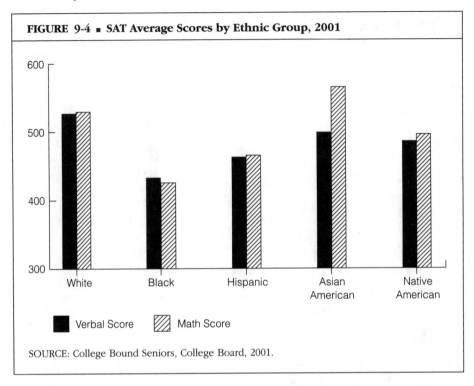

FIGURE 9-4 ■ SAT Average Scores by Ethnic Group, 2001

SOURCE: College Bound Seniors, College Board, 2001.

This provides support for the concern that American schools may not be providing an equal education to all groups of students.

Student performance on the ACT has remained stable over time. The ACT is a different type of test than the SAT. ACT scores range from one to thirty-six, and questions on the test are designed to reflect high school curriculum with scores reported in English, mathematics, reading, and science. ACT scores would not necessarily reflect a decline in the rigor of high school curriculum. Since 1970, the national average on the ACT, about twenty, has remained very stable, varying less than a half-point.

Minimum competency tests. Whatever the cause of the drop in student performance, parents and legislators have become more concerned over students' achievement levels. The result of this concern was the adoption of minimum competency tests (MCTs) in over forty states by 1990. States use these tests for a variety of purposes: as criteria for student promotion, and as diagnostic tools to determine the need for remedial training. Twenty-one states now require that students earn a passing grade on an MCT as a requirement for receiving a high school diploma. Most of the MCT exams require performance on an eighth- or ninth-grade level.[23]

The proliferation of MCT examinations traces back to the public's concern about the academic content of courses. Minimum competency testing has been advocated as a way to force schools to stress the basics of education. Many believe that imposing such tests on students as a requirement for a high school diploma will combat what they perceive as a trend toward lower academic standards and add value to the high school diploma by confirming the graduate has mastered specified levels of knowledge.

Educators tend to remain skeptical of the tests as a prerequisite for graduation. They charge that the examinations are biased, statistically unreliable, and a simplistic solution to a complex problem. Representatives of the African-American community charge that cultural differences and vestiges of segregation are the primary cause of African-American problems with the exam. Given their disproportionate impact on minority students, it is more likely that MCTs measure the impact of racial discrimination in education, not student achievement.[24]

Research indicates that between 60 and 80 percent of students pass these types of exams on their first attempt and that the vast majority of high school students (some 99 percent) eventually pass the test by the end of their senior year.[25] Critics argue that MCTs do not measure essential skills or even skills that are applicable to life outside the classroom.[26] The MCT program tends to emphasize a narrow range of academic abilities rather than providing a framework for establishing a sound education system. Several negative potential impacts for education resulting from an emphasis on student testing can readily be identified. These include an emphasis on teaching of test content materials and excluding nontested curriculum materials, which narrows the curriculum; devoting time to teaching test-taking techniques rather than developing critical thinking skills; contributing to the dropout rate of high school students; and, finally, teaching which is mechanical in nature, with a reduced emphasis on creativity and stirring student creativity.

Although MCTs have proliferated, there is no clear agreement about the validity of these tests and their consequences for student learning. There is an absence of evaluation literature that provides a foundation for assessing the impact of MCTs on the education system. One conclusion is certain: MCTs have become a fixture on the educational landscape and will continue to be a source of conflict.

Questioning Teacher Competency

Accompanying the concern for student performance has been a concern for the level of teacher competency in the nation's schools. Today, every state uses some form of competency testing for initial certification of classroom teachers. Most states rely on one of three test forms: The National Teacher Examination (NTE), the Preprofessional Skills Test, or a test developed and approved by a specific state. The Educational Testing Service, a major developer of standardized tests, developed the NTE. This test requires three hours to complete and attempts to measure general knowledge and the basic skills of reading, writing, and arithmetic.

The validity of the competency tests, however, remains under serious question. There is an absence of data to support the assertion that the tests actually measure competency. In fact, these tests may be biased toward middle-class white Americans just as MCTs are biased toward middle-class white high school students. There are two components to effective teaching: mastery of knowledge and mastery of teaching strategies. Even if competency tests do validly measure the mastery of academic material, their power to assess mastery of teaching skills remains unconfirmed. Despite the problems with determining teacher competency, the use of such testing will continue in this decade.

Another related problem centers on the starting salaries of college graduates. Average starting salaries for teachers range from $5,000 to $9,000 less per year than for other career fields such as business administration, engineering, sales and marketing, and liberal arts. This salary gap does not disappear as teachers gain experience and earn master's degrees. Many experts argue that, given the lack of financial rewards after graduation, teacher education programs have a disadvantage in recruiting students of the highest academic caliber.

The policy implications arising from this situation present genuine difficulties in any attempt to improve the quality of education. First, in order to enhance the appeal of teaching as a career, salary levels may have to increase. Second, projections indicate that the demand for teachers will exceed the supply in a number of disciplines. This is currently a problem in the areas of math and science. The challenge is to produce an adequate supply of high-quality teachers in an environment that makes it difficult to recruit and retain the best and the brightest. The issue of teacher competency is bound up in the policy of teacher compensation as reflected in the issues of merit pay and master teachers.[27]

Merit Pay and Master Teachers

Merit pay. The current emphasis on quality education has led to a widespread advocacy of merit pay as an appropriate way to attract and retain quality teachers. The Report of the National Commission on Excellence in Education *(A Nation at Risk)* recommended that merit pay plans be adopted across the nation. State governments have experimented with various types of merit pay provisions for teachers. A majority of states have developed some variant of teacher incentive pay plans.

Although merit pay does appeal to the public and the teaching profession, there are problems in implementing the concept. First, because the merit pay concept intends to attract and retain exceptional teachers, it is best implemented after teachers' salaries are elevated to levels competitive with those of the private sector. Merit pay is not a substitute for an adequate salary scale.

A second problem with the concept is the validity of merit pay as a motivating force in teacher behavior. Because many of the nation's quality teachers continue in the profession despite low salary scales, salary may not be the main factor in recruiting and retaining the highest-caliber teaching force.

A third problem is establishing an unbiased operational definition of merit as applied to teachers. No group, whether teacher organizations, school boards, state education commissions, or federal agencies, has been able to determine exactly what constitutes merit or effective teaching. For example, student performance is not an acceptable measure, because intelligence is widely viewed as an innate quality; therefore, teachers are very much captives of the students assigned to their classrooms.

A fourth problem with merit pay will arise if somehow it could receive a definition in specific, unambiguous terms and standards. In order to qualify for merit pay, teachers may abandon their own creativity in order to comply with a rigid set of standards. Merit pay may become a threat to teachers' experimentation and creativity if teachers follow established guidelines to meet merit standards.

A fifth problem with merit pay is cost. A genuine merit plan would increase costs to local districts. The federal government does not plan to expand its role in financing teacher salaries. Given the climate of opposition to local property taxes, school boards will find it more difficult to pass the tax increases necessary to fund a merit pay system. This means that state governments are the only viable source of revenues to pay for a merit plan. At the same time, because of fiscal limitations, state legislatures resist demands to assume greater responsibilities in financing programs.

A sixth problem with merit pay is that job status, not the contribution of the job to the organization, historically governs compensation.[28] Historically, salary reflects rank within both public- and private-sector organizations in the United States. Principals and Assistant Principals always will receive higher pay than teachers, just as executives are paid more than front-line employees in other companies. Merit pay advocates seem to ignore this historical pattern.[29]

Some policy advocates push merit pay as a major innovation and remedy for the nation's education system. However, during the 1920s, the concept of merit pay was widely supported in the United States,[30] and the rhetoric of that period closely resembled that of today. Nevertheless, merit pay plans failed to be adopted then because of the problems of defining merit and evaluating teachers. Only when these problems are solved can a truly effective merit pay plan be implemented.

Master teachers. The concept of classifying master teachers closely relates to the concept of merit pay. This system may include merit pay components as well as career ladders for teachers as they progress. Master teachers are to provide a variety of services and fill a range of roles, depending on the educational climate and needs of each school district. Typically, a master teacher plan includes the identification of exceptional teachers, a system of merit-based financial rewards, and the use of master teachers as resource personnel in a supervisory capacity over other teachers to encourage higher levels of teaching effectiveness.

The master teacher movement continues to expand across the nation as teacher organizations, universities and colleges, and state and local school districts develop this designation for teachers. Selection criteria, the role of teacher organizations in the process, and financial compensation procedures vary from state to state. The role and impact of the master teacher movement will continue to expand in the coming years.

Bilingual Education

Bilingual education programs grew out of Title VI of the Civil Rights Act of 1964 and the Equal Educational Opportunities Act (EEOA) of 1974. The U.S. Supreme Court interpreted these acts to mandate that states and local school districts set up programs to rectify language deficiencies of students from non-English-speaking families. These acts left program development and implementation in the hands of state and local education officials. The Bilingual Education Act of 1974 provided federal funds to meet the language needs of non-English-speaking students. Throughout the 1970s, bilingual education was favored as the appropriate method to remediate language difficulties.

School districts in areas with high concentrations of minority students developed these programs, with over 70 percent located in the Southwest and Pacific coast areas. When policy analysts evaluated bilingual programs, their effectiveness in improving educational achievement was challenged. Even though several studies found that bilingual programs were not effective, the issue remains unresolved. On the positive side, proponents argue that bilingual programs reduce dropout rates and facilitate the political socialization of non-English-speaking students into American culture.

Bilingual education is gradually developing into one among a variety of suitable programs to remedy language deficiencies. Bilingual programs are increasingly not a right or entitlement, but simply an available policy option. In the absence of federal mandates to provide bilingual programs, any reduction in federal funds for these programs would place their future entirely in the hands of the state governments. Given the costs of the programs, the lack of positive evaluations, and the financial pressures on state governments, the future of bilingual education programs remains uncertain. One indication of this uncertainty is the 1998 passage of Proposition 227 in California, which mandated that limited English proficiency students receive instruction in sheltered English programs, rather than bilingual education, unless their parents personally request bilingual education. Arizona enacted similar legislation two years later.

Multiculturalism

In order to establish a greater appreciation for the contributions of the various ethnic groups in the United States, the "multicultural" movement has emerged and is having a direct impact on education policy. The objective is to change public perceptions by reexamining traditional views of the Western European impact on the Americas. The resulting emphasis on redefining the diverse and disparate ethnic elements in American society and revising the history books accordingly will have significant consequences for curricula.[31] In fact, multicultural education has been defined in "Social Reconstructionist" terms,[32] as a program designed to create social changes beyond increasing tolerance and understanding. In 1973, the American Association of Colleges for Teacher Education (AACTE) defined multiculturalism as a rejection of "the view that schools should seek to melt away cultural differences or the view that schools should merely tolerate cultural pluralism."[33] The AACTE defined multiculturalism in terms of embracing such concepts as multilingualism, multidialectism, empowerment, equity, and cultural and individual uniqueness. The political dimensions of multicultural education are extensive, and any attempt to depoliticize it is inconsistent with its very nature.[34]

Redefinition of the African-American contribution, for instance, requires that African culture and values be identified and taught. Accordingly, a Portland, Oregon, syllabus stated that "Africa is the cradle of civilization," and an Atlanta, Georgia, syllabus stated, "Nothing in the twentieth century has touched humanity so totally as those things which were first accomplished by Africans." These curriculum revisions have the effect of expanding students' knowledge of cultures often ignored in education curricula. The emphasis on Afrocentrism arises from a conviction that African-American students' educational performance improves with a heightened sense of cultural pride.

The curriculum changes that accompany the multicultural movement generate considerable conflict. The emphasis on self-definition by various ethnic groups requires revision of both their contributions and the Western heritage. The result can be a significant alteration of traditional views. Some critics of the new trend argue that basic American values brought from Europe—democratic principles, the Anglo-Saxon legal system, the importance accorded the individual, and science and technology—will not receive sufficient attention in a revised curriculum.

Multiculturalism is also at odds with the view of America as a "melting pot," wherein an undeniable measure of political and social integration was synthesized from innumerable ethnic elements. The multicultural curriculum may be better characterized as a "salad bowl" view of America, stressing and encouraging diversity rather than homogeneity. Advocates of multicultural curriculum reject the concept of "mainstream America" as being nothing more than an attempt to foster an emphasis on Eurocentrism in education.

Opponents of the multiculturalist current note the ethnic conflicts accompanying the dissolution of the Soviet Union and the civil wars in Bosnia, Serbia, and Croatia following the disintegration of Yugoslavia. They fear that an emphasis on cultural diversity could lead to serious conflict, fragmentation, and weakness. Some critics argue that multiculturalism is a "poor substitute for the real inclusion" of all groups into the economic, social, and political system.[35] Multiculturalism has also emerged as an issue facing higher education with the concern for diversity.[36]

Minority teachers. Currently, minority teachers comprise slightly over 10 percent of the teaching profession. Some projections indicate that the low salary structure for teachers causes many minority college students to reject teaching as a profession. These projections continue to indicate that minority Americans continue to be underrepresented in the teaching profession. This occurs at a time when minority children attending public schools will increase from the current 25 percent to about 33 percent of the school-age population.

FUTURE ALTERNATIVES: COMMUNITY CONTROL, PRIVATE SCHOOLS, A CHANGING FEDERAL ROLE, AND CONFLICTING PRIORITIES

The questions regarding equality and education, the ability of schools to educate minority students, and the competence of both students and teachers have produced calls for alternatives to the public school system as it has been traditionally organized. Two frameworks dominate the current discussion of educational reform. *Liberals* tend to emphasize federal leadership in establishing education policies and programs. Such leadership is necessary if schools are to achieve their social purposes. An acceptance of a strong role for education professionals as policy experts marks this perspective. Liberals tend to combine an emphasis on public schools with a somewhat skeptical view of private and church schools. *Conservative* thought generally emphasizes local governance through the community control of schools. This orientation is skeptical of using schools to advance the social agenda of educational professionals, which may conflict with local values. Conservatives are also willing to deemphasize public schools through measures to strengthen private and church schools.

Community Control and Decentralization

Cutting across ideological lines, members of minority groups have begun to advocate effective local participation in school decision making in order to exercise power over the institutions that directly affect their lives. Other groups resisting federal and state intervention in local schools have made this same demand. Examples include controversies over textbooks, school prayer, and student drug abuse. Today, citizens expect education to be both technically advanced and responsive to the public. Often communities, angered by what they perceive as the failure of their schools to educate well, will balk at paying any more in taxes for a system that is outside their control.

The role of professional educators.   Professional educators resist the movement toward decentralization and community control. One reason they present is the public's alleged lack of expertise, which prevents the effective evaluation of educational alternatives. However, the public often has strong opinions about education and usually agrees on the general criteria for judging a school: qualified teachers, classroom discipline, and physical equipment.

Historically, professional educators tended to dominate state and local education bureaucracies and molded education policy. A professional education establishment is inclined to resist giving power to groups it perceives as less well informed and qualified. Yet, community participation in education also serves to move minority Americans into wider-ranging positions of power and responsibility. Other nonminority and conservative Americans have become more interested in local control as a way of challenging the educational bureaucrats who control the public education system.

District consolidation and decreased local power.   The issue of community control is linked to the evolution of the education power structure. The structures adopted during this century have progressively reduced the role of parents and the public while expanding that of professional educators and various governmental institutions at the state and federal level. The move to consolidate school districts weakened the power of the community. Nationally, the number of school districts fell from over 100,000 at the turn of the century to fewer than 16,000 today.

The emphasis of the consolidation movement was on operating efficiency, achieved by an economy of scale. Larger districts offer services at a lower cost than smaller districts. However, consolidation also has curtailed interaction between the public and school boards. Consolidation reduced the number of school boards, thereby dramatically increasing constituency size. These constituencies now number in the thousands and in large urban areas can include several hundred thousand. Consolidation also acted to diminish the ability of parents to influence education policy. The resultant sense of powerlessness has led some parents to turn to private schools, which they feel may be more responsive to their needs. While economic issues have historically driven the consolidation movement, an unintended and unanticipated consequence has been an increase of power of state government over local education policies. Economic considerations drive consolidation and the shift of power to state governments, and there has been little public debate about local control and accountability.

The Department of Education.   Another source of conflict over decentralization and community control is the role of the U.S. Department of Education (DOE). Congress created the department in 1979 during the term of President Carter. As originally proposed, the department would have consolidated virtually all programs relating to education then scattered among the various federal departments and agencies. As approved by Congress, however, the new department consisted only of programs housed primarily in what had been the Department of Health, Education and Welfare (HEW). Although the law transferred some 152 education-related programs, a significant number of education programs remain outside the present department's control. Among others, the Department of Energy, the Department of Defense, and the Department of Health and Human Services also administer federal education programs.

The DOE does have the potential to expand its role and become a major force in policy formulation. This potential power is an issue of concern, especially from the conservative perspective, for the department can expand its power only at the expense of state and local community control. Conservatives argue, quite forcefully, that the creation of the department extends the power of the federal government into an area in which it has no right to be involved. One example is the issue of "mainstreaming" (placing special needs children in the least restrictive environment, and the regular classroom when possible) in schools. The Education Department played a major role in initiating and mandating this approach to education without providing the necessary funding to support the added costs to local districts, creating an "unfunded mandate." This is one policy decision that directly contributed to calls for the abolition of the department, an issue that remains alive on the political agenda of some conservatives.

This point is much less important to liberals. They defend the department as primarily a coordinator for education programs and policies. Accordingly, the department gives the federal government the necessary organizational structure to address effectively the problems in this critical policy area on a national as opposed to a local level. Liberal thought tends to have a higher level of confidence in the ability of the federal government to provide leadership in education policy.

The Issue of Private Schools

Since the 1970s, there has been some shifting of students from urban and suburban public schools to private schools. Most parents justify the shift to private schools as a concern for quality education. Parents also often object to "mainstreaming," whereby students with disabilities (mental or physical) are integrated into regular classrooms to the fullest extent possible. This practice has led to charges that teachers have to spend excessive time with the special students and neglect the needs of others. Parents claim that their children are simply "warehoused through" the twelve grades. Evidence for these views came in the form of a study by James S. Coleman, cited earlier for his theories on educating minorities, which showed educational achievement scores by private school students of all races and classes to be higher than those of public school students.[37]

Parental concern over religious beliefs and values has added to the enrollment support of private schools. Approximately 80 percent of private schools have religious ties. Today over 9 million children attend private schools of various types. A major factor now appears to be a desire for an educational system that follows traditional curriculum and is committed to teaching moral values.

As reflected in Figure 9-5, the percentage of students attending private schools of all types has remained stable since 1980. This indicates that public schools have not lost ground; nevertheless, they will continue to face competition from private schools throughout this decade, especially under a voucher system. This competition will involve enrollment numbers, but also curriculum content, student achievement levels, social values, and financial support.

Education vouchers and tax credits. One proposed reform of education financing is a system of vouchers or tax credits that would allow parents to select the school best suited to the needs of their children. This reform has strong conservative support as well as support from private schools. Vouchers allow public tax dollars to be redeemed at private schools for education services. A voucher system would allow parents to use them as tuition payment at either public or private schools. The origin of the voucher concept can be traced to economist Milton Friedman's contention that the education system would be strengthened by

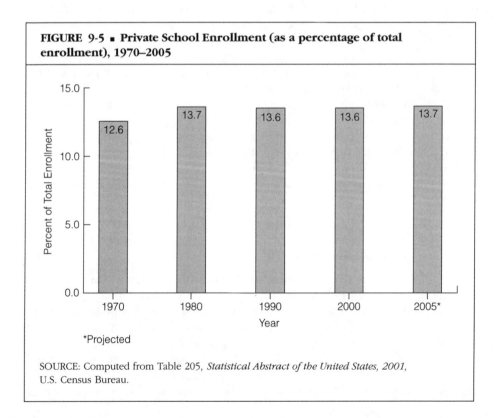

FIGURE 9-5 ▪ Private School Enrollment (as a percentage of total enrollment), 1970–2005

*Projected

SOURCE: Computed from Table 205, *Statistical Abstract of the United States, 2001,* U.S. Census Bureau.

free-market competition between public and private schools.[38] Public and private schools would either develop quality programs or cease to exist as their enrollments evaporated. Others have long supported vouchers or tax credits as a way of facilitating parental control over their children's education.

Proponents of the voucher plan argue that it is necessary to overcome the inflexibility of the existing local public school districts. This view holds that public schools, dominated by rigid professional education bureaucracies, are incapable of developing the programs and incentives necessary for an effective teaching and learning environment.

The concept of school vouchers enjoys significant public support. By 1999, some 60 percent of public school parents indicated support for the voucher system, with elected officials (both Republican and Democrat) evenly split on the issue.[39]

School choice plans vary significantly. Some choices concern public schools only and allow parents to send their children to any public school regardless of their district of residence. Other plans encourage the option of attending private schools (including religious schools) through grants, tax credits, or tax deductions. Tax credits would allow parents to deduct educational expenses from their actual federal or state income tax bill. In effect, parents would use money for private education expenses instead of paying it as income tax and would therefore be free from the burden of paying both tuition costs for a private education and contributing to the upkeep of public schools that their children do not attend.

The adoption of a system of vouchers or tax credits might spur an enrollment shift toward private schools, which liberals and public educators oppose on egalitarian grounds. Professional educators also have an interest in maintaining their control over local schools. Before desegregation, a duality existed in the education system based on race. If middle-class students are removed from the public system, a new duality could arise based on socioeconomic status, and a two-tiered educational system would be the final result. Private schools, funded with public tax monies, would constitute the upper tier, with public schools relegated to the bottom. Supporters of vouchers and credits counter that students from all economic classes would use the financial aids and that suburban/urban schools are already two-tiered, as well as socially and economically segregated.

The use of a voucher system might create nationwide social problems, according to opponents. The educational system acts as a major vehicle for political socialization through which the young achieve a common set of values and level of knowledge concerning the political and social system. A common curriculum and the opportunity to interact with students from diverse backgrounds achieve this result. A voucher system would segregate students in accordance with parental preferences, and the diversity of experiences available to public school students would disappear.

Private religious schools provide students with an educational environment in which religion is an integral part of the curriculum. Modern jurisprudence has no argument with such mixed secular and religious training. Rather, financial aid from the government for religious education instantly evokes the doctrine of separation of church and state. Here it is sufficient to say that the Court has struck down as unconstitutional state programs of general aid to religious schools. However, at the same time the Court has allowed public funding to support a variety of services to private religious schools. Proposals for assisting private and religious schools face a serious constitutional challenge, the outcome of which is in doubt.[40]

Crisis in Education

> If an unfriendly foreign power had attempted to impose on America the mediocre educational performance that exists today, we might have viewed it as an act of war. As it stands we have allowed this to happen to ourselves.[41]

The previous excerpt came from the 1983 report of the National Commission on Excellence in Education. The report was critical of the current state of the nation's education system and concerned about the implications for the future. The ability of the United States to maintain a preeminent position in commerce, industry, science, and technology was, in the words of the Commission, "at risk." Competition from Japan, South Korea, and Western Europe places a burden on our education system to produce skilled, creative individuals in order to ensure economic strength.

The Commission's concerns extended beyond economic matters to the role of education in strengthening the foundations of a free and open democratic society. The Commission shared Jefferson's conviction that an educated public is necessary to supply intellectual and moral strength to the Union. Education also offers an appreciation for a pluralistic society and fosters a common political culture. According to the Commission, the problems in education quality are the functional illiteracy of 23 million Americans, American students' lower performance than students from other industrialized nations on nineteen academic tests, the continued decline in achievement test scores, and the proliferation of remedial courses at the college level. In addition, for the first time in American history, the educational skills of the current student generation will be lower than those of their parents.

The Commission's report is significant because it reflected the concern of elected officials, education professionals, and the general public about the perceived decline in the quality of education. The commission's recommendations focused on curriculum reform, with a renewed emphasis on the basics of education (English, science, math, and social studies) and on a longer school day and year (seven-hour day, 220-day academic year). The Commission also endorsed the concepts of merit pay, competency testing for students and teachers, and the implementation of a master teacher program. It gave the primary responsibility for financing education to the local school districts and the states, limiting the federal government's fiscal role.

The failure of the United States to make significant progress toward overall educational excellence was documented again in October 1991, with the release of the report of the National Assessment of Educational Progress, prepared by the National Education Goals Panel, a group of governors and federal officials. The report depicts a bleak overall picture of nationwide academic achievement. Some specifics of the report follow:

> *Advanced math:* Less than 1 percent of fourth-graders and eighth-graders and 2.6 percent of high school seniors could perform at the advanced level.

Basic math: Only 60 percent of students in grades four, eight, and twelve could solve simple math problems. Fewer than 20 percent of the students could perform math skills on their grade level.

Student performance was equally poor in the areas of science, social studies, and language arts.

International competition overshadows the academic performance of American students. American students perform less well in science and mathematics than do students from other industrialized nations. Historically, the lack of rigor in the curriculum of American schools creates some of this difference.[42]

The high school dropout rate is another continuing problem, the magnitude of which appears in Figure 9-6. The national dropout rate of 13 percent is high, but the Hispanic rate is 33 percent. The failure of a significant proportion of the population to earn a high school diploma encourages the development of an undereducated minority class.

Changing Priorities in Federal Education Policy

The changing priorities of education policy are reflected in the changes of policy preferences at the federal level. The domestic policies of President Johnson, as embodied in his Great Society programs, took the lead in encouraging new and

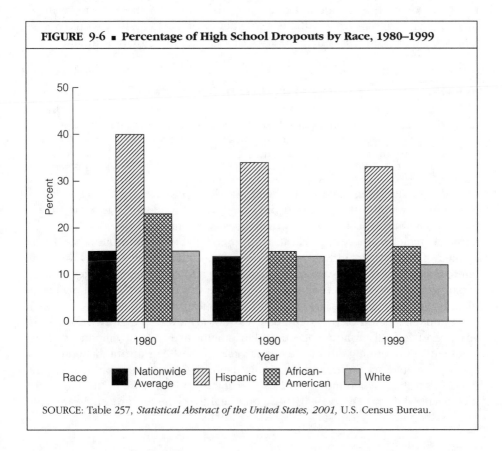

FIGURE 9-6 ▪ **Percentage of High School Dropouts by Race, 1980–1999**

SOURCE: Table 257, *Statistical Abstract of the United States, 2001,* U.S. Census Bureau.

innovative programs aimed at the educational needs of disadvantaged groups. Although the level of federal education spending did not increase dramatically, there was a general expectation that the proportion of federal aid would continue to increase. President Nixon sought to shift the direction of federal education policy by placing greater emphasis on the role of state and local governments. The Carter administration shifted slightly toward federal leadership in education policy. It created the Department of Education and renewed its emphasis on governmental involvement in fostering equal educational opportunity. Federal financial support for educational programs reached a high point during this administration.

President Reagan's administration led to another shift in education policy, with attempts to transfer responsibility for education policy back to the state level. The 1980s also saw debate over curriculum content and reform. The Education Department developed two model curricula. *James Madison High School* (1987) and *James Madison Elementary School* (1988), published by the DOE, embodied an emphasis on "classical" education with a college-preparatory focus. For example, the English requirement consisted of a four-year literature sequence: introduction to literature, American literature, British literature, and world literature. Three full years of mathematics included an emphasis on algebra, geometry, trigonometry, statistics, and calculus.

Although the approach pleased some, especially conservatives, because of its emphasis on traditional values, others were critical. Liberals, although commending the model's rigor, felt that it was overly narrow. While students were to read Homer, Shakespeare, the Bible, and other great literature, they would not be exposed to the works of contemporary women, minority, or ethnic authors.

Education Policy Priorities in the Twenty-First Century

> The centerpiece of our National Education Strategy is not a program; it's not a test. It's a new challenge: to reinvent American education—to design new American schools for the year 2000 and beyond.
>
> *—America 2000,* 1991

In mid-1991, President George H. Bush released *America 2000: An Education Strategy.* Although *America 2000* presented very broad goals for the United States, some very specific policy preferences were included: adoption of a nationwide achievement test, publication of annual national and state report cards by the U.S. Department of Education to document student achievement levels, differential teacher pay for teachers in "dangerous and challenging environments," expansion of school choice options through the use of vouchers, and maintaining a limited federal financial role in funding education initiatives.

Implementation of *America 2000* was not achieved, primarily because the absence of federal money made the plan unattractive. An unwillingness to increase federal spending during the deficit years of the 1990s meant that education spending would not increase dramatically. Figure 9-7 illustrates that total spending on education, when measured as a percentage of GDP, rose in the 1960s and then declined from 1970 to 1980, rising only slightly in the most recent years. This increase is primarily from state, not federal, funds.

FIGURE 9-7 ▪ U.S. Education Spending as Percentage of GDP, 1959–1999

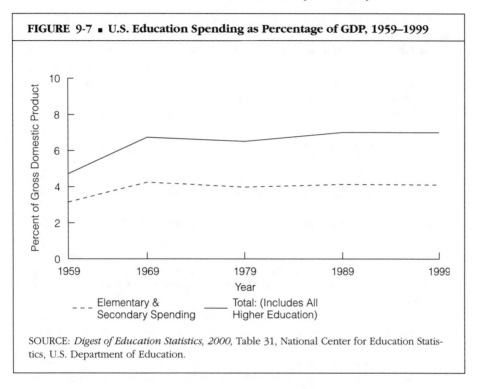

SOURCE: *Digest of Education Statistics, 2000,* Table 31, National Center for Education Statistics, U.S. Department of Education.

President Clinton proposed *Goals 2000* as the centerpiece of his education policy agenda. This program contained the same basic goals as those announced by President George H. Bush in his *America 2000* initiative. The importance of Clinton's education policy was to give the states participating in the program the option of either adopting the national standards developed by the National Education Standards and Improvement Council (NESIC) or developing their own standards, which must be of "equal or higher quality" than NESIC standards.

Box 9-2 shows *Goals 2000* highlights. They reflect a strategy of federal policy leadership in the areas of curriculum and education "outcomes," but with minimal federal funding. This policy initiative involved a greater role for the federal government, using mandated policy guidelines, than the very similar *America 2000* plan of President Bush. President Clinton's education policy initiatives emphasized increased federal control over education policy without a commensurate increase in federal funding. These goals generated considerable debate between conservatives and liberals. Conservatives supported many of the individual goals such as school choice and technological literacy, but they opposed the creation of national standards imposed by what they perceived as a remote federal education bureaucracy. Conservatives were concerned about the impact of mandatory national testing programs and of the cultural values that may be mandated for inclusion in the school curriculum. Liberals tended to support these initiatives, but had reservations about some components such as school choice and the creation of charter schools. Liberals tended to be less concerned about national standards and the values that educational professionals would include in

---

BOX 9-2
Major Education Policy Objectives of President Clinton's *Goals 2000*

Establish National Achievement Standards: Accompanied with national achievement tests at the fourth- and eighth-grade levels.

Talented Teachers in Every Classroom: National standards for excellence in teaching, emphasis on technology literacy, develop strategies to recruit talented teachers, and remove weak teachers.

Enable Every Child to Read by the End of the Third Grade: Recruit and train one million reading tutors to assist learning, encourage parents to read to their children each day, and create linkages between businesses and the schools to increase literacy.

Expand Head Start: Increase participation in Head Start from 800,000 to 1,000,000 children.

Expand School Choice and Accountability: Encourage states and local districts to provide school choice to parents, expand development of charter schools, encourage development of magnet schools, and publish an Internet report card on every school.

Safe, Disciplined, and Drug-Free Schools: Establish "zero tolerance" policies for weapons and drugs, consider adopting school uniforms, expand after-school and summer education programs, and develop a values-based curriculum.

School Construction and Modernization: Encourage states and communities to modernize existing facilities and build state of the art facilities primarily through limited federal interest subsidies on school bonds.

Expand Access to the First Two Years of College: Expand federal grant and loan programs, provide tax benefits to make tuition more affordable, and encourage colleges to control the cost of tuition.

Establish School-to-Work Programs: Create programs that link job skills to the high school curriculum, and encourage states and local districts to develop school-to-work programs for students not bound for college.

Technological Literacy: Provide access to computers for every teacher and student, connect every classroom to the Internet, and integrate educational software into the curriculum.

---

curriculum. Conflict over these policy initiatives provided a foundation for political conflict throughout the years of the Clinton presidency.

President George W. Bush developed an education policy initiative of his own. "The No Child Left Behind Act of 2001" was signed into law in January 2002 as a re-authorization of the Elementary and Secondary Education Act. Box 9-3 presents the significant provisions of his education initiative.

A review of these presidential initiatives reveals a consistent federal education policy pattern. First, federal funding levels do not grow significantly. Education programs will continue to primarily receive funding from states and local school districts. Second, there is an emphasis on improving the quality of education available to students across the nation combined with the use of student

---

BOX 9-3
President George W. Bush's Education Policy Initiative

THE NO CHILD LEFT BEHIND ACT OF 2001 (RE-AUTHORIZATION OF ESEA IN 2002)

Accountability and Assessment: Annual assessment of student achievement in reading and math in grades three to eight, accompanied by school and state report cards.

State and Local Flexibility: Reduces the number of ESEA programs from fifty-five to forty-five and allows states to transfer up to 50 percent of non-Title I funds into other ESEA areas without advance federal approval. Local districts may participate in "flexibility demonstration projects" to consolidate all federal funds in exchange for agreements to produce higher student achievement.

Expansion of Parental Choice: Parents of children in "failing schools" are allowed to transfer their child to a higher performing public school or charter school and to obtain supplemental education services from either public- or private-sector providers.

Emphasis on Reading: Provides federal funding assistance to local districts in order to achieve the goal that every child can read by the end of third grade.

Improvement of Teacher Quality: Provides federal grant funding to states to improve teacher recruitment and retention in exchange for agreements to improve student achievement.

Promoting English Proficiency: Consolidate bilingual and immigrant education programs with emphasis on improved teaching methods and testing of student achievement after a student has been in the school system for three consecutive years.

Safe Schools: Districts must use federal funding to implement drug and violence prevention programs with provisions that students in "persistently dangerous schools" be allowed to transfer to another public or charter school.

---

achievement tests. Third, states and local districts must agree to unfunded federally mandated requirements to improve student achievement in order to continue to receive federal dollars. Finally, there are continuing efforts to address the issue of increasing school choice for parents. School choice may be limited to other public schools or to charter schools under the federal initiative, but there remains a constant effort to expand this option to parents.

Unresolved Education Issues: Teachers and Curriculum

A number of unresolved issues remain on the education policy agenda. Figure 9-8 presents the most important educational issues facing the nation today as identified by the public.

Drug abuse remains a serious problem for schools today. Drug usage contributes to educational problems by interfering with learning; leading students to drop out; and creating a climate of fear, violence, and lack of respect for educational values. Violence and crime emerged in the 1990s and present significant challenges to the education system arising from the incidence of student violence and homicide at a number of schools. One response has been the development of "zero tolerance" codes for weapons, fighting, drugs, and other student behaviors in an effort to promote student safety.

National teacher certification. The qualifications of teachers are an increasingly important issue. Professional educators created the nongovernmental National Board for Professional Teaching Standards in 1987 in response to the publication of a report by the Carnegie Forum on Education and the Economy titled *A Nation Prepared* (1986). The primary focus of this report was the establishment of *national* standards to assess and certify teachers, as opposed to the uncoordinated process used by the fifty states today. If the quality of education is a national priority, proponents argue, teacher certification is too important to leave to the states to develop fragmented and uncoordinated standards.[43] Before 2000 there were only around 9,500 nationally certified teachers; by 2002, this number had increased to over 16,000.

Workforce preparation. Historically, the American public education system produced two types of graduates. One group consisted of students on a college track, who would later become managers, decision makers, and scientific or technical experts. The second group consisted of students who, after high school graduation, would assume non-technical positions in the nation's factories. Today,

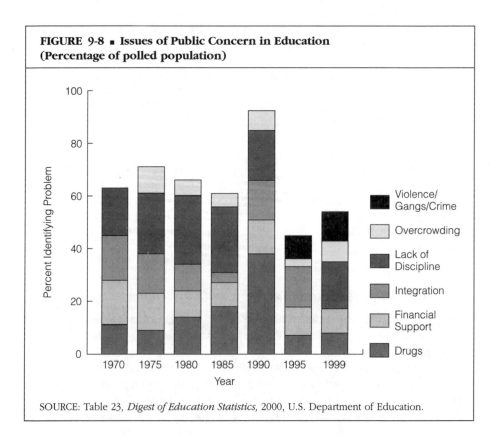

FIGURE 9-8 ▪ Issues of Public Concern in Education (Percentage of polled population)

SOURCE: Table 23, *Digest of Education Statistics,* 2000, U.S. Department of Education.

the nation requires workers who are capable of rapid and continuous learning to improve productivity and enhance the global competitiveness of the nation.[44]

Federal programs continue to provide limited financial assistance for developing and implementing partnerships between school districts, businesses, labor unions, and community groups, which provide high school students with work experience and insights into the education requirements for specific careers.

Proponents of these programs argue that students should be exposed to the relationship between education and careers while in high school, rather than after graduation. Such exposure will translate into increased student motivation in the classroom and an appreciation of the need for lifelong learning. Critics argue that the program simply provides academic credit for low-level, part-time jobs that have little relevance to a genuine career.

National student assessment standards. The National Assessment of Educational Progress (NAEP), mentioned earlier, gathers information on students in grades four, eight, and twelve. The program has been in place for almost twenty years. The *No Child Left Behind* policy initiative would strengthen this program considerably and use it as a foundation for issuing report cards for the nation's schools. Given the emphasis on standardized tests to measure student achievement and the increasing demand by parents and other groups for comparative data on school performance, national assessment will continue to be controversial.[45]

Moral education. Conservatives argue that the schools have an obligation to provide a moral foundation for the nation's children through an emphasis on traditional values. The Northwest Ordinance in 1787 clearly linked "religion, morality, and knowledge" to good government. Federal legislation in the twentieth century did not emphasize moral foundations, but stressed values such as national security, equality, and separation of church and state. Both liberals and conservatives are increasingly concerned that moral foundations are linked to the education process.[46] However, differences over substance are divisive. Conservatives emphasize values that stress the importance of the individual as shaped by institutions such as the church, the family, and traditional political values. These values then shape collective societal values. Liberals, however, place greater emphasis on social values that shape institutions such as the church, the family, and the political culture. These collective values then shape the values of the individual.

Back to the basics. This movement implies an increased emphasis on basic skills, such as reading, writing, and arithmetic, but also may incorporate the traditional values of respect, obedience, and moral content.[47] The movement first emerged in the late 1950s after the Soviet Union launched Sputnik. During this early period, the emphasis was on basic education as a foundation for national security. Basic skills of the 1950s did not focus on individual and personal goal attainment, but rather on the individual's responsibility to use basic skills to contribute to the national good. The current movement emerged during a period of inflation and economic instability. Concern over low student achievement was linked to individual, not national, economic survival. Critics charge that the current movement emphasizes employment skill levels rather than educational excellence and national advancement. Current debates over curriculum flow directly from the "back-to-the-basics" movement.

Outcome-based education (OBE). Outcome-based education has emerged as a major source of conflict in education policy. One reason is that both proponents and opponents define the concept differently. Proponents argue that OBE simply focuses education policy on the desired outcomes of the education system and is a method to achieve accountability within the education system. It is simply an education process that does not drive curriculum. Other proponents are concerned with creating an educational "system" that produces certain values through the education process. Opponents argue that OBE is an approach that will reduce local control over education and instill values that may not be consistent with those of parents.[48]

OBE produces conflict since it requires that the fundamental purpose of education be addressed: What should students know, and what is the ultimate purpose of education? Conservatives tend to oppose OBE on the grounds that the approach minimizes academic content of the curriculum in favor of such nonacademic values as personal well-being, interpersonal relationships, and group participation. Liberals tend to support OBE as an educational innovation that has the potential to improve the ability of students to master material.

Unresolved Education Issues: Structural Questions

Charter schools. The concept of the charter school was introduced in the mid-1980s and is designed to allow the creation of an independent legal entity with responsibility for delivery of education programs.[49] Under this concept, state boards of education grant a charter to either a public or private group to organize and operate a school. A charter school is a tuition-free entity that receives funding from the state and that provides an educational choice to students and parents. Charter schools blur the distinction between public and private school systems since they can be considered as either quasi-public or quasi-private entities. As indicated in Figure 9-9, the charter school movement has experienced significant growth. The number of charter schools is somewhat difficult to estimate because some schools cease to operate during any given year and because some schools receive charters but may not be in operation. Charter schools are in operation in over thirty states and have a total enrollment of over 550,000 students.

Local school boards tend to have minimal responsibility for the operation of a charter school within their jurisdiction. Some states eliminated their responsibility. Proponents of charter schools argue that they present a unique opportunity for education reform. Critics of charter schools see the movement as simply a modification of a voucher system for private schools.

Charter schools may serve as a new approach to create autonomous schools that can respond to specific educational needs and develop creative strategies to improve student performance that are unattainable by current school systems.[50] For example, some charter schools build their entire program around the arts; others emphasize the sciences; still others focus on multicultural education; and so forth.

Privatization. Another educational reform movement involves the creation of "for-profit" schools. Education Alternatives, Inc. (EAI) and what is now known as the "Edison Project" promoted this idea as a mechanism to improve the performance and quality of local schools.[51] Under this concept, the operation of either a single school or an entire district may be "contracted out" to a private firm. Proponents

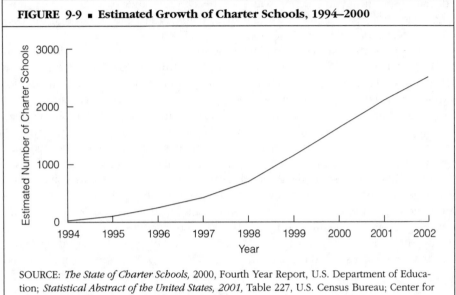

FIGURE 9-9 ▪ **Estimated Growth of Charter Schools, 1994–2000**

SOURCE: *The State of Charter Schools,* 2000, Fourth Year Report, U.S. Department of Education; *Statistical Abstract of the United States, 2001,* Table 227, U.S. Census Bureau; Center for Education Reform, *National Charter School Directory,* 2002.

argue that initiative provided by the private sector provides a mechanism to improve the performance of the nation's schools by reinventing the curriculum and teaching techniques. Proponents also believe that privatization is consistent with the charter school movement. Critics argue that there is no evidence that private commercial schools actually perform at a higher level than their public counterparts do and that concern for profit will require that student needs become a secondary priority.

In 1995, four school districts (Baltimore City Public School District-Maryland, Dade County Public Schools-Florida, Hartford School District-Connecticut, and Minneapolis School District-Minnesota) had contracts with private companies for school management. In 1996, five other districts (Boston-Massachusetts, Mt. Clemens-Michigan, Sherman-Texas, Wichita-Kansas, and Wilkinsburg-Pennsylvania) entered into management contracts with private companies. This process continued with the City of Philadelphia assigning the management of forty-two schools to the private sector in 2002. Often, privatization emerges as a last-ditch effort to salvage failing urban schools.

The authority granted to the private contractor varies from district to district. Mixed evaluation results produce significant conflict. Benefits include an increase in student attendance rates, a drop in suspension rates, increased access to computers in classrooms, and improved building maintenance. Privatization varies in scope, from contracting for limited services such as a cafeteria, maintenance, and transportation, to managing an entire school. Because privatization experiments are so small and diverse, it remains an unsettled issue on the education policy agenda.

Home schooling. Perhaps the ultimate form of privatization in education is the development of home schooling. Under this model, parents assume primary responsibility for the education of their children. Some parents undertake this effort from dissatisfaction with their local public schools; others wish to provide a religious education specifically in keeping with their beliefs. Still other parents wish to allow their children to develop their learning more naturally, instead of through the perceived artificial organization of standardized public school curricula.

Estimates are that over 2 million students participated in home schooling in 2001. Based on the limited evidence available, children participating in home schooling perform at a level higher than their public school contemporaries do. Parents involved in home schooling have organized at the state and national level to defend their right to educate their children at home with considerable success. Virtually all states now recognize the rights of parents to supervise their children's education in this setting, and increasingly colleges accept home-schooled students, despite the lack of conventional transcripts and recommendations.

Single-gender schools. Public education in the United States evolved from single-gender (boys only) to coeducational schools by the mid- to late 1800s. During the colonial period, formal education tended to be limited to boys, with girls receiving informal education at home. By 1890, coeducation was the norm across the nation. In 1972, Title IX of the Education Amendments prohibited discrimination against students based on sex and imposed limits on single-gender institutions. The Citadel and the Virginia Military Institute are two public universities forced to abandon their single-gender status and admit women students. Some educators now advocate single-gender schools as a viable alternative to increase student achievement. Proponents argue that single-gender schools for girls reduce distractions, provide greater self-confidence, enhance the development of leadership skills, and reduce the risk of educational failure. Since 1994, a number of bills have been introduced in Congress that would provide limited waivers to Title IX and other statutes that would allow experimentation with single-gender public schools.

Issues in Higher Education

Diversity. Justice Powell introduced the concept of diversity as a rationale for group preferences in the *Bakke* decision dealing with the issue of "reverse discrimination." (See Chapter 10 for a discussion of this term and of affirmative action in general.) The other members of the Supreme Court did not embrace Justice Powell's reasoning, but it became a value embraced by colleges and universities across the nation. Higher education flourishes when varieties of racial, economic, ethnic, and social groups interact on the same campus. Moreover, graduation from college is increasingly necessary for economic and social advancement in American society. Minority groups and women, historically held back in educational opportunity, see the pursuit of diversity in higher education as a way to remedy the effects of historical discrimination. Diversity thus served as the primary legal justification in the admissions process for over fifteen years. It continues to be a significant value in higher education.

Affirmative action. Affirmative action in admissions has been one of the primary means to achieve diversity in higher education (see Chapter 10). However, the future role of affirmative action admissions programs for colleges and universities is unclear. California's passage of Proposition 209 in November 1996 (an amendment to the state constitution that prohibits the use of race-based and gender-based preferences in hiring, contracting, and education) signaled a significant education policy shift. The amendment survived a challenge in the federal courts and affected 1997 to 1998 admissions policies. A few years earlier, following a U.S. Circuit Court ruling, the Texas Attorney General issued guidelines that eliminated race-based admissions policies at Texas institutions of higher education in admissions and financial-aid decisions for public universities. Other challenges to affirmative action are working their way through the federal courts.

Affirmative action programs have their greatest impact primarily in highly selective colleges and universities where there is considerable competition in the admissions process. At "non-elite" colleges, the impact of affirmative action in terms of granting an advantage based on race or gender is actually relatively minor. This means that the elimination of affirmative action programs in university admission standards will not have a uniform effect on all campuses. It does mean that some of the most selective public institutions may no longer be as accessible to some groups in society. Figure 9-10 indicates that minority groups continue to be underrepresented in higher education.

Cost of higher education. One issue on the policy agenda involves the ever-increasing cost of higher education. Tuition increased by nearly 258 percent between 1985 and 2000 (see Figure 9-11), a rate significantly greater than the median household income increase of 176 percent for the same period.

Two factors contribute most to the increase in tuition: spending increases by colleges and a greater dependency on tuition (as opposed to state funding)

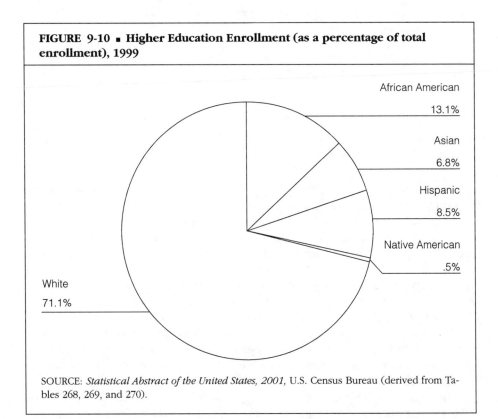

FIGURE 9-10 ■ **Higher Education Enrollment (as a percentage of total enrollment), 1999**

African American

13.1%

Asian

6.8%

Hispanic

8.5%

Native American

.5%

White

71.1%

SOURCE: *Statistical Abstract of the United States, 2001,* U.S. Census Bureau (derived from Tables 268, 269, and 270).

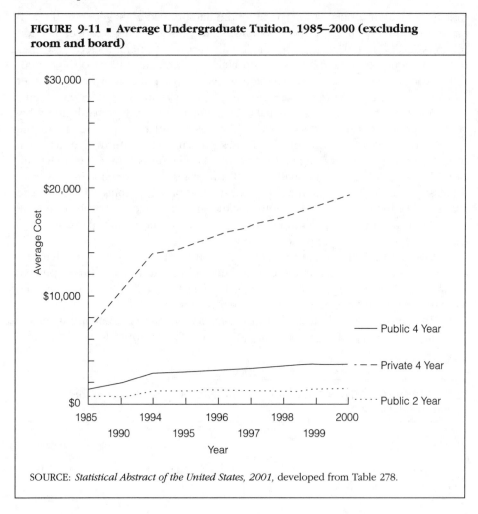

FIGURE 9-11 ▪ Average Undergraduate Tuition, 1985–2000 (excluding room and board)

SOURCE: *Statistical Abstract of the United States, 2001,* developed from Table 278.

as a source of revenue. Public universities are increasingly state-assisted as opposed to state-funded institutions. Figure 9-12 shows that state funding has decreased as a source of revenue. The decrease in public funding must be offset by an accompanying increase in tuition. Universities have been able to use research funding, gifts, and endowments only as a small buffer for tuition charge increases.

Yet spending patterns for colleges and universities exhibit a marked stability. Between 1980 and 2000, colleges and universities consistently spent between 78 and 81 percent of their revenues on the delivery of instructional programs, student services, and physical facility maintenance. Research spending remained a consistent 9 to 10 percent of revenues per year. This means that costs for university administration (often targeted as an area of excessive spending on campuses) has remained at a constant percentage spending level as well.[52]

If the goal of higher education for most Americans is attainable, it will have to be a major priority of state governments. State legislators will have to make dif-

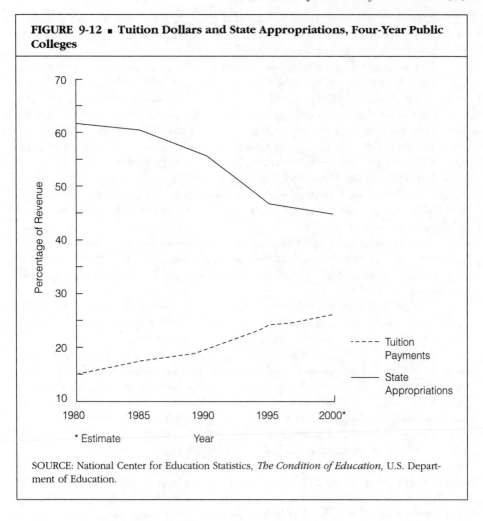

FIGURE 9-12 ■ **Tuition Dollars and State Appropriations, Four-Year Public Colleges**

SOURCE: National Center for Education Statistics, *The Condition of Education,* U.S. Department of Education.

ficult choices about raising taxes to fund higher education or cutting other programs to free up funds.

SUMMARY

The United States has a long tradition of free public education, traceable to the earliest periods of the American experience, when education was first utilized as part of the political socialization process to build a sense of national identity.

For nearly all its existence, the federal government exercised only a limited role in education. In fact, before 1965, that role was insignificant and indirect, with limited programs targeted for specific problems. With the enactment of the Elementary and Secondary Education Act (1965), the federal government began to expand its role. Federal aid became a more important source of revenue for both local school districts and the nation's universities.

Education has been used to further the struggle for equality in the United States. One concern has been the equality of opportunity and movement toward integration and racially balanced schools.

One unresolved problem that adversely affects educational equality is inequity in school finances. Because school districts rely heavily on the property tax as a source of revenue, the unequal distribution of resources results in a wide disparity in the level of per-pupil expenditures within the states and across the nation. Attempts to reform the school finance system have failed in the federal courts and have met with only limited success at the state level. The outlook for the future indicates the continued existence of financial inequities.

National standardized tests, such as the SAT, have indicated a progressive decline in student performance since the early 1960s, a phenomenon that some link to liberal curricular policies. A reaction to this has been the "back-to-basics" education movement.

Concern with the quality of education has led to the development of minimum competency tests for both students and teachers. MCTs attempt to measure student achievement; passing such an exam is required to receive a high school diploma in many states.

Competency tests for teachers are used by an increasing number of school districts to screen new applicants. Proposals for merit pay for teachers and for master teacher programs reflect the same concern for instructional competence.

Community control of education has always been a fundamental American principle. The federal government's reversal of this trend over the past two decades has brought many changes in how and who runs schools. State control also has grown. Local communities, fearing centralized control over education, resist this trend. The consolidation of schools into ever-larger districts has further reduced the influence of parents and the public over education policy, and the power and influence of professional educators continues to grow.

General dissatisfaction with the public school system has caused increasing numbers of parents to send their children to private schools. Parents have sought out these schools as educational institutions committed to traditional values and moral absolutes. The issue of vouchers and tax credits for private school tuition as a method of assisting the growth of private schools is hotly debated, raising serious ideological and constitutional questions.

Although presidential preferences in education policy have changed priorities in the last two decades, a general trend toward moderate federal intervention has prevailed. Policy options designed to reduce the role of the federal government in education have achieved only limited success.

Outcome-based education involves basic conflict over the values that should be taught in the curriculum and the emphasis on academic content. Groups opposed to OBE argue that this is the product of federal and state interference in the local control of education policy.

The policy of affirmative action and diversity is being challenged by state constitution amendments and in the federal courts. The U.S. Supreme Court has indicated a willingness to review cases that may have a significant impact on the future of these policies.

The cost of higher education is becoming an important policy issue as the cost of tuition continues to increase and as state funding fails to keep pace with the increased costs faced by universities.

NOTES

1. Quoted in S. E. Frost, Jr. and Kenneth P. Bailey, *Historical and Philosophical Foundations of Western Education,* 2nd ed. (Columbus, Ohio: Chas. E. Merrill, 1973), 340.

2. William M. French, *America's Educational Tradition* (Lexington, MA: Heath, 1964), 54–60.

3. Robert L. Church, *Education in the United States* (New York: Free Press, 1976), 420.

4. U.S. Bureau of the Census, *Statistical Abstract of the United States, 2001* (Washington, DC: U.S. Government Printing Office, 2001).

5. See Mary E. Moran, "Standards and Assessments: The New Measure of Adequacy in School Finance Litigation," *Journal of Education Finance,* 25 (Summer, 1999): 33–80, for an expanded discussion of court cases addressing financial disparities.

6. *Serrano v. Priest,* 5 Cal. 3d 584.

7. *San Antonio Independent School District v. Rodriguez,* 411 U.S. 1 (1973).

8. See Katharine L. Bradbury, "School District Spending and State Aid: Why Disparities Persist," *New England Economic Review* (January/February, 1994) for a discussion of some of the factors which affect local district spending.

9. See Debora A. Berstege and Richard A. King, "The Relationship between School Spending and Student Achievement: A Review and Analysis of 35 Years of Production Function Research," *Journal of Education Finance,* 24, No. 2 (Fall, 1998): 243–262, for a review of the literature relating to school spending and student achievement.

10. See Mary E. Moran, "Standards and Assessments," for a discussion of student performance in the education funding debate.

11. See National Center for Educational Statistics, "Do Rich and Poor Districts Spend Alike?" (Washington, DC, December, 1996); and "Disparities in Public School District Spending" (Washington, DC, February, 1995).

12. See Anne T. Lockwood, *The Future of School Finance* (Madison, WI: National Center for Effective Schools, 1994).

13. See D. Van Slyke, *School Finance Litigation: A Review of Key Cases* (ERIC Document Reproduction Service, No: ED394–195, 1995).

14. The National Commission on Excellence in Education, *A Nation at Risk: The Imperative for Educational Reform* (Washington, DC: U.S. Government Printing Office, 1983), 4.

15. N. F. Ashline, T. R. Pezzulo, and C. I. Norris, eds., *Education, Inequality and National Policy* (Lexington, MA: Heath, 1976), 49.

16. Christopher Jencks et al., *Inequality: A Reassessment of the Effect of Family and Schooling in America* (New York: Basic Books, 1972), 7.

17. James S. Coleman, *Equality of Educational Opportunity* (Washington, DC: U.S. Government Printing Office, 1966).

18. U.S. Commission on Civil Rights, *Racial Isolation in the Public Schools,* 2 vols. (Washington, DC: U.S. Government Printing Office, 1967).

19. The College Board, *Balancing the SAT Scales* (Princeton, NJ: 1994).

20. See Lawrence C. Stedman, "The Achievement Crisis Is Real," *Education Policy Analysis Archives,* 4, No. 1 (January, 1996).

21. See, for example, Donald Rock, et al., *Factors Associated with Decline of Test Scores of High School Seniors, 1972–1980* (Washington, DC: Center for Statistics, Department of Education, 1985).

22. See David C. Berliner and Bruce J. Biddle, *The Manufactured Crisis* (Reading, MA: Addison-Wesley, 1995).

23. See Norman Frederikson, *The Influence of Minimum Competency Tests on Teaching and Learning* (Princeton, NJ: Educational Testing Service, 1994).

24. Diana Pullin, "Minimum Competency Testing: The Denied Diploma and the Pursuit of Educational Opportunity and Educational Adequacy" (ERIC Document Reproduction Service No. ED 228–279, 1982).

25. J. S. Catterall, "Standards and School Dropouts: A National Study of Tests Required for High School Graduation," *American Journal of Education,* 98: 1–34.

26. Gerald W. Bracey, "On the Compelling Need to Go Beyond Minimum Competency" (ERIC Document Reproduction Service No. ED 223–645, 1982).

27. See Larry G. Daniel, "Predicting Teacher Performance: A Multivariate Investigation" (ERIC Document Reproduction Service No. ED 357–029, 1993) for a discussion of factors affecting teacher performance.

28. See Rosabeth M. Kanter, "Attack on Pay," *Harvard Business Review,* 65 (1987): 60–67, for a complete discussion of the impact of position status on compensation.

29. A. I. Ramirez, "How Merit Pay Undermines Education," *Educational Leadership,* 58, No. 5 (Feb 2001): 16–20.

30. See Susan M. Johnson, "Merit Pay for Teachers: A Poor Prescription for Reform," *Harvard Educational Review,* 54 (May 1984): 175–188.

31. See *Infusing Multicultural Education into Today's Schools. An Annotated Bibliography* (ERIC Document Reproduction Services, No. ED 369-703, 1993) for an extensive bibliography on multicultural education.

32. Nancy P. Greenman and Ellen B. Kimmel, "The Road to Multicultural Education: Potholes of Resistance," *Journal of Teacher Education,* 45, No. 5 (November–December, 1995): 360–368.

33. American Association of Colleges for Teacher Education Commission on Multicultural Education, "No One Model American," *Journal of Teacher Education,* 24, No. 4 (September–October, 1973): 264–265.

34. J. Garcia and S. L. Pugh, "Multicultural Education in Teacher Preparation Programs: A Political or an Educational Concept?" *Phi Delta Kappan,* 74 (4): 214–219.

35. Louis Goldman, "Misconceptions of Culture and Perversions of Multiculturalism," *Interchange,* 24, No. 4 (1993).

36. See Sonia Nieto, "Multiculturalism in Higher Education: Emerging Literature," *Equity and Excellence in Education,* 26, No. 3 (1993); and Lynne Goldstein, "Achieving a Multicultural Curriculum: Conceptual, Pedagogical, and Structural Issues," *The Journal of General Education,* 43, No. 2 (1994), for a discussion of some of the issues facing higher education.

37. James S. Coleman, *Public and Private Schools* (Chicago: National Opinion Research Center, March 1981); also James S. Coleman, "Social Capital and the Development of Youth," *Momentum,* 18 (November, 1987).

38. Margaret Hadderman, "Educational Vouchers" (ERIC Digest, Number 137, May 2000, ERIC Clearinghouse on Educational Management, Eugene, OR).

39. "Annual Phi Delta Kappa/Gallup Poll of the Public's Attitudes toward Public Schools," *Phi Delta Kappan,* 81, No. 1 (September, 1999): 41–55.

40. See Amy S. Wells and Stuart Biegel, "Public Funds for Private Schools: Political and First Amendment Considerations," *American Journal of Education,* 101 (May 1993), for a discussion of the legal issues in the voucher debate.

41. *A Nation at Risk,* 5.

42. C. McKnight, et al., *The Underachieving Curriculum: Assessing U.S. School Mathematics from an International Perspective* (International Association for the Evaluation of Education Achievement, 1987).

43. Lee Shulman and Gary Sykes, *A National Board for Teaching? In Search of a Bold Standard* (Palo Alto, CA: Stanford University School of Education, March, 1986).

44. Benjamin Duke, *Japanese Schools: Lessons for Industrial America* (New York: Praeger, 1986).

45. U.S. Department of Education, *The Nation's Report Card: Improving the Assessment of Student Achievement* (Washington, DC: U.S. Government Printing Office, 1987).

46. Carl Kaestle, "Moral Education and Common Schools in America: A Historian's View," *Journal of Moral Education* (May 1984).

47. Ellen V. Leininger, "Back to the Basics: Underlying Concepts and Controversy," *Elementary School Journal,* 79, No. 3 (1979): 167–173.

48. See Ron Brandt, "Is Outcome Based Education Dead?" *Educational Leadership,* 51 (March, 1994), for a discussion of various perspectives on OBE.

49. Louann A. Bierlein and Lori A. Mulholland, "The Promise of Charter Schools," *Educational Leadership,* 52 (September 1994): 34–40.

50. General Accounting Office, *Charter Schools: New Model for Public Schools Provides Opportunities and Challenges* (Washington, DC: U.S. Government Printing Office, 1995).

51. Benno C. Schmidt, Jr., "The Edison Project's Plan to Redefine Public Education," *Educational Leadership,* 52 (September 1994): 61–64.

52. *Digest of Education Statistics* (Washington, DC: U.S. Government Printing Office, 1996), Table 334.

SUGGESTED READINGS

Books

Bennett, William J. *James Madison Elementary School: A Curriculum for American Students.* Washington, DC: U.S. Department of Education, August 1988.

Bennett, William J. *James Madison High School: A Curriculum for American Students.* Washington, DC: U.S. Department of Education, December 1987.

Berliner, David, and Biddle, Bruce. *The Manufactured Crisis.* Reading, MA: Addison Wesley, 1996.

Bierlein, Louann A. *Charter Schools: Initial Findings.* Denver: Education Commission of the States, 1996.

Burstyn, Joan N., ed. *Educating Tomorrow's Valuable Citizen.* New York: State University of New York Press, 1995.

Coleman, James S. *Public and Private High School: The Impact of Communities.* New York: Basic Books, 1987.

D'Souza, D. *Illiberal Education: The Politics of Race and Sex on Campus.* New York: The Free Press, 1991.

Everhart, Robert, ed. *The Public School Monopoly: Critical Analysis of Education and the State in American Society.* Cambridge, MA: Ballinger, 1982.

Goldberg, David T. *Multiculturalism: A Critical Reader.* Cambridge, MA: Blackwell Publishing Co., 1994.

Jencks, Christopher et al. *Inequality.* New York: Basic Books, 1972.

Kozol, Jonathan. *Savage Inequalities.* New York: Crown, 1991.

National Commission on Excellence in Education. *A Nation at Risk: The Imperative for Educational Reform.* Washington, DC: U.S. Government Printing Office, 1983.

Nieto, S. *Affirming Diversity: The Sociocultural Context of Multicultural Education.* New York: Longman, 1992.

Odden, Allan R., and Picus, Lawrence O. *School Finance: A Policy Perspective,* 2nd ed. New York: McGraw-Hill, 2000.

Rasell, Edith, and Rothstein, Richard, ed. *School Choice: Examining the Evidence.* Arlington, VA: Public Interest Publications, 1993.

Schoem, D., Frankel, L., and Lewis, E. A., eds. *Multicultural Teaching at the University.* Westport, CT: Praeger, 1993.

Smith, Kevin B., and Meier, Kenneth J. *The Case against School Choice.* New York: Sharpe, 1995.

Wells, Amy S. *Time to Choose: America at the Crossroads of School Choice Policy.* East Rutherford, NJ: Putnam Publishing Group, 1993.

Web Sites

The American Federation of Teachers   www.aft.org
The Annenberg Institute for School Reform   www.annenberginstitute.org
The Ayn Rand Institute   www.aynrand.org
The Center for Education Reform   www.edreform.com/charter_schools

The Edison Project   www.edisonproject.com
The Educational Resources Information Center (ERIC)   www.ericsp.org
National Alliance for Safe Schools   www.safeschools.org
National Association for Bilingual Education   www.nabe.org
National Board for Professional Teaching Standards   www.nbpts.org
The National Center for Education Statistics   www.nces.ed.gov
National Center for the Study of Privatization in Education   www.tc.columbia.edu/ncspe/
The National Clearinghouse for Comprehensive School Reform   www.goodschools.gwu.edu
The National Education Association   www.nea.org
Regional Education Laboratory Network   www.relnetwork.org
The United States Department of Education   www.ed.gov

CHAPTER 10

Legal and Social Equality: The Struggle Against Oppression and Bigotry

Few concepts in the context of either domestic or international politics generate as much symbolic and emotional appeal as equality. Traceable in some form as far back as the concept of justice, its roots precede Plato. Equality is a familiar and recurring theme in the history of Western thought.

Yet despite its strong symbolism and cultural familiarity, the substantive content of the term has remained imprecise, inconsistent, or both. A central theme of this chapter is that there are three distinguishable conceptualizations of equality: equality under law, equality of opportunity, and equality of material well-being. Each conceptualization implies different goals for public policy, and the dominant reading of the term has changed over time. Indeed, definitional quarrels in the matter of race have become so pervasive that Stephen and Abigail Thernstrom, in their much-discussed book on "race in modern America," contend that "today we argue without a common language" in this area.[1] A generation ago, a widespread conception of racism involved judging the qualities of people by the racial group to which they belong and treating them accordingly. We will see later that a current conceptualization includes a demand that race be used as a factor in selecting people for employment or admission to selective universities. Terms in this area express emotional and symbolic content as much as precise meaning.

This chapter will demonstrate that an expanding sense of equality of material well-being has come to dominate the policy process. Meanwhile, the roster of groups identified by the policy process and the media as official victims of discrimination has expanded. To the evils of racism (referring to discrimination against African Americans, Hispanics, and Native Americans) and sexism (referring to discrimination against women) have been added ageism (discrimination against the elderly), ableism (discrimination against the handicapped), homophobia (discrimination against homosexuals), and nativism (discrimination against the foreign-born or immigrants). The law has further developed the concept of the rights of children independent of their families. Children have acquired the right to sue their parents and even to "divorce" their parents. Expanding on the concept of nativism, the status and rights of foreign-born citizens and legal immigrants to this country developed into the recent controversy of whether illegal immigrants have rights and whether these illegals should, as proposed by the Bush administration in 2002, be granted a blanket amnesty. This issue came to national attention with the 1994 passage of California's Proposition 187 referendum, a vote that amended the California Constitution to deny public benefits (including welfare), access to public health facilities, and even the right to attend public school to illegal aliens and their children.

ISSUE BACKGROUND: THE IDEA OF EQUALITY

Equality under Law

The first conceptualization, equality under law, is the minimum position. If equality means anything, it means at least this much. The concept of equality under law implies that government should treat people as individuals rather than as members of social groups, and that when those categorizations are made, they impose a heavy burden of proof on government to show that there is a valid and widely accepted public purpose behind them. This concept clearly implies that government should not allocate rewards and punishments to people based on the racial, ethnic, or religious groups to which they belong. Clearly, the law does make many categorizations of people. It distinguishes criminals from noncriminals, the psychotic from the sane, children from adults, and so forth. The reason why law permits these categories is that there is widespread consensus that these categories reflect behavioral distinctions. Thus, we assume that criminals behave differently from noncriminals, psychotics differ from those defined as sane, and children differ from adults. However, insofar as the law has now completely rejected the belief that there are behavior patterns or dispositions intrinsic to members of a given race, at the very least, classification by race is inconsistent with the concept of equality under law.

The law now presumes that categorization of people based on the group into which they are born, such as race and ethnicity, is unconstitutional, unless government can satisfy the burden of proof to demonstrate that they satisfy a "compelling public need." Therefore, such categorizations are not always unconstitutional. Government conceivably could satisfy the required burden of proof. One basis of recent controversy is disagreement as to what constitutes a "compelling public need."

Accordingly, some categorizations, such as sex, may be constitutional for some purposes but not for others. The law has come to reject the assumption that men are intrinsically more intelligent than women; therefore, laws banning women from occupations in which intelligence is the main qualifying criterion would violate the concept of equality under law. However, the law may protect some residual assumptions that women are intrinsically less aggressive than men are by excluding them from combat roles in the military. The recent acceptance of women for many combat roles in today's military, including that of combat pilot, has substantially eroded this assumption. It will become apparent from our discussion of sex discrimination that society's assumptions about the intrinsic properties of women are undergoing a process of evolution and that this process is affecting law and policy. Legal principles distinguishing the sexes that went unchallenged a generation ago now violate the right to equal protection of the law or are now banned by statute, and women increasingly appear in roles previously assumed to be beyond the competence of the typical woman. A similar flexibility of roles is beginning to emerge for men. Thus, one can now find women working as doctors, lawyers, or judges, and men working as nurses, flight attendants, or grade-school teachers. Despite the breakdown of the exclusive domination of certain roles by one sex or the other, many roles remain dominated by the gender conventionally associated with that role. Most lawyers, doctors, and professors are men despite the inroads of the feminist movement, and most housekeepers, raisers of children, secretaries, receptionists, and grade-school

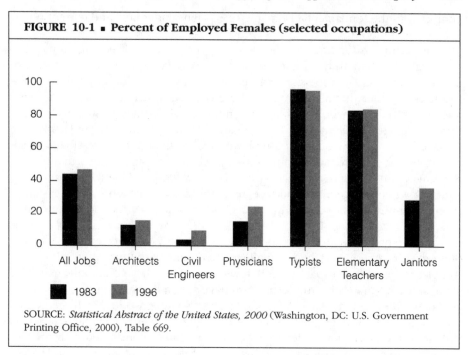

FIGURE 10-1 ■ Percent of Employed Females (selected occupations)

SOURCE: *Statistical Abstract of the United States, 2000* (Washington, DC: U.S. Government Printing Office, 2000), Table 669.

teachers are women (see Figure 10-1). The Former Speaker of the U.S. House of Representatives, Newt Gingrich, made a controversial speech in early 1995 in which he asserted that women were physically unfit for combat roles in which they would have to "roll around in the dirt and get infections," but naturally more aggressive men are disposed to go out and "hunt giraffes," indicating that sex-role stereotyping runs deep in high places.

Equality under law and racial profiling. Thus, an important issue in the acceptability of racial, ethnic, and gender categories is whether these categories reflect significant aggregate differences in behavior of which public policy might reasonably take account. There has been a normally unstated policy of *racial profiling* among many of America's police personnel. This terms refers to a greater tendency to be suspicious of African Americans and, to a lesser extent, Hispanics, and to investigate members of these groups more closely, based on the argument that members of these groups are statistically more likely to commit crime. This greater tendency to stop and interrogate target group people when whites in the same circumstances are left alone indicates an affront to the dignity of the many law-abiding members of these groups. In their protest against being singled out because of their race for closer police scrutiny, African Americans are asserting their right to equality under law.

Racial profiling came to the forefront of national attention shortly after the events of September 11, 2001, because airport security officials singled out young males with Middle Eastern looks (or features) for scrutiny. Those defending such policies point out that we have a sound basis in experience for assuming threats to airline security are more likely to come from such individuals than from, say, Scandinavian-looking people. However, the policy does seem to come in logical conflict with the fundamental principle of equality under law, and current policy is to screen randomly.

Equality under law in U.S. history. The concept of equality under law historically has had a liberal implication. For many years in Western history, political movements used the concept against legally mandated privileges of aristocracies or other dominant groups. These privileges included weighted voting and laws stipulating who could or could not own land, enter prestigious occupations, and so forth. Even in the United States, dominant groups were legally able to have laws—or rules supported by laws—that restricted the accessibility of social values to subordinate groups. It is well known that before the historic Supreme Court decision in *Brown v. Board of Education of Topeka, Kansas,* which struck down legally required racial segregation in public schools, laws existed to reserve the best public schools and facilities for whites. Furthermore, laws sanctioned discrimination in facilities licensed by the state to serve the public.[2] Inns and restaurants across the country freely and openly, with the blessing of the Supreme Court, restricted their clientele to the dominant groups. Although African Americans, women, Hispanics, and Jews were the most commonly excluded groups, Asians and Native Americans also have suffered severe discrimination, especially in the western states. Until a decade or so after World War II, many major law schools and graduate schools overtly or covertly maintained quotas restricting the admission of Jews—who, it was feared, constituted a disproportionate share of such professions—regardless of the credentials of the individual applicants. In the 1920s, Harvard University, under the direction of President A. Lawrence Lowell, attempted to reduce the number of Jewish students by various means. Harvard limited the amount of scholarship aid available to them, devised disguised quotas, required photographs on admissions applications, and made "character" a qualification for admission and then defined the term in such a way as to exclude negative attributes that Jews were considered to possess. It also tried a system of geographical balance to pass over applicants from New York City, which had a large Jewish population, to favor candidates from the South and West, regions with sparse Jewish populations. No method worked satisfactorily. In 1926, admissions officers began to reject candidates known or presumed to be Jewish without any stated reason. The number of Jewish students did in fact drop from 25 percent to 15 percent.[3]

It was alleged in 1988 that the University of California was using such an unofficial quota to restrict the proportion of high-achieving Asians among the students accepted to its several campuses. Although the university denied the charge, it was a fact that the percentage of Asians admitted was substantially lower than that of successful applicants whose objective qualifications (grade point averages and SAT scores) were inferior to those of the Asian students. According to Ernest Koenigsburg, a Berkeley professor who served on several admissions committees, African-American and Hispanic applicants were twenty times, or 2,000 percent, more likely to be admitted than Asians with the identical academic records. In 1989, Berkeley rejected more than 2,500 Asian and white students with straight A averages. Asians as a group suffer from this more than whites because a higher percentage of them attain such credentials.[4]

In mid-nineteenth century California, Chinese victims of crime were unable to obtain justice because the courts would not allow Chinese to testify against a white person. The legislature levied special taxes against their laundries. In the first half of the last century, laws prohibited intermarriage with Asians and segregated Asian schoolchildren. Policy virtually excluded Asians from immigration to the United States in the 1920s, and those already here were denied citizenship and were prohibited from owning agricultural land (see Chapter 11). Although legal discrimination against Asians is not as widely known to this generation of Americans as is discrimination against African Americans and Hispanics, "the intensity of discrimination against Japanese Americans in the first half of the twentieth century greatly exceeded that encountered by Mexican Americans."[5] This anti-Asian discrimination in official policy culminated in one of the most blatant examples of inequality under American law in this century, the compulsory internment during World War II of Americans of Japanese ancestry in what critics called concentration camps. The government euphemistically called them "relocation centers." In 1988, the U.S. Congress did belatedly authorize paying reparations to survivors of the Japanese internment, a move that generated pockets of vociferous opposition. This payment reflected a consensus among opinion leaders in the United States that the internment was a gross, racially motivated denial of legal equality and basic due process of law.

For much of American history there was an explicit legal denial to Native Americans of equal access to the values of our society, a fact manifested in herding them off their land and confining them to residual pieces of unwanted territory called reservations.

Of course, the denial of equality under law to African Americans has been a well-known and widespread phenomenon. The Black Codes were one of the more blatant examples of this. These were a series of laws passed in many parts of the Old South after Reconstruction to attempt to nullify the reality of the Thirteenth Amendment's prohibition of overt slavery. The effect of these laws was to restore the almost-complete black dependence on and subservience to the former slaveholders. These laws forbade African Americans to hold jobs, receive an education, or even walk the streets of cities and towns without permission from whites. General Colin Powell, Chairman of the Joint Chiefs of Staff during the Gulf War, recalls that in 1962 as he was driving through Virginia, about to leave for Vietnam, he and his wife were unable to find a bathroom they were allowed to use.[6] Until the impact of the *Brown* school desegregation case was finally established in the late 1960s, blacks continued to be singled out by law for specified disadvantages. They were routinely excluded from public facilities in the Old South.

Women have also been denied equality under law. Until the passage of the Nineteenth Amendment, they were not allowed to vote in national elections. Political wisdom was apparently held to correlate with gender. Many vestiges of the notion of female inferiority continued until recent decades. In seven of the eight states with community property laws, whereby husband and wife could hold property in common, the community property was under the control of the husband. Five states limited a woman's freedom to venture into business. Most states denied a woman the same rights as her husband to establish a separate domicile.[7]

Although the United States has never had a formal aristocracy to unseat and despite the commitment in American ideology to the idea of equality under law, there has been a more or less identifiable dominant group in this country, a group definable by gender and race or ethnicity. These groups directly or indirectly used the law in addition to social discrimination to maintain other groups in a subordinate status. This dominant group has been white, male, and largely Protestant, especially the older, non-evangelical sects such as Episcopal, Congregational, or Methodist—as opposed to Baptist, Church of Christ, and Pentecostal.

Inequality in the Western world. Dominant groups throughout the Western world create institutional arrangements to perpetuate their status and to minimize social mobility. The educational system has often functioned as this kind of selective institution in Western nations. In Great Britain and France, for example, rigorous competitive examinations determined who went on to a university. England had its "eleven plus" exams until the early 1970s, and France still uses the baccalaureate. These exams really test those skills and attributes passed from parent to child in middle- and upper-class families. In England, there is a select system of private and expensive secondary education that is the major avenue to Oxford and Cambridge, which educate most of Great Britain's elite. There is a similar system of preparatory schools in the United States that improves the chance of admission to prestigious higher education for the children of the affluent.

The culture defines dominant groups along ethnic, racial, or religious lines where there is diversity of such attributes. In nations where there is more ethnic or racial homogeneity, stratification is mainly along the lines of social class. Nations with distinct subcultures, such as Belgium, the Netherlands, Canada, and Austria, usually contain one such subculture perceived as dominant and others as subordinate. Frequently these divisions are along religious or linguistic lines. In general, whenever cultural, religious, racial, ethnic, or linguistic attributes are congruent with socioeconomic divisions, this intensifies the political conflict between dominant and subordinate groups.

Equality of Opportunity

Laws that treat each individual equally do not necessarily have an equal impact on each individual. The impact of a law on an individual is a function not only of the substance of the law itself, but also of the circumstances and attributes of the individual. Equality under law does not necessarily create genuine equality of opportunity. *Equality of opportunity* refers to the right of all individuals to realize their human potential to become whatever their personal abilities and desires allow them to become, free from barriers imposed by society and its institutions. When government reserves certain roles or rewards in society for particular groups or classes of individuals, irrespective of performance or behavior, this in effect impedes the goal achievement of others. This would constitute a violation of equality of opportunity as well as of equality under law.

It is clear, however, that social and economic barriers exist, even though neither law nor public policy assigns privileges or disabilities to specified groups or individuals. The unequal distribution of such resources as wealth, abilities, and health will bestow advantages or disadvantages on individuals in competition for social or material values even when law and policies are neutral. People acquire things they value through the successful investment of resources they already possess. Those who lack such resources cannot use them for self-improvement even when permitted to do so by law. This is especially true in a capitalist system in which capital (resources deferred from consumption to investment) generates more resources. One may need to be clever to succeed in the stock market, but one first needs capital to invest. Even such things as leisure time, transportation, and good health are resources that can be invested for self-improvement, but they are not evenly distributed throughout the population. Furthermore, people and institutions may make goal achievement more difficult for some than for others through mechanisms such as prejudice.

Thus, governmental or legal neutrality perpetuates the existing inequalities of opportunity by permitting those who have superior resources to use them to maintain or increase their status relative to the have-nots. Without governmental regulation of the market, the gap between those who have more and those who have less tends to increase.

It is clearly unrealistic to assert that a child born to and raised by a poor, semi-literate African-American single teenager in one of America's urban ghettos has the same chance of achieving high socioeconomic status as does the child of upper-middle-class, well-educated parents in an affluent suburb, even assuming that all legally imposed distinctions between these groups have been eliminated. The latter set of parents will impart skills, values, and resources to their offspring that the former parent cannot offer. The Coleman Report on educational achievement, discussed in Chapter 9, finds that the best single predictor of such achievement is the educational achievement level of one's parents. Although it is true that some individuals with superior talents and motivations may rise in Horatio Alger fashion from rags to riches, when genetically acquired properties are about equal, the child of affluence has a much higher probability of reaching his or her potential.

The principle in operation here is that *equal laws have unequal impacts on equal persons*. The French socialist, Anatole France, put it eloquently when he said, "The law, in its majestic impartiality, forbids the rich as well as the poor to beg in the streets, sleep under the bridges, and steal bread." Obviously, such laws do not prevent the rich from doing anything they are likely to do.

Consequently, the discrimination that makes a group of people socially and economically unequal will tend to cause the offspring of that group to continue to be socially and economically unequal after the original discrimination is discontinued and the current rules of the game apply equally to all. Thus, previous, legally imposed inequalities generate unequal opportunity. A somewhat different unequal opportunity stems from differences in the talents and values that one either is born with or acquires early in life, that do not stem from any socially or legally imposed discrimination.

A major controversy emerged in this regard with the publication of a book, *The Bell Curve*, by the late Harvard psychologist Richard Hernnstein and Charles Murray.[8] The essential argument is that whatever intelligence tests measure is more genetically determined than society admits. Since they further argue that IQ is a major determinant of wealth and social status, they offer the pessimistic conclusion that poverty and inequality are largely beyond the power of social policy to remedy. This conclusion deeply offends many Americans, but especially those on the social and political left, who have a more optimistic disposition to believe that social policy can remediate social problems. The book further offends those involved in the quest for racial equality by noting that racial groups significantly differ with respect to this putatively genetically acquired intelligence, with Asian Americans having the highest mean IQ scores, whites next, and African Americans the lowest of these three groups. Of course, there is a substantial overlap among these groups with respect to the distribution of intelligence. However, the suggestion that the gene pool of one group is genetically inferior to another group with respect to intelligence constitutes a challenge to the entire struggle for equality and its public policy implications. Here it is a question of whether the government has an obligation to remedy the lower probabilities that one will realize one's potential that stems from such personal qualities as lack of talent and ambition. Hernnstein and Murray suggest that, given their conclusions, welfare and affirmative action are useless policies. It should be clear, however, that their conclusions and the implications of them are vehemently challenged by a broad spectrum of scholars, writers, and policy analysts. Notably, when the prestigious journal of opinion, *The New Republic,* published an excerpt of the Hernnstein-Murray work, it felt obliged to preface it with seventeen attacks on the article, including most of the writers on the journal's staff, attacks that included charges of Neo-Nazism.[9]

The idea of meritocracy, essentially a conception of what is meant by social justice, holds that the allocation of social values and status should be on the basis of performance standards in part derived from perceived contributions to the public good. Meritocracy entails the following assumptions: (1) Some social roles contribute more to the good of the community than others do, and so rewards should be proportionate to such contributions; (2) the fulfillment of such roles frequently requires long and difficult training or rare talents; (3) special inducements are necessary to persuade people to fill these important and difficult roles; and (4) both justice and public need require that the occupants of some roles be rewarded a disproportionate share of social values. It is important to note that the concept of meritocracy entails the principle that people are rewarded based on what they do rather than who they are.

It is also important to keep in mind that the assumption that performance is a function of material reward is one that has not been conclusively or even, to some, convincingly demonstrated. People contribute to the social order for many reasons, and it is unclear how large a role the prospect of material reward plays in such behavior.

It might be said that a consensus exists in America that people ought to be differently rewarded on the basis of performance standards, based in turn on talent, effort, and contribution to the social good; there is, however, a lack of consensus on how performance or social contribution should be measured. There is the question, for instance, as to whether the standards for admission to higher socioeconomic status in the United States, such as success in the educational system, reflect talent and potential social contribution or merely the cultural experiences of the dominant middle-class group. Does a higher grade point average, a standard on which certain groups consistently fall short, indicate a probability of being a superior physician, lawyer, or scientist? For example, Linda Wightman argues that race-based selection to America's law schools has been successful because the graduation rates of African Americans admitted on race-based selection are not significantly different from those of whites. Stephen Thernstrom retorts, however, that since 89 percent of her whole sample graduates, this was a deceiving measure of African-American performance. A more accurate figure, he claims, is that whites were six times more likely to pass the bar examination on their first attempt.[10] To answer the question of who is better in certain roles, one would have to be able to precisely measure performance in such roles. Because such measurement is impossible to the satisfaction of everyone regardless of their values, it remains impossible either to demonstrate or to justify the social relevance of the performance standards that ground a meritocracy.

Equality of Material Well-Being

Because of the aforementioned difficulties in using the principle of meritocracy to legitimize the material inequalities that exist in all societies, spokespersons for relatively disadvantaged groups and individuals go on to argue that government has a moral obligation to engineer a more equal distribution of material values, irrespective of traditional performance standards. Furthermore, because one's actual opportunities for upward social mobility depend on the resources with which one starts life, advocates argue that equality of opportunity requires equality of material well-being. In short, equality of opportunity is inseparable from equality of result.

Proportional equality. The concept of equality of material well-being (sometimes called equality of result) requires precise definition for application to actual social policy. The extreme form of the concept, the idea that all individuals should possess the same income or wealth, has never found many advocates as a public policy goal in this country. Rather, the policy goal refers to proportional equality among designated social groups. Proportional equality refers to the idea that a social group's percentage in the overall population should be equaled by its share of certain benefits, such as income and wealth, or the holding of desired social roles, such as membership in the professions, high socioeconomic status, and admission to professional schools. According to this notion, for example, if African Americans make up 12 percent of the population, they should make up approximately 12 percent of doctors, lawyers, and executives. It is further inferred that if a group has less than its share of social values—for example, the 12 percent of African Americans contains less than 5 percent of the nation's physicians— this is evidence that institutional factors, such as systematic discrimination or its pervasive effects, are operating to bring about "underrepresentation." Therefore, the implicit assumption is that if discrimination were not present, each group would acquire its proportionate share of society's goods. Figures 10-2 and 10-3 illustrate the distance between proportional equality and the actual inequality of the races.

The concept of proportional equality is important because it ultimately became the key tool of the social reforms championed by the American civil rights movement. That movement, however, came to this consensus only after a lengthy period of trial and error with other political tactics.

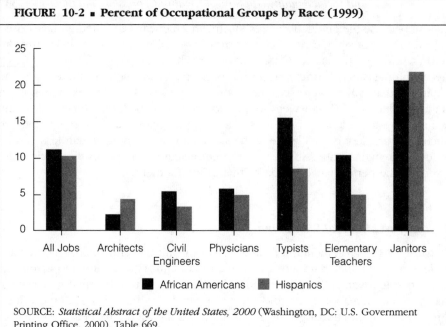

FIGURE 10-2 ■ Percent of Occupational Groups by Race (1999)

Legend: ■ African Americans ■ Hispanics

SOURCE: *Statistical Abstract of the United States, 2000* (Washington, DC: U.S. Government Printing Office, 2000), Table 669.

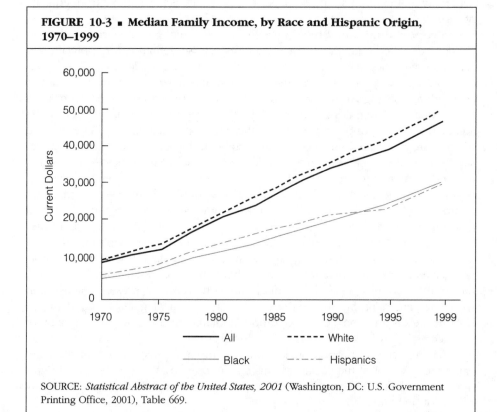

FIGURE 10-3 ■ Median Family Income, by Race and Hispanic Origin, 1970–1999

Legend: ——— All ------ White ——— Black — - — Hispanics

SOURCE: *Statistical Abstract of the United States, 2001* (Washington, DC: U.S. Government Printing Office, 2001), Table 669.

The Civil Rights Movement and Equality

The civil rights movement appears to have gone through three distinct stages in its political evolution. The first stage, dating from the early years of the twentieth century and the establishment of the National Association for the Advancement of Colored People (NAACP) and other organizations, was to attack denials of equality under law. Early cases attacked particular denials in law school admissions and public school facilities, culminating in the great school desegregation cases of the 1950s and 1960s. The goal was to eliminate Jim Crow laws that segregated African Americans and imposed legal disabilities on them.

Although this first stage was mostly successful, these policies did not realize expectations for a more profound change in the lifestyle of the typical African-American individual, leading to disappointment and dissatisfaction among civil rights leaders. With the goals of legal equality largely realized, the second stage of the movement, from the mid-1960s into the 1970s, concentrated on other goals, particularly equality of opportunity. The movement pressed for (1) legislation to secure access to jobs and to public facilities such as restaurants and places of accommodation (the 1964 Civil Rights Act); (2) legislation to secure the right to vote (the 1965 Civil Rights Act); and (3) legislation to end discrimination in the sale and rental of housing (the 1968 Civil Rights Act). In other words, the second stage largely had to do with access to values and facilities privately owned but ostensibly available to the public. Finally, the movement began to press for proportional equality, an effort that focused largely on bureaucratic agencies such as the Department of Health and Human Services (HHS).

CONTEMPORARY POLICY: STRENGTHENING CONSTITUTIONAL GUARANTEES OF EQUALITY

The Erosion of the Fourteenth Amendment

After the Thirteenth Amendment (1865) ended outright slavery in the United States, laws continued to single out African Americans and other racial and ethnic groups for discriminatory treatment. The Fourteenth Amendment (1868) intended to end such discriminatory legislation by state governments, but two important decisions by the Supreme Court, *The Civil Rights Cases* (1883) and *Plessy v. Ferguson* (1896), greatly weakened the amendment's role and in fact legitimized existing forms of discrimination, specifically in education and access to public facilities. It is important to understand this weak interpretation of the intent of the Fourteenth Amendment because, in varying ways, each of the policy areas discussed in this section—school desegregation and integration, equal opportunity in employment and higher education, and equal rights for women—was an attempt to circumvent this eroded interpretation.

Restrictions on the concept of state action. A key portion of the Fourteenth Amendment has been the subject of much litigation concerning the struggle for equality over the years. It reads, ". . . nor shall any state deprive any person of life, liberty or property without due process of law; nor deny to any person within its jurisdiction the equal protection of the laws." Among the important points to note about this passage are (1) that the language does not prohibit purely individual discrimination and (2) that the language is passive—it tells what the state cannot do, but it does not explicitly command the state to do something actively.

After the Civil War and the enactment of the Fourteenth Amendment, many assumed that the amendment intended to encourage state governments to take action per se and also to extend such actions to businesses licensed by the state to serve the public. Because established common law principles assume that such businesses perform a public function under state aegis, the law customarily considered them state agents. In other words, because they derive their income from the public, they have an obligation to the public. Such an interpretation would have brought this form of discrimination, the most pervasive in our society, within the purview of the Fourteenth Amendment. For instance, this conception of the Fourteenth Amendment would prevent restaurants, hotels, and stores from excluding African Americans and other nonwhites as they had done in the United States over the years.

The Supreme Court rejected this traditional interpretation of the amendment in *The Civil Rights Cases* (1883), when it ruled that businesses licensed by the state to serve the public did not come under the concept of state action for the purposes of the amendment, an interpretation that still is in effect.[11] This ruling emasculated the amendment's effectiveness in dealing with this form of discrimination.

Ending Segregation

The emasculation of the Fourteenth Amendment as an effective instrument against segregation soon went even further than it had under *The Civil Rights Cases.* The Court ruled in 1896 to legalize active state intervention to segregate public facilities, including public schools. In *Plessy v. Ferguson,* the Court held that the equal protection clause of the amendment did not forbid laws requiring separation of the races.[12] Separation, the Court held, did not necessarily mean inequality. The opinion of the Court argued that any implication of African-American inferiority derived from such Jim Crow laws was solely a function of the perceptions of African Americans themselves. Hence, in enunciating the so-called separate-but-equal doctrine, the Court officially legitimized such segregation laws. Moreover, in asserting that separation was legal, neither the Court nor society paid much heed to the equality portion of that doctrine. It was an accepted fact that the public facilities available to African Americans in localities where segregation was the official practice, the states of the Old South, were not at all equal to facilities for whites.

The *Plessy* separate-but-equal principle remained in effect until 1954. After a series of cases that made inroads on its logic, *Plessy* was formally overruled in the 1954 landmark case of *Brown v. Board of Education of Topeka, Kansas,* which held that any state-mandated segregation in the field of education inherently violates the equal protection clause of the Fourteenth Amendment.[13] That 1954 decision is now known as *Brown I.* Chief Justice Warren, speaking for a unanimous court, held that segregation was widely understood as a badge of nonwhite inferiority and that this perception was likely to have a permanent destructive impact on the psychological development of African-American children, irrespective of the physical equality of the facilities in question. In fact, those who brought the case deliberately selected Topeka because the physical inequality of African-

American schools was not a serious issue there. This selection, therefore, brought to the fore the issue of the inherent inequality of segregated schools. The courts eventually applied the unconstitutionality of Jim Crow laws to all other public facilities, such as parks, cemeteries, and hospitals.

It is one thing to hand down a principle of law; it is quite another to see that it is carried out. The step of policy implementation, as pointed out in the introductory chapter, is separate from policy adoption and is usually a difficult process in its own right. The response of the southern state governments was largely to resist the integration of their school systems as forcefully and as long as possible. Recognizing that the immediate dismantling of the dual school system would be disruptive and expensive, the Court, in a separate opinion (known as *Brown II*), ordered the implementation of its *Brown I* decision "with all deliberate speed."[14] There was sufficient ambiguity in that standard to permit those southern politicians who wished to do so to interpret the phrase as referring to the indefinite future, which in practical terms meant never. The South moved slowly toward the termination of its dual school systems. Mississippi did not make its first token integration of its public schools until 1964, ten years after *Brown*. By 1964, only about 2 percent of the African-American school children in eleven Old South states were attending integrated schools. As late as 1969, the Court in *Alexander v. Holmes County* had to inform a Mississippi school board that the time for "all deliberate speed" had run out and that further delays would not find approval.[15]

The *Holmes County* case ended the last legal justification for the operation of dual school systems. Meanwhile, the Civil Rights Act of 1964 placed pressure on local school districts to comply with the intent of *Brown I* by the threat of withholding federal funds from districts that did not satisfactorily respond. Under such pressures, desegregation in the Old South finally proceeded rapidly in the late 1960s. By 1970, a greater percentage of African Americans were attending schools with whites in that region than in the North. Thus, the first major goal of the civil rights movement, the elimination of Jim Crow laws, had succeeded. The movement had already turned its attention to the reality that the demise of state-mandated segregation failed to provide integration.

Enforcing Integration

Persisting discrimination against African Americans and Hispanics in the sale and rental of housing has exacerbated a widespread tendency in urban America toward racial and ethnic homogeneity in housing and residential patterns. Although each group of immigrants (Italian, Irish, Greek, Polish, and so forth) had displayed some tendency to seek out and live in neighborhoods peopled by those of its own derivation, housing discrimination against African Americans and Hispanics has added to the racial homogeneity of the neighborhoods of these latter two groups. Because assignment to public schools traditionally used neighborhood schools, the traditional policy perpetuated the reality of racially homogeneous public schools. This racial separation of students due to the effects of discriminatory housing patterns is a form of *de facto* segregation. (De facto segregation is that not caused by law or public policy. *De jure* segregation is that so caused.)

Dissatisfaction with the mere end of de jure (state-mandated) school segregation was given impetus by the Coleman Report of 1966, a study of the causes of educational achievement involving over a half-million students. This report, described in Chapter 9, found that among educational attributes, the one factor that had a significant effect on scholastic achievement was an intermingling of higher achievers and lower achievers. Peer group influence tended to upgrade the performance of the lower achievers without harming that of higher achievers. Moreover, the U.S. Civil Rights Commission found specifically that African Americans attending predominantly white schools had significantly higher levels of scholastic achievement than did African Americans attending predominantly African-American schools when family background was held constant.[16] Many interpreted these results to mean that actual intermingling of and interaction among African-American and white students would be the most effective technique for upgrading the educational performance of African-American students.

This interpretation, of course, assumes a correlation between race and educational performance, a correlation that is statistically significant but far from perfect. To a large extent, the apparent correlation between race and educational performance and other behaviors or attributes, such as crime rates and unemployment, actually reflects a correlation between race and social class. African Americans and Hispanics are more likely to be among the lower socioeconomic class than whites are, and lower-class individuals are more likely to be academic underachievers than are those from the middle and upper classes. Therefore, it is an oversimplification to assume that white students are always high achievers, whereas African Americans and Hispanics are always lower scholastic achievers. Coleman's study focused on school achievement levels, and others read into it the racial implications. It may be that simply mixing high- and low-achieving students, regardless of race, is what Coleman's data suggest, a policy contradicted by the widespread practice of "tracking," or grouping students by ability.

In any event, the goals of the civil rights movement with respect to education came to be redefined in terms of the racial balance of the student body and faculty of each school, a goal first stipulated by the Supreme Court in *Green et al. v. County School Board of New Kent County* (1968).[17] Once this standard becomes the accepted interpretation of the Fourteenth Amendment, an active governmental role in assigning students to schools on a racial basis is inescapable.

The explicit judicial mandate for compulsory busing came in *Swann v. Charlotte-Mecklenburg Board of Education* (1971).[18] The Court specifically stated that the lower courts may require busing as one means of achieving the racial balance goal, a goal that was expressed in terms of specific percentages (71 percent white to 29 percent nonwhite), but it held this up as a norm to be striven for rather than a rigid quota. The courts could not require busing to remedy racial imbalance that was purely de facto; that is, had occurred wholly independently of government action. However, any governmental activity, such as the opening or closing of schools, that contributed to such imbalance would justify a court-ordered busing remedy. Although the Court preserved a legal distinction between de facto and de jure segregation, in practice the broad range of governmental actions held to justify busing orders, irrespective of any showing of governmental intent, rendered the distinction unimportant.[19] In other words, the fact of racial imbalance itself has constituted grounds for inferring correctable segregation if any past government action can be shown to have somehow contributed to that imbalance.

Based on *Swann v. Charlotte-Mecklenburg,* many court-ordered busing programs were instituted in cities and smaller communities around the country, but the policy was very unpopular. Polls in the early 1980s showed that between 80 and 90 percent of whites (depending on how the question was worded) and even 48 percent of African Americans opposed the policy.[20] In recent years, courts have begun to remove requirements for busing. When districts achieve "unitary status," they move out from under court supervision. Following this, districts may decide for themselves when and how to use busing and other measures to achieve integration, and most over time decide to reduce the use of busing for racial balance. Oklahoma City achieved this status in 1991; Buffalo, Boston, and Little Rock achieved it soon thereafter, followed by many other school districts. More than any other means, busing was the essential tool for solving the problem of racial imbalance in public schools. Figure 10-4 shows progress in school integration. The sections that follow discuss the reasons for such limited progress.

The Struggle for Racial Balance in Employment and Higher Education

Civil Rights Act of 1964. Busing dealt with the integration of the public schools. This left the underrepresentation of the designated disadvantaged groups—usually African Americans and Hispanics, but occasionally including all

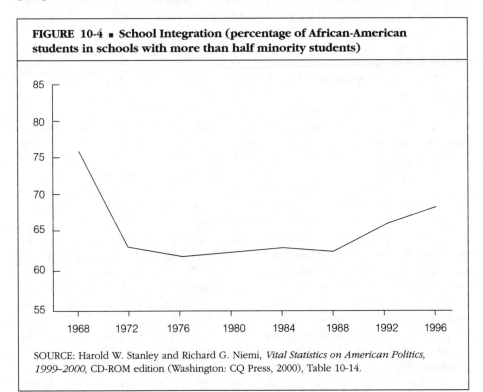

FIGURE 10-4 ■ **School Integration (percentage of African-American students in schools with more than half minority students)**

SOURCE: Harold W. Stanley and Richard G. Niemi, *Vital Statistics on American Politics, 1999–2000,* CD-ROM edition (Washington: CQ Press, 2000), Table 10-14.

nonwhites and women—untouched in various sectors of the American economy and in higher education. The Civil Rights Act of 1964, in its Title VII provisions, set up the Equal Employment Opportunity Commission (EEOC) to implement policy toward ending discrimination by any employer or labor union with twenty-five or more persons. Title VI of the same act requires that each federal agency take action to end discrimination in any program or institution to which it allocates federal funds. The Office of Federal Contract Compliance is responsible for implementing this policy. As discussed earlier, the goal of ending discrimination appears as the achievement of proportional representation for designated groups in various valued social roles. Although the EEOC cannot require either quotas or preferential treatment from the mere fact of racial imbalance, it can use such imbalance as evidence of discrimination. The assumption again is that if discrimination were not at work, these groups would be present in various sectors in rough proportion to their numbers in society.

Expanding the Constitution's "commerce clause."   Because *The Civil Rights Cases* weakened the Fourteenth Amendment, review of the constitutionality of the Civil Rights Act of 1964's provisions guaranteeing all citizens access to restaurants, motels, and other places of public accommodation required drawing on an expanded meaning of the Constitution's "commerce clause." Federal power to regulate interstate commerce forbade discrimination by businesses directly or indirectly involved in such commerce. The *Heart of Atlanta Motel* case in 1964 upheld this power. Another case that year, *Katzenbach v. McClung,* permitted the law's extension to businesses whose only connections to interstate commerce were purchases from a national market.[21] Thus, a restaurant well-removed from any interstate route was held to be included in the act's antidiscrimination provisions because if that restaurant could discriminate, so could all other such establishments. Cumulatively, that could have an impact on the interstate market that the single restaurant lacked.

Equality of result in education and employment.   The adoption of proportionality as a criterion of discrimination came into being largely because much discrimination is covert rather than overt and is thus hard to prove. For example, a school wishing to keep African Americans out may deliberately adopt entrance requirements that it knows African Americans will disproportionately fail; similarly, it is frequently difficult to establish why a particular applicant failed to obtain a job.

The remedies to imbalance in employment, in the composition of professions, or in admissions to higher education consist of some form of preferential treatment for members of the underrepresented groups or of an attack on the standards by which people are selected. Accordingly, the Office of Federal Contract Compliance and the EEOC laid down guidelines to the effect that any test for employment, promotion, or membership disproportionately failed by members of the designated groups constitutes evidence of illegal discrimination, unless the employer can demonstrate the test's job relevance. In other words, the employer must show that those who score higher on the test or selection criteria actually perform better in the roles for which they are being selected.

The Court upheld these guidelines in *Griggs v. Duke Power* (1971).[22] By holding that Congress had in Title VII outlawed criteria for employment disproportionately failed by a protected group, the Court in effect threatened the legality of any performance criteria. The job relevance of such criteria is nearly impossible to prove because it is rarely possible to precisely measure job performance. For example, how can one say that requiring particular academic credentials for a job serves to select better teachers unless one can precisely measure how good one is as a teacher, a judgment on which reasonable people usually disagree?

However, beginning with the case of *Washington v. Davis* (1976),[23] the Court tended to shift the burden of proof to the plaintiff to demonstrate the test was instituted with the intent to discriminate. Subsequent decisions in the appellate courts applied the latter standard of placing the burden of proof on the plaintiff alleging discrimination. It is this new rule of law that the controversial 1991 Civil Rights Act (described later) sought to overturn.

Another approach to proportionate equality is the idea of preferential treatment. Preferential treatment plans vary from using membership in one of the designated groups as one positive factor taken into consideration to rigid quotas that require a set proportion of members of such groups among those selected. Nevertheless, strict quotas generate considerable emotional hostility among some groups (for example, among Jews) because quotas once excluded them from prestigious schools and professions. Often preferential treatment finds support in federal affirmative action policies. These require businesses and educational institutions guilty of past discrimination or in receipt of federal funding to demonstrate by positive action that they do not discriminate and that they hire and admit minorities and women.

The challenge to race-based selection. The opposition to selection based on race, although frequently emanating from perceived self-interest, has been argued in terms of an interpretation of the equal protection clause of the Fourteenth Amendment. The argument is that preferential treatment for nonwhites unconstitutionally discriminates against whites.

Many observers approached the Alan Bakke case in 1978 with great expectation that the Court would resolve the constitutional issue. This case involved the admissions procedure for the University of California Medical School at Davis, which had rejected Bakke's application for admission. This school had set aside a fixed number, sixteen places out of one hundred, for nonwhites. Because the school compiled scores for each applicant on grade point averages (GPA), the Medical College Aptitude Test (MCAT), and a personal interview, the procedure created two separate applicant pools.

Although the applicants for the sixteen minority seats had to meet minimum standards on these criteria and in that sense were qualified, the records of those selected from the minority pool on the two objective scores (GPA and MCAT) were significantly inferior to those selected from the regular pool. Perhaps more significantly, they were well below the record of some of those, like Bakke, rejected under the regular admission process. In fact, the average percentile ranking on MCAT scores of those admitted under the special program were from 36 to 52 percentile points below those selected from the general applicant pool in the years studied.[24] The GPA of regular admittees averaged 3.5 and 3.4 for those years, where the special admittees averaged 2.6 and 2.4, respectively.

The Court found itself as divided as society itself on the legality of such a program. Four justices (Burger, Rehnquist, Stevens, and Stewart) held that the use of racial criteria violated Title VII of the Civil Rights Act of 1964. Therefore, they wished Bakke admitted, without considering whether such admissions policies violated the equal protection clause. By deciding the case on statutory rather than constitutional grounds, these justices gave Congress the opportunity of overriding the decision by ordinary legislation rather than constitutional amendment.

Four other justices (Blackmun, Brennan, Marshall, and White) argued that neither the Constitution's equal protection clause nor Title VII prevented the use of racial categories to remedy the effects of past discrimination.

Four-to-four stalemates do not make for constitutional decisions on a nine-person Court. Therefore, Justice Powell, as the swing vote, determined the outcome of the case. His opinion constituted the official Opinion of the Court, although none concurred with it, thereby reducing its force as legal precedent. Agreeing that racial categorizations are suspect categories that place a severe burden of proof on the state to show a compelling public purpose, Powell held that the need to secure "a diverse student body" satisfied this burden. However, Powell saw fit to distinguish a fixed quota of student slots assigned based on race—a policy he found incompatible with the equal protection clause—from the use of race as one among several factors in selecting from an open applicant pool—a policy known as *racial preference plans*. He approvingly endorsed preference plans based on the description of such a system at Harvard. Powell found the Davis program invalid on equal protection grounds, whereas the Burger group invalidated it on Title VII grounds; thus, Powell and the other group made a motley majority of five to order Bakke admitted.[25] We will later see an intensified effort from several sources to challenge the racial preference plans that Powell went out of his way to affirm in *Bakke*, challenges especially reflected in several cases at the level of Circuit Courts of Appeal that have not been resolved at the Supreme Court level.

Conclusion.   Today, government and educational institutions continue to strive to ameliorate the underrepresentation of targeted groups in the economy and in higher education. However, programs to do so inevitably displace nontargeted people, who increasingly challenge such programs. When the Piscataway School District in New Jersey fired Sharon Taxman rather than an African-American colleague, Debra Williams (who had been hired the same day), to give preference to targeted group teachers, Taxman sued. When Assistant U.S. Attorney General Deval Patrick filed an amicus brief in *Piscataway v. Taxman* supporting the school district's decision in the name of racial diversity, the Justice Department was ignoring the implication of Powell's decision in *Bakke* that race may not be the deciding factor in hiring and firing decisions. Patrick's brief argues that a racially diverse faculty satisfies the district's burden of proof that preference serves compelling public interest (diversity). However, in 1997 the civil rights groups feared a decision by the Court in favor of Taxman that could threaten a great deal of public policy designed to increase target group representation in valued socioeconomic roles; therefore, they avoided that decision by reaching an out-of-court settlement with Taxman allowing her to keep her job. The Court dealt affirmative action a serious blow in 1995, however, when it ruled unconstitutional a University of Maryland scholarship, the Banneker Scholarship, that was set aside for African Americans only. This is consistent with *Bakke* and other cases in that the scholarship went beyond racial preference by restricting competition to African Americans. The Court's 1997 decision in upholding the California Civil Rights Initiative, discussed later, struck another blow against affirmative action.

Equality and the Women's Movement

With the rise of the feminist movement in the United States, women have become a target group in many social policies designed to bar and redress the repression of women and their consequent underrepresentation in valued social roles. In *Craig v. Boren* (1976) the Court set standards for when gender may be used to classify people: The government must convince the Court that its purpose is an important one and that the sex classification is "substantially related" to achieving that purpose.[26] This case invalidated a law that set a higher legal drinking age for boys than for girls. The Court applied this standard in *Rostker v. Goldberg* (1981), when it upheld the right of Congress to exempt women from selective service.[27] However, some have said that the Court poorly applied, if not completely abandoned, the standard here. The defenders of the selective service law made no real effort to show that the exclusion of women is substantially related to the goal of raising an army. This case appears to leave the legality of classification by gender with an uncertain status. Many affirmative action programs and laws, such as Titles VI and VII of the Civil Rights Act of 1964, identify women as one of the beneficiary groups.

In the sense of proportional equality, women have been and remain underrepresented in higher-status positions (for example, doctors, lawyers, business executives, and professors) and overrepresented in lower-status positions (for example, elementary school teachers, secretaries, and nurses). (See Figure 10-1.) Even the minimal goal of equal pay for equal work has been difficult to obtain. The median income for women was only 60 percent that of men only two decades ago. By 1993, this gap had narrowed to the point where the median income for women was 77 percent that of men (see Figure 10-5), progress attributed more to the increased entry of women into occupations formerly dominated by men than

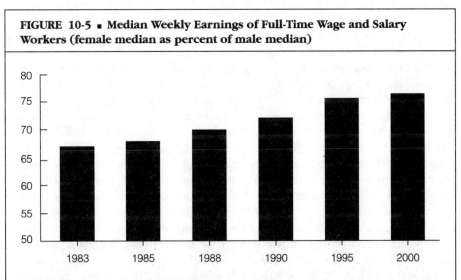

FIGURE 10-5 ▪ Median Weekly Earnings of Full-Time Wage and Salary Workers (female median as percent of male median)

SOURCE: *Statistical Abstract of the United States* (Washington, DC: U.S. Government Printing Office), Table 678 (1991), Table 665 (1994), Table 663 (1996), and Table 621 (2001).

to any increase in the pay for those occupational roles traditionally held by women. Although supporters of the feminist movement hailed this progress, they took pains to point out that the gap remains unjustifiably large. Part of this large differential still reflects the tendency of society to channel women into lower-status and thus lower-paying roles. Nevertheless, part of so large a difference probably also reflects the tendency to pay women less for some of the same jobs that men have. "Pink-collar" jobs, those traditionally held by women, often pay less than those jobs traditionally held by men when the levels of skill or training demanded by the respective sets of jobs are comparable. Although men increasingly occupy such pink-collar jobs and women increasingly move into traditionally male jobs, most people still occupy roles conforming to gender-based expectations. Therefore, the movement for sexual equality concentrates on requiring equal pay for jobs of *comparable worth* (equal pay for different jobs requiring equal levels of skill, training, or responsibility). There is no reason, it is argued, why secretaries should receive less pay than plumbers should, when comparable levels of training and responsibility are involved. The concept of "comparable worth," however, has not made progress at the federal legislative level.

Unemployment rates are higher for women than for men. This further reflects the overall economic discrimination against women that remains an ongoing reality in American society. However, the inferior status of women, as with other disadvantaged groups, is not entirely a function of public policy. Widely held stereotypes regarding the appropriate roles of each gender see prestigious tasks demanding intelligence, creativity, courage, or other admirable traits as being by definition "man's work," while a woman's natural role is seen as housekeeper and mother.

Overcoming these sex-role stereotypes is one of the most difficult tasks for the women's movement because they appear to retain a greater persistence in the public mind even than racial stereotypes. The fact that many Americans regard the National Organization for Women (NOW) as outside the American mainstream and dominated by extremists perhaps impedes the creation of a more favorable public perception of efforts to alter the status of women. In general, the major women's organizations do not take a negative stance against men, but rather concern themselves with the maximization of social and economic choices available to women and focus intently on marketplace equity and reproductive freedom.

Part of the subtle denial of marketplace equity to women traces to the fact that society long restricted access to business opportunities in male-dominated bastions. The effort of feminists to penetrate traditional male domains received a boost when the Supreme Court upheld a New York City ordinance that banned discrimination by private clubs based on race, gender, creed, or national origin in *New York State Club Association v. City of New York* (1988).[28] The clubs in question were those membership associations in which business deals were actually concluded, employment decisions made, and professional contacts established, thereby preserving an "old boys network" in the upper echelons of American business. The exclusion of women and minorities from membership in such associations served, therefore, to effectively exclude them from equal opportunities for success. Such clubs have not only been restricted to whites but have also generally excluded women. The law defined the clubs covered in terms of the size of membership and the fact that they offered regular meal service and regularly received dues or fees from nonmembers for the use of space and services. Such clubs were considered not "distinctly private." The state's compelling interest in ensuring equality of opportunity in business and professional life overrides First and Fourteenth Amendment values that might conflict with that interest.

Although sex-role stereotypes have had much to do with the formation of discriminatory laws against women, it is helpful to distinguish between their subtler effects and the blatant use of law to define the female role. The legal disabilities that women have faced should not be minimized. They did not obtain the right to vote, for example, until 1920, fifty years after African-American men received the right. Women also were once denied the right to serve on juries, work in bars, and pursue various other callings. Some laws with the ostensible purpose of protecting women—such as limiting the amount of weight they could be required to lift on the job or the maximum hours they could be required to work—had the negative effect of keeping women out of many jobs. Some critics have argued that this was deliberate. Such laws assume inexorable connections between men and physical strength and between women and less strength, relationships that exist but are far from certain. Nevertheless, most of the discrimination against women has been the product of social attitudes and sex-role stereotypes rather than the law per se.

It is not unusual, for instance, for men in hiring positions to avoid considering women for jobs in the belief that they will only quit to get married or have babies. Prospective employers can continue to apply such sexist standards surreptitiously as long as they do not have to justify not hiring any particular applicant. Furthermore, for years colleges and universities spent many times as much on men's athletics as on women's, principally for two discriminatory reasons. First, society in general regards athletic prowess as a male prerogative; that is, male athletes were admired, whereas their female counterparts were chided for being unfeminine. Second, given such attitudes toward women athletes, their sports have not been good collegiate revenue producers because, until recently, they did not attract large paying audiences. However, Title VII of the Civil Rights Act of 1964 bans discrimination based on sex as well as race, and Title IX of the Educational Amendment Acts of 1972 forbids any institution from receiving federal funds to engage in sex discrimination. Accordingly, the government now requires colleges and universities to equalize the amount spent on interscholastic athletics. This has caused vociferous opposition from supporters of expensive but profitable football programs, so the cost equation exempts these programs.

Issues central to the concerns of the leaders of the women's movement include the control of one's childbearing, which entails both access to information and support of effective contraception as well as the freedom to receive legal abortions and the achievement of equity in job status and material well-being. These are issues of symbolic and emotional as well as of substantive content. Control of one's fecundity is of crucial importance because becoming a parent is perhaps the most all-encompassing commitment that one can experience, one that will inevitably constrain one's life choices. Chapter 13 discusses in detail the complex issue of access to abortion. Feminists are also concerned with the issues of rape and sexual harassment. Chapter 6 discusses the former offense; later paragraphs in this chapter discuss the latter.

A proposed equal rights amendment (ERA) to the Constitution, rejected in 1982, was an issue of great emotional significance to the supporters of the women's movement. It was viewed as an instrument to eradicate most gender-based classifications in law and public policy as well as a symbolic public stand against such gender-based discrimination. Nevertheless, some of the strongest opposition to the amendment came from women, partly because they realized that women would lose not only burdens but also privileges. Laws and social policies in many situations favor women over men. For instance, courts and judges overwhelmingly award child custody to women whenever such custody is contested in divorce proceedings. Some states have laws stating that the woman automatically wins custody unless the father can prove that she is an unfit mother. Some states permit alimony payments to women but not to men, irrespective of the relative financial status of the divorcing spouses. An Illinois law allowed unwed mothers to acquire custody of illegitimate children, but did not even allow unwed fathers a hearing, automatically presuming them to be unfit.

Such policies are under increasing attack by men. In fact, women's liberation is also "men's liberation," and some women fear that the financial and other responsibilities that men assume toward the women they marry would be open to challenge if gender-based distinctions in the law were abolished. Although the gender-based distinctions heretofore found in law and public policy may hinder those women who aspire to fill what were traditionally male roles, such distinctions in some ways do protect women in traditionally female roles (for example, housewife and mother).

As was seen in our discussion of the expanded conceptualization of rape in Chapter 6, the asymmetrical relationship between the sexes defined by the dominant power position of men over women in our society gave rise to an effort by feminists to utilize law and policy to protect women from sexual harassment. Here again we encounter a fundamental shift in the meaning of terms, the lack of a common language. While traditionally sexual harassment referred to a situation in which a man who holds a position of dominance over a woman repeatedly attempts to establish a form of sexual relationship (broadly defined) with her, now sexual harassment appears in actions that offend the victim or render her uncomfortable, producing a perceived hostile environment. People have found themselves assigned real punishment because a woman has felt offended or uncomfortable when the alleged perpetrator had no intention to offend. For example, a sexual harassment suit was filed at the University of Nebraska because the plaintiff took offense at a photograph on a man's desk of his wife clad in a swimming suit. A professor filed a sexual harassment suit at Penn State University because a reproduction of Goya's painting "The Naked Maja" hung in one of her classrooms. The most famous such suit is the one filed by Paula Jones against former President Clinton. Assuming Ms. Jones' account of the facts is 100 percent accurate, as Jeffery Rosen wrote in *The New Republic,* the President "made a pass at her, took no for an answer and reassured her that he meant no harm." His putative behavior, while clearly boorish, placed no pressure on or implied any threats to Ms. Jones. Here again we have the concept of sexual harassment reinterpreted as a right to not be offended. Arkansas Judge Susan Webber accordingly dismissed Jones' lawsuit in a summary judgment. Jones appealed, and the case was eventually settled out-of-court for an undisclosed sum of money paid to Jones. In 1994, a jury slapped a $500,000 judgment on a radio station because, as one juror put it, the station managers "seemed to feel it was partly okay to make jokes about women."[29]

The classic conception of sexual harassment refers to a situation where one person, usually a male, having power over some aspect of another's life (usually a woman), uses the power persistently over time to extort sexual favors. In 1997, an oilrig worker sued his fellow workers (male) for such harassment. More recently, courts have expanded the meaning of the term to cover the creation of a "hostile workplace environment." Such a standard is vague in the extreme; what is actionable is a function of the perceptions and sensitivities of the observer. Not knowing what will bring a lawsuit makes people bend over backwards to avoid anything that could be offensive to the most sensitive person. Crude or boorish behavior has now become actionable. The effect is a dampening effect on the exercise of one's First Amendment rights, a prime purpose of which is precisely to protect speech that offends and upsets. It is not clear that the law, consistent with a meaningful First Amendment, can guarantee a right against being offended. Is there a responsibility in a free society to be thick-skinned?

Men charged with such harassment have recently filed a number of countersuits alleging frivolous or unfounded lawsuits by women, such as the suit won by political scientist C. Harmon Zeigler against his university. It is unclear whether this will discourage more frivolous litigation in this area. The Jones case against Clinton was not reassuring in this regard.

Female critics of the goals and policies of the feminist movement include not only traditionally oriented women who aspire to domestic and childrearing roles but also women who consider themselves feminists and are very active in professional roles. Women such as Camille Paglia and Katie Roithe argue that the feminist portrayal of women as a victimized group demeans them. Roithe, in her much-discussed book, *The Morning After,* argues that the concept of sexual harassment as an "actionable offense" (one over which one can file a lawsuit) implies that women, unlike men, are incapable of warding off unwanted sexual advances.[30] The legal protection of women against the broadened conceptualization of sexual harassment demeans the strength and independence of women. Thus, the feminist movement remains divided between "equality feminists"—those who wish to abolish sex-based classification in law and policy so that women can be treated equally with men—and "difference feminists," who wish to emphasize the distinct status and needs of women as a victimized group in need of special protection and treatment.

Bias against Homosexuals, the Handicapped, and Native Americans

Homosexuals ("gays" and lesbians) are another group claiming to have suffered discrimination in American society and increasingly asserting legal and constitutional rights to combat such discrimination. Homosexuals differ from the other targeted groups in that they are defined on the basis of implied behavior, not attributes.

One of the primary concerns of opponents of homosexual rights is the fear that homosexuals will somehow influence or recruit heterosexual but impressionable children to join their ranks. This fear conflicts with the prevailing psychological opinion that homosexuality is more an involuntary than a conscious choice, by either school-age children or adults. A study done in 1991, moreover, concluded that there are measurable genetic differences between the brains of homosexual men and those of heterosexual men. The implication of this study is that one is born with one's sexual orientation and that orientation will be unaffected by any system of rewards and punishments. Therefore, it does not make sense to regard homosexuality as something that criminal law can deter. The study also suggests that the danger of heterosexual minors being "recruited" into the homosexual community is overstated and virtually nonexistent.

An Oklahoma law typified the widespread efforts to bar or remove homosexuals from teaching positions. The law criminalized "advocating, soliciting, or promoting public or private homosexual activity in such a manner that creates a substantial risk that such conduct will come to the attention of school children . . . ." Note that the law criminalized the advocacy of homosexuality, not the attributes of being a homosexual. A U.S. court of appeals struck down the law on the grounds that advocacy cannot be criminalized (especially when it is not carried out in a context of incitement). The Supreme Court upheld this ruling in 1985.

However, efforts continue to bar homosexuals from leadership or role model positions relative to young people. For example, the Boy Scouts of America have a ban on avowed homosexuals in scout leadership positions. Gay rights advocates challenged this ban, but the Supreme Court upheld it in *Boy Scouts of America v. Dale*.[31] Dale was a gay activist who sought a position as assistant scoutmaster. He had an outstanding record as a former scout, reaching the rank of Eagle Scout, and was therefore otherwise well-qualified for the post. The Court treated the Boy Scouts as a private organization and the issue as one of freedom of association.

In 1993, incoming President Bill Clinton sought to gain acceptance for homosexuals in the military by executive order. This raised such a critical reaction in the country, not to mention among most military personnel, that Clinton had to back off from his original intention and accept a compromise plan. The plan was that the military would no longer inquire into the sexual orientation of their personnel or recruits; hence, gay recruits could elect to serve as long as they did not make that orientation public, the so-called "don't ask, don't tell" policy. However, gays are still subject to dismissal if they emerge "from the closet" or are caught in homosexual acts. In the course of the debate, it was revealed that many gay people had served with valor and distinction in this nation's wars; however, many feared that the presence of gays in such close and often intimate quarters would detract from the central mission of the military. Moreover, reports on the implementation of the policy indicate that some military officers have circumvented the intent of the policy by putting pressure on suspected homosexuals to reveal their orientation and then proceeding to discharge them on a less-than-honorable basis.

In the 1986 case of *Bowers v. Hardwick*, the Court upheld the Georgia sodomy statute with reference to its ban on homosexual behavior, a statute that criminalizes sex "against the laws of nature." A year later, the Court refused to review a case out of Texas upholding that state's more narrowly drawn ban on homosexual behavior.[32] Lower federal courts, however, have upheld the rights of homosexuals in a number of cases, particularly those of military personnel dismissed for revealing their sexual orientation. These cases challenge the "don't ask, don't tell" policy; they are moving toward the Supreme Court for final resolution.

The movement toward greater social tolerance of homosexuals and toward reducing the discrimination they suffer in law and social policy has received a setback in the past few years because of the spread of the contagious and nearly uniformly fatal disease, acquired immune deficiency syndrome, or AIDS. Homosexual men have constituted one of the high-risk groups in the United States, and they were widely perceived as one of the major sources of contagion, which generated widespread fear in the population. While there is a lack of certainty in this regard, the consensus among medical experts is that the disease spreads readily through a kind of sexual activity especially prevalent among male homosexuals and through sharing of contaminated needles among intravenous drug users. Medical experts reassure us that casual contact (drinking fountains, toilet seats, and so on) would not transmit the disease. However, because of perceived uncertainty about transmission and the fatal nature of the disease, the public is in many cases not reassured. This has led to public pressure to identify and isolate homosexuals, costing them their jobs and the right to function in the broader society. It has even led to the denial of the right to attend school to hemophiliac children who have contracted the infection through the transfusion of contaminated blood products. The question is whether the AIDS issue is perceived as a civil rights for homosexuals issue or a public health issue.

The perception of AIDS as a "gay disease," particularly in the 1980s, led some members of the public, fearful of the disease and seeking a scapegoat, to blame and want to punish this group. The shared use of needles by intravenous drug users is now the most important factor in the spread of AIDS. Although the incidence of AIDS among the general heterosexual population is still small, it is rising as a proportion of AIDS cases.

The specific policy issues related to AIDS and homosexuality involve the delicate balance of the right of homosexuals and of persons with AIDS to live out their lives free from harassment, with the public right to all possible protection against a usually fatal affliction. Yet, some people lack confidence in the thoroughness and reliability of such screening. Public identification of carriers of the virus and identification of their sexual partners would help people who are sexually active to protect themselves from contracting the infection, but it would subject such carriers to public harassment and social ostracism. Proposals for mandatory testing of some sectors of the population carry the same potential benefits and risks. Such proposals also raise the questions of whom to test and at what cost. Another problem with proposals for mandatory testing is the fact that the tests are imperfect. Not only would the test fail to detect some people carrying the virus, it would incorrectly turn out positive for some noninfected people. These noninfected "positives" would be subject to the same mental anguish and social ostracism as those who actually carry the virus. These issues involve the balancing of the right of persons with AIDS and of homosexuals to confidentiality regarding their sexual activity and the right of the public to protection.

Defining new victims: The handicapped and the new disability. Handicapped people have recently become a visible minority with an agenda of demands. The nature of their demands, however, differs considerably from those of the aforementioned groups. The demands of the handicapped concentrate on access to public places and various public benefits—for example, demands for ramps where only stairs had been present, the availability of material in Braille for the blind, closed-captioned television for the hearing impaired, and the like. There is much less concern for proportional equality, the placement of set or targeted proportions of handicapped people in valued roles. The concern of the leaders of the handicapped appears to fit the idea of equalizing opportunity and competition rather than the idea of equality of results. The goals are the amelioration of the present effects of their disabilities rather than any compensation for the effects of past discrimination, and so their claims have generated less controversy than have those of the other groups previously discussed.

The most important legislation protecting the rights of persons with disabilities is the Americans with Disabilities Act of 1990. Its primary provisions extend to handicapped persons the kinds of protection granted to minorities and women in the 1964 Civil Rights Act. This legislation prohibits discrimination because of disability in employment, public services, and public accommodations. In employment, a qualified disabled person is one who, with or without reasonable accommodations, can perform the essential functions of a particular job. The law also requires new buses and trains, as well as public buildings, to be accessible to the disabled, and it mandates communications companies to operate relay systems that will allow speech- and hearing-impaired persons access to telephone services.

As with the concepts of rape and sexual harassment previously discussed, the concept of disability has undergone a definitional expansion to cover not only the lame, the halt, and the blind, but a plethora of claims of learning disabilities and other dysfunctional attributes beyond the universally recognized and classically defined mental disorders such as schizophrenia and depression. The EEOC announced a ruling that the aforementioned Disabilities Act will cover not only physical, but also mental disabilities, including a range of learning disorders. For many of the newly claimed learning disabilities, there are no standard tests or indicators. The act defines learning disabilities as "a disorder in which one or more basic psychological processes involved in understanding or using language . . . may manifest itself in an imperfect ability to listen, think, speak, read, write . . . ." Accommodations have been mandated to covered individuals. For example, a college was required to waive a math requirement for a business major who was afflicted with dyscalculia—a math disability. The New York Board of Law Examiners was required in July 1997 to provide one Marilyn Bartlett unlimited time to take the exam, a special private room, and other amenities because she was putatively "afflicted" with a reading disability called "phonological processing." The issue here is whether a person who, for whatever reason, cannot read at a normal level should be certified as a competent attorney. Secondly, critics fear that colleges and employers must now accommodate failure and mental incompetence because it has been redefined in clinical terms. For example, "premature closure, belief perseverance, resistance to new ideas, dogmatism about beliefs," has been identified as "dysrationality" in the October 1993 *Journal of Learning Disabilities*. Professionals in the field disagree as to the reality of these newly conceptualized pathologies. Would the above person simply be closed-minded? The expansion of the conceptualization of a handicap to which society must provide accommodations is, to the critics of this trend, a way of shifting blame and responsibility for failure. It is less humiliating to claim that you are a victim of dysgraphia than to admit that you are poor at grammar.[33]

Native Americans. Native Americans constitute another group histori-cally subject to oppression by the dominant culture. From Plymouth, Massa-chusetts, to Wounded Knee, South Dakota, their numbers were systematically reduced, and they were forced onto desolate and often infertile reservations. Countless western films caricatured Native Americans as malevolent and igno-rant savages. Their standard of living is substantially below the national norm, and they suffer from structural unemployment, alcoholism, and other symptoms of alienation.

In 1991, Native Americans took up as a target of protest the names of cer-tain athletic teams. When the Atlanta Braves went to the World Series, and again in early 1992 when the Washington Redskins went to the Super Bowl, demon-strations were organized around the events. Defenders argued that the team names were traditional and had never been meant to disparage, and that, in any case, the protests begged the issue of the undeniably deep social and economic problems of the Native Americans. The five hundredth anniversary of Christopher Columbus's voyage of discovery also became an opportunity to debate the effect of American society on the original population.

POLICY EVALUATION: THE DRIVE
FOR PROPORTIONAL EQUALITY

The impact of public policy on the issues of inequality examined in the preceding section is complex, but focusing on two important areas—busing for racial balance and racial preference programs—will tell us much about present general trends.

Busing for Racial Balance

Some argue that because students have always been bused to school, court-ordered busing imposes no particular hardship or social cost. The opposition to such bus-ing to achieve racial balance must therefore reveal an opposition to the goal of school desegregation itself. Opponents of busing, regardless of their high-flown rhetoric, are widely regarded by proponents as thinly veiled bigots. Although this is doubtless an accurate description of many opponents of busing, it is not an ac-curate description of all of them.

First, there is a cost to busing for racial balance. In the case of Charlotte-Mecklenburg, the district court's order necessitated doubling the existing bus fleet at an additional cost of $1.5 million. Although only 27 percent of the pupils were bused to school before the order, 61 percent were bused after the order. To the monetary cost must be added the expenditure of time as a resource, an expendi-ture that can vary from around a half-hour each way in smaller communities to several hours per day for some of those bused in Los Angeles. The student either loses school time or must leave home earlier and return later, time that may be used more productively elsewhere. Thus, at best, busing is a brief inconvenience, and frequently it can make significant inroads into the pupil's day, curtailing time available for extracurricular activities.

Obviously, an important policy question is whether such busing produces social benefits that can justify the social cost. The answer may depend on what busing is supposed to achieve. Is it supposed to balance schools racially to bring about actual social interaction among racial groups? Alternatively, is its purpose restricted to upgrading the school performance of designated groups? Busing can bring about racially balanced schools without creating actual integration. Frequently, schools group students in classes according to previous test scores or grades (tracking) so that the higher-achieving middle-class students take college preparatory academic subjects, and lower-achieving minority students take vocational education or remedial courses. This practice, of course, defeats the purpose envisioned by believers in the Coleman Report, the intermingling of high and low achievers. The categorization of low achievers becomes a self-sustaining one as those students continue in school unexposed to the material they need to master to be reclassified on subsequent tests.

As to whether busing has had any impact on academic performance, the evidence is at best mixed and inconclusive. Sociologist David Armor published an empirical study that concluded that after several years of busing the academic performance of desegregated African-American students showed no significant improvement.[34] Others have criticized Armor's findings, claiming that his conclusions do not necessarily follow from the evidence and that his work does not recognize busing's importance for the goal of an integrated society. It is certainly true that Armor's work is not conclusive on this topic, but to attack his work because the conclusions are inconvenient for one's goals is not a rejection of those conclusions on scientific grounds.[35] Meanwhile, Christine Rossell has inquired into the question of whether objection to busing is merely a disguised objection to attending schools with African Americans. Rossell finds that considerations like travel distances and the achievement records of the receiving school are better predictors of resistance to busing than the percentage of African Americans in a school.[36]

It seems fair to say that busing has not yet provided the educational panacea for underachieving minorities that its supporters may have desired. Beyond the problem of tracking within the schools, the hostility and other negative emotions generated on this issue by those concerned could impede the kind of social interaction among the races that busing was supposed to bring about and that the Coleman Report suggested as a tool for upgrading the school performance of underachievers. Moreover, as Coleman himself warned a few years later, busing may exacerbate white movement out of the city school districts to the suburbs, a trend that has the effect of increasing segregation.

The impact of such de facto segregation is even greater today than it was in the 1960s, at least legally speaking, as the effectiveness of busing as a tool to achieve racial balance in the schools of many northern urban areas was severely curtailed by the more conservative Burger Court in the mid-1970s. In *Milliken v. Bradley* (1974), the Court held that busing could not be required across school district lines.[37] In many metropolitan areas, whites have moved to the suburbs with their own independent school districts, and so African Americans now dominate the population of the city proper, a phenomenon known as "white flight." In the famous and especially contentious case of Judge Arthur Garrity's imposition of busing on Boston, the percentage of white students attending the Boston schools plummeted from 64 percent when the busing order was handed down in 1970 to only 18 percent by 1994. After twenty-four costly and tumultuous years of busing, the index of racial isolation of the average African-American child in the Boston schools actually increased. A number of major American cities have African-American majorities or a very large African-American minority citizenry. Thus Chicago, with a population slightly less than 50 percent African American in 1989, has a public school population that is over two-thirds African American. Washington, D.C., had only 4 percent non-Hispanic whites in their public schools in the 1993 to 1994 school year, Detroit had 6.6 percent, and Chicago had 11.4 percent.[38]

Trends and projections show that inner cities are overwhelmingly African American, with the suburbs overwhelmingly white. Thus, because city boundaries frequently constitute the school district boundaries, moving students about within mostly African-American cities or nearly all-white suburbs will not contribute much to the racial balance of the schools. Moreover, some scholars express doubts that racial balance is the most important goal in engineering better schools. A majority of white parents and nearly half of the African-American parents in polls express a preference for the school closest to home to better facilitate parental involvement in their child's education.

Despite the foregoing doubts, supporters defend busing as the only available remedy to the widespread reality of racial isolation in America's public schools. Stating that busing is ineffectively implemented by allowing its purpose to be defeated by tracking or suburban de facto segregation does not necessarily condemn the potential of busing itself.

Whether or not it is actually a cost-efficient means of achieving widely agreed-upon goals of public policy, reliance on busing to achieve racial balance has declined in recent years in favor of alternative methods such as the use of magnet schools. Magnet schools are schools in target group neighborhoods that offer special or enriched programs and activities to attract students from outside those neighborhoods. Busing, however, remains an issue of great symbolic and emotional content: a commitment to busing has been widely perceived by African-American leaders and their supporters as inseparable from a commitment to the broader goal of racial equality, making it difficult to question the efficacy of one without seeming to oppose the other. Moreover, the courts have officially declared busing to be an imperative of the Constitution and have expended some of their capital of legitimacy for it. Busing is still the law of the land, and it would be difficult for the courts to back down and reverse themselves on this point without damaging their own legitimacy. Nevertheless, the Court does not have to turn around completely in order to make changes in the status of busing. For example, in a 1991 case, *Board of Education of Oklahoma City Public Schools v. Dowell,* the Supreme Court ruled that school districts can be freed from court desegregation orders if they have complied in "good faith" with such orders and have eliminated the vestiges of segregation "to the extent practicable."[39] The key issue will be the ability of school districts to convince federal judges that they have met this test but, as previously noted, the trend appears to be away from court ordered busing as a remedy for racial imbalance in the schools.

Retreat on Racial Preference Programs

The *Bakke* case, discussed earlier, appeared to cast doubt on the validity of direct quotas in educational admissions. In *Kaiser Aluminum v. Weber* and *United Steelworkers of America v. Weber* (1979), the Court confronted the legality of a voluntary quota to racially balance a training program leading to promotion at Kaiser Aluminum.[40] Weber's allegation was that Title VII of the 1964 Civil Rights Act forbade the company, with the union's concurrence, from voluntarily adopting such a racially preferential program that involuntarily excluded Weber from an opportunity to which he otherwise would have been entitled. That law forbade a covered employer from discriminating against any individual with respect to his compensation, terms, condition, or privileges of employment because of such individual's "race, color, religion, sex, or national origin; or to limit, segregate or classify his employees . . . in any way which would . . . adversely affect his status as an employee because of such individual's race, color, religion, sex, or national origin."

The Kaiser program, which led to promotions, selected individuals based on seniority. However, for every white selected, one African American had to be selected regardless of seniority. Thus, though Weber was not selected, some African Americans with less seniority than Weber were selected. There was no evidence or allegation of previous discrimination by either Kaiser or the union.

In holding that Title VII did not prohibit Kaiser's racial preference program, Justice Brennan, speaking for the Court, distinguished between the literal meaning of the law and the purposes that he inferred Congress had in mind in adopting that law. Brennan saw the purpose of Congress as correcting the problems of African-American unemployment and African-American underrepresentation in management or higher-status jobs. He reasoned that because the program aimed at this purpose, Congress could not have intended Title VII to preclude the program, even though that is what the words of the law say.

Careful examination of the legislative debate over the adoption of the law may lead to the conclusion that Congress intended Title VII to prevent race from being used as a basis for hiring, firing, or employment status, and at least one scholar, quoting the leaders of the House and Senate in this debate, made a powerful case for that interpretation.[41] The author cites extensive references from the *Congressional Record* showing that the bill's authors gave repeated assurances to congressional leaders that it was intended to outlaw all discrimination by race, for or against any given racial group. The bill's chief sponsor, Hubert Humphrey, offered to eat the bill if anyone could find a requirement in it for an employer to hire based on percentage or quota.

The apparent support for affirmative action in general, and even for the quotas that one might detect in *Weber,* was reinforced by the *Fullilove* decision (1980), which upheld a policy of setting aside 10 percent of all city contracts for businesses owned by minorities, regardless of who was the lowest bidder.[42] In *Johnson v. Transportation Agency of Santa Clara County,* the Court upheld the hiring of a woman as a truck dispatcher over admittedly better-qualified men to correct a general pattern of societal discrimination against women, even though there was no allegation of a pattern of past discrimination by the particular agency.[43] Yet, other cases in the 1980s did not support affirmative action in employment. For example, in the *Stotts* (1984) case, the Court rejected a claim that relying on a seniority principle to decide who to lay off from an Ohio fire department violated the equal protection rights of African Americans who, being the most recently hired in an affirmative action drive and thus the least senior, were disproportionately among those laid off.[44] The Court held in *Wygant v. Board of Education*[45] that a rule requiring nonminority teachers to be laid off before minority teachers regardless of other factors violated the equal protection clause of the Fourteenth Amendment, a ruling that put the Court clearly in opposition to racial preference plans. The *Wygant* opinion would appear to support the claims of Sharon Taxman in her suit against the Piscataway Board of Education discussed earlier. Because the African-American and white teachers in this case were very nearly equal, making it a clear case of racial preference without a pattern of previous discrimination by that institution, supporters of racial preference plans feared that the Court, in light of the *Wygant* precedent, would strike down racial preference itself. Therefore, they settled with Taxman to avoid a Court decision on what was for them a strategically bad case.

Three 1989 decisions (*Richmond v. Croson, Wards Cove Packing Co. v. Atonio,* and *Martin v. Wilks*) reinforced the trend of weakening support for affirmative action.[46] In these cases, the Rehnquist Court moved to limit the policy's force and effectiveness. For example, in *Martin v. Wilks,* the Court gave firefighters in Birmingham, Alabama, the right to challenge in court a consensual hiring and promotion plan negotiated between African Americans and the city personnel board and approved by a court. The ability of members of nontargeted groups to challenge voluntary affirmative action plans in court could discourage negotiating such plans.

The *Croson* case concerned a Richmond, Virginia, statute requiring that 30 percent of all city contracts go to firms in which a targeted minority controlled at least 51 percent. These targeted groups, according to the statute, include "citizens of the United States who are African American, Spanish-speaking, Oriental, Indians, Eskimos, or Aleuts." Apparently, Richmond modeled its statute after the *Fullilove* statute in choosing favored groups, although the groups other than African Americans amounted to just 1.82 percent of Richmond's population. The statute clearly aimed at African Americans, who account for about half of that city's population. The J. A. Croson Company challenged the law, and the Supreme Court overturned it. In July 1995, the Court reinforced *Croson* with their ruling in *Adarand Constructors v. Peña.*[47] A five-to-four majority, speaking through Justice O'Connor, held that affirmative action plans must satisfy a "compelling public interest." The parties involved must direct that interest at redressing specific discrimination. Merely creating "a more diverse society" will not pass that "strict judicial scrutiny." This criterion places much of the network of affirmative action programs in constitutional jeopardy. The case concerns a business challenging a construction contract awarded to a contractor that subcontracted guardrail construction to an African-American-owned firm that was not the low bidder. (Ironically, the challenger in this case was Hispanic.) The "rebuttable presumption" underlying minority set asides is that minority-owned businesses are necessarily disadvantaged. Thus, white-owned businesses may try to refute the presumption by showing they are more disadvantaged, a difficult task considering the ambiguous definition of the concept of "disadvantaged." The Court rejected that presumption.

The 1991 Civil Rights Act and the judicial assault on racial preference.
The issue of affirmative action or reverse discrimination remains far from settled. The key issue that emerged from the *Johnson* case and from the *Croson* case is whether employers or government may implement racial preference plans in the absence of evidence of specific discrimination by the firm or institution instituting

the plan. In addition, if past discrimination must be shown, what kinds of evidence may be used as the basis of that conclusion. The policy instituted by the city of Richmond rested on a statistical discrepancy between the percentage of contracts awarded to MBEs (minority business enterprises) and the percentage of the targeted groups in that community. Some argue that a more realistic policy might flow from any discrepancy between the percentage of contracts awarded to MBEs and the percentage of MBEs among the firms seeking such contracts. The issue is whether the first kind of statistical discrepancy justifies the inference that discrimination is the necessary cause. The *Croson* and *Wards Cove* cases showed that the Court was unprepared to accept simple statistical evidence to justify racial preference policies.

Congress, then controlled by the Democratic Party, sought legislative reversal of the *Croson* and *Wards Cove* decisions in the Civil Rights Act of 1991. The essential provision of the act is to reverse the burden of proof in charges of employment discrimination and thereby to render it easier for minorities to initiate and win litigation in such disputes. The law requires employers charged with discrimination on the basis of a statistical underrepresentation of targeted groups in their work force to justify their hiring criteria in terms of job relevance or "business necessity" as in the *Griggs* ruling previously discussed, a requirement that effectively negates the *Wards Cove* decision.

Critics branded the legislation "a quota bill," a charge its supporters denied. The bill specifically outlaws quotas. However, it made statistical disparities in the work force prima facie evidence of employment discrimination and placed the burden of proof on employers to show business necessity for such disparities. The underlying assumption of using statistical disparities as evidence of discrimination is that in the absence of such discrimination each social role would represent all groups proportionately; that certain people from certain kinds of cultural or religious backgrounds, for instance, are not more or less disposed than people from other backgrounds to pursue certain social or occupational roles. This may not be true. For example, the Cleveland Symphony was under pressure to increase its African-American membership in light of the large African-American population of the city. However, the talented musicians from the African-American community tended to pursue nonclassical forms of music; hence, the pool from which the orchestra could draw was not the African-American population of the city, but a very small pool of classically trained musicians.

The effect of the provision putting the burden of proof on employers to justify statistical imbalance, opponents of the bill argued, is to invite a deluge of litigation against employers in whose work force target group members are statistically underrepresented. The result would be lawsuits that are expensive, time-consuming, and stressful even if one wins. Therefore, it would be rational for employers to try to avert the increasing prospect of being sued by avoiding statistical disparities in their workplaces; in other words, to institute "voluntary" quotas. In this manner, the law that specifically stated that employers are not legally obliged to hire based on quotas in effect might place great pressure on employers to voluntarily impose such quotas. In effect, the *Wards Cove* and *Croson* decisions were overturned, and the burden of proof is upon employers to justify any statistical discrepancies in their work force.

Challenges to Racial Preference in Higher Education

A case emanating from the University of Texas Law School challenged the racial preference plans implicitly approved in the *Bakke* decision. In this case, Cheryl Hopwood and four others claimed the school's admission policy discriminates against whites.[48] The case grew out of the following facts: The Law School, with many more applicants than it can accept, is highly selective. The median LSAT score of white students admitted was the ninety-third percentile, and the mean GPA was 3.5. As of 1992, the median LSAT score for African Americans was the seventy-eighth percentile. These criteria would have admitted only one of the 280 African-American applicants, resulting in a virtually all-white student body. The admissions process passed over nearly seven hundred higher-scoring white applicants before denying the first African Americans admission; therefore, race was clearly the deciding factor in selecting African Americans over whites. The school set a different set of criteria for target group members in order to meet a goal of 10 percent Mexican Americans and 5 percent African Americans. These criteria had the result that the combined GPA/LSAT score that meant automatic rejection for a white applicant was higher than the score that meant automatic acceptance for an African-American applicant. Although race was one factor in the admissions process for the University of Texas Law School, the school insisted that it admitted African Americans that were qualified to meet the academic demands of a legal education. Yet, although some 90 percent of the regular admittees from that school passed the bar exam on the first try, the corresponding rate for the African Americans admitted under the race-sensitive selection criteria was a pass rate of less than 50 percent. According to an associate dean, it was an embarrassment that the school's pass rate was below that of "even lowly Texas Tech." The question for the courts here, as in the *Piscataway* case previously discussed, was whether race could, consistent with the Fourteenth Amendment, be the deciding factor in plaintiff Hopwood's rejection by the law school. The Supreme Court declined to review, thus letting stand a decision by the Fifth Circuit Court of Appeals that racial preference in admission to that school violated the equal protection clause, a decision that logically places many racial preference plans vulnerable to constitutional challenge. For the present, college admissions may not use race as a criterion in three states covered by the Fifth Circuit: Texas, Mississippi, and Louisiana. Without that factor, the University of Texas Law School became virtually an all-white institution as even well-qualified African Americans elected to apply elsewhere, and the percentage of target group students in other public universities in the circuit declined sharply.

Two cases involving the University of Michigan in 2001 and 2002 (*Grutter v. Bollinger* and *Gratz v. Bollinger*) challenge the *Hopwood* principle. These cases, emanating from the sixth judicial circuit, are not legally bound by the *Hopwood* decision in the fifth circuit. The trial courts differently decided the two *Bollinger* cases, which were argued before the Court of Appeals in December 2001. Experts expect the U.S. Supreme Court to grant *certiorari* (a court order for the lower court records, meaning the Supreme Court has decided to hear the case), and a decision is expected in late 2002. The university admits students on a point system. An excellent essay on the admission form is worth three points and an SAT score over 1360 out of a possible 1600 is worth twelve points, but being a member of the right target group is worth twenty points, more than any other single factor.

The "compelling public need" used to justify race-based selection, the criterion previously discussed for overriding the principle of equality under law and using the suspect category of race, is diversity defined in terms of race. Critics charge that race-based selection ignores other possible criteria of diversity such as religion, socioeconomic background, or even ideas. The most far-reaching assault on race-based selection, an assault led by African-American entrepreneur Ward Connerly, was in the form of a constitutional referendum in the state of California that passed handily in 1996 and was upheld by the Supreme Court in 1997. Proposition 209, known as the California Civil Rights Initiative, reads as follows:

> Neither the State of California nor any of its political subdivisions or agents shall use race, sex, color, ethnicity or national origin as criterion for either discriminating against, or granting preferential treatment to, any individual or group in the operation of the state's system of public employment, public education or public contracting.[49]

Clearly, this proposition, written by a professor of Anthropology at California State University at Hayward, effectively ends affirmative action in its most recognized forms (either quotas or racial preference plans for hiring and firing in state agencies) by the state of California and nationally if it is adopted in other states. Some argue that to increase target group numbers without using either quota or racial preference plans, state agencies will have to substantially lower their selection criteria. California has in the past been a bellwether for the rest of the country; hence, it is likely that other forms of it will begin appearing across the country, as most recently in Florida. As of 2002, Ward Connerly is leading a nationwide movement in opposition to race-based selection. His claim as an African American is that such policies demean the many African Americans who achieve on merit and ability and that they exacerbate opposition to other legitimate objectives of the civil rights movement.

The impact of challenging race-based selection. An empirical study by Linda Wightman on the effect of race-based selection on diversity in the nation's law schools reveals that in 1990 to 1991, of the 3,435 African Americans admitted to law schools that year, only one-fifth would have been admitted to the schools that accepted them without racial preference. Among the more prestigious law schools, 17.5 times as many African-American students were admitted as would have gotten in if race had not been a factor.[50] Advocates of affirmative action are angry that many target group members who would have had the opportunity to attend law school will not, making for a less ethnically diverse student body and profession. Critics of affirmative action argue that these data confirm that people who get in by race-based selection are less able academically, and the data on differential rates of passing the bar exam suggest that the weaker levels of preparation are handicaps that race-based admittees do not frequently succeed in overcoming. The supporters of affirmative action are correct in that the student body of the selective professional and graduate schools lost almost all of the African American and Hispanic student body after abandoning racial preference plans. Supporters of the *Hopwood* decision and California's Proposition 209 argue that minority students who can no longer be admitted to the highly selective programs under a racial preference plan can enroll in a less-selective institution where their chances of failure substantially lower. It is a fact that, although the percentage of African Americans admitted to higher education has greatly increased under affirmative action plans, they tend to drop out without getting their degree at a much greater rate than whites. It is uncertain what psychological costs the individual who enters a program beyond his or her abilities and skills and consequently fails incurs.

FUTURE ALTERNATIVES: THE CHANGING CONCEPTION OF EQUALITY

The Debate over Affirmative Action

The racial preference plans previously discussed are part of the entire spectrum of affirmative action programs that date from the late 1960s, when government instituted a number of specific policies to redistribute social benefits to those groups who had less than their share—the goal of proportional equality.

Affirmative action describes a series of policies or active government efforts to bring into valued roles members of designated disadvantaged groups in rough proportion to their percentage of the population at large. Advocates defend it primarily in terms of compensatory justice. That is, justice requires that these groups receive compensation for the harm done to them by previous social policies. It announced the intention of the national government no longer to be neutral toward disproportionate distribution of society's values, whether among racial or ethnic groups, between the sexes, or in the sense of underrepresentation of these groups in valued social roles. Sometimes affirmative action has taken the form of direct government action, as in the preferential hiring or promotion of government employees from among the groups designated for such benefits. More often, it has been the encouragement of others to take such steps, by the promise or threat of granting or withholding federal funds or by direct government order.

Affirmative action includes a number of government actions, regulations, and judicial decisions. The idea most identified with affirmative action and its most controversial manifestation is quotas, the setting aside a fixed percentage of social values for members of the target group, such as the requirement that a given percentage of those hired, promoted, or admitted to desired roles must be from designated groups. Members of the target groups pursue these values as members of a separate applicant pool. Secondly, affirmative action may mean granting some form of preferential consideration to members of target groups. In such racial preference plans, target group members receive benefits over nontarget group members only when other qualifications were equal. The possibility would still exist that no members of target groups would receive the values in question. Thirdly, the meaning of the term can include a readjustment of standards that define a society to accommodate the inability of a proportionate number of targeted groups to meet those standards. A 1979 California case, *Larry P. v. Riles,* banned the use of IQ tests for African Americans in the public schools. The judge reasoned that "Black children's intelligence may be manifested in ways that the tests do not show. . . ."[51] The decision by a Michigan federal judge to require courses in "Black English" as an alternative to conventional English in the Detroit public schools is an example of this. Another illustration is the court challenge to the tests of reading skills, passage of which is required for a high school diploma irrespective of high school grades. Most states now require minimum competency tests for students and teachers (discussed in Chapter 9). African Americans and Hispanics fail such tests at a disproportionate rate.

This implicit assumption that it is unfair to hold African Americans to the standards of the European or Western-based civilization on which this nation has operated also underlies the rationale for Afrocentrism, a movement that goes beyond stressing the role of African Americans in American history and culture to the claim that most of the great cultural, philosophical, and scientific advances in the world originated with Africans. Proponents of this theory contend that Alexander the Great stole these ideas from a library in black-dominated Egypt. Designed to enhance the self-esteem of African-American students accustomed to failure, Afrocentrist curricula influence the educational experience of a growing number of young African Americans. Critics express concern that this influence is done at the expense of those students acquiring the skills and knowledge they will need to function in this society. The academic qualifications of the leaders of these programs have been called into question. For example, Hunter Adams, who wrote the essay on science in the most widely used Afrocentric textbook, *African American Baseline Essays,* has only a high school diploma. Abena Walker, who was paid $165,000 to train Washington, D.C., teachers in Afrocentrism, had only a degree from a bogus "university" that she created herself. Critics of the Afrocentric curriculum also express concern that at root, Afrocentrism constitutes an attack on the fundamental Western concept that facts and science possess an objectivity that is independent of culture. As Marimba Ali writes in *Yurugu: An African Centered Critique of European Cultural Thought and Behavior,* "Our task is to throw into question European scientific epistemology." Martin Bernal of Cornell argues that evidence from cults and legends "is not categorically less valid than from archeology." Thus, instead of imparting the tools and the ability to use them that young African Americans will need to function in a modern Western society, Afrocentrists choose to use scarce educational resources attacking the validity of those tools.

The tactic of attacking selection criteria that are racially and gender neutral on their face, but that have a discriminatory impact, came to a head in early 1989 when the National Collegiate Athletic Association adopted a new rule, Proposition 42, regarding the eligibility of incoming freshmen for athletic scholarships. The new rule was that a student must have at least a 2.0 GPA in addition to 700 on the SAT or 15 on the ACT to be eligible for such a scholarship. This tightened up the old rule, which granted eligibility if the scholarship recipient met either one of these requirements. A number of African-American leaders, led by then-Georgetown University basketball coach John Thompson, charged that the new policy was discriminatory. An estimated 90 percent of those who would lose scholarships by failing to meet these standards would be African American. Thompson walked off the court before a scheduled game to protest the new policy. Defenders of the policy argue that under the existing standards, colleges admitted many young men for athletics without a reasonable chance of actually graduating, and the lower standards lead colleges to manipulate records to keep academically marginal athletes eligible to play. This controversy raised the old issue of whether such standardized tests disproportionally failed by members of target groups are racially biased or are valid predictors of the probability of academic success.

Support for affirmative action. Those who challenge such traditional performance standards claim that they do not really measure what they purport to measure. They frequently charge that such standards are attributes of the dominant groups in society. These standards perpetuate the existing stratification system. For instance, critics express skepticism that college grade point averages really show one's potential for becoming a good doctor, lawyer, businessperson, or scientist or that the general abilities test given as part of the civil service examination measures one's potential for becoming a good bureaucrat. In other areas such performance standards have been challenged in court, including whether a score on an IQ test is relevant to selecting a good police officer, whether a high school diploma is relevant to selecting power company employees,[52] or whether publications and prestigious degrees are relevant to selecting college teachers. These requirements are questioned in the first place because the targeted disadvantaged groups fail in disproportionate numbers to meet these performance standards, and the gap between those who have more and those who have less widens still further.

The basic defense of affirmative action rests on the continuing impact of previous discrimination. Because it is now recognized that poverty is self-perpetuating both for individuals and across generations, policies that place a group in a disadvantaged position can be blamed for that group's continuing disadvantaged position even after the discriminatory policies themselves have ended.

Another justification for affirmative action policies designed to place a number of members of targeted minorities in valued roles is that they become role models for the youth of their group. Young African Americans, for instance, may be motivated to aim higher if they can see African-American doctors, attorneys, teachers, and executives. Such role models may provide hope of success within the confines of the system and thereby head off pervasive alienation.

The zero-sum aspect of affirmative action programs, the fact that resources assigned to targeted groups must be taken from nontargeted groups (for instance, white men), is defended by claiming that the dominant position of the nontargeted groups was attained at the expense of the subordinate target groups. In other words, whites have become dominant by exploiting African Americans and Hispanics, so whites should pay the cost of correcting the consequences of that exploitation.

Affirmative action programs at professional schools and universities create a racially and ethnically diverse student body, which more closely mirrors that ethnically diverse population with whom the graduates of these schools will have to work and interact. That very process of interaction should lessen the tendency of people from different backgrounds to perceive one another in terms of stereotypes.

Opposition to affirmative action. Despite the compelling logic of the case for affirmative action, such policies remain among the most controversial of our time and generate persisting and often bitter opposition, which sometimes comes from the very people who supported the civil rights movement when its goal was primarily legal equality. The case against affirmative action draws on both logical arguments and the self-interest of groups not favored by the policy.

Perhaps the main logical or philosophical objection to affirmative action is that it seems to deny the principle of equality under law. In the final analysis, affirmative action policies reward or penalize individuals based on who they are— their racial, ethnic, or sexual attributes—rather than on the basis of what they do.

Furthermore, this aspect of affirmative action reintroduces the relevance of racial and ethnic categories as permissible in American legislation. Yet, as was noted in the discussion of equality under law, the struggle to label certain categories as suspect is a liberal and progressive struggle, and the triumph of meritocracy over privilege based on the accidents of birth has been traditionally one of the attributes of both a liberal and a more developed society. Some opponents of affirmative action warn that if race can be used for benign purposes, it will henceforth be more difficult to prevent race from being used in other ways. After all, defining what constitutes a "benign" policy is a judgment by those in power. Thus, critics claim, affirmative action works against the principles of individualism and meritocracy. Moreover, in technologically advanced societies with the high skill levels required to fill more complex social and economic roles, modification of the principles of meritocracy seems to threaten overall productivity.

Some opponents of affirmative action question the selection of its beneficiaries. They argue that many groups have suffered serious discrimination. It was described earlier how Asian immigrants once suffered worse discrimination and more disadvantages than Mexican immigrants did; yet the latter are designated as affirmative action beneficiaries, but the former are frequently classed with the white majority. Poles, Irish, Jews, and Italians all in their turn suffered social and/or legal discrimination; yet, none of these groups receives affirmative action benefits. By what criterion, affirmative action opponents ask, are some groups selected for benefits?

The attribute that distinguishes the target groups seems to be that statistically they have lower success levels than other groups do; they have lower mean incomes, lower mean indices of socioeconomic status, and higher levels of poverty. In other words, the recipients of affirmative action benefits are members of groups that, taken together, have been unable to overcome the impact of discrimination. It is a policy that rewards the lack of competitive success and achievement.

The definition of affirmative action recipients raises two key observations from critics. First, individual members of groups not targeted by affirmative action often suffer real penalties as the disadvantaged group receives compensation. The resources of society are finite; when a resource goes to one who would not have earned it by meeting society's performance standards, it must be denied to another who would have met them. For each African American, Hispanic, or other designated beneficiary admitted in law school, medical school, a management-training program, or some other upward-mobility program to which that person would not otherwise have been admitted, a member of a nontargeted group who may otherwise have "earned" admission must be kept out. To members of non-targeted groups who also see themselves as victims of systematic persecution, such as Jews and Asians, such policies generate particular hostility. These people see their group as, in effect, penalized for its success in overcoming the effects of past discrimination. This would seem to be inconsistent with the approval of competitive success widely identified as a basic attribute of American culture and a key feature of the equality of opportunity.

Members of such groups deny that their success is simply a result of exploiting African Americans and Hispanics. As we pointed out, many of the more successful groups have themselves suffered discrimination. Moreover, the cultural dispositions of some groups are more conducive to success in this system than others. For example, David McClelland notes that the childrearing patterns of some groups foster an "achieving personality."[53] In recent years, an explosion of illegitimate teenage pregnancies among members of the underclass in urban slum neighborhoods is both a social tragedy and a major impediment to upward mobility among members of the underclass. Some conservatives argue that persisting marginal socioeconomic status of the underclass is now more a function of their own behaviors than of past social oppression. If so, this weakens the argument for privileges to target groups in the name of compensatory justice.

Many critics ask whether affirmative action policies actually help those members of targeted groups who are most disadvantaged. Affirmative action programs, being race based, assume a perfect correlation between race and other attributes such as socioeconomic status and the ability to compete. Affirmative action policies stipulate that members of certain groups be selected for desired roles without specifically stipulating which individuals may be chosen or what attributes they may or may not possess; that is, these policies tend only to say that they must be members of the designated group. Because those who design and administer affirmative action programs are reluctant to abandon performance standards entirely, those members of the designated groups who are the best qualified by traditional performance standards tend to be the ones selected for desired roles. This means that middle-class African Americans and Hispanics, not hard-core unemployed school dropouts (who are mainly responsible for their group's statistically disadvantaged status), are often the ones who benefit most from affirmative action. This fact illustrates the often-observed weakness of the assumption that what is true for relationships among groups (the white race is better off than the African-American race as a whole) holds true for individuals within those groups. It is, in fact, quite likely that the best nonwhites selected for affirmative action positions may come from less-disadvantaged backgrounds than do those whites they displace, whites who would have only marginally succeeded in being selected by conventional performance standards.

Stephen and Abigail Thernstrom, in a much-discussed 1997 book on America's race problem, present a large body of data indicating a very large measure of African-American progress by social and economic criteria, progress that to a large measure antedated affirmative action. According to the Thernstroms, this progress indicates that African Americans are capable of effectively competing with whites. For example, they note that in 1940 the median annual income for African-American males was 41 percent of that for white males, while by 1970 it had risen to almost 60 percent. The corresponding figures for African-American women were 36 percent and 73 percent. Most of this progress antedated affirmative action, which dates from the mid-1960s. Moreover, while African-American families as of 1995 had only 61 percent of the income level of white families, if one includes only intact or two-parent families, African Americans had 87 percent of the income of whites.[54] Hence, one might infer that the greater tendency toward family instability in the African-American community might account for much of the gap between African Americans and whites rather than the lack of a level playing field that affirmative action programs are designed to rectify.

Underlying the goal of proportional equality that is at the heart of affirmative action is the presumption that in the absence of pervasive and continuing discrimination against target group members, they would attain a proportionate representation in valued social and economic roles. Yet, others suggest that different groups have cultural backgrounds and widely held values that dispose their members to seek certain roles more than others. Without denying that cultures are equally valid and of value, they are not identical and do not disseminate the same values, attitudes, and skills to their progeny. The example of the difficulty of the Cleveland Symphony in finding an African-American classical musician, as previously discussed, is an example of this problem.

It should be noted that some of the opposition to affirmative action programs reflects self-interest rather than principle. Those who are not members of the designated beneficiary groups, such as white men, find that with selected social rewards being set aside for members of designated minority groups, there are fewer rewards for white men to allocate among themselves. Thus, for instance, when corporate personnel departments in a given field succumb to governmental pressure to hire more nonwhites, it becomes harder for white men to find jobs in that field.

African Americans and Jews: A broken alliance. American Jews epitomize this successful minority phenomenon. They populate high-status roles well in excess of their proportion of the population. For example, although comprising only 3 percent of the total population, Jewish teachers constitute nearly half of all Ivy League faculties. Thus, when white men in general are restricted (by quotas favoring minorities) from competing for a stipulated number of academic positions, Jewish men are disproportionately excluded, as they are being partially barred from an area of traditional high employment. Therefore, although Jews helped lead the struggle for legal equality of African Americans—as many legally supported restrictions applied to them as well—Jewish writers and publications have often taken strong editorial stands against the affirmative action direction of the African-American civil rights movement. This opposition has generated tension between these formerly allied ethnic groups, as was manifested in the 1984 and 1988 presidential nomination bids of the Reverend Jesse Jackson. Many in the normally Democratic Jewish community were offended by incidents such as his reference to New York City by the anti-Jewish slur "Hymietown" and his physical embrace of Palestinian leader Yasir Arafat. African Americans currently manifest more anti-Jewish attitudes than do any other American ethnic or racial group, and these attitudes are more common among the younger and better-educated African Americans.[55] Anti-Semitism in other groups generally appears in older and less well-educated people; among African Americans, such attitudes are strengthening over time, whereas they are fading among other groups. It appears that the differences in interests between these two former allies are growing into an emotional, deeply felt antipathy between them.

The mutual hostility was highly visible in the 1990s. Jesse Jackson contributed an anti-Zionist statement to a book sponsored by the League of Arab States. At the City University of New York, paired incidents occurred: The Chair of the Black Studies Department, Leonard Jeffries, Jr., in the course of several anti-Semitic speeches, claimed that Jews had financed the slave trade and that Jews controlled the American media and film industry and conspired to exclude African Americans from both. A philosophy professor, Michael Levin, was telling his classes that African Americans are for genetic reasons less intelligent than whites and that African Americans should be segregated in the New York subways for reasons of public safety. In this same period, anti-Semitic lyrics, often violent, were turning up in the songs of popular rap groups. Neighborhood tensions were high in several cities, most notably in the Crown Heights section of Brooklyn, where large African-American and Hasidic Jewish neighborhoods intersect. Violent demonstrations took place after an African-American child was struck and killed by a van driven by a Hasidic Jew (ironically, an African-American driver had struck and killed a Jewish child in the same neighborhood two years before). A young Hasidic scholar from Australia, Yankel Rosenbaum, was killed by one of the roving mobs and an all-African-American jury released Lemrick Nelson, who bragged about killing Rosenbaum.[56] This mutual antipathy continued in November 1993, when a Nation of Islam leader gave a much-reported speech at Keane College in New Jersey. Among other things, he claimed the Jews owned 75 percent of the slaves in the Old Confederacy, that the Holocaust was justified by the actions of the Jews, and that Jews were "the bloodsuckers of the Black nation," a speech repeated at numerous other colleges in the following months.

Race and Equality

The most clearly discernible trend in the struggle for equality is the evolution of the generally understood meaning of the term, which has changed its goals and issues. The meaning of the term once referred to the struggle for eradication of discrimination based on racial, religious, sexual, or ethnic attributes and of laws or social policy that burden or penalize people on the basis of such attributes. In recent decades, it has come to imply that each identifiable racial or ethnic group and each sex has a right to a proportionate share of the benefits of society. The legitimacy of an uneven distribution of material well-being and of the dominance of certain groups over others has increasingly come under attack.

A changing conception of racism accompanied the changing conception of equality. Traditionally, racism referred to the disposition to classify people based on their race in order to allocate rewards and punishments to them and to make judgments about them. Such a conceptualization would almost seem inconsistent with affirmative action policies discussed in this chapter that identify who is disadvantaged and deserving of special help and allocate benefits on the basis of target group categories. More recently, supporters of target groups have been using the term *symbolic racism* to refer to opposition to programs and policies advocated by target group leaders or to statements not overtly racist as a racial or ethnic slur, but statements to which target group members nonetheless take offense to as "insensitive."[57] Thus, someone who criticizes busing for racial balance or some affirmative action policy may be accused of using such critiques as a cover for deeply held racist attitudes. Of course, the charge of symbolic racism is hard to avoid. One can with care avoid using direct racial slurs, but one may find it more difficult to anticipate those statements or opinions to which some target group member may take offense or regard as insensitive. For example, at the University of Pennsylvania in early 1993, a graduate student, an Israeli named Eden Jacobowitz, shouted to a group of African-American women celebrating beneath his dorm window, "Shut up, you water buffalo!" Jacobowitz had translated an Israeli term that connotes coarseness or crudeness, but has no particular racial connotations. Still, the university pursued Jacobowitz for an entire semester with charges of racist insults under Penn's rigorous speech code.

When a goal of social policy is the redistribution of material well-being, the redistribution of finite values is involved. The benefits accorded to some must be taken from others. What some gain, others must lose. Clearly, there are good arguments for some form of compensatory justice in view of the history of discrimination against certain groups. However, because of the confusion between the bigotry or discrimination directed toward groups and to individuals within those groups, the justice of the matter becomes muddled. The white race may, in the aggregate, be guilty of discrimination, but individuals such as Brian Weber, Cheryl Hopwood, Sharon Taxman, or Alan Bakke pay the debt, even though they may not personally have so discriminated. Nor do the benefits of affirmative action necessarily flow to the most disadvantaged individuals in society. The hard-core unemployed seldom reach professional school under such programs; rather, these programs often benefit middle-class members of designated groups. To change the rules of the game and to deny benefits to the Hopwoods, Webers, and Bakkes of society, benefits to which they were entitled under the old rules, is perceived by some as a denial of their rights.

Yet, minorities do have a right to combat the persisting impact of the history of social discrimination. The point is that rights conflict. The intractable difficulty of the equality issue is that it is not a clear case of right and wrong, but one of conflicting rights. Plausible ethical arguments can and have been constructed to support conflicting claims based on powerful interests. In addition, in an economy in which hopes of perpetual economic growth confront the reality of scarcity and the finite supply of resources, society is increasingly in a zero-sum situation. This means that to the extent that the total supply of benefits is finite, those benefits reallocated to some must come from others. Members of nontargeted groups increasingly perceive that they cannot help target groups without giving up something themselves. Thus, the strongest opposition to affirmative action frequently comes from those segments of white society most likely to be displaced by members of target groups, the middle or lower-middle classes. Members of the upper class are less likely to be so displaced, and therefore the support for affirmative action by so-called "limousine liberals" is without cost. Because of this conflict among plausible rights, issues concerning equality promise to continue to be among the most intractable and divisive of issues facing the country for the indefinite future.

The struggle for equality by African Americans has resulted in an inevitable rise in tensions between African Americans and the rest of society, many of whom perceive the progress of the targeted groups toward greater material well-being as coming at their expense. In particular, many deeply resent racial, ethnic, or gender preference plans. A new phase of the struggle of the less-well-off groups has begun, in which the goal of such groups has shifted from seeking integration or assimilation in the liberal democratic system, as symbolized by the renowned "I have a dream" speech of the Rev. Dr. Martin Luther King, Jr., to challenging the legitimacy of the system itself. Thus, the sympathy of such current African-American leaders as the Rev. Jesse Jackson for third-world antidemocratic leaders such as Fidel Castro or Hafez Assad seems a threat to the dominant system in a way that King's goals of assimilation were not. Thus, despite all of the progress toward equality documented throughout this chapter, tensions between the targeted less-well-off groups and the rest of society remain higher than ever. Highly publicized incidents, such as the conflict between African Americans and Jews previously discussed, exacerbate racial tensions. The question of whether African Americans can receive equal justice in the American judicial system is likely to remain salient for the near future.

Two housing studies in 1991 dramatically revealed just how difficult it is for African Americans and other racial minorities to achieve just treatment. One, conducted by the Federal Reserve Board, found that minority-group homebuyers experience much higher rejection rates than whites on mortgage applications in America's major cities (see Figure 10-6). The other study, conducted for the Department of Housing and Urban Development by Syracuse University, employed three thousand paired African American, white, and Hispanic prospective homebuyers and renters. It found that African Americans experienced some form of discrimination 56 percent of the time they sought to buy and 59 percent of the time they sought to rent a house. Comparable figures for Hispanics were 50 percent and 56 percent, respectively.[58]

The levels of racial antagonism and African-American frustration with continued discrimination and inequality of material well-being exploded in the 1992 Los Angeles riots following the acquittals of the four police officers involved in

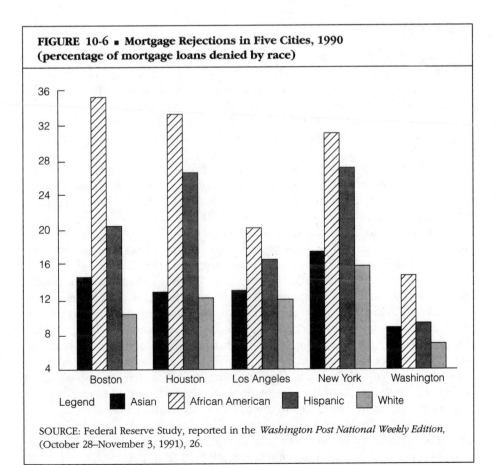

**FIGURE 10-6 ▪ Mortgage Rejections in Five Cities, 1990
(percentage of mortgage loans denied by race)**

Legend ■ Asian ▨ African American ■ Hispanic ▨ White

SOURCE: Federal Reserve Study, reported in the *Washington Post National Weekly Edition,*
(October 28–November 3, 1991), 26.

the beating of African-American motorist Rodney King. They appeared as well as in the celebrations, nearly confined to the African-American community, of the acquittal of accused murderer O. J. Simpson. Simpson's attorney, Johnnie Cochran, had urged the jury to send a message to the white community in the face of a mountain of incriminating evidence. The right of a jury to hand in a verdict in the face of contradictory evidence is known as "jury nullification," an option that was frequently used by southern white juries to free whites who committed crimes against African Americans. Now it appears in defiance of the white criminal justice system. It was also a factor in the acquittal of Lemrick Nelson despite his admitted role in the murder of Yankel Rosenbaum (discussed previously). Not only was there generalized outrage at the criminal justice system and at the living conditions of many African Americans in urban America, there was specific hatred directed at whites, Hispanics, and Asians. In particular, rioters attacked Korean-owned businesses in African-American neighborhoods in the 1992 Los Angeles riots. Here, the dilemmas of equality discussed in the present chapter intersect with the economic problems of unemployment, the inadequacies of the public assistance system, and the pathologies of the urban underclass discussed in previous chapters.

SUMMARY

There are three forms taken by the concept of equality: equality under the law, equality of opportunity, and equality of material well-being. Each conceptualization has its own implications for the imperatives of public policy. Thus, while the Voting Rights Act of 1965 originally aimed at securing the right of African Americans to cast ballots, its imperatives have been redefined in terms of a right to a proportionate number of minority office holders attained through the gerrymandering of safe districts.

Equality of material well-being, the main thread of this chapter, is the goal of proportional equality for targeted disadvantaged groups. The various policies designed to realize this goal are collectively designated as affirmative action or preferential treatment.

Affirmative action can be defined as compensatory justice for the persisting effects of past discrimination, a definition with which most of its supporters would agree. Its critics attack affirmative action because of its denial of meritocracy, its inconsistency with equality under law, its focus on groups rather than individuals, and its penalizing of competitive success and denial of performance standards. By the mid-1990s, opposition to affirmative action had grown so intense that major journals of news and opinion predicted its imminent demise. Many scholars believe that the California Civil Rights Initiative is a portent of things to come, as is the recent action led by an African-American member of the Board of Regents of the University of California system, Ward Connerly, to abolish racial preferences in that system. Because plausible arguments exist on both sides, the issue comes down to differences in the interests of the groups concerned.

Meanwhile, the race issue remains an open sore on the American political landscape. President Clinton took the initiative in 1997 to organize a national dialogue on the issue of racial discrimination. All people of good will want eradication of the poverty, misery, and crime victimization that continue to plague the African-American community. Reasonable people disagree on the causes of these plagues and hence of the best ways to address them. Liberals tend to emphasize the continuing levels of racism that undoubtedly still exists in America and the resulting lack of opportunity as the prime causes of these problems. Conservatives and centrists argue that while racism still exists, it is far less virulent now than it was a few decades ago. Moreover, they point to the huge gains by African Americans in the aggregate in terms of legal rights and material well-being despite the continuing misery of too many individual African Americans as evidence that African Americans can compete and that our society is not hopelessly oppressive. They note that much African-American progress occurred before affirmative action as we know it was instituted and, in fact, leveled off under that policy. Finally, they argue that much of the remaining gap between African Americans and whites in the aggregate (all but 13 percent) disappears when one controls the factor of family instability and illegitimacy. This finding leads them to suggest that the main cause of the remaining gap may lie in behaviors within the African-American community more than in any continuing level of white racism. Liberals counter that this is blaming the victim.

Women remain disadvantaged by proportional standards, and some policies identify them as a targeted group. Although some discrimination against women has been legal, much of it follows from sex-role stereotypes. The Civil Rights Act of 1964 also bans discrimination based on sex. Two issues of great emotional and symbolic significance to the women's movement, abortion and comparable worth, have generated much passionate controversy. We have seen the women's movement dividing between the more established victimization wings and the newer equality wings over the expanding conceptualization of rape and sexual harassment. We have seen a similar expansion in the conceptualization of disability that deserves special governmental dispensation. Meanwhile, gays have found that society still resists granting their lifestyle equal legitimacy with monogamous heterosexuality.

NOTES

1. Stephen and Abigail Thernstrom, *America in Black and White: One Nation Indivisible: Race in Modern America* (New York: Simon & Schuster, 1997): 14.
2. *The Civil Rights Cases,* 109 U.S. 3 (1883).
3. For a detailed account of admissions policies at Harvard, see Alan Dershkowitz, *Chutzpah* (Boston: Little, Brown, 1991): 66–74.
4. For a full treatment of Berkeley's policies to restrict the admission of Asians, see Dinesh D'Souza, *Illiberal Education* (New York: The Free Press, 1991), Chapter 2.
5. Peter Uhlenberg, "Demographic Correlates of Group Achievement: Contrasting Patterns of Mexican Americans and Japanese Americans," in Robert K. Yin, ed., *Race, Creed, Color or National Origin* (Itasca, Ill: Peacock Press, 1973): 86.
6. Colin Powell, *My American Journey* (New York: Random House, 1995): 72.
7. Elizabeth Koontz, "Women as a Minority Group," in Yin, ed., *Race, Creed,* 288–289.
8. Richard Hernnstein and Charles Murray, *The Bell Curve: The Reshaping of American Life by Differences in Intelligence* (New York: The Free Press, 1994).
9. *The New Republic,* October 31, 1994, especially 14–15.
10. Stephen Thernstrom, "The Scandal of the Law Schools," *Commentary,* 104 (December, 1997): 27–31.
11. *The Civil Rights Cases,* 109 U.S. 3 (1883).

12. *Plessy v. Ferguson,* 163 U.S. 537 (1896).

13. *Brown v. Board of Education of Topeka, Kansas,* 347 U.S. 483 (1954). The Court also struck down the constitutionality of government-required segregation in federally controlled territory, in this case. Washington, DC, in *Bolling v. Sharpe,* 347 U.S. 497 (1954). Recall that the Fourteenth Amendment only restricts state government; hence, the *Bolling* case was decided under the due process clause of the Fifth Amendment.

14. *Brown v. Board of Education of Topeka, Kansas,* 349 U.S. 294 (1955).

15. *Alexander v. Holmes County Board of Education,* 396 U.S. 19 (1969).

16. James Coleman, *Equality of Educational Opportunity* (Washington, DC: U.S. Government Printing Office, 1966); and U.S. Commission on Civil Rights, *Racial Isolation in Public Schools* (Washington, DC: U.S. Government Printing Office, 1967).

17. *Green v. School Board of New Kent County,* 391 U.S. 430 (1968).

18. *Swann v. Charlotte-Mecklenburg Board of Education,* 402 U.S. 1 (1971).

19. See the discussion of specific cases in Nathan Glazer, *Affirmative Discrimination* (New York: Basic Books, 1975), 100ff.

20. Cited in Thernstrom and Thernstrom, *America,* 330–331.

21. *Heart of Atlanta Motel v. United States,* 379 U.S. 241 (1964); *Katzenbach v. McClung,* 379 U.S. 294 (1964).

22. *Griggs v. Duke Power,* 401 U.S. 424 (1971).

23. *Washington v. Davis,* 426 U.S. 229 (1976).

24. Alan Sindler, *Bakke, DeFunis, and Minority Admissions* (New York: Longman, 1978), 59.

25. *Bakke v. Regents of the University of California,* 438 U.S. 265 (1978).

26. *Craig v. Boren,* 429 U.S. 190 (1976).

27. *Rostker v. Goldberg,* 453 U.S. 57 (1981).

28. *New York State Club Association v. City of New York,* 108 S. Ct. 2225 (1988).

29. *The New Republic,* June 23, 1997.

30. Katherine Roithe, *The Morning After* (Boston: Little, Brown, 1993).

31. *Boy Scouts of America v. Dale,* 530 U.S. 640 (2000).

32. *Bowers v. Hardwick,* 106 S. Ct. 2841 (1986).

33. This discussion of disability draws significantly from Ruth Shalit, "Defining Disability Down," *The New Republic* (August 25, 1997): 16–22.

34. David Armor, "The Evidence of Busing," *The Public Interest,* 28 (Summer, 1972): 90–126.

35. For example, see Thomas Pettigrew et al., "Busing: A Review of the Evidence," *The Public Interest* (Winter, 1973): 88–113. See the reply by Armor and the summation by James Wilson, 113–134.

36. Christine Rossell, "Is it Busing or the Blacks?" *Urban Affairs Quarterly,* 24 (September, 1988): 138–148. Rossell also finds that desegregation plans based upon magnet schools produce more interracial exposure than does mandatory busing. See Rossell, "The Carrot or Stick for School Desegregation Policy," *Urban Affairs Quarterly,* 25 (March, 1990): 474–499.

37. *Milliken v. Bradley,* 418 U.S. 717 (1974).

38. These data are drawn from Thernstrom and Thernstrom, *America in Black and White,* 334, 336.

39. *Board of Education of Oklahoma City Schools v. Dowell,* 498 U.S. 237 (1991).

40. *Kaiser Aluminum v. Weber* and *U.S. Steelworkers of America v. Weber,* 443 U.S. 193 (1979).

41. Carl Cohen, "Justice Debased: The *Weber* Decision," *Commentary,* 68 (September, 1979): 43–53.

42. *Fullilove v. Klutznick,* 448 U.S. 448 (1980).

43. *Johnson v. Transportation Agency of Santa Clara County,* 480 U.S. 616 (1987).

44. *Firefighters Local Union 1784 v. Stotts,* 104 S. Ct. 2576 (1984).

45. *Wygant v. Board of Education,* 476 U.S. 267 (1986).

46. *Richmond v. J. A. Croson Co.,* 488 U.S. 469 (1989); *Wards Cove Packing Co. v. Atonio,* 493 U.S. 802 (1989); and *Martin v. Wilks,* 492 U.S. 932 (1989).

47. *Adarand Constructors v. Peña,* 515 U.S. 200 (1995).

48. *Hopwood v. Texas,* 78 F. 3rd 932 (1996) and 116 S. Ct. 2580 (1996).

49. Quoted from *The New Republic* (January 30, 1995), 18.

50. Linda Wightman, "The Threat to Diversity in Legal Education: An Empirical Analysis of the Consequences of Abandoning Race as a Factor in Law School Admissions Decisions." *New York University Law Review,* April 1997.

51. *Larry P. v. Riles,* 495 F. Supp. 926 (1979).

52. *Washington v. Davis* and *Griggs v. Duke Power.*

53. David McClelland, *The Achieving Society* (New York: The Free Press, 1967).

54. Thernstrom and Thernstrom, *America,* 194–195.

55. See the A.D.L. surveys cited in Nathan Perlmutter and Ruth Ann Perlmutter, *The Real Anti-Semitism in America* (New York: Arbor House, 1982), Chapter 8. See also Arthur Liebman, *Jews and the Left* (New York: John Wiley, 1979): 564–568. The 1978 Harris Survey also found anti-Semitism higher among African Americans than among other groups.

56. A detailed account of these events may be found in *The New Republic,* (October 14, 1991): 21–31.

57. Paul Sniderman, "The New Racism," *Journal of Political Science,* 35 (May, 1991): 423–424.

58. *The Baltimore Sun,* August 31, 1991.

SUGGESTED READINGS

Books and Articles

Bell, Daniel. "Meritocracy and Equality." *Public Interest,* 29 (Fall 1972): 29–68.

Bernstein, Richard. *The Dictatorship of Virtue: Multiculturalism and the Battle for America's Future.* New York: Knopf, 1994.

D'Souza, Dinesh. *Illiberal Education: The Politics of Race and Sex on Campus.* New York: The Free Press, 1991.

_____. *The End of Racism: Principles for a Multiracial Society.* New York: The Free Press, 1995.

Dworkin, Ronald. *Taking Rights Seriously.* Cambridge, MA: Harvard University Press, 1977.

_____. *A Matter of Principle.* Cambridge, MA: Harvard University Press, 1985.

Edsall, Thomas B. *The New Politics of Inequality.* New York: W. W. Norton, 1984.

Glazer, Nathan. *Affirmative Discrimination.* New York: Basic Books, 1975.

Greer, Germaine. *Sex and Destiny.* New York: Harper & Row, 1984.

Hacker, Andrew. *Two Nations: Black and White, Separate, Hostile, Unequal.* New York: Scribner, 1992.

Kristol, Irving. "About Equality." *Commentary,* 54 (November 1972): 41–47.

Lefkowitz, Mary. "Not Out of Africa." *The New Republic.* (February 10, 1992).

Millet, Kate. *Sexual Politics.* New York: Doubleday, 1969.

Roithe, Katherine. *The Morning After.* Boston: Little, Brown, 1993.

Shipler, David. *A Country of Strangers: Blacks and Whites in America.* New York: Alfred Knopf, 1997.

Thernstrom, Stephen, and Thernstrom, Abigail. *America in Black and White: One Nation Indivisible, Race in Modern America.* New York: Simon & Schuster, 1997.

Web Sites

American Civil Liberty Union's Lesbian and Gay Rights Freedom Network   http://aclu.org/issues/gay/hmgl.html

Center for Equal Opportunity (anti-affirmative action)   www.ceousa.org/

The Feminist Majority Foundation www.feminist.org/

The Manhattan Institute (conservative think tank)   www.manhattan-institute.org/html/race_and_ethnicity.htm

National Association for the Advancement of Colored People (NAACP)   www.naacp.org

National Organization for Women (NOW)   www.now.org

U.S. Supreme Court Multimedia Database   www.oyez.org/

CHAPTER 11

Immigration Policy: The Barely Open Door

Reflecting its new world heritage, the United States often is defined as a nation of immigrants. Indeed, the romanticized notion of America is that anyone could come to the United States and succeed through hard work. Immigration represented a means for the nation to expand westward and helped to fuel the industrial revolution that defined the U.S. economy for over a century. Beneath the romanticization of immigration, however, there always lurked fear of the impact of immigrants on the social, cultural, economic, and political fabric of the nation. Even in colonial days, the nation's founders feared that immigrants might foster challenges to the political system of the new country.[1] Nonetheless, it was not until the late nineteenth century that significant debate developed over immigration. Since that time, the issue has waxed and waned as a major concern. Beginning in the 1970s, immigration policy commanded a great deal of attention in political debate, as it has been tied to issues of the rate of immigration flow, effects on racial/ethnic mix of the population, economic well-being of citizens, and demands for public services. In the 1990s, the issue dominated public policy debates in many parts of the country and in national elections.

Michael LeMay notes that every shift in immigration policy followed a major recession or depression and came during a period of social unrest and turmoil.[2] According to LeMay, each major shift also resulted from one or more of the major political parties including such a change in policy as part of its party platform and after the formation of interest groups focusing on the issue. In most instances, groups used immigrants as scapegoats for the problems they identified; on occasion, however, the groups advocated greater support for immigration. This chapter examines immigration policy in light of the forces advocating either opening the doors to or advocating limitations on immigration.

ISSUE BACKGROUND: FROM AN OPEN DOOR TO INCREASING LIMITS

The Open Door

Traditionally, people viewed the United States as a nation of immigrants, implying that it was open to immigrants from around the world. As part of that view, the expectation arises that immigrants are part of the social contract the nation has with its citizens. The social contract "implies that citizens (and, in certain instances, other residents) who work hard and obey the law are eligible for government assistance in the form of health and education benefits and other social services at certain points in their lives, including those times when they are especially economically vulnerable."[3] The poem by Emma Lazarus inscribed inside the pedestal of the Statue of Liberty,

> "Give me your tired, your poor,
> Your huddled masses yearning to breathe free,
> The wretched refuse of your teeming shore.
> Send these, the homeless, tempest-tost to me,
> I lift my lamp beside the golden door"

symbolizes the values of liberty and opportunity that attract many immigrants and that reflect the openness of American society. For most of its history, U.S. government policy officially reflected these ideals. Nonetheless, implementation of policy did not always live up to the ideal, and there always has been sentiment to restrict entry.

Although some founders of the nation expressed concern about the effects of immigration, such as the potential for undermining the political values of the new nation, little formal policy emerged during the developing years of the United States. Instead, immigrants were welcomed to populate the country and aid in its economic development. Early concerns focused mostly on moral character and loyalty to the country. Some of these concerns arose from colonial days when authorities objected to the acceptance of criminals, paupers, or others of undesirable character. For example, in 1717, the Pennsylvania Colony imposed a fine of five pounds on every criminal brought in and made shipmasters post a year's bond for the good behavior of some passengers. Religious compatibility also affected colonial acceptance of immigrants. Beginning in Massachusetts in 1637, all colonies but Rhode Island imposed limits on settlers based on religious belief. Massachusetts, for example, restricted the settlement of non-Puritans. Still, economic development and the abundance of land overshadowed these other concerns and little regulation took place.[4] Citizenship could be acquired in state courts after five years of residence. This laissez-faire approach to immigration held until the mid-nineteenth century.

Use of Quotas

From the 1780s until 1819, approximately 250,000 immigrants arrived in the United States. Beginning in 1820, the pace of immigration quickened with over 140,000 arriving during the 1820s and an annual average of almost 164,000 from the 1830s until 1860. A total of 5.1 million arrived during the 1860s and 1870s.[5] The increasing pace of immigration created the conditions for opposition to arise. However, since more than 80 percent of the immigrants came from western and northern Europe, opposition was not widespread before 1820. As most of the immigrants who came after 1820 looked for work in the developing factories and textile mills, most of them settled in the northeast, especially in New York and Pennsylvania. Because many of these immigrants were different from the existing population, coming from southeastern Europe, being non-English speaking, and being predominantly Catholic and Jewish, opposition began to arise and quotas were imposed.[6]

Immigrants were ghettoized, and many urban pockets of poverty developed. To many of the "native" population, these ghettos were spawning grounds for social problems such as poverty, housing deterioration, lack of social cohesion, and crime.[7] Violence erupted in some places such as in Philadelphia, which experienced a riot in 1844. The Native American Party (also known as the Know Nothing Party) arose in the 1850s out of anti-immigrant sentiment and enjoyed success in electing governors and members of Congress in the northeastern states. The party built on the beliefs of many native-born citizens that immigrants were a threat to their job security and threatened their religious foundations and the political culture.[8]

After the 1850s, negative responses of native-born citizens continued to build, and states expanded their exclusionary policies. The Civil War created a temporary diversion from the immigration issue and split the Know Nothing Party, but after the war, sentiment against immigrants grew again. California, in particular, excluded people based on their nation of origin, focusing on the Chinese who arrived in large numbers in the West. California also imposed fees on Chinese immigrants, but various decisions of state and federal courts invalidated this policy and all other state laws restricting immigration because immigration was a matter of national and not state law. In 1882, the U.S. Congress acceded to the pressure from California and the Asian Exclusion League by passing a law setting a quota on the number of Chinese who could immigrate to the United States. In 1888, Congress further targeted Chinese immigrants through the Chinese Labor Exclusion Act. Congress also established a national policy on immigration through the Immigration Act of 1882, excluding ex-convicts and the mentally ill. These policy initiatives foreshadowed the bases for future limitations to immigration. The notion of excluding undesirables led to a long list of those to be excluded. Subsequent laws restricted polygamists, those convicted of crime, and those with certain illnesses.[9] Congress also responded to the concerns of organized labor with the Alien Contract Labor Act of 1885, banning the importation of contract labor, which often commanded lower wages than domestic labor.

By the end of the nineteenth century, Japanese immigration to the United States emerged as an issue, again in California. Efforts to limit Japanese immigration resulted in cities such as San Francisco segregating Japanese from the white population in schools. California again turned to the national government to stem the tide of Japanese immigrants. With pressure from President Theodore Roosevelt, Japan agreed to limit the issuance of passports for nonlabor individuals going to the United States.[10] California went so far as to prohibit Japanese from owning agricultural land, and eventually, from even owning leases or any other real estate interests. A few other states, such as Arizona, Texas, and Washington, followed suit.

In 1881, Congress established the Office of Immigration in the Treasury Department to coordinate the evolving immigration policies. The 1906 Naturalization Act renamed the office to the Bureau of Immigration and moved it to the Commerce and Labor Department. The act also established the requirement that immigrants be able to speak English to gain citizenship. Reflecting continuing growth of anti-immigrant sentiment, Congress passed the 1917 Immigration Act, which incorporated all the earlier exclusions, required a literacy test, and specifically banned immigration of most Asians and Pacific Islanders. During the first

FIGURE 11-1 ■ **Legal Immigration Trends, 1820–2000**

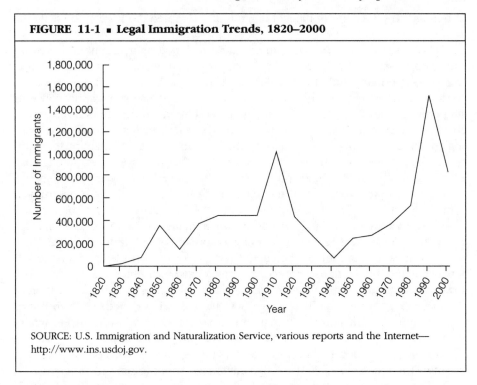

SOURCE: U.S. Immigration and Naturalization Service, various reports and the Internet—
http://www.ins.usdoj.gov.

two decades of the twentieth century, immigration averaged over 700,000 per year. During World War I, immigration dropped off, but it resumed at a higher pace after World War II (see Figure 11-1).

Social problems such as unemployment, economic sluggishness, and a shortage of housing fueled anti-immigrant sentiment. Groups such as the Ku Klux Klan, the American Coalition, the Immigrant Restriction League, and the American Protective League of True Americans arose to advocate greater restriction on immigration. At the same time, others such as the Hebrew Sheltering and Immigration Aid Society and the Anti-National Origins Clause League opposed the restrictions. Congress passed the 1921 Quota Act, restricting the number of immigrants, and established a quota limiting those of any given nationality immigrating to 3 percent of those of the same nationality living in the country in 1890 as the base year for the quotas. The National Origins Quota Act of 1924 helped enforce the provisions by requiring any immigrants to obtain visas from U.S. embassies in their native country. These acts attempted to maintain the ethnic balance of the United States and made it especially difficult for people from Italy, Spain, Russia, and Africa, because their proportions in the population already living in the United States were small compared to Western or Northern Europeans. Thus, the intent of the act was to shift the balance of immigration flow back to Northwestern Europe by establishing low quotas for others. An unintended consequence of these new policies emerged in the illegal immigration through Mexico and Canada by those from countries with very low quotas, because they had no other way of entering the country. Unlike the economies of the affected nations, the economy of the United States was very strong and opportunities abounded. The increase in illegal immigration prompted the Bureau to create the Border Patrol.

Because of the Depression, immigration declined dramatically in the 1930s. Most people seeking residency in the United States during the 1930s were attempting to flee Germany and other Nazi-dominated countries, although the quota acts led to restrictions on the number to be admitted. By 1940, national security concerns further limited immigration, and Congress passed the Alien Registration Act, which required fingerprinting and registration of new immigrants. It also required deporting criminals and subversives. The bombing of Pearl Harbor by Japan led to internment of Japanese living in the United States. Whether they were new immigrants, long-time residents, or citizens, public officials considered Japanese potentially disloyal. The national government moved them from the West Coast to internment camps, primarily in Arizona, and confiscated their property. Many also were imprisoned. In addition, in 1940, the Bureau of Immigration was moved to the Department of Justice and renamed the Immigration and Naturalization Service (INS).

World War II and the draft created shortages of labor resulting in a policy allowing temporary workers (especially from Mexico) to enter the country. The lower wages paid to these workers led to industries pressuring for continuation of the program after the war. The United States and Mexico signed a Migrant Labor Agreement in 1951 making the program permanent. Called the Bracero Program, it survived until 1964. In 2001, some businesses and political leaders, especially in the Southwest, argued for a return to allowing temporary workers to enter the country. The recession of 2001 to 2002 eliminated support for such programs.

The many applications of refugees just before and during World War II called attention to the problem of refugees and the fact that the United States did not differentiate among potential immigrants (see Table 11-1). Eventually, the 1948 Displaced Persons Act addressed the issue by setting up a separate refugee system. During the 1950s, the act accommodated those fleeing Communist countries. The refugee system permitted people to be accepted outside the quota system for their nations of origin. These refugees were granted permanent resident status and were permitted to apply for citizenship. The Cold War and anti-Communist frenzy stimulated scrutiny of immigrants as well to ensure exclusion of suspected subversives. After the terrorist attacks of September 11, 2001, similar pressures arose for greater scrutiny of immigrants and visitors.

Transition to a Preference System

In 1952, Congress enacted the Immigration and Nationality Act, which consolidated much of the earlier policy into one general policy. The act maintained the quota system and alien registration. It also gave preference to skilled labor and relatives of citizens and resident aliens. The Immigration and Nationality Act of 1965 abolished the national origins quota system and established numerical limits in order of preference to:

1. Unmarried children of U.S. citizens,
2. Spouses and unmarried children of permanent resident aliens,
3. People in the professions and exceptional scientists and artists,

---

TABLE 11-1 ■ Glossary of Terms Concerning Immigrants

Asylee: a person in the United States unable or unwilling to return to his or her country of origin because of persecution or fear of persecution; eligible to become a permanent resident after one year of continuous residence in the United States. T/F

Immigrant: an alien admitted to the United States as a lawful permanent resident.

Investor Immigrant: individual permitted to immigrate based on a promise to invest $1 million in an urban area or $500,000 in a rural area and to create ten new jobs.

Legalized Aliens: illegal aliens eligible to apply for temporary resident status under provisions of the Immigration Reform and Control Act of 1986; to be eligible, individuals must have lived continuously in the United States since January 1, 1982. T/F

Naturalization: act of making a person who was not born a citizen into a citizen.

Nonimmigrant: an alien seeking temporary entry to the United States for a specific purpose such as foreign government officials, tourists, students, temporary workers, exchange visitors, and so on.

Permanent Resident: a noncitizen allowed to live permanently in the United States who can travel in and out without a visa and to work without restriction; person is also permitted to accumulate time toward becoming a citizen. T/F

Refugee: same as asylee. T/F

---

4. Married children of U.S. citizens,
5. Siblings of U.S. citizens,
6. Workers with skills needed in the U.S. labor market, and
7. Refugees.[11]

The act set a limit of 170,000 immigrants annually from the Eastern Hemisphere. It also established a limit of 120,000 annually for the Western Hemisphere after July 1968. A special commission was created to study the factors affecting immigration in the Western Hemisphere. The new policies resulted in large increases in illegal immigration and mounting pressure within the country for policies dealing with it. Much of the illegal immigration increase resulted from the fact that employers, especially in the agricultural sector, still welcomed many of the Braceros who worked legally in the United States until the unilateral termination of the program by the United States. The workers instead just came across the border illegally to work in the same jobs. The deterioration of the Mexican economy also contributed to the increase.

After 1965, immigration again surged and backlogs developed in applications because of the ceilings imposed, especially on immigration from the Western Hemisphere. To some, the reforms of 1965 represented a method of maintaining the same effect of the national origins quota system without being overt about it, since Asians and Africans would still find it difficult to immigrate because relatively few of them had relatives here.[12] The concept of family reunification drove the development of the new system that still underpins much of today's policy. The huge backlogs led to long waits for applicants, especially from Mexico. In 1976, Congress responded by creating the appearance of equality of treatment by establishing a limit of 20,000 immigrants from each country in the Western Hemisphere. Another change in 1978 imposed a ceiling of 290,000 visas per year for the world as a whole, thus deleting the differentiation between the Eastern and Western Hemispheres. The preference categories established in 1965 provided the basis for immigration under the 1978 policy.

Congress addressed the refugee issue again in 1980, separating refugee policy from overall immigration policy. The Refugee Act of 1980 created a separate admissions process for refugees and established a ceiling of 50,000 per year. It also gave the president, in consultation with Congress, the power to act in emergencies involving refugees.

In 1986, Congress also confronted the illegal immigration issue through the Immigration Reform and Control Act of 1986. The act granted amnesty and temporary resident status to illegal immigrants who had lived in the United States continuously after January 1, 1982. It also attempted to address the employment of illegal aliens by banning the employment of undocumented workers and imposing sanctions on employers who knowingly hired illegal aliens. It created a program to help alleviate labor shortages that might result from the sanctions on employers. The act also strengthened the Border Patrol and inspections.

The Immigration Act of 1990 built upon the 1965 reforms and serves as the foundation for current policy. The act provided that, after 1995, immigration would be limited to 675,000 per year for all types of immigration. Family reunification remained the primary criterion for the policy, but some new categories also were created. For example, those who would invest $1,000,000 in urban areas or $500,000 in rural areas and create at least ten new jobs would be eligible above the overall ceiling. The act created a classification of "diversity immigrants" to allow people from countries with very low representation in the U.S. population to immigrate through a lottery process.

Illegal Immigration

The Illegal Immigration Reform and Immigrant Responsibility Act of 1996 addressed numerous issues concerning illegal immigration. The act responded to growing pressures among the public, especially in states along the Mexican border, to stem the flow of illegal immigration. To achieve that objective, the act almost doubled the size of the Border Patrol and provided resources to acquire sophisticated technology and otherwise improve the tools for securing the border and for detection and apprehension of those entering the country illegally. The law enacted stiffer penalties for smuggling illegals into the country and for the production and use of fraudulent documents. Illegal aliens who are caught also face stiffer penalties under the law.

The 1996 reform also attempts to deal with the problem of employment of illegal aliens. Specifically, the act creates some pilot projects to assist employers in confirming the eligibility of the "employee" to be hired. The programs emphasize the need for the Immigration and Naturalization Service, Social Security Administration, and the Attorney General to work together to develop systems for speedy confirmation of information to employers.

The law requires family members who sponsor immigrants to earn 125 percent of the federal poverty income guideline in order to sponsor a relative. The law also addresses some of the provisions of the 1996 welfare reform affecting immigrants. In particular, the provisions make clear distinctions between legal and illegal immigrants relative to benefits states can or may provide. Generally, illegal immigrants may be denied benefits, but some benefits also will be denied to legal immigrants. Specifically, Social Security benefits may not be paid to aliens not legally present in the country, higher education benefits to illegal aliens are restricted, food stamps and Supplemental Security Income are phased out for most noncitizens, and states are permitted to deny benefits such as nonemergency Medicaid to illegal aliens and sometimes to legal permanent residents. By 1997, Congress and the president faced pressure to change some of the provisions to assure benefits to legal immigrants in the country who worked and paid taxes. SSI benefits were restored for legal immigrants in the country before the enactment of the 1996 reforms. Congress also approved changes that allow immigrants with green card applications filed by January 4, 1998, to remain in the country while the application paperwork is processed. Congress also passed legislation making Nicaraguan and Cuban refugees automatically eligible for permanent status and allowing refugees from El Salvador, Guatemala, and Eastern Europe to apply for suspension of deportation under pre-1996 provisions less stringent than those in the 1996 act. In 2002, the U.S. Senate considered legislation extending amnesty to Mexican aliens while they are applying for citizenship. President Bush supports the legislation.

Many of the recent policies stimulated unprecedented citizenship applications and approval in 1995 and 1996, resulting in criticism of INS because of the more than 2 million naturalizations. Approximately 2,000 people attained citizenship even though they had criminal backgrounds. Congressional critics charged that the INS streamlined the procedures and encouraged large numbers to attain citizenship so that they would be able to vote in the 1996 and 2000 presidential elections, presumably to the benefit of the Democrats. The criticisms led to more stringent procedures for background checks and a slowing down of the naturalization process. In 2002, INS came under intense criticism again because of slowness of its operations and concerns about not knowing what happens with visitors after they enter the country. The agency was embarrassed by the disclosure that it had sent approval of student visas for two of the terrorists six months after they committed suicide in the September 11, 2001, terrorist attacks. The reaction to the disclosures included calls for reorganizing the agency and for reengineering its processes.

CONTEMPORARY POLICY: RESPONDING TO CHANGING IMMIGRATION DYNAMICS

As with all public policies (Chapter 1), contemporary immigration policy serves diverse purposes. Most pieces of immigration policy reflect attempts to deal with a particular concern rather than a comprehensive approach, thus resulting in a complex patchwork of items. Thus, efforts to limit immigration often are justified in terms of meeting the security and prosperity needs of people. Specifically, many opponents of immigration argue that immigration is an internal threat to the extent that it causes social problems such as crime and poverty and to the extent that it undermines the political and social covenants on which American society is built. At times immigration also is linked to external threats such as terrorism or, as during the Cold War, to subversion. These threats to security provide one rationale for limiting immigration. The threats became very real with the September 11, 2001, terrorist attacks in New York and Washington, D.C. In response, Congress passed the U.S.A. Patriot Act of 2001, officially known as the Uniting and Strengthening America by Providing Appropriate Tools Required to Intercept and Obstruct Terrorism Act of 2001. The act enhanced immigration enforcement with particular attention to potential terrorist threats.

Regulation of immigration also is often based upon prosperity needs. Many of the arguments against immigration are couched in terms of economic impact. Opponents argue that immigrants take away jobs of the native born and put downward pressure on citizen wages and standard of living. Others contend that immigration should be encouraged because our economy needs people to take jobs which have to be done, but which native-born people are unwilling to take. In addition, many supporters of immigration point to the many highly skilled immigrants in technical fields as important to our ability to compete in the global economy. Thus, both proponents and opponents of immigration point to effects on the prosperity needs of the society to support their positions.

Policies on illegal immigration also rest on arguments about security and membership purposes. The same contentions as those regarding immigration generally are used, but others emerge as well. Membership is used as a basis for limiting access to various social programs. For example, denying noncitizens and/or illegal aliens education and welfare benefits is based on membership as defined by citizenship.

The myth of immigration in United States history claims that the country opens its doors to the world and represents the best and most generous aspects of humankind. It has become a part of what is known as the American spirit. Some label it a myth because the specifics of immigration policy, as they developed, support anti-alien sentiment arising from people's anxieties and self-interest.[13] Despite the restrictions imposed, the United States ranks "as the principal immigrant-receiving nation in the world."[14] Others, however, argue that, while absolute numbers of immigrants place the United States at the top, other nations such as Australia, Canada, and Germany, among others, admit more immigrants as a ratio of their total population.[15]

Part of the debate over immigration policy emanates from the national origin of immigrants and the large concentrations of some ethnic groups. Current policy gives preferences to those who have family already in the country, reflecting the family reunification philosophy of the policy. Approximately 69 percent of immigrants were admitted in 2000 on this basis, a slight drop from previous years. The family reunification policy supports maintaining the ethnic balance of the country and makes immigration from Africa particularly difficult. Furthermore, perceptions are that the number of Hispanics, and especially Mexican Americans, has increased dramatically in recent years. Data indicate that immigration from Mexico and other Latin American countries has remained stable since the 1920s at 35 to 45 percent of immigrants.[16] The concentration of immigrants from Central America and Mexico in the Southwest and of Cubans in Florida gives the appearance of huge waves of immigrants from these areas and results in their being targets for the frustrations of native-born citizens.

The 1965 Immigration and Nationality Act with modifications made in the 1990 Immigration Act and the Illegal Immigration Reform and Immigrant Responsibility Act of 1996 is the foundation of current policy. The policy establishes family reunification as the primary criterion for immigration and sets limits on the flow of immigrants. The 1996 act, in particular, attempts to control the influx of undocumented persons and imposes penalties on employers of illegal immigrants. Immigration to the United States peaked at an all-time high of 1.8 million in 1991. Tougher policies reduced those numbers dramatically in succeeding years. The reforms of 1990 provided a ceiling of 675,000 beginning with fiscal year 1995. The ceilings have been exceeded because of various exceptions granted and because the family reunification philosophy allows immigrants to include their immediate families beyond the limit. In 1996, for example, total immigration numbered 915,900, dipped to 647,000 in 1999, and went back up to 850,000 in 2000 (see Table 11-2). Family sponsored immigrants account for roughly 70 percent. Included are parents and children of U.S. citizens and resident aliens and siblings of U.S. citizens.

Approximately 13 percent of immigrants are admitted under employment-based preferences. These include people with advanced degrees or of exceptional ability, skilled professionals, unskilled workers filling special needs, and other special categories, including students covered under the Chinese Student Protection Act, who might face persecution if they return to China. The category also includes investor immigrants. Employment-based immigration often is justified in terms of the increasingly global economy and the need for the United States to remain competitive. Often, highly technical skills are available in other nations; these approaches also address the ability to communicate and penetrate other economies through language and culture.

Refugees and asylees constitute another category. They are people who face persecution in their native countries. Refugees usually are people displaced from their countries because of political instability or persecution by a political regime against a particular group. Asylees are individuals who claim political persecution for their ideas or political activities. They may be granted political asylum because of the harm they face by going back to their native countries. Refugees and

TABLE 11-2 ■ Immigration in the 1990s

Year	Number of Immigrants Admitted
1991	1,827,167
1992	810,635
1993	880,014
1994	804,416
1995	720,461
1996	915,900
1997	798,378
1998	654,451
1999	646,568
2000	849,807

SOURCE: U.S. Immigration and Naturalization Service; information posted on the Internet.

TABLE 11-3 ▪ Legal Immigrants by Top Ten Countries of Origin, FY 2000

All Countries	*849,807*
Mexico	173,919
China	45,672
Philippines	42,474
India	42,046
Vietnam	26,747
El Salvador	22,332
Jamaica	22,004
Canada	21,475
Cuba	19,322
Dominican Republic	17,441

SOURCE: *2000 Statistical Yearbook of the Immigration and Naturalization Service,* Table 17, www.ins.usdoj.

---

asylees make up about 8 percent of immigrants. Diversity immigrants represent a very small portion of immigrants.

More than half of the immigrants since the 1960s have come from seven nations: Mexico, the Philippines, China, Vietnam, Korea, India, and the Dominican Republic. The top countries in terms of ethnic origin in 2000 were Mexico, China, the Philippines, India, and Vietnam (see Table 11-3). Until the 1960s, Europe dominated in sending immigrants to the United States. With the new face of immigrants, especially the large numbers of Asians and Hispanics, public attitudes have changed as well. Assimilation is not as easy as it was for the Europeans of early immigration waves. Resentment grows and is exploited by many interest groups and political opportunists. Anti-immigrant attitudes seemed to peak in 1995 and have declined since then. Polls by the Knight Ridder Newspapers in 1995 showed that 65 percent of respondents believed that legal immigration should be reduced. In 1996, 50 percent responded that way. By the time of the poll in June of 1997, only 42 percent responded that they believed that recent immigration is bad for the country.[17] Not surprisingly, sentiment varies by area of the country, but the overall results indicate that the high level of anti-immigrant feeling is subsiding as the political rhetoric also has cooled. The improving U.S. economy, especially in the southwestern states, contributed significantly to the decline in anti-immigrant sentiment. The September 11, 2001, terrorist attacks in New York and Washington, D.C., and economic downturns resulted in a rise in anti-immigrant views.

Immigration patterns are different today than they were before the 1970s.[18] As noted before, most immigrants during the nineteenth century and into the 1960s came from Europe, primarily Northern and Western Europeans, followed by Southern and Eastern Europeans. Generally, they settled in the Northeast and Midwest. The urban areas that had jobs in the industrial sector attracted them. Since the 1970s, however, more immigrants have come from Asia and the Caribbean and Latin American countries. Their settlement patterns are different as well. Generally, they settle in the coastal states, with the Pacific states and Southwest attracting Asians and Mexican Americans. Florida and the northeast coast are the destinations of most of those from Cuba and the Caribbean. Currently, Cali-

TABLE 11-4 ▪ Concentration of Immigrant Populations by Top Ten States of Intended Residence, FY 2000

All States	*849,807*
California	217,753
New York	106,061
Florida	93,391
Texas	63,340
New Jersey	40,013
Illinois	36,180
Massachusetts	23,483
Virginia	20,087
Washington	18,486
Pennsylvania	18,148

SOURCE: *2000 Statistical Yearbook of the Immigration and Naturalization Service,* Table 17, www.ins.usdoj.

fornia, New York, Florida, Texas, New Jersey, and Illinois attract the largest numbers of foreign-born people (see Table 11-4).

Racial and ethnic origins of immigrants also have changed over recent decades.[19] Prior to 1970, 86 percent of the foreign-born population was white, while during the 1990s, only 62 percent of those arriving were white. Hispanics increased from 32 percent pre-1970 to 43 percent in the 1990s, and Asians increased from 9 to 29 percent of new immigrants in the same periods. African Americans posted a modest change, going from 4 percent before 1970 to 9 percent of arrivals in the 1990s.

The education level of immigrants varies somewhat from the native-born population as well. Interestingly, more than twice the percentage of foreign born (37 percent) than native born (16 percent) lack a high school degree, but approximately 12 percent of foreign born have graduate or professional degrees compared to about 8 percent of those native born. Immigrants also are a little more likely to have a bachelor's degree (17 percent) than are native born (16 percent). However, native born are almost twice as likely to have graduated from high school and have some college (60.4 percent) than foreign born (34 percent).[20] Data for 1999 indicate that the education level of immigrants overall is dropping.[21]

The Illegal Immigration Reform and Immigrant Responsibility Act of 1996 addressed the problem of illegal immigration, which reached a head in the 1990s. Much of the pressure for reform of immigration arose out of the frustration many people felt about illegal immigration and their beliefs that illegal immigrants are the cause of many of the country's social ills. The 1996 reforms aimed directly at this problem. Figures on illegal immigration are difficult to ascertain with accuracy. Census data estimate there were approximately 6 million illegal aliens residing in the United States in 2000, but others claim that there is twice that number.[22] The number of illegal aliens apprehended (currently approximately a million per year) by the U.S. Immigration and Naturalization Service serves as one measure of the magnitude of the problem. As Table 11-5 indicates, illegal immigration, as measured by INS apprehension of undocumented persons, skyrocketed from the 1960s

TABLE 11-5 ▪ Illegal Aliens Apprehended	
Years	*Number*
1961–1970	1,608,356
1971–1980	8,321,498
1981–1990	11,883,328
1991–1997	6,211,000*

*estimate

SOURCE: U.S. Immigration and Naturalization Service, various reports and the Internet.

to the 1980s and declined slightly during the 1990s. Increased enforcement and Mexico's improving economy are reasons for recent declines, and the 1996 Act and 2001 U.S. Patriot Act are expected to have an impact that is even more significant. Apprehension of undocumented persons grew from a little more than one and a half million during the 1960s to over 8 million in the 1970s, and to almost 12 million in the 1980s. Clearly, the tougher policy on legal immigration has stimulated illegal immigration. Illegal immigration is a very emotional issue as many Americans are convinced that immigrants are a burden to society and create economic problems by taking jobs away from native workers. Additionally, the distinction between legal and illegal immigration is not always clear. The law has allowed undocumented persons to become legal; many families in the United States contain some legal and some illegal members, and the status of many is unclear, awaiting adjudication. The next section explains the different views about the effects of current immigration policy.

POLICY EVALUATION: CONTRASTING PERCEPTIONS

Current Policy Concerns

Immigration policy is a very emotional issue, but one that does not lend itself easily to ideological splits. Instead, people's views are shaped by their family ties, their experiences with immigrants, their fears of the impact of immigration, and the areas of the country in which they live, to name a few. LeMay argues that economics, race, nationalism, and foreign policy play pivotal roles in all U.S. immigration policy.[23] The opposing perspectives presented in the following discussion bear out LeMay's contention. Negative or positive perspectives on immigration revolve around several issues including the impact on the economy with special emphasis on employment, dependence on public services such as welfare and education, quality of life, and impact on the social and political culture.

Economic Concerns

Much of the debate over immigration policy focuses on the impact on the economy, with those favoring a more restrictive policy claiming that immigrants are a drain on the economy and take jobs away from the native population.[24] Those who support immigration and even argue for more immigration point to many positive effects on the economy and the need for the labor provided by immigrants.[25] Certainly, traditional immigration provided a supply of labor, which helped develop the United States into a leading economic power. Even during the nineteenth and early twentieth centuries, however, the arrival of many immigrants led to resentment and policy changes attempting to limit or exclude some groups, as noted in the first part of this chapter. During economic boom times, the issue usually is not as visible as during periods of economic sluggishness.

Opponents of immigration argue that immigrants take jobs held by natives or are willing to work at very low wages, thus depressing the income of the native population.[26] This argument has a lot of emotional appeal and seems very logical. The critics use examples of Vietnamese who fish on the Gulf Coast of Texas or the prevalence of Hispanics in hotel and food service industries in Florida and California to support their contentions that immigrants take jobs from the native born. While these examples illustrate real problems in specific locales, they do not reflect the overall impact on the labor market. Critics of immigration argue that the unemployment rate is evidence of the availability of native-born labor. Labor unions cite the inability of people to live on the minimum wage and blame immigrants for depressing wages because of their availability in the work force. Additionally, it has become a popular position of labor unions, which oppose immigration as a means of protecting their own interests. Cheap labor might undermine the efforts of labor unions to share in the profits of business. Additionally, they argue that cheap immigrant labor does not reflect the type of skills the United States should be encouraging to help it in global competitiveness.[27]

People on the other side of the issue argue that immigration has a negligible impact on the labor market and that rather than taking jobs from others, immigrants actually help create jobs.[28] Employment opportunity still attracts immigrants. As they take jobs, they become productive participants in the economy and spend money, thus helping to create demand for more products and thus more employment. Proponents of immigration also note that immigrants tend to have very strong work ethics because they were motivated to come to the United States to seek opportunity. They do not differ from nonimmigrants in their rates of unemployment, contrary to the claims of many opponents.[29]

Proponents of immigration also cite the entrepreneurial activities of immigrants and how those activities contribute to the growth of the economy and employment. Julian Simon refers to Canadian studies that suggest that nearly 5 percent of immigrants to Canada started businesses within their first three years in Canada, creating nearly 30 percent more jobs than all the immigrants held during that time.[30] He argues that the Canadian experience should reflect what happens in the United States, although the U.S. experience has not been documented to the same extent as the Canadian experience. Available data indicate that minorities and immigrants start businesses at a much higher rate than members of the native population do.[31] Though the enterprises tend to be small, small enterprises are the source of nearly a quarter of all new jobs since the early 1970s.

Although many immigrants work in low-wage jobs, many also are highly talented and skilled professionals. Clearly, many industries depend upon the unskilled laborers who harvest produce and work in the garment, restaurant, and hotel industries. Significant numbers of immigrants also are scientists and engineers and have been important parts of the success of high-technology industries. Additionally, as noted earlier in the chapter, the children of immigrants tend to achieve college education and enter the professional ranks at very high rates. Asians appear to be the most successful and arrive with high levels of education and skills. Indians and Arabs also tend to be highly educated and skilled. Not surprisingly, Mexicans tend to be less educated and unskilled, as they generally are immigrating to escape poverty and the lack of opportunity in their society. Generally, facts suggest that immigration has positive impacts on the economy. At the same time, the negative impact in a given community with high concentrations of immigrants can be very significant and can put a strain on resources in that community.

Impact on Public Services

Opponents of immigration raise the specter of overloaded public services as another major issue. They argue that our schools are overrun with children of immigrants and that immigrants burden the welfare system. The issue created much pressure in many states and in national politics to limit the access of immigrants, especially illegal immigrants, to these governmental benefits. California, in particular, led the nation in many of the restrictions, where Governor Pete Wilson used the immigration issue to gain attention for his presidential aspirations. Proposition 187 in California passed overwhelmingly in the early 1990s and denied all public benefits to illegal immigrants. While Wilson's campaign for the nomination of his party failed, his views on immigration and the passage of Proposition 187 helped him get reelected as governor and helped place the issue squarely on the national political agenda, leading to welfare and immigration reforms which limited many benefits.

Immigration poses many challenges to public school systems in the areas in which there are large concentrations of immigrants. Clearly, these challenges have existed for long periods in the major cities such as New York and Chicago. Recent immigration patterns, however, have brought the challenges to new areas, especially in Florida, Texas, California, and generally the southwest.[32] School districts in these areas have trouble in handling the numbers of students and in meeting their needs because of language barriers and the lack of resources to serve many of their students, immigrant or nonimmigrant. Typically, the most-affected school districts are the large urban districts that long have suffered most from lack of adequate funding and from overcrowding in poorly maintained facilities. These problems mean that they cannot meet the educational needs of immigrant and native-born children alike. All the problems of large urban school districts make the assimilation of immigrant children more difficult than it otherwise would be. Because immigration law, specifically the 1996 act, permits states only to limit higher education benefits, public schools are required to provide education for immigrant students. The Supreme Court in *Plyler v. Doe* (1982) ruled that illegal immigrants could not be denied public education. Restrictions do apply, however, to some students, particularly those who live on the Mexican border and enter the United States for their education. Under visa restrictions, they are denied access to public schools. Nonetheless, studies indicate that children of immigrants are less likely to drop out and more likely to do better in school than U.S.-born children.[33] While not much research exists on the subject, a few studies indicate differential performance by immigrant groups. A study of San Diego high school students indicated that, with the exception of Hispanics, performance of children of non-English-speaking immigrants had higher test scores than all other students. Other studies indicate that students from immigrant families from China, Korea, Japan, Vietnam, the Philippines, Laos, and Cambodia outperform native-born students. In addition, Mexican-born immigrant students tend to outperform U.S.-born students of Mexican descent.[34]

According to many opponents of immigration, the welfare state is a major attraction of immigration to the United States. State government officials raise many of the concerns because state and local governments bear much of the cost of social services, especially as the national government has cut back in recent years (see Chapter 2). Studies indicate that recently arrived immigrants are slightly more likely to use public services than the general population, but that over time, they are less likely to do so.[35] Most recent research suggests that immigrants are not much different from the rest of the population in the use of social services.[36]

All immigrants are eligible for public school education, but eligibility and use of other benefits differs somewhat by category. Until 1996 reforms in welfare and in immigration, most legal immigrants were eligible for most benefits. With the 1996 reforms, higher education benefits and welfare benefits such as food stamps and disability benefits are denied to some legal immigrants. Some states are considering legislation to ensure medical and financial assistance to legal immigrants by replacing the federal funds with state money. Refugees and asylees generally are treated like legal immigrants when it comes to benefits. Illegal immigrants, however, are unlikely to see any support for their access to services.

In addition to pointing out the lack of difference in the rate of immigrants and U.S. born using the social services system, proponents of immigration also present data on the taxes paid versus the costs of services. By these calculations, immigrants represent a very positive investment for the country. Immigrants contribute more to the system in taxes than they use in benefits and thus pay their own way. Ironically, illegal immigrants contribute at an even higher rate than others do because they work and pay taxes, but are less likely to be eligible for or to apply for public services because they fear deportation.[37] A disproportionate share of the taxes, however, is paid in income tax to the national government while the burden of providing services falls to state and local governments.

Much has been made of older relatives of immigrants coming to the United States to take advantage of Social Security or SSI benefits in recent years. (See Chapter 7 for a description of these programs.) After the 1965 immigration legislation, it appears that there was an increase in such immigration, but some observers suggest that immigrants actually provide support for the survival of Social Security programs. Given the fact that the native population is aging and increasingly qualifying for Social Security benefits, workers are faced with increasing taxes to support the system. Many argue that the system will be bankrupt by the time the baby boomers retire. Some scholars argue that immigrants usually come to the country while they are in their prime working years and that they will help ensure the survival of the Social Security system by their contributions to the Trust Fund.[38]

Clearly, many state and local governments feel the pressures of immigration, both legal and illegal. The pressures on social services, roads, and bus systems can be very heavy, leading to frustration on the part of the taxpayers who have to pay for the services and for those needing the services when they are unavailable. The burden is distributed unevenly. Because of large numbers of immigrants in states such as Florida, California, Arizona, and Texas, and especially in major cities such as Miami, San Diego, and Los Angeles, the pressures on these states and cities are especially large. At the same time, the contributions of working immigrants to the tax base support the economy and society as a whole. Both supporters and opponents of immigration have pointed out the uneven distribution of the costs and make suggestions for federal government support for the services that cannot be denied because of the Constitution or other federal policy. The restriction of many benefits to citizens or legal immigrants resulted in part from this pressure as well.

Quality of Life

Quality of life issues arise relative to immigration mostly among those who oppose more immigration. They argue that continued immigration will lead to overpopulation of the country resulting in increasing poverty and harm to the environment. Opponents also argue that the culture of the society is being changed and that the social fabric is being destroyed. In particular, they hearken back to the idea that the United States has been a melting pot, but that with the new waves of immigration, the society is being fragmented. Assimilation occurs more slowly because larger concentrations of people of similar background sustain old customs and traditions. Some suggest that the United States no longer is a melting pot, but a pluralism of ethnic groups that do not become assimilated. In recent years, many groups have tried to preserve their ethnic identities by celebrating their ethnic and cultural traditions. These developments lead to resentment by people who believe they should make efforts to assimilate more fully. Immigrants often become scapegoats for many of the problems of society.[39]

Overpopulation. Those opposing more immigration often cite overpopulation as a problem. Some people fear the sheer growth in numbers of population as putting a strain on all aspects of American society.[40] Many social critics blame immigrants for the decline of some of the major cities, citing crime statistics, fleeing of whites to the suburbs, housing deterioration, poverty, and loss of business and jobs in the central cores at the same time that immigrants moved into those areas.[41] The rhetoric often is very inflammatory and leads to policy proposals that might not necessarily address the real problems. Blaming immigrants for threats to economic security, for example, diverts attention away from the causes of the slow wage growth, as the data indicate that immigrants have little overall impact on the issue. Closing the doors to immigrants seems like an easy solution, but the problems of America's major cities are much more complicated than merely the presence of immigrants.

One of the issues raised concerning population growth is the impact on the environment. Some critics suggest that the pressures on food production and the waste produced will lead to everything from global warming, air pollution, and water pollution to the destruction of the physical environment (see Chapter 5).[42] There is no question that the increasing population puts a strain on many environmental factors. What those on the other side of the issue say, however, is that the United States is nowhere near its capacity to handle the population and that efforts should be made to improve environmental policy to protect the environment rather than using immigrants as the scapegoat. They also counter that the native birth rate is declining and that immigration is barely replacing the decline in population due to the declining birth rate.[43]

Crime. Crime is another issue used by opponents of immigration to get the attention of the populace. They blame immigrants for a high crime rate, especially in the major cities. Although immigrants themselves appear to be less likely than the rest of the population to be involved in crime, critics still blame them for crime by their argument that they take the jobs of U.S-born people, thus increasing the unemployment rate. High unemployment in the urban centers then contributes to a life of crime by people who are disenfranchised from the system.[44] Given the evidence on the negligible impact of immigrants on employment issues, proponents of immigration note that the argument does not follow. They also cite the vitality of many ethnic neighborhoods fostered by immigrant groups and how those neighborhoods foster a sense of community, which helps discourage crime.[45]

Social and political culture. Perhaps the most controversial issue raised about the impact of immigration on the quality of life is the impact on social and political culture. Many opponents of immigration claim that immigration threatens the values of our society and that ethnic groups have separatist notions that lead to the balkanization of American society. Some claim that these developments lead to culture wars and that our borders must be closed to stop the disappearance of America's distinctive social and political culture.[46] These arguments are not new. The founders of our nation raised the issue at the very beginning, as did many of the colonists. The Know Nothing Party of the 1850s and 1860s brought the ideas to the electorate. Depending on the time and circumstances, critics perceived threats to religious homogeneity, family structure, and social cohesion of communities, to name a few. Thus, these critics of immigration continue a long tradition of appealing to the fears and anxieties of citizens. Clearly, the concentrations of Mexican Americans in the Southwest, and Haitians and Cubans in Miami, are examples to many people of the ability of new immigrants to hold on to their cultures. Because they have distinct cultures, they are easy targets for those who have an idealized view of Americans as a homogenous culture. Sometimes it is easier to strike out at the identifiable group than to accept that society evolves constantly. There is much evidence of identifiable ethnic groups attempting to continue their homeland cultural traditions, but there is no evidence that it undermines the political democracy of the United States.

Because of the cohesion of some groups, critics also fear the political power they represent. During and after the 1996 and 2000 elections, the INS came in for much criticism because of its procedures for processing citizenship applications. Some claim that the Clinton administration sped up the process to get people sympathetic to it on the voter rolls.[47] Former California Congressman Robert Dornan claimed that he lost his reelection bid to a Mexican-American female because of the concentration of Hispanic voters and fraudulent participation by noncitizens. He had many sympathizers in the House of Representatives. Of course, immigrants in the past helped political machines of both political parties in many major cities. Their support was given in return for services provided by the machines, and the process helped assimilate many immigrant groups into the political culture. Modern-day immigrants are unlikely to have the same close relationship with political leadership, but political parties certainly can exploit the opportunity to address their interests in the hopes of gaining their support. It is unlikely, however, that the type of patronage the nineteenth and early twentieth centuries witnessed will arise. Politicians, however, will pay attention to issues that affect new citizens. President George W. Bush, for example, has been criticized for his support of renewing the policy to allow immigrants to stay while they apply for citizenship even though their visas have expired or they are here illegally.

Some proponents of immigration charge that the culture issue is a code for racism.[48] They are concerned that opponents are worried primarily that the white majority is declining and that opponents fear competition with the many ethnic groups that are emerging as serious social and political forces. They claim that the effects of immigrants on jobs and on public services create divisiveness and pit groups against one another.[49] These efforts create what the opponents of immigration claim is a culture war, but in many ways the opponents themselves provide the fuel for the culture wars through the rhetoric they use to support their positions.

FUTURE ALTERNATIVES: OPENNESS OR RESTRICTION?

While there is much disagreement about whether immigration *per se* is a problem, there seems to be consensus that immigration policy needs improvement. Depending upon whether people believe that there is too much or not enough immigration or fall somewhere in between, views on future policy options range from closing down immigration to encouraging more immigration, with options between the two extremes as well.

Some people argue that immigration should be stopped completely. Political commentator and third-party presidential candidate Pat Buchanan spoke for them when he suggested that the borders of the United States be closed down and that the military be used to enforce the policy. In some instances, he seemed to support a temporary suspension while, at other times, he seemed to be suggesting a permanent closure to immigration. His arguments usually focused on preserving the national culture and on preserving jobs for the native born. Congress has been debating proposals to use the military to seal the border. Many critics of militarizing the border claim that the military is not equipped for law enforcement. The terrorist strike of September 11, 2001, however, led to the military being involved in many activities to deal with terrorist activities as well as border security.

Terrorism produced immediate effects on immigration, with much tighter security at U.S. borders and scrutiny of immigrants, particularly those from the Middle East. Moreover, the apparent ease with which terrorists entered and lived in the United States accelerated calls for reform of the Immigration and Naturalization Service. The INS has had great difficulty in keeping track of persons who enter on temporary student or tourist visas and then overstay their limits, slipping into the margins of American society. Although associated with the immigration options discussed later, how to prevent terrorism is a distinct issue with dimensions going well beyond questions of how many and what type of persons to admit legally to the United States on a permanent or semipermanent basis.

Most people recognize that a complete stop to immigration is impractical and maybe impossible even if the present degree of immigration troubles them. Thus, they advocate a moratorium[50] or a reduction.[51] The reasons vary according to the way they define the problem. For the most part, advocates of a moratorium or reducing immigration believe that the nation needs to catch up with the absorption of those who have already arrived. They also see a moratorium or reduction as an opportunity to consider improvement in immigration policies to deal with the problems they believe immigration has created. The reforms in 1991 and 1996 took cues from some reduction advocates by attempting to address concerns about the numbers of immigrants entering the United States. However, the current policy has not stemmed the flow to any great extent and leaves the proponents of reduction calling for more reform with lower caps on immigration and fewer exceptions to the caps.

Some of the specific recommendations for limiting immigration suggest that the policy should focus on what needs the country has, especially in job skills. It is argued that the majority of immigrants are unskilled and do not help revitalize the economy or support U.S. competitiveness in the global economy.[52] To correct this perceived problem, advocates suggest that immigrants be allowed in, based primarily on having skills that will contribute to advancing the economy.

Others argue that immigration should focus primarily on people who are committed to becoming U.S. citizens.[53] Applications for citizenship give some indication of the prevalence of commitment to citizenship. After enactment of the Immigration Reform and Control Act of 1986, granting amnesty to illegal aliens who had lived in the United States continuously since January 1, 1982, and providing for restrictions and renewal of green cards allowing employment, applications for citizenship increased. Similarly, when California debated Proposition 187, many people applied for naturalization so that they could vote in the election. Applications for citizenship numbered about 200,000 in 1991 and were more than 1.4 million in 1997. They decreased to 933,000 in 1998 and to 700,000 in 2000. The concern of people arguing that citizenship should be the focus is that most debates over immigration take a short-term perspective on the problems and contributions of immigration. The long-term view considers the assimilation of immigrants and their becoming citizens as having positive outcomes, because they imply commitment to the system and greater likelihood of learning the language and culture of the United States. Most studies indicate that the issue of language and culture is not nearly as important as many critics of immigration contend. In fact, children of immigrants prefer English and adapt very quickly to American culture.[54] It appears that those groups that come to the United States with little hope or intent of returning to their native lands (e.g., the Vietnamese, Laotians) achieve citizenship and adapt to the culture more quickly. Those who expect to return to their homelands some day are less likely to do so (Central Americans and those from the Caribbean, for example).[55]

Still others contend that the various criteria for determining who can immigrate are not realistic and that immigration should be based on a "first come, first served" basis.[56] People taking this position suggest that some spots should be reserved for family reunification and other criteria, but the majority of slots should be based on review of applications as they are received. The position harkens back to the ideological basis for immigration; namely, that the country opened its doors to people from around the world primarily because Americans believed that everyone should be given a chance. Proponents of this position contend that other bases for including or excluding immigrants have not worked and should be scrapped for this more rational approach, which does not accept the premises of the proposals at either extreme of the debate.

The arguments over immigration often appear driven by anxieties that actually have nothing to do with immigrants. Immigration is easy to exploit as the cause of many of the nation's problems, because immigrants are an easily identifiable and usually relatively powerless element of society. The nativist arguments resonate with people who fear what they do not know or understand. Those who suffer economic dislocation or fear poverty and crime find an easy target in immigrants. Immigrant rights groups also often oversimplify the issues and see immigrants as victims in every effort to gain some control over the problems related to immigration. Most observers of immigration policy recognize that some regulation of the flow of immigration is desirable. How to achieve that regulation and how to ensure fairness and humane considerations are at the root of the controversies over immigration policies.

SUMMARY

Political and economic environments shape U.S. immigration policy; thus, the policy evolves over time. Several common themes characterize the shifts and the causes of the shifts in policy. The colonial settlers and the early experience of the original states presaged some of the types of concerns that have driven immigration policy over the entire history of the United States. Specifically, the early settlers expressed concerns about economic, social/cultural, public order, and services issues. These issues and the added issues of security and environmental concerns arise today in discussions of immigration.

Residents of the colonies and original states restricted immigrants based on religion, political culture, moral character, and impacts on public order and safety. After the 1820s, quotas were developed to limit immigration by nation of origin. These quotas favored Western and Northern Europeans. Policies in the late nineteenth century actually excluded some groups, especially Asians. There were dramatic increases in the number of immigrants in the late nineteenth century and early twentieth century. Immigration dropped off during World War I and reached a low point during World War II. After World War II, immigration grew gradually until the early 1980s when it grew dramatically until about 1991, after which a gradual decline set in until it reached 915,900 in 1996 and then began another gradual decline. The increases and decreases in immigration resulted from changing economic circumstances, wartime strife, and specific policy changes.

Quotas provided the basis for most immigration policy until the 1950s when preference systems began to emerge. The early preferences were based on skills needed in the work force and on relatives. Eventually in 1965, family reunification became the foundation of immigration policy and remains the basic criterion for admitting immigrants, although occupations and other considerations such as refugee status also govern. Illegal immigration grew after 1965 and became the subject of legislation, especially in 1986, 1990, and 1996. Much of current policy focuses on controlling illegal immigration.

The sources of immigrants have changed over time as well. Early immigrants came primarily from Northern and Western Europe. The next waves came from Southern and Eastern Europe. Now most immigrants come from Asian and Central American nations. These shifts in the makeup of the immigrant population have resulted in changes in some of the arguments against immigration. The early immigrants were more easily assimilated into the United States because they were much like the citizens. The second wave differed in national origin, religion, and culture; thus, they were much more visible. Groups developed in opposition to them (especially during the 1920s) on the basis that they threatened the social and political fabric of the nation. While these arguments had been used earlier, they became more pronounced after this time. The same concerns about more contemporary immigrants emerge as they are also very visible. They become scapegoats for the fears of many people concerning their economic security and because of the changes they bring to society and politics.

Debates about immigration policy revolve around the impacts of immigration on the economy, public and social services, quality of life, and social and political culture. To resolve the problems people associate with these issues, suggestions range from banning any immigration to setting limits to encouraging more immigration. Those who argue against any immigration or setting limits raise concerns about the society being able to absorb immigrants and the negative effects they see for the economy, costs of government, and the environment. Those advocating immigration cite the contributions immigrants make to the economy, contributions to tax revenues, and the fact that immigration as a proportion of the total population places the United States at the low end compared to other nations.

The debate over immigration policy is certain to remain an important item on the political agenda for the near future. It is an emotional issue that does not lend itself to consensus.

NOTES

1. The CQ Researcher, "Immigration Policy: A Historical Overview," in Scott Barbour, ed., *Immigration Policy* (San Diego: Greenhaven Press, 1995): 11–16.
2. Michael LeMay, *From Open Door to Dutch Door: An Analysis of U.S. Immigration Policy Since 1820* (New York: Praeger, 1987): xiii–xiv.
3. Frank D. Bean, Robert G. Cushing, Charles W. Haynes, and Jennifer V. W. Van Hook, "Immigration and the Social Contract," *Social Science Quarterly,* 78 (June 1997): 263.
4. Chilton Williamson, Jr., *The Immigration Mystique: America's False Conscience* (New York: Basic Books, 1996): 24–27.
5. Phillip Q. Yang, *Post-1965 Immigration to the United States: Structural Determinants* (Westport, CN: Praeger, 1995): 10.
6. Michael LeMay, *From Open Door to Dutch Door,* xiii.
7. Barry Edmonston, ed., *Statistics on U.S. Immigration: An Assessment of Data Needs for Future Research* (Washington, DC: National Academy Press, 1996): 10–11.
8. Vernon M. Briggs, Jr., *Immigration Policy and the American Labor Force* (Baltimore, MD: Johns Hopkins University Press, 1984): 19–22; Thomas J. Curran, *Xenophobia and Immigration, 1820–1930* (Boston: Twayne Publishers, 1975): 21; David Bennett, *The Party of Fear: From Nativist Movements to the New Right in American History* (Chapel Hill: University of North Carolina Press, 1988); and James Lincoln Collier, *The Rise of Selfishness in America* (New York: Oxford University Press, 1991).
9. U.S. Immigration and Naturalization Service, *An Immigrant Nation: United States Regulation of Immigration, 1798–1991* (Washington, DC: Immigration and Naturalization Service, 1991).

10. Chilton Williamson, Jr., *The Immigration Mystique,* 47–49.

11. Michael LeMay, *From Open Door to Dutch Door,* 111–112.

12. Vernon M. Briggs, Jr. and Stephen Moore, *Still an Open Door? U.S. Immigration Policy and the American Economy* (Washington, DC: The American University Press, 1994): 16–17.

13. As noted by Chilton Williamson, Jr., *The Immigration Mystique,* 47–49.

14. Michael Fix and Jeffrey S. Passel, *The Door Remains Open: Recent Immigration to the United States and a Preliminary Analysis of the Immigration Act of 1990* (Washington, DC: The Urban Institute, 1991); and Michael Barone, *The New Americans* (Washington, DC: Regnery Publishers, 2001).

15. Stephen Moore, "Part Two—The Economic Case for More Immigrants," in Vernon M. Briggs, Jr. and Stephen Moore, *Still Open Door?* 84–85; and Julian L. Simon, *The Economic Consequences of Immigration* (Cambridge, MA: Basil Blackwell, 1990).

16. Stephen Moore, "Part Two—The Economic Case for More Immigrants," 87; and U.S. General Accounting Office, *Immigration: The Flow of Legal Immigration to the United States* (Washington, DC: U.S. Government Printing Office, 1988).

17. "Acceptance Grows for New Immigrants," *The Arizona Republic,* June 16, 1997.

18. Heather Dewar, "Wave of Immigration Altering Nation's Face," *The Arizona Republic* (June 16, 1997): A1–A2.

19. Michael Barone, *The New Americans*; and Michael LeMay, *From Open Door to Dutch Door.*

20. Stephen Moore, "Part Two—The Economic Case for More Immigrants," 115–118.

21. Dirk Chase Eldredge, *Crowded Land of Liberty: Solving America's Immigration Crisis* (Bridgehampton, NY: Bridge Works Publishing Company, 2001).

22. The Federation for American Immigration Reform, "Census Data Shows That Illegal Alien Population Much Larger than Estimated by INS," http://fairus.org/html/07445102.htm.

23. Michael LeMay, *From Open Door to Dutch Door,* xiv.

24. Roy Beck, *The Case against Immigration* (New York: W. W. Norton, 1996), especially Chapters 5 and 6; and Otis L. Graham, "The Unfinished Reform: Regulating Immigration in the National Interest," in Roger Daniels and Otis L. Graham, eds., *Debating American Immigration, 1882–Present* (Lanham, MD: Rowman & Littlefield Publishers, 2001).

25. Roger Daniels, "Two Cheers for Immigration," in Roger Daniels and Otis L. Graham, *Debating American Immigration, 1882–Present,* 5–69; and John R. Logan, Richard D. Alba, and Michael Dill, "Ethnic Segmentation in the American Metropolis: Increasing Divergence in Economic Incorporation, 1980–1990," *International Migration Review,* 34 (Spring 2000): 98–132.

26. George Borjas, *Friends and Strangers: The Effect of Immigrants on the U.S. Economy* (New York: Basic Books, 1990); Otis L. Graham, "Unfinished Reform;" and Lawrence E. Harrison, "Immigration Should Be Reduced to Strengthen U.S. Competitiveness," in Scott Barbour, ed., *Immigration Policy,* 34–37.

27. Lawrence E. Harrison, "Immigration Should Be Reduced"; and Julie R. Watts, *Immigration Policy and the Challenge of Globalization* (Ithaca, NY: Cornell University Press, 2002).

28. Barry Edmonston, ed., *Statistics on U.S. Immigration,* 19–29; Stephen Moore, "Part Two—The Economic Case for More Immigrants," 77–80; and Julian L. Simon, "Immigration to the United States Should Be Increased," in Scott Barbour, ed., *Immigration Policy,* 55–66.

29. David M. Kennedy, "Can We Still Afford to Be a Nation of Immigrants?" *The Atlantic Monthly Atlantic Unbound,* http://www.theatlantic.com/atlantic/issues/96nov/immigrant/kennedy.htm.

30. Julian L. Simon, "Immigration to the United States Should Be Increased," 60–61.

31. Alejandro Portes and Ruben G. Rumbaut, *Immigrant America* (Berkeley: University of California Press, 1990).

32. Lorraine M. McDowell and Paul T. Hill, *Newcomers in American Schools* (Santa Monica, CA: Rand, 1993).

33. Ruben G. Rumbaut, *Immigrant Children in California Public Schools: A Summary of Current Knowledge* (Baltimore, MD: Center for Research on Effective Schooling for Disadvantaged Students, Johns Hopkins University, 1990).

34. Ruben G. Rumbaut, *Immigrant Children.*

35. Stephen Moore, "Part Two—The Economic Case for More Immigrants," 81–90.

36. George Borjas, *Friends or Strangers?*; Hiromi Ono and Rosina M. Becerra, "Race, Ethnicity and Nativity, Family Structure, Socioeconomic Status and Welfare Dependency," *International Migration Review,* 34 (Fall 2000): 739–765; Ellen Seghal, "Foreign Born in the U.S. Labor Market: Results of a Spe-

cial Survey," *Monthly Labor Review* (July 1985): 18–24; and Julian L. Simon, "Immigration to the United States Should Be Increased."

37. Roger Mahony, "Roman Catholics Should Work for Liberal Immigration Policies," in Scott Barbour, ed., *Immigration Policy*, 95–99; and Julian L. Simon, "Immigration to the United States Should Be Increased," 60.

38. Stephen Moore, "Part Two—The Economic Case for More Immigration," 95–96; and Julian L. Simon, "Immigration to the United States Should Be Increased," 62.

39. Elizabeth Martinez, "The U.S. Should Not Make Immigrants Scapegoats," in Scott Barbour, ed., *Immigration Policy*, 17–20; and La Resistencia, "Ethnic Cleansing by Attacks on Immigrants Must Be Stopped," in Scott Barbour, ed., *Immigration Policy*, 108–111.

40. George F. Kennan, "Immigration to the United States Should Be Reduced," in Scott Barbour, ed., *Immigration Policy*, 17–20; and Dan Stein, "The Federal Government Should Enact a Moratorium on Immigration," in Scott Barbour, ed., *Immigration Policy*, 21–24.

41. Gregory Fossedal, "Immigration Juggernaut," *San Francisco Chronicle* (March 28, 1990); Daniel James, "Big Immigrant Wave Swamps Assimilation," *Wall Street Journal* (July 2, 1992): A9; and Michael Myer, "Los Angeles 2010: A Latino Subcontinent," *Newsweek* (November 9, 1992).

42. Leon F. Bouvier, "Immigration Should Be Restricted for Environmental Reasons," in Scott Barbour, ed. *Immigration Policy*, 38–40.

43. Stephen Moore, "Part Two—The Economic Case for More Integration," 82–84; and John Isbister, *The Immigration Debate: Remaking America* (West Hartford, CT: Kumarian Press, 1996), especially Chapter 5.

44. Louis Uchitelle, "America's Army of Non-Workers," *The New York Times* (September 17, 1987): F1 and F6; and William Julius Wilson, *The Truly Disadvantaged: The Inner City, the Underclass, and Public Policy* (Chicago: University of Chicago Press, 1987).

45. Elizabeth Bogen, Testimony before the Joint Economic Committee, U.S. Congress, *Hearings on the Economic and Demographic Consequences of Immigration* (Washington, DC: U.S. Government Printing Office, 1986).

46. Patrick J. Buchanan, *The Death of the West: How Dying Populations and Immigrant Invasions Imperil Our Country and Civilization* (New York: Thomas Dunne Books, 2001).

47. Patrick J. Buchanan, *The Death of the West*.

48. Julian L. Simon, "Immigration to the United States Should Be Increased;" Elizabeth Martinez, "The U.S. Should Not Make Immigrants Scapegoats"; and La Resistencia, "Ethnic Cleansing by Attacks on Immigrants Must Be Stopped."

49. Roy Beck, *The Case against Immigration*, Chapter 8.

50. Dirk Chase Eldredge, *Crowded Land of Liberty*; and Dan Stein, "The United States Should Enact a Moratorium on Immigration."

51. George F. Kennan, "Immigration to the United States Should Be Reduced;" Lawrence E. Harrison, "Immigration Should Be Reduced to Strengthen U.S. Competitiveness;" Leon F. Bouvier, "Immigration Should Be Restricted for Environmental Reasons;" and Roy Beck, *The Case against Immigration*.

52. Otis L. Graham, "The Unfinished Reform"; Lawrence E. Harrison, "Immigration Should Be Reduced to Strengthen U.S. Competitiveness"; and Roy Beck, *The Case against Immigration*.

53. John Kotkin, "U.S. Immigration Policy Should Be Based on Citizenship," in Scott Barbour, ed., *Immigration Policy*, 84–89.

54. Alejandro Portes and Ruben G. Rumbaut, *Immigrant America*.

55. Ruben G. Rumbaut, *Immigrant Children*.

56. Peter D. Salins, "U.S. Immigration Policy Should Not Discriminate," in Scott Barbour, ed., *Immigration Policy*, 72–76.

SUGGESTED READINGS

Books

Barbour, Scott, ed. *Immigration Policy*. San Diego: Greenhaven Press, Inc., 1995.
Barone, Michael. *The New Americans*. Washington, DC: Regnery Publishers, Inc., 2001.

Briggs, Vernon M. Jr. *Mass Immigration and the National Interest,* 2nd ed. Armonk, NY: M. E. Sharpe, 1996.

Buchanan, Patrick J. *Death of the West: How Dying Populations and Immigrant Invasions Imperil Our Country and Civilization.* New York: Thomas Dunne Books, 2002.

Daniels, Roger, and Graham, Otis L. *Debating American Immigration, 1882–Present.* Lanham, MD: Rowman & Littlefield Publishers, Inc., 2001.

Eldredge, Dirk Chase. *Crowded Land of Liberty: Solving America's Immigration Crisis.* Bridgehampton, NY: Bridge Works Publishing, 2001.

Foner, Nancy, Rumbaut, Ruben G., and Gold, Steven J., eds. *Immigration Research for a New Century: Multidisciplinary Perspectives.* New York: Russell Sage, 2000.

LeMay, Michael. *Anatomy of a Public Policy: The Reform of Contemporary American Immigration Law.* New York: Praeger, 1994.

LeMay, Michael, and Barkan, Elliot Robert, eds. *U.S. Immigration and Naturalization Laws and Issues: A Documentary History.* London: Greenwood Press, 1999.

Suro, Roberto. *Strangers among Us: How Latino Immigration Is Transforming America.* New York: Knopf, 1998.

Watts, Julie R. *Immigration Policy and the Challenge of Globalization: Unions and Employers in Unlikely Alliance.* Ithaca: Cornell University Press, 2002.

Web Sites

Center for Comparative Immigration Studies   www.ccis.ucsd.org
Center for Immigration and Refugee Studies   www.csupomona.edu~iris/irisimm.htm
Center for Immigration Studies   www.cis.org
Center for Migration Studies   www.cmsny.org
Center for Research on Immigration Policy   www.rand.org/education/crip.html
Ellis Island Immigration Museum   www.ellisisland.com/intro.html
Federation for American Immigration Reform   www.fairus.org/
Immigration and Naturalization Service   www.ins.usdoj.gov
National Immigration Forum   www.immigrationforum.org

CHAPTER 12

Foreign and Defense Policy: Security and Interests in a Dangerous World

The events of September 11, 2001, brought home to America the realization that retreat to a "fortress America," the recurring isolationist approach to foreign policy in American history, is no longer (if it ever had been) a realistic option. The apparently ongoing threat of massive terrorism cast this country into the maelstrom of world conflicts with a suddenness and a degree for which we, as a nation, were quite unprepared.

The natural borders on our east and west coasts, provided by two major oceans, together with nonthreatening neighbors on our northern and southern borders seemed for much of our history to insulate us from the need for active involvement in the affairs and conflicts of the world outside of the Western Hemisphere. Two world wars in the twentieth century did much to puncture our belief in such insulation. Yet America's insulation from the currents of diplomacy and conflict through much of its history left it with a distinctive perspective and style in the formulation of the aims and applications of foreign and defense policy compared to other Western powers.

ISSUE BACKGROUND: COMPETING APPROACHES TO FOREIGN POLICY

Realism or Classical Diplomacy

There is a style in the conduct of international diplomacy that characterized relations among European and other Western powers for much of the modern era. This style, based upon a set of assumptions about the nature of the world order and about the nature of humanity, is widely known as *classical diplomacy*. This approach to foreign policy is also known as *political realism or power politics*. Scholars such as Hans Morgenthau, E. H. Carr, and Kenneth Thompson most clearly articulated this approach.[1]

This chapter will show that a different perspective from realism has primarily influenced the foreign policy of the United States in the twentieth century.

The first premise of classical diplomacy is that there are no universally self-evident principles of justice, right and wrong, or truth that nations are morally obligated to pursue. Hence, the national interest is not only a legitimate goal of foreign policy, but, in the view of political realists, the only defensible goal. States function and are morally obligated, in this view, to protect the interests of their societies. Realists point to the widespread public support that has existed for policies that we in the mainstream West regard as obscene such as genocide

401

(the systematic slaughter of an entire racially, religiously, or ethnically defined people).[2] Regimes based on widespread public support carried out such genocide not only in World War II, but in the former Cambodia (now called Kampuchea), in the former Yugoslavia, and in parts of Africa since World War II. As this is written, the defiant lack of remorse by Slobodan Milosevic, the former president of Serbia now on trial in an international tribunal for a policy of "ethnic cleansing" against Bosnian Muslims, as well as the aforementioned other acts of modern genocide, cast doubt on the assumption that universal principles of justice are self-evident to all reasonable persons.

Because of considerations of geography, demography, resources, and history, each nation develops a set of interests, some of them considered vital, that are unique to that nation. Moreover, the interests of nations naturally come into conflict. Hence, conflict among nations is normal. What is good for some nations logically conflicts with what is in the interests of other nations. The goals of foreign policy, therefore, ought to be framed in terms of such interests, rather than in terms of abstract principles of justice or universal morality.

For example, the American Cold War policy of containment, the resistance to any expansion of communist control or influence between World War II and 1990, was based more on the presumption that communism was a "bad" thing, the antithesis of many of the fundamental values of the West, than upon any consideration of how much a particular expansion of communist influence affected our national interests. Many realists criticized our involvement in the Vietnam War on the basis that we did not have enough at stake in who controlled the Indochinese Peninsula to justify the costs of keeping South Vietnam in the hands of an anticommunist regime. Foreign policy goals, in the realist perspective, can be framed in terms of whether the national interests in question are achievable and in terms of an analysis of the costs of achieving them in relation to the benefits to be derived. The unsavory nature of the North Vietnamese dictatorship would be beside the point in this kind of analysis. The aims of foreign policy, to the realist, should not be separated from the consideration of the relative power of the concerned nations.

Power politics. Force, in this classical or realist perspective, is neither moral nor immoral in itself, but rather an extension of diplomacy intended to pursue the national interest. *Power* is a central concept in the realist perspective.[3] Power is defined here as a relationship between two or more actors such that the power wielder can get others to do what the power wielder wants them to do and which they otherwise would not have done. The powerful accomplish this by manipulating the threat or promise of potential rewards and punishments to make the others perceive that they would be better off doing what the power wielder wants. Such use of power is the essence of politics.

Realists define broadly the resources involved in creating the threat of rewards or punishments; they may include such things as economic power, the appeal of one's principles, or the intensity or degree of one's commitment to the goals in question, as well as military might. Given the natural conflict of interests among nations, politics or the use of power is inescapable in this perspective. Diplomacy or negotiation is not a substitute for the application of power or force, because diplomacy without an understood ability and willingness to back up one's goals with force or power becomes equivalent to supplication (begging).

Nations, in this view, must be perceived as willing to use force or power to pursue their interests to the extent that the likely benefits of achieving one's goal exceed the costs. This cost-benefit analysis does not include a moral judgment of the inherent goodness or evil of one's opponents. Realists, therefore, are willing to engage in limited war for limited objectives, something with which we, as Americans, have traditionally felt uncomfortable, because we have defined our conflicts in moral terms.

Spheres of influence. Since principles of justice are not universal, the legitimate interests of nations are greater in some parts of the world than in others. Normally, nations have a greater interest in territories contiguous to their borders than in other parts of the world. Hence, in the "Monroe Doctrine," the United States proclaimed to the world that we had a vital interest in the politics of the Western Hemisphere. Similarly, at Yalta we yielded to the claims of the Soviet Union that they had a greater interest in the affairs of Eastern Europe than we did. This was not, as critics of the Yalta agreements charge, a case of selling out the freedom of Eastern European people as much as a case of not having as great an interest and a willingness to expend as many resources in shaping the politics of that region as did the Soviets.

In a reaction against our participation in the Vietnam War, many people identified the lessons of Vietnam as indicating that we ought not to attempt to shape the internal politics of other countries as we did in trying to prevent South Vietnam from becoming part of the communist orbit. These "lessons" were the basis of a scathing critique of our opposition to the pro-Marxist Sandinista regime in Nicaragua during the 1980s. Yet, the sphere of influence principle was also used to argue that America had a legitimate interest in the affairs of Central America that we did not have in the affairs of Indochina. After all, an anti-American regime in Central America, able to influence if not subvert other regimes in the region, including Mexico, which shares a long, porous border with the United States, could pose a realistic threat to American interests that did not exist from a small, nonindustrialized country in Southeast Asia.

It seemed heartless, or at least ethnocentric, that we did not commit blood and treasure to contest the mass slaughter between the Hutus and Tutsi tribes in Rwanda in Central Africa in the early 1990s, while we did commit such resources to halt ethnic cleansing in the former Yugoslavia. Critics of the failure of America to act more decisively to halt the slaughter in Africa have suggested it was because the victims were black. Yet one could make the argument that we had more interests at stake in the affairs of Central Europe, a region that provided the spark to ignite the two world wars in which we engaged in the twentieth century, than we did in Rwanda. Such a conclusion would be an implementation of the concept of spheres of influence as opposed to the idealist conception that America should fight injustice with equal vigor wherever it occurs.

The concept of spheres of influence provides a criterion for the rationing of the expenditure of scarce resources. Political realists argue that if we appoint ourselves as a world police force or guardian of international justice, we would have to raise and support a considerably expanded defense and military establishment. By confining our efforts to the protection of the vital interests of our own country, the expenditure of our resources becomes more manageable. George W. Bush may have been articulating this position in the 2000 presidential campaign, when, in reaction to the unsuccessful insertion of our military forces in Somalia during the Clinton administration, he argued against our assuming a role of the world's policeman.

This kind of realism is not equivalent to the isolationist sentiment of the interwar period (between the two world wars), which asserted that events outside of our borders were none of our concern. The spheres of influence concept acknowledges that we have vital interests at stake in the Western Hemisphere and Western Europe, among other places. However, due to modern technology, our interests are no longer defined only geographically. The economic affairs of an economic superpower like Japan may have a serious economic impact on Americans.

The Balance of Power

Another major concept of this realist or power politics approach to foreign policy is that of *the balance of power*. The key principle of this concept is that no one power or coalition of powers should be allowed to gain such dominating power as to be able to dictate terms of the relationships among nations without having to compromise its interests with the demands of competing interests. *Hegemony* designates a situation in which one state so dominates other states that it may dictate the terms of the relationship between them without the need to compromise its interests. When one nation acquires hegemonic power over other nations, the other nations lose their ability to protect the vital interests of their citizens.

Nations that pursue the balance of power strategy do so by shifting alliances so that one power always allies with the weaker of competing states or alliances. If a nation joined the stronger alliance, once that alliance eliminated the competing weaker alliance, the strongest power in the victorious alliance would have hegemonic power. However, by joining the weaker alliance or power, and thereby increasing the strength of the weaker forces or diminishing the strength of the strongest power, the balancing nation could force the strongest power in the stronger alliance to bargain and come to terms with competing powers and interests.[4] The idea is to check the imposition of the goals and values of the strongest and potentially hegemonic powers by establishing equilibrium among the nations.[5]

For several centuries in European history, beginning around the sixteenth century, Great Britain played the balancing role in the recurring conflicts involving France, Spain, and the Holy Roman Empire. Henry VIII, who allegedly said, "He whom I support will prevail," and Elizabeth I played this role especially well. The balancing power has as its objective the maintenance of balance or equilibrium irrespective of concrete policy considerations. This balancing power has neither permanent friends nor permanent enemies and is thus in a state of self-imposed "splendid isolation."[6] Great Britain thus allied itself with the Low Countries, especially the Netherlands, and the Hapsburgs of the Holy Roman Empire against the powerful Louis XIV of France, most notably in the War of the Spanish Succession (1702–1713). The roles of Britain and eventually the United States in World War I were an exercise in balance of power politics with the goal of checking Germany's Second Reich under Kaiser Wilhelm from obtaining a hegemonic domination of Western Europe. Thus, Nicholas Spykman, late Professor of International Relations at Yale and a staunch political realist, wrote that,

"Twice in one generation we have come to the aid of Great Britain in order that the small offshore island might not have to face a single gigantic state in control of the opposite coast of the mainland."[7] Of course, United States idealists did not see it that way. Instead, they defined the American mission in apocalyptic and idealistic terms, such as "the war to end all wars" and "saving the world for democracy."

The balancing strategy epitomizes classical diplomacy in that policy considerations are irrelevant and power considerations are everything.

Deterrence. As opposed to the strategy of avoiding aggressive action by potential foes by reconciling differences through negotiation, realists avoid attacks on their vital interests with a strategy known as *deterrence*. Deterrence is a strategy based purely on power politics considerations without concern for the relative merits or justice of the respective policy goals. This strategy involves the possession of sufficient and varied power to survive the best first strike by a potential foe with enough power and willingness to inflict unacceptable damage on such an attacker.

There are psychological dimensions to the strategy of deterrence. The implied threat of the use of power or force against the potential foe must be credible. That is, the potential foe must believe in one's willingness to actually use the deterring force. Thus, the United States' Cold War strategy of relying on massive nuclear power to deter Soviet encroachment on our vital interests did not deter the Soviets from numerous encroachments on our interests, because they did not believe in our willingness to launch a thermonuclear strike and risk nuclear retaliation for any interest short of the very survival of our country.

The second psychological dimension is the question of what damage to a potential foe their leadership considers "unacceptable." Authoritarian leaders in some countries have shown a willingness to accept a considerable amount of misery and even death among large segments of their citizenry in order to pursue their policy goals. Both Stalin and the rulers of Communist China were willing to accept massive starvation in order to collectivize agriculture. Saddam Hussein of Iraq was willing to accept considerable deprivation among his people to ride out American sanctions and protect his weapons programs. These leaders have provisions such that they could survive even nuclear retaliation against their countries. There is therefore a serious question as to whether the prospect of massive losses among their populations would be enough to deter such men.

Nevertheless, deterrence has a record. Despite an announced desire to do so, the Soviet Union never attacked the West directly during the Cold War, the longest period in modern history without a general war in the West. However, the strategy used between 1919 and 1939 to avoid future wars was negotiation unsupported by the credible threat of power, combined with mutually negotiated disarmament.[8] World War II attests to the colossal failure of this latter strategy.

THE AMERICAN STYLE IN FOREIGN POLICY: WILSONIAN IDEALISM

The previous discussion of classical diplomacy or power politics implicitly contrasted that approach to foreign policy with a different American style. Scholars characterize that American style as *idealism*. Because President Woodrow Wilson's

"Fourteen Points" speech in 1918, in which he proposed the League of Nations to Congress, epitomized this approach, it is often called *Wilsonian Idealism.*

Universal Justice and the Nuremburg Principle

To the idealist perspective, the pursuit of the national interest is an inadequate justification for resorting to the horrors of armed conflict. There are, for idealists, knowable and universal principles of justice over and above the laws and policies of any particular state. Hence, the governments and people of nation states can be held accountable for the protection and pursuit of those principles. Thus, the leadership and even the population of the sovereign nations of the world are morally obligated to disregard and disobey the laws and policies of their countries to the extent that these laws and policies violate these knowable principles of justice. This position is sometimes called *the Nuremburg Principle,* because without the assumption of such knowable universal principles of morality and justice, the War Crimes Trials of top Nazi leadership in Nuremburg, Germany, would have made no sense. The Nazi élites, after all, were obeying the laws and orders of the lawful superiors of their nation state.

The universal harmony of interests. With this assumption of knowable universal good, idealists view human nature as essentially good and cooperative. Most people share basic values (health, prosperity, family). The world, therefore, possesses a universal harmony of interests marred only by the selfish motives of a small group of nonaccountable rulers. This view was propagated by the antiwar left in the 1960s in such venues as the film *The Russians Are Coming . . .,* the theme of which was a Russian submarine running aground in Maine. The negatively portrayed superpatriots run around in a panic, while the calm hero finds out that the Russians are just ordinary folks like the rest of us who want the same things out of life. In the same way, American leaders reassured the American public in the wake of the attacks on the World Trade Center and Pentagon on September 11, 2001, that these events were the work of a few extremists who distort Muslim principles and that the vast multitudes of ordinary people in the Muslim world would never condone such attacks. In positing the clear distinction between the allegedly selfish and out-of-touch rulers and their ordinary masses, the idealist perspective rejects the claim of scholars like Harvard's Samuel Huntington that Islamic civilization has been based upon pursuing values and goals in direct conflict with the West for 14 hundred years and that the Muslim masses increasingly see the West as "materialistic, corrupt, decadent and immoral."[9]

Because of this universal harmony of interests, calm reasoning or negotiation can generally resolve conflicts, and war is usually wrong and unnecessary. When war becomes unavoidable, however, it becomes a crusade against these selfish and autocratic rulers. War is never justified in terms of a pursuit of the national interests, but only as a moral crusade. President Bush in his 2002 "State of the Union" speech defined conflict in such moral terms, when he characterized Iran, Iraq, and North Korea—nations whose professed aims and whose potential weaponry render them a threat to the vital interests of the United States—as "the axis of evil."

When one defines conflicts in such normative terms, the goals of the utilization of force frequently become unconditional surrender or the total destruction of one's opponents. After all, one does not bargain and compromise with pure evil. When it was obvious by the fall of 1918, following America's 1917 entry into World War I, that Germany would be unable to obtain the hegemony that she sought over Europe, Germany sought a negotiated peace. The American president, however, insisted upon the abdication of the "evil" Kaiser Wilhelm and the creation of a democratic republic that was completely incongruent with the German culture and experience. The war dragged on for another year before the capitulation of the Second Reich. The inevitable failure of the Weimar Republic that followed created a power vacuum in Central Europe that would be filled by Hitler's Third Reich some fourteen years after the abdication and armistice.

Because these principles of justice are universal, idealists reject the premise of the "spheres of influence" principle of classical diplomacy. Thus, to the idealist, "the lessons of Vietnam" are that we should not meddle in or try to shape the internal politics of another country, not because the costs of doing so in Vietnam far exceeded potential benefits, but because such interference is wrong. It was equally wrong to meddle in the internal affairs of the Marxist government of Nicaragua in the 1980s, despite that nation's possible capacity to influence Mexico into an anti-American position on key issues.

The converse conclusion of this assumption of universal justice is that the same moral imperatives that led to our intervention in the former Yugoslavia against the Serbian "ethnic cleansing" should have led to our intervention in the mass slaughter in Rwanda. Evil is evil whether it occurs in central Europe or in Africa.

Diplomacy, Force, and American Optimism

In the American idealist perspective, diplomacy is an alternative to the use of force. Since people are essentially cooperative by nature and motivated by the same basic values, mutual reasoning and persuasion can resolve differences among peoples. From the Kellogg-Briand Pact of 1928 that renounced war as an instrument of national policy and the mobilization of antiwar sentiment by Charles Lindbergh and others on the eve of World War II, to the mobilized opposition to our entry into the Gulf War and the conflicts in the former Yugoslavia, Americans have been reluctant to commit military force for any purpose short of the survival of the country. The disappointing outcome of our intervention in the Vietnam War reinforced this reluctance to the point where American hesitancy to use force is sometimes called "the Vietnam syndrome."

This persisting faith in diplomacy rests upon the deep-seated American faith that all conflicts are ultimately resolvable by reasoned negotiation. Henry Kissinger has written of the American confidence in the bargaining process in which negotiators view themselves as mediators between Washington and the country with which they are negotiating.[10] All of this presumes that there is a scenario to which all parties, given their values and goals, can plausibly agree. For example, it will shown later that advocates of the Middle East "peace process" in which America has been so heavily engaged assume that all of the major parties ultimately would be satisfied with a two-state solution. This perspective also assumes that the conflict is really about borders rather than mutual acceptance by Palestinians and Israelis of the right of the other to exist. Yet, it is not self-evident that all relevant parties would agree to such an outcome regardless of the borders.

Besides divorcing diplomacy from power, idealists tend to divorce the formulation of foreign policy goals from the costs and possibilities of achieving them. Our Cold War goal of *containment,* the policy that we should resist any further encroachment of governments labeled communist in whatever form or context, framed foreign policy in terms of the moral presumption that communism was a bad thing. Although, other things being equal, the United States would have been better off with a noncommunist government in place in a given country than an avowedly communist one, it is not clear that all regimes labeled communist pose an equal threat to American interests. Therefore, the costs of preventing the expansion of a communist regime may or may not be justified in terms of those interests.

Moreover, aside from considerations of cost, it is not clear that all foreign goals are ultimately achievable. It will be posited later that regardless of the desirability of having a stable and legitimate noncommunist and pro-Western government ruling South Vietnam, knowledge of the history of Vietnamese nationalism suggests that goal was never achievable.

This disposition to define foreign policy goals independently of the costs and possibility of achieving them is a result of defining international conflict in the normative terms of the pursuit of some conception of universal justice, rather than in terms of the pursuit of the national interests. American idealists have tended to seek an alternative to power politics and to define military conflict as "a holy crusade against evil incarnate . . . holy wars of 'unconditional surrender' against solitary infidels. . . ."[11]

Collective Security and Institutional Solutions to World Conflict

Idealists reject the balance of power strategy for deterring aggressive behavior and its underlying premise that war is a normal instrument of policy. Among the institutional means of preventing conflict offered by idealists is the principle of *collective security.* This system assumes that the preponderance of states in the world share values of peaceful coexistence and wish to prevent aggression by one state on another. It assumes that the states in the system will subordinate their particular national interests to the collective good. It further assumes that there is agreement among the states as to the status quo that is to be preserved. It also assumes there is agreement about what constitutes an act of aggression.[12] Given that the term is normative (the other fellow's military action is aggression; mine is self-defense), identifying acts of aggression could be a problem. Is an act of terrorism aggression or an act of war? Such regional alliances as the North Atlantic Treaty Organization (NATO) and the Southeast Asia Treaty Organization (SEATO) are examples of the principle of collective security, where each participant declares that an attack on one is an attack on all.

Policymakers in the American idealist tradition have thus sought an alternative to what they regarded as the corrupt power politics of classical diplomacy. We will now turn to how the formulation and implementation of major foreign policies in the post-World War II world reflected these assumptions and dispositions and how these policies differ from the classical style of diplomacy.

RECENT AND CONTEMPORARY POLICY: COLD WAR, CONTAINMENT, AND AFTER

The alliance of the United States and the Soviet Union quickly fell apart at the close of World War II, when the Soviets engineered the installation of regimes in Eastern and Central Europe hostile to the West and its values. What Winston Churchill called "the iron curtain" descended across Europe, separating the democratic states of Western Europe from these Soviet puppet regimes united in a collective security arrangement called *The Warsaw Pact*. Meanwhile, the Western democracies formed their own collective security arrangement, *The North Atlantic Treaty Organization* (NATO).

This arrangement seemed necessary in light of the failure of the collective security provisions of the newly established United Nations. Collective security in the UN depended upon the unanimous agreement of the great powers (as noted in the previous discussion of collective security). The effective veto power of the Soviet Union over decisions of the Security Council of the United Nations meant that the organization could not mobilize a response to Soviet aggression.

After World War II, the success of the communist revolution in China and other parts of Asia did not initially seem to alter the apparent bipolar nature of the post-war world order. The essential nature of that order was perceived in the West as the freedom-loving, democratic states of the West threatened by a monolithic bloc of communist nations directed from the Kremlin.

The reality of the Chinese-Soviet split and the emergence of a wave of newly independent nations in Africa and Asia in the 1950s and 1960s following the breakup of European-dominated imperialistic empires modified this initial perception. These newly emergent states, however, appeared to many Americans as a similarly monolithic "third world" independent of the communist and noncommunist blocs of nations.

Nevertheless, the United States viewed the post-war world as dominated by the threat of the aggressive communist bloc of nations to the security of the democratic West. While ideological tension between the putatively capitalist West and what the Soviets called communism goes back to the Bolshevik Revolution of 1917, these ideological stances were more of a justification for action in pursuit of national interests than a cause of conflict. The ideological conflict, however, took on a life of its own once the Cold War became a reality.[13] Fear of communist expansion and assaults on the vital interests of Western nations was not unrealistic in this early Cold War period. Aggressive action by communist bloc nations did occur (for example, the invasion of South Korea by its northern neighbor in 1950), as did instances of Soviet-directed espionage and undermining of noncommunist regimes. However, this bipolar view of the world dominated all other interests and became normatively defined as a struggle against what President Ronald Reagan called "the evil empire."

It was clear that the publics of the West were not ready to undertake military action to wrest control of the communist bloc nations from Soviet control, especially when it became clear that the Soviet Union had acquired the capability to manufacture and deliver nuclear weapons. The alternative that we adopted as the defining principle of American foreign policy during the Cold War was what George Kennan, a diplomat in the U.S. embassy in the Soviet Union, called "*containment*."[14] Kennan and those who thought like him believed that the Soviet

Union was going to be an aggressively expansive power, a conclusion reinforced by Soviet leader Joseph Stalin's speech in February 1946, in which he discussed "the inevitability of conflict with capitalist powers."[15] The essence of the concept of containment was that the United States would act to resist the expansion of the influence of communist powers over previously noncommunist powers. The policy glossed over the distinctions among the nation states in each of these broad categories. Clearly, some structures bearing the label communist posed a very different level of threat to American interests than other such structures. Hence, a hard line Stalinist regime such as the one that headed the Democratic Republic of Germany (East Germany) would challenge American interests much more than a nominally communist party that had declared its independence of the Kremlin line, such as the Italian Communists. Moreover, noncommunist states vary greatly with respect to whether they support or challenge American interests. The United States supported some very authoritarian and unsavory regimes during the Cold War because such regimes identified themselves as being anti-Communist. For example, we supported a military junta in Greece headed by an autocratic Colonel Papadopoulos because the elected Greek head of government was a leftist too closely associated with a Marxist point of view. This simplistic division of the world into the good-guy capitalists and the bad-guy communists reflects a characteristically American moralistic perspective that ignores the national interest in particular cases.

The war in Korea that began when the North Korean regime invaded the south in 1950 was a classic implementation of the principle of containment. When the communist North Korea launched its invasion, President Truman, under UN auspices, ordered American forces into battle to save South Korea. There was little or no discussion of how communist control of the Korean peninsula would affect American interests, other than to invoke the Munich analogy. Munich refers to the infamous appeasement of Adolf Hitler on the eve of World War II, as if Europe under the control of the Nazi war machine posed no greater threat to American interests than the Korean peninsula under the control of the less-modernized north. The American effort was successful in saving the noncommunist status of South Korea, because our military had a stable, legitimate, and relatively effective political system to defend. We will see that was not the case in the next major American military commitment in Vietnam.

The Failure of Containment in Vietnam

The success of the individual known as Ho Chi Minh in gaining control of first the government of the north and the support of much of the population of the south was that he co-opted the strong nationalist and anti-imperialist passion among the Vietnamese people for his political and communist purposes.[16] Indeed, the success of the communist movement in Southeast Asia was proportional to its ability to become identified with the struggle for national independence.[17] While we perceived the struggle there as between the yoke of communist oppression and the freedom of the noncommunist world, many Vietnamese saw the struggle as between Western imperialism and national liberation.

The Leninist modifications of Marxism in fact offered an ideal ideological vehicle for mobilizing movements of national liberation. Lenin explained the failure of capitalism to collapse as Marx predicted by imperialism. Imperialism, he argued, gave capitalism artificial life by providing cheap foreign raw materials and captive markets to siphon off the "surplus value" that Marx predicted would bring down capitalism. Leninism appealed to the colonial subjects of Western empires by identifying the entire colonized world as Marx's oppressed victims of Western capitalism. Thus, this third world "proletariat" can claim Marx's "scientific" certainty of ultimate redemption that gives hope to these oppressed people. Leninism in this context "confers upon its believers absolute confidence in the ultimate victory of their cause."[18] Furthermore, Leninism appealed to third world nationalists because it transferred blame for the economically less-developed state of their nations to imperialistic exploitation by Western powers rather than on attributes of their own society. It was therefore not hard to combine a passion for Marxism-Leninism and nationalism in the same movement.

Ho Chi Minh, born Nguyen-Ai-Quoc, worked his way aboard a French ship from Indochina to Paris, where he worked as a chef and campaigned actively for Vietnamese independence. Rebuffed by the French at the Versailles Conference at the end of World War I, he joined the French Socialist Party (then called the French Section of the Workers' International or SFIO).[19] When the SFIO supported the French empire, he joined the Marxist wing of the party and was sent to Moscow for training in the nationalism issue. The front of various opponents of French rule that he headed when smuggled back into Indochina, the *Viet Minh* (*Vietnam Doc Lap Dong Minh Hoi*—The League for the Independence of Vietnam), was essentially a nationalist organization (*Doc Lap* means independence). Was Ho Chi Minh (meaning he who enlightens), as he now called himself, a nationalist or a Marxist? Clearly, he was both.[20] The Indochinese Communist Party was a well-organized veteran of operating clandestine antisystem activities since the 1930s and was able to co-opt the *Viet Minh*.

The Japanese in World War II threw the French out of Indochina. Because we identified Ho Chi Minh as a communist, the United States financed and supported a French invasion of Indochina to resume French colonial control after the war. When the French armies were defeated, we gradually assumed the role of fighting the Viet Minh for control of South Vietnam under the presumption that we were fighting communism. Many of the Vietnamese, however, saw our role as a defense of Western colonial control of their homeland.

At this point in history, Western imperialism was not a defensible system; yet, that defense appeared to be our role in Vietnam. Because much of the native population perceived South Vietnam as an instrument of Western colonialism, it lacked internal legitimacy. Our military can certainly defend a sovereign, legitimate government, but it cannot create one. Hence, the putative goal of participation in the Vietnamese War, the maintenance of a stable, effective, noncommunist and pro-Western government in South Vietnam, was probably never attainable.

American political leaders seldom asked questions about the feasibility and costs of our goals. Southeast Asia experts, whose sense of history made them skeptical about our policies, had been squeezed out of the State Department by young, inexperienced people characterized by the typically American unbounded optimism that any goal could be achieved with sufficient commitment.[21] The realists' position that some goals are unachievable seems to be supported by the frustrating outcome of our Vietnam War, the loss of South Vietnam to the North in the mid-1970s.

The Search for a Comprehensive Peace in Palestine

The United States has been actively engaged on several occasions to broker a comprehensive peace agreement between the state of Israel, the various Arab and Muslim countries that occupy the area, and the various groups that support the nationalist aspirations of the people known as the Palestinians. From the active role played by President Carter to engineer a peace agreement between Israel and Egypt to the intense effort by President Clinton to broker a comprehensive settlement between the Israelis and the Palestinian Authority represented by Yasir Arafat, the United States has expended a considerable amount of diplomatic capital on this effort. This effort is justified by the recognition that we have important interests in the region, by the presumption that a settlement is desired by both parties and is possible, and by an American disposition to end violence and correct perceived injustices throughout the world.

POLICY EVALUATION: REALISM VERSUS IDEALISM IN THE MIDDLE EAST

The contemporary foreign policy challenges that stem from American policy in the Middle East particularly involve the conflict between Israel and the Palestinians, the politics of oil, and the terrorism directed at the United States and its allies, partly in response to American policy.

America perceives that it has several important interests at stake in the region, interests that could be threatened by an eruption of the tension in the area to a general conflict. We, of course, have an interest in access for ourselves and our Western allies to the world's largest proven reserves of crude petroleum; hence, we feel we need to maintain a working relationship with those Arab and Muslim states in the area that control those reserves. Actually, our European and Japanese allies are even more dependent on Mid-East oil than we are, but we have an interest in the health of their economies. Secondly, the Middle East is geographically at a strategic crossroads in the world. Therefore it is to our benefit if we have reliable allies who can provide logistical support for forces we may have in the area (for example, to land and refuel planes, store supplies, dock ships, and give liberty to crews) as well as to share intelligence about movements and forces in the area that affect our interests. For example, the United States used bases in Saudi Arabia during the Gulf War of 1991. Middle East policy, then, tests the limits of classical diplomacy and of foreign policy idealism.

Oil, U.S. Foreign Policy, and the Middle East

The premise of our efforts to broker peace and stable relations in the Middle East reflect the tension between traditional American idealism and realism. For example, the idealist position assumes that there is a just and legitimate Palestinian nationalism and a just and legitimate Israeli nationalism. We assume that the goal of a peace process is a Palestinian state that would coexist with the Jewish state of Israel and that this goal can be achieved by trading for peace land that Israel illegitimately seized in 1967. Therefore, efforts to broker peace presume the conflict is essentially where to draw the borders between a Jewish and a Palestinian state, and that there is some scenario or outcome to which all contending parties might conceivably agree.

Just as important is American (and other Western) access to the oil reserves of the Middle East, which makes it an important national interest. How an American-brokered settlement would enhance that access or whether the continued tension between the parties would impair that access is another question. The Arab world has sold oil to the West since the value of that resource became manifest. This has occurred despite the fact that the 14-hundred-year history of relations between the Muslim world and the West has been one of tension.[22] The Arabs sell oil to the West because that is the only way that resource is of much value to them, not because they like the West. Iraq, despite the Gulf War of 1991 and the continued tensions between that country and the West, has been fighting for the right to sell its petroleum to the West.

Moreover, it is arguable that the United States has an interest in the preservation of the one nation in that part of the world that is democratic and has been consistently pro-Western. The Arab world has yet to produce a single transition to democracy despite a wave of such transitions in other parts of the world. America, partly out of a feeling of kinship to a Western-style democracy, partly out of sympathy for a nation born out of the Holocaust, and partly out of the domestic power of the American Jewish community, has felt obliged to offer considerable financial support to the beleaguered state of Israel, without which that nation could not survive. This support angers the Muslim world, which refers to the establishment of the Jewish state as "the catastrophe." Yet, for the reasons previously stated, we seek to maintain a working relationship with the Muslim nations of the Middle East.

Palestinian Nationalism as a Just and Achievable Cause

The argument for the justice of the Palestinian cause reflects a widespread assumption that the Israelis are "settlers" that have occupied land that has been Arab or Palestinian since "time immemorial." This widely held assumption about that area was most succinctly stated in a work by Joan Peters. She refers to "the myth that 'the Jews arrived only in 1948 where they displaced a teeming Arab population from its rooted homeland since time immemorial.' "[23] In a profusely documented work culminating years of research, she came to a different conclusion than the one she set out to prove. She found that while some Arabs and some Jews had always lived in the area of the Palestine Mandate, it was sparsely settled and run down. Many of the people we call "Palestinians" descend from people who migrated to the area about the same time as the Zionists in the early twentieth century, taking advantage of an expanding Westernized economy.[24] Characterizing the Israelis as "settlers" and the territories they control as "occupied" implies the land belongs in some sense to the Muslim people and that the Jews have no right to be there. The facts of history show a more complicated reality. Secondly, the argument for the justice of a borders-based settlement to the conflict reflects the widespread belief that all national groups deserve self-determination and a sovereign state that allows them to act in the world as an identifiable people. The difficulty is that both Israel and the Palestinian people claim the same territory as their base of sovereignty.

When the Ottoman Turks took Constantinople in 1453, the Ottoman Empire displaced Byzantium and ruled Palestine until the close of World War I. Being on the losing side in that war cost the Turks their empire, and Palestine became a League of Nations mandate, in effect international territory. After World War II, the mandate was under the auspices of the United Nations, with Great Britain continuing as the mandatory power. There never was an Arab state of Palestine; hence, the legal rights of Arabs and the Jews to live in the unincorporated parts of the mandate are equal.

When the British abandoned their mandate after World War II, the United Nations Security Council voted to partition the mandate into three states: a small Jewish state on the shores of the Mediterranean, an Arab state east of the Jordan River called Trans Jordan to be governed by the Hashemite Monarchy, and another Arab state between the West Bank of the Jordan River and Israel. Israel and Trans Jordan accepted the partition and declared their states. The rest of the Arab world rejected the partition and mobilized to destroy the Jewish state by armed force. The point here is that a Palestinian state was formally offered by the UN and Israel and rejected. This is the first of three times a formal offer of a Palestinian state was rejected. Although the Arab attempt to destroy the Jewish state did not succeed, Jordan occupied the West Bank of the Jordan River, leaving the Jewish state eight to twelve miles wide at its neck, which was not a defensible position.

The second rejection of such an offer came in the wake of the 1967 Six Day War. Declaring once again their intention to destroy the Jewish state, the Muslim states massed their troops on its borders. Israel's ports were blockaded, an act of belligerency under international law. Facing this situation with their indefensible borders, Israel launched a preemptive strike, destroyed the Egyptian air force on the ground, and defeated the combined Arab powers in six days. The Israelis thus controlled the West Bank, the Sinai Desert through which the Egyptians had launched three armed attacks against Israel in twenty years, and the Golan Heights through which Syria had launched their assaults on Israel. Though Israel now had defensible borders, its government offered to return the territories it had captured in return for peace treaties and formal recognition from its neighbors. The immediate Arab response was "no negotiation, no recognition, no peace." However, after Egyptian president Gammel Nasser died, President Anwar Sadat negotiated a peace treaty with Israel. The entire Sinai, with its valuable oil reserves and strategic passes, returned to Egyptian control. Relations between the two states, however, remain cold and hostile.

The third refusal of an explicit offer of a state for the Palestinians came after weeks of intense negotiations under the mediation of American President Clinton in late 2000. The offer included the return to Palestinian control of over 90 percent of the West Bank, the Gaza Strip, and the holy parts of old Jerusalem, which are highly sacred to Jews and Muslims. This offer went further than anyone familiar with Israel thought its government would ever go. Nevertheless, Chairman Arafat of the Palestinian Liberation Organization (PLO) refused the offer, believing that the offer did not grant sufficient territory and sovereignty to the Palestinian people. Subsequently, he either ordered or permitted his followers to launch a new wave of intense violence against Israeli civilians, following various perceived injustices on the part of the Israeli occupation of parts of the West Bank and the Gaza Strip.

The Clinton-led negotiations were the culmination of a lengthy process known as the Oslo Process after an agreement negotiated in that city. The agreement committed the Israeli and Palestinian parties to a land-for-peace process. The Palestinians committed themselves in this pact to recognize Israeli's right to exist and to curb violence against Israeli citizens. The Israelis committed themselves to withdrawal from territories occupied in the 1967 war. The PLO has not formally changed its charter provisions that commit the organization to seek the complete destruction of Israel, although its chairman, Yasir Arafat, has personally stated that recognition. The escalating violence involving numerous suicide bombers in public places through this writing in the spring of 2002 speaks to the unwillingness of many Palestinians to recognize that right. Meanwhile, the Israelis have withdrawn from over 90 percent of the West Bank and all of Gaza. However, a number of Israeli settlements remain in this contested territory. These settlements in formerly Palestinian territory, the refusal of the Israeli government to permit Palestinian building in territories under dispute, and the strikes ordered by hard-line Israeli Premier Ariel Sharon against purported leaders and sources of the suicide bombings in Israel are regarded by the Palestinian leadership as provocative. These leaders demand that Israel withdraw to the 1967 borders before negotiations can take place, while Israel demands all violence cease before such negotiations.

Given the offer rejected in 2001, it is hard to see any plan on which the parties can agree. While classical diplomacy involved mutual concessions in which no party got all of what it wanted, the Arab position, in the wake of their having launched and lost at least three wars in less than half a century, seems to be to demand that the victorious target of those attacks surrender to Arab demands unconditionally. Moreover, several strong and well-armed Palestinian groups have never wavered in their declared intention to completely destroy the Jewish state: Hamas, Islamic Jihad, The Popular Front for the Liberation of Palestine, Black September, and even Arafat's Fattah movement. On the other side, a significant Jewish minority claims the right of Israel to the entire territory of Palestine as a biblical mandate.

In 2002, the Kingdom of Saudi Arabia floated a peace proposal in the wake of escalating violence with repeated Palestinian suicide bombings of Israeli civilians and Israeli retaliatory strikes against targets associated with the groups claiming credit for the attacks. Substantial civilian casualties have resulted. The Saudi plan calls for Israel to withdraw to its pre-1967 borders in return for a promise to recognize Israel's right to exist. These, however, are indefensible borders, leaving Israel just a few miles wide. Given the doubts about the intentions of several Arab states and the assorted militant groups previously mentioned, it is almost inconceivable that Israel would ever accept anything resembling the Saudi plan. In fact, were Israel to withdraw to such borders, the temptation would be great for some

Arabs to take advantage of the situation and to attempt to eliminate the Jewish state entirely. Such an Israeli concession would make war more likely.

American Options in the Region

It is therefore hard to imagine the basis for any conceivable settlement. Yet, at this writing, the American government continues to dispatch representatives to the region to try to broker a settlement that will bring peaceful coexistence and harmony among these bitter enemies. Israel seems most amenable to American pressure, so the temptation is to lean on them to make additional concessions. Yet, others argue that this encourages the instigators of the *Intifada,* the Palestinian war of terror on Israel, that their policies are succeeding. Moreover, if the process leaves Israel with indefensible borders, the temptation of the Arab militants to launch another attack on Israel will be great.

America may be able to physically guarantee a cessation of the violence; however, for the reasons given, it is unlikely that we can broker a comprehensive peace in the foreseeable future. The continuation of tension and stalemate between Israel and the Palestinian and Arab forces opposing it does not in itself harm American interests, which consist of access to Middle East petroleum reserves and maintaining the existence of the single consistently pro-Western democratic state in the area.

FUTURE ALTERNATIVES: CONTROL OF TERRORISM

The events of September 11, 2001, brought the specter of terrorism to the forefront of American consciousness to a greater extent than ever before. Although Americans have suffered acts of terrorism on several occasions in recent years, including the deliberate destruction of the Pan American airliner over Lockerbie, Scotland, the first bombing of the World Trade Center in 1993, and the destruction of the building housing American military personnel in Saudi Arabia, foreign terrorism had never struck so violently so close to home. Terrorism appears to be an increasingly popular tool for militarily weak but disaffected forces against the democratic West. In the wake of the events of September 11, our government fully committed itself to a "war on terror." In order to assess the effectiveness of that war, we need to examine the nature of terrorism and the policy options for confronting it.

Defining Terrorism

Terrorism is not merely violence to achieve political objectives. War, and even guerilla tactics by irregular troops, uses violence for political goals, but these are not normally designated as terrorism. Rather, terrorism consists of *random, devastating violence against noncombatant populations* (civilian and off-duty military) to compel another power to change its policies. Thus, the events of September 11 were clearly terrorism, as was the attack in June 1996 on the Khobar Towers in Saudi Arabia housing sleeping military personnel in a noncombat mode. This tactic appeals to weaker forces with grievances against stronger powers, because such acts are unpreventable. Because of their random nature, no nation can constantly guard every possible target of such attacks. Moreover, when terrorists are willing, as they frequently are, to risk or sacrifice their own lives, there is really no defense against these tactics. The use of terrorism creates a state of anxiety and fear and disrupts the lives of the citizens of the stronger power. (The increased "inconvenient" airline security and widespread fear to fly since September 11, 2001 illustrates such anxiety and disruptions.)

While September 11 brought terrorism to the forefront of American consciousness, America, as the world's strongest power, has been the target of terrorist tactics numerous times in recent decades. Iranian militants seized fifty-two hostages from the American embassy in Tehran in 1979. In 1983 a Hezbollah ("Army of God") suicide bomber blew up his truck at the American embassy in Beirut, Lebanon, killing sixty-three employees. Two Americans were murdered when a Kuwaiti airliner was hijacked in 1984, and Hezbollah hijacked a TWA airliner the same year. Pan Am flight 103 was blown up over Lockerbie, Scotland, in December 1988, killing 270 people, and car bombs blew up American embassies in Kenya and Tanzania in August 1998, killing 200 people, including twelve Americans. The World Trade Center had also been bombed in February 1993, in which "only" six Americans died, and the Federal Building in Oklahoma City was blown up in 1999 with massive loss of life. Even the strongest military power in the world has been unable to prevent such attacks.

Options for Confronting Terrorism

Some policy analysts and political activists urge that we try to assuage and remedy the grievances of those who commit or are likely to commit such acts. They argue that although we cannot stop people from committing acts of terror if they are determined to do so, we can remove the incentive by remedying the injustices and the poverty that breed suicidal rage at American interests. From this perspective, a just peace in the Middle East and economic development in the Islamic world would reduce the conditions of terrorism.

Realists, however, dispute this. They note that the head of the leading *Islamist* terrorist organization, Osama Bin Laden, came from a wealthy family and that most of the perpetrators of the events of September 11 were not poor. (Islamism refers to the militant aspects of Islam, not to the entire Muslim world.) These realists argue that one should never grant the grievances of terrorists even to the extent of not doing something one might have been disposed to do if such policy was a terrorist demand, and even to the extent of refusing to negotiate with the terrorists or discuss their grievances. These realists argue that the first principle in preventing acts of terror is to remove the incentive to commit them by making it clear that the potential terrorists cannot realize their agenda with these acts. They further argue that the strategy of granting their demands and remedying their grievances is impossible, because such grievances tend to be infinitely expansive and conflict with the vital interests of the stronger power. Thus, Daniel Pipes argues that the agenda of the Islamist militants (not all Muslims) is to impose an Islamic theocracy on the United States, which is obviously not a viable policy option.[25] To create the impression that weaker powers can advance their agenda by committing acts of terror invites such acts in the future, according to the realist position.

To take this position means that the potential target nation must consider victims and potential victims of terror as expendable. When terrorists seize hostages, the media always consults the families of the hostages, who of course urge that we meet all of the terrorists' demands. Realists argue that these are the last people to have any perspective on balancing the concern for the victims with the interests of the whole nation and the prevention of future acts of terror.

The second realist principle in fighting terrorism is to impose costs on those who make the decision to commit such acts and who plan and support them. This means that one should hold accountable not merely the perpetrator, such as the suicide bomber, but the states or large organizations who increasingly plan and sponsor such acts. Until the 2001 "war on terror," the United States was reluctant to take action against such states or organized terrorist networks.[26] The United States has known for some years about the Al Qaeda Network that planned and sponsored not only the September 11 attacks, but also a number of the other acts against the United States previously listed. Increasingly, complex acts of terror involve either the sponsorship of nation states or well-organized networks like Al Qaeda. This is a phenomenon known as "*state-sponsored terrorism*." A related version of this has been terrorism sponsored by the governing authority in the Palestinian-controlled territories or the organizations affiliated with them such as Hamas, Islamic Jihad, and Black September. These organizations, including an arm of Chairman Arafat's own political group, unleashed a rash of nine suicide bombings in nine days in the heart of Israeli cities, killing dozens of men, women, and children in March 2002. A sense among the Arab world that such a strategy is effective was encouraged by a wave of anti-Israeli and anti-Semitic violence throughout Europe. Israel, following the realist formula, responded with a military push into the West Bank against the headquarters and leaders of these groups. Israel also refuses to discuss the grievances of the Palestinians while the suicide attacks continue, because they do not want to appear to reward this kind of terrorism. This exacerbated the level of tension and violence in the area. At this writing, both sides appear intransigent in their respective positions, and it is hard to foresee their peaceful coexistence.

However, it is not at all clear that the realist strategy alone is effective in the end. Israel employed such tactics against Palestinian terror for many years; yet, we are witnessing the escalation of terrorism against Israel. Until the March 2002 attacks, Israel had been backing off from their hard line stance on terror. They did withdraw from most of the disputed West Bank and Gaza in the wake of the first *Intifada*. The realist tactic of imposing costs and withholding benefits on terror may be frustrated by the depth of the hatred that those who lead the terrorist assault feel for the essence of Western civilization itself. It has now been reported that Islamist academies not only in the Middle East, but in the United States as well, are teaching children that it is their sacred duty to kill Jews and convert other Americans. The realist strategy views terrorism as an essentially rational act to achieve certain goals. However, it may be that such acts are just as much an expression of raw hatred and shame at one's powerless situation. The danger here is magnified by recent efforts by the leaders of states and organizations sponsoring terrorism to acquire chemical, biological, and nuclear weapons of mass destruction.

It may well be that only a skillful combination of realism and idealism over a long time can reduce terrorism in the modern world. The appeal of terrorism as a strategy to the weaker forces consumed by intense passions such as hatred of the West and a sense of monumental injustice suggests that terrorism will pose a continuing danger to the West for the foreseeable future.

SUMMARY

Realism and idealism are the most common approaches to foreign policy. American foreign policy historically has tended toward idealism.

The most important assumption of realism, sometimes called classical diplomacy, is that nations do and should follow their self-interest instead of putative universal moral norms. Its most important components are power politics, spheres of influence, balance of power, and use of power to deter actions against the nation's interests.

The most important assumption of idealism, sometimes called Wilsonian idealism, is that interests divorced from moral principles are destructive, both to other nations and ultimately to one's own nation. There is a universal harmony of interests, and the goal of foreign policy is through negotiation and pursuit of peace to find that harmony. International organizations, such as the United Nations, and collective security agreements among nations can provide the structure for harmonious relations among nations.

Following World War II, American foreign policy focused on containment of communism, developing collective security agreements, especially the North Atlantic Treaty Organization (NATO), to realize this goal. American idealism divided the world into good (allies) and evil (communist states and movements). Failing to distinguish genuine interests and differences between communist movements, America was drawn into questionable alliances and distant regional conflicts. American failure in Vietnam demonstrated the limits of containment.

The eventual collapse of communism two decades ago presented a new situation for American foreign policy. Conflict in the Middle East illustrates this new situation. Idealist perspectives suggest that it will be possible to discover a peaceful, two-state solution to the Israeli-Palestinian conflict. In such a scenario, the goal of American diplomacy is to mediate between the two parties and to bring them to this solution. Realist perspectives suggest the impossibility of such a solution and the incompatible interests of Israel and the Palestinian Authority. If this is true, the United States should aim to keep the conflict from exploding into regional war, thus protecting its interest in Middle East oil and in strategic bases in the region.

Terrorism (random, devastating violence against noncombatant populations to compel another power to change its policies) presents one of the most important future challenges to American foreign policy. September 11, 2001, brought terrorism's devastation and challenge to the United States. Idealist approaches suggest responding to terrorism by discovering and remedying its root causes in poverty and injustice. Realist approaches argue that terrorism must be fought without compromise. The longer experience of terrorism in the Middle East casts doubts on either approach by itself.

NOTES

1. Hans Morgenthau, *In Defense of the National Interest* (New York: Alfred Knopf, 1951); Edward H. Carr, *The Twenty Years' Crisis, 1919–1939,* 2nd ed. (New York: St. Martin's Press, 1964); and Kenneth Thompson, *Political Realism and the Crisis of World Politics* (Princeton, New Jersey: Princeton University Press, 1960).

2. Daniel Jonah Goldhagen, *Hitler's Willing Executioners: Ordinary Germans and the Holocaust* (New York: Vintage Books, 1997) presents a mountain of documentation that the Nazi's systematic extermination of the Jews in World War II was not only widely known but enthusiastically supported by millions of ordinary Germans.

3. On the concept of power in political science, see Harold Lasswell and Abraham Kaplan, *Power and Society* (New Haven: Yale University Press, 1950); and Lasswell, *Politics: Who Gets What, When, How* (Cleveland and New York: Meridian Books, 1958).

4. See Hans Morgenthau, *Politics among Nations: The Struggle for Power and Peace,* 3rd edition (New York: Alfred Knopf, 1960), Chapter 12, 178 and following.

5. See the discussion of balance and equilibrium in Ernst Haas, "The Balance of Power: Concept, Prescription, or Propaganda," *World Politics,* 5 (1953): 459–474.

6. Morgenthau, *Politics among Nations,* 194.

7. Nicholas J. Spykman, *America's Strategy in World Politics* (New York: Harcourt Brace, 1942), 460.

8. The failure of American policy during this period is the theme of Carr's classic, *Twenty Years' Crisis.*

9. Samuel Huntington, *The Clash of Civilizations* (New York: Simon & Schuster Touchstone Books, 1997): 209–213.

10. Henry Kissinger, *American Foreign Policy,* expanded edition (New York: W. W. Norton, 1974): 31–32.

11. Thompson, *Political Realism,* 68.

12. Morgenthau, *Politics among Nations,* 414ff; Thompson, *Political Realism,* 189–197.

13. John Lewis Gaddis, *The United States and the Origins of the Cold War, 1941–1947* (New York: Columbia University Press, 1972).

14. Kennan first stated the doctrine of containment in a now celebrated "anonymous" article, X, "The Sources of Soviet Conduct," *Foreign Affairs,* 25 (July, 1957): 566–582; see also Kennan, "The United States and the Soviet Union, 1917–1976," *Foreign Affairs,* 54 (July, 1976): 570–590.

15. Reported in Charles Kegley and Eugene Wittkopf, *World Politics: Trend and Transformation,* 4th ed. (New York: St. Martin's Press, 1993): 93.

16. Sir Malcom Kennedy, *A Short History of Communism in Southeast Asia* (London: Wiedenfeld and Nicolson, 1957): 19, argues, "Communism and Nationalism in South and East Asia have become so intertwined as to be almost indistinguishable one from the other."

17. Virginia Thomson and Richard Adloff, *The Left Wing in Southeast Asia* (New York: Sloan for the I.P.R., 1950): 205.

18. J. Brimmel, *Communism in Southeast Asia: A Political Analysis* (London: Oxford University Press, 1959), 8.

19. The most widely respected general treatise on the Vietnamese struggle for independence up to the Americanization of the war is Bernard Fall, *The Two Vietnams: a Political and Military Analysis* (New York: Praeger, 1967). Fall himself was killed observing the later stages of that war. On Ho's background, see p. 87ff.

20. See Ruth Fisher, "Ho Chi Minh: Disciplined Communist," *Foreign Affairs,* 33 (1954): 86–97.

21. James Thompson, Jr. "How Could Vietnam Happen: An Autopsy," in Charles Kegly and Eugene Wittkopf, eds., *Perspectives on American Foreign Policy* (New York: St. Martin's Press, 1983): 379ff.

22. The strongest case for this conclusion is made by Huntington, *The Clash of Civilizations,* 209ff.

23. Joan Peters, *From Time Immemorial: The Origins of the Arab Jewish Conflict over Palestine* (New York: Harper & Row Perennial Library, 1984): 221.

24. Peters, *From Time Immemorial,* especially Chapters 11–14.
25. Daniel Pipes, "Who Is the Real Enemy?" *Commentary,* 113 (January, 2002).
26. See the analysis of this trend in Norman Podhoretz, "How to Win World War IV," *Commentary,* 113 (February, 2002): 19–30.

SUGGESTED READINGS

Books

Huntington, Samuel. *The Clash of Civilizations.* New York: Simon & Schuster, 1997.
Morgenthau, Hans. *Politics among Nations: The Struggle for Power and Peace,* 3rd ed. New York: Alfred A. Knopf, 1960.
Pipes, Daniel. *Militant Islam Reaches America.* New York: WW Norton, 2002.
Russett, Bruce, and Starr, Harvey. *World Politics: The Menu for Choice,* 5th ed. New York: W. H. Freeman and Company, 1996.
Thompson, Kenneth. *Political Realism and the Crisis of World Politics.* Princeton: Princeton University Press, 1960.

Web Sites

American Enterprise Institute   www.aei.org/
The Brookings Institution   www.brookings.edu
The Century Foundation   www.tcf.org/
Ethics and Public Policy Center   www.eppc.org/
MSNBC news and analysis of the Mideast   www.msnbc.com/news/MIDEAST_Front.asp
Terrorism Research Center   www.terrorism.com/index.shtml
Thomas Friedman on terrorism—six columns   www.nytimes.com/timestopics/

Private Morality and Public Policy: Family Values, Social Issues, and the Open Society

The election of President Ronald Reagan in 1980 heralded a process of transformation of the American right that had been occurring for decades. The traditional Republican Party of Calvin Coolidge, Herbert Hoover, and Robert Taft, a party whose principles included a hierarchical sense of human nature and a commitment to neoclassical (free market and pro-business) economics, has been transformed into a neo-populist party of the right. This "blue-collar" Republicanism reflects a well-established populist tradition in American history and transformed the issue focus of the American right from a preeminent concern with the protection of the self-regulating market and the interests of the business and capitalist classes of society to a preeminent concern with social issues and the protection of their view of public morality.

THE IDEA OF THE OPEN SOCIETY

The Emergence of Neo-Populism on the Right

Populism is one of those social science terms without precise meaning or content; however, there is widespread agreement on several attributes associated with the concept. Rather than accepting the hierarchical view of human nature associated with traditional conservatism, populism presumes a common sense wisdom of the working class and average person. It further perceives that conspiratorial elites such as bankers, big business, bureaucrats, and politicians oppose the interests of these common people. This antielitist faith in the common-sense wisdom of the masses frequently degenerates into anti-intellectualism.

The populist tradition in the United States mobilized in 1892 with the first nominating convention of the People's Party, which was a movement of midwestern and southern farmers. It eventually found expression in such charismatic mobilizers of the marginalized masses as Huey Long, William Jennings Bryan, and Tom Watson. The American right evolved into a new right distinct from the old Republicanism. The populist tradition appealed to marginalized individuals such as unskilled workers, small shopkeepers, smaller farmers, and others whose economic roles and well-being seemed threatened by the forces of modernization. By contrast, big business, professionals, and other examples of the social and economically successful in our society dominated the clientele of the old right. With the new clientele of the right, evangelical and fundamentalist Protestants and traditionalist Catholics joined such mainstream Protestants as Congregationalists, Episcopalians, and Presbyterians as the core support of the GOP.

The populist revolt on the American right was largely a revolt against modernity, especially against the secularization of the American culture. In particular, the extent to which this secularization became a goal of official policy offended the evangelical and fundamentalist clientele of the new populism. Thus, we will see later that religious conservatives are not so much offended by the fact that some people are homosexual as by official policy equating and legitimizing the formal union between gays as the moral equivalent of conventional heterosexual marriage. Thus, the GOP changed from the party of big business, the well-to-do, and the professional classes to a party whose clientele is more middle class and to a party that emphasizes social issues and government-mandated restoration of traditional Christian morality. The emergence of a resurgent populism brought these social issues to the forefront of the American political agenda in a state of tension with another emerging force in American politics: the legitimation of a multicultural and open society.

The Open Society and the Tolerance of Diverse Public Ideas

The concept of *the open society* entails tolerance of diversity in social, political, and religious points of view; that is, acknowledgment that different judgments on these subjects all have a right to be held and advocated. At a minimum, genuine, regular competition among alternative political elites for the occupancy of decision-making roles characterizes democratic political institutions in the modern world.[1] This open—and orderly—competition should render governing elites accountable to the governed by compelling them to justify the results of their acts in terms of the public interest.

It is therefore presumed that the different conceptions of the public good, emanating from different interests, will be resolved by a process of bargaining and compromise in which no one group or interest will completely get its way. Competing interests will restrain each. The concept of an *open society* thus means that in matters of social, political, or ethical judgments, no one has a monopoly on truth or wisdom; therefore, it makes sense to leave the channels of communication open. As Justice Oliver Wendell Holmes said in perhaps one of the most eloquent of all expositions of the concept of freedom of thought:

> . . .when men have realized that time has upset many fighting faiths, they may come to believe more than they believe in the very foundations of their own conduct that the ultimate good desired is better reached by free trade in ideas—that the best test of truth is the power of thought to get itself accepted in the competition of the market.[2]

The notion here is that if opinions or philosophies are untrue or pernicious, an open society aware of competing ideas will reject them. It should not be necessary to use the enforcement machinery of the state to repress any set of ideas. Rather, differences in opinion should be dealt with by discussion—the interchange of ideas. The open society further entails the principle that each perspective on these essentially subjective matters on which reasonable persons will always disagree are equally legitimate—that there is no official position on matters of morality and religion. The new politics of social issues, however, appeals to such concepts as family values, community, and political correctness that entail the assumption that some positions on such issues are preferable to competing positions and thus ought to be protected or encouraged by public policy. More importantly, competing positions are penalized and therefore not tolerated by public policy.

The various parts of the First Amendment all may be seen as protecting the concept of the open society, that dominant majorities may not suppress some perspectives and values. The whole point of the concept of civil liberties is that there are some things that majorities may not do, no matter how politically dominant they may be. This position that majorities may need to be restrained is in a state of tension with the populist perspective which places great faith in the wisdom of the masses and generally seeks procedures to guarantee that majorities of the moment can determine the course of public policy, procedures such as referenda, plebiscites, and recall of public officials.

Community and Family Values versus the Open Society

The central precept of the open society and of multiculturalism, that all perspectives are equally legitimate, exists in a state of tension with the recently rediscovered concept of community. The principle of community, as advocated by such communitarian spokespersons as Amitai Etzioni, entails the idea that a set of shared values and assumptions defines the essential nature of society.[3] Thus, it may be argued by conservative communitarians that the United States is a Western society defined by the traditions of Western political thought and the Judeo-Christian religious tradition and that competing religious and philosophical perspectives, while tolerated, are not equally legitimate in defining this social system. In the wake of the events of September 11, 2001, a widespread perception exists that the radical Islamist movement poses a direct threat to Western civilization and its values. This perception created a challenge for the multiculturalist view that all religious perspectives are equally valid and should receive equal tolerance. Thus, some scholars were arguing that radical Islam is an enemy of the West,[4] while other scholars were advocating that Americans should avoid stigmatizing Muslims.

Communitarians in general argue that shared values are the cement that binds the social system together as a coherent entity and gives it meaning. America, in this perspective, stands for something; it is not merely the collection of individuals who happen to reside there. Moreover, opponents argue that multiculturalism carried to its logical conclusion can lead to a *segmented society*— a society in which the different cultural segments are mutually isolated from one another. Such societies in the world with mutually isolated and alienated segments have not generally fared well as coherent entities able to effectively resolve issues. Our neighbor Canada has been beset with secessionist sentiment among its French-speaking subculture for some time. Belgium has gone from a unitary state to a confederation. Nigeria has experienced a civil war between its Muslim elite and one of its Christian tribes and is proving ungovernable. The list could go on, but the message is that some level of community may be necessary in order for a political system to retain stability and effectiveness. The Christian right in the United States, although in disagreement with the communitarians on a number of issues, has advocated widespread acceptance of traditional, bourgeois moral values—what are referred to as *family values*—as precisely this kind of social "cement."

Family values is a somewhat imprecise term that has acquired a great deal of symbolic content as a code word for many of the values that characterize America as a community defined by its Western heritage. It appears to refer to the principles of the Judeo-Christian tradition that underlies America as a community. Family values has therefore been used in contradistinction to equal moral and social status for homosexuals, against toleration of sexual promiscuity, against redefinition of appropriate gender roles (and therefore for the traditional two-parent family with a male breadwinner and a female bearer and nurturer of children), and even against the promotion of effective contraception. In other words, family values has come to symbolize a defense of middle-class morality against the forces of secularization and change that seem to follow modernization. To its opponents, the concept of family values suggests a kind of "monism" as opposed to pluralism and the open society—the idea that only a particular set of values are legitimate and that there are distinct limits to the extent to which contradictory values will be tolerated. The issues generated by the defense of family values are particularly divisive in the United States because the process of *secularization* has affected that nation to a significant extent, but much less than in other Western nations. Secularization refers to the decline of conventional religion, regular church attendance, and professed belief in traditional religious doctrines, along with restriction of religion to private spheres of life. Thus, while a 1989 survey showed that 20 percent of the British citizens and 29 percent of the Germans attend church at least once a month, 54 percent of Americans do so. While over 80 percent of the British accept the Darwinian explanation of human origins, less than half of Americans do so. Thus, Americans are more likely to support policies designed to reinforce Christian doctrine symbolized by the concept of family values.

On another front, the partial secularization of American society has emboldened many homosexuals to emerge from "the closet" and to demand treatment in various walks of life that is equal to that accorded heterosexuals, a movement discussed in some detail in Chapter 10. Among the demands in most recent years are the demand to serve in the armed forces without regard to their sexual orientation, and the demand, closely approximated in Vermont, for legal recognition of homosexual marriage. For our purposes here, it is important to note that the agenda of the homosexual rights movement aims to receive official imprimatur as an equally acceptable alternative lifestyle, rather than a life regarded as somehow deviant and less moral than heterosexuality. This goal offends supporters of "family values," resulting in such phenomena as the constitutional referendum in Colorado banning laws and actions that forbid discrimination against homosexuals, a referendum subsequently struck down by the Supreme Court in the *Roemer* case.

The concept of the open society is therefore in logical conflict with the support of family values. A theme of this chapter will be how this tension generates political issues. Among these issues, the following ones will be dealt with: (1) reproductive freedom or the right to control one's fecundity, including access to effective contraception and medically supervised abortion; (2) the suppression of pornography and the pursuit of sexual pleasure, including the suppression of homosexuality; (3) protection of the practice of traditional institutional religion including religion in public schools and government aid to religious schools; and (4) opposition to those aspects of feminism that challenge "family values."

Meanwhile, it is important to recognize that the concept of the open society is not merely a philosophical question, but an important bulwark for the structure of democracy itself. Without acceptance of the legitimacy of positions with which one disagrees, those in power will tend to use the powerful administrative tools at their disposal (e.g., command of law enforcement and the tax structure) to suppress those who advocate unpopular positions and thereby to suppress political opposition itself. Yet, democracy by definition entails regular and meaningful competition for political office. *Therefore, liberals hold that governmental imposition of a particular perspective on social and moral issues threatens the political competition that is one of the cornerstones of a democratic system. Conservatives, however, hold that granting equal status to all perspectives on such issues threatens the sense of community that is the glue binding society and enabling it to function as a coherent entity.*

The Role of the Court and the Presumption of Constitutionality

There is a philosophy concerning the role that the law and courts ought to play in the democratic political process. This philosophy holds that when there is doubt about the legality or constitutionality of the actions of the political process, judges ought to accept the values implied by that political action rather than impose their own values on society. In other words, when there is doubt as to whether the actions of the political or administrative sectors of society are constitutional, such doubt should be resolved in favor of these actions. This is called the *presumption of constitutionality.*[5]

This presumption conflicts with the idea that the Constitution entails unambiguous principles that the Court is duty-bound to protect against intrusion by a government reflecting a current of popular opinion. When a court, using an interpretation of law or the Constitution on which reasonable people might disagree, nullifies a law or governmental action, we say the court is practicing *judicial activism.* Both conservatives and liberals have relied upon an activist court to protect principles that they regarded as fundamental to the American system against governments with which they disagreed. Conservatives relied on the Court to protect a nearly absolute right of property from the Founding Fathers to the late 1930s. In the post-World War II era, liberals relied upon the Court to protect individual values such as First Amendment freedoms or racial equality. Scholars and activists refer to such limits on what government may or may not do to people as *rights.* Controversy arises when the finding of such rights does not rest on an unambiguously stated constitutional principle.

Government actions to encourage and protect "family values" have come into conflict with variously interpreted "rights" from the First Amendment, as well as with the right of *privacy,* a right NOT stated as such in the Constitution but inferred by judicial interpretation. The fact that the right of privacy is based upon judicial inference weakens its legitimacy. The inferential basis of the right of privacy is in the Fourth Amendment protection against "unreasonable searches and seizures" and in the much-overlooked Ninth Amendment, which tells us "the enumeration in the Constitution of certain rights shall not be construed to deny or disparage others retained by the people." This is nothing less than an invitation for future generations and courts to find unlisted rights by inference, an "elastic clause" for the Bill of Rights. The concept of a right of privacy—that there are some areas of behavior or life that are none of the government's business—is one of the core attributes by which a relatively liberal society differs from one with totalitarian tendencies or aspirations.

Among the purposes for which the right of privacy has been used is to protect access to information and technology for effective contraception and to professionally performed abortions, goals that conflict with the principle entailed by the family values belief that human sexuality should be strictly confined within the bonds of marriage. The Court first explicated the privacy right in *Griswold v. Connecticut,* a case that struck down Connecticut's ban on the practice of "artificial" contraception. When the Court later used this inferred or "penumbra" right to resolve the sensitive and controversial issue of the legal status of abortions by judicial fiat, this resolution proved unacceptable or illegitimate to the antiabortion or "pro-life" forces on the losing side. The legal status of abortion is perhaps the issue that generates the most passion and intensity of conflict of all the issues that involve the clash of "inviolable" moral principles on the one hand and the secularized, more libertarian concept of the open society on the other.

ABORTION, BIRTH CONTROL, AND THE LAW

Before 1973, most states criminalized most abortions. The common exceptions were abortions permitted when necessary to save the life of the mother. *Roe v. Wade* (1973) overturned these laws as a violation of the right of privacy, a right not specifically mentioned in the Constitution, but inferred from the Fourth, Fifth, and Ninth Amendments and applied to the states through the *due process* clause of the Fourteenth Amendment.[6] Specifically, the opinion said that states cannot ban abortions in the first trimester (three months) of pregnancy; states may regulate abortions in the interest of the health of the mother in the second trimester; and the state may choose to ban abortions in the final trimester unless the health (broadly considered) of the mother is in danger. The Court found that states had no "compelling interest" to intervene during the first trimester in the private decision of a pregnant woman to abort. Abortions are statistically safer than childbirth for the mother during the first trimester, when performed by competent medical personnel in sanitary surroundings. However, abortions become progressively more dangerous during the second trimester; this gives states a compelling interest in protecting the health of the mother. At around the beginning of the third trimester, the fetus becomes viable outside the womb, and the now potentially independent new life becomes another compelling interest. These three time distinctions are, of course, approximations. Fetuses born in the second trimester have survived, and fetuses born after the second trimester sometimes do not live. Moreover, the trimester division comes increasingly under question as medical advances place the viability of fetuses earlier in pregnancy. A Missouri law upheld in 1989 requires fetal viability tests on any fetus over twenty weeks old.[7] Critics argue that no fetus could survive at that early age and that the tests are dangerous and inconclusive. Antiabortion, or pro-life, forces have alleged that the *Roe v. Wade* decision has resulted in a "holocaust" of killing the unborn (appropriating the imagery of the Nazi slaughter of the Jews and thereby drawing an inference of equivalence between a sixty-cell blastocyst shortly after conception and the slaughter of conscious, active human beings). Pro-choice forces and Jews who feel that the Holocaust was a unique event resent this inference. The recorded rate of abortion has almost doubled since *Roe v. Wade* from around fifteen per 100,000 live births to around twenty-six. However, the pre-*Roe* figure might be low because illegal abortions were not accurately recorded.

Despite charges that *Roe* grants the right to "abortion on demand," that case affords no absolute constitutional right to a third-stage abortion. In addition, despite the imagery employed by pro-life forces, as in Bernard Nathanson's film, *The Silent Scream,* well over 95 percent of all abortions are performed in the first trimester. Second-trimester abortions occur principally because of the availability of amniocentesis, a procedure that shows whether a fetus is seriously flawed, as with spina bifida. Amniocentesis is possible only in the fourth month of the gestation period. Although hundreds of third-trimester abortions do take place, it is difficult to find physicians willing to perform them. *The New York Times* reported that as of January 5, 1992, only three physicians in the United States were performing late-stage abortions on a regular basis.

However, pro-life activists drew attention in 1997 to a particularly brutal form of late-stage abortion known as "partial birth abortion," a procedure in which the unborn baby is extracted from the womb except for the head. The abortionist then pierces the base of the baby's skull and sucks out the brain, collapsing the size of the head, at which point the head is removed from the woman. Proponents justify this procedure as being less threatening to the health and well-being of the mother, although these details did not serve to enhance public support of the pro-choice positions. Proponents of the availability of this procedure argue that there may be circumstances in which the health problems of the pregnant woman could not have been known until late in the pregnancy and that alternative methods are effectively unavailable or unnecessarily risky to the pregnant woman. However, even those who support "a woman's right to choose" to have a legal abortion were repulsed by the details of this procedure, as well as by the claim that many of these procedures are performed on healthy women bearing healthy fetuses. The Republican Congress passed a bill outlawing this procedure in 1996 and again in 1997, but President Clinton vetoed the bill, causing pro-life supporters to label him as a proabortion "extremist." Clinton argued that serious health imperatives make the availability of late-stage abortions necessary, although late-stage abortions constitute only a very small fraction of all abortions. Disagreements exist as to the frequency with which this procedure occurs; estimates range from a few hundred to a few thousand. The widespread public revulsion to partial birth abortion resulted in a Nebraska statute that criminalized that procedure. A Nebraska physician, Leroy Carhart, challenged this law, and in 2000, the Supreme Court overturned it as presenting "an undue burden" on the ability of a woman to choose the safest abortion procedure when necessary to protect her health.[8] This decision casts doubt on the willingness of the presently constituted Court to sustain a ban on the procedure. It is not yet clear whether this controversy will influence the judicial appointments of President George W. Bush, who favors a ban on the procedure.

The ease by which a pregnancy may be terminated was enhanced in 1988 by the development of a pill (RU-486) in France that induces a spontaneous expulsion of a newly implanted embryo without the necessity of any further medical procedure. The Roman Catholic Church in France forced the pharmaceutical firm, Roussel-Uclaf, which produced the pill to withdraw it from the market, but then-President Mitterand ordered the pill placed back on the market. Faced with a threatened boycott of its other pharmaceutical products organized by the American pro-life forces, the firm was reluctant to introduce the pill into the United States. However, it finally donated the patent on the pill to the New York-based World Population Council, a contraceptive research group. The Food and Drug Administration has approved the pill as safe and effective. Because of opposition by pro-life forces and because use of the pill is more complex than originally thought, requiring three to four visits to a physician, it has not yet come into widespread use.

The Supreme Court's *Roe* decision does not require any physician to give an abortion or require any medical personnel to participate in the procedure. Rather, it says in effect that when physicians decide to give abortions to patients who freely seek them at a time when the procedure is safer than childbirth itself, it is none of the state's business. Hence, the agenda of the pro-life forces is to coerce others into acting according to the moral principles and values of those pro-lifers. Many hospitals, especially religiously sponsored ones, refuse to permit abortions in their facilities. In some areas, this makes legal abortions unavailable to persons who want them and who are willing and able to pay. Pro-choice forces have introduced legislation in Congress and a number of state legislatures to force Catholic hospitals to provide the "full range of reproductive services," measures that in effect would force religious groups to conform to pro-choice moral values!

The administration of President George H. Bush supported two controversial attempts to circumscribe the right to legal abortion in the "abortion gag rule" and in the Pennsylvania abortion law. The former situation involved a 1988 administrative ruling by the Department of Health and Human Services that prohibited doctors, or other health care professionals working in medical clinics receiving Title X federal funds, from providing any information regarding the availability of abortion to their patients, regardless of the circumstances of the pregnancy, on the penalty of losing their nearly indispensable funding. Since clinics funded under Title X predominantly serve the poor who cannot pay for private medical care, the gag rule operated to render knowledge of medical options a function of one's economic well-being. The Clinton Administration rescinded the gag rule.

Meanwhile, Pennsylvania enacted a law erecting a number of barriers to the exercise of abortion rights: a mandatory twenty-four-hour waiting period for women seeking abortions, a requirement that a doctor inform the patient of the development of the fetus and of alternatives to abortions, and that minors seeking an abortion obtain the consent of one parent or a judge. The federal appeals court upheld that law in *Planned Parenthood of Southeastern Pennsylvania v. Casey,*[9] citing the standard enunciated earlier by Justice Sandra Day O'Connor that restrictions on abortions were constitutional if they did not place "an undue burden" on women seeking abortions. Both pro-choice and pro-life forces saw the case as providing an instrument for the Supreme Court to issue a definitive reevaluation of the constitutionality of *Roe*.

The strategy of pro-choice groups was either to procure a definitive reaffirmation of *Roe* or to compel a reversal of *Roe* right before the 1992 presidential election. They hoped that either outcome would energize what they saw as the pro-choice voting majority against the reelection of President Bush and for involvement in state-level politics, where access to legal abortions in many states was likely to remain protected for the near future. In June 1992, the Supreme Court upheld the Pennsylvania law's abortion restrictions, with several justices citing the "undue burden" standard. The Court also, however, explicitly upheld *Roe's* right to abortion.

Of course, abortions are not cheap, and economic considerations limit their availability to the poor. Congress has perpetuated this situation by forbidding the use of *federal* Medicaid funds for abortions (which during much of the 1970s were provided under the program) except to save the life of the mother, even in cases of rape or incest. However, it is important to note that one study showed that the cutoff in Medicaid funds has not substantially reduced the incidence of legal abortions. Apparently, women who want legal abortions will undergo other sacrifices or find other means to pay for them, and some states fund Medicaid abortions with *state* dollars.

Access to abortion is not merely a matter of the legal right to abortion, but of actually having access to medical personnel and facilities willing and able to perform them. Clinic access has become a contentious political issue. An increasingly aggressive pro-life movement has been led by such groups as Operation Rescue, whose tactics include the physical obstruction of clinics performing abortions, and a "Nuremburg Files" Web site inciting viewers against 225 identified physicians who performed abortions. Two operators of abortion clinics sought injunctive relief from the Web site induced harassment under the RICO antiracketeering statutes. The demonstrators claimed the freedom of speech clause of the First Amendment protected their right to such activity. In *Planned Parenthood of Columbia* v. *American Coalition of Life Activists,* the ninth Circuit Court of Appeals upheld the freedom of speech claims against a court injunction prohibiting harassment in the form of mobilizing hatred of abortion providers through the Internet.[10] The Supreme Court has not ruled on these conflicting claims.

Congress and some states in the early 1990s enacted laws designed to protect access to abortion facilities by restricting the activities and distances of protesters. The Supreme Court in *Hill* v. *Colorado*[11] had upheld a state law establishing restrictions on antiabortion protesters within 100 feet of the clinic, commanding an eight-foot space between the protester and the abortion clinic client. The difference between the cases is that the Colorado law involved physical impediments to abortion clinic clients, while the Columbia case did not involve physical force, a distinction that the Court has long used.[12]

Pro-life forces have responded in many cases by escalating their tactics. People disagree as to whether these increasingly aggressive tactics lead to violence against medical personnel performing abortions. Since 1993, three individuals who at some point have been associated with the organized harassment of abortion clinics and their patrons murdered five people, including two physicians, at abortion clinics. In 1993, Michael Griffen of Rescue America shot and killed Dr. David Gunn; in 1994, Paul Hill murdered Dr. John Britton and his escort; and in 1995, two receptionists at abortion clinics in Massachusetts were slain by an individual who had been associated with picketing abortion clinics. Pro-choice people were outraged that a number of people in the pro-life movement suggested that the number of aborted unborn children somehow justified these killings. John Burt of Rescue America said that the shootings were "unfortunate," but a large number of "babies' lives will be saved." Mainstream pro-life groups unequivocally condemned such killings. Many medical personnel offering abortion services saw these events as an implicit threat to the health and safety of themselves and their families. In some cases, the threats were explicit. This violence continued through 1996 with the bombing of a Planned Parenthood clinic that performed abortions in Spokane, Washington, and a fatal bombing in Birmingham, Alabama, in early 1998. As a result, numerous doctors who were performing abortions are no longer willing to do so. Fewer medical students elect to learn the procedure, although a couple of states now require training in abortion procedures of medical residents in obstetrics-gynecology. It is still true, however, that although abortion may be technically legal, in many parts of the United States it is difficult to find medical personnel willing and able to perform the procedure. This is particularly true in rural areas.

Contraception.   The same logic that impels concern over the availability of safe, legal abortion applies to the availability of effective contraception. The argument of pro-life forces that abortion should not be used for birth control is plausible if effective contraception is available. Yet, some conservative forces have opposed the promotion of effective contraception. One example of this is the opposition of such groups to sex education in the schools on the grounds that it encourages promiscuity and that "abstinence-only" programs are more effective. Another is the example of the so-called squeal rule established by the Reagan administration and avidly supported by forces of the religious right. This was the executive order denying federal funds to any clinic that provided contraception aid to minors unless the parents of such minors were notified. Supporters pointed to the value of parental responsibility and control of minors, a quintessential *family values* position, involving not only parental control, but also the protection of middle-class moral principles, especially with regard to extramarital sexual activity. Opponents argued that such a rule would only discourage minors from seeking such aid, not from engaging in sexual activity. This would result in exacerbating the already critical level of unwanted teenage pregnancy.

Conservatives assume that the ability to have illicit sex without the risks of pregnancy encourages promiscuity. The liberal position is that sexual activity is inevitable; therefore, denying access to abortion and birth control merely produces the spillover effect of unwanted pregnancy. The squeal rule was defeated after a two-year struggle. The struggle over encouragement of contraception erupted again when President Clinton's controversial Surgeon General, Dr. Jocelyn Elders, advocated the distribution of condoms to high school students to quell the crisis level escalation in illegitimate births among teenagers and to limit the spread of AIDS. This suggestion incited the wrath of conservative forces that object to any policy facilitating unmarried sex without consequences. These forces finally succeeded in obtaining the resignation of Dr. Elders when in 1995 she overstepped the bounds of the dominant moral values of our society in opining that it would be appropriate for high schools to teach about masturbation. Conservative forces were more recently mobilized when, in February 1996, the FDA approved a "morning after pill," a pill that would prevent a fertilized egg from being implanted in the womb. Antiabortion forces argue that a fertilized egg is equivalent to human life, since they consider human life to begin at conception. This group regards as immoral anything that enables people to engage in sexual activity for mere pleasure while avoiding its natural consequences. Promotion of family stability and traditional sexual morality are inseparable, they argue. Supporters of the condom policy, many of whom are also concerned with the availability of safe, legal abortions, argue that abstention from sexual activity may be desirable, but that it is not realistic to expect it. They point to survey data indicating that most teenagers are in fact sexually active. President Clinton's nominee to replace Dr. Elders failed confirmation in the U.S. Senate because he had performed abortions during his career as a gynecologist, showing the continuing passion and determination of pro-life forces.

The Moral Issue

Opponents of abortion base their opposition mainly on the premise that the fetus is in fact a human being; therefore, legal abortions are tantamount to the legalization of murder. The point of disagreement is whether life begins at the point of conception. Many aver that human life commences at birth or when the fetus becomes viable outside the womb. Opponents of abortion—led by many New Right conservatives and religious groups—argue that legalized abortions encourage greater use of this procedure, to the point that the procedure becomes a form of birth control. Moral considerations require the state to take a stand against what these opponents see as legalized killing. The data seem to support the claim that the number of abortions has increased considerably since abortion was made legal, and it is undeniable that many fetuses are aborted by pregnant women simply because they do not want the child, rather than for reasons of health.

However, pro-abortion forces—who tend to be liberal, better educated, and religiously secularized—object to the contentions of pro-life groups on two grounds. First, whether legal or not, women who need abortions will seek them out. Second, the availability of legal abortions is fundamentally an issue of protecting the civil right of women (like men) to make their own decisions about themselves—in this case, the right not to have the state dictate what choices they make about their own bodies.

First, the pro-choice activists point out that abortion has long been a widespread reality, legal or otherwise. By criminalizing the procedure, the state may reduce the number of abortions, but it cannot prevent many abortions from occurring. Criminalizing abortion may have the impact of driving many pregnant women to incompetent and untrained abortionists, with disastrous effects on the lives and health of the women involved, although pro-life forces dispute these claims. When abortion was against the law, many women died each year, from crudely performed, unsanitary, illegal abortions—women who in many cases would have lived had legal abortions been available. Therefore, supporters of legal abortion emphasize that the number of unborn children saved by criminalizing abortion must be balanced against the number of pregnant women killed or seriously maimed.

To pro-life groups, these considerations pale in the face of their strongly held beliefs that readily available, affordable, and safe abortion (1) constitutes a form of murder and (2) encourages sexual promiscuity. The feelings here are so strong that the arguments on this issue are antithetical moral assumptions unresolvable by discussion. What pro-choice groups call choice or freedom, pro-life groups call promiscuity or irresponsibility. Yet, both groups refer to the ability to engage in sexual activity without suffering undesired consequences. In the same way, what pro-life forces call the inconvenience of an unwanted child, pro-choice forces see as something that irrevocably changes the entire course of a woman's life. The essential facts are not in dispute; rather, the moral interpretation of such facts is the essence of the issue. Second, the issue of legalized abortion affects equality for women, as the legal availability of abortions gives women greater decision-making power over their lives. They have greater freedom to pursue sexual activity—as men do—without suffering the consequences of childbearing, and they need not retire from economic pursuits to raise children from unwanted pregnancies. Abortion and birth control offer greater alternative possibilities to women than do their traditional roles of homemaker and raiser of children. However, many opponents of abortion see such greater sexual freedom as leading to sexual irresponsibility and increased rates of adolescent pregnancy. It should also be noted that not everyone sees the issue of legalized abortion as a woman's equality issue. The opponents of legalized abortion see it as a fundamental moral issue, a question of human life and dignity and a defense of the "family values" that defined the United States as a community. Yet, the Court as constituted at this writing does not appear disposed to reject the right to abortion as such.

If *the Court reconsidered Roe,* however, the decision would be vulnerable on the inferential nature of the right of privacy that underlies it and on the justification of when the fetus acquires life. The Court's justification for allowing states to ban abortion in the third trimester rests on the presumed point at which the fetus becomes independent of the mother in the sense of survival outside the womb. However, since the decision in 1973, medical technology enables fetuses to survive a miscarriage in the second trimester, in rare cases as early as twenty-three weeks.

The determination of pro-life forces to criminalize abortion remains unabated despite opinion polls indicating that a majority of Americans supports access to legal abortion in certain circumstances. The incidence of direct physical impediment to the operation of clinics or medical facilities performing abortions has intensified. Pro-choice forces have responded by advocating laws and injunctions severely restricting pro-life speech and demonstrations near abortion facilities. The Supreme Court, it will be recalled, upheld such a law in the *Hill* case, but also upheld the free speech rights of pro-life activists to mobilize opposition to abortion providers through their Web site. Pro-life forces argue that this is an assertion of their free speech rights, rights that are asserted on both sides of the morality and family values debate.

THE FIRST AMENDMENT AND PUBLIC MORALITY: SUPPRESSING OBSCENITY

Freedom of Speech

The attempt by socially conservative forces such as the Christian Coalition to reverse the liberalization of the laws permitting the distribution of literature, films, and other materials with strong sexual content further manifests the attempt to defend, if not impose, a set of values reflecting middle-class morality, so-called "family values." They regard this material as obscene, and it is generally referred to as pornography. The concept of obscenity refers to that which offends widely accepted basic values or one's sense of decency. In the American context, obscenity for the most part refers to sexual content, although, more recently, liberal forces have attempted to stress the graphic display or depiction of violence as obscene. Of course, the attempt to suppress material on obscenity grounds comes into conflict with the constitutional protection of freedom of speech as well as with the concept of the open society. The extent of that conflict depends on the interpretation that the courts give to the phrase "freedom of speech." Judges have developed a set of principles or criteria by which they may consistently interpret that phrase.

Once one rejects the absolute position, which holds that the freedom of speech clause encompasses all utterances, it follows that the clause refers to some utterances and not to others. Courts then must address the task of making the distinction. Courts operate most legitimately when deriving their decisions from some generic principle, a standard or criterion that applies to a whole category of cases. Courts have been engaged in devising such principles or criteria to distinguish those utterances encompassed by the phrase "freedom of speech" from those that are not.

Traditionally, in the English common law, the concept of freedom of speech merely entailed a restriction on the right of government to suppress what was said or written in advance of the utterance; in other words, it prohibited censorship.[13] This doctrine, that freedom of speech merely meant the absence of previous or *prior restraints,* gave government full authority to punish speakers or writers for "seditious libel;" that is, false criticism of the government.

Freedom of speech now means more than the absence of prior restraint, but the concept has always meant at least that much. In that sense, the absence of prior restraint is a minimal conception of freedom of speech. An exercise of prior restraint, or censorship, places a particularly heavy burden of justification on a government taking such action. Denial of licenses to speak, injunctions not to publish, and the like are strongly presumed to be unconstitutional unless clearly demonstrated otherwise. However, even prior restraint is not an absolute doctrine. The burden of proof, however heavy, may be satisfied. One may conceive of some utterances whose effects are so pernicious (for example, revealing military secrets in a time of war) that the government is under no obligation to allow their dissemination. This means that there is a strong presumption in the law against censorship. This is significant because policy to protect public morality has frequently involved censorship of materials thought to be morally corrupting.

Although exercises in prior restraint require a particularly heavy burden of justification, to say that a governmental action is prior restraint is not automatically to say that it is unconstitutional. It is, however, especially difficult to reconcile censorship with the concept of an open society. Censorship, after all, allows a small elite, often self-designated, to tell the general population of presumably rational adults what they might read, hear, or view and what values or thoughts they may safely absorb without being morally corrupted. The concept of an open society, however, entails the assumptions that rational adults are the best judges of their own interests and that they are able to choose among the many ideas and values to which they are exposed. Here again we see that the concept of the open society comes into apparent conflict with the protection of family values and public morality.

Beyond this minimalist "no prior restraint" position, the Court, under the famous Justice Oliver Wendell Holmes in the *clear and present danger test,* held that the freedom of speech clause protected the arena of public discussion, the exchange of ideas that is thought to be a necessary foundation for the democratic process.[14] Unless unpopular positions have a right to a hearing, the competitive foundation of a democratic political system is threatened. Freedom of speech in this perspective has a *political purpose,* the protection of the democratic institutions by which all rights are protected. The so-called "fighting words" principle accordingly held that the protection of the freedom of speech clause is limited to speech that is relevant to such discussion. The erosion of this principle with the emergence of expressive or "artistic" utterance generated strong conflict in recent decades between the First Amendment and the effort to protect public morality by suppressing material with strong sexual content.

From discussion to expression: The decline of the fighting words test. Perhaps the best illustration of how much judicial interpretation has expanded the freedom of speech clause to protect expressive utterance is the demise of the "fighting words" doctrine. As laid down in the *Chaplinsky* case (1942), this doctrine held that:

> There are certain well-defined and limited classes of speech, the prevention and punishment of which has never been thought to raise any Constitutional problem. These include the lewd and obscene, the profane, the libelous and the insulting or "fighting" words—those that by their very utterance inflict injury or tend to incite a breach of the peace. Such utterances are no essential part of any exposition of ideas and are of such slight value as a step to the truth that any benefit derived from them is clearly outweighed by the social interest in order and morality.[15]

The erosion of the fighting words principle became apparent in the *Cohen v. California* case (1971), in which the Court overturned Cohen's conviction for inciting a disturbance of the peace (Cohen had worn a jacket in the halls of the Los Angeles County Courthouse bearing the epithet "Fuck the draft").[16] The Court held that times change and that words that offend at one time and place may not offend elsewhere; in other words, no phrase is inherently and necessarily beyond First Amendment protection. In this case, there was no evidence that Cohen intended to offend anyone or that anyone was actually offended.

The coup de grace to the fighting words doctrine came in the 1978 controversy surrounding the attempt by the Chicago branch of the American Nazi party to conduct a parade and rally, complete with swastikas, SS uniforms, and jackboots, in Skokie, Illinois, a community with a preponderantly Jewish population and numerous survivors of Nazi extermination camps. Clearly, no persuasion was likely to take place in this context. What was being protected was the symbolic and explicit expression of racial and anti-Semitic slurs. The city of Skokie attempted to prevent the march by several means, including the requirement of a confiscatory bond against potential damage and, perhaps more significantly, an injunction against utterances that castigated any racial or religious group. The U.S. district court held that racial slurs are a protected form of speech, and the Illinois Supreme Court held that ". . . the display of the swastika in Skokie cannot be enjoined under the fighting words exception to free speech, nor can the anticipation of a hostile reaction justify prior restraint."[17]

This overrules the fighting words doctrine, for if anti-Semitic slurs by avowed Nazis to concentration camp survivors are not fighting words in the *Chaplinsky* sense of the term, it is hard to imagine any other utterance that would so qualify. In striking down the injunction against racial slurs, the district court reasoned as follows:

> The question is not whether there are some ideas that are unacceptable in a civilized society. Rather the question is which danger is greater: the danger that allowing the government to punish "unacceptable" ideas will lead to the suppression of ideas that are merely uncomfortable to those in power; or the danger that permitting free debate on such unacceptable ideas will encourage their acceptance rather than discouraging them by revealing their pernicious quality.

The district court found the former danger the greater, a decision affirmed by the U.S. Supreme Court.[18] The *Cohen* and *Skokie* cases transformed the political interpretation of the freedom of speech clause to embrace any form of expressive utterance, regardless of its relevance to the democratic process.

Protection against Insensitive Speech

Yet, the *Skokie* case did not lay to rest the issue of the constitutional protection of inflammatory speech, especially with regard to the protection of "racial slurs." Although the courts have not negated the Skokie decisions, growing public pressure from practicing lawyers and constitutional scholars has suggested reconsidering the constitutional status of such slurs. The heightened sensitivity of the racial or religious groups that are frequent targets of racial slurs renders such speech increasingly illegitimate or unacceptable in public discourse. To this end, some communities have enacted laws that specifically ban speech inciting racial or religious hatred, so-called "hate speech" laws. Critics of such laws claim that the behaviors that such laws are intended to proscribe are rendered punishable under other existing, conventional statutes such as those penalizing destruction of property, incitement to violence, and so forth. In a case involving the burning of a cross in the lawn of an African-American family, the Court struck down a Minnesota hate speech ordinance banning speech that "arouses anger, alarm or resentment in others" as an overly broad infringement on freedom of speech.[19] Obviously, speech that arouses anger or offends is exactly the kind of speech that the First Amendment is designed to protect; one does not need constitutional protection to say what everyone wants to hear.

The "political correctness" controversy. Academe has taken the lead in the attempt to suppress speech regarded as insensitive to targeted racial and ethnic groups. In some cases, conservative critics of such suppression charge that the leaders in academic communities and the media have imposed a criterion of "political correctness" on permissible expression. Some see the vagueness of the definition of racial or ethnic insensitivity as allowing its use as a tool to limit the expression of positions that contradict a liberal perspective. In some instances, it has virtually come to include anything to which target group members take offense.

For example, Harvard University defined "racial harassment" as any actions or words "which cause another individual or group to feel demeaned or abused because of their racial or ethnic background." The offense, in this reading, consists not in what the speech in question actually says, but how some people feel about it. In February 1988, Stephan Thernstrom, Winthrop Professor of History at Harvard, was charged with racial insensitivity because during his lectures he had quoted southern plantation owners on the subject of black character. Although his tenure was not threatened, university officials chastised Thernstrom and warned him to avoid "possible insensitivity in lecturing." He claimed that he was quoting for analytical purposes, not expressing his own views, and that he was unaware of having given offense. A similar event occurred at the University of Maryland when a professor of Latin American History read to his class a description of Native Americans written by Spanish conquistadors. The professor was required to read a formal apology to his class for "racist speech." Such examples of insensitivity rest upon subjective perceptions of those most easily offended and insensitivity appears impermissibly vague by any interpretation of the First Amendment.

Similarly, an editor of the student newspaper at California State University at Northridge was suspended from school for printing a political cartoon critical of affirmative action, and another student was suspended for writing a letter to the paper criticizing the editor's suspension. There was no suggestion that either the letter or the cartoon was outside the bounds of taste and propriety; the sin seems to be the substance of the position rather than an inflammatory style in presenting it. This is very close to the concept of "symbolic racism" discussed in Chapter 10.

The campaign to suppress speech offensive to some oppressed groups arose from a spate of racial insults on American college campuses. At the University of Michigan, for example, in 1987, a radio talk show host at the university-run station called for listeners to contribute their favorite racial jokes. In 1988, an African-American student walked into his French class and found scrawled on the board, "A mind is a terrible thing to waste—especially on a nigger." In 1988, at Yale University, someone painted a swastika and the phrase "white power" on the Afro-American Center.

The University of Michigan took the lead in 1988 in adopting a rule restricting speech that members of targeted groups found offensive, raising again the question previously posed with regard to hate speech laws, whether one can, consistent with the concept of freedom of speech, grant anyone the right to not be offended. The policy adopted defined as punishable "any behavior, verbal or physical, that stigmatizes or victimizes an individual on the basis of ethnicity, religion, sex, sexual orientation, creed, national origin, ancestry, age, marital status, handicap, or Vietnam-era veteran status." University officials averred that freedom of speech does not include the right to harass or injure others. Harassment or injury is further described as a situation in which a person perceives that he or she is in "a hostile learning environment." Sanctions may vary from reprimand to expulsion. The significant departure in such policies on "insensitive speech" is to define the offense as how the listeners perceive or react to the speech rather than the content of what is said or the tone and style of the writer or speaker. The incident discussed in Chapter 10 involving a student using the term "water buffalo" to several black women illustrates how a phrase might be perceived as a racial slur even though the speaker did not intend it as such. The punishing of speech because of the way others perceive it or react to it violates an established rule of law called *scienter* (roughly, "knowledge")—that the distinction between what is permissible and what is sanctioned must be specified in advance of the act in question. One cannot be sure at what others will take offense.

Several other schools have adopted policies of speech censorship patterned after the Michigan model. They include Middlebury College, Brown University, Pennsylvania State University, Tufts University, Stanford University, and the Universities of California, Connecticut, North Carolina, Pennsylvania, and Wisconsin.[20] Clearly, the protection of minorities against being offended by hate speech is taking priority over more rigorous interpretations of freedom of speech. Moreover, the diversity sought by proponents of race-based college admissions (discussed in Chapter 10) apparently does not include diversity of opinion. The "political correctness" movement intends to guard against insensitivity to the feelings of affected groups. Carrying this goal a step further, a movement known as *multiculturalism* claims as a goal the protection of the self-esteem of members of these groups, a goal accomplished by the "cultural legitimation" of the background of nonwhite, non-European heritage groups, especially through changes in curricula to reflect the contributions of such groups. Chapter 9 discusses multicultural issues in education.

The campaign to restrain expression is not limited to insensitivity to racial and ethnic groups, but has at times required conformity to the values of the intellectual left in general. During the 1991 war in the Persian Gulf, for instance, administrators at the University of Maryland ruled that students might not fly the American flag in support of the war effort because such displays might offend those (including many administrators) who opposed the resort to arms. Such codes also forbid expressed antipathy to homosexuals. A University of Connecticut student was banned from her dormitory and dining hall for displaying a poster on the door of her room referring to "homos," a pejorative epithet.

Many charge that the nation's universities, heretofore counted on to defend the unfettered exchange of ideas, have now taken the lead in suppressing the expression of ideas that are regarded as "politically incorrect." The range of matters considered too insensitive to be permitted is both broad and expanding. For example, Clinton administration Secretary of Health and Human Services Donna Shalala, at the time when she was University of Wisconsin Chancellor, instituted a revised "code of conduct" (U.W.S. 17) that stipulated that students may be disciplined for:

> . . .racist or discriminatory comments, epithets, or other expressive behavior directed at an individual or on separate occasions at different individuals [that] intentionally demean the race, sex, religion, color, creed, disability, sexual orientation, national origin, ancestry, or age of the individual or individuals; and create an intimidating, hostile, or demeaning environment for education, university-related work, or other university-authorized activity. [21]

It may be inferred, in light of the Skokie incidents, that the First Amendment protects the right to express pejorative claims about a group; therefore, codes like the one quoted above are carefully drawn to proscribe only insults directed at individuals. Yet, the incidents that gave rise to these codes frequently involved insults to groups as a whole. In the Wisconsin instance, a fraternity had held a mock slave auction with white students performing in blackface and Afro wigs, an example of bad taste that nevertheless did not single out an individual.

Obscenity and the marketplace of ideas. It should be noted that the material in question in obscenity legislation rarely contributes to the free exchange of ideas. Much of it does not even qualify as worthwhile artistic expression by the standards of most critics. Controversial examples include Andres Serrano's photograph of a crucifix in a glass of urine, nude dancer Karen Finley smearing herself with chocolate and moving her hands on her body in a highly suggestive fashion, and performance artist Annie Sprinkle who invited the audience to closely examine her sexual organs. But a great deal of material regarded as artistically valuable has in some places been suppressed on obscenity grounds, some of which are listed later; good literature, attempting to deal with life in a realistic way, does not ignore the reality of human sexuality. The origin of obscenity legislation, however, never rested on critical measures of aesthetic worth; instead, it sought to protect communities from the perceived social evils of sexually explicit material in any context. Essentially, such legislation had two goals: the reduction of sexual stimulation and the perpetuation of the view sometimes found in Christianity that sex for pleasure is an avoidable and undesirable aspect of human personality and interaction. The origins of this principle trace, if not to St. Paul, then clearly to the second- and third-century church fathers who felt that physical indulgence was inconsistent with spiritual well-being. The Puritan tradition in America, once characterized by H. L. Mencken as the nagging fear that somewhere someone may be enjoying himself, was the heir of this view. The suppression of information about sex, however, has been a spillover effect of obscenity legislation.

One source of controversy in this arena is that different individuals have differing levels of tolerance for sexually related material. Some are greatly offended by any four-letter expletive; others are untroubled by graphic depictions of sex acts. Those who are most easily offended tend to be the most active in trying to obtain legislation and ensure its enforcement of their more restrictive moral standards on others. People who are less easily offended are generally less concerned about pornography, and they have left the field to the wishes of the moralists. Moreover, there is an additional pressure that tends to prevent those with a more tolerant attitude from defending pornography too vigorously, for there is a certain stigma attached to taking such a position; one risks being identified as a consumer of pornography and an oversexed deviant. Thus, the censor's position seems more legitimate than that of the defenders of freedom of speech and expression.

Obscenity and the Law: The Roth Rule

The courts have never taken the position that obscenity, defined here as materials whose primary purpose is to arouse erotic impulses, should itself be granted First Amendment protection. The difficulty is that much material that might otherwise be deserving of such protection contains sexually explicit elements. The constitutional problem has been to devise principles that will allow society to shield its citizens from being unduly sexually stimulated or offended without closing off their access to art, literature, and ideas that are protected by the freedom of speech clause. The common-law interpretation of the freedom of speech clause gave wide latitude to the discretion of the censors in the suppression of sexually relevant material. The nineteenth-century *Hicklin* test (1868) judged matter to be obscene if any isolated passage in the material has a "tendency to corrupt and deprave those who are open to such immoral influence. . . ."[22] In other words, material that contains any passage that is likely to arouse someone who is particularly susceptible to being so aroused may, by this test, be censored. Because it is possible to find some individuals who are offended and aroused by the most innocuous material and because many pieces of serious writing contain some isolated passage that may offend such people, the *Hicklin* test puts freedom of speech on very tenuous grounds. Consequently, there was pressure to liberalize this standard to afford greater protection to art and literature against suppression by the censors.

The *Roth* case in 1957 finally handed down a more liberal standard. The so-called *Roth* rule has become the standard that subsequent obscenity decisions either assume or modify. It modified the *Hicklin* test in three important ways. First, the test no longer focused on any isolated passage or words, but rather on whether "the dominant theme of the material, taken as a whole, appeals to prurient (sexual) interests." Second, its standard of measure became whether the material appeals to the prurient interests of the "average" person, not a particularly susceptible segment of society. Third, the treatment of sex in the material under question was not to justify censorship unless it was "utterly without redeeming social importance."[23]

Now authorities may no longer censor material because of some isolated passage or because some individual can find a sexual innuendo, where the thought would not occur to most people. However, the stipulation that only works "utterly without redeeming social importance" can be censored leaves very little material without First Amendment protection. Material that most people would find to be predominantly trash may have some small measure of social value. Although *Roth* suggests that a small, peripheral part of sexually relevant material would not condemn a work, it also appears to say that a small, peripheral amount of worthwhile material might save an otherwise worthless piece of sexual exploitation. This part of the *Roth* rule appears inconsistent with its dominant theme.

The *Miller v. California* case (1973) later modified the *Roth* rule in two important ways.[24] The Supreme Court dropped the key problematic phrase previously quoted in favor of saying that, in order to be legally censored, material must lack *serious* literary, artistic, political, or scientific values (LAPS values). This seems more in line with judging the work as a whole rather than because of some isolated passages. Presumably, under the *Miller* criterion of serious LAPS values, an isolated article in an otherwise provocative "girlie" magazine or a discussion of the healthful benefits of sunshine in an illustrated nudist publication would not, in and of itself, save such material from censorship.

The second way in which the *Miller* case modifies the *Roth* rule has especially serious implications. Miller defines the concept of community as local rather than national. The Court explicitly rejected the idea that there can or should be a national standard for what can or cannot be censored. Yet, the very purpose of the First Amendment is to provide some national standards for freedom of speech. The Constitution is national law, and law by definition must apply uniformly throughout its realm. The Constitution cannot mean one thing in one state and something else in another state or it would not be law.

Publishing, film, and broadcasting are examples of national commerce, and the legal status of their enormous investments must be predictable throughout the country. One cannot profitably produce the output of such media only for liberal East and West Coast cities; one must also be certain, to borrow a phrase from former presidential advisor John Erlichman, that "it will play in Peoria." Without national standards, the standards for the nation as a whole become the standards of what the most prudish local prosecutors or juries are wont to censor, the lowest common denominator, in effect completely negating the average-person criterion of *Roth*. By the *Miller* standard, any community should be able to censor whatever sexually explicit material dominant groups choose to censor without violating the Constitution. To the question of what the standards are for the material the Constitution protects, the answer is that there are no standards. *Miller* is not merely bad law; it is no law!

The Court backed off from the implications of the local community standard in *Jenkins v. Georgia* (1974) when it ruled that Georgia could not ban the critically acclaimed film *Carnal Knowledge* on obscenity grounds. The Court rejected a reading of *Miller* "that juries have unbridled discretion to determine what is 'patently offensive'."[25] Thus, a community is not free to censor the mere depiction of sex; the material had to be "patently offensive." The Court even offered a list of the kinds of things that may be censored. However, this implies national standards that constrain community discretion. In 1987, the Court backed further away from community standards, substituting a "reasonable man" test, a criterion that would allow the repression of speech that is obscene to ordinary, sane individuals.

There may be a useful distinction between obscenity and pornography. One may accept the concept that the avoidance of sexual stimulation is not a value of sufficient weight to justify the discretion given to censors; yet, one may still argue that there remains a category of material beyond mere salaciousness—it is "patently offensive." In 1989, the Court further elaborated on the distinction between what may be censored in obscenity cases and what the First Amendment in the "dial-a-porn" case, *Sable Communications v. Federal Communications Commission,* protects from such challenges. The Court struck down an amendment to the communications act that banned "indecent" interstate calls. The Court said that while obscene calls may be banned, the denial to adults of access to calls that are merely indecent violates the First Amendment.[26] The Court extended the same logic in *Reno v. ACLU* to the regulation of the Internet by the Communications Decency Act, signed into law by President Clinton and designed to control children's access to sexually explicit material on that medium. The Court found the proscribed categories, indecent and patently offensive, as constitutionally vague.[27]

There is, of course, a problem in drawing the line, but most know intuitively where it is. Justice Stewart put it best in the *Jacobellis v. Ohio* case (1964):

> I have reached the conclusion that . . . under the First and Fourteenth Amendments, criminal laws in this area are limited to hard-core pornography. I shall not today attempt to further define the kinds of material I understand to be embraced within that short hand description; and perhaps I shall never succeed in doing so. But I know it when I see it. . . .[28]

Regardless of which test one prefers, the use of either still constitutes censorship. Earlier, the chapter noted that the origins of obscenity legislation aimed at controlling sexuality, not somehow ensuring that only "artistic" products intelligently and maturely reflected that area of human behavior. To this day, society's goals in regulating sexually explicit material are very mixed.

Censorship, sex, and the arts. The expansion of the concept of protected expression generated controversy over government funding of artistic work with sexual content that was offensive to the moral sensibilities of significant segments of the population. Here the issue was one of government funding, not government suppression. In the one instance, the government funded a photographic exhibition produced by a well-known photographer, Robert Mapplethorpe, including some explicit homoerotica and some photographs involving the genitalia of children. Other funded projects that were offensive to many Americans include the Serrano, Finley, and Sprinkle works mentioned earlier.

The debate over funding such projects demonstrated the absence of any objective criteria over what constitutes artistic merit that would override the public interest in the preservation of public morality. Those who opposed funding these projects argued that they went beyond the bounds of common perceptions of artistic value and that, in any event, whatever rights may exist to freedom of expression do not extend to a right to public funding, especially when the material in question is deeply offensive to a majority. Those who support funding of these projects argue that representatives of the artistic community should determine what is art and what deserves funding. Since market forces do not identify and reward genuine artistic merit, the issue of public funding is an important one. An atonal rap group will sell many more recordings than a classical violinist. Without public subsidies, many widely respected creators of classical music, dance, drama, and the like could not survive. Some conservative politicians, such as North Carolina Senator Jesse Helms, used this controversy as political capital in election campaigns to mobilize the constituency that fears the erosion of conventional moral standards. Congress has debated cutting off funding to the arts through the National Endowment for the Arts, or at least severely limiting such arts funding. The NEA narrowly escaped fiscal death in 1997. It is apparent that as the frontier of what is perceived as having artistic value expands, public tolerance of extending protection to such expression may continue to weaken.

The Conflict between Pornography and Public Morality

A lingering question in the ongoing controversy over obscenity legislation is what social value is preserved by allowing the censorship of patently offensive, hard-core pornography, even assuming that such material can be adequately defined. Is the goal of obscenity legislation to protect people from being offended, or is it to prevent certain preventable, harmful behavior and events that flow from unrestricted dissemination of hard-core pornography? If the former is the value guarded, government is in the business of controlling thought rather than restricting itself to the control of behavior. Of course, so-called kiddie porn, the use of children to produce pornographic books and films, goes beyond thought control, raising issues of the exploitation of those unable to exercise independent judgment. The law has always distinguished the protection needed by children from the needs of adults. However, in 2002 the Court struck down a ban on computer-generated virtual reality images of children in sexually suggestive depictions.

The issue of child pornography and pedophilia in general has become especially sensitive in 2002 in the context of the widespread and notorious scandals surrounding pedophilia by Catholic priests and especially the protection and retention of such priests by church leadership. The question of privacy and other civil rights of those accused of such offenses versus protection of the public and of children in particular became highly salient in the wake of these events. For example, a number of states have enacted laws mandating notification of the neighbors of the residence of convicted child molesters, a law known after one of the victims of such a crime as "Megan's law."

Some decades ago, Justices Black and Douglas took the position that control of thought is not compatible with an open society. In their dissent from the *Roth* decision, they attacked the central premise of obscenity legislation, that it is permissible to "punish mere speech or publication that the judge or jury thinks has an undesirable impact on thought but is not shown to be part of any unlawful action. . . ." They disagreed with the *Roth* rule because it permits the state to censor material that arouses sexual impulses, whether or not it results in particular forms of behavior. They were suggesting that utterances or ideas that have not been shown to have a likely impact on some unlawful behavior or to cause the physical impeding of some lawful activity are protected by the First Amendment, no matter how much they may offend the moral standards of any particular part of the community. They were essentially rejecting the inferred right not to be offended, as previously discussed.

The distinction between the impact of material on thought and its impact on action is easier to make in practice than that between hard-core pornography that is patently offensive and soft-core pornography that is mildly offensive. Because these two liberal justices did not believe that material could be censored based on its content, they were the only justices who did not read or review the material at issue in obscenity cases. To them, the material was constitutionally protected, regardless of what it contained.

Some data are available on pornography's impact on behavior. A commission established under President Johnson and reporting years later during the Nixon administration systematically searched for a causal connection between exposure to sexually explicit material and the disposition to engage in antisocial behavior.[29] The commission used both experimental techniques and aggregate data analysis with a large, representative sample of the population. It failed to find any systematic evidence of such a connection. The commission recommended the abolition of all laws that proscribe the dissemination of sexually explicit material among consenting adults.

Arguments for censorship. Opponents challenged these findings on several grounds. The studies were carried out on volunteers who, to that extent, were unrepresentative of the population at large. They did not consider the effects on children. Nor did they take into account long-term effects. Sociological and anthropological research on the long-range effects of sexual permissiveness leans toward the conclusion that such permissiveness is dysfunctional for creative energy and cultural development.[30]

Late in the Reagan administration, Attorney General Edwin Meese released a Justice Department-sponsored study purporting to show the harmful effects of pornography. Critics charged that it lumped together a wide range of sex-related material and did not prove the connection it alleged between pornography and criminal actions. It seems fair to say that there is some systematic evidence that pornography does not in fact produce undesirable behavior, but that the evidence is not without flaws and there is a fair amount of thought to the contrary. The issue has not been resolved.

Despite such data, a majority of the population clings to the belief that pornography leads people to commit sex crimes. A 1978 survey by the Roper organization found that 57 percent of a national sample agreed with the statement, "Sexual materials lead people to commit rape." Only 36 percent disagreed, and 7 percent did not know.[31] These findings are consistent with the popularity of the solicitor general for the county encompassing Atlanta, Georgia, who defended his concentrating the resources at his disposal on driving pornography out of the city with the bald assertion, "I'm convinced that the use of obscene materials results in many antisocial acts . . . rape, sodomy, and the molesting of young children."[32] Such persistent beliefs are a political reality that can both affect and undermine whatever legal principles may protect sexually relevant material. Here again, commitment to community moral standards conflicts with belief in an open society.

Arguments against censorship. Given the weakness of evidence to support an alleged causal effect of pornography on antisocial behavior, liberals argue that what consenting adults read or view is none of the state's business. This concept of the "consenting adult" implies that people do not have such material involuntarily foisted on them and that the probability is very remote that they could naively or unwittingly place themselves in contact with such material. For example, a theater showing X-rated films should be clearly identified, and no one should be pressured or even implored to enter. The notion of consenting adults also implies a distinction between what is available to adults and what is available to minors. The Court clearly upheld this distinction when it struck down a law banning the sale "to the general reading public" of any book "tending to incite minors to depraved or immoral acts" or "tending to the corruption of the morals of youth." The Court held that this law reduced the adult population of Michigan to reading only what is fit for children.[33] The argument that individuals must be presumed able to decide for themselves what material is fit for them to read or view does not apply with equal force to minors. Assuming that the availability of sexually explicit materials is effectively limited to consenting adults and that there is no demonstrated causal connection between adult exposure to pornography and socially disruptive behavior, why not allow rational adults to choose for themselves what materials they can view without becoming morally offended or depraved? The Supreme Court came close to this position in *Stanley v. Georgia* (1969), which involved the seizure of sexually explicit films in a private home. The Court held that "if the First Amendment means anything, it means that a state has no business telling a man, sitting alone in his own house, what books he may read or what films he may see."[34] One may read into this decision the principle that consenting adults have the right to read or view whatever they choose as long as they do not force such material on unwilling adults or allow its availability to minors. The Court, however, refused to adopt this logical entailment of *Stanley* when, in the *Reidel* case (1971), it upheld a state ban on the buying and selling of pornography by consenting adults.[35] The Court explicitly rejected the position that if someone has a right to read what he or she wants in private, he or she also has a right to buy it from someone willing to sell it. Because it was also held in the *Twelve 200 Foot Reels* case (1973) that one may be prosecuted for importing salacious materials for one's own personal use, one has no legal right to acquire the materials that *Stanley* gives that person a right to read or see.[36]

The Court more explicitly rejected the consenting adults argument in *Paris Adult Theater v. Slaton* (1973), in which it upheld the right of the state to close down a theater specializing in X-rated films.[37] It was admitted that the theater was so clearly marked that it was impossible to enter it unaware of the sexual nature of the films shown. It was further admitted that minors were effectively excluded. Nevertheless, the Court still perceived some legitimate state interests in permitting censorship to override any First Amendment values involved. These state interests include "the interest of the public in the quality of life and total community environment, the tone of commerce in the great city centers and, possibly, the public safety itself." The Court further held that even though it had not been shown that there is a causal relationship between exposure to pornography and deviant or objectionable behavior, a state may nevertheless reasonably assume that such a relationship exists in asserting a legitimate interest in regulating what consenting adults may view or read. The Court did not discuss why a state may "reasonably assume" something to be true contrary to available evidence.

Supporters of censorship correctly point out that much of the material in obscenity cases is obviously pornographic trash and hardly worth protecting. Indeed, despite the Supreme Court's obscenity rulings, opponents point out, all forms of mass entertainment have become far more sexually explicit. Such material contributes very little if anything to the political purpose of the First Amendment, the free trade in socially relevant ideas. Moreover, although censorship in effect imposes the moral standards of dominant groups on other members of society, such principles may be part of the essence of that society. Even if unwilling adults do not actually see pornography, opponents argue that its very presence lends an unsavory moral climate to the environment. In neighborhoods characterized by widely available pornography, crime rates tend to be significantly higher than average. Furthermore, the suppression of pornography would, many believe, bring about the diminishment if not the disappearance of some notorious abuses associated with the production of pornography. Child pornography is one of the more egregious examples of such abuses.

Feminist attacks on pornography. A group of feminists, led by law professor Catharine MacKinnon and writer Andrea Dworkin, mounted an attack on pornography from a different direction. Their strategy was to obtain legislation to the effect that such material demeans women and thereby violates their civil rights. The remedy invited by such legislation is civil action against either the producers or the distributors of such material, including the bookseller. Because the criminal process is not involved, the burden of proof shifts from previous strategies of criminalizing the production and distribution of sexually explicit material.

The first example of this was a 1984 law passed by the Minneapolis city council, but vetoed by the mayor. Other such ordinances were introduced in Indianapolis and Los Angeles. These ordinances came under severe criticism on freedom of speech grounds. The critics charged that the standards for determining what may be considered demeaning to the dignity of women are left very imprecise and therefore any bookseller, publisher, or other disseminator of sexually relevant material may find himself or herself the defendant in a lawsuit initiated by any woman who was so offended. Even if the defendant wins, the costs of being party to such litigation would be great, and so such litigation could cause a severe dampening effect on the willingness of people to handle any sexually relevant material that may offend those most easily offended. The public would then almost be limited to having access only to material inoffensive to the most sensitive women. Laws granting women the right to sue booksellers who distribute salacious material that the plaintiff believes demeans women were tested in *The American Association of Booksellers v. Hudnut* (1984), a case challenging the Indianapolis law. The district court judge, a woman, found that the law presented an unconstitutional deterrent to free speech.

These feminists argue that pornography does promote and legitimate the image of women merely as sex objects rather than as complete and equal persons. Moreover, some sadomasochistic, hard-core pornography fosters the idea of the physical abuse of women as a manly thing to do. Such material characterized by simulated rape and violence toward women is increasingly typical of hard-core pornography today, whereas material formerly considered hard-core (explicit but normal sexual activity) is now relegated to soft-core status, such as that found in such mainstream outlets as *Playboy*. The dissemination of such sadomasochistic material thus may actually pose a physical danger to women. Pornography in general depicts sex as a conquest, something that men do *to* women rather than as a mutual expression of affection that men and women do *with* each other. Studies after the 1970 President's Commission Report discussed earlier do indicate that exposure to the new violent, hard-core pornography does soften attitudes toward rape and the sexual exploitation of women. Indeed, men exposed to such material become more tolerant of sexual violence. Of course, to the extent that it can be shown that the violent forms of pornography make men more tolerant of such violence, the argument is no longer simply one of competing moral perspectives but rather a question of the right of the state to protect the well-being of its female citizens. However, whatever the case for censorship on moral grounds, censorship of the kinds of material that can be shown to pose a physical danger to women is another matter.

MacKinnon in particular has led the feminist attack on pornography arguing that the relationship between the portrayal of women as sexual objects and male subjugation of women is so strong that the distinction between material that merely offends and is thus protected by the First Amendment and material that causes behavior that is preventable does not apply to sexually explicit material. MacKinnon would give such broad powers of censorship that her critics charge she would virtually abrogate the First Amendment in these matters.[38]

The concept of blaming the source—producers or sellers of reading or viewing material—for the acts performed by consumers of such material, which was struck down in the *Hudnut* case, was resurrected in 1992 by Senate sponsors of the Pornography Victim's Compensation Bill, which would allow civil litigation against the purveyors of pornography by the victims of sexual violence. The bill makes three assumptions. First, as in the MacKinnon-Dworkin laws struck down in *Hudnut,* it assumes that sellers of books, magazines, or videocassettes should be acquainted with the content of everything they sell. If the basis of the litigation intended by the bill is that the material in question may incite lust, that charge could be made of much serious adult material. The second assumption, given some support by the claims of confessed serial killer Theodore Bundy, is that viewing or reading sexually relevant material causes people to commit sexually violent acts, an assumption in conflict with the 1970 President's Commission Report. Third, the bill assumes that violent sex crimes are an expression of uncontrollable lust. Current research indicates, however, that such crimes are expressions of misogyny or hatred of women and a desire for power over them. If so, the bill would be useless in curbing a tragic social malady whose incidence is growing. Congress has not passed this bill.

Censorship and the open society. The problem with censorship because material is immoral or offensive is that one cannot appoint a censor to selectively stamp out this particular worthless piece of trash or that particular despicable point of view. By definition, censorship means delegating the power to one or more persons to decide for everyone else in the jurisdiction which of all future utterances they may see, hear, or read. The adult members of society lose the right to decide for themselves what material is trash and what materials have value, what ideas are legitimate and worthy of consideration, and what ideas are so heinous as to be outside the democratic political arena.

To give a censor power is to give that person discretion to choose what material to suppress. The record does not support optimism about judicious use of such discretion. Although most Americans can agree that some materials are offensive and worthless, the record is replete with examples of overzealous censors suppressing material that most Americans would find harmless and often of considerable artistic value. The critically acclaimed films *Midnight Cowboy* and *Carnal Knowledge* were censored in some places, even though the Supreme Court found that the latter film did not "depict sexual conduct in a patently offensive way." Another critically acclaimed film, *Paper Moon,* a comedy involving very little that was even implicitly sexual, was challenged because of the use of profane language. The 1960s saw numerous attempts to ban the well-respected novel *Catcher in the Rye* from school libraries. John Steinbeck's *East of Eden, The Grapes of Wrath, The Red Pony,* and *Of Mice and Men* have all been banned in various places in the United States on obscenity grounds, as were several Hemingway novels.

Boycotts. One recent tactic used to protect society from putatively salacious material is not direct censorship by a public official but rather a boycott of the products of firms that sponsor television shows allegedly containing such material. These boycotts are organized and promoted by nongovernmental sources. The chilling effect of the threat of such a boycott has caused sponsorships to be withdrawn in more than one instance. The extent to which producers have altered the selection and content of shows because of the boycott threat is unclear. These boycotts are not formally censorship in the traditional sense of a public official banning the dissemination of certain material by law or edict; instead, they constitute a less-formal kind of censorship, whereby the mechanism of socioeconomic pressure eliminates materials from dissemination.

Another version of these less-formal tactics is the pressure to eliminate certain kinds of material from public school textbooks. Those who want material expurgated from the books seem to dominate the testimony at textbook adoption hearings; live-and-let-live people who welcome new ideas tend to vacate this field. Some people have almost become fixtures at such hearings in the attempt to make textbooks reflect their view of the world. It is the familiar case of a vocal and passionate minority controlling policy over the more passive majority.

Norma and Martin Gabler of Texas gained considerable notoriety in the 1970s by devoting their lives and fortunes to the cause of having what they consider a liberal view of the world expurgated from schoolbooks. They attacked books that contain references to sex, evolution, feminist values, or suggestions that the United States may not always have been right in its foreign affairs. In anticipation of such attacks, many publishers self-censor their textbooks in advance. For example, Scott Foresman expurgated four hundred potentially offensive lines from its high school version of Shakespeare's *Romeo and Juliet* in an effort to eliminate any suggestion of carnal lust between those star-crossed lovers.

The right wing does not have a monopoly on such attempts to control the content of textbooks. Feminists, for example, show up to complain about demeaning depictions of women. African Americans have caused the censorship of such works as *The Adventures of Huckleberry Finn* and *Gone with the Wind* because they used the word *nigger,* and Jews have caused the removal of Shakespeare's *The Merchant of Venice* from school districts because of the portrayal of Shylock as a wicked Jew.

Liberal groups, though less concerned with sexual morality, have tried to pressure the networks to reduce the violent content of television shows. Network executives claim to have reduced such content, although it is difficult to tell from current programming. There is some circumstantial evidence, mostly of an illustrative variety, that exposure to television violence can result in violent behavior. (A case in point is the man who set fire to his wife in October 1984, after watching The TV movie *The Burning Bed.*) However, the evidence is inconclusive and the debate continues.

If a major premise of an open society is that reasonable adults are capable of assessing the value of competing ideas, should they also be presumed capable of making moral choices for themselves, if such choices do not harm others? When a censor presumes to tell such reasonable, consenting adults what material is too immoral for them to see or read, is that censor not presuming to make moral choices for others? If so, by what criteria can a censor be presumed to be more fit to make moral choices for other people than the people themselves? Thus, the central premise of censorship, that reasonable adults cannot be trusted to make social, political, and moral choices for themselves, is a denial of the essence of an open society. Proponents of censorship argue, however, that an unqualified adherence to the principle of an open society may weaken the commitment to moral and family values that define the essence of America as a community.

CONFLICT OVER THE ROLE OF RELIGION IN THE UNITED STATES

A general trend toward the secularization of society in the Western world affects the United States less strongly than other nations. The prevalence of evangelical and fundamentalist churches in America such as the Southern Baptists, Assemblies of God, and smaller "Bible Belt" churches promote the continuing relevance of religiosity in American society. The salience of religiosity in American political life has been promoted by the emergence of such religious advocacy groups as the Moral Majority and the Christian Coalition, the latter being the creation of former presidential candidate and televangelist Reverend Pat Robertson and its former Executive Director, Ralph Reed.

These groups have applied pressure on both Congress and the Republican Party platform writers to incorporate the imperatives of fundamental Christian social doctrine into policy proposals. The strong antiabortion plank in recent Republican Party platforms illustrates their success. In addition to efforts to re-criminalize abortion and suppress contraception, the "New Christian Right" has focused on reintroducing devotional observance in the public sector, especially in the public schools.

Freedom of and from Religion

Previous sections have shown how the First Amendment protects pluralism, the legitimate coexistence of various points of view and belief systems. The religion clauses of the First Amendment protect the legitimacy of divergent religious orientations, including agnosticism and atheism. If the right to choose one's own views and to evaluate ideas for oneself is a hallmark of the concept of the open society, surely this principle also applies to religion, which touches fundamental and intensely held sets of values and beliefs. It is therefore fitting that the religion clauses of the Bill of Rights are included in the First Amendment, which is devoted to the protection and legitimacy of pluralism and the open society. Precisely because religious beliefs are so intensely held, however, dominant groups will seek to impose values from those beliefs on their society. Many of the values that the social conservatives and religious right define as part of the essence of the American community are religiously based. The social and religious right therefore seeks to impose conformity to these values through law and social policy, an objective that comes into conflict with the concept of the open society.

There are two distinct religion clauses in the First Amendment: the establishment clause and the free exercise clause, which read as follows:

> Congress shall make no law respecting an establishment of religion, or prohibiting the free exercise thereof . . . .

The *establishment clause* is concerned with preventing the government from promoting or aiding religion; the *free exercise clause* is concerned with preventing the government from interfering with the practice of religion. To the extent that government implements either of these clauses to its logical extreme, it may violate a conception of the other clause. For example, when government does nothing that may indirectly aid religion, such as not permitting religious practices in public schools even when a decisive majority desires such activity, government may be seen as preventing the dominant forces in the community from practicing their religion as they see fit. In short, these clauses may come into conflict with each other; therefore, to uphold one clause absolutely would endanger the other.

The Establishment Clause

Public schools. There is, of course, considerable ambiguity in the phrase "Congress shall make no law respecting an establishment of religion." Reasonable people can and do disagree about precisely what government is prohibited from doing. At a minimum, government may not sanction a particular religious sect as the official state religion, a practice common in most European nations. In England, the Anglican Church is the state church; in Scotland, it is the Presbyterian Church; in France, Italy, and Spain, the Catholic Church has official status; and in Scandinavia, the Lutheran church is the official state religion. A state church or religion means that the head of state normally must be a member of that church, that he or she officially appoints the leading clerics in that church (usually on the advice of political and religious leaders), and that the church and its schools receive overt financial support from the state. In some places, it may mean that the religion's moral views have the force of law, as exemplified by the bans on divorce, contraception, and abortion in some Catholic countries. Although it has meant in the past that members of minority or nonofficial religions lost their religious freedoms and even their property and lives, members of the nonofficial religions are no longer so threatened in Western democracies. The Western world, on the official level at least, is now generally a model of toleration of religious pluralism, despite the continued existence of established churches.

Beyond this prohibition of an official national church, scholars generally agree that government in the United States may not legislatively bestow advantages on one or more sects over other religions. That is, any government activities that aid one religious sect must similarly aid all religions. This is the "accommodationist" interpretation of the establishment clause. If the clause meant no more than this, this interpretation would allow government to promote religion in general as long as one sect was not favored over others.

The Supreme Court has taken the position, however, that the establishment clause does mean more than this, that it is more restrictive of government activities having the effect of aiding or promoting religion. The Court has come to the position that government may not directly aid or promote religion in general over nonreligion. This position is sometimes called the "wall of separation" position, using the words of Thomas Jefferson. Not only does this position itself generate controversy, as it is not self-evident that the establishment clause forbids government aid to all religions equally; the wall of separation doctrine also generates controversy even among its ostensible adherents concerning precisely what the government may do without breaching the wall. For example, in the 1947 *Everson* case, the Court ruled that it is constitutional to use public money to reimburse parents for bus transportation to both public and parochial schools.[39] Justice Black's opinion explicitly used the wall metaphor in upholding the legislation, although the four dissenters thought the policy in question breached the wall. The case implicitly established the precedent that the wall of separation doctrine does not prevent some government activities that provide some secondary or spillover benefits to religion if the primary purposes of the policy are secular ones and, in the case of parochial education, if the primary beneficiary is the schoolchild. Thus, the question of where to draw the line went unanswered by the wall of separation position.

The wall of separation interpretation of the establishment clause has been used to oppose public aid to private parochial schools. In general, the Court has taken the principle laid down in *Lemon* that such aid is permissible if the primary purpose is secular (teaching courses like math, language, or science) and the primary beneficiary is the child rather than the church.[40] More recently, the no preference attitude has been gaining a majority of the Court, as shown in *Mitchell v. Helms,* upholding the distribution to parochial schools of library and media materials, as well as computer hardware and software on secular subjects.[41]

The problem of parochial schools as an alternative to secularized public schools for parents who want religious content in their child's education remains their affordability for most middle-class families. Hence, many parents continue to press for religious content in the public school curriculum. The argument for the complete secularization of public schools discussed below may seem stronger if parents had a realistic parochial school alternative, an alternative that depends on some measure of public support.

Prayer in school. The solution seems on the surface to be simple: the public schools may sponsor no devotional activity, no matter how voluntary or nondenominational it may be. Of course, the concepts of devotional activity and school sponsorship are not unambiguous. In two separate decisions—the Bible-reading cases, *Schempp* and *Murray* (1963), and the New York regents prayer case *Engle v. Vitale* (1962)—the Court seemed to take an unequivocal position. In the first case, the Court ruled that devotional reading, without comment, from the New Testament is inconsistent with the establishment clause, even when objecting students are excused from class.[42] In the second it ruled that prayer sponsored by school authorities, regardless of who actually reads it and regardless of how nonsectarian or voluntary the prayer may be, is in violation of the establishment clause.[43] In fact, the prayer in question may be the most innocuous, nonsectarian, and inoffensive prayer conceivable. In striking down such a prayer, the Court made clear that any prayer sponsored by public school officials is on its face unconstitutional. There is no way that any amount of tinkering with the nature of a school prayer or the mode of its presentation can render that prayer logically consistent with the constraints imposed by the school prayer decision. In the summer of 1985, the Court struck down an Alabama law requiring silent meditation or prayer as an organized activity in its public schools. The Court's opinion did hint, however, that some form of silent meditation might pass constitutional muster. The Court has also ruled that it is unconstitutional to distribute Gideon Bibles in public schools, even though students have the right to refuse to accept one, and that the Ten Commandments may not be posted in the classroom.

Both President Reagan and the 1984 Republican Party platform explicitly supported both a constitutional amendment to overturn the *Vitale* decision and to establish the right to "voluntary prayer" in the public schools, a goal that was reaffirmed by Republican Speaker of the House Newt Gingrich after the massive GOP victory in the congressional elections of November 1994. In a sense, students still have the right of voluntary prayer. It is important to realize that the courts have in no way limited the right of individuals in school to pray in any private manner they choose. Rather, decisions have banned only organized devotional activity, sponsored by the school. Some religious leaders have held that such private prayer is actually more meaningful, as it comes from within an individual by choice rather than from compulsion as part of a group exercise. The advantage of the school-sponsored group prayer that the proposed constitutional amendment would ostensibly protect, according to its supporters, is that it gives official recognition and support to the Judeo-Christian moral values they feel are the core of the American community. More skeptical opponents suspect that the dominant group wants the advantage the amendment would give them to compel others to pray and to do so in a manner determined by the dominant group. As Justice Frankfurter observed in the *McCollum* case, "The law of imitation operates, and nonconformity is not an outstanding characteristic of children."[44] Peer pressure to participate will be strong and, accordingly, in the case of organized, school-sponsored religious activities, participation is never genuinely voluntary. Some fundamentalist religious leaders still argue that such organized prayer in the schools is essential to restoring the nation's moral foundations, though other religious leaders contend that prayer must be private and voluntary in order to be meaningful. The Senate in 1984 rejected a proposed constitutional amendment to permit such prayer, but congressional Republicans place the issue back on the agenda in almost every session, and Religious Right victories in local school board elections in recent years signal the issue's continued vitality.

The prayer and Bible-reading decisions reinforced a tendency for the Court to compel the complete secularization of America's public schools that had previously been apparent in the *McCollum v. Board of Education* case (1948), which struck down "voluntary" religious training by leaders of the major religions during the school day and on school time. Both the hostile public reaction and noncompliance to this decision and the prayer and Bible-reading cases were extensive in many public school districts throughout the nation. For instance, one national sample of schoolteachers found that 28 percent continued to recite classroom prayer two years after the *Engle* decision.[45] Noncompliance was heaviest in the "Bible Belt" South. For example, a survey of 121 of Tennessee's 152 school districts found that only one had eliminated such Bible reading.[46] Estimates are that almost half of the released-time programs continued after *McCollum*, although they were clearly inconsistent with the decision. In the face of such public resistance, the Court backed off somewhat from the implications of *McCollum* and held in a New York case that students could be released for religious instruction during the school day if the instruction took place off the school campus. In doing so, they implicitly rejected much of the logic in the *McCollum* decision.

The *McCollum* rationale held that the voluntary aspect of such religious practices was more formal than real. As the concurring opinion in the case pointed out, because school children are not noted for their tolerance of nonconformity, there is a definite peer group pressure on the school-aged members of minority religious persuasions to go along with the practices. Given this pressure, the promotion of religious practices during the school day provides religious leaders with a captive audience gathered by the enforcement machinery of the state (like truant officers). The school audience will be larger than the audience they could gather for religious instruction after school, especially as the students' choice will be between religious training and algebra or study hall.

Those who seek to ban religion in public schools argue that a related function of mass public education is socialization into a common culture and promotion of a sense of unity among all citizens. Religion, however, can be a divisive phenomenon, appealing as it does at the level of people's most fundamental values and beliefs. Thus, the introduction of religious practices in the public schools can detract from the integrative function of those schools.

However, not all agree with the socialization argument. The trend toward noncompliance with bans on public school religious observances has been a continuous obstacle to the Court-mandated secularization of those schools. Not only were there periods of strife following each of the major policy decisions, but pressures for noncompliance also continue today. The theoretically simple solution to the degree of religious activity constitutionally allowable (none) has proved more complex than anticipated.

The secularization of public schools by judicial fiat generated widespread hostility and noncompliance. Recall the general observation that the constitutional principles in Supreme Court decisions are not self-implementing. This means, for instance, that although any school-sponsored or school-sanctioned prayer in any school district is logically irreconcilable with the original Supreme Court school prayer case, the legal force of the initial Court order banning prayer applies only to the parties in that particular lawsuit. Persons concerned about the religious practices in other school districts would have to file separate lawsuits citing the original school prayer case as a precedent. Given this reality (widespread misinformation about the imperatives of the decisions), and the social and political pressure of extensive popular opposition to secularizing the public schools, the existence of many pockets of noncompliance is not surprising.

Other establishment clause issues. The forces that have promoted the secularization of the public schools have broadened their efforts to promote the secularization of other aspects of public life. These efforts came to a head in the lawsuit challenging the right of Pawtucket, Rhode Island, to display a life-sized nativity scene at city expense. The Supreme Court continued its tradition of permitting Christmas pageants, Easter celebrations, and the like in public schools (and therefore presumably in public life) on the grounds that these holidays have become so much a part of the American culture that they have significance beyond their sectarian religious meaning. In *Lynch v. Donnelly* (1984), the Court ruled that the Pawtucket display merely "engenders a friendly community spirit of good will in keeping with the season."[47] Yet the conservative majority (Scalia, Kennedy, Rehnquist, White, and O'Connor) in 1989 struck down the public display of a nativity scene with overt Christian messages (e.g., "Jesus is Lord") while in a separate decision it upheld the public display of a Jewish menorah (the candle holder commemorating the Chanukah season). The menorah was accompanied by symbols of the secular aspects of Christmas in "the spirit of religious pluralism." Thus, this ostensibly conservative Court has handed down several First Amendment decisions that reflect the liberal perspective on these matters.

The issue of prayer in the schools arose again in *Lee v. Weisman.*[48] Ironically, this case involved a challenge by a Jewish parent to a prayer offered at 1991 graduation ceremonies by a Jewish rabbi. Despite this unusual circumstance, in the overwhelming preponderance of cases, such prayers are offered in the dominant religion of the community. The suit raised the distinction between private prayers and prayers or other devotional activities sponsored by the government. The administration of the elder George Bush filed a brief for the school district, arguing that government promotion of religion should be considered valid unless the practice at issue provides direct benefits to a religion in a manner that threatens the establishment of an official church, or if it compels persons to participate in a religion or religious exercise contrary to their consciences. This interpretation would have reversed *Engle, Schempp, McCollum,* and other cases, undoing three decades of precedent. It would have abandoned the wall of separation position in favor of the no preference or accommodationist position and would have legitimized an increase in officially mandated sectarian religious activity in public schools. In 1992, the Supreme Court decided the case, ruling such graduation prayers unconstitutional, thereby maintaining exclusion of officially sponsored prayer in public schools. More recent attempts to insert prayer into the public schools have involved prayer services initiated by students, rather than by school officials, and instituted at extracurricular functions. This phenomenon came before the Court in 2000, involving a well-established practice in countless small-to-medium-size communities: public prayer at high school football games. In *Santa Fe Independent School District v. Doe,* the Court considered a student-led prayer delivered on the public address system prior to each game, a practice approved by a substantial majority of the student body in an annual vote.[49] Community opinion was so strongly supportive of the prayers that the two plaintiffs were permitted by the lower courts to proceed anonymously. Nevertheless, the Court struck down the practice by a six-to-three vote as a violation of the establishment clause. The Court found that in addition to those who had to attend—players, cheerleaders, and band members—there was strong peer pressure on others to attend the high school football game in that small Texas town. Once again, the Court was pointing out that in the area of school-sponsored devotional activities, voluntary is not really voluntary due to peer pressure to conform.

A recent issue in the area of religious material in public places in general, and public schools in particular, has been the controversy over the display of the Ten Commandments in public school classrooms and other public venues such as courtrooms. The Ten Commandments are of course a nonsectarian symbol of the Judeo-Christian tradition that is an important aspect of our culture.

The Free Exercise Clause

The beginning of this section discussed the tension between the establishment clause and the free exercise clause ("Congress shall make no law . . . prohibiting the free exercise" of religion). In light of this tension, the latter clause is most frequently mentioned in conjunction with values threatened by the vigorous enforcement of the former. Thus, opponents invoke the free exercise clause to challenge the effort to secularize the public schools, an effort justified by the establishment clause.

In general, the free exercise clause most often protects the religious practices of unconventional groups. The clause had been used to protect the right of believers to proselytize door-to-door, to refuse to pledge allegiance to the flag, and to refuse to work on Saturdays for religious reasons—while still receiving unemployment benefits.[50] Of course, the free exercise clause protects such daily religious practices as worship, preaching, and religious education.

The clause does not protect some practices performed in the name of religion, especially those that would be otherwise illegal or would violate strongly held moral imperatives. The courts have tended to reject the free exercise argument in such cases and to allow the states to ban such practices. Among the illegal or objectionable practices for which free exercise protection has been denied are polygamy, the use of mind-altering drugs, sexual license, and exposure to poisonous snakes as a test of faith.[51] Furthermore, the free exercise clause does not give parents the right to withhold vaccinations, essential medical care, or education in the name of religion.[52] For instance, a couple was convicted of involuntary manslaughter after they refused medical treatment on religious grounds for their daughter, critically ill with pneumonia, who later died. Only the absence of evidence that the parents were aware of the seriousness of the illness prevented the convictions from standing.[53] In 1984, a faith-healing couple from Albion, Indiana, was sentenced to ten years in prison for withholding medical care from their nine-year-old daughter who had died a "preventable death" from meningitis. The superior court rejected their free exercise claim in finding them guilty of reckless homicide.

Faith healers or cult leaders using the free exercise clause to counter charges of fraud present a difficult issue. Clearly, the courts cannot inquire into the truth or falsity of beliefs, or all religions would be in trouble. However, the Supreme Court did hold in the case of a preacher who claimed that he could cure all ailments and take the spots off clothing that it is permissible to inquire into the *sincerity* of one's beliefs.[54] With the growing popularity of religious and political cults—highlighted by the tragedy of the Branch Davidians in Waco, Texas—the efforts of unorthodox movements to use the free exercise clause as a shield will increase. There have been calls to curb the antigovernment rhetoric of such groups, especially since the bombing of the Oklahoma City federal building by persons resentful of the killing of the Branch Davidians. The pattern of decisions thus far raises considerable doubt of the extent to which the free exercise clause can block the regulation in the public interest of harmful behavior or movements.

Yet, such decisions place tremendous burdens on unconventional or unpopular, yet sincerely and deeply held, religious beliefs and traditions. A 1993 case drew a great deal of attention in this regard when the City of Hialeah, Florida, passed ordinances to bar animal sacrifices by a religious group (the Afro-Cuban religion, Santeria) in that city. In *Church of Lukumi Babalu Aye v. City of Hialeah,* a unanimous Court held that the city had singled out that church with the ban on sacrifices; hence, the regulation was a violation of the free exercise clause.[55] This decision was in line with the "compelling interest" test and brought a noticeable shift in such free exercise cases, because in recent cases the Court had generally held against religious plaintiffs.

If the free exercise clause does not protect such convictions, what is its point? A case that made many religious persons very wary in this regard was removal of special protection for religion in the "peyote" case, *Employment Division v. Smith.* Here, the Court upheld the dismissal from employment of two Native Americans who used peyote in Indian religious ceremonies, using the argument that actions otherwise illegal do not receive protection on free exercise grounds.[56] Justice Scalia for the Court held that government does not need a "compelling interest" to burden religion as long as the limitation was an "incidental effect" rather than an exercise of clear intent to target an individual person or a particular faith. Supporters of free exercise, including religious groups across the political and theological spectrum, argued that such a principle would unduly impede the free exercise of religion, views that led to bipartisan passage in 1993 of the Religious Freedom Restoration Act (RFRA). This act forbad policies and rules that burden the exercise of religion, unless government can show that the burden furthers a "compelling public interest" and that the challenged action is "the least restrictive means of doing so."

However, in the 1997 case of *City of Boerne v. Flores,* the Supreme Court struck the act down as an unconstitutional infringement by Congress on the province of the federal courts. Conservative and religious groups across the board reacted strongly to this decision, arguing that it was an extreme case of judicial activism and an attempt to impose secularization on all aspects of life. Reverend Oliver Thomas claimed the decision would hurt "every religious person in America," and David Saperstein of the Union of American Hebrew Congregations declared that the decision would "go down in history with *Dred Scott* and *Korematsu* among the worst mistakes the Court has ever made."[57] Congress reacted by House of Representative passage in 1999 of a substitute bill, the Liberty Protection Act.

The bill failed to pass the Senate, however, in the light of opponents of these bills who argued that they would open a floodgate of litigation from all kinds of marginal cults or allow religious conservatives to deny rights to gays and lesbians in the name of religion. In fact, prison inmates sued under RFRA for the right to use drugs as part of their "religious experience," and an Amish group won an exemption from posting orange safety triangles on its buggies. In fear of such a flood of claims, sixteen states joined the city of Boerne in challenging RFRA.

Conscientious objection. The free exercise clause has also justified an expansion of the grounds for conscientious objection to compulsory military service. It was once a settled rule that to claim religious grounds for excusal from military service one had to be a member of a sect that explicitly disavowed military service, such as the Quakers. Pressures to expand this definition became intense during the Vietnam War, when some of the strongest opposition to the war came from leftists who tended to be nonreligious in the conventional sense. The Court allowed an expansion of the grounds for conscientious objection in the case of war protester Daniel Seeger.[58] The law states that such an exemption may be granted based on "religious training and belief" based on "an individual's belief in relation to a Supreme Being involving duties superior to those arising from any human relations." Seeger admitted that he did not believe in God "except in the remotest sense," but based his objections to military service on a "purely ethical creed." In this and other cases, the Court allowed such vague ethical justifications for refusal to submit to induction.

The dual meaning of the religion clauses. The resistance to the Bible-reading and prayer decisions, previously discussed, was justified by the argument that in forcibly taking "religion out of the schools," the courts were violating the free exercise clause. Yet, these decisions did not prohibit people from reading the Bible or praying. Children are in school for about seven hours per day. Presumably, this leaves nine waking hours in which to practice religion to whatever extent they or their parents wish. There are many things the children are presumably free to do but cannot do during school time because such things would interfere with the functions schools are supposed to perform. Although a person is free to practice religion, one may not necessarily do so whenever and wherever one pleases. Moreover, others have a right not to exercise a given religion. Accordingly, the adherent of any religion may not use the powerful enforcement machinery of the state to pressure others to exercise that religion or religion in general. One of the entailments of the religion clauses is that we have both freedom *of* and freedom *from* religion.

Opposition to the removal of religion from the public schools has come from conservatives and religious people, but not all conservatives share this perspective. For example, libertarians and the New Christian Right support similar policies in some policy areas, but the former oppose government-sponsored religiosity, whereas the latter strongly support it. Supporters of religion in the public schools argue that religion is a necessary part of our heritage and that schools should reflect the dominant culture. They further contend that the secularization of the school is tantamount to teaching a "religion of humanism," a vague concept implying the elevation of humanity to the place of God.

Aid to Parochial Schools

Recall that the *Everson* case (1947), in upholding the reimbursement of public funds to parents for the costs of busing their children to sectarian schools, laid down the child benefit standard. This means that if the primary effect of the aid is to benefit the pupil in the attainment of a secular education, a spillover effect of some benefit to a religious institution does not in itself make the legislation unconstitutional.

The Court applied this principle in the *Allen* case (1968) in holding that it is legal for the state to lend textbooks on secular subjects approved by public school officials to pupils in sectarian schools.[59] It was argued in dissent that books are a major instrument in propagating a creed and that religious school officials would choose books suitable to their purposes and place powerful pressures on secular school officials to approve them. Such textbooks might reflect the dominant religious creed in that community, thus infringing on both secular rights and rights of minority religious persuasions. Although the Court was willing to approve the loan of textbooks, it drew the line in another case on state reimbursement for the purchase of books and payment of teachers' salaries by sectarian schools.[60] The Court could accept the claim that secular authorities would exercise control in ensuring the religious neutrality of lent textbooks. However, it faced the reality that the state could not ensure the religious neutrality of sectarian schoolteachers, whose salaries they would be paying, when they worked under independent religious school administrations in the protected environment of their classrooms. However, the Court appeared to reverse direction when it voted five-to-four to uphold a Minnesota law allowing parents a state income tax deduction for certain expenses of a private parochial education as well as for public education.[61]

The Court appeared in 1993 to retreat from the extreme secularizing position manifested in cases such as the 1985 *Aguilar* decision.[62] In *Aguilar,* the Court struck down a New York City after-school program in which public school teachers had provided remedial assistance to underclass children in public and private religious schools alike. However, eight years later in *Zobrest v. Catalina Foothills School District,* the Court held that the establishment clause did not require the school district to deny the services of a sign language interpreter to a hearing-impaired student at a Catholic school, since the district provided the service to students at public and nonreligious private schools. The Court reversed *Aguilar* itself in 1997.[63] The proponents of school secularization were outraged at this decision in a case that had attracted more *amicus curiae* briefs (opinions filed by groups not party to the suit) than any other case in that term.

The uncertainty in devising a precise legal principle for dealing with state aid to sectarian schools reflects the practical political and social dilemma presented by this issue. Like most of the social and political issues discussed in this book, advocates can frame persuasive arguments both for and against public aid to sectarian schools.

Arguments for aid.   First, arguments for such aid begin with the fact that sectarian schools do a respectable job in providing a secular education; that is, training pupils in subjects like mathematics, English, science, and geography. In fact, many people believe that in general sectarian schools do a better job in that regard than do most public schools. Thus, because sectarian schools perform an important public function, they deserve public support. Moreover, if sectarian schools were to cease to function tomorrow, the existing public school systems would be unable to handle the large number of religious school pupils they would discharge into the public schools. The money not spent on sectarian schools would then have to be spent on a substantial expansion of the public schools.

Second, parents of parochial school pupils carry a double burden: They must pay the property taxes that support public schools and must finance the parochial education of their own children. In effect, they are financially penalized for choosing a religious school education for their children. Therefore, advocates argue that the lack of public support for parochial education goes beyond neutrality toward religion. Although it is true that parochial school pupils are free to take advantage of the public school system, if any great number of them did so, that system would collapse if not supported by greatly increased taxation. Presidents Reagan and the elder Bush supported a plan for tax credits or vouchers for parochial school tuition, a plan that would alleviate the double taxation burden.

Third, arguments for aid to religious schools draw upon the desire to return to the traditional value of strong parental responsibility for the education of children. This responsibility is particularly strong with regard to the religious upbringing of children in the faith of their parents. Because many evangelical and fundamentalist parents believe that modern, secular education in the public schools undermines traditional Christian teachings, they assert a free exercise right to support for their educational duties.

Arguments against aid.   Emotion and symbolism frame the argument against public aid to parochial schools. For example, some of the most vigorous opposition to such aid comes from portions of the Jewish community. This opposition rests on a perception, however right or wrong, that the theology taught in many Christian schools contributes to anti-Jewish feelings among their pupils. They question why they should have to finance the teaching of anti-Semitism. In some nations, however, Jews support public financing of sectarian education, as it also supports a network of Jewish day schools, or Yeshivas. This is part of the reason for the large Jewish population in Montreal; predominantly Catholic Quebec generously supports all religious schools.

Other opponents of aid to parochial education see such aid as the first potential break in the symbolic wall that separates church and state, a breach that will make subsequent breaches more likely. Their objection expresses the principle of a secular political system for its own sake, rather than any adverse effect such aid would have on their interests and well-being.

In light of the intense emotion surrounding religion, the danger of parochial school aid is that the benefits will not be allocated equally among all religions, not to mention between organized religion and nonreligion. Any aid policy will benefit the members and institutions of some religions to the exclusion of those who do not belong to those religions, as different religions have different levels of commitment to parochial education. Perhaps this is one justification for a secularized school system in a society with a variety of religious orientations.

Scientific Creationism and Secular Humanism

Creationism. The removal of prayer and Bible reading from public schools does not complete their secularization. Public schools still engage in Christmas pageants and related exercises that have clear religious content. Christmas is clearly a Christian holiday, and other celebrations observed in public schools, such as Halloween and Saint Valentine's Day, have their genesis in Christian traditions. The Court backed away from barring such exercises by ruling that they are a fixture in the American cultural tradition, not religious exercises. Therefore, the law now says that although atheists, Moslems, and Jews are protected from exposure to an innocuous, nonsectarian prayer, they may be compelled either to isolate themselves or to participate in an extensive Christmas pageant under the Court declaration that Christmas is not a religious holiday! Moreover, federal law gives students the right to organize religious clubs and activities on school property outside school hours. Clearly, the establishment clause is imperfectly successful in resisting the social pressures placed on others to adhere to the imperatives of a dominant religious orientation.

The extent of noncompliance with Court dictates in the religion cases described earlier illustrates the difficulty in attempting by judicial fiat to secularize the institutions of a nonsecularized culture. Communities have come to expect that the schools that teach their children should reflect the values of the community, and a mere pronouncement by a distant tribunal, a pronouncement that they may well not have heard of and that they almost certainly have not read or studied, is not going to change that expectation. Thus, the famous *Scopes* "monkey trial" involved the question of whether a community can bar the teaching of the theory of evolution—a theory almost universally accepted by the scientific establishment—because it conflicts with the dominant religious doctrine of that community. As late as 1968 the Court had to rule such efforts unconstitutional, as Arkansas had brazenly passed a law nearly identical with the one challenged in the *Scopes* trial.[64] Despite this, Arkansas and Louisiana passed laws in the early 1980s requiring instruction in "scientific creationism." The Supreme Court declared such laws unconstitutional in 1987.

Such establishment clause cases are a classic example of how the Court prevents a clear majority from exercising its strongly felt will. At the very least, such religious majorities feel that the biblical account of creation should be taught in addition to evolution, and they continue to exert pressures to have this done. Yet, the point of civil liberties is that there are some things that a majority cannot do to a minority, no matter how strong that majority may be and no matter how intensely it may want to do so. The efforts to reverse the Court on the prayer issue and to circumvent rulings on pornography suggest that there is no permanent resolution of issues involving morality and religion. Such issues will continue to occupy the public in the decades ahead.

Secular humanism. A major issue raised in recent years is the right of religious fundamentalist parents to shield their children from the influence of what they call "secular humanism." This vaguely defined term has almost become symbolic of everything many fundamentalists disdain about the modern world. Its general connotation, however, is that humans control their fate and are not subject to the will of a deity. Moreover, it is a legitimate and worthwhile enterprise to strive to improve the quality of life on earth independent of the assistance of God and independent of considerations of salvation. The declining importance of religion in the modern world has created a perceived threat of the encroachment of secular humanism on traditional religious values. The issue is whether secular humanism merely symbolizes the declining salience of traditional religious observance and belief or is an alternative religious perspective.

The issue was manifested in the refusal of a group of fundamentalist parents to allow their children to participate in the assigned reading in their public schools because, the parents argued, the books promoted the philosophy of secular humanism and thereby interfered with the right of these parents to raise their children in the religious orientation of their own choosing. The school officials, however, argued that the educational goals of the school would suffer if parents refused to allow their children to share a common set of readings and educational experiences. The federal district court upheld the rights of the parents, but a federal appellate court overruled that decision.

The case of the parents was weakened in the eyes of many nonfundamentalist Americans by the innocuousness of some of the passages to which the fundamentalists objected. For example, one of the offending passages merely declared that people ought to strive for self-improvement and to gain increasing control over their own destiny. This decision reinforces the principle that one of the values of the educational system is to socialize children into shared or common sets of values or a common identity. Nevertheless, the decision does not end the dispute over the extent of recognition of religious values in the public schools.

FAMILY VALUES AND FEMINISM

The beginning of this chapter suggested that the concept of family values appears to entail the traditional two-parent family. The moral and religious underpinnings of this value have been reinforced by recent research that concludes that the children of traditional two-parent families do much better, other things being equal, than children from broken homes, particularly children from the growing proportion of female-headed families in this country. In fact, research shows that the significant income gap between African Americans and whites in the United States would be far more narrow if one controlled whether the family was single-parent or two-parent. In other words, if as large a proportion of African-American children were raised in traditional two-parent homes as white children, family incomes would be closer.

A decade ago, former Vice President Dan Quayle generated substantial controversy when he criticized a television show in which the lead character, a single woman named Murphy Brown, chose to have a child without any intention of marrying the natural father. While this plot development was supportive of the feminist position that women do not really need a man, Quayle argued that single-parent options for raising children are less satisfactory and should not be encouraged. Liberals and feminists vigorously attacked Quayle for being hopelessly out-of-date in his values. However, the recent data suggests that Quayle was correct in his assertion that the children of two-parent families fare significantly better in income, school achievement, and lower rates of crime and drug addiction.

Chapter 10 discussed feminism at length. However, it is important to note in this context that in their effort to liberate women from their traditional domestic roles, feminists fought for policies to make women more free of the imperatives of those roles, policies such as reproductive freedom and the suppression of pornographic material that contributes to a demeaning and simplistic image of women. In this effort, feminists come into direct conflict with the supporters of "family values," values that favor the traditional roles for women and that oppose on moral grounds the freedom to engage in sexual activity outside of marriage and independent of the reproductive function of such activity. Insofar as traditional religious institutions have promoted a supportive rather than equal or leadership role for women, feminists do not favor the religiosity entailed by the concept of "family values." Hence, the movement to resurrect and support family values comes into direct conflict with the leaders of the feminist movement. This conflict came into focus in a massive gathering in Washington in October 1997 of a conservative Christian group of men calling itself "Promise Keepers." Although their surface or ostensible goal was the unassailable one of resolving to be responsible husbands and fathers, it was clear to many that their view of the family was the traditional one in which men exercised authority and carried responsibility. The women were to be cared for and, in most cases, should stay at home with children. Hence, leaders of the National Organization for Women (NOW) vigorously criticized Promise Keepers for seeking to perpetuate a subordinate role for women. The conflict here was another manifestation of the broader conflict that has been this chapter's focus, the conflict between the perspective advocating family values (a set of moral principles based largely on the Judeo-Christian ethic and bourgeois morality) and the concept of the open society (advocating the equal legitimacy of all moral perspectives on which reasonable people continue to disagree).

The moral principles entailed by the concept of family values came into the spotlight in 1998, when the sexual harassment lawsuit by Paula Jones against President Clinton erupted into a broader inquiry into the president's alleged sexual behavior. In particular, Mr. Clinton used his position to solicit sexual favors from a White House intern, Monica Lewinsky. The case raised significant issues of the relationship between morality and politics. Did the president lie under oath and attempt to have Ms. Lewinsky lie as well, thereby obstructing justice? Is the president a moral role model for the nation, and is his sexual behavior symptomatic of the kind of moral decline alleged by the supporters of traditional morality in politics? Does the behavior in question relate to broader attributes of character such as trustworthiness, integrity, self-control, and judgment? Curiously, feminists, who might be expected to be in the forefront of the fight against sexual predators, were unexpectedly tolerant of President Clinton, a president whom they liked on policy grounds.

SUMMARY

First Amendment freedoms protect the legitimacy and tolerance of different social, political, and religious perspectives. The environment in which such different perspectives can legitimately coexist is pluralism, or an open society. In protecting this pluralism, First Amendment freedoms are essential to the maintenance of a democratic system.

As important as these freedoms are, they inevitably come into conflict with competing values such as the protection of property, civil order, and national security. Among the most important values with which the concept of the open society and its concomitant First Amendment freedoms are in conflict are those entailed by the somewhat imprecise term "family values." This term, which has had a prominent place in political dialogue in recent years and has become pregnant with social and political symbolism, refers to those values generally associated with middle-class or bourgeois morality. These are the traditional two-parent family centered on the woman assuming the primary role of bearing and raising children, circumscribing sexual activity toward its primary function of procreation with the traditional family context, and encouraging religiosity in its traditional and institutional sense.

Family values, thus conceptualized, form the basis of a community. This last term refers to the aggregate of individuals that make up the United States united by some level of shared values and symbols that in turn promote a shared sense of belonging. Individualism, rights, and tolerance carried to an absolute can come into conflict with this sense of community based on family values. This chapter has described the most important of these conflicts.

These conflicts primarily come in four areas. First, morality policy debates the restriction of human sexuality to the domain of traditional marriage and hence restrictions on materials that promote lust, such as the censorship of pornography. Second, debate focuses on whether to discourage practices that ameliorate the consequences of inappropriate sexual behavior, such as the availability of information and material to support contraception and the availability of medically performed, relatively safe abortions. Third, the question arises if society should promote the exercise and practice of traditional religiosity. Fourth, liberals and conservatives differ over the feminist movement, particularly the extent that it might threaten the traditional two-parent family structure. These areas of controversy will continue to be difficult to resolve because they rest on differences in deeply held beliefs and values.

NOTES

1. This minimal definition may be found expostulated most notably in Joseph Schumpeter's classic, *Capitalism, Socialism and Democracy* (New York: Harper Torchbooks, 1942 and 1962), Chapter 22.

2. Dissenting opinion in *Abrams v. United States,* 250 U.S. 616 (1919), at 630.

3. Amitai Etzioni, *The Spirit of Community* (New York: Crown Publishers, 1993).

4. For example, Samuel Huntington, *The Clash of Civilizations: The Remaking of the World Order* (New York: Simon & Schuster, 1996): 263–272.

5. Justice Stone's now famous footnote 4 in *U.S. v. Caroline Products,* 344 U.S. 144 (1938), at 152.

6. *Roe v. Wade,* 410 U.S. 113 (1973).

7. *Webster v. Reproductive Health Services,* 109 S. Ct. 3040 (1989).

8. *Stenberg v. Carhart,* 530 U.S. 914 (2000).

9. *Planned Parenthood of Southeastern Pennsylvania v. Casey,* 505 U.S. 833 (1992).

10. *Planned Parenthood of Columbia Inc. v. American Coalition of Life Activists,* 244 F. 3d. 1007 (2001).

11. *Hill v. Colorado,* 530 U.S. 703 (2000).

12. *Adderly v. Florida,* 385 U.S. 39 (1966).

13. For a scholarly inquiry into the meaning of the freedom of speech clause for its authors, a study that concludes that the authors merely understood it to embrace this common law definition, see Leonard Levy, *The Legacy of Suppression* (Cambridge: Harvard University Press, 1960).

14. *Schenck v. United States,* 249 U.S. 47 (1919).

15. *Chaplinsky v. New Hampshire,* 315 U.S. 568 (1942).

16. *Cohen v. California,* 403 U.S. 15 (1971).

17. *Village of Skokie v. National Socialist Party of America,* 46 LW 2396 (1978). For a full discussion of this episode, see Phillipa Strum, *When the Nazis Came to Skokie: Freedom for the Speech We Hate* (Lawrence: University Press of Kansas, 1999).

18. *Smith v. Collin,* 99 S. Ct. 291 (1978).

19. *R.A.V. v. City of St. Paul,* 505 U.S. 377 (1992).

20. The discussion of the Michigan policy is drawn from Dinesh D'Souza, *Illiberal Education* (New York: The Free Press, 1991): 140–144.

21. The discussion of the Wisconsin policy relies on Ken Emerson, "Only Correct," *The New Republic* (February 18, 1991): 18–19.

22. *Regina v. Hicklin,* L. R. 3 Q.B. (1868).

23. *Roth v. United States,* 354 U.S. 476 (1957).

24. *Miller v. California,* 413 U.S. 15 (1973).

25. *Jenkins v. Georgia,* 418 U.S. 153 (1974).

26. *Sable Communications of California v. Federal Communications Commission,* 49 U.S. 115 (1989).

27. *Reno v. American Civil Liberties Union,* 521 U.S. 844 (1997).

28. *Jacobellis v. Ohio,* 378 U.S. 84 (1974).

29. *The Report of the Commission on Obscenity and Pornography* (Washington, DC: U.S. Government Printing Office, 1970).

30. James Q. Wilson, "Violence, Pornography and Social Science," *The Public Interest,* 22 (Winter, 1971): 45–61; J. D. Unwin, *Sex and Culture* (London: Oxford University Press, 1934). These arguments are well summarized in Harry M. Clor, "Commentary on the Report of the Commission on Obscenity and Pornography," in Clor, ed., *Censorship and Freedom of Expression* (Skokie, IL: Rand McNally, 1971): 119–129.

31. U.S. Department of Justice, *Sourcebook for Criminal Justice Statistics, 1980* (Washington, DC: U.S. Government Printing Office, 1980): 223.

32. Quoted in *Newsweek* (May 25, 1981), 46.

33. *Butler v. Michigan,* 352 U.S. 380 (1957), at 383–384.

34. *Stanley v. Georgia,* 394 U.S. 557 (1969).

35. *U.S. v. Reidel,* 402 U.S. 351 (1971).

36. *U.S. v. Twelve 200 Foot Reels of Super 8mm Film,* 413 U.S. 123 (1973).

37. *Paris Adult Theater v. Slaton,* 413 U.S. 439 (1973).

38. Catherine MacKinnon, *Only Words* (Cambridge: Harvard University Press, 1993).

39. *Everson v. Board of Education,* 390 U.S. 1 (1947).

40. *Lemon v. Kurtzman,* 403 U.S. 602 (1971).

41. *Mitchell v. Helms,* 530 U.S. 793 (2000).

42. *School District of Abington Township v. Schempp* and *Murray v. Curlett,* 374 U.S. 203 (1963).

43. *Engle v. Vitale,* 370 U.S. 421 (1962).

44. *Illinois ex. rel. McCollum v. Board of Education,* 33 U.S. 203 (1948), at 227.

45. Frank Way, "Survey Research on Judicial Decisions: The Prayer and Bible Reading Cases," *Western Political Quarterly,* 21 (June 1968): 189–205.

46. Cited in Stephen Wasby, *The Impact of the United States Supreme Court: Some Perspectives* (Homewood, IL: Dorsey Press, 1970): 134–135.

47. *Lynch v. Donnelly,* 104 S. Ct. 1355 (1984).

48. *Lee v. Weisman,* 505 U.S. 577 (1992).

49. *Santa Fe Independent School District v. Doe,* 530 U.S. 290 (2000).

50. *Cantwell v. Connecticut,* 310 U.S. 296 (1940); *West Virginia State Board of Education v. Barnette,* 319 U.S. 624 (1943); and *Sherbert v. Verner,* 374 U.S. 398 (1963).

51. See, among such cases, *Reynolds v. U.S.,* 98 U.S. 145 (1879); and *Hardin v. Tennessee,* 188 Tenn 17 (1949).

52. For example, *Jacobson v. Massachusetts,* 197 U.S. 11 (1955).

53. *Craig v. Maryland,* 220 Md. 500 (1959).

54. *U.S. v. Ballard,* 322 U.S. 78 (1944).

55. *Church of the Lukumi Babalu Aye v. City of Hialeah,* 113B S. Ct. 2217 (1993).

56. *Employment Division v. Smith,* 110B S. Ct. 2605 (1990).

57. *City of Boerne v. Flores,* 117 S. Ct. 2157 (1997).

58. *U.S. v. Seeger,* 380 U.S. 163 (1965).

59. *Board of Education v. Allen,* 392 U.S. 236 (1968).

60. *Lemon v. Kurtzman,* 403 U.S. 602 (1971).

61. *Mueller v. Allen,* 463 U.S. 388 (1983).

62. *Aguilar v. Felton,* 105A S. Ct. 3248 (1985).

63. *Zobrest v. Catalina Foothills School District,* 113B S. Ct. 2462 (1993).

64. *Epperson v. Arkansas,* 393 U.S. 97 (1968).

SUGGESTED READINGS

Books

Abraham, Henry J. *Freedom and the Court,* 5th ed. New York: Oxford University Press, 1988.

Alley, Robert S., ed. *The Constitution and Religion: Leading Cases on Church and State.* Amherst, NY: Prometheus Books, 1999.

Bickel, Alexander. *The Least Dangerous Branch.* Indianapolis Bobbs-Merrill, 1962.

Bork, Robert. *Slouching toward Gomorrah: Modern Liberalism and the American Decline.* New York: HarperCollins, 1996.

Chaffee, Zachariah. *Free Speech in the United States.* Cambridge: Harvard University Press, 1954.

Chopper, Jesse. *Judicial Review and the National Political Process.* Chicago: University of Chicago Press, 1980.

Clor, Harry M., ed. *Censorship and Freedom of Expression.* Skokie, IL: Rand McNally, 1971.

Conway, M. Margaret, Ahern, David W, and Steuernagel, Gertrude A. *Women and Public Policy: A Revolution in Progress,* 2nd ed. Washington: The CQ Press, 1999.

Ducat, Craig R. *Modes of Constitutional Interpretation.* St. Paul: West Publishing, 1978.

Emerson, Thomas I. *The System of Freedom of Expression.* New York: Vintage Books, 1970.

Etzioni, Amitai. *The Spirit of Community.* New York: Crown Publishers, 1993.

MacKinnon, Catharine A. *Only Words.* Cambridge: Harvard University Press, 1993.

Meikeljohn, Alexander. *Free Speech in Relation to Self-Government*. New York: Harper & Row, 1948.

Monsma, Stephen V. *Positive Neutrality: Letting Religious Freedom Ring*. Westport, CT: Greenwood Press, 1993.

Mooney, Christopher Z., ed. *The Public Clash of Private Values: The Politics of Morality Policy*. New York: Chatham House, 2001.

Segers, Mary C., and Jelen, Ted G. *Wall of Separation? Debating the Public Role of Religion*. Lanham, MD: Rowman & Littlefield, 1998.

Shapiro, Martin. *Freedom of Speech: The Supreme Court and Judicial Review*. Englewood Cliffs, NJ: Prentice-Hall, 1966.

Witte, John, Jr. *Religion and the American Constitutional Experiment: Essential Rights and Liberties*. Boulder, CO: Westview Press, 2000.

Wolfe, Christopher, ed. *The Family, Civil Society, and the State*. Lanham, MD: Rowman & Littlefield, 1998.

Web Sites

Americans United for Separation of Church and State   www.au.org
Christian Coalition   www.cc.org
Communitarian Network   www.gwu.edu/~ccps/
Interfaith Alliance   www.interfaithalliance.org
National Abortion and Reproductive Rights Action League (NARAL)   www.naral.org
National Catholic Educational Association (Public Policy Department)   www.ncea.org/publicpolicy/
National Education Association (Legislative Action Center)   www.nea.org/lac/
National Organization for Women (NOW)   www.now.org
National Right to Life   www.nrlc.org

CHAPTER 14

The Continuing Policy Debates: A Conclusion

The first edition of this text was written during the early months of the first Reagan administration. This edition was written during the first years of George W. Bush's presidency. Ironically, the heady promises of substantial reduction in the federal government and in federal deficits that so elated conservatives with the 1980 election became possible only with a Republican majority in Congress and a moderate Democrat, Bill Clinton, holding the presidency in the mid-1990s. Yet the victory of government cutters is partial at best. The goals of security, prosperity, needs, and membership remain. To address them, national and state government continue to create and administer public policy. The economic uncertainty of the early 1980s gave way to a long period of prosperity, low inflation, low unemployment, and steady economic growth, until the recession and terrorist attacks of 2001. Material prosperity brought neither political consensus nor reduced questioning of national purpose. The gap between wealthy and average workers widened. Despite economic growth, the number of workers without health insurance grew. Racial turmoil is more open and heated than when this book first appeared. Fierce moral and ideological struggles over sex, gender, family, and national identity rage in ways only hinted at twenty years ago.

POLITICAL ACTORS

On the domestic front, President Reagan's 1980 promise to balance the budget within three years turned into eight years of the largest budget deficits in American history. Promises to reduce taxes produced some early cuts, but the mid-1980s saw tax increases, and finally a tax reform bill that contained only part of what the president had wanted. Spending-cut proposals in health, education, public assistance, housing, environment, revenue sharing, transportation, and other domestic programs were partially successful, particularly in the first years of the Reagan presidency. But later years brought increasing resistance to such cuts and budget stalemates that colored the elder Bush administration from 1988 to 1992. The "Reagan Revolution" was successful only at the margins. President George Bush increased spending in some areas targeted for deep cuts by his predecessor. The 1980s demonstrated that an activist Democratic Congress may resist Republican presidential cuts, but not initiate new programs. The 1990s demonstrated that a conservative, Republican Congress finds it easier to talk about major program cuts than to enact them over the threat of a presidential veto. Yet the conservative mood of the country pushed a Democratic president into major programmatic changes in welfare and into a budget agreement in 1997 that deeply troubled liberals. The administration of the younger Bush followed the Reagan strategy of reducing taxes to make fewer funds available for government spending.

The first point to take from this history is that, although the president is the most visible actor on the American political stage, he is not the dominant actor. From time to time it may seem that way, but others, especially Congress and sometimes the Supreme Court, frequently take the leading role. However, given its size and the independence of its members, it is also very difficult for Congress to dominate the agenda. Although the Reagan and Bush administrations had a substantial impact on public policy, the direction of that impact was shaped by other agents as well, often in directions that these presidents did not particularly foresee. President Clinton was not able to dominate the public agenda, even during his first two years when there was a Democratic majority in Congress.

During his second term, having failed in his first to make health care reform his legacy, President Clinton struggled to find issues to define his presidency's place in history. Welfare reform was a major change, but he had to share credit with the Republicans for it. The same was true of the Balanced Budget Agreement of 1997. The younger Bush became the preeminent national leader only because of the domestic and foreign policy challenges of responding to the terrorist attacks of September 2001.

IDEOLOGY, DEMOGRAPHY, AND POLICY STALEMATE

One legacy of the policy changes of the 1980s and 1990s is renewed vitality in *federalism* (see Chapter 2). Both liberal and conservative state governors and legislatures have undertaken significant policy experiments in environmental regulation, health care provision, work programs for public assistance recipients, education, and economic development. Federal legislation, such as the 1996 welfare reform law, assumed and built upon state and local policy experimentation. Legislation to forbid "unfunded mandates" and the welfare and health care reform debates of the mid-1990s turned in part on the desirability of giving the states larger responsibilities for policy creation and implementation. Because these emphases run in cycles, it is difficult to predict just how long this renewed emphasis on federalism will last. However, state responsibilities do not come without costs. Sharp state spending increases for crime control, prison construction, unemployment compensation, and health care meant sharp reductions in many states for transportation, public assistance, parks, and other state programs. The general national mood of fiscal conservatism affects all levels of government, but the states do not have the federal government's borrowing capacity to cushion the shocks of budgetary shortfalls, as occurred during the last recession. The ultimate mix of federal and state responsibility for "homeland security" has yet to be determined.

These budgetary pressures in the states mean that highly principled debates about the separate and intertwining responsibilities of the national and the state governments are also debates about who will pay for programs. Conservative rhetoric counsels delegating as many programs as possible to the states, which are more flexible, more efficient, and closer to the actual problems. Democrats have also been important voices in this direction. The "reinventing government" movement at the federal level was spearheaded by Vice President Al Gore. Federal programs have been consolidated and federal payrolls sharply reduced. Yet citizens demand services. If they are not available at the federal level, gaze may shift to financially strapped state governments. Moreover, it is not at all clear that citizens are more trusting of state than of federal government, that states are in fact more efficient in delivering services, or that turning responsibility to the states is not simply a smoke screen for neglecting responsibilities. Federalism debates have focused not so much on elimination of programs, but on whose responsibility it is to control funding or to provide the services that meet needs, ensure prosperity, provide security, and ensure equal membership. These debates also are not without their ironies. Conservatives and Republicans, eager ideologically to return power to the states, have not hesitated to impose new mandates on states or to take away state responsibilities when it suits other interests. TANF, for example, came with substantial federal directives to the states on how welfare reform was to be accomplished. The Bush-sponsored education bill that passed Congress in 2001 imposed substantial federal testing requirements on state and local schools.

The demographic shifts described in Chapter 1 and their policy consequences have been significant themes in many of the substantive policy chapters. The economy must contend with a work force that contains more women and single parents than ever before, and with an aging "baby boom" generation as well. The aging of the population places intense pressure on the social insurance and health care systems. The frequency of divorce places many children and their mothers in poverty. Crime policy, too, has to respond to the economic and social pressures that changes in family structure place upon adolescents. The educational system must respond to a generation with a substantial portion of its numbers growing up in broken homes, immigrant families, and poverty.

The increasing numbers of racial minorities, especially Hispanics, and the failure of public policy to address the problems of the underclass and the effects of racial discrimination continue to demand a response from the policy system. There is a danger that the United States is becoming a two-tiered society, with many citizens achieving unprecedented levels of affluence and a significant minority moving deeper into poverty. Competitive pressures on our economic system generated by newly emerging economic powers overseas exacerbate these trends. The late 1990s saw increasingly acrimonious debate over immigration, with its implications for the racial composition and economic well-being of the United States (see Chapter 11).

In the new century, Americans must reassess the commitments of one generation to another. What are the obligations of the generation of workers to the aged, to children, and to generations to come in the form of stewardship of the environment? This question pervades Medicare, Social Security, and education, but it also runs through policy debates over day care, environmental protection, economic revitalization, and the size of the national debt.

Another set of compelling issues has to do with limits on individual liberty in a nation that prides itself on its commitment to freedom. With the emergence of the new religious right and with public policy impinging upon the traditional institutions of church and family, new moral questions have emerged to prominence in the last twenty years. Abortion policy poses questions of an unborn child's right to life and of a woman's freedom; medical technology produces dramatic questions of the right to die. The epidemic of drug addiction and drug-related crimes generates pressure for drug-testing programs that raise substantial privacy questions, as do the increased police and FBI intelligence-gathering activity as a result of September 11.

These last issues recall the moral and cultural conflicts that run through many of the policy areas discussed in this book, especially in Chapters 10 and 13. The "culture wars" intensified during the 1990s. Deciding how to respond to poverty, child neglect, teen pregnancy, urban unrest, drug addiction, AIDS, women's equality, and multicultural education are not simply questions of the best means to achieve agreed-upon goals. Instead, they touch on the deep divisions in beliefs, principles, and behavior characterizing America today. What is the role of government (if any) in promoting family stability and encouraging good character? Indeed, what is the meaning and importance of the family itself, and just what constitutes good character? What obligations does society have to the poor, and how great can it allow divisions of income to grow? Is America still the land of freedom and opportunity for immigrants from all nations, or must it preserve an Anglo-European racial and cultural dominance? The very principles themselves are hotly debated, as well as the capability of government to affect such values positively. Liberalism, conservatism, the religious right, feminism, and other ideological movements strive to define national identity and moral principles to guide the United States in the twenty-first century.

On one thing, however, most Americans are unified—they possess a deep distrust of politicians and political institutions. This frustration with government produced a backlash against Presidents George H. Bush and Clinton, demands for tax reduction, and term limitation efforts. It also did much to produce the Republican landslide in 1994 and the Republican Congressional victory in 1996. It is yet to be seen whether the initial favorable attitudes toward government produced by the terrorist attacks will have lasting effects.

This distrust has had a significant impact on many policy areas. It has produced an economic policy stalemate in which the taxes needed to pay for desired government programs or deficit reduction are difficult to find, but reducing spending in expensive programs like Medicare and Social Security is political suicide. The failure of a significant economic stimulus package in late 2001 reflected this stalemate. Voters worry about crime, health care, and the state of the economy. They doubt that government can or will do anything about it, but nevertheless hold elected officials, especially the president, responsible. An electorate that fundamentally distrusts its leaders is unlikely to look to them for creative approaches to health care, poverty reduction, improved education, or environmental protection. There is serious question whether American political institutions that have endured for more than 200 years can cope with this new distrust and cynicism about politics and public service.

It should be clear after reading this book that public policy in the United States is affected by many factors in the political environment. Although some people perceive policy and pursue policy goals from a conservative, liberal, or radical perspective, it is highly unlikely that any individual or group will always be satisfied with the policy results. Rather, it is likely that each participant in public policymaking will realize only some of his or her desired outcomes. Partial fulfillment of the desired goal leads participants to continue to attempt to influence policy.

PLURALISM

Because the United States is a pluralistic political system, political reality dictates compromise in the policymaking arena. In order to move toward their ultimate policy goals, participants must be able to build support with other participants in order to succeed in legislative or other decision-making units. Building support normally requires modifying positions so that the resulting policy is a compromise of alternative proposals. Welfare reform illustrates such compromise; health care reform in 1994 illustrates its failure. Some issues, such as abortion and the death penalty, seem intractable to compromise. Even though they may compromise in the short run, most policy advocates see the compromises as a temporary step as they work toward the ideal goal they have set for themselves. Of course, goals also change as people change their values and become aware of different issues and alternatives.

Values are at the base of different perspectives on how problems should be resolved. An important difference in values is that people differ on whether government ought to intervene in many problems at all. The debate over the role of the federal government has been intense in many policy areas. The continuing debates during the 2000s over taxes and government spending, assistance to agriculture, and abortion rights also are, at least partly, issues of the extent of government intervention into economic, personal, and social life.

Even where there is agreement on the need for intervention, differing values dictate how people view what should be done and how it should be accomplished. For example, it is agreed that there is a governmental obligation to provide education. Beyond that agreement, however, there is a wide diversity in opinion about what should be provided. Should it be for elementary and secondary levels only, or should public universities be supported as well? Should education be only the "three Rs," or should it also include vocational education and education in the arts? Which level of government should have the dominant voice? People also differ on whether public education should refer only to the actual operation of public schools or whether it should also include vouchers and tuition tax credits, which can be used to pay for tuition at private schools. Every policy area is subject to differing perspectives on the appropriateness and forms of intervention.

The question of government intervention also asks whether free-market forces or government regulation should be used to accomplish public goals. The debates over economic regulation and the move to deregulation, reduction of federal deficits, and tax reform, for example, question which kinds of government policy can best work with and stimulate market forces for economic prosperity. The debate over cost control in health care policy means deciding whether to rely on market forces or public regulation. Similarly, TANF marks an era of greater confidence that the free market can provide decent jobs and wages for persons formerly dependent upon public assistance. Even in education policy, market models of choice and privatization captured policy attention. The proper mix of market forces and government action lies at the heart of the most contentious policy debates.

In addition to the political realities of public policymaking and issues of government intervention, forces of policy demand are also important. If a policy is developed and no one is aware of or interested in it, the policy will not be very effective. Most policies are established as a result of a demand to do something about a particular problem; thus, there is already a market for the policy. But the size of the market may be critical. There is no guarantee that a policy advocated by an environmental group which may, in fact, be beneficial to a large portion of the population will be enacted into policy. It is just as likely that it will be strongly opposed by interests that would be negatively affected.

THE LIMITS OF PUBLIC POLICY

Yet another aspect of public policy is its cost. Any government program has costs, and in this day of downsizing and cutback management, there are conflicts over the ability of government to underwrite new activities or to maintain old programs. The debate over the deficit dominated economic policy for over a decade and brought the cost question and cost trade-offs to the forefront. There are conflicts over which programs are to survive and at what level of activity. As long as governmental funds are limited and public officials are under pressure to cut expenditures, such conflicts are likely to escalate. Thus, the policies discussed in this book should not be examined in isolation from one another. Time, attention, and money devoted to Medicare mean less of these available for transportation, crime, or education, for example. Devoting large sums of money to Social Security for the aged means less money is available for the education of the young.

It should also be clear that there are interdependencies among policies and that policies do not have only the effects they are created to have. Instead, many unintended consequences occur that may affect other policies or require modifying their approaches in order to accommodate some new difficulty. Many of the interdependent features of policy become apparent in the debates over a given policy. For example, environmentalists struggle with those worried about the effects of environmental protection on economic development. The conflicts between industrialists and environmentalists are well known, but accommodations have been made by both sides. Less-commonly understood, however, are unintended consequences. Examples of unintended consequences are the stiff enforcement of drug laws leading to increased crime, cheap energy policy encouraging wastage and pollution, and deductions for health insurance driving up health care costs.

The interrelatedness of policies does not stop at the borders of a country. Foreign policy is closely intertwined with economic and other domestic policies. Economic policies that affect the strength of the American dollar affect our relations with other nations on many other fronts. A strong American dollar and high American interest rates encourage foreign investments and imports into the United States and discourage American exports.

"PROBLEM" AND "SOLUTION"

When something is a "problem," Americans believe it must have a "solution." Citizens often approach public policy with a characteristically American problem-solving mentality, and they can become very disillusioned when, for example, new anticrime programs do not solve the problem of crime or when cities continue to decay after billions of dollars are spent on urban renewal. Indeed, such disillusionment may produce significant misperceptions. The Crime Bill of 1994 dominated public debate for months with most citizens believing that crime was rapidly increasing while Congress and the president fought, even though the crime rate actually declined in 1993 and 1994, a drop that continued into the present.

A public policy may fail to achieve improved conditions for a variety of reasons. First, there is often no general agreement on what the issues are. For example, some believe that the primary economic challenge is inflation, others feel it is unemployment. The Federal Reserve Board during the 1990s worked to control inflation with high interest rates, though the president and many in Congress saw little inflation danger. By the early 2000s, the Fed had to cut interest rates to the lowest point in decades. Second, when the perceptions of issues differ so much, it is likely that any policies formulated will have conflicting goals or will have goals that are too limited to deal adequately with the conditions demanding a response. Third, the costs of a complete solution may be too high or public resources too few, even if such a total solution is theoretically possible. Fourth, the dilemma being faced may change before a policy has had time to have its intended impact. (Economic policy is particularly subject to this difficulty. Given the time lag between adoption and impact, the original problem may have diminished by the time the effect is felt; thus, the program may create a new problem of its own.) Fifth, some problems are inherently unsolvable. Crime will never be totally prevented; there will always be citizens in need of public assistance. The difficulty is keeping crime and need at manageable levels. Sixth, government is limited in its rationality, efficiency, and authority. Bureaucracy, departmental jealousies, petty politicking, and the simple limits of time, attention, and information all prevent government from formulating fully rational policy, even when the conflict over goals is minimal.

Additionally, government is constitutionally prevented from adopting certain kinds of policies to attack issues. The U.S. Constitution reflects what is culturally and politically unacceptable in America—for example, it forbids torture as a means of deterring crime or terrorism. Not all such limits are constitutional, however. Letting the poor starve to death to "solve" the problem of poverty would be politically and socially unacceptable. Finally, although issues that become matters of public concern often have more than one cause, government response is limited to acting on only those causes within its scope of authority. For example, one cause of the financial problems of Social Security is the aging of the population, a factor not under government control. Many of these same limitations temper policy evaluation and issue understanding. The study of public policy rapidly teaches the lesson that not all problems have solutions. Public policy has so many inherent limitations that it may be best not to speak of solving problems at all but, rather, of facing dilemmas, addressing issues, improving conditions, or responding to challenges. To expect too much of public policy is to face certain disappointment and disillusionment, conditions that may obscure the real, though limited, accomplishments of public programs.

Often voters assume that if a policy is developed, it will automatically solve the problem to which it is addressed. Unfortunately, such is not the case. Instead, implementation is necessary, and there can be as many disagreements about the method of implementation as over the content of the policy. Furthermore, implementation depends on the administrator charged with carrying out the policy. Different administrators and agencies have different interpretations of what a policy means, and these will affect its development.

Similarly, the evaluation of policies produces different results. Because people have different perspectives on policies, they also view the results differently. Personal values affect the way citizens view the effects of any policy or program. Understanding of the intent of the policy also varies and thus leads to different evaluations of the effectiveness of that policy.

Ultimately the question is whether American public policy is in the best interests of its citizens. In order to make that assessment, it is necessary to know the public interest, a concept on which there is little agreement. Because of variation in the interests of the citizens, evaluations also vary widely. For these reasons and because of the sharp ideological disagreements over the role of government, the necessary trade-offs between policy areas, and the compromises necessary within an issue area, public policy always diverges from the ideal, both in procedure and substance. Those who expect a policy to completely solve a public concern will always be disappointed. They should not be surprised when, as has happened frequently in the last decade, stalemate characterizes numerous policy arenas. The task of policymakers and citizens alike is not to expect perfection or immediate action, but to develop a way of keeping policymakers and implementers accountable for their actions. In this way policy can be adjusted when failures occur. Adjustment in response to citizen demand is a central feature of a democratic political system.

Index

A Nation at Risk, 302

A-95 review process, 34–35; *See also* Reagan administration
   importance of, 35

Abortion, 427–433, 468–469
   Department of Health and Human Services, 429
   gag rule, 429
   moral issue, 432–433
   partial birth, 428
   pro-choice strategy, 430–431
   and RU-486, 429

Accused
   and Bill of Rights, 158
   and constitutional rights, 158
   and crime, 158
   right to counsel, 159–160

Achieving personality, 367

Acid rain, 127–128

Acidity, 127–128

ACIR (Advisory Council on Intergovernmental Relations), 28, 38
   regulations, 31–32

Acquaintance rape, 176

Actionable offense, 351

Adams, Hunter, 364

Adult Theater v. Slaton (1973), 445

Advertising, and free-enterprise system, 46

Advisory Council on Intergovernmental Relations (ACIR); *See* ACIR

Advocacy, 3

AFDC; *See* Aid to Families with Dependent Children

Affirmative action; *See also* Racial preference plans; Reverse discrimination
   and higher education, 321
   future of, 363–372
   opposition to, 365–368
   reverse discrimination, 359
   support for, 365
   zero-sum aspect, 365

African American Baseline Essays, 364

African Americans
   and capital punishment, 165
   and crime, 152, 154–157
   equality under law and, 333

Afrocentrism, 364

Against Our Will, 176

Age
   and poverty, 202–203
   and public policy, 14

Agenda-setting, 8

Agricultural Adjustment Administration, 47

Agriculture, and regulation, 65

Agricultural economy, 47

Agricultural wastes, 124

Aid to Families with Dependent Children (AFDC), 219

AIDS, 353

Air pollution, 121–124
   policy for, 129–130

Air Pollution Control Act of 1955, 129

Alcohol, Drug Abuse, and Mental Health, 262

Alexander the Great, and Afrocentrism, 364

Alexander v. Homes County, 341

Ali, Marimba, 364

Alien Contract Labor Act of 1885, 378

Alien Registration Act, 380

Alkalinity, 127–128

Alternative medicine, 265

America 2000: An Education Strategy, 312

American Bar Association, 55

American Coalition, anti-immigrant sentiment, 379

American Health Security Act, proposal of, 268

American idealism, and foreign and defense policy, 405–408

American Protective League of True Americans, anti-immigrant sentiment, 379

American Revolution, and economic policies, 47

Americans with Disabilities Act of 1990, 354

Analysis, and public policy, 3

Anglo-Iranian Oil Company, 103

Anti-merger act, 52

Anti-national Origins Clause League, 379

Antitrust Division, 52–53

Antitrust laws, 50

Antitrust policy, 52
   defined, 53
   and energy, 101
   international approach, 57
   weaknesses of, 56–57

Arab Oil embargo, 104–105
Arabian American Oil Company (Aramco), 103
Aramco; *See* Arabian American Oil Company
Armor, David, 356
Artic National Wildlife Refuge, 120
Articles of Confederation, 25
Artistic expression, and freedom
    of speech, 439
Asians, equality under law and, 332–333
Asylee, 381
AT&T, 53
Authoritarian leaders, 405
Atomic Energy Commission (AEC), 102
Automobiles
    Corporate Average Fuel Economy (CAFE),
       108–109
    National Energy Act of 1978, 108–109

Back to the basics, 317
Bakke, Alan, 345
Balance of power; *See* Diplomacy; Foreign
    and defense policy; Power
Balanced Budget Act of 1997, 80, 91–92
    and Medicare, 258, 273
Balanced budget amendment, 95
Balanced Budget and Emergency Deficit
    Control Act of 1985, 88; *See also* Gramm-
    Rudman Act
Banking, and Federal Reserve Board, 76–77
Bartlett, Marilyn, 354
Bechofer, Laurie, 176
Bell Curve, The, 335
Benign policy, 366
Bernal, Martin, 364
Bias, Len, 175
Bilingual education, 303–304
Bill of Rights, 158, 427
Bituminous Coal Act, 101
Black English, 363–364
Block grants; *See* Funding
Booth v. Maryland (1987), 171
Bowers v. Hardwick, 352
Boy Scouts of America v. Dale, 352
Boycotts, and censorship, 447–448
Bracero Program, 380
Brady bill, 184
British Petroleum, 103
British Royal Commission, and capital
    punishment, 162
Brookings Institution, 94
Brown I, 340
Brown II, 341
Brown v. Board of Education (1954), 288,
    332, 340
Brown v. Illinois, 168
Brownmiller, Susan, 176
Bubble concept, 131

Budget deficit
    elimination of, 89–92
    and Gramm-Rudman Act, 88–89
    history of, 88–89
    1980s and 1990s, 80–83, 86–87
    and privatizing social security, 216–217
    and social security, 214–215
Budget Enforcement Act (BEA), 90
Budget surplus, 94–95
Bureau of Immigration, naming of, 378
Burger Court, 168
Bush, George H. administration, 466–467
    and abortion, 429
    deficit spending, 78
    deregulation, 60–61
    and education, 312
    fiscal policy, 86–89
    and FTC, 55
    international trade, 61–62
    and mergers, 55–56
    Supreme Court justices, 157–158
Bush, George W. administration, 31, 477
    education, 314–315
    environmental policy, 132
    Kyoto Protocol, 134
    oil exploration, 109, 120
    and partial birth abortions, 428
    tax reform, 83–84
Business, government assistance, 62
Busing, and education, 342–343, 355–357
Butler, Paul, 157

CAFE; *See* Corporate Average Fuel Economy
California, and Asian immigrants, 378–380
California Civil Rights Initiative, 362
California Medical School at Davis, University
    of, 345–346
California, University of, and equality, 332
Capital gains taxes, reduction of, 94
Capital punishment, 161–167, 169–172; *See*
    Capital punishment; Crime; Future
    Alternatives; Policy evaluation; U.S.
    Constitution
    and African-Americans, 165
    Booth v. Maryland (1987), 171
    Death Penalty Act of 1994, 172
    as deterrent, 162–164, 170
    and *Furman v. Georgia,* 166, 169
    Gregg v. Georgia (1976), 170
    and the law, 164–166
    limitations of, 171–172
    Maynard v. Cartwright (1988), 171
    McCleskey v. Zant (1991), 171
    of minors, 170–171
    as retribution, 161
    South Carolina v. Gathers (1989), 171
    Sumner v. Shuman (1987), 171

Capital punishment *(continued)*
  Thompson v. Oklahoma, 170–171
  and women, 166
Capitalism; *See* Free-enterprise system
Capitation, 246
Carbon dioxide (CO_2), 122–123
Carbon monoxide (CO), 121
Carhart, Leroy, 428
Carnal Knowledge, 441
Carr, E. H., 401
Carter administration
  deregulation, 60–61
  solar energy, 111–112
  superfund, 131
Cash assistance, 218, 219–222
Cash-flow tax, 94
Cash Management Improvement Act of 1990,
    and cross-cutting requirements, 31
Categorical grants, 27; *See also* Funding
  and administrative issues, 33–34
Categorization, of people, 330–331
CDC; *See* Centers for Disease Control
Censorship; *See also* Freedom of Speech; Law;
    Obscenity; Pornography, 442
  arguments against , 444–445
  arguments for , 443–444
  and boycotts, 447–448
Centers for Disease Control (CDC), 124
Centers for Medicare and Medicaid Services
    (CMS), 259
CFCs; *See* Chlorofluorocarbons
Charitable Choice, 221
Charter schools, 318
Chevron; *See* Standard Oil of California
Childcare assistance, 220
Chinese Labor Exclusion Act, 378
Chinese Student Protection Act, 385
Chlorofluorocarbons (CFCs), 123–124
Christian Coalition, 17
Circular A-95 of the Office of Management and
    Budget; *See* A-95 review process
Citizenship, 4
Civil Rights Act of 1964, and cross-cutting
    requirements, 31
Civil rights cases, 339–342, 344
Civil rights laws, 5
Civil rights movement, and equality, 339
Civil War, 340
Civilian Conservation Corps, 47
Class action suit, 53–54
Classification, and public policy, 4–6
Clean Air Act of 1963, 129
Clean Air Act Amendments of 1977, 130
Clean Air Act Amendments of 1990, and partial
    preemption, 32
Clean Waters Restoration Act of 1966, 129
Clinton, Bill, administration, 131, 143, 147, 467
  and abortion, 429
  and deficit spending, 78

  and education, 313
  and enterprise zones, 57
  and FTC, 55
  and logging, 132
  and the Middle East, 14–415
  and partial birth abortion, 428
  and Supreme Court, 158
  and universal health care, 268–269
CMS; *See* Centers for Medicare and Medicaid
    Services
Coal, 101, 105, 138
  National Energy Act of 1978, 108
Coal liquefaction, 112
Cocaine, 175
Cohen v. California, 435
Coinsurance, 257
Cold War, 409–412
Coleman, James, 296, 308
Coleman report of 1966, 342
Collective goods, 6
Collective security, 408; *See also* Foreign and
    defense policy
  post-World War II
Colorado River Authority, 28
Commerce clause, 344
Commerce Department, 75
Commonwealth of Independent States, 25
Communications Decency Act, 441
Communists, 18
Communitarians, and public policy, 18, 424
Community Development Block Grants, 30
  spending pattern, 35
Community Health Centers, 262
Community, principle of, 424
Community rating, 272
Community revitalization, 68
Comparable worth, 348
Comprehensive Environmental Response
    Act, 131
Condit, Gary, 147–148
Confederation, 25
Conference of State Legislatures, 38
Confusions, 167–168
Congress
  and economic policy, 75
  and intergovernmental relations, 27
Conservation, 120–121
Conservatism
  and freedom, 17
  and public policy, 17
Consumer
  and deregulation, 61, 64
  and FTC, 55
  oversight committee, 68
Containment, 408
  and Cold War, 409–410
  and Korean War, 410
  non-communist nations, 410
  Vietnam failure, 410–412

Contraception, 431–432
Contracts, 5
Conyers, John, 165
Corporate Average Fuel Economy (CAFE), 108–109
Correctional facilities, 190
Cost-push inflation; *See* Inflation
Council of Economic Advisers, and economic
    policy, 75, 76
Council on Environmental Quality, 130–131
Courts
  and intergovernmental relations, 27
  and open society, 426–427
Crack, 175
Craig v. Boren (1976), 347
Cranston-Gonzalez National Affordable
    Housing Act, 236
Creationism, teaching of, 459–460
Crime, 143–144; *See also* Capital punishment;
    Future Alternatives; Policy evaluation; U.S.
    Constitution; Violence
  and African-Americans, 154–157
  capital punishment, 161–166, 169–172
  and confusions, 167–168
  constitutional rights, 157–167
  cost of, 148–149
  decriminalization of, 186–187
  demographic change, 152–153
  deterrence of, 157–167, 172–173, 186–187
  drugs, 150–151, 174–176
  and education, 315–316
  and ethnicity, 154–157
  and exclusionary rule, 160–161, 168–169
  growth and decline of, 145–157
  and ideology, 157
  and illegally obtained evidence, 168–169
  and immigrants, 393
  index of, 145
  and Miranda rights, 167–168
  and police, 187–188
  and population, 152–153
  punishment of, 190–192
  and racism, 156–157
  reasons for, 149–157
  reduction of, 174–192
  reporting of, 149
  and search and seizure, 168–169
  statistics of, 143–144, 145–146
  street, 148, 174–176
  support of drug habit, 150–151
  and Supreme Court, 157–158
  victimless, 150
  of violence, 178–186
  and warrantless search, 169
  white-collar, 146–148
Crime bill, 188–190
Crime index, 145
Criminal justice system; *See* Capital punishment;
    Crime; Future Alternatives; Policy
    evaluation; U.S. Constitution; Violence

Cross-cutting requirements, and
    intergovernmental interactions, 31
Crossover sanctions, and intergovernmental
    interactions, 32
Crude Oil Windfall Profit Tax Act of 1980, 109
Cruel and unusual punishment, 161
Cultural context, and public policy, 19–20, 469
Cultural legitimation, 438
Currency; *See also* Federal Reserve Board;
    Money supply
  circulation of, 76
  strength of, 83
  supply of, 76
  value of, 76

Dahmer, Jeffrey, 161
Date rape, 176
De facto segregation, 341
De jure, 341–342
Death Penalty Act of 1994, 172
Debt management; *See* Fiscal policy
Deductible, 257
Defense policy; *See* Foreign and defense
    policy
Defense spending, 92–93, 94–95
Deficit spending, 77
Delaware River Basin Compact, 28
Deliberation, 9
Demand-pull inflation; *See* Inflation
Demand-side theory, 78–79
Demographic context, and public policy,
    14–17, 468
Department of Agriculture, 256
Department of Agriculture's Economy Food
    Plan, and Poverty, 198
Department of Education (DOE), 307
Department of Energy (DOE), 114
Department of Health, Education and Welfare
    (HEW), 129, 307
Department of Health and Human Services, 257
Deregulation, 60–61, 67
  and supply-side economics, 80
Deterrent
  and authoritarian leaders, 405
  and capital punishment, 162–164
  and foreign and defense policy, 405
Development, of policy; *See* Policy
    development
Diagnosis Related Groups (DRGs), and
    Medicare, 259
Dial a porn, 441
Diggle, Angus, 178
Diplomacy
  classical, 401–404
  realism, 401–404
Direct cost, 11; *See also* Policy evaluation
Direct impact, 11; *See also* Policy evaluation
Direct orders, and intergovernmental
    interactions, 31

Disadvantaged Minority Health Improvement
    Act of 1990, 262
Discount rate, 77
Discrimination; *See also* Equality
  covert, 344
  overt, 344
  reverse, 359
Dismantlement, and nuclear power
    plant, 115
Displaced Persons Act, 380
Distributive policies, 5
Diversity, and higher education, 320
Doc in a Box, 244
Doc Lap, 411
Domestic violence, 177
Domestic wastes, 124
Don't ask, don't tell policy, 352
DRGs; *See* Diagnosis Related Groups
Drug formularies, 245
Drug Free Workplace Act of 1988, and
    cross-cutting requirements, 31
Drugs
  attacking demand, 175–176
  attacking supply, 174–175
  and automatic weapons, 175–176
  and education, 315–316
  and gang warfare, 175–176
  reducing of crime, 174–176
  relationship to crime, 174–176
  statistics and use of, 150–152
  and violent crimes, 178
Dual eligible, 258
Dual school system, 341
Due process, 158, 427
Dworkin, Andrea, 176
Dysrationality, 354

EAI; *See* Education Alternatives, Inc.
Earned Income Tax Credit (EITC), 222
Earth in the Balance, 131
Economic context, for public policy, 13
Economic development; *See* Economics
Economic expansion, and federal
    deficits, 89
Economic forecasts, 75
Economic Growth and Tax Relief
    Reconciliation Act of 2001
    (EGTRRA), 83–84
Economic policy, 74–75
  conflict of goals, 75
  fragmentation of, 74–75
  obstacles of, 75
  outcomes of, 75
  participants in, 75
Economic regulation, 50–51, 63–66;
    See also Economics
  antitrust policy, 52
  and FTC, 52–60
  and regulatory agencies, 50–51

Economics; *See also* Economic policy; Economic
    regulation; Funding; Intergovernmental
    relations; Macroeconomic policy
  and abortions, 430
  business assistance, 62
  community revitalization, 68
  concepts and issues, 43, 73–78
  consumer choice, 46
  consumer oversight, 68
  contemporary policy, 78–84
  defense spending, 92–93
  deregulation, 60–61, 67
  and development, 57–58
  enterprise zones, 57–58, 62, 66
  fiscal policy, 86–89, 89–92
  free-enterprise system, 44–46
  future of, 66–69, 93–96
  globalization of, 66, 68–69
  government involvement, 48, 65–66,
    66–69, 73–79
  government monopolies, 45
  governmental history, 46–48
  Great Depression, 47–48
  growth of, 74
  ideology, 74
  and immigration policy, 388–390
  incentives, 67
  inflation and recession, 48–49, 85–86
  international trade, 59–60, 68–69
  macroeconomic approaches, 75–78
  microeconomic approaches, 49–51
  nationalization, 68
  policy evaluation, 84–93
  policy obstacles, 74–75
  quality of, 74
  regulation, 50–51, 63–66
  revenues and spending, 89
  revitalization programs, 57–58
  and social issues, 57–58
  socialist, 44–45
  social and political values, 73–74
  and social order, 84–85
  and social regulation, 51
  and social security, 214–215
  and solid-waste pollution, 125
  supply and demand, 43, 46
  tax reform, 83–84
  unevenness of, 46
Edison Project, and education, 318
Education, 236–237, 285, 468; *See also* Equality
  aid to parochial schools, 457–459
  and ACT scores, 300
  back to the basics, 317
  bilingual, 303–304
  and busing, 342–343, 355–357
  charter schools, 318
  contemporary policy, 291–297
  cost of higher, 321–323
  crisis with, 310–311

decentralization, 306
district consolidation, 306–307
emotional growth, 298
and equality, 295–297, 332–333, 340–341
federal involvement, 287, 311–312
free public, 286
future alternatives, 305–323
goals 2000, 313–314
and higher, 291
home schooling, 319–320
and immigration, 387, 390–391
inequality in funding, 292–295
and integration, 341–343
issues with, 286–291
issues with higher, 320–323
local control of, 286, 287–288, 306–307
master teachers, 303
merit pay, 302–303
minimum competency tests, 300–301
moral, 317
multiculturalism, 304–305
NAEP, 317
national teacher certification, 316
outcome-based education, 317–318
and private schools, 307–310
privatization, 318–319
quality of, 297–305
and racial preference plans, 361–363
and religion, 450–454
and SAT scores, 298–300
speech censorship policies, 437–438
state government role, 287
structural issues, 318–320
student achievement, 298–301
teacher competency, 301–302
and teachers, 300–303
teaching of creationism, 459–460
teaching of secular humanism, 460
vouchers and tax credits, 308–310
workforce preparation, 316–317
Education Alternatives, Inc. (EAI), 318
Education Commission of the States, 28
Educational Testing Service, 301
EEC; *See* European Economic Community
EEOC; *See* Equal Employment Opportunity
    Commission
Effective governance, 2
EITC; *See* Earned Income Tax Credit
Elementary and Secondary Education Act of
    1965, 287–290
Elite model; *See* Models
Emergency Banking Act, 47
Empirical dimension, 10; *See also* Policy
    evaluation
Employment
    and equality, 343–346
    and immigration policy, 389–390
    and unemployment, 73–74
    and women, 347–348

Employment Act of 1946, 76
Employment issues, 236–237
Energy, 96; *See also* Energy policy
Energy policy
    antitrust, 101
    complacency, 119–120
    decentralization, 101
    decontrol, 109
    economic stability, 107
    Eisenhower administration, 105
    and environment, 137–139
    fossil fuel dependency, 106–107
    future of, 119–120
    legislation, 108–109
    National Energy Act of 1978, 108–109
    1990s, 111
    Nixon administration, 105, 108, 109
    oil dependency, 117–119, 119–120
    oil imports, 105–106
    post-1973, 105–111
    post-1980, 109–111
    pre-1973, 100–105
    price regulation, 109
    problems with, 105–106
    Project Independence, 108
    Reagan administration, 109–111
    unrestricted competition, 111
Energy policy and Conservation Act
    of 1975, 109
Energy policy post-1973, 100–105, 105–111; *See
    also* Energy; Energy policy; Energy policy
    post-1973
    import quota, 105
Energy policy pre-1973; *See also* Energy;
    Energy policy; Energy policy pre-1973
    Arab oil embargo, 103–105
    coal, 101
    natural gas, 102
    nuclear power, 102
    oil, 101–102
    OPEC, 103–105
    taxation, 101
    Western oil companies, 103
    Yom Kippur War, 104
Energy Research and Development
    Administration (ERDA), 108
Energy Security Act, 112
Enron, 54
    and white-collar crime, 147
Enterprise zones; *See* Economics
Entitlement programs and Omnibus Budget
    Reconciliation Act of 1990, 90
Entombment, and nuclear power
    plant, 115
Environment; *See also* Environmental policy
    abuse of, 121–128
    air pollution, 121–124
Environmental Equity Workgroup, 134
Environmental law, 5

Environmental policy, 120–139, 468
 air-pollution, 129–130
 conservation, 120–121
 contemporary solutions, 128–131
 current direction, 131
 enforcement of, 133
 future of, 133–139
 and health care, 265–266
 history, 120–121
 legal action, 135–136
 politics of regulation, 132–133
 and popular opinion, 132, 137
 reduced concerns, 132
 reduced regulation, 134–135
 and social justice, 134
 state government, 136
 taxes, 135–136
 water-pollution, 129
Environmental Protection Agency (EPA), 130
Environmentalists, and public policy, 18
EPA; *See* Environmental Protection Agency
Epstein, Julian, 165
Equalitarian social order, 85
Equalitarian values, 85
Equal Employment Opportunity Commission
 (EEOC), 344
Equal Rights Amendment (ERA), 350
Equality, 329
 and African Americans, 333
 and AIDS, 353
 and Asians, 332–333
 categorization of people, 330–331
 and civil rights movement, 339
 creating inequality, 334–337
 and education, 295–297, 332–333, 340–343
 and educational busing, 342–343, 355–357
 employment, 343–346
 enforcing integration, 341–343
 future alternatives, 363–372
 and handicapped, 351–355
 higher education, 343–346
 and homosexuals, 351–355
 issues with, 330–339
 and learning disabilities, 354
 material well-being, 337–339
 and Native Americans, 333, 351–355
 of opportunity, 334–337
 policy evaluation of, 355–366
 proportional, 337
 and race, 369–372
 and racial profiling, 331–332
 and segregation ending, 340–341
 and sexual harassment, 350–351
 strengthening constitutional guarantees,
 339–355
 U.S. history of, 332–334
 under law, 330–334
 and women, 333–334, 347–351

Equality feminists, 351
Equality of Educational Opportunity, 296
Equality of result; *See* Equality, material
 well-being
ERA; *See* equal rights amendment
ERDA; *See* Energy Research and Development
 Administration
Erlichman, John, 441
Establishment clause, 449, 450–454
 other issues, 453–454
 prayer in school, 451–453
 and public schools, 450–451
Estrich, Susan, 178
Ethics
 euthanasia, 276–277
 and health care, 276–280
 medical research and development, 277–279
 and public policy, 3, 7
Ethnic cleansing, 402
Etzioni, Amitai, 424
European Economic Community (EEC), 60
Euthanasia, 276–277
Evaluation; *See* Policy evaluation
Exclusionary rule, 168–169
Executive branch
 and economic policy, 75
 and intergovernmental relations, 27
Experience rating, 272
Exxon; *See* Standard Oil of New Jersey

Faith-Based and Community Initiative, 221
Family values, 425, 460–462
 and freedom of speech, 434
Fast-track authority, 60, 62
FCCC; *See* Framework Convention on Climate
 Change
FEA; *See* Federal Energy Administration
Fed; *See* Federal Reserve Board
Federal Agriculture Improvement and Reform
 Act of 1996, 65
Federal Communications Commission
 (FCC), 1
Federal Death Penalty Act, 164
Federal Emergency Relief Act, 47
Federal Energy Administration (FEA), 108
Federal Energy Regulatory Commission
 (FERC), 115
Federal funding; *See* Funding;
 Intergovernmental relations
Federal Power Commission (FPC), 102
Federal Reserve Act of 1913, 76
Federal Reserve Board
 and banking, 76–77
 board members, 76
 and economic policy, 75
 and monetary policy, 76
Federal Reserve Note, 76
Federal revenues and spending, 89

Federal system, 25–28
  intergovernmental policies, 26–27
  issues of, 25–27
Federal Trade Commission (FTC), 1, 50, 52–60
  consumer rights, 55
  and economic regulation, 50, 52–60
  hearings, 54–55
  mergers, 55–57
  political appointees, 55
  weaknesses of, 56–57
Federal Trade Commission Act of 1914, 52
Federalism, 25, 29, 467; *See also* Federal
    system; Intergovernmental relations
Fee-for-service (FFS), and health care, 244
Feminism, 460–462
Feminists
  and equality, 347
  and public policy, 18
Feminization of poverty, 16, 203
FERC; *See* Federal Energy Regulatory
    Commission
FFS; *See* Fee-for-service
Fighting words, 435–436
Fiscal policy, 77–78, 86–89
Fission, 113
Flat-tax proposal, 94
Food and Drug Administration, 256
Food pantries, and welfare reform, 230
Food stamps, 222–223
  accomplishments of, 226
  and PRWOR, 222
Foreign and defense policy
  American idealism, 405–406
  balance of power, 404–405
  and deterrence, 405
  diplomacy, 407–408
  evaluation of, 412–416
  force, 407–408
  institutional solutions, 408
  Middle East, 412–416
  Nuremburg principle, 406–407
  optimism, 407–408
  Palestine peace, 412, 413–414
  realism or classical diplomacy, 401–404
  recent and contemporary policy, 409–412
  relationship with Israel, 413
  Rwanda, 403
  security, 408
  spheres of influence, 403–404
  terrorism control, 416–419
  universal justice, 406–407
  Vietnam containment failure, 410–412
  Yugoslavia, 403
Foreign policy; *See* Foreign and defense policy
Fossil fuels
  alternatives, 111–117
  dependency on, 106–107, 111–119
Fourteen Points speech, 406

Framework Convention on Climate Change
    (FCCC), 133
France, Anatole, 335
Free exercise clause, 449, 454–457
  conscientious objection, 456
  religion clauses, 456–457
Freedom of speech, 433–436; *See also*
    Censorship; Law; Obscenity; Open Society;
    Pornography
  and artistic expression, 439
  arguments against censorship, 444–445
  arguments for censorship, 443–444
  and boycotts, 447–448
  censorship policies, 432, 437–438
  fighting words, 435–436
  hate speech laws, 436
  Hicklin test, 440
  LAPS values, 440
  Megan's law, 443
  and obscenity legislation, 439, 442–448
  racial slurs, 435–436, 436–439
  Roth case, 440–442
  Roth rule, 440–442
  U.S. Constitution First Amendment, 177, 351,
    424, 426, 433–448
Free-enterprise capitalism, 44
  control of, 45
Free-enterprise system, 44–46
  and advertising, 46
  Friedman, Milton, 45–46
  and immigration policy, 389
Freestanding surgical units, 244
Friedman, Milton, 45–46, 66, 84, 308
FTC; *See* Federal Trade Commission
Funding; *See also* Intergovernmental
    relations
  administrative issues and, 32–34
  block grants, 27, 30, 34, 36
  categorical grants, 27, 30, 33–34, 35
  community development block grants, 30
  community health centers, 262
  education, 292–295
  future of, 39–40
  general revenue sharing, 27, 30, 34, 36
  grant-in-aid program, 30
  health care, 245–246
  higher education, 321–322
  Joint Funding and Simplification Act
    of 1974, 34
  Medicaid, 259–260, 264
  Medicare, 257–259, 264, 273
  monitoring of, 34–35
  parochial school aid, 457–459
  and SCHIP, 261
  shift of, 36
  state and local governments, 37
  structural effects, 37
  and TANF provisions, 220–221

Funding *(continued)*
　unfunded mandates, 27, 32, 36–37
　and welfare reform, 219–220, 227
Furman v. Georgia, 166
Fusion, 113
Future alternatives
　crime reduction, 174–192
　deficit, 93–96
　and education, 305–323
　energy policy, 119–120
　environmental policy, 133–139
　and equality, 363–372
　government and economy relationship, 66–69
　and health care, 267–280
　and health care ethics, 267–280
　immigration policy, 394–396
　intergovernmental system, 38–40
　and long-term care, 267–280
　public assistance, 232–237
　social security reform, 214–218
　spending, 93–96
　taxes, 93–96

Gacy, John Wayne, 161
Galbraith, John Kenneth, 43, 84
Galston, William, 18
Game models; *See* Models
Gang warfare, 175
Garrity, Jude Arthur, 356
Gases, and air pollution, 121–123
Gas-guzzling, 108
Gatekeepers, 245
GATT (General Agreement on Tariffs and
　Trade), 59–60
Gay and lesbian community, and public
　policy, 18
GDP (Gross Domestic Product), 74
Gelles, Richard, 177
General Agreement on Tariffs and Trade
　(GATT); *See* GATT
General assistance, 222
General revenue sharing; *See* Funding
*General Theory of Employment, Interest, and
　Money,* 48
Genocide, 401–402
George Washington University Law School, 157
Geothermal energy, 112–113
Germany, and antitrust policy, 57
Ghettoized, 378
Gideon v. Wainwright, 159
Giuliani, Rudy, 188
Glendening, Parris, 38
Gore, Al, 131
Government
　cynicism towards, 12–13
　economic influences of, 47
　economic stimulation and, 47
　intervention of, 49–51
　and membership, 4

microeconomic approaches, 49–51
　mistrust of, 12–13
　and needs, 5
　and prosperity, 4
　purpose of, 4–5
　and security, 4
Government spending; *See* Fiscal policy
Graduate Medical Education, 262
Gramm-Rudman Act, 88–89
　failure of, 89
Great Britain, and antitrust policy, 57
Great Depression, 47
　government intervention, 47–48
*Green et al. v. County School Board of New
　Kent County* (1968), 342
Greenhouse gas, 122–123
Gregg v. Georgia (1976), 164, 170
Grigg v. Duke Power (1971), 344
Gross Domestic Product (GDP); *See* GDP
Group model; *See* Models
Gulf Oil, 103
Guns, 179–186; *See also* Semi-automatic
　weapons
　opposition to control of, 180–182
　proliferation of, 180
　regulation of, 182–184

Handicapped, equality and, 351–355
Harris v. New York (1971), 168
Harvard Center for Educational Policy
　Research, 296
Harvard University, and equality, 332
Hatch Act, 29
Hate speech laws, 436
Hawaii Volcanoes National Park, 112
Hazardous and Solid Waste Amendments of
　1984, and partial preemption, 32
Hazardous waste, 125–127
　radioactive, 126–127
Head Start, increase funding for, 233
Health care
　and age, 254
　and alternative medicine, 265
　American health, 247–249
　clinics and hospital mergers, 244
　covering the uninsured, 271
　and ethics, 276–280
　failure of universal, 268–270
　federal government involvement, 256, 261–262
　fee-for-service, 244
　high cost of, 251–255, 263
　incremental reform, 270
　inequities of, 249–251, 263
　insurance market reform, 272
　international examples, 246–247
　issues with, 243–256, 262–267
　labor coast, 253
　and long-term care, 267–280
　maldistribution of resources, 250–251

managed care, 244–245, 266–267
mandated coverage, 272–273
Medicaid, 259–260, 263–264
Medicare, 257–259, 263–264
new business approach, 244
overspecialization, 256
policy evaluation, 262–267
prescription drugs, 253–254, 262–264,
    273–274
public expectations, 254–255
and public health measures, 265–266
quality of, 255–256
reform of, 267–280
regulation of, 265
research and development, 277–279
right to, 267–268
SCHIP, 261
and specialist, 256
state reform of, 271–273
structure of, 243–245, 264–266
and technology, 252–253
third party payments, 252–253
two main types, 246
uninsured, 249–250
Health Careers Opportunity Training, 262
Health Insurance Portability and Accountability
    Act (HIPAA), 270
Health Insurance Purchasing Cooperatives
    (HIPC), 268
Health insurance vouchers, 269
Health Security Act, 269–270
Heart of Atlanta Motel, 344
Hebrew Sheltering and Immigration Aid
    Society, 379
Hegemony, 404
Hernnstein, Richard, 335
Heroin, 175
HEW; *See* Department of Health, Education and
    Welfare
Hicklin test, 440
Hill, Anita, 177
HIPAA; *See* Health Insurance Portability and
    Accountability Act
HIPC; *See* Health Insurance Purchasing
    Cooperatives
Hispanics, and crime, 152–153
Ho Chi Minh, 411
Holmes, Justice Oliver Wendell, 423
Home schooling, 319–320
Homeland security, 96
Homelessness, 235–236
Homosexuals, equality and, 351–355, 425
Hoover, President Herbert, 47
Horizontal intergovernmental relations; *See*
    Intergovernmental relations
Horizontal merger, 53
Hospital, and DRGs, 259
Hospital Insurance Trust Fund, 264
Hospital insurance, and Medicare, 257

Hostile takeover, 53, 61
Housing, 223–224
    and racial equality, 371–372
    programs for, 235–236
Hydrocarbons (HC), 121

Idealism, and foreign and defense policy,
    405–408
Ideological context, and public policy, 17-19
Illegal immigration, 379–380, 382–383, 388
Illegal Immigration Reform and Immigrant
    Responsibility Act of 1996, 382–383, 387–388
Illegally obtained evidence, 168–169; *See also*
    Exclusionary rule; Search and Seizure
Immigrant Restriction League, anti-immigrant
    sentiment, 379
Immigration; *See also* Immigration policy
    and education, 387
    patterns of, 386–387
    and public policy, 14–15, 468
    racial and ethnic origins, 387
    top ten countries, 386
Immigration policy, future alternatives, 394
Immigration Act of 1882, 378
Immigration Act of 1917, 378
Immigration Act of 1990, 382
Immigration and Nationality Act, 380, 385
Immigration and Naturalization Service (INS),
    380, 387–388
Immigration policy
    American spirit, 384
    anti-immigrant sentiment, 379
    and California, 378–379
    Chinese exclusion, 378
    contemporary, 383–388
    current concerns, 388
    depression affect on, 380
    economic concerns, 388–390
    employment based preference, 385
    ethnic balance, 379–380
    evaluation of, 388–394
    and family reunification, 381–382, 384–385
    ghettoized, 378
    illegal immigration, 379–380, 382–383
    issue of, 376–383
    limitations on, 378–380, 394–396
    myth of, 384
    open door, 376–377, 394–396
    preference system establishment, 380–382
    public service impact, 390–392
    quality of life concerns, 392–394
    and refugee policy, 382
    refugees and asylees, 385–386
    social problems, 379–380
    use of quotas, 377–380
Immigration Reform and Control Act of 1986, 382
Immigrants, 381
    and crime, 393
    and overpopulation, 392–393

Immigrants *(continued)*
  and social security, 391–392
  and welfare, 391
Imperialism, 410–411
Implementation; *See* Policy implementation
Incentives, 67
Indeterminate sentencing, 190
Indirect costs, 11; *See also* Policy evaluation
Indirect impacts, 11; *See also* Policy evaluation
Industrial wastes, 124
Inequality, equality created, 334–337
Inequality: A Reassessment of the Effect of Family and Schooling in America, 296
Infant mortality, 256
Inflation, 48–49
  cost-push, 49
  demand-pull, 49
  policy evaluation, 85
  and interest rates, 73–74, 76–77
In-kind assistance, 218, 222–224
  accomplishments of, 225
Innocent, and justice system, 158
INS; *See* Immigration and Naturalization Service
Insanity, 191
Institutional context, for public policy, 12–13
Institutional model; *See* Models
Institutional solutions, 408; *See also* Foreign and defense policy
Insurance market reform, 272
Insurance, and Medicare, 257–258
Integration; *See also* Equality
Intended consequences, 10; *See also* Policy evaluation
Interest rates
  and budget deficit, 82–83
  and inflation, 73–74
  and recession, 76–77
  and strength of the dollar, 83
Intergovernmental interactions, 38–40; *See also* Intergovernmental policies; Intergovernmental relations
  and Federal system, 26
  forms of, 31–32
Intergovernmental policies; *See also* Intergovernmental interactions; Intergovernmental relations
  and Federal system, 25–28
  future alternatives, 38–40
  interactions, 26, 31–32
  issues and concerns, 25–27
  and Medicaid, 259–260
  relations, 26, 27–28
  and TANF provisions, 220–221
Intergovernmental relations, 27–31, 38–40; *See also* Funding; Intergovernmental interactions; Intergovernmental relations; Policy evaluation
  A-95 review process, 35
  administrative problems, 32–34

Bush administration, 31, 38
current trends, 31
and education, 289–290
and federalism, 29
and Federal system, 26
horizontal, 28
and interactions, 31–32
modern, 29–31
participants in, 27–28
Reagan administration, 30–31, 32, 34, 37, 38
state and local control, 38–40
Intergovernmental system; *See* Intergovernmental interactions; Intergovernmental policies; Intergovernmental relations
International
  and antitrust policies, 57
  EEC, 60
  GATT, 59–60, 62
  NAFTA, 59–60, 62
  and trade, 59–60, 61–62
  WTO, 59–60
International treaties, and environmental policy, 133–134
Intifada, 418
Investment, and social security, 216
Investor immigrant, 381
Islamist militants, 417–418
Islamist terrorist, 417–418
Issue-oriented approach, 1

James Madison Elementary School, 312
James Madison High School, 312
Japan, and antitrust policy, 57
Jawboning, 78
Jefferson, Thomas, 286
Jencks, Christopher, 296
Jenkins v. Georgia (1974), 441
Jewish state; *See* Middle East
Jews, 368–369
Jim Crow laws, 340–341
Job Corps, 224
Job Training Partnership Act, 224
Job Training, and PRWOR, 224
Jobs first, 230
Job-training programs, 224, 236–237
Johnson v. Transportation Agency of Santa Clara County, 358
Joint Funding and Simplification Act of 1974, 34
Jones, Paula, 350
Journal of Learning Disabilities, 354
Judicial activism, 426
Jury nullification, 157
Justice Department, Antitrust Division; *See* Antitrust Division
Juveniles, and crime, 153

Kaczynski, Ted, 191
Kaiser Aluminum v. Weber, 357–358

Katzenbach v. McClung, 344
Keynes, John Maynard, 48, 78
Keynesian economics, 78–79
Know Nothing Party; *See* Native American
  Party, 378
Koenigsburg, Ernest, 332
Korean War, 410
Ku Klux Klan, anti-immigrant sentiment, 379
Kyoto Protocol, 133–134

Labor Department, 75
Lack serious literary, artistic, political, or
  scientific values (LAPS values), 440
LAPS values; *See* Lack serious literary, artistic,
  political, or scientific values
Larry P. v. Riles, 363
Law; *See also* Equality; Freedom of Speech;
  Obscenity; Open Society; Pornography
  and capital punishment, 164–166
  and democratic political process, 426–427
  environmental, 5, 135–136
  and obscenity, 439–448
  and public policy, 1–2
  equality under , 330–334
Lay, Ken, 147
Lazarus, Emma, 377
Learnfare, 219
Legalized Aliens, 381
LeMay, Michael, 376
Leninism, 411
Liberalism
  and freedom, 17
  and public policy, 17
Libertarians, and public policy, 18
LILCO; *See* Long Island Lighting Company
Lineberry, Robert, 187
Line-item veto, 95–96
Long Island Lighting Company (LILCO), 115
Long-term effects, 11; *See also* Policy evaluation
Love canal, 126
Lowell, Lawrence, 332
Lower-class, and crime, 152–153

MacRae, Duncan, 2
Macroeconomic policy, 49–51
  approaches of, 75–78
  managing the economy, 78–84
Magnetic Resonance Imaging (MRI), 252
Managed care, 244–245
Managed competition, 266–267
  and universal health care, 268
Mandates; *See also* Funding
  and congress, 27
  unfunded, 27, 32
Mandatory sentencing, 188–189
Mandatory spending, caps on, 96
Mapp v. Ohio (1961), 160, 168
Market capitalism; *See* Free-enterprise system
Market forces, 85

Market system, 43; *See also* Economics
Market-oriented social forces, 85
Marriage and family, and public policy, 16
Marxism-Leninism, 411
Master teachers, 303
Maternal and Child Health Services, 262
Maynard v. Cartwright (1988), 171
McClelland, David, 367
McCleskey v. Zant (1991), 171
McKinney Homeless Assistance Act, 236
McNaughten Rule, 191
MCT; *See* Minimum Competency Test
McVeigh, Timothy, 161
Mead, Lawrence, 2
Means test, 207, 219, 228
  punitive features of, 228
Medicaid, 29, 259–260
  and abortion, 430
  problems, 263–264
  success of, 263
Medical savings accounts (MSA), 269
Medicare, 257–259, 468
  cost of, 258–259
  and hospital insurance, 257
  long-range prospects, 274–275
  plus choice, 258, 266, 274
  prescription drugs, 253–254, 262–264, 273–274
  problems, 263–264
  reform of, 273–275
  success of, 263
  and supplementary medical insurance, 257–258
Medigap, 258
Membership, and government, 4
Merger, 53, 55–57, 61, 65
Meritocracy, 336
Merit pay, 302–303
Methadone, 175
Microeconomic policy, 49–51
Microsoft®, 53
Middle East
  brief history of, 413–416
  foreign and defense policy and, 412–416
  Jewish and Palestinian states, 412–413
  oil reserves of, 413
  Palestinian nationalism, 413–416
  Palestinian state rejection, 414–415
  Six Day War, 414
Migrant Labor Agreement of 1951, 380
Miller v. California (1973), 440
Milliken v. Bradley (1974), 356
Milosevic, Slobodan, 402
Mineral Leasing Act of 1920, 100–101
Minimum Competency Test (MCT); 300–301
Minor care clinics, 244
Miranda rule, 159–160, 167–168
Miranda v. Arizona, 167–168
Models
  elite, 7
  game, 7

Models *(continued)*
  group, 7
  institutional, 6–7
  pluralist, 7
  of policymaking, 6
  public choice, 7
  public policy, 2, 6–7
  rational-comprehensive, 7
  stages, 7
  sub government, 7
Monetary policy, 76–77, 95
Money supply, 76; *See also* Currency
Monopolies, and antitrust policies, 52
Monopoly, 53
Monroe Doctrine, 403
Moral education, 317
Morgenthau, Hans, 401
Morning After, The, 351
Morrill Act, 29
Mothballing, and nuclear power plant, 115
Motor Vehicle Air Pollution Control Act of
  1965, 129
MRI; *See* Magnetic Resonance Imaging
MSA; *See* Medical Savings Accounts
Multiculturalism, 438
Municipal wastes, 124
Murray, Charles, 335

NAACP; *See* National Association for the
  Advancement of Colored People
Nader, Ralph, 55
NAEP; *See* National Assessment of Educational
  Progress
NAFTA; *See* North American Free
  Trade Act
Nagel, Stuart, 169
Naked Maja, The, 350
Nation Prepared, A, 316
National Academy of Sciences, 201
National Assessment of Educational Progress
  (NAEP), 317
National Association for the Advancement of
  Colored People (NAACP), 288
National Commission on Excellence in
  Education, 302–303, 310–311
National debt, 77, 82, 86–87
National Education Standards and
  Improvement Council (NESIC), 313
National Energy Act of 1978, 108
  failure to comply, 109
National Environmental Policy Act
  (NEPA), 130–131
National Governors Association, 38
National Health Service Corps, 262
National Industrial Recovery Act, 47
National Institutes of Health
  (NIH), 256–257
National Labor Relations Board, 61
National Origins Quota Act of 1924, 379

National Organization for Women
  (NOW), 348
National Rifle Association (NRA), 180
National Science Foundation, 257
National teacher certification, 316
National Teacher Examination (NTE), 301
Nationalization, 68
Native American Party, 378
  and civil war, 378
  and equality, 351–355
  equality under law and, 333
  and poverty, 202–203
NATO; *See* North Atlantic Treaty Organization
Natural Gas Act of 1938, 102
Natural gas, 102, 105
  National Energy Act of 1978, 108
Natural monopolies, 45
Naturalization Act, 378
Naturalization, 381
Needs, and government, 5
Neoconservatives, 17
Neo-populism, 422
NEPA; *See* National Environmental
  Policy Act
New Deal, and intergovernmental relations,
  29–30
New England Journal of Medicine, 183
New Jersey Port Authority, 28
New Republic, The, 336, 350
New Right, 17
New style regulation; *See* Social regulation
New York Port Authority, 28
*New York State Club Association v. City of New
  York* (1988), 348–349
Nichols, Terry, 161
NIH; *See* National Institutes of Health
Nitrogen oxide (NO), 121
Nix v. Williams (1984), 160–161
Nixon administration
  and drug crimes, 174
  and energy policy, 105–106, 108, 109
  and fiscal policy, 78
No Child Left Behind Act of 2001, 314–315
Nonimmigrant, 381
Normative dimension, 10; *See also* Policy
  evaluation
North American Free Trade Act (NAFTA), 59
North Atlantic Treaty Organization (NATO),
  408, 409
Northwest Ordinance, and education, 317
NOW; *See* National Organization for Women
NRA; *See* National Rifle Association
NRC; *See* Nuclear Regulatory Commission
NTE; *See* National Teacher Examination
Nuclear power, 102, 105, 113–117, 138
  future of, 116–117
  plant age and decommissioning, 114–115
  safety, 114
  waste, 114

Nuclear Regulatory Commission (NRC), 114
Nuclear-fission technology, 113
Nutrition, and food stamps, 226

OASDI; *See* Old Age, Survivors, and Disability
    Insurance; Social Security
OBE; *See* Outcome-based education
Obscenity, 439–448; *See also* Freedom of
    Speech; Law; Open Society; Pornography
    and legislation, 439
    suppressing of, 433–447
O'Connor, Justice, 158
    and abortion, 429
Office of Federal Contract Compliance, 344
Office of Immigration, formation of, 378
Office of Management and Budget (OMB);
    See OMB
Oil, 101–102; *See also* Energy policy; Energy
    policy pre-1973; Energy policy
    post-1973; Oil dependency; OPEC
    Arab oil embargo, 104–105
    Crude Oil Windfall Profit Tax Act
        of 1980, 109
    decontrol of, 109
    dependency on, 106–107, 117–119
    faulty demand projections, 119
    National Energy Act of 1978, 108
    1970 shortfall, 119–120
    and OPEC, 103–105
    prices of, 105, 109
    Western companies, 103; *See also* Energy
        policy; Energy policy pre-1973; Energy
        policy post-1973; Oil; OPEC
Oil dependency, 117–119
    trade deficit, 118
    hidden cost of, 118
    political impact, 117
Oil depletion allowance, 102
Old Age, Survivors, and Disability Insurance
    (OASDI), 208
Old Faithful, 112
Old style regulation; *See* Economic regulation
OMB (Office of Management and Budget), and
    economic policy, 75
Omnibus Budget Reconciliation Act of 1990
    (OBRA-90), 90
Omnibus Crime Bill, 166, 185
Omnibus Trade Act of 1988, 59
OPEC (Organization of Petroleum Exporting
    Countries), 103–105, 118–119; *See also*
    Energy policy; Energy policy pre-1973;
    Energy policy post-1973; Oil; Oil
    dependency
    Arab oil embargo, 104–105
    limiting strength, 103
    oil prices, 105
    origins of, 103–104
    political disunity, 118
    unity erosion, 118

Open market operations, 77
Open society, 423–424
    and abortion, 427–433
    and censorship, 447
    and communitarians, 424
    communitarians vs. family values, 424–426
    and contraception, 431–432
    creationism, 459–460
    family values, 425–426, 460–462
    freedom of speech, 433–436
    and obscenity, 438–439
    parochial education funding, 457–459
    political correctness, 436–438
    presumption of constitutionality, 426–427
    and racial slurs, 435–436, 436–439
    religion, 448–460
    role of court, 426–427
    secular humanism, 459–460
    segmented society, 424
Oregon v. Haas (1975), 168
Organization of Petroleum Exporting Countries
    (OPEC); *See* OPEC
Osama Bin Laden, 417
Oslo process, 415
OTA; *See* U.S. Office of Technology Assessment
Ottoman Empire, 414
Outcome-based education (OBE), 317–318
Outpatient surgeries, 244
Ozone layer, 123–124

Quayle, Dan, 461
Quota Act of 1921, 379

Race; *See also* Equality; Freedom of speech
    and busing, 355–357
    and education, 288–289, 291–292, 295–297
    and environmental policy, 134
    and higher education, 320–321
    and immigration, 387
    and IQ scores, 336
    and MCT, 301
    and multiculturalism education, 304–305
    and public policy, 14–15, 468
    and teachers, 305
Race-based selection, 345–346
Racial harassment, 436–437
Racial preference plans, 346; *See also*
    Affirmative action; Reverse discrimination
    and higher education, 361–363
    retreat of, 357–359
Racial slurs, and freedom of speech, 435–436,
    436–439
Racism, and crime, 156–157
Radioactive waste; *See* Hazardous waste
Rape, 176–178
    crime of violence, 178–179
Rasmussen Report, 114
Rational-comprehensive model; *See* Models
RBRVS; *See* Resource-based relative value scale

Reagan administration, 466–467
    A-95 review process, 34
    antitrust policy, 61
    and the Cold War, 409–410
    and deficit spending, 78
    deregulation, 60–61, 80
    and education, 312
    and EEC, 61–62
    energy policy, 109–111
    fiscal policy, 86–89
    and FTC, 55
    and inflation, 85–86
    intergovernmental relations, 30–31, 38
    international trade, 61–62
    and mergers, 55–56, 61
    power to the states, 37
    and supply-side economics, 79–80
    Supreme Court justices, 157–158
Reagan revolution, 466
Reagan, Ronald, 26, 30–31; *See also*
    Intergovernmental relations; Reagan
    administration
Reasonable costs, and Medicare, 259
Reasonable man test, 441
Re-authorization, TANF, 230–232
Recession, 49
    and depression, 49
    and monetary policies, 76–77
Recidivism, 188–189
Red tape, 26, 32–33
Redistribution, 6
Reeves, Mavis Mann, 38
Reform, economics, 66–69
Refugee; *See* Asylee
Refuse Act of 1899, 129
Refugee Act of 1980, 382
Refugee policy, 382
Regulation, 63–66
    changes in, 64–66
    community revitalization, 68
    consumer oversight, 68
    and deregulation, 67
    and environmental policy, 132–133
    future of, 66–69
    incentives, 67
    nationalization, 68
    sunset laws, 68
    trade, 68–69
Regulatory agencies, 50–51, 63–66
    abolishment of, 66–67
    independence of, 50
    structure of, 50–51
Regulatory policies, 5, 50–51
Rehnquist, Chief Justice, 158
Reilly, Walter, 132
Reinventing government, 467–468
Religion, 448–460
    establishment clause, 449, 450–454
    free exercise clause, 449, 454–457

    and freedom, 449
Reno v. ACLU, 441
Research and development, fossil fuel
    alternatives, 111
Reserve requirement, 77
Resource-based relative value scale (RBRVS), 259
Retirement, and social security, 215–216
Revenues and spending; *See* Federal revenues
    and spending
Reverse discrimination, 359
Revitalization programs, and economy, 57–58
Right to counsel, 159–160, 167–168
Rivlin, Alice, 31
Roe v. Wade (1973), 427
Roithe, Katie, 351
Roosevelt, Franklin D., 47, 208
Rossell, Christine, 356
Rostker v. Goldberg (1981), 347
Roth case, 440–442
Roth rule, 440–442
Royal Dutch Shell, 103
RU-486, 429
Rural Development Councils, 28

*Sable Communications v. Federal
    Communications Commission,* 441
Safe Drinking Water Act, 31, 129
Safe storage; *See* SAFSTOR
SAFSTOR, 115
*San Antonio Independent School District v.
    Rodriguez,* 293
SAT scores
    declining of, 298–299
    recentering of, 298
Scalia, Justice, 158
SCHIP; *See* State Children's Health Insurance
    Program
Schools of crime, 190
Scienter, 437–438
Scottsboro opinion, 159
Search and seizure, 160–161, 168–169
SEATO; *See* Southeast Asia Treaty Organization
Secular humanism, teaching of, 460
Securities and Exchange Commission, 47
Security, 4
Segmented society, 424
Segregation, ending of 340–341; *See also*
    Equality
Selective incapacitation, 192
Self-regulatory policies, 5
    and self-regulatory politics, 5
Self-regulatory politics, 5
Sellin, Thorsten, 162
Semi-automatic weapons, 184–186
    control of, 184–186
Separate but equal, 288, 291, 340
Service intensity, 256
Services, 5
Sex-role stereotypes, 348–349

Sexual harassment; *See* Equality; Women; Crime
Sherman Antitrust Act, 52, 54
Short-term effects, 11; *See also* Policy evaluation
Silent Spring, 121
Silver Certificate, 76
Simpson, O.J., 156–157, 177
Single parent families, and poverty, 232–234
Single-gender schools, 320
Single-payer, and health care, 269
Social contract, 376–377
Social culture, and immigrants, 393–394
Social hierarchy, 85
Social insurance programs, 208–211
  social security, 209–210
  unemployment insurance, 210–211
Social justice, and environmental policy, 134
Social orders, 84–85
  and immigration policy, 392–394
  market-oriented, 85
Social regulation, 51
Social Security Act of 1935, 208
  and intergovernmental relations, 29
  federal programs, 218
Social Security Administration (SSA), poverty
    defined, 198
Social Security, 209–210, 468
  administration of, 209
  conservative view, 213
  dilemma with, 212–213
  fairness of, 213–214
  future of, 214
  and Illegal Immigration Reform and
    Immigrant Responsibility Act of 1996,
    382–383
  and immigrants, 391–392
  investment of funds, 216
  liberal view, 213
  pay-as-you-go, 212–213
  privatizing of, 216–217
  quick fixes, 215–216
  success of, 211–212
Social welfare; *See* Intergovernmental relations;
    Poverty
Socialism, 44
Socialist economies, 44–45
  control of, 45
Socialists, 18
Society; *See* Open society
Socony-Vacuum (now Mobil), 103
Solar energy
  Carter administration, 111–112
  decline of, 111
  fossil fuel alternative, 111
Solar Heating and Cooling Demonstration Act
    of 1975, 112
Solid-waste pollution, 125
Souter, Justice, 158
South Carolina v. Gathers (1989), 171
Southeast Asia Treaty Organization (SEATO), 408

Sovereignty, 25
Soviet Union, and Warsaw Pact, 409
Special interest groups, and intergovernmental
    relations, 28
Spheres of influence, 403–404
SSA; *See* Social Security Administration
SSI; *See* Supplemental Security Income
Standard Oil Corporation, 53
Standard Oil of California (Chevron), 103
Standard Oil of New Jersey (Exxon), 103
Standard Oil Trust, 101
State Children's Health Insurance Program
    (SCHIP), 261, 271
State and local control; *See* Intergovernmental
    relations; Reagan administration
State-sponsored terrorism, 418
Statue of Liberty, 377
Steward, Justice, and pornography, 441
Stone, Deborah, 17
Strauss, Murray, 177
Street crime, 148
Sub-government model; *See* Models
Subsidies, 5, 65–66
Suburban population, and public policy, 16
Sulfur dioxide (SO2), 121
Sumner v. Shuman (1987), 171
Sunset laws, 68
  and Economic Growth and Tax Relief
    Reconciliation Act of 2001 (EGTRRA), 84
Superconducting Supercollider Project, 1–2
Superfund, 131
Supplemental Security Income (SSI), 218,
    221–222
Supplementary medical insurance, and
    Medicare, 257–258
Supply and demand, 43, 46
  and health care, 256
Supply-side economics, 79–80
  and budget deficit, 80–83
Supportive Housing Demonstration Program, 236
Supreme Court, and immigrant education, 390
Suspend, 191
*Swann v. Charlotte-Mecklenburg Board of
    Education* (1971), 342
Swift and certain punishment, 162
Symbolic impacts, 11; *See also* Policy
    evaluation
Symbolic racism, 437
Synthetic Fuels Corporation, 112

Takeover, 53
TANF; *See* Temporary Assistance to Needy
    Families
Tangible impacts, 11; *See also* Policy evaluation
Tax cut, 77, 93–94
Tax, and environmental policy, 135–136
Tax incentives, 77
Tax policy; *See* Fiscal policy
Tax Reform Act of 1986, 83–84

Tax reform, 83–84, 93–94
Technology, and health care, 252–253, 256
Temporary Assistance to Needy Families
    (TANF), 218, 219
  earnings, 230
  evaluation of, 229–232
  poverty rates, 230
  Re-authorization of, 229–232
  reform provisions, 220–221
  time limits, 220
Terrorism
  and realist principles, 418
  confrontation of, 417–419
  control of, 416–419
  defined as, 416
Texaco; *See* Texas Company
Texas Company, 103
Texas Railroad Commission, 102
Thermal pollution, 124
Thernstrom, Stephen, 337, 437
Third-party payments
  Medicaid, 252
  Medicare, 252
Thomas, Clarence, 177
Thomas, Justice, 158
Thompson v. Oklahoma, 170–171
Thompson, John, 364
Thompson, Kenneth, 401
Thompson, William, 170–171
Three Mile Island, 114
Times Beach, MO, 126
Title IX, 349
Title VII, 344
Toxic waste, 125–127
Trade; *See also* International
  international, 59–60, 61–62
  reform of, 68–69
Trans-Alaska pipeline, 108
Treasury Department, 75
Treatment protocols, 245
Trickle-down theory, 78
Trust, 53
Tucker, Karla Faye, 166
Twelve 200 Foot Reels, 445

U.S. Chamber of Commerce, and white-collar
    crime, 147
U.S. Civil rights Commission, and education, 342
U.S. Constitution
  Eighth Amendment, 161, 164, 170
  Fifth Amendment, 427
  First Amendment, 177, 351, 424, 426, 433–448
  Fourteenth Amendment, 158, 160, 168,
      339–340, 342, 344, 427
  Fourth Amendment, 160, 426, 427
  Ninth Amendment, 426–427
  Thirteenth Amendment, 333, 339–340

U.S. Office of Technology Assessment (OTA), 128
U.S. Supreme Court
  and California Civil Rights Initiative, 362
  and crime, 157–158
  and race-based selection, 345–346
U.S. v. Leon (1984), 161
U.S.A. Patriot Act of 2001, 384, 388
Underclass, 205, 234
Unemployment
  and employment, 73–74
  and insurance, 210–211, 214
Unfunded mandates, 27, 32, 36–37
Unfunded Mandates Reform Act of 1995, and
      intergovernmental interaction, 32
Uniform Crime Report, 145
Uninsured
  and health care, 249–250
  maldistribution of resources, 250–251
  number of, 255
Unintended consequences, 11; *See also* Policy
    evaluation
Unitary system, 25
United Mine Workers (UMW), 101
United Nations, 25
United States–Canada Free Trade Agreement of
    1988, 59
United Steelworkers of America v. Weber (1979),
    357–358
Uniting and Strengthening America by
    Providing Appropriate Tools Required to
    Intercept and Obstruct Terrorism Act of
    2001, 384
Universal health care, failure of, 268–270
Urbanization, and crime, 152
Urban population, and public policy, 16
Utilization review, 245

Value-added tax, 94
Vertical merger, 53
Victimless crime, 150, 186
Viet Minh, 411
Vietnam War, 12, 403
  early history, 410–412
  failure of, 410–412
Violence; *See also* Capital punishment; Crime;
    Future Alternatives; Policy evaluation; U.S.
    Constitution
  and guns, 179–186
  crimes of, 178–186
  drug-related crime, 178
Violence against Women Act, 178

Wage and price controls, 78
Walker, Abena, 364
Wall of separation, 450–451
War on terror, 416
Warrantless search, 169

Warren, Chief Justice, 340–341
Warren, Earl, 157
Wasby, Stephen, 168
Washington v. Davis (1976), 345
Waste; *See* Acid rain; Air pollution; Solid-waste pollution; Hazardous Waste; Toxic waste; Water pollution
Wastewater treatment, 125; *See* Water pollution
Water pollution, 124–125
  policy for, 129
  primary treatment, 125
  secondary treatment, 125
  tertiary systems, 125
  wastewater treatment, 125
Water pollution Act of 1948, 129
Water Pollution Control Act, 129
Water Pollution Control Act Amendments of 1972, 129
Water Quality Act, 129
Watergate, 148
Weapons; *See* Guns; Semi-automatic weapons
Webber, Judge Susan, 350
Welfare reform, 37, 219–220
  adequacy, 227–228
  administration of, 227
  children, 228–229
  cost of, 227
  marriage and family, 229–230
  and public assistance, 228–229
  punitive features, 228
  success of, 226–229
  unfairness, 228
  and TANF
  work disincentives, 229
Welfare state, 207–208
  capitalism, 44
Western world, and inequality, 334
White-collar crime, 146–148
  and political figures, 147–148
Whitewater, 147–148
Wightyman, Linda, 362
Wildavsky, Aaron, 84–85
Wilde, James A., 2
Wilson, James Q., 148, 172, 191

Wilson, Pete, 390
Wilson, Woodrow, 405
  Fourteen Points speech, 406
Wilsonian idealism, 405–408
Windfall profits, 109
Wisconsin works, 219
Wolfgang, Marvin, 153
Women
  and childbearing, 349
  equality and, 333–334, 347–351
  and equality under law, 333–334
  and pornography, 445–447
  and rape, 176–178
  right to vote, 349
  and sexual harassment, 176–177, 350–351
  violence against, 176–178
Women's liberation, as men's liberation, 350
World Trade Organization (WTO), 59–60
World War II, and intergovernmental relations, 30
Wright, Deil, 29
WTO; *See* World Trade Organization
Wygant v. Board of Education, 358

Yellowstone National Park, 112
Yom Kippur War, 104
Young Adult Conservation Corps, 224
Youth
  and absent fathers, 233
  Balanced Budget Agreement, 233
  and capital punishment, 170–171
  and crime, 152–153, 191–192
  and food stamp program, 226
  and guns, 180
  and poverty, 203, 232–234
  SCHIP, 261, 271
  and welfare reform, 228–229, 229–230
Yurugu: An African Centered Critique of European Cultural Thought and Behavior, 364

Zero tolerance, 190
Zero-sum game, 6